WESTERN EUROPE

A HANDBOOK

HANDBOOKS TO THE MODERN WORLD
  General Editor: Andrew C. Kimmens

WESTERN EUROPE
THE SOVIET UNION AND EASTERN EUROPE
THE MIDDLE EAST
AFRICA
ASIA
LATIN AMERICA AND THE CARIBBEAN
AUSTRALIA, NEW ZEALAND AND THE SOUTH PACIFIC
THE UNITED STATES AND CANADA

HANDBOOKS TO THE MODERN WORLD

WESTERN EUROPE

Edited by

RICHARD MAYNE

Facts On File Publications
New York, New York ● Oxford, England

First published in Great Britain in 1967 by Anthony Blond Ltd.
This completely revised and updated edition published in the
United States in 1986 by Facts on File Publications, 460 Park Avenue South,
New York, N.Y. 10016, in association with Muller, Blond & White,
55 Great Ormond Street, London WC1N 3HZ.

ISBN 0-8160-1251-X

10 9 8 7 6 5 4 3 2 1

Printed in Great Britain at The Bath Press, Avon

CONTRIBUTORS

TONY ALDOUS, a graduate of the University of Bristol, has been a journalist since 1960 and a freelance writer on environmental issues since 1974, contributing articles on urban conservation, architecture and landscape architecture, and town planning to newspapers, periodicals and professional journals. A frequent lecturer, he has also appeared on radio and television. He is at present editorial consultant to the Civic Trust and consulting editor and contributor to the English Tourist Board's monthly *Tourism in Action*. His books include *Battle for the Environment* (1972), *Goodbye, Britain?* (1975), *The World's Cities: London* (1978), *Landscape by Design* (1979), *Changing Bristol* (1979) and *The Illustrated London News Book of London's Villages* (1980).

RICHARD BAILEY is an economist who has worked in the public and private sectors. He was formerly director of Political and Economic Planning, now the Policy Studies Institute, and economic adviser to the London Chamber of Commerce. He has worked on projects for the World Bank, the U.N. Center on Trade and Development (UNCTAD) and the U.N. Industrial Development Organization (UNIDO). His books include *Energy—the Rude Awakening* and *The European Connection*.

COLIN BEEVER holds a diploma in Economics and Political Science from Oxford University. He was a research Fellow in the Council of Europe in 1957–58 and published a thesis "European Unity and the Trade Union Movements." He has worked as shop steward and trade union officer for the Engineering Union and the Local Government Officers Union, and has held various industrial relations and personnel directorships since 1971. A manager of the Social Democratic party's Euro-centre, he was a candidate for the European Parliament in 1984. Beever currently writes and lectures on the European Community and on personnel matters.

TONY BURGESS read economics at London University. After working in advertising he turned to economic journalism in 1957. He was appointed to the staff of the European Communities Information Service in Luxembourg, 1962, as editor of English-language publications. From 1964 to 1966 he was press officer in the Information Service's London office. Currently, he is an official of the Foreign and Commonwealth Office.

WILLIAM M. CLARKE read economics at Manchester University. He was financial and industrial editor of *The Times*, 1962–66, and has been editorial consultant to *The Banker* since 1966. Currently he is Director and Deputy

Chairman of the British Invisible Exports Council. His publications include *The City's Invisible Earnings* (1962), *The City in the World Economy* (1965), *The World's Money: How It Works* (1971), and *Inside the City* (1979).

MICHAEL DURAND is an official of the OECD in Paris, who prefers to remain pseudonymous.

CHARLES FORD is a graduate of the London School of Economics and Political Science. He has been secretary (1957–71) of the Trade Union Advisory Committee (TUAC) of the Organization for Economic Cooperation and Development (OECD) in Paris; at the same time he served as assistant general secretary of the European Regional Organization of the International Confederation of Free Trade Unions (ICFTU). Since 1971 he has been general secretary of the International Textile, Garment, and Leather Workers' Federation (ITGLWF) in Brussels.

MARIANNE GELLNER read economics at the London School of Economics. She was on the staff of the Royal Institute of International Affairs, London, 1951–62, specializing in international economics. She began work in the steel industry in 1965 and retired in 1976 as Manager, Overseas Assessment, in the Commercial Division of the British Steel Corporation. A free-lance consultant to the OECD Secretariat for the setting up of their Steel Committee, she currently sits as member on industrial tribunals.

VIC GEORGE has been professor of social policy and administration and social work at the University of Kent since 1973. Prior to that, he was a senior lecturer at the University of Nottingham. His publications include *Ideology and Social Welfare* (with Paul Wilding), 1976; *Poverty and Inequality in the Common Market Countries* (with Roger Lawson), 1980; *Socialism, Social Welfare and the Soviet Union* (with Nick Manning), 1980; and *The Impact of Social Policy* (with Paul Wilding), 1984.

BRIAN HOLMES holds a B.Sc. in physics from University College, London and a Ph.D. in comparative education from the University of London Institute of Education. He has taught physics and was a lecturer in education at the University of Durham from 1951 to 1953. Since 1953 he has been on the staff of the Institute of Education, London, becoming head of the department of comparative education in 1977. He has held several visiting professorships in the United States, Canada and Japan. Besides numerous articles in professional education journals, he is the author of *Problems in Education* (1965) and *Comparative Education: Some Considerations of Methods* (1981), and editor of *Diversity and Unity in Education* (1980) and *Equality and Freedom in Education* (1985).

NEVILLE MARCH HUNNINGS, LL.M., Ph.D. (Lond.), Diplômé of the Hague Academy of International Law, is a barrister and editorial director of European Law Centre, Ltd. He is the editor of *Common Market Law Reports*, founder and coeditor of *European Commercial Cases* and *Commercial Laws of Europe*, and European law editor of *Journal of Business Law*. He is the author of *Gazetteer of European Law* (1983).

MALCOLM J. MACMILLEN holds a B.A. from the University of Keele and an M.A. from the University of Sussex. Since 1970 he has been a lecturer in economics at the University of Exeter. He has written several articles on European migrant labor.

JACQUES MALLET studied at the Ecole Nationale d'Administration and the Institut d'Etudes Politiques, Paris. He was a staff member of the Information Service of the Common Market in Paris and a member of the Council of the French Association for the Atlantic Community. Has written widely on international affairs, particularly on the problems of the Third World and European integration. He has made a special study of relations between the Common Market and the United States. He is now a Member of the Euopean parliament.

J. S. MARSH was educated at St. John's College, Oxford and the University of Reading. From 1977 to 1984 he was professor of agricultural economics at the University of Aberdeen and since 1984 has been professor of agricultural economics and management at Reading. A member of the Potato Marketing Board (1977–84) and the Economic Development Council of the Food and Drink Manufacturing Association, he is president-elect of the Agricultural Economics Society. He has written many articles on British and European agriculture.

RICHARD MAYNE was educated at Cambridge University. He has served on the staffs of the European Coal and Steel Community and has been director of the documentation center of the Action Committee for the United States of Europe and personal assistant to Jean Monnet. From 1973 he headed the United Kingdom office of the Commission of the European Communities and was later special adviser to the Commission. He is currently coeditor of *Encounter*. He is author of *The Community of Europe, The Recovery of Europe, The Europeans* and *Postwar*.

RICHARD MOORE was educated privately and at Trinity College, Cambridge, where he was president of the Cambridge Union. He was an editorial writer for the *News Chronicle*, 1956–60. Moore was Liberal parliamentary candidate at Tavistock, 1955 and 1959; Cambridgeshire, 1961 (by-election) and 1964; and North Antrim, 1966. A member of the Royal Institute of International Affairs and the Institute for Strategic Studies, London, he is now on the staff of the Liberal and Democratic Group of the European Parliament, Brussels.

KEITH L. R. PAVITT was educated at the University of Cambridge (engineering and industrial management) and Harvard University (economics and public policy). From 1961 to 1970 he worked on science and technology policy problems for the OECD Directorate for Scientific Affairs. From 1971 to 1984 he was Senior Fellow at the Science Policy Research Unit (SPRU), a research group of natural and social scientists working on problems of developmental policy in industrial and developing countries. Currently, he is Deputy Director of SPRU and director of studies for postgraduate research. His numerous publications include *The Conditions for Success in Technologi-*

cal Innovation (with S. Wald, 1971) and *World Futures: The Great Debate* (coeditor, 1978).

JOHN PINDER is former director of the Policy Studies Institute, London, and a professor at the College of Europe in Bruges. He is also president of the European Union of Federalists. His publications include *Britain and the Common Market* (1961), *The Economics of Europe* (editor, 1971), *Policies for a Constrained Economy* (with Charles Carter, 1982) and *National Industrial Strategies and the World Economy* (editor, 1982).

ROY PRYCE, Ph.D. (Cantab.), was a Fellow of Emmanuel College, Cambridge, and of St. Antony's College, Oxford, 1955–57. He was head of the London office, European Communities Information Service, 1957–64, and an officla of the EC in Brussels, 1973–81. Since 1983 he has been a visiting professor at the Institute of Public Administration, University of Maastricht, and director of the Federal Trust for Education and Research.

ANTHONY SHARP read international politics at University College of Wales, Aberystwyth. He is now a writer and lecturer on international affairs.

DAVID SPANIER was educated at Cambridge University, where he read English under Dr. F. R. Leavis. He has been a foreign correspondent for *The Times* (London) and its diplomatic correspondent from 1973 to 1982. He is now diplomatic correspondent of Independent Radio News. He was awarded the European Journalists' Prize in 1971 for his book *Europe Our Europe*. He is also the author of *Total Poker* (1977) and *Total Chess* (1984); he is writing a book on gambling.

CHRISTOPHER STEVENS holds the B.Sc, Econ. from the University of Wales, an M.A. from the London School of Oriental and African Studies, a Ph.D. from the London School of Economics and Political Science. He holds research appointments at the Centre of European Policy Studies, Brussels; the Overseas Development Institute, London; and the Institute of Development Studies at the University of Sussex. He specializes in analyzing the impact of the European Community's economic policies on the Third World. The editor of the annual *EEC and the Third World: A Survey*, he has also written extensively on North–South relations.

PIERRE URI studied at the Ecole Normale Supérieure, the Faculté de Droit of the Sorbonne and Princeton University. He was economic and financial counselor to the Commissariat Général du Plan, 1947–52; member of the United Nations Committee of Experts on Full Employment, 1949; economic director of the ECSC, 1952–59; chairman of the Experts Group on the Longterm Development of the EEC, 1960–64; economic consultant to the Atlantic Institute near Paris. His publications include *La Crise de la zone de libre-échange* (1959), *Dialogue des continents* (1963), *From Commonwealth to Common Market* (editor, 1968), and reports on the Schuman Plan (1951) and on the economic situation of the EEC (1958).

C. M. W. VASEY read history at Oxford University, studied European institutions at the College of Europe in Bruges, and was research assistant in political science at the University of California, Berkeley. He spent several years as a journalist with Agence Europe, and was later attached to the Secretariat of the Council of Europe, Strasbourg, as secretary to the Political Committee of the Consultative Assembly. He is a member of the Spokesman's Group of the Commission of the European Communities in Brussels.

ANTHONY VERRIER, who was formerly defense correspondent for *The Observer* and *The New Statesman*, and wrote for many other journals, was a Senior Associate Member of St. Antony's College, Oxford, 1967–73. He lectures regularly at the Foreign Office Conference Centre, Wilton Park. Author of *An Army for the Sixties* (1966), *The Bomber Offensive* (1968), *International Peacekeeping* (1981), and *Through The Looking Glass—British Foreign Policy In The Age of Illusions* (1983), he is currently writing a study of the background to Zimbabwe's independence.

CAROLE WEBB, holder of a B.A. in political studies from Leeds University and an M.Sc. from the London School of Economics and Political Science, has been a lecturer in European studies at the University of Manchester Institute of Science and Technology since 1972. She has been a coeditor of *Policy-Making in the European Communities* (1977; rev. ed., 1983) the *The European Community: An Exercise in Decision-Making* (1978). Publications to which she has contributed include *A Common Man's Guide to the Common Market* (1978) and *West European Politics Today* (1983).

GLEN GARFIELD WILLIAMS is a graduate of the universities of Wales, London and Tübingen. He served as Baptist minister in St. Albans, Hertfordshire, in 1955–59. He was divisional area secretary for Europe of the World Council of Churches in 1959–68, and general secretary of the Conference of European Churches from 1968.

PHILIP WINDSOR read modern history at Oxford University and did research on German history at Oxford and the Free University of Berlin. He spent three years at the Institute for Strategic Studies, London, and is currently reader in international relations at the London School of Economics. His publications include *Arms and Stability in Europe* (with Alastair Buchan, 1962), *Czechoslovakia 1968* (with Adam Roberts, 1969), *Germany and the Management of Détente* (1971) and *Change in Eastern Europe* (1981).

SALOMON WOLFF was born in Minsk, and read politics at Hamburg University. He was economic correspondent of the *Frankfurter Zeitung* for France, 1923–34; was with the bankers Mendelssohn and Co. in Amsterdam, 1934–39; and from 1940 to his death was economic correspondent of the *Neue Zürcher Zeitung* for France, covering European economic integration and monetary questions.

CONTENTS

PART ONE: THE COUNTRIES OF WESTERN EUROPE

Basic Information *compiled by Anthony Sharp, William Golightly and George Kurian*

PART TWO: GENERAL

PART THREE: WESTERN EUROPEAN INTEGRATION

MAPS

INTRODUCTION

RICHARD MAYNE

The present volume is an entirely revised and largely rewritten edition of *Western Europe: A Handbook*, edited by the late John Calmann, which appeared in 1967. Much of what Calmann wrote in his Introduction to that edition is still valid and relevant today. "In 1945," he declared,

> most of the countries described were at war with each other, and when the war was over their future was as bleak as their devastated cities and their abandoned farms and factories. Now Western Europe—which we have taken to include all the noncommunist countries of Europe and Turkey—has become a rich, highly integrated, recognizable unit, with a variety of more or less free institutions, and a vast spread of prosperity, surpassed only in North America. Politically and economically, it has become separated from the communist countries of Europe, and while that separation may now be drawing to its close, the gap between the two areas is still a strong factor in the condition of Europe. Thus Western and Eastern Europe can still be treated as distinct and recognizable regions, with their own economic and political systems, their own cultural development, and their own diversity.
>
> This book, unlike the others in the series, emphasises the similarities of the problems which the various countries face, rather than their national characteristics. Indeed, the oddest thing about Western Europe is that it still has such a variety of structures to deal with what is really much the same business; thus, while each country is still expected to cope with its own problems, it finds this less and less easy to do without the support and interest of its neighbors. Just as during the prewar depression it was gradually realized that even the rich were to some extent dependent on the well-being of the poor, so governments in Western Europe have come to regard each other as having the same objectives rather than necessarily being in competition with each other. ... If the object of a handbook on Western Europe is to give the basic facts about the area, then it must stress the interdependence of the nations of which it is made up, and the community of needs and expectations formed by its peoples.
>
> This is not to ignore the survival of the nation-states—they are amply covered in the section providing basic information—but rather to show how they have changed since prewar days, in spite of the continuity of their institutions. ... In fact the essays in this book bring out two opposed.elements common to all the nation-states: first, that they are bound to act in concert in a large number of fields because their interests are complementary; and second, that their national structures impose limitations on their joint action which are detrimental to their prosperity and progress. What Western European countries have been seeking since the war—and this includes Britain—is to find a method or methods of resolving this contradiction. It is certainly not a proof of the eternal vigor of the nation-

state that the difficulty of doing so remains. The feebleness of the states was revealed during World War II itself, when they nearly all collapsed before Hitler's armies. (Their interdependence was also revealed in this catastrophe.) A more intelligent and more constructive change in their relationships is being wrought more slowly today by a common recognition of economic circumstances and by some common institutions.

Part Three of this book covers these institutions, and more particularly the European Community. The reason for this emphasis on the Treaties of Paris and Rome is that they represent a revolutionary challenge to the traditional concept of the European state. Their effects as well as their aims go far beyond the large number of other organizations, such as the OECD or EFTA, which group Europeans together. Their aim, unlike that of Bismarck's "blood and iron," is to marry states to each other without individual loss of life or property. Their success is proved by the fact that they have survived some rather violent crises, more or less intact. ... Indeed, the presence of the European Community is felt in the formulation of nearly every major decision which the countries described in this book take. Quite apart from broad generalities of economic policy, in the discussion of specific industrial, argricultural, transport, energy, or even social questions, all Western European governments, whether they are inside the Community or outside, look to see what is being done in Brussels. Naturally the influence of the Community is largest in the member countries, but in the others there is a constant preoccupation with knowing how to "fit in" with Community policies.

All this is still true; but, were he writing today, John Calmann might be less emphatic. Europe and the world have changed rather markedly in the past generation—not only materially, but psychologically too.

The biggest, most obvious change is the world recession—"stagflation"— triggered off (or hastened, according to other interpretations) by the oil crisis of 1973. As this book goes to press, there are intermittent signs of recovery, even in Europe. But the recession has made a deep wound, affecting attitudes and policies that superficially appear unconnected with it.

One such effect has been to heighten doubts about whether the recession itself is only cyclical, one of the periodic downturns of confidence and economic activity that used to occur more frequently, for reasons still not fully fathomed by economists. Already in the 1950s, there was much talk about the consequences for employment which might result from the spread of "cybernetics" and "automation," as they were then called. When the 1970s recession began, there was similar concern as to whether the silicon "chip" (the next buzzword) would not make labor increasingly redundant. Coupled with sharpening competition from lower-wage countries outside Europe, many of them engaged in fairly high-technology industries, this led to fears that Europe might be facing the "crisis of capitalism," which Marxists had long predicted. The erosion of confidence made confidence erode still further. Only now, and rather shakily, are Europeans beginning to recover from that paralyzing nightmare.

A further effect of recession has been to enhance nationalism. When the oil crisis began, with a fivefold increase in oil prices and the threat of a blockade, European countries presented an unedifying spectacle. Each hurried to save itself, hastily courting its favorite sheik, or Shah. The oil "majors"—the international companies—saved the situation by supplying the fuel; but a nationalistic mood had begun. As recession deepened, there were further pressures to return to protectionism, both in Europe and in the United States. Formally, these were resisted fairly successfully; but if tariffs and quotas were not used to stave off foreign competition, "self-limitation" agreements were, particularly on textiles and other sensitive products, and particularly also with Japan. And where trade policy was no longer allowed to operate, monetary policy was sometimes invoked. Currency parities, it soon appeared, were still very much treated as mainly national, not collective, concerns.

This was all the more serious in that in 1971, hard pressed by the effects of the Vietnam war and by the growing unwillingness of others to continue financing the American deficit, the United States had floated the dollar, thereby removing the last shreds of the international monetary system established at Bretton Woods. The resultant instability was further increased by the vast quantities of petrodollars accumulated by the oil states after the first and second price rises. These sums of money, too great to be easily absorbed into indigenous investment, began to move about the world markets in search of both profits and stability. Easily frightened, quickly shifted, and formidably large, such "flight money," as it came to be called, made life very difficult for European and other central bankers, no longer able to exert the control they had once maintained, even when they combined their forces. The huge debts owed to private banks by less-developed countries added even more instability to the world monetary scene.

In the circumstances, it is perhaps surprising that the postwar international system has resisted resurgent nationalism as well as it has. That nationalism is indeed resurgent has been shown fairly conclusively in Britain and the United States by the choice, and the rhetoric, of respective national leaders. Here, at least, Gaullism may be said to live on. Yet despite understandable appeals to wounded national pride, and occasional forays into justified military action on a safely small and conventional scale, both Prime Minister Thatcher and President Reagan have proved in practice far more responsible than they are often painted by their opponents or their speech-writers. If Gaullism lives on, so too does Keynes; so too does the system built by Dean Acheson, Harry Truman and the other postwar giants.

That is not to say that the system is immune from strains—especially in the vital areas of security and defense. Anthony Verrier, in a rewritten chapter, traces the political crisis in the Alliance provoked by controversies over Cruise and Pershing II missiles; and although on this the dust appears to be settling, there are fresh disputes and perhaps misunderstandings over the U.S. Strategic Defense Initiative, or "Star Wars."

If in these respects there is now more gloom than in 1967, there are also many more encouraging signs. A generation ago, President de Gaulle was still excluding Britain, Denmark and Ireland from the European Community (EC), and he had only recently thrown it into crisis by his "policy of the empty chair"—a crisis patched up only by an equivocal compromise whose effect was to discourage majority voting. The European Parliament was still appointed, not elected. A number of policies still hung fire.

Today, the EC has been enlarged not once, but twice. By 1973 a community of 10, by 1986 it numbered 12. As a result, there are now exactly as many new members as founder members; and many fear that sheer numbers, as well as policy problems, will tend to slow it down. Hence current debates about a "two-tier" Community or "variable geometry"—allowing some member states to take action together without waiting for the others. In a common market, this might be dangerous: but in new fields for integration it might prove the way ahead. At least, now, progress is being discussed, rather than consolidation or retrogression.

And progress has undoubtedly been made. The Community now has, at last, a common fisheries policy. It has the beginnings of a monetary system, if little more. It has formal links, through the Lomé Convention, with African, Caribbean and Pacific countries, instead of only with largely francophone Africa. Britain, for long an uneasy partner threatening withdrawal, has confirmed its membership by referendum, and appears to have turned opponents of the Community into a minority, even within the Labour party. After years of damaging squabbles about the Community budget, the British government has tabled encouraging positive proposals—notably to sweep away the remaining nontariff barriers which still divide what should be a common market. At the same time, the Community's national governments are studying ways to achieve what is called a "citizen's Europe"—a community, that is, whose benefits are obvious and immediate as well as obscure and profound.

In foreign policy, the Community countries have not adopted Community-type institutions, and seem unlikely to do so, despite a draft treaty prepared by the European Parliament. But the degree to which national foreign ministries now share information and discuss policy together would surprise the outsider. Only part of this process comes to the surface at meetings of foreign ministers and heads of state—regularized now in thrice-yearly sessions of the European Council, which the Commission also attends. The European Parliament, now directly elected, monitors this "political cooperation" no less keenly than the specific operations of the EC. To many, it looks like the Community's growth area.

Western Europe, then, still has claims on any reader's attention. One of the many ironies of history is that in 1967 fears were still expressed that the EC would be diluted and perhaps divided if it established a free-trade area coterminous with Western Europe. Today, that "vast free-trading zone" exists, with four of its original members inside the Community. The Community has not collapsed, despite enlargement and despite the industrial free-trade area of which it is now the more closely-integrated nucleus. It has even survived the biggest economic crisis since the Depression of the 1930s. To say the least, there must be something in it after all.

Users of this Handbook's previous edition may appreciate a final note on how the present version was compiled. Where possible, the original contributors were asked to rewrite or revise their own work. In some cases, where this has proved impossible, the editor has taken the liberty of doing it for them. He also takes, of course, full responsibility for the resulting text. In certain cases, where far more drastic rewriting proved necessary, and where the original authors were unable to undertake it, new and often younger experts were invited to contribute. Their credentials, with those of the other contributors, are to be found on pp. v–viii. One of the gratifying discoveries, in updating these brief biographies, is how eminent some of the original contributors have now become. Later editions will no doubt provide further pleasant surprises concerning the second generation of contributors. Many of them, in fact, have written what are virtually new chapters. In three other cases, entirely new chapters have been included: on Spain and Portugal, with a glance at Turkey, by David Spanier; on the environment, by Tony Aldous; and on communications, by the editor. These replace, in space if not in subject matter, the original volume's chapters on the arts. The sections of Basic Information and Comparative Statistics, compiled originally by Anthony Sharpe, have been updated by William Golightly and George Kurian.

In conclusion, thanks are due to Anthony Blond, for his helpful suggestions and support; to Hilary Whyte, for her imperturbable efficiency; and above all to the general editor of the series Handbooks to the Modern World, Andrew C. Kimmens, without whose cheerful enterprise, drive and attention to detail nothing would have been done on time, or perhaps at all.

PART ONE

THE COUNTRIES OF WESTERN EUROPE

BASIC INFORMATION

ANDORRA

Features: A mountainous country seldom below 2,500 ft/760 m. *Area:* 180 sq. miles/465 sq. km. *Total population:* About 42,000, of whom about 66% are foreigners. *Capital;* Andorra la Vella (16,200). *Language:* Catalan. *Religion:* Roman Catholic.

Constitution: Andorra has existed as an independent principality since 1278. It is now ruled by two co-princes, the Spanish bishop of Urgell and the president of the French Republic.

Executive and legislature: The permanent delegate of the French co-prince to Andorra is the prefect of the Pyrénées Orientales, resident in Perpignan. The delegate of the bishop is his vicar-general, resident in La Seu d'Urgell. Both delegates are represented in Andorra by locally resident civil servants (*veguers*). Under the Political Reform Law approved in November 1981, a true head of government (*cap del govern*) was inaugurated, and the former first and second syndics lost their executive functions and were redesignated as syndic and subsyndic, respectively. The General Council of the Valleys sits for four-year terms; its membership was expanded to 28 by splitting the former joint parish of Andorra la Vella and Les Escaldes-Engordany (which together account for 70% of the population) into separate parishes. Women were enfranchised in 1970 and were permitted to stand for public office in 1973. Second-generation Andorrans were permitted to vote in 1971; first-generation Andorrans were given that right in 1977. The president of the Council is the syndic, assisted by the subsyndic, both of whom are elected by the Council, but are not members of it. In an effort at institutional reform, in January 1982 the General Council appointed an Executive Council for the first time. *Head of government (cap del govern):* Josep Pintat Solens.

Local government: Seven parishes are administered by municipal authorities (*comúns*) of about 10 members. Each *comú* elects a senior and junior consul as mayor. Villages are administered by *quarts*.

Judicial system: Civil law is exercised in the first instance by four civil judges (*batlles*), two appointed by each co-prince. The litigant may apply to a judge appointed by either. Appeals are heard by the appeal judge, who is appointed for life by the two co-princes alternately. Final appeal is to the Supreme Court of Andorra in Perpignan or to the court at Urgell. Criminal law is administered by the Tribunal des Corts, consisting of two members of the Council, the *batlles*, the two *veguers* and the appeal judge; it is based on the French and Spanish legal codes.

ECONOMY

Main agricultural products are cereals, potatoes, vegetables and tobacco. Lead, stone, alum, timber and iron are also produced. Sheep-rearing and tourism—between six and seven million visitors in 1984—are the main industries. As there are no customs duties, apart from 3% on the invoice price of exports, Andorra has become a great market for European goods. There is no income tax, sales tax or death duty, and only a 5% levy on alcohol and motor fuels.

SOCIAL SECURITY

Andorra's first social-security scheme was introduced in 1966 to cover the 4,000 Andorran, 3,500 Spanish and 500 French employees in the country. Its annual cost is met by a return of half the profits on the sale of French stamps in the principality. A new modern clinic, primarily for maternity care, provides mainly free services. There is also a private clinic and there are several resident doctors and dentists as well as ambulance and fire services.

EDUCATION

Primary schools teach mainly in French and Spanish. The General Council has constructed primary schools in the nine parishes and a secondary school in Andorra la Vella, all teaching in Catalan. Previously, children were compelled to go to Barcelona or Toulouse for secondary education. Whereas in the past all teachers were supplied by France and Spain, the Council now reserves the right of selecting its teachers from any nationality. There were 305 teachers in 1982. In 1983, the principality's 18 schools had 8,356 pupils.

MASS MEDIA

The press: The first Andorran weekly, *Poble Andorra*, began publication in 1974. It has a current circulation of 3,000. The only Catalan magazines are *Serra d'Or*, published by the Catalan Monks of Montserrat in Catalonia, *Vida Nova*, published in Montpellier, and the skiing quarterly *Neu*, published in Barcelona.

Broadcasting: In 1984 Radio Andorra was founded. It is Andorran-owned and replaces two stations, one French and one Spanish, that closed in 1981. In 1984 there were approximately 4,000 television sets and 7,000 radios in use.

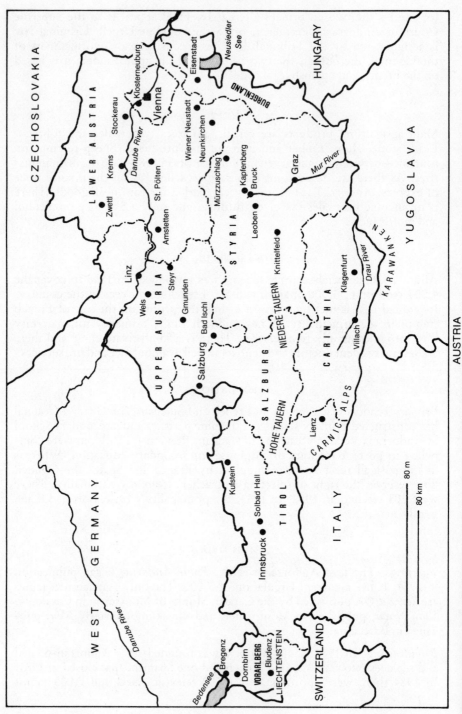

AUSTRIA

Features: Austria is essentially an Alpine country, although it contains sections of other major European physical regions. North of the Danube is an area of rolling granite uplands and elevations of 1,200–2,500 ft/365–760 m. and incised valleys. South of the Danube is the Alpine foreland, which is covered with glacial material and contains a number of lakes. The loess-covered Vienna basin, an eastern continuation of this region, provides a lowland break between the Alps and the Carpathians. Southeast is the Styrian lowland, centered on Graz. The largest geographical region is the Alpine zone, with Vienna and Salzburg standing on its northern edge. Variations between limestone, sandstone and crystalline rocks give the variations in scenery for which the Alps are famous. Heights of over 10,000 ft/3,000 m. are common, and the only major areas of level ground are to be found along the river valleys.

The most fertile areas are the loess regions of the Vienna and Styrian basins, and some parts of the Alpine foreland area; in the Alpine zone agriculture is concentrated on the alluvial and glacial fans and terraces of the latitudinal valleys. In the mountainous areas, however, there is much summer pasture. Principal natural resources are hydroelectric power, oil (from a field in the east), lignite and iron ore (Styria and Linz). Industry is concentrated mainly around Vienna, Salzburg and Linz, and in Styria.

Area: 32,355 sq. miles/83,850 sq. km. *Mean max. and min. temperatures:* Vienna (48° N, 16° 30′ E; 660 ft/200 m.) 75°F/24°C (July), 26°F/−3°C (Jan.); Innsbruck (47° 30′ N, 11° 30′ E; 1,900 ft/580 m.) 78°F/26°C, 20°F/−7°C; Graz (47° N, 15° 30′ E; 1,200 ft/370 m.) 87°F/31°C, 10°F/−12°C. *Relative humidity:* Vienna 82%; Innsbruck 87%; Graz 84%. *Mean annual rainfall:* Vienna 59 in./1,500 mm.; Innsbruck 34 in./860 mm.; Graz 34 in./860 mm.

Total population: (1984 est.) 7,600,000. *Chief towns and populations:* (1981) VIENNA (1,580,600), Graz (247,150), Linz (208,700), Salzburg (140,000), Innsbruck (123,100). *Distribution:* In 1981 about 30% of the population lived in municipalities and communes of over 120,000 inhabitants. *Language:* 99% of the population speaks German, and minorities speak Czech, Croat and Slovene. *Religion:* 89% Roman Catholic, 6% Protestant.

CONSTITUTIONAL SYSTEM

Constitution: Austria is a federal republic. The 1929 constitution was reintroduced in 1945 unaltered. *Head of state:* President Dr. Rudolf Kirschshläger. *Head of government:* Federal Chancellor Dr. Fred Sinowatz (Socialist Party of Austria).

Executive: The federal president is elected by popular vote for six years. Although invested with special emergency powers, he normally acts on the authority of the government. The government is composed of chancellor, vice chancellor and ministers. The president selects the chancellor from the party with the greatest representation in the National Council and appoints the other ministers on the chancellor's advice. Ministers need not be members of the National Council and must resign after a personal vote of no confidence.

Legislature: Legislative power rests with the National Council (Nationalrat), which is composed of 183 members elected for four years by all Austrians over 19 by proportional representation, and the Federal Council (Bundesrat). The latter is composed of 63 members representing the Länder. Legislation originates exclusively in the Nationalrat. The Bundesrat has delaying powers but no power of veto over legislation, except in matters relating to its own composition. *Referendum:* The constitution provides for the use of the referendum. Further, any petition to the government having the support of 200,000 electors must be laid by the government before the National Council.

Political parties: The two main parties are the Catholic-conservative Austrian People's party and the Socialist party of Austria. The only other party represented in the Nationalrat is the liberal Freedom party of Austria. There are four other small parties—the Communist party of Austria, which upholds a policy of strict neutrality and good relations with the Soviet Union and bordering Soviet-bloc countries; the Austrian Alternative List, advocating an antinuclear policy and connected to the Green party in West Germany; the National Democratic party of Austria, advocating extremely right-wing policies; and the United Green party of Austria.

Election results:

| | 1979 | | 1983 | |
Party	Percentage of poll	Seats	Percentage of poll	Seats
People's party	41.9	77	43.22	81
Socialist party	51.0	95	47.65	90
Freedom party	6.1	11	4.98	12

Leading political figures: Austrian People's party—Dr. Alois Mock and Dr. Michael Graff. Socialist party—Dr. Fred Sinowatz (Federal Chancellor).

Local government: Each *Land* has its own parliament (*Landtag*) elected in the same way as the Nationalrat. The Landtag elects its own government (*Landesregierung*), consisting of the governor (*Landeshauptmann*) and his councillors (*Landesräte*), which is responsible to the Landtag. The Landeshauptmann acts in a dual capacity as chief provincial officer for the central administration, and as Land premier. The administration of the Land is the responsibility of prefectures (*Bezirkshauptmannschaften*), composed of civil servants and of the mayors and executive committees responsible to elected communal councils.

Judicial system: The constitution provides for the separation of the judiciary from the legislative and administrative authorities. Professional judges are appointed by the president on the recommendation of the minister of justice and may be neither dismissed nor transferred. Some cases are heard by non-professional magistrates (*Schöffen*). The lowest courts are the local courts (*Bezirksgerichte*), which are competent in minor civil cases and cases involving minor misdemeanors. All other civil cases and criminal cases involving sentences up to 10 years are heard by the provincial and district courts (*Landes-* and *Kreisgerichte*). These also act as appeal courts for the Bezirksgerichte. The more serious criminal cases are heard by the jury courts (*Geschworenengerichte*), composed of three judges and eight jurors; the jury determines the sentence together with the judges. The four higher provincial courts (*Oberlandsgerichte*) sit with three judges and hear appeals from the lower courts in civil and criminal cases. The final court of appeal for civil and criminal cases, from both the commercial courts (*Handelsgerichte*) and the juvenile courts (*Jugendgerichte*), is the Supreme Court (*Oberster Gerichtshof*) sitting with five judges. The Constitutional Court (*Verfassungsgerichtshof*) deals with all matters concerning the interpretation of the constitution and with disputes between the Länder and the central government, and examines the legality of administration and legislation. There is no death penalty.

RECENT HISTORY

After World War II, Austria was occupied by the United States, France, the Soviet Union and Britain. An abortive Communist putsch took place in 1950. In May 1955 Austria regained its independence under the Austrian State treaty, and in October 1955 opted for permanent neutrality. Austria was a founder-member of EFTA and as such is linked in a free trade area with the EC. The Socialists came to power in 1970 and have remained in office since.

Defense: The federal president is commander-in-chief of the armed forces. The State Treaty forbids Austria the possession of atomic, biological and chemical weapons, missiles, and heavy bombers. Compulsory national service for all men between 18 and 50 lasts for six months. The defense forces of Austria totaled about 50,000 in 1984; the army numbered about 45,300 and the air force 4,700. The Austrian air force is an integral part of the defense forces. The 1982 defense budget was Sch 12.86 billion ($870 million), which represented 1.1% of GNP. In 1984, the defense budget totaled Sch 14.844 billion ($740 million).

ECONOMY

Background: In the 1950s, the base of the Austrian economy shifted from agriculture to industry, and in the process a consistently high rate of economic growth was achieved. The movement of the working population from agriculture to industry (especially manufacturing) and services was accompanied by greater diversification of industry. After a boom in 1960, price-rises accelerated, and in 1964–65 short- and long-term countermeasures were introduced. Budgetary policy was tightened and a more liberal import policy adopted.

From 1980 to 1982, the average annual growth rate of GNP at constant prices was 3.9%. The main growth industries in recent years have been iron and steel, hydroelectric power, electrical engineering, paper and wood processing, and building. The origin of GDP at factor cost in 1982 was:

Sector	Percentage
Agriculture	4
Industry	39
Services	57
GDP	100

Industrial production increased by over 3.0% in volume over 1970–82 (compared to 5.4% during 1960–70); agricultural production by 1.5% (1.2% during 1960–70). The main agricultural products are cereals, potatoes, sugar beets, wine, cattle and pigs.

Foreign trade: There was a balance of payments surplus in 1982 of $300 million. Exports of manufactured products accounted in 1982 for 84% of total exports, the remainder consisting of raw materials and energy 11%, and food, tobacco and beverages 5%. Imports in 1982 were: manufactured products 65% of total imports, raw materials and energy 19%, and food, tobacco and beverages 7%. Exports amounted to 17% of GNP and imports to 22%. Industrial market economies received 67% of Austrian exports, East European countries 12% and developing economies 18%. The relative shares of imports were 69%, 11% and 17% respectively.

Employment: The total labor force in 1980 was 3.1 million, of whom 18% were employed in agriculture, 37% in industry and 45% in services. In 1983, unemployment averaged 4.5%. The government, which advocates a policy of full employment, has instituted a number of job-creating measures.

Price and wage trends: From 1970 to 1982 consumer prices rose by about 6.1%. In 1981 the hourly wage of industrial and building workers in the Vienna region was $3.75, largely due to negotiated adjustments and shortage of labor.

Consumption: Private consumption rose steeply in 1979 (9%); it was 3% in 1978 and 11% in 1977. Private consumption accounted for 57% of GNP in 1982 and public consumption for 19%. Public consumption rose by 5.4% in 1970–82, compared with increases of 3.9% during 1960–70.

SOCIAL SECURITY

The Ministry of Social Administration supervises health, pensions and accident insurance and directly administers unemployment insurance through provincial and local unemployment offices.

Health insurance: Insurance with funds is compulsory for employees earning Sch 2,105 or more a month, the self-employed (except in agriculture), apprentices and pensioners. There are special funds for railway employees, public employees and the agricultural self-employed. There is a voluntary affiliation for noncovered residents. All funds are self-governing bodies managed by elected representatives of insured persons and employers. Financing is provided by employees and employers. Maximum earnings for contribution and benefit purposes are Sch 18,600 a month. This is subject to automatic annual adjustment for changes in national-average covered earnings. The government provides 50% of cash maternity benefits. Pension insurance institutes contribute 10.5% of pensions paid for medical insurance of pensioners. Medical benefits are provided without limit, usually by services under contract to the funds. Patients pay Sch 5 per prescription and up to 20% of dental care; there is some cost sharing for appliances. Exceptions are made for patients of limited means. Employers pay 100% of earnings for the first four to 10 weeks for wage earners; and six to 12 weeks (plus four additional weeks at 50%) for salaried employees, according to worker's length of service in the establishment. Thereafter, sick funds pay 50% of covered earnings. Employers are reimbursed by the sick funds for the full cost of benefits paid under the 1974 legislation (cash benefits for wage earners). Maternity benefits are 100% of earnings, paid for eight weeks before and eight weeks after childbirth (12 weeks after in special cases) and a lump-sum maternity grant of Sch 1,000. Dependents receive the same medical benefits as the insured, except that they pay 10% of costs during first four weeks of hospitalization (except for maternity). A housewife receives the same maternity care and nursing benefits as an insured woman; the maternity grant is subject to a minimum contribution period by the insured.

Accident insurance: Benefits are paid by the General Accident Insurance Institute. There are separate institutes for the agricultural and nonagricultural self-employed, railway employees and public employees. Contributions are collected by sick funds, which pass them on to accident insurance institutes. Accident insurance covers all employed and self-employed persons, students and apprentices. Employers pay 1.5% of payroll. The self-employed pay flat annual amounts. The Family Allowance Equalization Fund reimburses Work Injury Funds for accident insurance of students. The maximum earnings for contribution and benefit purposes are Sch 22,800 a month. This is subject to automatic annual adjustment for changes in national-average covered earnings. Temporary disability benefit is provided by the sickness funds in the form of ordinary sickness benefits. The employer pays 100% of earnings for at least 30 weeks. Thereafter, for permanent disability, the insured receives a pension from the accident institute amounting, for employed persons, to two-thirds of average earnings during the last year plus a supplement of 20% of total disability pension, with supplements of 10% for each child under 18 (26 if a student, no limit if an invalid) up to a maximum of Sch 1,050 for each child, and an allowance of 50% of pension if the insured is in need of constant attendance. For partial disability, a proportion of the full pension in paid corresponding to loss of earning capacity (converted into a lump sum if it is less than 25% of the full pension). Widows' pensions, also payable to dependent widowers, amount to 40% of the insured's earnings if she (or he, if dependent widower) is aged 60 or invalid; otherwise, 20%. Orphan's pensions are 20–30% of earnings. Other eligible survivors may receive 20% of earnings.

Pensions insurance: This covers compulsorily all wage earners and salaried employees, for whom there are separate but similar systems, as well as the self-

11

employed (except in agriculture) and apprentices. There are special systems for the agricultural self-employed, miners, notaries and public employees. Contributions are collected by sick funds, which transmit them to pension insurance institutes, and maintain contribution records for individual workers. These autonomous institutes are managed by elected representatives of the insured and employers. Wage earners and salaried employees, respectively, pay 9.75% of earnings; the employer pays 11.35% of payroll. The government pays any deficits and the cost of income-tested allowance.

Old-age pensions are paid at 65 for men (60 for women); they are paid at 60 (for men) and 55 (for women) after a year of sickness or unemployment. One hundred and eighty months of contribution, including 12 months in the last three years, are required. Pensions are also paid after 35 years of contribution (with 24 months in the last three years).

Pensions are reduced by any earnings greater than Sch 5,369 a month (as automatically adjusted) or Sch 2,878 for early retirees. Bonuses of one month's pension are paid twice a year. Old-age pensions amount to 30% of average earnings in the last five years, or if higher, the last 60 months before age 45. Up to 10% is added if pension plus supplements is below 50% of earnings. The maximum pension is 79.5% of covered earnings. Other supplements are for constant attendance (50% of pension with a monthly minimum of Sch 2,110 and a monthly maximum of Sch 2,533) and for each child (5% of earnings).

Widow's or dependent widower's pensions are 60% of basic pension of insured. Orphan's pensions are 40–60% of the widow's or dependent widower's pension, payable to each orphan under age 18 (26 if a student, without limit if an invalid). Maximum survivor pensions are 110% of the pension of the insured. The income-tested allowance can raise the survivor pension to Sch 4,173 a month plus Sch 1,558 for orphans or Sch 2,341 for a full orphan under the age of 24; thereafter, an eligible orphan gets Sch 2,767 and a full orphan Sch 4,173 a month.

Unemployment insurance: This covers all employed persons earning Sch 2,105 or more a month, and apprentices; it excludes public employees. There is a special system for construction workers. The employer pays 2% of payroll; the insured person pays 1.5% of earnings. The government pays any deficit and cost of emergency assistance. Benefits are about 30% to 60% of earnings, inversely according to 43 wage classes. The maximum benefit is Sch 6,192 a month, plus a housing allowance (Sch 30 a month). There is a Sch 420 per month supplement for each dependent, up to a maximum of 80% of the insured's earnings. Benefits are payable, after a three-day waiting period, for up to 12 weeks, 20 weeks (if there were 52 weeks of coverage in the last 24 months), or 30 weeks (if there were 156 weeks of coverage in the last five years). Unemployment assistance is available for the needy unemployed citizen when insurance benefits have been exhausted; this assistance is 92% to 100% of unemployment benefit, according to the number of dependents.

Other benefits: The Ministry of Finance administers the family allowance scheme through its Family Allowances Equalization Fund. The scheme covers all permanent residents with one or more children; there is a special

12

system for most public employees. It is financed by the insured (through a portion of income tax or land tax), the employers (5% of payroll) and government. Family allowances are paid at the monthly rate of Sch 1,000 a month for each child up to age 11, thereafter Sch 1,050 a month, Sch 2,100 for a permanently disabled child. A lump-sum grant of Sch 8,000 is paid for each birth and the same sum after the child's first birthday.

EDUCATION

The Federal Ministry of Education and the Arts has control over primary and secondary schools. Higher education and research are under the control of the Federal Ministry of Science and Research. In each of the nine federal districts, provincial boards (*Landesschulräte*) oversee education in the district schools. Education is free and compulsory from the age of six to 15.

Primary education: This is given in the *Volksschule*. In the first four years of "basic school" (*Grundschule*), all children receive the same education. Those not admitted to secondary education go on to the *Hauptschule* for four more years, where they receive a general and practical education in preparation for vocational training. Admission to the Hauptschule is dependent upon the satisfactory completion of the fourth year of Grundschule and a certificate stating that the pupil is capable of attending the Hauptschule. There is provision for a ninth year of compulsory schooling: a one-year polytechnic course to consolidate basic general education with a special emphasis on the future occupation of those who neither remain at primary school nor take intermediate or secondary education. This course is organized either as an adjunct to primary or vocational schools, or as a separate school.

Secondary education: Admission to secondary schools is dependent upon the successful completion of the Grundschule and passing an entrance examination. Secondary education generally lasts for nine years—four years in the lower and five in the upper divisions. Secondary schools are of four main categories: the arts grammar school (*Gymnasium*); the science grammar school (*Realgymnasium*); the domestic science college (*Wirtschaftskundliches Realgymnasium*) for girls; and special categories of general secondary schools. The latter include the *musisch-pädagogisches Realgymnasium*, which admits pupils who have successfully completed primary education for five-year courses, preparing them for entry into teacher training colleges and social service occupations; the intermediate grammar school (*Aufbaugymnasium* and *Aufbaurealgymnasium*), which provides a one-year transition grade and a five-year upper division for pupils who have successfully completed Volksschule and wish to attain secondary education standards; the grammar school for employed persons (*Gymnasium* and *Realgymnasium für Berufstätige*), which provides 10 half-yearly courses for persons over 18 who have completed vocational education or are employed. Other special secondary schools provide courses for noncommissioned officers and physically handicapped children. All secondary education terminates with a leaving examination (*Reifeprüfung*), which is the qualification for entry into the universities and the institutes of higher education. Since 1977–78, some trade-oriented or career-oriented university courses have been open to all Austrians who have professional experience and are over the age of 24.

13

Special education: There are special schools, organized either as separate institutions or attached to primary schools, for mentally or physically handicapped children, as well as some sanatorium schools.

Technical and vocational education: There are four types of vocational school: part-time, intermediate, secondary and those for social work. For those serving apprenticeships in commerce and trade, attendance is compulsory at a part-time vocational school (*berufsbildende Pflichtschule*). Intermediate schools (*berufsbildende mittlere Schulen*) generally admit as students those who have completed primary school and passed the entrance examination. Courses last from one to four years. Trade, technical, and arts and crafts schools have four-year courses ending either with a final proficiency examination (*Abschlussprüfung*) or—after a special course—the master craftsman's examination (*Meisterprüfung*). Other schools exist for domestic science, business and commerce and for social workers. In the last case, courses last from one to two years, and students must be at least 18. Secondary schools (*berufsbildende höhere Schulen*) have the same entrance qualifications as the berufsbildende mittlere Schulen; courses last for five years and end, like those at the secondary schools, with the Reifeprüfung, which qualifies the pupil to study a related discipline in a higher educational institute. The School for Social Work (*Lehranstalt für gehobene Sozialberufe*) offers courses lasting four semesters to students who have passed the Reifeprüfung.

University and higher education: Austria has 20 institutions of university standard empowered to grant degrees of equivalent standing. All are self-governing public institutions. The four universities proper—Vienna, Graz, Salzburg and Innsbruck—are run on the principle of freedom of studies, but attendance at a certain number of lectures is obligatory. There are two technological universities, in Vienna and in Graz. There are 14 other specialized institutes, each with university status; these include schools of agriculture, veterinary medicine and commerce, all in Vienna; a school of mining in Loeben; a university for educational studies at Klagenfurt; a Hochschule for industrial design at Linz; the Hochschule für Angewandte (applied studies) in Vienna; a university for economics at Vienna; and the Johannes Kepler University at Linz. In addition, there are three academies of music—in Vienna, Salzburg and Graz—and one each of fine arts and applied art, both in Vienna. Students must meet the costs of university fees. Scholarships are available.

Educational Institutions, 1983–84:

	Institutions	Staff	Students
Primary	3,775	32,094	359,908
General secondary	1,714	50,694	524,067
Compulsory vocational	1,183	22,009	377,205
Teacher training:			
second level	45	517	8,366
third level	26	1,431	8,838
Universities and other higher			
schools*	18	9,414	134,621

* 1982–83 figures. Source: Austrian Office of Central Statistics.

14

Adult education: This is provided mainly by adult education regional and local centers. In addition, there are a few public boarding schools maintained by the church and the trade unions. In 1979 there were over 426 public libraries.

MASS MEDIA

The press (1983):

Dailies: Kurier, Vienna, independent, 428,646, *Neue Kronen-Zeitung*, Vienna, ind., 856,667, *Arbeiter-Zeitung*, Vienna, organ of Socialist party, 67,940; *Kleine Zeitung*, Graz, ind., 146,988; *Oberösterreichische Nachrichten*, Linz, ind., 94,349; *Neue Zeit*, Graz, Socialist, 78,229, *Wiener Zeitung*, Vienna, official government paper, 50,000; *Die Presse*, Vienna, ind. liberal, 67,838; *Südost Tagespost*, Graz, organ of People's party, 45,300; *Tiroler Tageszeitung*, Innsbruck, ind., 90,900; *Salzburger Nachrichten*, Salzburg, ind., 64,758; *Volkstimme*, Vienna, organ of Communist party, 41,361 (all weekday sales).

Periodicals: Neue Illustrierte Wochenschau (w), Vienna, illustrated, 158,600; *AT Auto-Touring* (f), Vienna, motoring, 726,100; *Die neue IW-Internationale Wirtschaft*, Vienna, economics, 10,300; *Niederösterreichische Nachrichten*, Vienna (w), 135,385; *Oberösterreichische Rundschau*, Linz (w), 112,500; *Wiener Wochenblatt*, Vienna, 91,000; *Samstag*, Vienna (w), 117,500; *Wochenpresse*, Vienna, news magazine, 48,988; *Austria-Ski*, Innsbruck, journal of the Austrian Skiing Association, 60,000; *Die Frau*, Vienna, women's weekly magazine, 85,711; *Hör Zu*, Vienna, radio, TV, and entertainment weekly, 155,100.

Broadcasting: Popular demand for reform of the Austrian Broadcasting Corporation (Österreichische Rundfunk GmbH), a state-supported private company, in particular to free it from the political appointments of the coalition period, led to a new law governing the corporation from January 1, 1967. The supreme authority of the corporation is a convention on which both Federal and Länder governments are represented. This body appoints a board of directors representing the nine Länder, religion, science, art, education and sport, and the main parties (proportionately) in the Nationalrat. The board chooses the director-general and departmental directors of the corporation. None of these may concurrently hold any political office, and the director-general must not have held any such office in the five years prior to appointment. Proportional broadcasting time is given to the parties represented in the Nationalrat. Daily commercial broadcasting is limited to 20 minutes on TV and two hours on radio.

There are two television channels; they broadcast on average seven to 10 hours daily. In 1983 there were 572 radio transmitters; there were two national programs and an overseas program (on shortwave), as well as 10 local programs. In 1983 there were 864 television transmitters. There were 2,341, 223 registered television receivers and 2,524, 315 radio receivers.

BELGIUM, THE NETHERLANDS AND LUXEMBOURG (BENELUX)

BELGIUM

GEOGRAPHY

Features: Belgium may be divided into a series of NE–SW bands. Southeast is a continuation of the low plateau and scarplands of the Province of Luxembourg. To the north lie the Ardennes, a dissected plateau that is a western continuation of the German Rhine uplands; at its greatest elevation it reaches nearly 2,000 ft/610 m., but much is no more than 1,000 ft (Low Ardenne). The narrow but deep Sambre-Meuse Valley, following the line of the coalfield outcrop, is marked by a series of important industrial towns and marks a divide between the Ardennes and the lower plateau areas to the north—Hainaut, Brabant, and Hesbaye, largely loess-covered chalk areas of about 250 ft/75 m. that slope gradually to the lower lands of Flanders to the north. Flanders consists of an inner, undulating, partly sandy plain, and an outer flat maritime plain immediately behind the coastal dunes. Finally, in the north lies the area of coarse gravels and sands known as the Campine (Kempenland), drained by the Scheldt River. This was largely a waste area until reclamation was undertaken in the 19th century.

Agriculture is mainly concentrated in the low loess-covered plateau and in Flanders. The chief mineral is coal, worked in the Sambre-Meuse Valley and the Campine coalfield. Industry is concentrated around both these coalfields and around Brussels and Antwerp.

Area: 11,780 sq. miles/30,500 sq. km. *Mean max. and min. temperatures:* Brussels (51° N, 4° 30′ E; 330 ft/100 m.) 73°F/23°C (July), 31°F/–1°C (Jan.); Ostend (51° N, 3° E; 13 ft/4 m.) 69°F/21°C (Aug.), 33°F/1°C (Feb.). *Relative humidity:* Brussels 94%; Ostend 86%. *Mean annual rainfall:* Brussels 33 in./840 mm.; Ostend 31 in./790 mm.

POPULATION

Total population: (1984) 9.9 million. *Chief towns and populations of cities proper:* (1980) BRUSSELS (1,008,715), Ghent (242,609), Charleroi (223,071), Liège (222,160), Antwerp (195,689). *Distribution:* In 1981 about 19% of the population lived in communes with more than 150,000 inhabitants. *Langugages:* Both French (Walloon) and Dutch (Flemish) are official languages. There are German-speaking minorities of about 100,000 around Eupen and Malmédy in the eastern part of Liège. In 1984, the Flemish-speaking provinces (East and West Flanders, Antwerp, Limburg and Northern Brabant) had about 5,643,000 inhabitants and the Walloon provinces (Hainaut, Namur, Liège, Luxembourg and Southern Brabant) 4,257,000. Brussels is officially bilingual but has a strong French-speaking majority. In all, the Flemings form about 55% of the total population and the Walloons about 44%. Both population density and birthrate are higher in the Flemish-speaking areas. *Religion:* The population is overwhelmingly Roman Catholic.

Constitution: Belgium is a constitutional monarchy with a constitution dating from 1831. As of 1971, Belgium's constitution was rewritten to provide the Dutch-speaking, French-speaking and German-speaking communities with powers in economic and cultural matters at the regional level. The present parliament was elected in 1981. *Head of state:* King Baudouin. *Head of government:* Prime Minister Dr. Wilfried Martens (Christian Social party, [CVP]).

Executive: Power is vested in the king and his ministers. The king may dissolve or prorogue parliament. He appoints and dismisses his ministers and implements legislation by royal decree, but such acts are only effective if countersigned by a minister, thereby ensuring ultimate governmental responsibility. The government cannot function unless supported by a majority of members in both houses.

Legislature: Legislative powers are vested equally in the Chamber of Representatives and the Senate. Either house may introduce legislation, but this becomes effective only when passed by both houses and promulgated by the king. The Chamber of Representatives consists of 212 members elected for four years by proportional representation. The Senate has 183 members, two-thirds of whom are elected on the same basis as the lower house; the remaining third consists of individuals elected by provincial councils and others who are chosen or coopted by the Senate itself.

Political parties: Belgium has three traditional parties: the Roman Catholic-conservative Christian Social party, with a Flemish section (CVP) and a Walloon section (PSC); the Socialist party—French-speaking wing (PS) and Fleming-speaking wing (SP); and the liberal Freedom and Progress party (PVV). The smaller parties are the Communist party; Vlaams Blok (Flemish Nationalist party); Volksunie (People's Union [VU]), a party representing Flemish nationalist interests; two parties representing Walloon interests, the French-speaking Front (FDP) and the Walloon Federalists (RW); the German-speaking party (PDB); the Parti Féministe Unifié (PFU)—Vereenigde Feministiche Partij (VFP); Parti Réformateur Libéral (PRL); and Union Démocratique pour le Respect du Travail (UDRT). The current Martens government is a coalition of four parties, PSC, CVP, PRL, and PVV.

Election results (1981):

Party	% of poll	Chamber of Representatives Seats	Senate Seats
CVP	19.3	43	22
PSC	7.1	18	8
PS	12.7	35	18
SP	12.4	26	13
PRL	8.6	24	11
PVV	12.9	28	14
VU	9.8	20	10
FDF/RW	4.2	8	4
Communist party	2.3	2	1
UDRT	2.7	3	1
Others	8.0	5	4
Total	100.0	212	106

In the Senate there are an additional 75 members, 50 elected by provincial councils and 25 chosen by the elected members.

Leading political figures: CVP—Dr. Wilfried Martens (prime minister), Léo Tindemans (minister of foreign affairs). PSC—Charles-Ferdinand Nothomb (deputy prime minister, minister of the interior, and minister of the civil service). PRL—Jean Gol (deputy prime minister, minister of justice and institutional reform, and minister of foreign trade). PVV—Frans Grootjans (deputy prime minister, minister of finance, and minister for the middle classes).

Local government: Each province elects a provincial council for a period of four years, headed by a governor who is appointed and dismissed by the king. From among its own members the council elects a permanent deputation to manage its everyday affairs. Each province is divided into several administrative districts (*arrondissements*), each headed by a district commissioner appointed by the governor, who supervises all communes within the arrondissements having less than 5,000 inhabitants. The communes (*communes*) are administered by town councils, elected for six years, which in turn elect their aldermen. Each mayor is appointed by the king on the basis of proposals submitted by the town council.

Judicial system: The supreme authorities are the five regional civil and criminal courts of appeal, the five regional labor courts, and the supreme Court of Cassation (Supreme Court of Justice) in Brussels. A law passed in 1967, in effect since 1970, reorganized Belgium's judicial system. The nine provinces of Belgium are divided into judicial districts. The four levels of the judiciary are the canton, district, regional and national courts. The courts of the justices of the peace and the police tribunals are the lowest courts; next are the district courts, which include the labor tribunals, the tribunals of the first instance and the tribunals of commerce; then there are the regional courts of appeal and labor courts; and finally the national Court of Cassation. There is also a military court in Brussels.

RECENT HISTORY

After the second German violation of its neutrality and its subsequent occupation in World War II, Belgium signed the Brussels Treaty (later to become the WEU) in March 1948 with the Netherlands, Luxembourg, Britain and France, and in 1949 became a founder member of NATO. Belgium has also been a leading exponent of European integration through its membership of Benelux and the EC. In 1922, Belgium signed a 50-year customs agreement with Luxembourg (Belgo-Luxembourg Economic Union—BLEU). Belgium's colonial disengagement from the Congo and the former Trust Territory of Rwanda-Urundi involved bloodshed in all three countries. The communist-inspired strikes of 1947–48, growing strife between Walloons and Flemings, frequent government changes and strikes by doctors and police have troubled the domestic scene in postwar Belgium. In 1966 there were attempts to expel the Walloon elements of the University of Louvain from Flemish territory. In June of the same year it was decided to transfer SHAPE and the HQ of NATO's Central Command to Brussels. By constitutional amendment in 1980, three cultural communities—the Dutch, French and German—were recognized, and four linguistic areas were established, the fourth including the 19 bilingual boroughs of Brussels. Linguistic parity in the central government was achieved in 1973. In 1983 regional self-governing councils were established in Wallonia and Flanders.

Defense: The sovereign is titular commander-in-chief of the armed forces. Military service lasts eight to 10 months. Total armed forces number 89,600, of whom fewer than half are conscripts: army 60,000, air force 20,100, navy 4,400 and medical service 5,100. The air force and navy are assigned to or reserved for NATO service. The 1982 defense budget was BF121.76 billion ($3.56 billion), representing 3.3% of GNP.

ECONOMY

Background: Belgium is a highly industrialized country. In 1959 a labor shortage and the slow rate of recovery from the 1958 recession led to the setting up of a Bureau of Economic Planning. Latterly, the problem of diversifying and increasing production has been tackled by a policy of redeployment of labor resources, heavy investment toward modernization, improvement of the competitive position of exports and continued controlled expansion of private consumption. An effort has also been made to intensify investment in underdeveloped regions that depend upon unprofitable industries. The basis of recent policy has been the Economic Expansion Laws of July 1959, offering tax exemptions, low-interest-rate loans and preferential treatment to foreign investors. To further industrial development, a National Investment Corporation was set up in 1963, authorized to invest capital in business enterprises on temporary and specially favorable terms. In the face of a shortage of investment capital (although foreign investment has remained strong) that brought on a serious crisis in public finance in 1965, subsequent policy was one of careful economy designed to keep the increase in total public expenditure below the growth in value of GNP, and to protect individual purchasing power by controlling prices and public spending.

In 1982 the Belgian GNP amounted to $119.77 billion. From 1970 to 1979 the annual average rate of growth was 2.9%. Main growth industries are chemicals, rubber, heavy metallurgical and metal products, food and beverages. In 1982 the origin of GDP at factor cost was:

Sector	Percentage
Agriculture	2
Industry	35
Services	63
GDP	100

Annual average rate of industrial growth in the period 1970–82 was 2.2%, representing a decline from the 5.5% for 1960–70. The principal industries are coal mining, coke and electricity production, oil processing, steel, textiles, mechanical engineering, non-ferrous metals, cement, food, beverages, tobacco, wood and paper. Owing to specialized farming, Belgium's agricultural industry can provide 80% of the nation's requirements. Expansion is taking place in horticulture and the production of vegetables. The main crops are sugar beets, potatoes, wheat, barley and oats.

Foreign trade; As a member of the EC, Belgium participates in the Community's free movement of goods and capital between member states as well as in its joint tariff, agriculture and transportation policies. Belgium is also a partner in the Benelux free-trade agreement and subscribes to the General Agreement on Tariffs and Trade (GATT). Since 1921, Belgium has been linked with Luxembourg in BLEU, which provides for tariff-free trade between the two countries and for a single external tariff and excise tax system, mutual acceptance of currencies, and coordinated monetary and foreign trade policies. The countries' economies are similar in many ways, although, as the larger of the partners, Belgium has suffered more from BLEU's widening trade deficit. In March 1981, BLEU was formally extended for a 10-year period. Under the new agreement, Luxembourg established its own central monetary authority, the Luxembourg Monetary Institute (LMI), and became an autonomous member of the International Monetary Fund, where it was formerly an observer.

Belgium's transportation, communications and port facilities make it the crossroads of Western Europe's international trade. Brussels is the headquarters of numerous international organizations, including the EC and NATO. Over 80% of Belgium's international trade is with industrialized countries, particularly West Germany. In the past decade it has lost some of its markets in developing countries while recently gaining more customers in the oil-rich Middle East. Trade with centrally planned economies of Eastern Europe has historically been small, but in 1980 the Soviet Union agreed to purchase $500 million worth of steel products and Belgium provided $1 billion in credit to develop the Soviet Union's 2,800-mile natural gas pipeline from Siberia to Western Europe. The credit is to be replaced with supplies of natural gas.

In 1980 BLEU's imports of goods and services amounted to 57.3% of GNP and exports to 51.5%. BLEU's main imports in 1980 were food 12%, fuels 20%, other primary commodities 10%, machinery and transport equipment 20%. The main exports in the same year were fuel, minerals and metals 14.1%, other primary commodities 12.1%, textiles and clothing 7.1%, machinery and transport equipment 2.2%. The trade deficit widened from $273 million in 1963 to $5.65 billion in 1980.

Employment: In 1980 the total working population in Belgium was 4.15 million, of whom 3% were employed in agriculture, 41% in industry, and 56% in services. Unemployment in the same year was 9.8%. There continued to be a labor shortage. Increased mechanization, an increased number of labor permits for foreign workers and a crash technical program with the aim of redirecting workers to areas with a particularly marked labor shortage were then introduced. The bulk of the 700,100 foreign workers are employed in mining and manufacturing industries.

Price and wage trends: Average hourly wages in 1981 were $5.24 for a bus driver, $6.25 for a construction worker, $3.75 for a printing press operator and $5.01 for a textile worker. The average monthly salary of a personnel manager was $2,862, of a bank teller $851 and of a secretary $992. The index of consumer prices in 1981 was 219 with 1970 = 100. The average annual rate of inflation for 1970–82 was 7.1%, as against 3.6% for 1960–70.

Consumption: In 1982 private consumption amounted to 67% of GNP at market prices and public consumption to 19%.

SOCIAL SECURITY

General supervision is exercised by the National Office of Social Security, except in the case of unemployment insurance, which is under the Ministry of Employment and Labor.

Health insurance: Contributions are collected by the National Social Security Office and benefits are paid by approved mutual benefit societies and a Public Auxiliary Fund for persons not belonging to a society. All employed persons must enroll with either a society or the Auxiliary Fund. Pensioners and other social security beneficiaries are also covered for medical benefits. There are special systems for self-employed persons, miners and seamen. The insured person contributes 1.8% of earnings for medical benefits and 1.15% of earnings for cash benefits. The employer contributes 3.8% of payroll for medical benefits and 2.2% of payroll for cash benefits. The government contributes proceeds from a 5% surcharge on automobile insurance premiums.

Accident insurance: This covers all employed persons and is administered by the Employment Accident Commission and by local accident boards and inspectors. There are special systems for public employees and seamen. The insurance is funded by the employer and the government. The employer contributes 0.3% of payroll for occupational injuries plus insurance premium, and 0.65% of payroll for occupational diseases. The government provides a subsidy for certain accidents in hazardous employment and for specified occupational diseases. Maximum earnings for temporary benefit purposes are BF689,160 a year. Widows' pensions are also payable to dependent widowers. There are provisions for orphans' pensions.

Pensions insurance: The National Social Security Office collects and distributes contributions. All employed persons and apprentices are covered, with special provision for miners and seamen. There are special systems for self-employed persons and public employees. The insurance is financed by the insured, who contributes 7% of earnings; the employer, who contributes 8.86% of payroll; and the government, which contributes annual subsidies (about 20% of expenditures in 1982). Old-age pensions are payable at age 65 (men) or 60 (women); they are payable up to five years earlier, with 5% reduction per year. Disability pensions are paid to all persons losing two-thirds of their earning capacity in their usual occupation. Survivor pensions are payable to widows and orphans.

Unemployment insurance: Local agencies handle benefit payments of unemployment insurance under the supervision of the National Employment Office. Insurance covers all employed persons and apprentices except public employees, nonboarding domestic servants, and casual and family labor. There are special systems for miners, seamen and construction workers. The insurance is financed by the insured person, who contributes 0.87% of earnings; the employer, who contributes 1.23% of payroll and the whole cost of prepension supplement; and the government, which contributes to cover any deficit, plus proceeds of special taxes on large personal incomes.

Other benefits: Family allowances are available to all gainfully occupied persons and social insurance beneficiaries with one or more children. There are special systems for public employees and self-employed persons. Families not covered under the family allowance system are eligible for means-tested allowances. These allowances are financed by childless workers, who in 1983 contributed BF900 a month; the self-employed, who contributed varying amounts according to income and occupation; the employer, who contributed 7% of payroll; and the government, which contributed subsidies to employee and self-employed programs covering any deficits. Generally, for family allowances the child must be under age 14. The income limit for means-tested allowances is BF43,074 a quarter for one child, increasing by 20% for each additional child.

EDUCATION

Freedom of education is guaranteed by the constitution. Two complete networks of educational establishments coexist: one is organized by the state and the municipalities and is generally known as the "official schools system," and 45% of the population are registered with it; the second was set up by private initiative—generally Catholic bodies—and is called the "free schools system," with which 55% of the population is registered. After a long period of rivalry between the two systems, they are now organized and state-financed along more or less identical lines. Expenditure on education increased greatly in the period 1970–80, amounting in 1980 to BF193 billion

23

($6.9 billion). Education is free and compulsory for all children between the ages of six and 18. The 1963 Language of Instruction Act mandated that teaching be provided in the language of the region. In the Brussels district the native language of the student determines the language of instruction.

Primary education: All municipalities are obliged to establish at least one primary school. Primary education lasts from the ages of six to 12, divided into three levels each of two years, and is generally completed by an examination for a certificate of primary studies.

Secondary education: All forms of secondary education begin at 12. The system is being directed toward a structure in which all pupils between 12 and 15 can study together in comprehensive secondary schools, and afterwards go on to higher secondary schools or secondary technical schools. In this period there are four major sections—humanities, science and commerce and two practical/technical streams; changes from one section to another are permitted. The system that is being replaced is that of an ordinary three-year secondary school on the one hand and six-year courses in the humanities at either state secondary schools (*athénées* for boys and *lycées* for girls) or private Catholic secondary schools (*collèges*) on the other. The six-year courses end with a certificate of humanities which is the main qualification for university entrance.

Special education: A number of institutions provide special education for physically and mentally handicapped pupils and students.

Technical education: This begins at the age of 12. The maximum six-year courses may lead to higher technical education, preparing students for very diverse professions and finalized by diplomas equivalent to university degrees in commercial sciences.

University and higher education: Belgium's growing need for executive and scientific personnel has resulted in a rapid expansion of higher education and its adaptation to modern requirements. There are state universities at Ghent and Liège and four state-subsidized private universities including the Catholic University of Louvain (Dutch and French) and the Free University of Brussels. Besides these, there are state colleges at Antwerp and Mons, agricultural colleges at Gembloux and Ghent, a polytechnic college at Mons, the State School of Veterinary Medicine in Brussels, and the Catholic university schools of St. Louis in Brussels and of Notre-Dame de la Paix in Namur. The universities are composed of five traditional faculties—philosophy and letters, law, science, medicine and applied science—as well as the schools and colleges of higher education attached to them. Courses last from four to seven (medicine) years and are generally divided into two parts, the *candidature* and the *licence*—the latter being comparable to a master's degree.

In 1980 state expenditure on scholarships was $809 million and on higher education $1.174 billion.

Educational institutions, 1981–82:

	Institutions	Students
Preschool	4,300	386,807
Primary	5,035	835,586
Secondary	2,272	849,502
Technical	250	81,816
Teacher training	169	25,293
Universities and Higher Institutions	19	95,882

Source: Belgian Education Ministry.

Adult education: There is a vast network of facilities for adult and self-education involving both public authorities and a number of private bodies. In 1982 there were 2,446 public libraries.

MASS MEDIA

The press (1984):
Dailies: Le Soir, Brussels, independent, 224,394; *Het Laatste Nieuws*, Brussels, ind., 311,068; *De Standaard/Nieuwsblad/De Gentenaar*, Brussels, Catholic, 356,875; *Het Volk*, Ghent, Catholic, 204,621; *La Meuse/La Lanterne*, Brussels/Liège, ind., 132,871; *Gazet van Antwerpen*, Antwerp, PSC, 185,448; *La Dernière Heure*, Brussels, ind. liberal, 110,000; *La Libre Belgique*, Brussels, Catholic, 188,432.

Weeklies and periodicals: Panorama/Ons Land, Antwerp, general interest, 91,000; *Le Soir illustré*, Brussels, ind. illustrated, 111,337; *Pourquoi pas?*, Brussels, news, 80,762; *Knack*, Brussels, ind. cultural magazine, 90,000; *Femmes d'aujourd'hui*, Brussels, women's, 148, 200.

Broadcasting: Belgian broadcasting is a state monopoly, funded by taxes on radio and TV receivers. Broadcasting in French is controlled by Radio-Télévision Belge de la Communauté Culturelle Française, and in Flemish by Belgische Radio en Televisie. There were approximately 2,981,497 TV receivers and 4,607,257 radio licenses in Belgium in 1983.

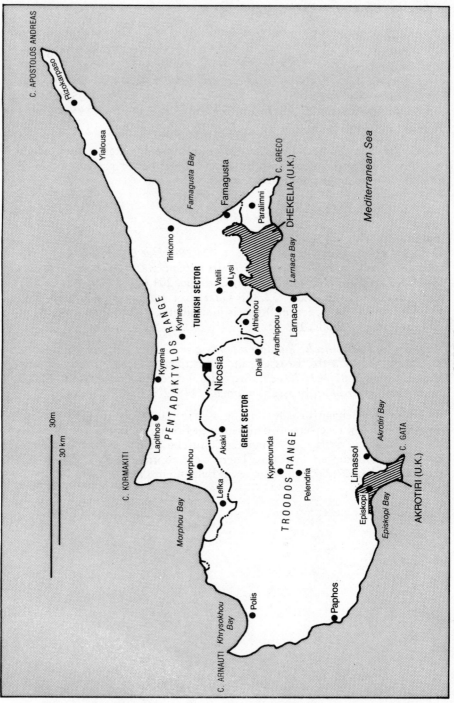

CYPRUS

CYPRUS

Features: This diamond-shaped island has a low, narrow chain of mountains in the north and a rather broader and higher range in the south, with a lowland area between. Agriculture is concentrated in the central plains; industry, of which there is little, is concentrated mainly in and around the large towns. *Area:* 3,570 sq. miles/9,300 sq. km. *Mean max. and min. temperatures:* Nicosia (35° N, 33° 30' E; 720 ft/220 m.) 97°F/36°C (July and Aug.), 42°F/6°C (Jan. and Feb.); Famagusta (35° N, 34° E; 75 ft/23 m.) 95°F/35°C, 43°F/6°C. *Relative humidity:* Nicosia 67%; Famagusta 71%. *Mean annual rainfall:* Nicosia 15 in./380 mm.; Famagusta 17 in./430 mm.

Total population: (1984) 700,000, composed of 75% Greek Cypriots, 23% Turkish Cypriots and the remainder of minorities such as Armenians and Maronites. *Main towns and populations:* (est. 1982) NICOSIA (149,100 [excluding Turkish occupied part]), Limassol (107,200), Larnaca (48,300), Famagusta (39,500), Paphos (20,800). *Language:* Both Greek and Turkish are official languages. *Religion:* About 76% of the population belongs to the Greek Orthodox Church, 19% adheres to Islam and the remainder to Armenian, Gregorian Catholic and Maronite minorities.

Constitution: Cyprus is a republic and a member of the Commonwealth since 1960. The 1960 constitution attempts to safeguard the interests of the two communities. The basic articles of the constitution cannot be amended; other articles may be amended by a two-thirds majority of the representatives of both communities in the House of Representatives; it is obligatory for all Cypriots to join either the Greek or Turkish communities. *Head of state:* President Spyros Kyprianou.

Executive: Executive authority is vested in the president, elected for five years by direct vote. He works through a Council of Ministers, who are not members of the legislature but are appointed by the executive. In January 1964, the Turkish members left the council and were replaced by Greeks. The president may veto legislation concerning foreign affairs and certain questions of security or defense, and may return part or all of other legislation for reconsideration.

Legislature: Legislative authority other than that reserved to the Communal Chambers is vested in the House of Representatives, whose 50 members are elected for five years. After the outbreak of civil strife in December 1963, the Turkish deputies ceased to attend the House, and both Greek and Turkish representatives extended the statutory tenure of office both for themselves and the executive after July 1965 for a period of one year at a time. The House of Representatives—in which only the Greeks were present—also legislated to dispense with the separate electoral rolls.

Election results: In the 1981 election, the Democratic Rally and the Progressive party of the Working People gained 12 seats each, the Democratic party eight seats and the Unified Democratic Union of the Cyprus–Socialist party three seats. In a 1982 by-election, the Democratic party increased its seats by one at the expense of the Democratic Rally. The current government is a coalition of the Democratic party and the Progressive party of the Working People.

Leading political figures: Spyros Kyprianou, president; Ezekias Papaioannou, leader of the Progressive party of the Working People; Georgios Ladas, president of the House of Representatives; Glavcos Clerides, former president and leader of the Democratic Rally; and Dr. Vassos Lyssarides, leader of the Unified Democratic Union of the Cyprus–Socialist party.

Local government: There was provision in the 1960 constitution for separate Greek and Turkish municipal councils in the five largest towns. But since the withdrawal of the Turkish members from the House of Representatives, the Greek members have legislated to unify the administration of the municipalities.

Judicial system: The lowest courts of criminal and civil jurisdiction are the six assize and six district courts. The High Court of Cyprus was amalgamated with the Supreme Constitutional Court in the period after December 1963. It now comprises a president and nine other judges. The Supreme Court was empowered under the constitution to amend, confirm or return to the House of Representatives any law or decision of the house that either the president or the vice president of the republic deemed to be discriminatory against either community. The Supreme Court is also the highest court of appeal and has final and exclusive jurisdiction in all cases. Judges are appointed by the Supreme Council of Judicature. There are also communal courts and an ecclesiastical tribunal of the Greek Orthodox church. Cyprus maintains capital punishment.

RECENT HISTORY

Cyprus became a British Crown Colony in 1925, having been administered by Britain since 1878. The constant demand of the Greek majority for Union with Greece (ENOSIS) erupted in 1955 into a campaign of violence led by the Greek underground army (EOKA). The British government imposed a state of emergency on the island until the signature of the London and Zürich agreements between Greece, Turkey, Cyprus and Britain in February

1959, providing for Cyprus to become independent. In December 1959, Archbishop Makarios was elected the island's first president and Dr. Fazil Küçük vice president. Cyprus became an independent republic in August 1960, and in March 1961 it joined the Commonwealth. In December 1963, after the Turkish rejection of Makarios' 13 points for constitutional amendment, fighting broke out between the Greek and Turkish communities, which led to the introduction of a U.N. Peacekeeping Force and a mediator.

Following more violent ethnic conflicts in 1967, the Turkish Cypriots formed the Turkish Cypriot Provisional Administration, constituting a *de facto* government. From 1967 until 1974, they withdrew from the Makarios government and formed a virtual state within a state. On July 15, 1974, the Greek Cypriot National Guard, led by Greek army officers, launched a coup against the Makarios government and installed Nikos Sampson, a right-wing extremist and former newspaper publisher, as president. Five days later Turkish troops invaded the island and occupied 39% of the national territory (1,400 sq. miles) before agreeing to a ceasefire. On July 23 Sampson resigned and the presiding officer of the Cypriot House of Representatives, Glavcos Clerides, was sworn in as acting president. On the same day the military government of Cyprus fell, and two days later the representatives of Greece and Turkey met at Geneva and reached an agreement concluding hostilities but leaving broader issues unresolved. Makarios returned to the island and resumed the presidency on December 7.

On February 13, 1975, Turkish leaders in the occupied zone proclaimed a Turkish Federated State of Cyprus, with Rauf Denktaş, as president. Eleven days later the formation of a Turkish Cypriot Legislative Assembly was announced. Archbishop Makarios died on August 3, 1977 and was succeeded by Spyros Kyprianou as acting president. In 1983, Kyprianou was reelected to a five-year term.

Defense: Under the February 1959 agreements, Britain retains full sovereignty over two military base areas, Akrotiri and Dhekelia. British sovereignty is guaranteed by a treaty between Britain, Cyprus, Greece, and Turkey, by which Cyprus undertakes not to unite with any other state, and to prohibit activity designed to promote either such a union or a partition of the island. Britain, Greece and Turkey are also signatories of a treaty of military alliance, whereby each guarantees the independence, territorial integrity and security of the Republic of Cyprus, and agrees to consult if there is a breach of these provisions. If they cannot agree on joint action, any one of them is entitled to take unilateral action with the sole aim of restoring the status quo.

The constitution provides for an army. Military service is now compulsory in the National Guard for 26 months for all Greek Cypriots between 18 and 50. The (Greek) National Guard is staffed by Greek army officers and totals some 10,000 men. The strength of the U.N. Peacekeeping Force in 1984 was 2,322. Estimated defense expenditures in 1981 were $27.3 million.

CYPRUS: TURKISH SECTOR, known as "Turkish Republic of Northern Cyprus" (TRNC). (Note: The Turkish "Kibris" was officially substituted for "Cyprus" as the English form of sector's name in 1979.)

Area: 1,400 sq. miles (3,626 sq. km.).Population: 122,000. President: Rauf R. Denktaş (National Unity party); *Prime Minister:* Mustafa Çagatay (National Unity party).

The Turkish Federated State of Cyprus was established on February 13, 1975, following the Turkish occupation of the northern 39% of the island. The state has not claimed international recognition; Denktaş has said that the Cypriot Turks are "merely reconstituting their internal administration to be ready for the birth of a federal state." The constitution was approved by the voters in a referendum held June 8, 1975, and is to remain in effect until superseded by the constitution of a proposed Federal Republic of Cyprus. It established a presidential parliamentary system headed by a popularly elected president who can serve no more than two successive five-year terms. The president appoints a prime minister from among the 40 members of the Turkish Cypriot Legislative Assembly. The Supreme Court is composed of a president and four or five additional judges.

The principal and ruling political party is the National Unity party, built upon the former National Solidarity Movement. Its current leader is the prime minister, Mustafa Çagatay. The principal opposition party is the Communal Liberation party, also known as the Socialist Salvation party. Its leaders are Alpay Durduran and Ziya Rizki. The minor parties include the Democratic People's party, led by Osman Orek; the Turkish Unity party, led by Ismail Tezer; and the Republican Turkish party, led by Ozer Özgür. In the Legislative Assembly elected in 1981, the National Unity party held 18 seats, the Communal Liberation party 13 seats, the Republican Turkish party six seats, the Democratic People's party two seats and the Turkish Unity party one seat.

The Turkish Cypriot Security Force consists of 4,000 men.

ECONOMY

Cyprus is heavily dependent upon agriculture, mining and receipts from the supply of goods and services to the British bases. The estimated GNP in 1981 was $2.21 billion and the GNP per capita $3,560, the sixth lowest in Europe but much higher than the rates for the Middle East and Turkey. In 1982 agriculture contributed about 10% of GDP and employed 25% of the active working population. The main products are wheat, barley, olives, citrus fruits, carrots, potatoes, carobs and grapes. In 1982 manufacturing industry contributed 17% of GDP and employed 16% of the active working population. Minerals account for over 40% of total domestic exports; main deposits are iron pyrites, copper, salt, asbestos. There is no heavy industry, but a wide variety of light manufacturing industries and increasing interest in the establishment of new industries and expansion of existing ones. Tourism is becoming an increasingly important source of revenue.

The main exports are mining products, fruit, vegetables and wine. In 1981 the main imports were motor vehicles, fabrics, fuels and building and construction materials. The main export markets in 1981 were the EC (39% of total exports), Britain (49%) and the Commonwealth (2%). Imports were distributed as follows: Britain 25%, the EC 43% and the Commonwealth 5%.

Health insurance: Medical benefits include free medical treatment, hospitalization, maternity care and medicine. The Ministry of Health administers the medical services. All employed and self-employed people aged 16 to 64 are covered. The insurance is funded by the insured, the employer and the government. Most employees contribute 6% of earnings, the employer contributes 6% of payroll and the government 3.5% of earnings. The government pays the remaining cost of medical care. Weekly sickness benefits are also paid.

Accident insurance: All employed persons are covered by the accident insurance scheme. The insurance is financed by the insured, the employer and the government; each contributes the same amount as under the health insurance scheme outlined above. There are temporary disability benefits and permanent grants, as well as survivor grants.

Pensions insurance: All employed and self-employed persons aged 16 to 64 are covered under this scheme, which provides old-age pensions, disability pensions and survivor pensions. The insurance scheme is financed by the insured, the employer and the government, each contributing the same amount as under the health insurance scheme described above. For old-age pensions, age 65 must be reached. Retirement is unnecessary. A widow may substitute her husband's insurance record for her own for a period prior to his death. Disability pensions are given if the insured is permanently incapacitated for work. Survivor pensions are payable to widows and orphans.

Unemployment insurance: All employed persons aged 16 to 64 are covered under this scheme, with the exception of certain categories of part-time and family employment. This scheme is financed by the insured, the employer, and the government, each contributing the same amount as under the health insurance scheme.

In 1982, 89% of the population over the age of 15 was literate. *Primary education:* This is free and compulsory from five to 11. *Secondary education:* This lasts six years. Secondary education is offered by technical schools, trade schools, the Agricultural Gymnasion, the Gymnasion-Lykeion (economics, science and classics) and the Upper School of Options, which was established in 1977. At technical schools at the secondary level education is free; at all other schools secondary education is free for the first four years. Although Cyprus has no universities, higher education is provided by vocational and technical colleges.

In the Turkish section of Cyprus, the TRNC administers the schools. Education is in two divisions—one for nursery, primary, secondary and higher education, and one for adult education.

Educational institutions, government-controlled area, 1983–84:

	Institutions	Teachers	Students
Preprimary (private and state schools)	333	546	13,960
Primary	417	2,218	46,766
Secondary (public)	67	2,237	38,741
Secondary (private)	22	369	5,330
Vocational and technical (public)	12	487	5,203
Teacher training	1	30	270
Other postsecondary	15	211	1,931

Source: Statistics and Research Department, Ministry of Finance, Nicosia.

Educational institutions, Turkish section ["Turkish Republic of Northern Cyprus"], 1982–83:

	Institutions	Teachers	Students
Nursery schools	5		
Nursery classes (attached to a primary school)	26	46	1,440
Total	31	46	1,440
Primary	165	678	19,580
Secondary and technical	39	894	12,812
Adult education	51	76	2,046
Turkish teachers' training college	1	6	143
Higher technical institution	1	26	304

Source: Office of the London Representative of the "Turkish Republic of Northern Cyprus."

MASS MEDIA

The press (1983):

Dailies (Greek): Havavgi, AKEL, Nicosia, 14,384; *Philelefthesos,* independent, moderate, Nicosia, 18,212; *Agon,* ind., right-wing, Nicosia, 7,500.

Dailies (Turkish): Halkin Sesi, ind. Turkish nationalist, Nicosia, 5,000; *Kibris Postasi,* Famagusta, 5,200.

Weeklies (Greek): Demokratiki, ind., left of center, Nicosia, 18,000; *Ergatiko Vima,* organ of Pancyprian Federation of Labor, Nicosia, 13,000; *Anexarctitos,* ind. socialist; Nicosia, 17,000.

Weeklies (Turkish): Demokratik Halk Gazetesi, Nicosia, 4,000; *Kibris (in English),* organ of the TRNC, Mersin, 4,000.

Broadcasting: In the government-controlled areas, approximately 170,000 radio receivers and 88,000 TV receivers were in use in 1983. The Cyprus Broadcasting Corporation Controls all radio and TV broadcasting in the government-controlled section. Radio transmissions are in Greek, Turkish,

English, Armenian and Arabic. Bayrak Radio and TV Corporation is an independent Turkish Cypriot company for the Turkish section. There is another Turkish TV Company, Türkiye Radyo Televizyon. The British Forces Broadcasting Service, Cyprus, broadcasts in English.

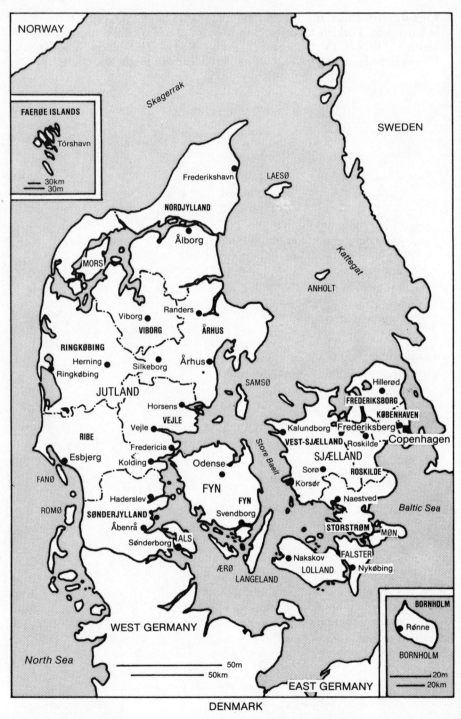

DENMARK

Features: Almost all the country lies below 500 ft/150 m. The area of greatest elevation is the north–south moraine that divides the Jutland peninsula into a rather shady and less fertile western part and a much more fertile eastern part. Eastern Jutland and the islands that constitute the rest of the country (of which some hundred are inhabited) are boulder- and clay-covered, with the exception of the granite island of Bornholm off the coast of Sweden. Apart from western Jutland, Denmark is covered mainly by soils that support an intensive agriculture. Minerals are lacking. There are modest offshore reserves of oil and natural gas. Industry is concentrated around Copenhagen and to a lesser extent Esbjerg, Odense and the other major towns. *Area:* 16,600 sq. miles/43,000 sq. km. Overseas Territories: Greenland and Faerøe Islands. *Mean max. and min. temperatures:* Copenhagen (55° 30′ N, 12° 30′ E; 40 ft/12 m.) 72°F/22°C (July), 28°F/−2°C (Jan.). *Relative humidity:* Copenhagen 84%. *Mean annual rainfall:* 23 in./580 mm.

POPULATION

Population: (1984 est.) 5.1 million. Overseas Territories: Greenland (1984) 51,000, Faerøes (1984) 45,000. *Chief towns and populations:* (1984) COPENHAGEN (1,206,622), Århus (245,565), Odense (169,183), Ålborg-Nørresundby (154,385), Esbjerg (79,694), Randers (62,232). *Distribution:* In 1981 about 85% of the population was living in towns and the remainder in rural communes. *Language:* Danish is the official language. In North Schleswig there is a German-speaking minority of 30,000. The main language of the Faerøes is Faroese, which is akin to Norwegian and Icelandic.

Religion: The overwhelming majority of the population adheres to the state Evangelical-Lutheran Church.

CONSTITUTIONAL SYSTEM

Constitution: Denmark is a constitutional monarchy. The present constitution dates from 1953. *Head of State:* Queen Margrethe II. *Head of government:* Prime Minister Poul Schlüter (Conservative People's party).

Executive: Executive authority is vested in the queen and her ministers. The queen appoints as prime minister the leader of the party likely to obtain a majority in parliament. The queen then appoints the other ministers on the advice of the prime minister. No act of the queen is valid without minister-ial responsibility. No minister may remain in office after a vote of no confi-dence. If a vote of censure on the prime minister is approved, the whole government must resign, unless a new election is ordered.

Legislature: Denmark has a unicameral parliament (Folketing) consisting of 179 members elected by proportional representation for four years. Both Greenland and the Faerøe Islands send two representatives each to the Folke-ting.

Referendum: Since 1953 certain bills may be submitted to referendum at the initiative of one-third of the Folketing. *Ombudsman:* The Public Affairs Commissioner (*ombudsman*) appointed by parliament observes the activities of the ministers, the civil service and parts of local government administration with a view to bringing defects in the system to the attention of the responsible authority, and investigating complaints of abuses against personal liberty.

Political parties: The four government parties are: Conservative People's party, founded in 1916, led by Prime Minister Poul Schlüter and Torben Rechendorf; Liberal party, founded 1870 as the Agrarian party, led by Hen-ning Christophersen and Kurt Sørensen; Center Democrats, founded in 1973 as a dissident Social Democratic group and led by Erhard Jacobsen and Yvonne Herløv Andersen; Christian People's party, founded in 1970 and led by Flemming Kofod-Svendsen. The opposition parties are: Social-Democratic party, founded in 1871, led by former Prime Minister Anker Jørgensen and Einer Hovgaard Christiansen; Progress party, founded in 1972 by maverick Mogens Glistrup, who was convicted in 1978 of tax evasion after the longest trial in Danish legal history. It is currently led by P. S. Hansen; Socialist People's party, founded in 1959, by former Communist party chairman Aksel Larsen: it is currently led by Gert Petersen and Lilian Ubbesen; Radical Liberal party, founded in 1905, led by Thorkild Møller; Left Socialist party, founded in 1967, led by Ebbe Skov Hansen; Justice party, also known as the Single Tax party, or the Georgists, after economist Henry George, founded in 1919, led by Poul G. C. Kristiansen; Danish Communist party, founded in 1919, led by Jørgen Jensen; European Center Democrats, founded in 1974, led by Erhard Jacobsen.

Party representation in the Folketing, January 1984
(metropolitan Denmark only)

Social Democratic party	56
Conservative People's party	42
Liberal party	22
Socialist People's party	21
Radical Liberal party	10
Center Democrats	8
Progress party	6
Left Socialist party	5
Christian People's party	5

Note: Greenland and the Faerøe Islands each send two members to the Folketing. They are not shown here.

Local government: Under a major reform enacted in 1970, the former 25 regional districts were reduced to 14 counties (*amtskommuner*), each governed by an elected council (*amtsråd*) and mayor (*amtborgmester*). The counties, in turn, are divided into 277 local administrative units, each governed by an elected communal council (*kommunalbestyrelse*) and mayor (*borgmester*). The city of Copenhagen is governed by a city council (*borger repraesentation*) and an executive consisting of a chief burgomaster (*overborgmester*), five burgomasters (*borgmester*), and five aldermen (*rådmaend*).

Judicial system: The lower courts (*underretter*) are usually constituted by one to 22 judges. Only one judge tries a case. All cases not falling within the lower courts' jurisdiction are initiated in the two high courts (*landsretter*). The Eastern High Court has jurisdiction over the islands, and the Western High Court over Jutland. At least three judges try a high court case. In criminal cases that are not minor police cases (*politisager*), the judges are assisted by lay assessors (*domsmaend*)—three in high court cases, two in lower court cases, and in those that may involve sentences of eight years or more by a jury of 12. The Supreme Court (Højesteret) functions only as a court of appeal; it is constituted by at least five judges. There are two special courts—the Commercial and Maritime Court, and for labor disputes the Permanent Arbitration Court. Judges are appointed by the crown and may be dismissed only by judicial sentence. There is no death penalty.

RECENT HISTORY

In 1948 Denmark granted home rule to the Faerøes. In 1949 it became a founder-member of NATO. In 1953 a new constitution was introduced abolishing the upper house and permitting female succession to the throne. In the same year Greenland became an integral part of the Danish Kingdom and Denmark joined the Nordic Council. In 1960 Denmark joined EFTA and the next year negotiated for full membership in the EC. After a referendum, Denmark entered the EC in January 1973. Denmark has provided troops for U.N. forces in Sinai and Cyprus. From 1953 to 1968 Danish politics were dominated by the Social Democrats led by Jens Otto Krag. Their influence began to decline by 1970. Krag resigned and withdrew from public life in 1972 after overseeing the installation of Queen Margrethe II and Denmark's entry into the EC. By 1973, voter support for Denmark's traditional parties had eroded and several splinter parties secured Folketing representation for the first time. Most governments since then have been coalitions in which no party had a dominant position. Greenland was granted home rule in 1979, and opted out of the EC in 1984.

Defense: The queen is head of the armed forces. Military service lasts nine months. All front-line Danish forces are assigned to or earmarked for NATO service. Strength of the services: army 19,300, navy 5,700, air force 7,600. There are no foreign bases or nuclear weapons on Danish soil. The 1981 defense budget was Dkr10.05 billion ($1.53 billion), representing 2.6% of GNP in 1981. All Danish and German forces in the Baltic area are under a unified NATO command (COMBALTAP).

37

ECONOMY

Background: Denmark is basically an agricultural country with a comprehensive cooperative marketing system. Economic growth since 1957 has been characterized by a change of emphasis from agriculture to industry, with improved utilization of labor and rapid growth of industrial investment. However, the economy has suffered inflationary tendencies for most of this period, leading to competitive losses in industry and strong pressures on foreign exchange reserves since 1964. Economic growth has involved a substantial redistribution of labor and other resources from agriculture to manufacturing industry. In 1980 the value of GNP was $66.35 billion and GNP per capita $12,950. Between 1970 and 1979, GNP per capita grew at the rate of 2.1%.

The origin of GDP at factor cost in 1982 was:

Sector	Percentage
Agriculture	5
Industry	24
Services	71
GDP	100

From 1970 to 1982 industrial production increased by an annual average of 0.9% as against 5.2% during 1960–70. The chief industrial products are machinery, manufactured foodstuffs (including beverages and tobacco), chemicals and ships. The main agricultural products are livestock, barley, sugar beets, potatoes and dairy products.

Foreign trade: Foreign trade is conducted largely with other members of the Organization for Economic Cooperation and Development (OECD). In 1980, for example, 85% of Danish trade was with OECD countries, and of that more than half was with the EC countries within OECD. Only 5% of the trade was with the centrally planned economies of Eastern Europe.

Because agriculture is crucial to the Danish economy, the Danes have been pressing their EC and Nordic Council partners to permit freer trade in farm products. Denmark is a member of the GATT as well as the EC, joining the latter in 1973 as its only Nordic member. There are no tariffs within the EC, which has an industrial free trade area with the European Free Trade Association (EFTA) and special arrangements with many developing countries. The EC's own tariff is quite low, with raw materials usually admitted duty free.

Denmark's exports in 1982 amounted to $15.527 billion and imports to $17.162 billion, leaving a trade deficit of $1.635 billion. During 1970–82, the average annual growth rate was 4.8% for exports and 2.1% for imports. Of the merchandise exports, fuels, minerals and metals accounted for 5%, other primary commodities for 39%, textiles and clothing for 5%, machinery and transport equipment for 25%, and other manufactures for 26%. Of the merchandise imports, food accounted for 12%, fuels for 24%, other primary commodities for 7%, and machinery and transport equipment for 21%.

Employment: From 1976 to 1981, unemployment rose from 5.1% of insured workers to 9.2%. In 1981 the latter was 2.62 million, of whom 7% were employed in agriculture, 35% in industry and 58% in services. During part of 1981, unemployment was a record 9.2%.

Price and wage trends: During 1970–81, consumer prices rose by an annual average of 10.3%. The main contributory factors to these rises were a shortage of labor, a rise in export prices and increased home demand.

During 1977 the Jørgensen government initiated the first of a series of austerity measures to cut down inflation. In 1977 and 1978 the biannual cost of living increases were withheld and transferred to workers' retirement accounts. In 1979 and 1980 they were canceled. In 1979 the government also intervened in wage-contract negotiations, extending current contracts at the same levels. At the end of the year, the government imposed a freeze on wages, rents and prices. Wage contracts negotiated in 1980 averaged increases of 7% to 8%, with workers suffering a 3% to 4% annual loss in real income. As part of a legislative crisis package, the government enacted a number of measures in 1979 to slow domestic demand. The value-added tax was raised to 22%, other indirect taxes were increased and the krone was twice devalued against other currencies of the European Monetary System by a total of 10%. The remedial effects of these policies were mixed: private consumption fell in 1980, the overall GDP declined by 1% and federal budget deficits continued to grow.

Consumption: In 1982 private consumption amounted to 55% of GNP at current prices and public consumption to 28%. Public consumption grew by 4.0% during 1970–82 and private consumption by 1.7%. The relative figures for 1960–70 were 5.9% and 4.1%.

SOCIAL SECURITY

The Ministry of Social Affairs and National Social Security Office exercises general supervision over health, accident and unemployment insurance and direct national administration over the pension scheme.

Health insurance: This is administered by approved self-governing sickness funds directly supervised by the Health Insurance Directorate within the Ministry of Social Affairs. All residents of Denmark are provided with free medical care with restricted choice of doctor, or they pay part of the expenses with a free choice of doctor. There are cash sickness benefits for wage earners after eight weeks with the same employer (as of April 1, 1983). Others may insure voluntarily. There are cash maternity benefits for employees and the self-employed. The insurance is financed by a voluntary cash benefit insurance against the first three weeks of incapacity. The employer provides the whole cost of the first 13 weeks (as of April 1, 1983) of cash benefits; thereafter, the employer provides none of the costs. The government provides all other costs, including the whole cost of cash benefits after the 14th week. Sickness benefits for employees and the self-employed are 90% of earnings, up to 335 kroner a day, six days a week. Homemakers caring for others are paid at 50% of the above sickness benefits rate (voluntary insurance only). Maternity benefits are 90% of earnings, up to Dkr 335 a day, six days a week, up to 18 weeks, for employees. Other earners and nonearners are on a voluntary basis, payable four weeks after birth.

Accident insurance: This is directly supervised by the National Social Security Office and financed by employers who carry the whole cost of disability insurance through private carriers and the government, through a portion of the income tax. The permanent disability pension (work injury) is 75% of average earnings, if a worker is totally disabled. The partial disability pension is a percentage of full pension proportionate to loss of earning capacity, if 50% to 99% disabled. A lump sum equal to commuted value of partial pension is paid, if 15% to 49% disabled. Medical benefits are mostly covered under ordinary health insurance. At age 67, pension is discontinued, and a lump sum of two years' benefits paid. Widows' pensions—also payable to widowers—are 30% of earnings of the insured, up to 10 years. Orphans' pensions are paid at 10% of earnings for each orphan, up to 40% maximum. Each full orphan receives 20% of earnings, up to 50% maximum. Orphans' pensions are payable through age 18 (21 if a student).

Pensions insurance: Universal and assistance pensions are administered at the national level by the Ministry of Social Affairs and National Social Security Office, and at the local level by local authorities. Employment-related pensions are administered by the Ministry of Labor. Universal pensions are funded by 3.5% of taxable income from the insured. Employment-related pensions are funded by the insured contributing Dkr 8.10 a week or Dkr 32.40 a month, and the employer contributing Dkr 16.20 per employee a week or Dkr 64.80 a month. Disability pensions are funded by the employer contributing Dkr 31 per employee a year. For universal pensions, the government contributes about 90% of cost; for disability pensions, all costs in excess of employers' contributions. Old age pensions are of two forms. At age 67 for men and married women and at age 62 for single women, a universal pension is granted. At age 67, an employment-related pension of three years' contribution is granted. Retirement is unnecessary for either pension. Universal old-age pension benefits are Dkr 2,589 a month (single) or Dkr 4,756 (aged couple); this increases 5% at each six-month deferment until age 70. Employment-related pension benefits are up to Dkr 10,800 a year after 40 years, or 35 years if covered in 1965; there is a 5% increment per half-year deferral of pension until age 70. A basic survivor's pension of Dkr 2,589 per month (income-tested) with a supplement (also income-tested) of Dkr 455 per month is payable to the widow only under the universal pension scheme. There are supplements for children. The employment-related survivor pension is 50% of the employment-related old-age pension paid or payable to the deceased.

Unemployment insurance: This covers most employed persons between the ages of 16 and 65. The Ministry of Labor and National Employment Office offer general supervision. The insurance is financed by an annual contribution of six times the rate of highest daily cash benefit from the insured; an annual contribution of $11\frac{1}{4}$ times the maximum rate of highest daily cash benefits per employee per year from the employer; and the cost above the insured person's and employer's contributions provided by government. Unemployment benefits are 90% of earnings, up to Dkr 335 per day, payable from the first day of unemployment, six days a week. There are supplementary benefits for travel and relocation allowances, rent allowances, etc.

Other benefits: Family allowances are entirely funded by the government and cover all resident citizens and many resident aliens. The regular family allowance is Dkr 2,184 a year for each child. This may be increased to Dkr 3,290 per child under certain conditions, plus Dkr 2,580 a year in single-parent families (reduced by 6% of income in excess of Dkr 156,000 a year). Full orphans are given a special allowance of Dkr 9,612 a year. There are special allowances for half-orphans and children of old-age and disability pensioners; these are Dkr 5,781 a year each. These family allowances are administered by local communal (municipal) governments.

EDUCATION

Primary and secondary education: Education is mainly public and is compulsory for nine years, although after seven years, an exemption may be given. The government must provide a preschool class and a tenth voluntary year. Nearly 90% of students attend municipal schools, although there are private schools with state subsidies. In August 1976, the 1975 Education Act became law. A comprehensive curriculum for the first 10 years was initiated and parents were given greater influence. Options on final tests of a leaving certificate thereafter were offered. Students at the age of 16 or 17 may now either transfer to an upper secondary school (*gymnasium*), leading to the upper secondary school leaving examination (*studentereksamen*) after three years, or they may enroll in a two-year program, leading to the higher preparatory examination. Both these programs allow the student admission to university. At this point, students may transfer to a vocational program or an apprenticeship.

Special education: Special education is provided at government boarding schools, which also accept day-pupils, for all children with severe physical handicaps. The State Welfare Service for Mental Defectives provides education for mentally defective children.

Vocational education: Apprentices must be at least 14 before beginning their training, which is combined with general and vocational education. Additional technical education takes place in evening classes. At the conclusion of the apprenticeship there is for some the opportunity for training at technical colleges (*technika*) for three-year courses. Technical schools (*techniskeskoler*) offer six- to twelve-month courses to skilled industrial workers, as do the colleges of technology in Copenhagen and Århus. Commercial schools (*handelsskoler*) run by trade organizations lead to examinations that when passed offer advancement for business people through business colleges. Having

41

gained a diploma here or having passed the *realeksamen* or studentereksamen, the student may proceed to an advanced business college. Success in a one- or two-year course may lead to one of the two higher commercial colleges (*handelshøjskoler*) in Copenhagen and Århus.

University and higher education: The University of Copenhagen provides five faculties—theology, law and economics, medicine, arts, and science. It is administered by the Ministry of Education but retains extensive autonomy. Århus University has the same five faculties. It is a private foundation whose activities are subjected to regulations laid down by statute, decree or ministerial order after discussions with the university authorities. Entry to the universities is open to all who have passed the studenter-eksamen and education is generally free. Attendance at lectures is to a large extent voluntary and there is no prescribed period before the examinations. Both universities draw on private grants and the government's Youth Education Fund for allocation of grants or loans to students of limited means.

Higher technical education takes place at the Technical University of Denmark and the Danish Academy of Engineering, both in Copenhagen. Other higher education institutes are the Royal Veterinary and Agricultural College in Copenhagen, the two independent dental colleges in Copenhagen and Århus, the Royal Danish School of Pharmacy in Copenhagen, the Danish College of Education for teacher training and the Royal Academy of Fine Arts, also in Copenhagen.

Educational Institutions, 1981–82:

	Institutions	Teachers	Students
Primary and secondary schools	2,690	72,208	852,154
Universities	5	2,802*	45,136

* 1979–80. Source: *Danmarks Statistik.*

Adult education· The folk high schools (*folkehøjskoler*), of which there were some 85 in 1983, are private institutions receiving large state grants. They offer five- to six-month winter courses. Students, who are generally between 18 and 25, may obtain state grants. The schools are free to arrange their own syllabuses within the terms of reference of general education, and they hold no examinations and give no certificates. Continuation schools (*efterskoler*) are similarly organized and offer similar education, but with greater emphasis on elementary school and practical subjects to the 14–18 age-group. Grants can be obtained from the state or the local authority. There were 118 of these schools in 1983. Youth schools (*ungdomsskoler*), maintained by local authorities, cater to the same age-group but are slanted more towards the problems of youth and have a vocational bias. In 1983 there were 570 youth schools. Evening schools and evening high schools provide very varied education, which is free save for a small registration fee. In 1981 there were nearly 251 public libraries.

MASS MEDIA

The press (1983):
Dailies (weekday circulation): *Berlingske Tidende*, Copenhagen, independent-Conservative, 120,000; *Ekstra Bladet*, Copenhagen, Liberal, 250,000; *B.T.*, Copenhagen, ind., 220,000; *Politiken*, Copenhagen, Liberal, 150,000; *Aktuelt*, Copenhagen, Social-Democratic, 114,000; *Aalborg Stiftstidende*, Ålborg, Liberal, 73,000.

Periodicals: Familie Journalen, Copenhagen, family, 337,093; *Hjemmet* (w), Copenhagen, fam., 200,000; *Sondags BT* (w), Copenhagen, ind.-Cons. fam., 200,000; *Se og Her* (w), Copenhagen, fam., 270,000; *Flittige Haender* (w), Copenhagen, women's, 145,000; *Finanstidende* (w), Copenhagen, financial, 6,000.

Broadcasting: Sound and TV services are the monopoly of Radio Denmark (Danmarks Radio). Radio Denmark is directed by a Radio Council responsible to the minister for cultural affairs. The minister appoints a majority to the Council as representatives of viewers, listeners and government, and the political parties represented on the Parliamentary Finance Committee appoint one member each. Radio Denmark is financed out of a Broadcasting Fund derived from radio and TV licences. In 1983 there were 1,889,297 licenses (including both television and radio).

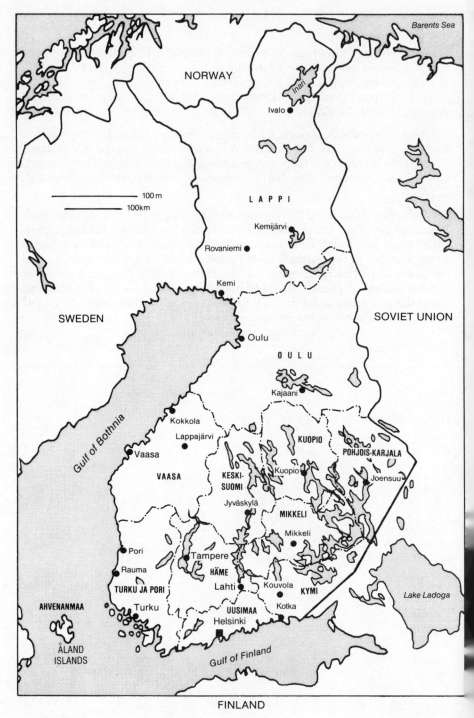

FINLAND

FINLAND

Features: The whole country, consisting geologically of metamorphic rock of the Baltic Shield, is of low relief, only a few areas in the extreme northwest reaching over 1,500 ft/450 m. and most of the center and south lying below 600 ft/180 m. The country is much affected by glaciation. There are two main regions: the south, with innumerable lakes and islands, short streams and low relief; and the region north of about latitude 64°N, which has few lakes, longer streams and is of greater altitude.

Almost the entire country is forest-covered, providing the main source of wealth. Agriculture is largely confined to the coastal plain areas. Iron ore is mined at Kolari in the north and copper from Lake Juo; other minerals are sparse and no fuels of importance are present, most power being derived from hydroelectric sources. Industry is concentrated in the coastal towns, e.g., Helsinki and Turku, the only large inland center being Tampere. *Area:* 117,800 sq. miles/305,400 sq. km. (excluding inland water areas amounting to an additional 12,200 sq. miles/31,600 sq. km.). *Mean max. and min. temperatures:* Helsinki (60° N, 24° E; 30 ft/9 m.) 71°F/22°C (July), 15°F/−9°C (Feb.); Sodankylä (67° 30′ N, 26° 30′ E; 590 ft/180 m.) 68°F/20°C, −5°F/−21°C. *Relative humidity:* Helsinki 85%; Sodankylä 85%. *Mean annual rainfall:* Helsinki 28 in./710 mm.; Sodankylä 22 in./560 mm.

POPULATION

Total population: (1984) 4.9 million. *Chief towns and populations:* (1984) HELSINKI (484,104), Tampere (166,235), Turku (163,507), Lahti (94,646), Oulu (93,822). *Distribution:* In 1984, 64% of the population lived in urban areas and 36% in rural districts. *Language:* Both Finnish and Swedish are official languages. The Swedish-speaking minority comprises about 7% of the population. *Religion:* More than 90% adhere to the state Evangelical-Lutheran church; 1.3% belong to the Eastern Orthodox church.

CONSTITUTIONAL SYSTEM

Constitution: Finland is a republic; the constitution dates from 1919. *Head of state:* President Dr. Mauno Koivisto. *Head of government:* Prime Minister Kalevi Sorsa (Social-Democrat).

Executive: The president is chosen for six years by an electoral college elected by direct suffrage. He appoints the ministers and usually acts on their advice. He has, however, considerable independence on such issues as the dissolution of parliament and the appointment of certain senior officials. The president determines foreign policy, making his decision in the Council of State (Valtio-neuvosto) upon the report of the foreign minister. The president also has power to initiate legislation, and every law passed by parliament must be confirmed by him. The prime minister and ministers, who together form the Council of State, are responsible to parliament. Presidential acts must be countersigned by the competent minister, except in cases involving the prosecution of the president or ministers.

Legislature: Parliament (Eduskunta), consisting of one chamber of 200 representatives elected by proportional representation for four years, is the ultimate source of legislative power. Parliament appoints an ombudsman to supervise the observance of the law.

Political parties: No political party in Finland has had an absolute majority since the Social Democrats in 1916–17. Consequently, cabinets are either coalitions or minority governments. The current government is a coalition of four parties: the Center party, the Social Democratic party, the Swedish People's party and the Finnish Rural party. The Socialist parties are:

The Finnish Social Democratic party, the dominant party in Finnish politics since 1907. It is led by Prime Minister Kalevi Sorsa and Olli Helminen, chairman of the parliamentary group.

Finnish People's Democratic League, a leftist electoral and parliamentary alliance founded in 1944. It withdrew from the Sorsa coalition in December 1982. It is led by Kalevi Kivistö, party chairman.

Finnish Communist party, comprising both the pro-Moscow and the pro-Peking factions, reconciled in 1982. It is led by party chairman Arvo Aalto.

The non-Socialist parties are:

Center party, founded in 1906 as the Agrarian party. It now draws support from both rural and urban constituents. It is led by Paavo Väyrynen, chairman.

Liberal People's party, formed in 1965 through a merger of the Finnish People's party and the Liberal Union. It became a wing of the Center party in 1982.

Finnish Rural party, a breakaway group of the Center party. It is led by Pekka Vennamo, party chairman.

National Coalition party, a conservative party founded in 1918, led by Ilkka Suominen.

Swedish People's party, representative of the Swedish minority interests. Its leader is Pär Stenbäck, a former foreign minister.

Constitutional party of the Right, founded in 1973, led by Georg C. Ehrnrooth.

Finnish Christian Union, founded in 1958, led by Esko Almgren.

In the 1983 elections, the Social Democrats won 57 seats, the National Coalition party 44, the Center party 38, the Finnish People's Democratic League 26, the Swedish People's party 10, the Finnish Christian Union three, the Finnish Rural party 17 and other parties five seats.

In addition to the party leaders named above, the leading political figures include President (and former Prime Minister) Dr. Mauno Koivisto and speaker of the Eduskunta, Erkki Pystynen.

Local government: Finland is divided into provinces (*läänit*) each under a governor (*maaherra*) appointed by the president. The provinces exert general supervision, particularly in financial matters, over the communes (*kunnat*), the basic units of local government whose councils (*kunnanvaltuustot*) are elected for four years. The provincial administration also has a judicial personality, particularly as court of appeal in taxation matters. Regarding internal matters, the Province of Åland is self-governing.

Judicial system: The lowest courts are the district and municipal courts (*kihlakunnanoikeudet* and *raastuvanoikeudet*). In towns, these are administered by the mayor (*pormestari*) and assessors (*asessorit*). In the country the decision depends upon a judge and a jury of from five to seven jurors with the judge alone deciding unless the jury unanimously differ, in which case their decision prevails. Appeal from these courts is to the superior courts (*hovioikeudet*) composed of a president and an appropriate number of members, and finally to the Supreme Court (*Korkein oikeus*) composed of a president and 23 justices. The Supreme Administrative Court (*Korkein hallinto-oikeus*) consists of a president and 21 justices appointed by the president of the republic, and is the highest appeal court for administrative cases. The judiciary is independent of the executive; the Supreme Court appoints the judges and they may only be removed by judicial sentence. There is no capital punishment.

RECENT HISTORY

Finland was at war with the Soviet Union in 1939–40 (the Winter War) and again from 1941 to 1944. By the terms of the armistice it ceded 12% of the land area to the Soviet Union, and 10% of its population was displaced. Since then it has maintained a policy of neutrality qualified by a special emphasis on preserving good relations with the Soviet Union. This is epitomized by the 1948 Finnish-Soviet Agreement of Friendship and Mutual Assistance, which was renewed in 1955 for a further 20 years. In 1955 Finland joined both the United Nations and the Nordic Council and in 1961 became an associate member of EFTA. Following President Urho Kekkonen's incapacitation in 1981, Mauno Koivisto was named president.

Defense: The president is commander-in-chief of the armed forces. The 1948 Finnish-Soviet Agreement forbids Finland to permit the use of its territory as a base for aggression against the Soviet Union, and commits Finland to defend its territory, if necessary with Soviet aid, in such an event. However, aid is not given automatically, since a separate agreement regulates the form and extent of assistance. Should the Soviet Union be involved in a war that does not affect Finnish territory, Finland is committed not to enter any alliance directed against the Soviet Union. Finnish defense forces are limited by the 1947 Peace Treaty with the Allies to 41,900. In 1984 there were 36,500: an army of 30,900, an air force of 2,900 and a navy of 2,700. Reserves were about 200,000 and there were 3,500 frontier guards. The treaty also forbade the possession of nuclear weapons, guided missiles, bombers and submarines. The ban on missiles was revoked in 1963. Compulsory military service is for eight to 11 months, and for officers, NCOs and specialized personnel, 11 months. The defense estimates for 1981 were Fmk2.874 billion ($713 million).

ECONOMY

Background: Finland has vast supplies of timber and water power but very few other national resources. It is heavily dependent upon foreign trade. The economy is based on a narrow range of products and has suffered serious inflation since World War II. The Finnish mark was devalued in 1949 and 1957, chiefly as a result of economic stagnation. By the end of 1958 the economy had started to expand again, but in 1961 the rate of growth had once more slowed down. Recovery during 1963 was followed by a boom in 1964. From 1970 to 1982 GNP at current prices increased by an annual average of nearly 11.7%. The 1970s were characterized by a slower annual average growth rate, severe inflation and acute balance of payments deficits. The main growth industries in recent years have been building and construction, metals and engineering.

The origin of GDP at factor cost in 1982 was:

Sector	Percentage
Agriculture	8
Industry	35
Services	57
GDP	100

Between 1970 and 1982 the annual rate of increase of industrial production was over 3.3%. The chief industries are wood, paper and pulp, mining, and power. In the same period the growth of agricultural output was less than 0.5% per year. The chief agricultural sectors are cattle, hay, fodder, roots, barley and vegetables.

Foreign trade: Finland has supported liberal trade policies, participating in the GATT and other multinational institutions. It joined EFTA in 1961 as an associate member, a year after the organization was founded. To allay resulting Soviet fears, Finland also extended similar tariff-free arrangements with Moscow. In 1973 Finland continued its balancing act, establishing industrial free-trade connections with both the COMECON and the EC, but without formally joining either. In recent years Finland's trade with both blocs has been exactly 20% each. In addition to its five-year barter deals with the Soviet Union, Helsinki has signed a long-term agreement of economic cooperation with Moscow and a five-year economic cooperation treaty with China. The Soviet Union remains Finland's largest trading partner, accounting for $4 to 5 billion of industrial exports. In the past few years, trade with developing nations has expanded to 11% of total. A free port located at Hanko and several free-trade zones permit duty-free storage for exporters and importers.

In 1982, total exports amounted to $13.132 billion and imports to $13.387 billion, leaving a trade deficit of $55 million. During 1970–82, the average annual growth rate was 4.7% for exports and 2.4% for imports. Of the merchandise exports in 1981, fuels constituted 8%, other primary commodities 20%, textiles and clothing 7%, machinery and transport equipment 21% and other manufactures 44%. Of the merchandise imports, food constituted 7%, fuels 31%, other primary commodities 7%, machinery and transport equipment 21% and other manufactures 28%.

Employment: The total labor force in 1981 was estimated to be nearly 2.3 million. Between 1960 and 1980 manpower in the service sector increased by nearly 19%, in industry by 4%, and in agriculture there was a decline of 25%. In 1982, agriculture, forestry and fishing employed an estimated 11% of the total labor force, industry 35% and services 54%. Unemployment in the same year rose to about 4.8%, being highest in forestry.

Price and wage trends: From 1970 to 1980, the most notable contributory factor to the rise in the domestic price level was the increase in labor costs. The increase in the average price level in 1980 was over 13%. The cost of living index rose by an annual average of nearly 12% from 1970 to 1981.

Consumption: In 1982 private consumption amounted to 55% of GDP at market prices, and public consumption to 20%.

SOCIAL SECURITY

Health insurance: Under the general administration of the Ministry of Social Affairs and Health, this insurance is compulsory for the whole population. The insured person contributes 1% of income subject to communal (municipal) tax; the employer contributes 1.35% of payroll if a private employer or 2.35% of payroll if a public employer; the government contributes the remaining cost. Sickness benefits are 80% of earnings, with a minimum of Fmk30.10 a day. Maternity benefits are 80% of earnings, with a minimum of Fmk30.10 a day. Medical benefits are cash refunds of part of medical expenses. These include 60% of doctors' fees and 75% of the cost of laboratory services over Fmk15. Free hospitalization is available in public hospitals. The medical benefits for dependents are the same as those for the family head.

Accident insurance: All employed persons and their families are covered against occupational accidents and diseases. The employer pays for this insurance through contributions to appropriate licensed private insurance companies. The temporary disability benefit (work injury) is 100% of earnings, for up to 12 months after the accident. The permanent disability pension (work injury) is a basic pension equal to 85% of earnings, plus a supplement up to 60% of earnings depending on degree of disability. There is also a constant-attendance supplement. Medical benefits for permanent disability (work injury) include medical attendance, surgery, hospital treatment, medicines and appliances. Survivor pensions (work injury) are 40% of earnings of the insured for one dependent, 55% for two and 65% for three or more dependents. These pensions are payable to widow, dependent invalid widower and orphans. The maximum survivor pension is 65% of earnings of the insured.

Pensions insurance: There are universal pensions and means-tested allowances for all residents. There are also employment-related pensions for all regular employees (each employer must establish a pension system for his or her own employees). Special pension systems exist for seasonal maritime and public employees, as well as for farmers and the self-employed. The insured person contributes to the universal pension scheme 1.75% of income subject to communal (municipal) tax. The employer contributes from 4.1% to 5.6% of payroll to the universal pension scheme, plus an average of 11.1% of payroll to the employment-related pension scheme. The government contributes about 20% of means-tested allowances. For the universal pension, retirement is unnecessary. Age 65 and five years of residence qualify the insured. For employment-related pensions, retirement from covered employment is necessary, and age 65 must have been reached. For full employment-related pension, there must be 40 years' coverage. The universal old-age pension benefits are Fmk268 a month, or Fmk536 for an aged couple. There is an increment of 12.5% of pension for each year deferred after 65; maximum is 62.5%. There are supplements for blind or disabled pensioners and those needing constant attendance. The universal survivor pension provides up to Fmk785 a month for all widows for the first six months after a husband's death. Thereafter, Fmk268 a month is provided for a widow supporting a child under age 16. Half-orphans are allowed up to Fmk158 a month, a full orphan up to Fmk315—both must be under age 16 (or 21 if a student). Survivor benefits of employment-related pensions provide widows with 50% of pension paid or payable to the insured, if the widow is aged 40 when widowed or caring for a child. Orphan benefits are allowed at 25% for one, or 50% for two or more orphans under age 18 (no age limit if the orphan is disabled). For the first or only full orphan, 50% of pension is allowed.

Unemployment insurance: This is administered by the state-recognized unemployment funds organized in individual industries. Unemployment assistance is entirely funded by the government and is available to all gainfully employed workers aged 16 to 64. The voluntary unemployment funds are available to employees aged 17 and over who voluntarily join the unemployment funds established by their trade unions. Wage earners contribute to unemployment fund sums to cover 7% of each fund's benefit costs. The employer contributes to a central fund 0.9% of payroll; this central fund contributes 70% of benefits available to unemployment fund's. Both employer and government contribute to costs of administering unemployment funds. The government subsidizes 23% of the benefits of each unemployment fund. Unemployment fund benefits vary among funds. Maximum unemployment fund benefits are Fmk87 a day. Unemployment assistance benefits are Fmk41.50 to Fmk61.50 a day, according to family status and local cost-of-living levels, plus Fmk3 a day per child under age 18.

Other benefits: Family allowances are available to all residents with one or more children. The government funds the entire cost. Family allowances are Fmk1,632 a year for first child, Fmk1,888 for second, Fmk2,200 for third and Fmk2,804 for fourth and each additional child, plus Fmk940 a year for each child under age three. There is a birth grant of Fmk440.

EDUCATION

Finland adopted a new, comprehensive educational system beginning with the 1977–78 school year. Education is free and the course work is the same for all students. A six-year lower level and a three-year upper level comprise the compulsory course. Upon completion of compulsory education, a student can enroll in either an upper secondary school or other vocational school or institute for three years. A student sits for a matriculation examination after three years in upper secondary school. Students can apply for admission to one of the 22 universities and colleges if they pass this examination.

Primary education: Education is free and compulsory from the ages of seven to 15. For the first four years, all children undergo virtually the same basic education. Then on the basis of the primary school certificate and an entrance examination, about 50% pass on to secondary education. The remainder continue in primary school and are given an education that has an increased bias towards civics and prevocational training. Primary schools are maintained by the municipalities, with the state paying the bulk of the costs; the size of the contribution depends upon the location of the school, a larger contribution being paid in rural areas. School meals are free.

Secondary education: Secondary schools are divided into five-year junior secondary and three-year senior secondary grades. Junior secondary education prepares children for higher vocational education, such as technical and business colleges, and for apprenticeships in certain branches of government service. Those who continue to senior secondary school have a choice between a language and a mathematics division, ending with the student examination (see under *University and higher education*). Secondary schools are maintained by the state and the municipalities, and although the bulk are private schools, the state covers about 70% of their expenses by subsidy. Secondary education is not free; fees are relatively low at state schools, but higher at private schools. Annual state boarding grants are awarded on merit.

Vocational education: This takes place through training in vocational schools and through apprenticeship. Vocational schools give training in commercial, technical, agricultural and other occupations. Most are owned—with substantial state aid—by municipalities, but the state, employers and other associations also maintain them. Courses last on average from 18 months to two years. Generally, students must pay their own tuition and lodging fees. However, grants may be obtained from many communes and numerous private associations and foundations, and there are state training grants and interest-free loans for persons of small means pursuing studies in state-owned or state-supported vocational schools, or other approved courses, or apprenticeship training.

Special education: Children with physical disabilities or who are mildly retarded are taught in special classes of elementary schools. The more severely retarded are free from compulsory education, but where possible are taught in special institutions maintained on a day-school basis by the state, the communes and voluntary associations. There are six residential schools for hearing-impaired and three for blind and visually handicapped children, organized under the public education system. Teacher training for special education is provided at the Pedagogical University in Jyväskylä.

University and higher education: Entrance to the universities is through the student examination and special entrance examinations. The University of Helsinki is an autonomous institution. The Finnish-language University of Turku is privately founded; its Swedish-language counterpart, the Åbo Academy (Turku), is also privately founded. The state-founded University of Oulu has an attached teacher training college. The (Finnish) Helsinki School of Economics and its Swedish counterpart are independent colleges, as are Turku's two corresponding institutes. Further institutions in Helsinki are an institute of veterinary medicine, a school of education offering two-year courses for elementary school teachers and an institute of technology under the jurisdiction of the Ministry of Commerce and Industry. The Institute of Pedagogics at Jyväskylä trains teachers, offers doctorates and confers the same degrees in humanities as the universities of Helsinki and Turku. The School of Social Science at Tampere is under the jurisdiction of the Ministry of Education.

Undergraduate courses last from four to seven years. Annual state grants are provided for students of small means.

Educational institutions, 1982–83:

	Institutions	Staff	Students
Primary	4,238	24,752	365,965
General secondary	1,078	22,279	325,763
Vocational			106,998
Universities and other higher education	556	21,437	127,657

Source: Finnish Statistics Office.

Adult education: Adult education is provided by People's High Schools and Workers' Institutes. People's High Schools are boarding schools providing courses in the winter months. Workers' Institutes provide evening courses. The main emphasis is upon a general education in civics for young people. These institutes are privately managed, but a large proportion of expenses is covered by state subsidies. In 1981 there were over 464 public libraries in Finland.

MASS MEDIA

The press (1984):

Dailies: Helsingin Sanomat, Helsinki, independent, 377,203; *Uusi Suomi*, Helsinki, National Coalition, 82,096; *Aamulehti*, Tampere, Nat. Coal., 130,646; *Turun Sanomat*, Turku, Finnish People's party, 129,182; *Satakunnan Kansa*, Pori, Nat. Coal., 56,244; *Sanomalehti Kaleva*, Oulu, ind., 74,076; *Hufvudstadsbladet*, Helsinki, Swedish People's party, 61,521; *Ilta-Sanomat*, Helsinki, ind., 122,611; *Kansan Uutiset*, Helsinki, Social Democrat, 55,613; *Savon Sanomat*, Kuopio, Center party, 76,782; *Vaasa*, Vaasa, Nat. Coal., 61,306; *Karjalainen*, Joensuu, Nat. Coal., 49,516; *Suomen Sosiaalidemokraatti*, Helsinki, Soc. Dem., 42,731; *Keskisuomalainen*, Jyväskylä, Center party, 66,580.

Periodicals (Helsinki): Apu (w), illustrated, 302,422; *Seura* (w), illus., 261,235; *Me Naiset* (w), wom., 131,575; *Eeva* (m), wom., 86,410; *Suomen Kuvalehti* (w), illus., 113,187; *Hopeapeili* (m), wom., 52,496; *Metsälehti* (w), forestry, 45,000; *Talouselämä* (w), economics, 35,288.

Broadcasting: The Finnish Broadcasting Company (Oy Yleisradio Ab) controls most radio and TV, including commercial broadcasting. Broadcasting is financed by radio and TV license fees and by profits from TV advertising. There were approximately 2,515,000 radio receivers and 2,200,000 television receivers in use in Finland in 1983. Cable television was received by about 100,000 households. Cable is provided by the independent commercial TV company MTV Oy.

FRANCE

Features: France is the largest country in Western Europe. The most extensive of its regions, and the most important economically, is the Paris basin, bounded in the west by Brittany, in the south by the Massif Central and in the east by the Vosges. The greater part of the area lies below 600 ft/180 m. and, particularly in the east, is composed of a series of alternating ridges and valleys. The Brittany peninsula is a low dissected plateau mainly below 600 ft. The Aquitaine basin to the south is triangular in shape; its general altitude increases away from the Garonne both towards the Massif Central and the Pyrenees.

The Massif Central is upland with an average height of 3,000 ft/900 m., with parts rising to over 6,000 ft. The eastern region is composed of alternating fault-guided uplands and depressions; the central area includes the volcanic zone of Auvergne and Cantal; in the south are the limestone plateau of the Causses and deep gorges, e.g., Lot and Tarn; in the northwest is the extensive plateau of Limousin.

To the east of the Massif Central lies the lowland corridor of the Rhône-Saône Valley, which provides a vital communication link between the Mediterranean and northern France. This corridor opens out onto the Mediterranean and there is a wider coastal plain to the west than to the east. Southwest lies the east–west band of the Pyrenees. East of the Rhône are the French Jura and Alps. In the northeast lie the Vosges (the French counterpart of the Black Forest).

As France covers a considerable latitudinal range, a wide variety of crops can be grown. The chief agricultural areas are the loess-covered chalk and limestone lands of the Paris basin (e.g., Artois, Picardy and Beauce), the terraces of the Garonne, the coastal lands of Brittany and scattered parts of the eastern Mediterranean lands and the Rhône Valley. The principal coalfields are in Lorraine, and the Franco-Belgian coalfield of the north; a number of small coalfields also produce good-quality coal in the Massif Central. Oil and natural gas are worked in the Rhône Valley and Aquitaine. The country has considerable resources of hydroelectric power; its chief minerals are the low-grade Jurassic iron ores of Lorraine. The principal industrial regions are on the Lorraine ore field, the northern coalfield and around the towns of Paris, Marseilles, Lyons, Clermont-Ferrand, St. Etienne and Bordeaux.

DEPARTMENTS

1. AIN
2. AISNE
3. ALLIER
4. ALPES-DE-HAUTE-PROVENCE
5. ALPES-MARITIMES
6. ARDÈCHE
7. ARDENNES
8. ARIÈGE
9. AUBE
10. AUDE
11. AVEYRON
12. BAS-RHIN
13. BELFORT
14. BOUCHES-DU-RHÔNE
15. CALVADOS
16. CANTAL
17. CHARENTE
18. CHARENTE-MARITIME
19. CHER
20. CORRÈZE
21. CORSE-DU-SUD
22. CÔTE-D'OR
23. CÔTES-DU-NORD
24. CREUSE
25. DEUX-SÈVRES

26. DORDOGNE
27. DOUBS
28. DRÔME
29. ESSONNE
30. EURE
31. EURE-ET-LOIRE
32. FINISTÈRE
33. GARD
34. GERS
35. GIRONDE
36. HAUTE-CORSE
37. HAUTE-GARONNE
38. HAUTE-LOIRE
39. HAUTE-MARNE
40. HAUTES-ALPES
41. HAUTE-SAÔNE
42. HAUTE-SAVOIE
43. HAUTES-PYRÉNÉES
44. HAUTE-VIENNES
45. HAUT-RHIN
46. HAUTS-DE-SEINE
47. HÉRAULT
48. ILLE-ET-VILAINE
49. INDRE
50. INDRE-ET-LOIRE

51. ISÈRE
52. JURA
53. LANDES
54. LOIRE
55. LOIRE-ATLANTIQUE
56. LOIRET
57. LOIR-ET-CHER
58. LOT
59. LOT-ET-GARONNE
60. LOZÈRE
61. MAINE-ET-LOIRE
62. MANCHE
63. MARNE
64. MAYENNE
65. MEURTHE-ET-MOSELLE
66. MEUSE
67. MORBIHAN
68. MOSELLE
69. NIÈVRE
70. NORD
71. OISE
72. ORNE
73. PARIS
74. PAS-DE-CALAIS
75. PUY-DE-DÔME

76. PYRÉNÉES-ATLANTIQUES
77. PYRÉNÉES-ORIENTALES
78. RHÔNE
79. SAÔNE-ET-LOIRE
80. SARTHE
81. SAVOIE
82. SEINE-ET-MARNE
83. SEINE-MARITIME
84. SEINE-SAINT-DENIS
85. SOMMES
86. TARN
87. TARN-ET-GARONNES
88. VAL-DE-MARNE
89. VAL-D'OISE
90. VAR
92. VAUCLUSE
91. VENDÉE
93. VIENNE
94. VOSGES
95. YONNE
96. YVELINES

FRANCE

Area: Metropolitan France 212,740 sq. miles/551,200 sq. km. The Overseas Departments are French Guiana, Guadeloupe, Martinique and Réunion. Overseas Territories: French Polynesia, New Caledonia, Saint-Pierre and Miquelon, Southern and Antarctic Territories, Wallis and Futuna Islands.

Mean max. and min. temperatures: Paris (48° N, 2° 30' E; 160 ft/50 m.) 76°F/ 24°C (July), 32°F/0°C (Jan.); Bordeaux (45° N, 0° 30' W; 160 ft/50 m.) 80°F/ 27°C (July and Aug.), 35°F/2°C (Jan.); Nice (43° 30' N, 7° 30' E; 40 ft/12 m.) 81°F/27°C (July and Aug.), 40°F/4°C (Jan.); Grenoble (45° N, 5° 30' E; 735 ft/22 m.) 81°F/27°C (July), 27°F/−3°C (Jan.). *Relative humidity:* Paris 87%; Bordeaux 90%; Nice 68%; Grenoble 82%. *Mean annual rainfall:* Paris 22 in./560 mm.; Bordeaux 33 in./840 mm.; Nice 32 in./810 mm.; Grenoble 38 in./965 mm.

POPULATION

Population: (1984—Metropolitan France only) 54.8 million. *Chief towns and populations:* (1962) PARIS (2,299,830), Marseille (908,600), Lyon (456,716), Toulouse (373,796), Nice (344,481), Nantes (255,693), Strasbourg (253,384), Bordeaux (223,131). *Distribution:* In 1982, 79% of the population lived in urban centers, of which 34% lived in cities of over 500,000, and 23.1% in Paris.

Language: French is the official language. Breton, Corsican (akin to Italian), Spanish, Basque, Catalan, Flemish and German are also spoken in parts of the country, mainly border areas. *Religion:* About 60% of the population belong to the Roman Catholic church. There are numerous other Christian, Jewish and Muslim communities.

CONSTITUTIONAL SYSTEM

Constitution: France is a republic. The constitution was adopted by referendum in 1958. *Head of state:* President François Mitterand. *Head of government:* Prime Minister Laurent Fabius.

Executive: The president is elected (since 1962) by direct universal suffrage for seven years. He appoints and dismisses the prime minister, and on the prime minister's advice the other members of the Council of Ministers. He presides over the Council of Ministers and signs its ordinances and decrees. He may return legislation to parliament for reconsideration. Like parliament and on the advice of the prime minister, he may initiate a revision of the constitution. The president dissolves the National Assembly, but may not dissolve it again within one year of its reelection. During parliamentary sessions he may submit draft laws to referendum and he has emergency powers in time of crisis, but he may not dissolve parliament during this period. He communicates with parliament by means of messages that are read but not debated.

The government, supervised by the prime minister, decides and directs general policy. The members of the government may not hold parliamentary or any other national office. The government is responsible to the Assembly, and that responsibility may be challenged only on a motion of censure, signed by one-tenth of the Assembly's members and voted for by an absolute majority, or if the government asks for a vote of confidence. If defeated by either method, the prime minister must hand in the resignation of the government to the president.

Legislature: Parliament consists of the National Assembly and the Senate. The Assembly comprising 491 deputies (including 17 for the Overseas Departments and Territories) is elected for five years by *scrutin d'arrondisse-ment* (two-ballot single-member constituency system). The Senate has 317 members representing Metropolitan France, Overseas Territories and Departments, and French citizens living abroad. It is elected for nine years by indirect suffrage by an electoral college formed of deputies, general coun-cillors (see *Local government*) and the representatives of municipal councils. One-third of the Senate is reelected every three years.

Legislation may be initiated by members of either the government (*projets de loi*) or of both houses of parliament (*propositions de loi*). Finance bills must originate in the National Assembly. Legislation must be passed by both houses before being submitted to the president for promulgation. There are three types of legislation. Parliament has the right of full and detailed legislation in such matters as civil rights, nationality, criminal law and proce-dures, and the parliamentary electoral system. Parliament determines the fundamental principles only regarding legislation in such matters as educa-tion, social security, national defense and civil law. All remaining legislation may be dealt with by the government by executive order. If parliament should invade these residual powers of the government by legislating beyond its specified powers, the government—after consultation with the Council of State and a favorable ruling by the Constitutional Council (see below under *Specialized bodies*)—may modify or annul such legislation. The gov-ernment may also rule by decree for a limited period by permission of parlia-ment; decree laws may be applicable to parliament's field of legislation and are enacted in the Council of Ministers after consultation with the Council of State. At the end of the limited period, parliament may revoke or amend decree laws that fall under its normal legislative power. Parliament authorizes any declaration of war.

Specialized bodies: A Constitutional Council (*Conseil Constitutionnel*) com-posed of three appointees each of the president of the republic, the president of the Assembly and the president of the Senate, and including as honorary members all previous presidents of France, has the duty of deciding whether laws conform to the constitution, examining the regulations of the two chambers, judging disputed elections and supervising referenda. The Econo-mic and Social Council (*Conseil Economique et Social*) is a consultative body whose 200 members are nominated for five years by business and trade union organizations. The High Court of Justice (*Haute Cour de Justice*), composed of an equal number of members elected from among the two chambers, has the power to try the president if indicted for high treason, and members of the government for crimes or misdemeanors committed in their term of office. The High Council of the Judiciary (*Conseil Supérieur de la Magistrature*), of nine members appointed by the government on the president's nomination, is an advisory and disciplinary body on judicial appointments. The Council of State (*Conseil d'Etat*) advises the government on the drafting of bills, ordinances and decrees; it is the highest administrative court in France. The Audit Office (*Cour des Comptes*) is formed of independent economic experts nominated for life, and supervises the execution of finance laws.

Political parties: France's unusually vigorous multiparty system is characterized by periodic groupings and regroupings in which major political ideologies continue to manifest themselves under different labels. Following the socialist victory in the 1981 elections, the parties underwent a series of realignments. The picture that emerged was as follows:

Leftist Parties

Socialist party (PS). Founded in 1905 as the French section of the Workers' International, it gained power in 1981 under François Mitterrand, and became the country's largest party. Its other leaders are Prime Minister Laurent Fabius, Michel Rocard, and Lionel Jospin, first secretary.

United Socialist party (PSU). A group of various socialist splinter groups, founded in 1960 under the leadership of Huguette Bouchardeau.

French Communist party (PCF). An offshoot of the Socialist party, PCF assumed a separate identity in 1920. The party remains a powerful force in local government and dominates the labor sector through the Confédération Générale du Travail (CGT). From 1968 to 1980, it disowned many Soviet policies, but under Secretary General Georges Marchais effected a reconciliation that led to its endorsing the Soviet invasion of Afghanistan.

Rightist Parties

Rally for the Republic (RPR). Founded in 1976 as successor to the Union of Democrats for the Republic (UDR), which itself had been formed in 1967 as the Gaullist Union of the New Republic (UNR). Under its current leader, Jacques Chirac, mayor of Paris, RPR's dominance of French politics has gradually eroded along with its membership in the National Assembly.

Union for French Democracy (UDF). Composed of a number of Giscardist centrist parties, it is led by Jean Lecanuet. UDF's component parties include:

Republican party (PR). Founded in 1977 through the merger of Giscard d'Estaing's National Federation of Independent Republicans and several smaller pro-Giscard groups, it is led by Michel Poniatowski.

Social Democratic Center (CDS). Formed in 1976 by the merger of the Democratic Center (CD) and the Democratic and Progressive Center (CDP), the latter of which was Christian in orientation. It is led by Pierre Mehaignerie and André Diligent.

Radical party (RRRS). The leading party of the prewar Third Republic, RRRS shares the anticlericalism of the left but is more conservative than the Socialists in economic matters. It is led by Olivier Bariani and Olivier Stirn.

Democratic Socialist Movement (MDS). Led by Max Lejeune.

National Center of Independents and Peasants (CNIP). The strongest free-enterprise party, it joined the RPR and UDF in the electoral alliance called Union for the New Majority in 1981.

National Front (FN). A neofascist party, anti-immigrant and anti-Semitic, it is led by Jean-Marie Le Pen. It came to prominence only after the socialist victory in 1981, and has no deputies in the National Assembly, but won several seats in the European Parliament in 1984.

There are numerous smaller parties, of which the most active are: The Ecology Political Movement; the rightist New Forces party and Movement of Democrats; and the leftist Workers' Struggle, Revolutionary Communist League, Marxist-Leninist Communist party and Revolutionary Marxist-Leninist Communist party.

The political party scoreboard in the legislature in 1984 was as follows:

National Assembly:
Socialist   269
Communist   44
Left Radical Movement   14
Other Leftist   6
Rally for the Republic   85
UDF—Republican   32
UDF—Social Democratic Center   19
UDF—Radical   2
UDF—Unaffiliated   9
National Center of Independents and Peasants   5
Other Rightist   6

Senate:
Socialist   70
Centrist Union   72
Union of Republicans and Independents   49
Democratic Left   39
Rally for the Republic   58
Communist party   24
Unaffiliated   5

President of the National Assembly: Louis Mermaz
President of the Senate: Alain Poher

Local government: On completion of the present administrative reform, France will be divided into 91 departments (*départements*), which are both state administrative districts and local communities, plus the Ville de Paris having a quasi-departmental personality. A government-appointed prefect (*préfet*) heads all state administrative services in the department.

The prefect is assisted by civil servants, and executes, or may initiate the cancellation of, the decisions of the General Council (*conseil général*) of the department. The General Council is elected by the population of the department for six years. It meets twice a year, approves the department's budget, and with the communes of the department (see below) has certain rights of oversight, particularly in financial matters.

The departments are grouped together in 21 regions. In all regions except Paris a regional prefect (*préfet de région*), chosen from the prefects of the departments in that region but maintaining his departmental powers, acts as a coordinating agent. He is advised by two regional bodies: the Inter-Departmental Administrative Conference, composed of the various prefects of the region, the inspector general of the national economy and the coordinating chief treasurer and paymaster; and the Regional Economic Development Commission, composed of representatives of the *conseils généraux* within the region (at least 25% of the Commission's membership), appointees of the prime minister (at most 25% of membership) and representatives of social, professional, economic and trade union organizations, nominated by the organizations themselves (50% of membership). The Commissions vary in size from 20 to 50 members according to the size of the region.

In the Paris region, the chief official is the administrator-general of the Paris region. He will not have a prefecture of his own, but will have authority over all the prefects of the region, and be empowered with considerable administrative and economic competence. He will be president of the Regional Administrative Conference and be advised by a regional assembly similar to those existing in the other regions.

The 38,000 communes of France are not artificial structures like the departments and enjoy a wide degree of local autonomy. Each is administered by a Municipal Council (*conseil municipal*) elected by the list system of proportional representation for six years, which in turn elects a mayor (*maire*) for the same period. Communes may group themselves into urban districts and zones.

The judicial system: Under the 1958 constitution, the president and the High Council of the Judiciary guarantee the independence of legal authorities. There is a clear distinction between civil and penal justice. There are four types of court corresponding to the major branches of French law: civil courts, penal courts, professional courts and administrative courts. Minor civil cases are heard by *tribunaux d'instance* and more serious cases by *tribunaux de grande instance*, which also act as appeal courts for the courts of first instance. Police tribunals judge petty offences (*contraventions*). Minor offences (*délits*) are judged by *tribunaux correctionnels*. The *cours d'assises* try *crimes* and are empowered to pronounce the death penalty; a mixed jury of nine jurors (chosen by lot) and three magistrates must give its verdict by at least eight votes. Appeal from this court is to the Cour de Cassation only, which decides whether the judgment is in conformity with the law; if the decision is negative, the case is sent back to another court of the same instance. Appeal from the other courts, including the specialized courts, is with the *cours d'appel* and then to the Cour de Cassation.

RECENT HISTORY

A provisional government was constituted in 1944 after the liberation of France, of which General Charles de Gaulle was head until his resignation in 1946. In 1946 the constitution of the Fourth Republic was adopted by referendum. Under the Fourth Republic, France became a founder-member of the ECSC, the EEC and Euratom. A search for guarantees of collective security against, first, the resurgence of Germany and, later, the threat of Soviet aggression, led France to sign the Dunkirk Treaty with Britain in 1947; the Brussels Treaty with Britain and the Benelux countries in 1948; and, in 1949, to join NATO. After the French parliament failed to ratify proposals for the European Defense Community, it agreed to the expansion of the Brussels Treaty into the Western European Union Treaty to permit German accession to NATO.

France's withdrawal from its colonial past was bloody. A prolonged war in Indo-China (1946–54) was followed by the Algerian war of independence (1954–62). Tunisia and Morocco were granted independence in 1956, Guinea in 1958 and all remaining African possessions, bar French Somaliland, in 1960; riots in Djibouti during the president's world tour in August 1966 led to French proposals on the future of French Somaliland. France's former African dependencies, plus the Malagasy Republic, are linked with France by bilateral agreements providing for a customs union, mutual cooperation in cultural and technical fields and in defense, and the provision of French development aid.

Domestically, while the French and the Community bureaucracy provided continuity and economic growth, the body politic witnessed a succession of 26 cabinets, which provided frequent periods of executive weakness and political frustration. During a period of near civil war brought on by an army rebellion in Algeria, this dissatisfaction with the Fourth Republic led to the return of General de Gaulle as prime minister in May 1958. In September of the same year the constitution of the Fifth Republic was approved by referendum.

Since that date, France has increasingly followed a policy designed to maximize its freedom of action and enhance its status as a world power. In 1962 the Algerian war was brought to an end by the Evian agreement. In January 1963 France vetoed Britain's application for membership of the Common Market and signed a Treaty of Friendship with West Germany. In 1965 de Gaulle was reelected president on the second ballot. French policy toward NATO reached its climax in early 1966 when France gave notice that it was withdrawing from the organization, though not the alliance, of the North Atlantic Treaty. Withdrawal of French air force units from Germany began in June 1966. French military policy under de Gaulle saw the development of an "independent" atomic strike force, the *force de frappe*, and France has not signed the Nuclear Test-Ban Treaty.

The Fifth Republic was shaken by a nationwide general strike and student agitation in May–June of 1968. De Gaulle, however, was able to ride the storm by holding new elections in June that resulted in a decisive Gaullist majority in the National Assembly. Georges Pompidou stepped down as premier and was succeeded by Maurice Couve de Murville. The recovery of the French economy in 1969 boded well for de Gaulle, but he surprised the nation by resigning in 1969 following the rejection of a series of constitutional amendments in a referendum. In the presidential election of 1969,

Pompidou was an easy winner over Alain Poher. Under a low-key Pompidou presidency, France regained a measure of tranquillity, but the Gaullist dominance was dissipated through rivalries and jealousies among the leaders and a recrudescence of scandal and corruption in public life. In the election of 1973, the Gaullist majority was reduced to 31. President Pompidou's death in 1974 led to a three-way presidential race among François Mitterrand, the candidate of the combined Socialist and Communist left, Jacques Chaban-Delmas, the heir to the Gaullist mantle, and Valéry Giscard d'Estaing, the candidate of the Independent Republicans. Giscard won the election with 50.7% of the vote.

Giscard's first premier was Jacques Chirac, who resigned in the face of mounting problems, including renewed student demonstrations, a growing export deficit, spiraling inflation and substantial gains by the left. Chirac's resignation left France for the first time in nearly three decades without a Gaullist as either president or premier. Chirac, out of office, reorganized the Gaullist party as the Rally for the Republic (RPR), and won election as mayor of Paris. In 1978, helped by dissensions in the left, the government parties, including RPR and a new Giscardian coalition, the Union for French Democracy (UDF), helped to recapture the legislature. But within the next two years, Giscard failed to consolidate his gains and allowed his popularity to slip. As a result, he lost the 1981 presidential election to François Mitterrand. In subsequent National Assembly balloting, the Socialists received a commanding legislative majority. Mitterrand's first cabinet included four Communist ministers, but they resigned in 1984 over policy disagreements.

Defense: The president is commander-in-chief of the armed forces. France has selective military service for 12 months (18 months for overseas service). The strengths of the armed forces are: army 321,320, navy 69,600, air force 103,460. Defense expenditure for the year 1982 represented approximately 3.3% of GNP. The defense estimates for 1982 were F104.44 billion ($21.23 billion). Military bases of other NATO powers on French territory are reverting to French control as France's withdrawal from the military organization of NATO becomes effective.

ECONOMY

France is well endowed with natural resources and over 80% of its land is productive. It is the largest agricultural producer in Western Europe and is virtually self-sufficient in food. The process of economic recovery and development in the period after World War II has been achieved through various four-year national plans. The government has regularly imposed a series of stabilization measures aimed at keeping down consumption, prices and incomes, while maintaining growth in certain key industries. These measures, including credit squeezes, industrial price freezes and the balancing of public finance, have succeeded in slowing down the upward movement in prices and wages, and have reduced pressure upon resources. The Fifth Plan (1966–70) envisaged a minimum annual average growth rate of 5% for GDP through modernization of the structure of agriculture, industry and commerce; it also aimed at the implementation of an incomes policy, the shortening of the working week by $1\frac{1}{2}$ hours, a heavy increase in foreign trade and an increase in all forms of investment.

In 1981, French GNP was $627.7 billion, and the GNP per capita was $11,730, the eighth highest in Europe. During the 1970s GNP per capita grew by 3%. During 1970–82, the services sector grew fastest, by 3.9%, where industry grew by 2.4% and agriculture by 0.8%. The main growth industries in recent years have been consumer goods—especially cars and textiles—and chemicals, fuels and building materials. The state controls about 40% of all industry. The relative importance of the major sectors of the economy in terms of their contributions to GDP at market prices in 1982 were:

	Percentage
Sector	of GDP
Agriculture	4
Industry	34
Services	62
Total	100

France's principal industries are textiles, fuel and power, iron and steel, mechanical engineering products (especially cars), and wood and paper-pulping. Agriculture varies according to regions because of wide differences of climate; the major products are cereals, livestock and poultry, wine and vegetables. In terms of land usage, France remains very much an agricultural nation with more than 60% of its total land area devoted to agriculture.

Foreign trade: Since 1972 France has been the fourth largest exporter in the world. Because of changes in economic policy, the direction and composition of foreign trade have been subject to shifts during this period. Official trade policies have promoted certain exports, such as farm and processed food products, industrial and high technology goods, and the shipment and servicing of whole industrial plants. As an importer, the country has become more self-sufficient in food, while nonfuel primary commodities have declined from one-fourth of total imports in 1960 to less than one-tenth in 1980. In the same period, the share of imported consumer goods, industrial components, and machinery and related products has nearly doubled. Successful conservation efforts have held the share of fuel and energy products to a level only marginally above that of 1960.

Commerce with the industrial economies has risen from about half of the 1960 total to some two-thirds in the 1980s. The EC is by far France's most important trading area, accounting for half of imports and exports. Trade with African and other developing nations, other than oil exporters, has declined. About a quarter of oil imports are paid for through arms sales to the Middle East, where France is competing effectively against British and U.S. arms exporters. In 1980 the government negotiated long-term trade agreements with East Germany, the Soviet Union and India, which is altering the composition of French trade in the 1980s.

Although committed to fairly liberal trade policies within the EC, OECD, and GATT and to the continuation of special trading relationships with its former colonies, protectionist pressures from organized labor have moderated these policies in practice. Where French jobs are at stake, the socialist government has generally been protectionist.

In 1982, total imports amounted to $115.645 billion and total exports to $92.629 billion, leaving a trade deficit of $23.016 billion, or about $2 billion per month. The annual growth rate during 1970–82 was 6.1% for exports and 6.2% for imports, both well below the relative rates of 8.1% and 11% for 1960–70. The percentage share of exports in 1981 was 8 for fuels, minerals and metals; 19 for other primary commodities; 5 for textiles and clothing; 34 for machinery and transport equipment; and 34 for other manufactures. The percentage share of imports in the same year was 10 for food, 29 for fuels, 8 for other primary commodities, 22 for machinery and transport equipment, and 31 for other manufactures. The relative importance of tourism is steadily declining.

Employment: Of France's total working population of nearly 23.2 million in 1982, 8% were employed in agriculture, 39% in industry and construction, and 53% in services. From 1960–80, the agricultural working population decreased by 64% and the number of persons employed in administration, transport, commerce and other services increased by 39%. Up to 1964 there was a mild labor shortage, but in 1965–66 the trend was reversed owing to the leveling-off of demand, the arrival on the labor market of school-leavers from the postwar "bulge" and the repatriation—begun in 1963—of settlers from Algeria.

More than four million guestworkers lived in France in the late 1970s, a fifth from Algeria, another fifth from Portugal, nearly 15% each from Italy and Spain, 8% from Morocco, and 4% from Tunisia. They filled a disproportionate number of jobs in construction, sanitation and heavy industry. New immigration of non-EC workers was terminated in 1974. However, most of the guestworkers remained in the country, despite government-sponsored efforts at repatriation. In 1980 they made up 8% of the labor force and 10% of the unemployed.

Price and wage trends: In 1983 the upward movement of prices and incomes slowed owing to the stabilization policy. Incomes showed a similar trend during the same period. Consumer prices are being used as the key indicator for the minimum guaranteed wage policy, which is part of the government's efforts to introduce a form of incomes policy.

The trade deficit halved between 1982 and 1983, and the price and wage growth decelerated. Profit margins have improved, particularly in industry. Given wage restraint and expected slow rises in import prices, inflation should be down for 1985 to the OECD average, compared with a differential of nearly four points in 1983. The growth of general government expenditure including interest payments slowed from 19% in 1982 to 11.5% in 1983.

Consumption: Private consumption expenditure amounted to 67% of GNP in 1982 and public consumption to 16%.

SOCIAL SECURITY

Health insurance: The general system, under the overall supervision of the Ministry of Social Affairs and National Solidarity, covers 72% of all employees. There are special systems for agricultural, religous, mining, railroad, public utility and public employees; seamen; nonagricultural self-employed; and agricultural self-employed. Health insurance is financed by the insured person, who contributes 5.5% of earnings; the employer, who contributes 5.45% of earnings below F88,920 a year, plus 8% of total earnings; and the government, which contributes its 12% surcharge on automobile insurance premiums, plus its proceeds of taxes on pharmaceutical advertising costs, alcohol and tobacco. Sickness benefits are from 50% to 66% of covered earnings. Medical benefits are cash refunds of part of medical expenses. Medical benefits for dependents are the same as for the insured person.

Accident insurance: The general system, under the supervision of the Ministry of Social Affairs and National Solidarity, covers about 72% of employees, vocational education students and certain unpaid members of social service organizations. There are special systems for most other employees and the self-employed. The insurance is financed by the employer, who contributes the whole cost. Temporary disability benefits (work injury) are 50% of earnings during first 28 days; maximum F445 a day. Thereafter, they are 66% of earnings; maximum, F593 a day. Permanent disability pension (work injury) is 100% of average earnings during last 12 months. Medical benefits (work injury) cover all necessary care. Survivor pensions (work injury) are payable to widow, widower or orphan.

Pensions insurance: The general system, under the supervision of the Ministry of Social Affairs and National Solidarity, covers about 70% of all employees. There are special systems for most other employees and the self-employed. The insurance is financed by the insured person, who contributes 4.7% of pensionable earnings (plus 0.1% of total earnings for a surviving spouse's allowance); and the employer, who contributes 8.2% of payroll. The old-age pension is 50% of average earnings in the 10 highest-paid years since 1947. Past earnings are revalued for wage changes. Disability pensions are 50% of earnings in the 10 highest-paid years, if totally disabled. Minimum pension is F11,300 a year. There are survivor pensions and child's supplements.

Unemployment insurance: The general system, under the supervision of the Ministry of Health and Social Security, covers all employed persons except domestic and seasonal workers. There are special systems for building and dock workers, merchant seamen and aviators. The insurance is financed by the insured person, who contributes 1.32% of earnings; the employer, who contributes 3.48% of payroll; and the government, which contributes a general revenue subsidy, plus the proceeds of a special tax on earnings of old-age pensioners. Unemployment benefits are F25 a day plus 42% of earnings (minimum, F66).

Other benefits: Under the general supervision of the Ministry of Health and Social Security there are systems of family allowances, family supplements, and prenatal allowances and birth grants. These are funded by employers, who contribute 9% of payroll, and the government, which in 1983 contributed 1% of 1982 personal income tax. Family allowances start at 23% of "base wage" (F1,093 a month) for a second child. Family supplements are F455 a month. Prenatal allowances are 22% of "base wage" for nine months. There is also a guaranteed family income system for resident families with three or more dependent children; the cash benefits vary with family income and number of children.

EDUCATION

Apart from a few advanced technical institutes and professional establishments, all public teaching is the responsibility of the state. Twenty-three educational districts (*académies*)—each embracing two to eight departments—administer primary, secondary and technical education. Each is headed by a state-appointed rector who controls the education inspectorate and is assisted by various consultative bodies formed of local government representatives, administrators and teachers. Public education is free and nonreligious. Private education is state-aided. Education is compulsory from the ages of six to 16. In 1980 educational reforms took place in order to decentralize the state school system. A more flexible system and a greater choice of curricula were introduced. The school calendar now differs according to zone, of which there are now three. In 1982, several new diploma courses were added.

Primary education: All children receive the same primary education until the age of about 11.

Secondary and vocational education: Children are graded according to their development during their first two years of secondary education (*cycle d'observation*). The first cycle of secondary education lasts from 11 to 15, and is divided into preuniversity, ordinary secondary and practical secondary levels. On the basis of their primary school record, or by examination—compulsory for pupils from private primary school—children are admitted to either a general section or a transitional section. The general section is divided into an A stream, educated in classical and modern lycées, and a B stream that is taught, in addition to those who failed the examination for secondary education—the transitional section—in general education colleges. The secondary education college brings together all three streams under one roof. Those in the transitional section of first cycle education who show sufficient ability may later rejoin the general section; the alternative is two years of terminal practical education of a more general and practical nature, ending at 15 with an end of studies diploma (*diplôme de fin d'études*), which mentions the child's professional speciality. Some may then proceed to the B general stream for two years of specialized professional training, ending with the certificate of professional proficiency (*certificat d'aptitude professionnelle*).

At the end of the fourth year the general section goes on to the second cycle of education—both short and long—which takes place between the ages of 15 and 18. Short education is for two years, leading to either the certificate of professional proficiency, or—through wider education given in technical and agricultural colleges and special sections of technical lycées—to the *brevet d'études* in industry, commerce, agriculture or administration, and possibly further to the *brevet d'agent technique*. Long education, lasting for three years, takes place in classical, modern, technical and agricultural lycées and leads on the one hand to a *brevet de technicien* in industry, commerce or agriculture and on the other to the *baccalauréat*. The reforms of second-cycle education envisage that a student, having obtained the *baccalauréat*, may take either an examination for an advanced technical institute, or a course in higher education, or enter an institute for advanced professional education. A pupil with the *brevet de technicien* may either embark on higher education or enter an institute for advanced professional education for a two-year course leading to the advanced technician's diploma (*brevet de technicien supérieur*).

Special education: Mentally and physically handicapped and maladjusted children are taught in special classes in primary schools, in small groups in secondary education colleges, and in 80 new *écoles nationales de perfectionnement*.

University and higher education: Higher education is also undergoing reform. There are both private and public institutes for higher education. Although admission to university education is unrestricted, the *baccalauréat* is the normal qualification necessary to study for a degree. Only the universities are empowered to confer state diplomas. There is a university in the chief town of most *académies* (see above). Generally, they include faculties of science, letters and human sciences, medicine, and pharmacy. But faculties, law institutes, and scientific and literary colleges have been set up in many towns not possessing universities. Strasbourg University has faculties of Catholic and Protestant theology. There are Catholic higher educational institutes in Paris, Lille, Toulouse, Angers and Lyon. The *grandes écoles* are advanced technical institutes that prepare highly selected students for careers in the civil service (Ecole Nationale d'Administration), education (Ecole Normale Supérieure), business and commerce (Ecole des Hautes Etudes Commerciales), engineering (Ecole Polytechnique), the army (St. Cyr) and several others. This education is financed entirely by the state.

Universities: Aix-Marseille, Besançon, Bordeaux, Caen, Clermont-Ferrand, Dijon, Grenoble, Lille, Lyon, Montpellier, Nancy, Nantes, Nice, Orléans, Paris (Sorbonne), Poitiers, Reims, Rennes, Strasbourg, Toulouse.

Educational institutions, 1982–83:

	Institutions	Teachers	Students
Preprimary	16,992	83,326	2,481,700
Primary	51,057	266,678	4,571,000
Secondary	11,171	410,596	5,307,000
University	—	—	1,000,000+

Source: Europa Year Book 1985.

Adult education: This is organized by the Ministry of Education with increasing state grants. The universities and other specialized institutes run advanced classes for technicians, engineers and executives.

MASS MEDIA

The press 1984:

Dailies: France-Soir, Paris, independent, 510,000; *Le Parisien Libéré*, Paris, ind., 438,300; *Ouest France*, Rennes, ind., 676,311; *Le Dauphiné Libéré*, Grenoble, ind., 362,000; *Le Figaro*, Paris, ind., liberal-conservative, 330,000; *L'Aurore*, Paris, ind., 220,000; *Libération*, Paris, left-wing, 109,000; *La Voix du Nord*, Lille, progovernment, 389,000; *Le Progrès*, Lyons, progov., 436,000; *Sud-Ouest*, Bordeaux, ind., 400,000; *Dépêche du Midi*, Toulouse, radical-socialist, 272,000; *Le Monde*, Paris, ind., 550,000; *La Nouvelle République du Centre Ouest*, Tours, progov., 274,193; *L'Est Républicain*, Nancy, ind., 263,000; *Le Provençal*, Marseilles, soc., 345,000; *Le Républicain Lorrain*, Metz, ind., 220,000; *L'Humanité*, Paris, Communist party organ, 150,000; *La Croix*, Paris, ind. Catholic, 120,000; *Les Echos*, Paris, economic-financial, 62,500.

Periodicals (Paris): L'Echo de Notre Temps (m), Catholic women's, 876,000; *Paris-Match* (w), illustrated, 645,000; *France-Dimanche* (S), popular, 736,785; *Nous Deux*, pop. romance, 1,121,000; *L'Echo de la Mode* (w), wom., 405,000; *Marie-Claire* (2m), wom., 677,772; *Marie-France*, wom., 532,189; *Elle* (w), wom., 412,000; *Le Journal du Dimanche*, Sunday edition of *France-Soir*, 510,000; *La Vie Catholique Illustrée*, Catholic illus., 500,000; *L'Express* (w), left-center, 585,000; *Le Canard Enchaîné* (w), satirical, 500,000; *Le Nouvel Observateur* (w), left-wing political and literary, 367,101.

Broadcasting: In 1975, the Office de Radiodiffusion-Télévision Française (ORTF) was replaced by seven independent state-financed companies. In July 1982 a broadcasting law was passed that modified the broadcasting organization's structure, freeing it from any direct political pressure. This ended the state monopoly of broadcasting. In 1983, approximately 50 million radio receivers and 19.5 million TV receivers were in use. The Haute Autorité de la Communication Audiovisuelle administers all French broadcasting.

FEDERAL REPUBLIC OF GERMANY

GEOGRAPHY

Features: Running across the north of West Germany is the North German Plain, stretching from Poland to the Netherlands, mainly below 300 ft/90 m. and with numerous morainic ridges, intervening valleys and marshlands. South of this area lies the Rhine massif, consisting of four plateaus divided by the Rhine, Mosel and Lahn: the Hunsrück, Taunus, Westerwald and Eifel, all rising to 1,500–3,000 ft/450–900 m. and composed largely of volcanic material. Between Mainz and Coblenz the Rhine has cut a spectacular gorge. South and east of this upland area are the sedimentary scarplands of Swabia and Franconia, consisting of an alternation of scarps and vales and seldom rising to more than 1,000 ft/300 m. In the far south, bounded by the Danube, is the Alpine foreland, a plateau of outwash material from the main Alpine ridges and dissected by the streams flowing northward to the Danube. It rises steadily in elevation as far as the Alps.

Germany has a wide variety of geology, soils and climate and thus a varied agriculture. The best of the agricultural lands are in the embayments that flank the Hercynian uplands lying south of the North German Plain, e.g., the Cologne area and other parts of Westphalia and Saxony; then come the Rhinelands and the more fertile parts of the scarpland zone. The country has considerable resources, the most important of which is the rich Ruhr coalfield (bituminous); Cologne lies on a coalfield (lignite); and there are other smaller fields. There is oil in the Rhine Valley. Iron ore is mined, especially in the Salzgitter area, though its quality is poor. There are extensive salt and potash deposits in various parts of the country. The main industrial regions are associated with the Ruhr coalfield and the Salzgitter-Braunschweig, Frankfurt, Mannheim, Stuttgart, Cologne and Hamburg areas, and West Berlin.

Area: Federal Republic 96,000 sq. miles/248,530 sq. km. West Berlin 185 sq. miles/480 sq. km. Together, these areas constitute about 53% of the area covered by the German Reich in 1937. The Soviet Sector of Berlin (East Berlin) and Soviet Zone of Occupation in Germany (East Germany or the German Democratic Republic) cover 155 sq. miles/400 sq. km. and 41,630 sq. miles/107,900 sq. km. respectively (23% of the 1937 Reich territory). The territories placed by the Potsdam Conference of 1945 under Polish and Soviet administration—the territories east of the Oder-Neisse

Line—together total 43,130 sq. miles/114,300 sq. km. (24% of Reich territory).

Mean max. and min. temperatures: Frankfurt-am-Main (50° N, 8° 30' E; 340 ft/104 m.), 75°F/24°C (July), 29°F/−2°C (Jan.); Bremen (53° N, 9° E; 50 ft/15 m.) 71°F/22°C (July), 30°F/−1°C (Jan. and Feb.); Munich (48°N, 11° 30' E; 1,740 ft/530 m.) 72°F/22°C (July), 23°F/−5°C (Jan.). *Relative humidity:* Frankfurt-am-Main 86%; Bremen 87%; Munich 87%. *Mean average rainfall:* Frankfurt-am-Main 24 in./610 mm.; Bremen 26 in./660 mm.; Munich 34 in./860 mm.

POPULATION

Total population: (1984) 61.4 million. (The number of Germans remaining in the Eastern Territories is perhaps 700,000.) Expellees and refugees from the Eastern Territories, the Sudetenland, East Germany and East Berlin, and other areas of German settlement in Eastern Europe comprise about a quarter of the population of the Federal Republic (including West Berlin and the Saarland).

Capital: BONN (286,184) is the seat of the Federal Government. *Main towns and populations:* (1984) West Berlin (1,898,900), Hamburg (1,648,800), Munich (1,298,900), Cologne (976,800), Frankfurt (829,200), Essen (650,200), Dortmund (609,400), Düsseldorf (592,200), Stuttgart (582,400), Duisburg (559,066), Bremen (555,700), Hanover (535,100), Nuremberg (484,184). *Distribution:* In 1982, 85% of the population lived in cities and 45% of this group in cities of over 500,000 inhabitants.

Language: The official language is German. There is a small Danish-speaking minority in Schleswig-Holstein. *Religion:* About 44% of the population adheres to the Evangelical-Lutheran church and about 45% are Roman Catholics.

CONSTITUTIONAL SYSTEM

Constitution: West Germany is a federal republic composed of 10 *Länder* and Berlin. The 1949 Basic Law (*Grundgesetz*) is the constitution of the Federal Republic, but ceases to be in force on the free adoption of a constitution for the whole of Germany. The constitution may be amended only by a two-thirds majority of both houses of parliament. *Head of state:* Federal President Dr. Richard von Weizsäcker. *Head of government:* Federal Chancellor Dr. Helmut Kohl (Christian Democratic Union).

Executive: The federal president (*Bundespräsident*) is elected for five years by a Federal Convention (*Bundesversammlung*) consisting of the members of the lower house of parliament (*Bundestag*) and an equivalent number of representatives of the Länder parliaments elected on a proportional representation basis.

The president nominates the federal chancellor (*Bundeskanzler*)—who determines general government policy—for election by the Bundestag, and appoints and dismisses the federal ministers on the chancellor's advice. The chancellor-nominee is elected by the Bundestag—without debate—by a simple majority, and must then be appointed by the president. If the nominee is not elected, the Bundestag has 14 days in which to elect another chancellor by simple majority. If there is no election in this period, a new vote must take place immediately in which the person receiving the largest number of votes is elected; if this number constitutes a majority, the president must appoint him, but if not then the president may either appoint him or dissolve the Bundestag. This procedure ensures that the chancellor has the confidence of the Bundestag.

The Bundestag may only express no confidence in the chancellor by a majority election of a successor, in which case the president is obliged to dismiss the incumbent and appoint the person elected as chancellor. If the Bundestag refuses the chancellor's request for a vote of confidence, or if the vote goes against him, the president, on the chancellor's request, may dissolve the Bundestag within 21 days, which right of dissolution lapses if the Bundestag elects a new chancellor. If the Bundestag does not elect a new chancellor and refuses to pass a bill that the government deems urgent, then the chancellor may request that instead of dissolution the president proclaim a six-month "state of legislative emergency" (*Gesetzgebungnotstand*; it may be declared once only in the same chancellor's term of office) to which president and *Bundesrat* must agree. During this period, the government, with the support of the *Bundesrat*, may pass any bill (except a constitutional amendment) rejected by the Bundestag.

The federal government (*Bundesregierung*) is composed of the federal ministers and the chancellor, who may not hold any other salaried office, engage in a trade or profession, or be managers of or—without the consent of the Bundestag—directors of a profit-making concern. The Basic Law makes no provision for a vote of confidence in individual ministers.

Legislature: The present Bundestag has 498 deputies elected for four years by a mixed system of proportional representation and the single-member simple majority method. A party must obtain at least 5% of the national vote or gain three seats by direct election in order to qualify for representation in the Bundestag. In addition, there are 22 members representing West Berlin who have consultative, nonvoting status only. The upper house (Bundesrat) has 41 members representing the Länder, apportioned on a population basis, and four with consultative status only for West Berlin. The members of the Bundesrat serve for no fixed period of time, being subject to appointment and recall by the Länder governments. The votes for each Land must be cast uniformly according to a prior resolution of the respective Land government. The *Bundesrat* discusses every bill that is introduced by the federal government before it is presented to the Bundestag and may itself in certain circumstances introduce legislation. The approval of the Bundesrat is necessary for such federal legislation as that affecting Länder administrative arrangements, important financial legislation and certain other matters. The Bundesrat gives its approval by a majority, otherwise differences between the two chambers may be settled by a joint committee. If the committee proposes any amendment the bill must be again voted by the Bundestag.

The federation (*Bund*) legislates exclusively in foreign affairs, defense, currency, post and telecommunications, customs, etc. Upon certain other matters, both Länder and Bund are permitted to legislate (concurrent legislation); the Länder may legislate to the extent that the Bund makes no use of its rights. In such matters as the press, cinema and the public services, the Bund lays down the general framework within which the Länder may legislate. Legislative matters reserved exclusively to the Länder are education, radio and TV broadcasting, and control of the police, although in grave emergency situations the federal government may place the police of any one Land or number of Länder under its own jurisdiction.

Political parties: The present government is a coalition of the Christian Democratic Union (CDU); its Bavarian wing, the Christian Social Union (CSU); and the Free Democrats (FDP). The Social Democrats (SPD) constitute the official opposition. Coalitions formed in the Länder do not always follow the federal prototype, even where the election results would permit. The principal West German political parties are:

Christian Democratic Union, CDU. Founded in 1945, and led by Konrad Adenauer until 1963, CDU dominated West German politics until 1969 and returned to power in 1982 under Chancellor Helmut Kohl. Its general secretary is Dr. Heiner Geissler.

Christian Social Union, CSU. The Bavarian affiliate of CDU, it tends to espouse more conservative policies under its leader Dr. Franz Josef Strauss.

Free Democratic party, FDP. A moderately rightist party that advocates economic liberalism and free enterprise, it was a coalition partner of the Social Democrats from 1972 to 1982 but joined CDU following the 1982 elections. Its leader, Hans-Dietrich Genscher, stepped down in 1985 and was succeeded by Martin Bangemann.

Social Democratic party, SPD. The oldest German political party, SPD was founded in the 19th century and reestablished in 1945. Under Willy Brandt, the party's original Marxist outlook was largely discarded in favor of a more pragmatic social-welfare approach to domestic affairs and détente with the Eastern bloc in foreign affairs. SPD is led by Hans-Jochen Vogel; former Chancellor Helmut Schmidt stepped down as vice chairman in 1984.

Green party (Die Grünen). Described as the "Antiparty party," the Greens gained their first representation in the Bundestag in 1983 with 27 seats. The party holds a melange of leftist and environmental ideas and basically serves as a gadfly in German politics. It is led by Rebekka Schmidt, Rainer Trampert and Wilhelm Knabe.

Liberal Democratic party, LDP. Founded in 1982 by dissident FDP members who opposed coalition with CDU, it is led by Ulrich Krueger.

National Democratic party, NPD. It was formed in 1964 through the merger of a number of neo-Nazi and rightist groups, but has carefully avoided the constitutional ban on Nazism. It is unrepresented in the Länder parliaments or in the Bundestag. Its leader is Martin Mussgnug.

German Communist party, DKP. Heir to the former Communist party led by Max Reimann that was banned as unconstitutional in 1956, it was formally reestablished in 1969. It is unrepresented in the Länder Parliaments and in the Bundestag. It is led by Herbert Mies.

In the current Bundestag, the party lineup after the 1983 elections was as follows:

CDU/CSU 244 seats
FDP 34 seats
SPD 193 seats
Greens 27 seats

President of the Bundestag is Richard Stucklen.

Local government: The Länder are autonomous but not sovereign states. Each Land has its own constitution. Each Land elects a parliament for four years, which is generally called the *Landtag*, but in Bremen and Hamburg, where the function of Land and Municipality is combined (a holdover from the days of the Hanseatic League), it is the city council (*Bürgerschaft*). In Bavaria there is a second chamber (*Senat*) of 60 members, representing professional and religious interests. Each Land has a government (*Landesregierung*) presided over by a *Ministerpräsident* (the corresponding organs for Bremen and Hamburg are an executive *Senat* headed by a mayor, *Bürgermeister*, and deputy mayor). Generally, the ministers of the Länder are appointed by the mayor or Ministerpräsident and are responsible to the Land parliament. There is a Constitutional Court (*Verfassungs-* or *Staatsgerichtshof*) in Bavaria, Hesse, Bremen, Rhineland-Palatinate, Baden-Württemberg and the Saar, whose members are professional and lay judges and persons elected by the Länder parliaments. North Rhine-Westphalia, Lower Saxony, Bavaria, Hesse, Rhineland-Palatinate and Baden-Württemberg are divided into from three to eight governmental districts (*Regierungsbezirke*), each headed by a *Regierungspräsident* appointed by and responsible to the Land government. These bodies supervise all the smaller units of local government. There are no separate legislative and judicial bodies at this level.

Functions—such as road construction, secondary education, police administration and hospitals—that are too large for the basic unit of local government in Germany, the commune (see below), are the concern of the Regierungsbezirke and the counties (*Landkreise*). A metropolitan community with a minimum population of 25,000 to 100,000 may detach itself from the Landkreis in which it is situated and constitute itself a city-county (*Stadtkreis*) or county-free city (*Kreisfreie Stadt*) and combine under a single authority those functions otherwise divided (within the county) between the county and the communes. Each Landkreis elects a county council (*Kreistag*), which in turn elects a chief executive officer called the *Landrat*. The corresponding authorities in the Stadtkreis are the city council (*Stadtverordnetenversammlung*) and the lord mayor (*Oberbürgermeister*), who is assisted by a number of deputies (*Beigeordneten*).

The communes (*Gemeinden*) have considerable autonomy. Although they execute the legislation of both Bund and Länder, they are supervised by the latter only, through the Regierungsbezirke. Villages, towns and cities are all communes—unless populous enough to become a Stadtkreis—and each elects a communal council (*Gemeinderat*, *Gemeindevertretung*, or in the city-communes *Stadtrat*) and in some cases an executive body (*Magistrat*) headed by a mayor (*Bürgermeister*), or in the city-communes by an Ober-bürgermeister. Most city-counties and city-communes as well as the city-states of Berlin, Bremen and Hamburg are further divided into boroughs or administrative districts (*Bezirke* and *Ortsämter*).

Judicial system: The court of first instance is the district court (*Amtsgericht*) in minor civil and criminal cases, with a single professional judge sitting either alone or with two lay judges (*Schöffen*) in criminal cases, according to the degree of seriousness. The next highest court, the regional court (*Landgericht*), has in civil cases original jurisdiction as a court of first instance in more important matters and also acts as an appeal court in cases decided by the Amtsgerichte. In criminal matters, the Landgericht also has original and appellate jurisdiction. For original jurisdiction in serious criminal cases the Landgericht is composed of three professional and two lay judges, or of three professional and seven lay judges when constituting a *Schwurgericht* in the most serious cases. The lay judges (known as *Geschworene* in a Schwurgericht) deal with both law and fact in conjunction with the professional judges, and decide by majority vote.

The appeal courts (*Oberlandesgerichte*) are the highest Land courts and are composed of criminal and civil sections made up of three judges each. The Oberlandesgericht is the final instance for district courts and the second instance for regional courts. It does not retry cases, but either confirms the verdict of a lower court or sends it back for retrial. The final court of civil and criminal jurisdiction is the Federal Court of Justice (*Bundesgerichtshof*). It is the final court of appeal for all cases originating in the Landgerichte, except those tried by the Schwurgericht, for which it is the first court of appeal, there being no intermediate review by the Oberlandesgericht. The Federal Court of Justice also has original jurisdiction regarding treason, which comprises both internal treason (*Hochverrat*)—offences against the internal constitutional order—and external treason (*Landesverrat*)—aid to a foreign power.

Other federal courts deal with administration, labor, social and financial matters. The Federal Constitutional Court (*Bundesverfassungsgericht*) checks constitutionality of executive, legislative and judicial action, advises in Bund/Länder disputes and safeguards individual liberties. Its members are elected by Bundestag and Bundesrat and may not hold federal/Land executive/legislative appointments.

Other federal judges are appointed by the president on selection of committees of federal and Land ministers. Länder judges are appointed by the Land justice minister and a similar selection committee. Federal judges may be dismissed only by the president after judicial sentence by a two-thirds majority of the Constitutional Court. There is no capital punishment.

Berlin: Berlin has a special legal status, governed by agreements (revised) of May/July 1945, as an area of four-power occupation. Since 1948, when the Soviet representative walked out, the authority of the Four-Power Kommandatura has in practice been applied only by Britain, the United States and France in the Western Occupation sectors. Similarly West Berlin's own municipal organs acting in subordination to the Kommandatura exist de jure as the government for the entire city, but operate de facto only in the three Western sectors. Although Berlin is defined by the Basic Law as a Land of the Federal Republic, federal legislation is not binding on Berlin; it may, however, be adopted and applied by the West Berlin government. There are also the restrictions upon the Berlin representatives in the Bundestag and Bundesrat (see above, *Legislature*).

Berlin's constitution dates from 1950. The executive authority of Berlin is the Senate (*Senat*) headed by the governing mayor (*Regierender Bürgermeister*) with a Bürgermeister as his deputy and a maximum of 16 Senators (*Senatoren*) as administrative departmental heads. The Senat is responsible to the House of Representatives (*Abgeordnetenhaus*). The House is elected for four years by the list system of proportional representation with the same 5% minimum as in national elections, and numbers 200 members; in fact, only 140 members are elected by the West Berlin electorate, the remainder being reserved for the East Berlin electorate.

The judicial system in Western Berlin is identical to that of the Federation. There are nine Amtsgerichte and one Landgericht. The supreme court of Berlin is the *Kammergericht*. Final appeal in civil and criminal cases is to the Bundesgerichtshof. The court structure is the same for administrative courts, the final court being the *Bundesverwaltungsgericht*. Like certain Länder, West Berlin has a Constitutional Court. West Berlin comprises 12 of the 20 traditional boroughs (Bezirke) of Greater Berlin. Each Bezirk has a borough council (*Bezirksverordnetenversammlung*) with some financial and local administrative powers, composed of 45 members elected by proportional representation for the same period as the House of Representatives. Each council elects a borough office (*Bezirksamt*), composed of a mayor (*Bezirksbürgermeister*) and a number of salaried officers (*Bezirkstadträte*).

RECENT HISTORY

After World War II the German Reich was divided into four Occupation zones administered by the United States, the Soviet Union, Britain and France; Berlin was constituted a separate area of occupation under the same four powers. Parts of the Soviet Zone were placed under Soviet and Polish administration pending a final peace conference. With the advent of the cold war, four-power cooperation virtually ceased and instead two states, the Federal Republic, comprising the occupation areas of the three Western powers, and the German Democratic Republic, formed from the Soviet Zone, were set up in September and October 1949 respectively. In the period 1948–49, the Soviet Union blockaded the Allied land routes to the Western sectors of Berlin and brought about a split in the city administration.

West Germany joined the Council of Europe in 1951 and became a founder-member of the ECSC in 1952 and in 1957 of Euratom and the EEC. After the failure in 1954 to set up a European Army under the European Defense Community, the Brussels Treaty was revised in October 1954 (Paris Agreement) to permit the membership of the Federal Republic and Italy, and to facilitate the former's rearmament and membership in NATO. At the same time, the Federal Republic was recognized by the United States, Britain and France as the only state entitled to speak for Germany in international affairs, and the Occupation Statute was rescinded. With the ratification of these agreements in May 1955, West Germany regained its state sovereignty and became a member of NATO. In January 1957 the Saarland returned to full German control.

After the breakdown of the foreign ministers' conferences on the joint administration of Germany in 1949, four-power contact on German reunification continued, but Stalin's proposals of March 1952 were not considered serious by the West. The next foreign ministers' conference (in Berlin) did not take place until early 1954, and followed upon the East German uprising of June 1953, Soviet suppression of which entailed increased Soviet commitment to a separate East German regime.

There have been subsequent major conferences on German reunification and related subjects at Geneva—twice in 1955 and again (when both the Federal Republic and East Germany were represented as advisers) in 1959. The last Geneva Conference took place during a sustained Soviet and East German offensive against Berlin in 1958–63, which had as one result the building of the Berlin Wall in August 1961, aimed at stopping the flow of refugees from East Germany. In January 1963, France and the Federal Republic signed a treaty of friendship. In the same year the Federal Republic ratified the nuclear test ban treaty.

Because of the division of Germany, the Federal Republic was not until 1973 a member of the United Nations. Until 1967 it was the policy of the Federal Republic either not to recognize, or to withdraw recognition of, any state that recognized the German Democratic Republic (the Hallstein Doctrine); the only full exception to this was the Soviet Union, with which diplomatic relations were established in September 1955. In 1970, for the first time, representatives of the Federal Republic and the German Democratic Republic met for formal talks. In 1972 they concluded a basic treaty outlining their relationship. In 1973 both became members of the United Nations.

Following the 1969 elections, Willy Brandt, the Social Democratic leader as well as foreign minister of the CDU-SPD government, became chancellor at the head of an SPD-FDP coalition. Brandt's chancellorship was cut short in 1974 by the revelation that one of his top aides was an East German spy. Brandt was replaced by Helmut Schmidt. In the elections of 1976 and 1980, the coalition majority was retained, but at reduced levels. In 1982 the FDP broke with its SPD partner over defense and economic policies and precipitated a vote of no confidence that led to the return to office of the CDU under Helmut Kohl. The new CDU-FDP coalition made significant gains in the 1983 elections against a badly split SPD.

In 1984 the government was embroiled in the Flick scandal. Economics Minister Otto von Lambsdorf was accused of accepting $50,000 from German industrialist Friedrich Flick in exchange for tax exemptions to Friedrich Flick Industrieverwaltung. Hans-Dietrich Genscher, leader of the FDP, stepped down as chairman in 1985 but remained as foreign minister.

The Federal Republic has provided large-scale compensation—in both cash and kind—to the victims of Hitler's Germany, and in particular to Israel.

Defense: The commander-in-chief of the armed forces is the defense minister in peacetime and the federal chancellor in wartime. Under the Paris Agreements (October 1954), the Federal Republic bound itself not to construct on its own territory atomic, biological or chemical weapons. Service in the Federal armed forces (*Bundeswehr*) is for 15 months. Total strength in 1982 was 513,700: army 335,200, navy 36,500, air force 106,000, territorial and local defense forces about 36,000. All operational forces except those of the last category are NATO-assigned. Other NATO forces in West Germany are mainly British, U.S. and French. The 1981 defense budget was DM42.09 billion ($20.17 billion), representing nearly 2.5% of GNP.

West Berlin: About 11,000 Allied troops are stationed here. Articles 5 and 6 of the North Atlantic Treaty define an attack upon the occupation forces in Europe of any member of NATO as an attack upon the Alliance as a whole. Berliners are not liable for military service with the Bundeswehr, and the Federal Republic has scrupulously observed the occupation status since there are no West German soldiers there, nor is advertising for the Bundeswehr permitted. Within Berlin itself there is a special police force (*Bereitschaftspolizei*), as well as regular police, to provide additional internal security.

ECONOMY

Background: After World War II the German economy recovered quickly following financial reforms. Since then the rate of economic growth has consistently surpassed that of any other European country. This "economic miracle" has taken place under the government's policy of a "social market economy"—a system of free competition subject to social obligations, with considerably more state involvement than is generally admitted. Between 1970 and 1979 GNP at constant prices grew at an annual average rate of 2.6%. In 1983 GNP was $827.790 billion. The average annual rate of industrial growth in 1970–82 was nearly 2.0%. The contributions of the different sectors of the economy to GDP in 1982 were:

Sector	Percentage of GDP
Agriculture, forestry and fishing	2
Industry including construction	46
Services	52
GDP	100

The Federal Republic is predominantly industrial. Its principal industries are coal mining, iron and steel production, machine construction, electrical, steel and metal, chemicals, textiles and food. Its main growth industries are manufacturing, coal mining, building and services; next in importance come trade and transport. Agriculture, forestry and fishing have expanded less rapidly, and Germany remains, both in absolute terms and in proportion to population, by far the largest food importer in the EC. The main emphasis of agricultural production is on animal products. The main crops are oats, wheat and potatoes, and there has been a considerable rise in eggs and poultry production. Germany also produce nearly five hectoliters of wine a year. Forestry is another important part of the country's economy.

In spite of its underlying strength, the West German economy has had its problems in recent years. In 1979, for the first time since 1965, the current account of the balance of payments registered a deficit. The following year, the deficit tripled to $16 billion. This situation has since been corrected. Between 1975 and 1978, unit manufacturing costs rose to a level exceeding that of the Federal Republic's main competitors, stimulating an outflow of capital. Monetary policy remained very restrictive. The Deutsche Bundesbank kept interest rates high in order to curb the outflow of funds and maintain a low rate of growth in the money supply. In 1983 the rate of growth of GNP was 5.9%; the annual growth rate of the consumer price index for 1970–81 was 5%

Foreign trade: Although West Germany is the world's largest trader, many major export industries are facing stiff international competition. Trade deficits pose a constant threat to the economy because exports generate 27% of GDP, but they are concentrated in industries that generate a disproportionate share of income and employment.

More than three-fourths of West German exports go to the OECD countries and more than half to the EC. West Germany has been particularly susceptible to oil-price increases. Although energy consumption is declining, fuel accounts for 24% of total import costs and the retail price of gasoline is very high. The Federal Republic has also increased exports to developing countries and to communist states. Among the latter, East Germany is treated as a special case. The growing volume of transactions between the two Germanies is not entered in the foreign accounts. West Germany is one of the strongest advocates of free trade in the world, although the Japanese penetration of European markets causes periodic concern among West German policymakers.

Except for a few years in the late 1970s, West Germany has always maintained a favorable balance of trade. In 1982, exports amounted to $176.428 billion and imports to $155.856 billion, leaving a favorable balance of $20.572 billion. The annual growth rate during 1970–82 was 5.6% for exports and 5.2% for imports (compared to 10.1% and 10.0% respectively during 1960–70). The percentage share of merchandise exports in 1981 was fuels 7%, other primary commodities 7%, textiles and clothing 5%, machinery and transport equipment 45% and other manufactures 36%. The percentage share of merchandise imports in 1981 was 12% food, 24% fuels, 9% other primary commodities, 20% machinery and transport equipment, 35% other manufactures.

Employment: Full employment was maintained from 1949 until the early 1980s. In 1982 the total labor force was nearly 28.3 million, of which 4% was employed in agriculture, 46% in industry and 50% in the services sector. The main countries of origin of the large numbers of foreign workers are

Italy, Spain and Greece. The heavy flow of labor from East Germany in the postwar years has been stopped. Unemployment was 5.5% in 1982.

Price and wage trends: Between 1967 and 1983, the average annual rise in net earnings far exceeded the rise in the cost of living index. In the period 1967–83, average hourly earnings rose by 66.4%, prices by 5% and real income by 24.1%.

Consumption: In 1982 private consumption accounted for 55% of GNP and public consumption for 21%. In 1970–82 private consumption rose by 2.5% and public consumption by 3.2%.

West Berlin: The rate of economic growth in West Berlin has matched and often exceeded that of the Federal Republic, particularly in industrial production. West Berlin suffers from an acute shortage of labor. The trend in prices, incomes and consumer expenditure corresponds to that of the Federal Republic. Unemployment is higher.

SOCIAL SECURITY

Health insurance: Under the general supervision of the Federal Ministry of Labor and Social Affairs, the scheme covers most employed and self-employed persons. It is funded by the insured, the employer and the government. The sickness benefit is 100% of total earnings for the first six weeks, paid by the employer; thereafter, sickness funds pay 80% of covered earnings for up to 78 weeks over three years. There are maternity benefits and maternity grants under the program. Medical benefits cover services provided to patients by doctors, hospitals and pharmacists under contract with and paid by the sickness fund. Medical benefits for dependents are the same as for the insured person.

Accident insurance: Under the general supervision of the Federal Ministry of Labor and Social Affairs, the scheme covers employed persons, most categories of the self-employed, apprentices, students, children in kindergarten and family helpers. There is a special system for public employees. The insurance is financed by the employer and the government. Temporary disability benefit (work-related injury) is the same as for ordinary sickness under the health insurance program. Permanent disability pension (work injury) is 66⅔% of the latest year's earnings, if the insured is totally disabled. There are supplements available, as well as a comprehensive plan for medical benefits. Survivor pensions (work injury) are available to widows, dependent widowers, orphans and parents or grandparents (if they are needy). Maximum survivor pensions are 80% of the insured's earnings.

Pensions insurance: Under the general supervision of the Federal Ministry of Labor and Social Affairs, the scheme covers most employed and self-employed persons. It is financed by the insured person, the employer and the government. Old-age pensions are generally available at age 63 with 35 years of coverage, or at age 65 with 15 years of coverage, for both men and women. Partial retirement benefits are available up to age 65. Disability pension is available if the insured person is incapable of any gainful activity (general disability), or has suffered a 50% reduction of earning capacity in his or her usual occupation (occupational disability). Old-age pension is 1.5% of the worker's assessed wages times the years of insurance coverage.

Disability pension for general disability is 1.5%, for occupational invalidity 1%, of the worker's assessed wages times years of insurance coverage. There are child's supplements. Survivor pensions are available for widows, dependent widowers and orphans. Maximum survivor pensions are 100% of the general disability pension of the insured.

Unemployment insurance: Under the general supervision of the Federal Ministry of Labor and Social Affairs, the scheme covers employed persons, with certain exceptions. It is financed by the insured person, the employer and the government. Unemployment benefits are 69% to 41% of earnings, varying inversely with the wage level. There are supplements for dependents. Unemployment assistance (means-tested) is 60% to 35% of earnings, varying inversely with the wage level, payable to workers ineligible for regular benefits, and after exhaustion of their regular benefits. Maintenance allowances are available.

Other benefits: Under the general supervision of the Federal Ministry of Labor and Social Affairs, family allowances are available to eligible residents with one or more children. The government contributes the entire cost.

EDUCATION

Education is entirely the responsibility of the Länder governments. Although the Länder systems vary in detail, the basic features are uniform, and the meetings of the permanent conference of Länder ministers of culture—which has a general secretariat in Bonn—facilitates coordination. Education is compulsory from six to 18, at least eight years of which must be spent in full-time education. Most schools are state-supported, and private schools are state-supervised. Primary and vocational education is free; at the other levels where fees are payable—and free schooling is becoming increasingly common here also—grants are provided, and fees are waived for the needy. Primary education is coeducational, but at intermediate and secondary schools the sexes are taught separately. Religious education given under church supervision is compulsory where parents wish it.

Primary education: The majority of children receive their entire compulsory education from six to 15 at the primary schools (*Volksschulen*). All children have a common education from six to 10 (to 12 in Bremen, Berlin and Hamburg) at the basic school (*Grundschule*). Those who pass the entrance examinations (about 22%) go on to intermediate schools (about 15%) and secondary schools (about 7%). The remainder (about 78%) go on to the upper classes of primary school (*Volksschuloberstufe*).

Secondary education: At the intermediate school (*Realschule* or *Mittelschule*) courses last for six years and provide a high level of general education. At the end of the course students take the intermediate examination (*Mittlere Reife*). Courses at the secondary schools (*Gymnasien*) last for nine years, ending with the final examination (*Abitur* or *Reifeprüfung*), which is both a leaving certificate and a qualification for university entrance. About 88% of successful students go on to university. The Gymnasien are of three types, emphasizing the classics, modern languages or mathematics and natural science. There are also secondary schools specializing in domestic science (*Frauenoberschulen*) and economics (*Wirtschaftsoberschulen*), and those successful in the final examination of these schools are entitled to attend a particular university faculty. In the city-states of West Berlin, Hamburg and Bremen, the "unified school" (*Einheitsschule*) system has been started, combining primary and secondary schools and providing a uniform basic grade with an upper grade consisting of practical, technical and economics branches. Private boarding schools such as the Waldorf Schools also provide different school programs for the compulsory period of education.

Vocational education: Basically, this is organized into the practical side, the apprenticeship (*Lehrzeit*), and the theoretical side, which is a part of the general educational syllabus. It is given mainly in four types of school—the part-time vocational school (*Berufsschule*), the full-time vocational school (*Berufsfachschule*), the full-time specialist school (*Fachschule*) and the full-time senior specialist school (*Höhere Fachschule*). Apprenticeships generally last for three years and conclude with the journeyman's examination in the trades and agriculture (*Gehilfenprüfung*) and industry (*Facharbeiterprüfung*). After further practical experience, the master's examination (*Meisterprüfung*) may be taken. Attendance at the Berufsschule is compulsory for six to 12 hours per week for students from 15 to 18 years, and courses are intended to supplement their full-time professions. At the same time, within the Berufsschule, they may attend for further general education at the continuation school (*Berufsaufbauschule*). At the end of the course, students may sit a vocational training examination (*Fachschulreife*), success in which permits them to go to the Höhere Fachschule.

The Berufsfachschulen provide full-time courses of one to three years orientated toward a specific profession, particularly in commerce, office and domestic occupations. About one-third of the Berufsfachschulen are privately run. The Fachschulen cover some 50 different professions and in general provide supplementary theoretical training to students of a minimum of 18 years of age, who have already had full-time vocational training. Courses last from one to eight six-monthly periods, the average course lasting for four. The Höhere Fachschulen and the engineering schools (*Ingenieurschulen*) provide courses of from two to three years for students over 18 who possess either the Mittlere Reife or the Fachschulreife. They prepare students for intermediate and senior positions in professions, insofar as a university or equivalent education is not required.

Special education: The mentally backward are taught either in special classes attached to the Volksschulen (*Hilfschule-Klassen*) or in special schools (*Hilfschulen*). There are schools for physically handicapped children and those with adjustment difficulties.

University and higher education: There are in West Germany and West Berlin 48 universities and nine technical colleges. The universities and technical universities are ensured the right of self-administration under a chancellor and senate. They confer their own doctorates, acknowledge the right to teach and recruit their own staff by proposing candidates to the appropriate Land minister of culture. According to the Basic Law, the equipment and maintenance of the higher educational institutions is a responsibility of the Länder in which they are situated, with the right of general supervision belonging to the Land minister of culture.

A university building program, begun in 1971, has failed to relieve a severe crisis of space in the Federal Republic's universities. Consequently, legislation has been passed limiting numbers of students and length of courses. This restriction applies especially to such subjects as medicine.

Universities, technical universities and faculties:

Universities: Free University of Berlin, Bochum, Bonn, Cologne, Erlangen-Nuremberg, Frankfurt, Freiburg, Giessen, Göttingen, Hamburg, Heidelberg, Kiel, Mainz, Marburg, Munich, Münster, Saarbrücken, Tübingen, Würzburg. There are new universities in Bremen, Constanz and Regensburg.

Technical universities: Aachen, Berlin Technical University, Braunschweig, Clausthal Mining Academy, Darmstadt, Hanover, Karlsruhe, Munich, Stuttgart.

Faculties of university status: Düsseldorf Academy of Medicine, Hanover Academy of Medicine, Hanover College of Veterinary Science, Hohenheim Agricultural College, Mannheim College of Economics.

Educational institutions, 1982–83:

	Institutions 1982	Teachers 1982	Students (000) 1982	Students (000) 1983
Primary	18,468	243,093	4,501.0	4,246.7
General Secondary:				
Intermediate schools	2,639	64,414	1,278.1	1,214.4
Grammar schools	2,489	123,754	2,050.5	1,960.7
Comprehensive schools	285	26,555	226.3	224.7
Special	2,820	41,429	319.3	301.9
Vocational secondary[1]	7,281	75,683	2,493.5	2,519.3
Trade and technical	2,970	9,065	207.1	205.6
Higher:				
Universities etc.[2]	n.a.	105,915	931.9	976.6
Colleges of art and music	n.a.	4,363	19.9	20.4
Vocational	n.a.	20,465	251.4	276.1

[1] Including part-time students.
[2] Universities and other institutions of similar standing, including colleges of theology and colleges of education.
Source: Statisches Bundesamt, Wiesbaden.

Adult education: The peoples' universities (*Volkshochschulen*) require no entrance qualifications and confer no leaving certificates, but provide evening courses emphasizing general knowledge and practical subjects. Most are maintained by the municipalities, but some in South Germany are run by voluntary associations. In 1980 there were 904 Volkshochschulen catering to more than 4.14 million people. In addition, there were about 30 residential universities (*Heim-Volkshochschulen*), educational centers offering a home and community life, combining normal adult education with a greater emphasis on political education and civics, and also providing intensive courses of advanced instruction. In 1983 there were about 12,700 public libraries maintained by the communes and a further 900 run by the churches.

MASS MEDIA

The press (1984):

Dailies: Bild-Zeitung, Hamburg, independent, 5,400,000; *Westdeutsche Allgemeine*, Essen, ind., 62,000; *Hamburger Morgenpost*, Hamburg, ind., 236,000; *Ruhr-Nachrichten*, Dortmund, ind., 250,000; *Hamburger Abendblatt*, Hamburg, ind., 278,000; *BZ*, West Berlin, ind., 323,000; *Rheinische Post*, Düsseldorf, ind-CDU, 400,000; *Die Welt*, Hamburg, ind., 230,000; *Frankfurter Allgemeine Zeitung*, Frankfurt, ind., 350,000; *Westfälische Rundschau*, Dortmund, ind., 145,000; *Süddeutsche Zeitung*, Munich, ind., 337,000; *Neue Ruhr Zeitung (NRZ)*, Essen, ind., 215,000; *Berliner Morgenpost*, W. Berlin, ind., 183,000; *Nürnberger Nachrichten*, Nuremberg, ind., 343,000; *Kölner Stadtanzeiger*, Cologne, ind., 245,000; *Rhein-Zeitung*, Koblenz, ind., 210,000; *Die Rheinpfalz*, Ludwigshafen, ind., 240,000; *Augsburger Allgemeine*, Augsburg, ind., 316,000; *Münchner Merkur*, Munich, ind., 175,000; *Kölnische Rundschau*, Cologne, ind-CDU, 163,000; *Stuttgarter Zeitung*, Stuttgart, ind., 156,000.

Weeklies: Hör Zu, Hamburg, illustrated and broadcasting, 4,300,000; *Bild am Sonntag*, Hamburg, ind., Sunday, 2,400,000; *burda-moden*, Offenburg, women's, 2,300,000; *Brigitte*, Hamburg, women's, 1,642,400; *Frau im Spiegel*, Lübeck, women's, 1,280,000; *Quick*, Munich, illus., 976,000; *Stern*, Hamburg, illus., 1,700,000; *Bunte Illustrierte*, Offenburg, illus., 1,350,530; *Neue Revue*, Hamburg, illus., 1,250,000; *Für Sie*, Hamburg, women's, 1,048,000; *Der Spiegel*, Hamburg, ind., political/cultural, 1,100,000; *Welt am Sonntag*, ind., Sunday, 336,000; *Die Zeit*, Hamburg, ind. pol./cult., 398,000.

Broadcasting: The Working Association of German Radio Stations under Statutory Regulations (Arbeitsgemeinschaft der öffentlich-rechtlichen Rundfunkanstalten Deutschlands—ARD) is the coordinating body for West German radio and TV. To it belong nine regional radio stations (nonprofit public corporations) and the two independent national radio stations, Radio Germany (Deutschlandfunk) and German Wave (Deutsche Welle), and the First German Television Channel (Deutsches Fernsehen—DF). RIAS (Rundfunk im Amerikanischen Sektor, which provides radio programs from West Berlin for East Berlin and East Germany, is represented via observer status in ARD. All regional stations provide local radio programs, and together they contribute TV programs to DF. The Second Television Channel (Zweites

Deutsches Fernsehen—ZDF) is not a member of ARD; it provides no regional programs and is partly funded by advertising revenue.

The organization of regional broadcasting is a responsibility of the Länder, and radio and TV installations are the property of the radio stations and are managed by them. Deutschlandfunk has the task of organizing radio broadcasts for and to the whole of Germany and other European countries, while Deutsche Welle broadcasts in many languages to all parts of the world. Broadcasting is financed by license fees and advertising revenue. There are several foreign radio stations: the American Forces Network; British Forces Broadcasting Service, Germany; Radio Free Europe/Radio Liberty Inc.; and Voice of America. In 1984 there were 22,340,623 TV sets and 24,856,997 radio receivers in use in the Federal Republic.

GIBRALTAR

Features: The territory consists mostly of a mass of rock. *Area:* 2.12 sq. miles, 5.5 sq. km.

Population: (est. 1983) 30,000.

Language: English is the official language but Spanish is spoken also.

Religion: 74.5% Roman Catholic, 8.5% Muslim, 8% Anglican, 2.5% Jewish.

CONSTITUTIONAL SYSTEM

Constitution: Gibraltar is a British Crown Colony deriving a great deal of internal self-government from the 1964 Gibraltar (Constitution) Order in Council. A new constitution came into effect in 1969. It contains a code of human rights. *Head of state:* Admiral Sir David Williams (governor, representing Queen Elizabeth II). *Head of government:* Chief Minister Sir Joshua A. Hassan.

Executive: Executive authority is vested in the governor, who is advised by the Gibraltar Council of five elected and four ex-officio members. The elected members are appointed from the Legislative Council by the governor in consultation with the chief minister. The chief minister is president of the Council of Ministers, which discusses policy matters in detail. Its recommendations are forwarded to the Gibraltar Council by the chief minister for formal approval. The chief minister may appoint such additional members to the Council of Ministers as he deems necessary.

Legislature: The Legislative Council consists of a speaker, two ex-officio members—the attorney-general and financial and development secretary—and 15 members elected by proportional representation for four years. From its number, five are appointed to the Gibraltar Council. *Political parties* are the Gibraltar Labor party and Association for the Advancement of Civil Rights, founded in 1942, led by Sir Joshua A. Hassan; the Gibraltar Socialist Labor party, founded in 1976, led by Joe Bossano; and the Democratic party of British Gibraltar, founded in 1978, led by Peter Isola. In the January 26, 1984, general election, the Gibraltar Labor party won eight seats in the House of Assembly and the Gibraltar Socialist Labor party won seven seats.

Local government: Municipal affairs are conducted by the elected City Council presided over by a mayor. *Judicial system:* There is a Supreme Court presided over by the chief justice, a court of appeals, a court of first instance, and a magistrates' court.

RECENT HISTORY

Britain acquired Gibraltar under the Treaty of Utrecht, 1713. The long-standing Anglo-Spanish contention over the exact status of the colony has not yet been resolved, although direct negotiations resumed in 1985 between the two governments. Gibraltar is, along with Britain, effectively within the EC.

Defense: There is a volunteer reserve unit, the Gibraltar Regiment, a local defense force. Conscription has been abolished. There is also a Royal Navy Reserve unit. Gibraltar is a NATO subcommand. Stationed at Gibraltar are British naval, army, and air force units.

ECONOMY

Owing to a lack of natural resources, the economy depends upon the transit trade, the tourist industry and revenue from British service spending. The construction industry is also important as is Gibraltar's banking and financial center. There are small light industries such as clothing manufacture, fish and fruit canning, tobacco and beverages. In 1982–83, Gibraltar's GNP was about £84 million.

SOCIAL SECURITY

There are two contributory schemes covering accident (work-related) insurance and social insurance benefits, such as maternity and death grants, old-age pensions, widows' benefits and unemployment benefits. There are noncontributory schemes funded by government to cover retirement pensions, family allowances, etc.

EDUCATION

Education is compulsory and free from five to 15 in government schools, of which there are eight at primary level and five at middle. There are two schools for children of military personnel. There are also several private schools. The government and private sources provide scholarships for university study. A special school exists for handicapped children.

MASS MEDIA

The press (1983): Gibraltar Chronicle, English daily, 3,000; *Vox*, Spanish and English weekly, 2,800; *Gibraltar Evening Post*, independent weekly, 1,500; *Panorama*, English, independent weekly, 2,000. *Broadcasting:* The Gibraltar Broadcasting Corporation is responsible for radio and TV broadcasting. GBC-Radio broadcasts 17 hours a day in Spanish and English. GBC-TV broadcasts five hours a day in English.

GREECE

Features: Greece is largely a mountainous area composed of ancient rocks (especially in the north), limestones and young volcanics. Much of the country lies over 5,000 ft/1,500 m., the only true lowland being the narrow coastal plains, Thessaly and the area northwest of Thebes. The country is divided into two main parts by the Gulf of Corinth and there is a large number of islands. Southern Greece is Mediterranean in climate and vegetation; the north is more continental, with greater temperature extremes. The chief island groups are the Ionian Isles off the west coast and the Cyclades and the Dodecanese in the east, between Greece and Turkey. In the south lies the largest island, Crete.

Although agriculture has traditionally been important, and has produced self-sufficiency and exports, less than 25% of the land surface is cultivable. The main cultivated areas are the lowlands and the river valleys. As in many parts of the Mediterranean region, sparse water supply frequently limits agriculture. A wide variety of minerals is produced, including iron ore, pyrites, manganese, oil and small amounts of lignite. Industry is largely concentrated around the main towns, especially Athens and its port Piraeus and around Thessaloniki

Area: 50,600 sq. miles/132,000 sq. km. *Mean max. and min. temperatures:* Athens (38° N, 23° 30' E; 350 ft/107 m.) 90°F/32°C (July and Aug.), 42°F/6°C (Jan.); Thessaloniki (40° 30' N, 23° E; 80ft/24 m.) 90°F/32°C (July), 37°F/3°C (Jan. and Feb.); Rhodes (36° 30' N, 28° 30' E, 290 ft/88 m.) 83°F/28°C (July and Aug.), 51°F/11°C (Jan.). *Relative humidity:* Athens 68%; Thessaloniki 71%; Rhodes 68%. *Mean annual rainfall:* Athens 16 in./405 mm.; Thessaloniki 19 in./485 mm.; Rhodes 21 in./73.5 mm.

POPULATION

Total population: (1984) 10 million. *Main towns and populations:* (1982) ATHENS (885,136), Thessaloniki (402,443), Patras (140,878), Larisa (103,263), Iraklion (101,668), Volos (70,967). *Distribution:* In 1982 64% of the population lived in urban areas.

Language: 98% of the population speaks one of the two forms of modern Greek—*katharevousa* (purist), an artificial attempt to return to classical Greek used for official and press purposes; or *demotiki* (demotic), the spoken language and generally used in literature. There is an increasing compromise

GREECE

between the two. The main minority language is Turkish. *Religion:* 97% of the population professes the established Eastern Orthodox faith. Freedom of faith and worship is guaranteed by the constitution, but proselytizing is forbidden.

Constitution: Greece is a democracy. At a plebiscite in 1974 the electorate rejected the monarchical constitution of 1952, which had been reintroduced following the restoration of civilian rule. The republican constitution, adopted on June 7, 1975, provides for a presidential system of government. Under the new basic law, the president has the power to name and dismiss cabinet members, to dissolve parliament and to veto legislation. He is elected for a five-year term by a two-thirds majority (three-fifths on a third ballot) of the parliament, and he can be reelected only once. He can also exercise certain emergency powers, suspend portions of the Constitution with the cabinet's approval and issue legislative decrees. The president is assisted in the exercise of these extraordinary powers by a Council of the Republic, composed of former presidents, former prime ministers, the current prime minister, the president of the parliament and the leader of the opposition. *Head of State:* President Christos Sartzetakis. *Head of Government:* Prime Minister Andreas Papandreou.

Legislature: The unicameral parliament (*Vouli*) consists of 300 members elected by direct universal suffrage for four-year terms subject to dissolution. The electoral system is governed by a special law rewarding larger parties by providing for a secondary allocation of parliamentary seats.

Political parties: The Greek political party system has historically been very fluid, shifting on the basis of personalities rather than ideologies. In 1984, there were at least 11 parties, of which only four were represented in parliament. The parties are as follows:

Panhellenic Socialist Movement, Pasok. Founded in 1974 by Andreas Papandreou, who led the party into office in 1981. Papandreou continued in power after the 1985 elections. Pasok is leftist in both domestic and foreign policies.

New Democracy, ND. Formed in 1974 by Constantine Caramanlis, prime minister and later president, ND is a broadly based pragmatic party committed to parliamentary democracy, social justice, an independent foreign policy and free enterprise. Its leader is Constantine Mitsotakis.

Communist Party—Exterior, KKE—Exterior. Refounded during the 1966–74 military dictatorship, KKE—Exterior evolved from the pro-Moscow wing of the earlier Greek Communist party. The party suffered mass defections during 1980 following the leadership's support of the Soviet invasion of Afghanistan.

Progressive party, KP. Right-wing party founded in 1979.

National Front, EP. Launched in 1977 as a more conservative alternative to the New Democracy by a former prime minister, Stefanos Stefanopoulos.

Communist Party—Interior, KKE—Interior. Founded in 1968 and outlawed until 1974, KKE—Interior is nationalist in orientation. Greece's principal Eurocommunist group, it is led by Yannis Banias.

United Democratic Left, EDA. Formerly a communist front organization while the KKE—Interior was outlawed, it subsequently evolved into a separate party. It is led by Ilias Iliou.

Democratic Unity, DE. A centrist alliance led by Ioannis Pesmazoglou.

Union of the Democratic Center, EDEK. Formed through the merger of the Center Union and the New Political forces, EDEK was weakened in 1978 by internal dissent. It is led by Ioannis Zigdis.

Center Rally, KS. Organized by George Mavros, following his resignation from EDEK.

Liberal Party, FK. Founded by former EDEK deputy Nikitas Venizelos to revive the political heritage associated with his grandfather, former prime minister Eleftherios Venizelos.

In 1985, the party lineup in the Vouli was as follows:

Pasok 161 seats
New Democracy 126 seats
Communist Party—Exterior 12 seats
Communist Party—Interior 1 seat

Local government: This is modeled on the French system. The country is divided into 52 prefectures (*nomoi*) headed by government-appointed prefects (*nomarchai*). There is a minister of Northern Greece—based in Thessaloniki—who is a full cabinet member. Each municipality (*demos*) and rural commune (*kenotis*) elects an urban council (*demarchiakon symvoulion*) and a rural council (*kenotikon symvoulion*) headed by a mayor for four years. Mount Athos is a self-governing community subject to the spiritual jurisdiction of the Ecumenical Patriarch in Istanbul.

Judicial system: The lowest court is that of the justices of the peace (*erenodikeon*). Each court of first instance (*protodikeon*) has a criminal court at its seat. The Court of Appeal (*Efetion*) has jurisdiction in both civil and criminal cases. Final appeal is to the Supreme Court (*Areios Pagos*), which has six sections—four civil and two criminal—and adjudicates in quorum. There are no commercial courts; all commercial cases are tried by ordinary courts. There are tax courts in some towns, however. Judges are appointed by the president—high court judges are appointed for life and other justices are irremovable except for criminal offences. Greece maintains capital punishment.

RECENT HISTORY

In 1944 and again in 1946–49 the Greek government fought a civil war against the Greek communists who were actively supported by members of the Soviet bloc. Greece became a member of NATO in 1952, and an associate member of the EC in 1962. The problem of Cyprus complicated relations with Britain and Turkey in the late 1950s, and relations with Turkey have been strained since the renewed strife in Cyprus in 1964 and 1974. Under the first premiership of Constantine Caramanlis (October 1955–June 1963), Greece made considerable economic and social progress. In 1965, a political crisis between the king and Prime Minister George Papandreou over the investigation of a secret organization within the army (ASPIDA) led to the latter's resignation, mob demonstrations and the defection of 45 members under Stephanopoulos from the Center-Union party.

In 1967 a military junta seized power in opposition to King Constantine, whose unsuccessful efforts to dislodge the junta led to his flight to Rome and the appointment of a regent. The government was reorganized with Col. George Papadopoulos as prime minister. A subsequent coup by the navy to restore the monarchy failed, resulting in the formal deposition of the king and the proclamation of a republic on June 1, 1973. Papadopoulos was ousted in 1974 when he tried to form a civilian cabinet and schedule a popular election. The new leader, Brig. Gen. Dimitrios Ioannides, was in office only for a short while before the crisis in Cyprus forced him to call on Caramanlis, the elder statesman of Greek politics, to form a caretaker government preparatory to a return to civilian rule. Caramanlis was confirmed as prime minister following a parliamentary election. A republican constitution was approved by the electorate in 1975, and Constantine Tsatsos was installed as the country's first elected president. Caramanlis resigned as prime minister in 1980 on his election as president. He was succeeded by George Rallis, whose poor showing led to the rout of the New Democracy in the general election of 1981. With a decisive majority in parliament, Andreas Papandreou, leader of Pasok, formed Greece's first Socialist government in October 1981. He continued in office with a reduced majority after the elections of May 1985.

Defense: The president is commander-in-chief of the armed forces. Military service is compulsory for 22 months in the army, 26 months in the navy and 24 months in the air force. Most of the army and air force is assigned to NATO. The strengths of the defense forces are: army 150,000, navy 19,000, air force 24,500. The 1981 defense budget was Dr71.25 billion ($1.77 billion), representing 4% of GNP.

ECONOMY

Background: The economy is still in the process of industrialization. Postwar political instability retarded economic growth, but in recent decades production has expanded rapidly. In 1965, the value of industrial production exceeded that of agriculture for the first time, and the disparity between the sectors has since widened. The cost of rapid expansion has been the loss of internal and external equilibrium; prices have accelerated upward, there have been consistent balance of payments deficits and foreign exchange reserves have fallen. From 1970 to 1979 GNP increased at an average annual rate of 4.1%. The five-year development plan of 1978–82 was devised to reduce inflation. Price freezes were introduced in electricity and other services and restraints were placed on government expenditure and the import of luxury goods. Notwithstanding these measures, the annual rate of inflation during 1970–82 was 15.4%. The main growth industries include iron and steel, textiles, chemicals and cement; agricultural output has declined relatively to industry, but diversification has occurred, including the introduction of cotton and rice.

The origin of GDP at factor cost in 1982 was:

Sector	Percentage	Growth rate 1970–82
Agriculture	19	1.9
Industry	29	3.9
Services	52	4.9
GDP	100	

The main agricultural products are olives, raisins, wine, tobacco, fruit, wheat and livestock (especially sheep).

An associate member of the EC since 1962, Greece became a full member in 1981, having formally concluded a treaty of accession in 1979. While the agricultural sector benefited directly from EC membership, much of the gain was overshadowed by a 30% rise in domestic food prices. Prime Minister Papandreou was able to exploit anti-EC sentiment to gain his mandate from the electorate, and he has called for Greece's membership to be submitted to a national referendum. Adding fuel to the anti-EC movement is the fact that the effect of lower import duties on manufactured goods for both industry and consumers has been offset by further declines in the drachma's relative value against foreign currencies. Moreover, imports from more competitively organized, large-scale EC producers have flooded the Greek market, undercutting domestic producers. Nevertheless, the $2 billion in anticipated EC assistance over the five-year transition period is a powerful inducement for Greece to remain in the Community.

Foreign trade: Greece's trade relations are undergoing major shifts following the country's entry into the EC. All EC tariffs on Greek goods have been removed, while Greek tariff reductions are to be phased in over five years. More immediate adjustments have included the removal of import licensing requirements and the gradual termination of bilateral barter arrangements with the Soviet bloc. The turmoil in Lebanon has been financially beneficial to Greece, with many multinational businesses moving their Middle East headquarters from Beirut to Athens. Greece is not technically a tax haven, but the government increasingly welcomes multinationals and grants them some tax concessions.

In 1982, exports amounted to $4.297 billion and imports to $10,023 billion, leaving a large trade deficit of $5.7 billion. There is little short-term prospect of a substantial reduction in Greece's balance-of-payments deficits. However, exports grew at a faster rate than imports during 1970–82: by 9.4% versus 4.5%. The percentage share of merchandise exports was 18% for fuels, minerals and metals; 28% for other primary commodities; 20% for textiles and clothing; 5% for machinery and transport equipment; and 29% for other manufactures. The percentage share of merchandise imports was 11% for food, 22% for fuels, 7% for other primary commodities, 28% for machinery and transport equipment, and 32% for other manufactures.

Employment: The total working population in 1982 was 3.2 million, of whom 37% were employed in agriculture, 28% in industry and 35% in services. The level of unemployment in that year was 2.4%. The average annual emigration has declined.

Price and wage trends: The relatively favorable trend in consumer prices in the 1960s was offset by the fast increase in money incomes. The rise in the consumer price index was about 15.4% during 1970–82, compared with 2.2% for 1960–70. The liberal social policy of the government, the drift from the land and the scarcity of skilled industrial and agricultural labor all contributed to wage increases in agriculture, industry and services, a trend that has shown little sign of slackening.

Consumption: In 1982, private consumption accounted for 69% of GNP, and public consumption for 18%. Private consumption rose by 4.2% in volume during 1970–82, compared with an increase of 7.1% in 1960–70. Public consumption increased by 6.3% during 1970–82 compared with 6.6% during 1960–70.

SOCIAL SECURITY

Health insurance: Under the general supervision of the Ministry of Social Security, this scheme covers most employees and self-employed workers. It is financed by the insured, the employer and the government. Sickness benefits are 50% of earnings, according to 22 wage classes. There are dependents' supplements. Medical benefits include medical services ordinarily provided directly to patients through facilities of the Social Insurance Institute. Medical benefits for dependents are the same as for insured workers. There are maternity benefits as well.

Accident insurance: This covers most employees and is under the general supervision of the Ministry of Social Security. It is entirely paid for by the employer. Temporary disability benefit (work injury) is 50% of earnings, according to 22 wage classes. There are dependents' benefits as well. Permanent disability pension (work injury) is the same as for ordinary disability pension, with a few exceptions. Medical benefits (work injury) are generally the same as ordinary health insurance sickness benefits. There are survivor pensions.

Pensions insurance: Most employees and self-employed persons are covered under this scheme, which is under the general supervision of the Ministry of Social Security. It is financed by the insured, the employer and the government. Old-age pensions begin generally at age 65 (men) and age 60 (women). Disability pensions are given if there is a loss of 67% of normal earning capacity. Old-age pensions are basically 30% to 70% of earnings during the last two years, varying inversely according to 22 wage classes. Minimum pension is Dr16,992 a month. There are dependents' supplements and medical benefits. There are also survivor pensions for widows, dependent disabled widowers and orphans.

Unemployment insurance: Under the general supervision of the Ministry of Labor, this scheme covers most employees. It is financed by the insured and the employer. Unemployment benefits are 40% of wages, or 50% of salary, according to 22 wage classes. There are dependents' supplements.

Other benefits: Under the general supervision of the Ministry of Labor, family allowances are available to most eligible employees with one or more children. Family allowances begin at full annual allowance of Dr6,240 for one child.

EDUCATION

Education is free at all levels, including university, higher and special education, and is compulsory for all children from six to 15. About 10% of the adult population is illiterate; this represents a sharp decrease in the proportion over the last half-century. The state allocates about 9.3% of the annual budget to education.

Primary education: This lasts from the ages of six to 12 in primary schools, and children then pass on to secondary education without taking an examination. *Secondary education:* A three-year course at the *gymnasium* may be followed, on passing an entrance examination, by a further three years at the *lyceum*, ending with a leaving examination that is the entry qualification for university. Secondary school teachers are university graduates. *Vocational and technical education:* There are both private and state schools. Courses begin at the age of 12 and generally last for about three years. *Special education:* There are centers in the main towns of Greece.

University and higher education: There are seven universities, including the National and Capodistrian and the National Technical (Polytechnic) universities, both in Athens, and the Aristotelian University in Thessaloniki. Four new universities have opened in Ioannina, Patras, Thrace and Crete. Other institutes at university level are graduate schools for economics and commercial sciences, political science, agriculture and fine arts in Athens; and for industrial studies in Piraeus and Thessaloniki. All are autonomous organizations governed by senates of professors, supported by and under the general supervision of the state. Courses last from four to six years. In addition, there are a number of higher schools, including pedagogic academies offering three-year courses for elementary-school teachers. There are government scholarships for undergraduates, postgraduates studying abroad, and also for secondary education.

Educational institutions, 1981–82:

	Institutions	Teachers	Students
Preprimary	4,743	6,901	151,666
Primary	9,400	37,947	891,488
Secondary:			
General	2,291	33,613	669,812
Vocational	766	7,410	108,212
Higher:			
Universities	13	7,489	87,476
Other	128	3,821	37,218

Source: National Greek Statistical Service, Athens.

Adult education: This is not greatly developed and is chiefly in the hands of such private organizations as the Greek YMCA and Boy Scouts.

MASS MEDIA

The press (1983) (Athens–Piraeus area):

Dailies: Ta Nea, liberal, 139,271; *To Vima,* liberal, 35,000; *Acropolis,* independent-conservative, 43,851; *Kathinerini,* conservative, 24,970; *Apoyevmatini,* ind., 130,000; *Estia,* 7,978; *Avgi,* communist, 7,481; *Vradyni,* right-wing, 71,914; *Rizospastis,* communist, 48,513; *Ethnos,* 203,216; *Eleftherotypia,* 98,888; *Avriani,* 72,445.

Periodicals: Gynaika (f), women's, 94,654; *Aktines* (m), political/cultural/scientific, 10,000; *Viomichaniki Epitheorissis* (m), industrial/financial, 25,000; *Pantheon* (f), 74,141; *Tahydromos* (w), illustrated, 177,182.

Broadcasting: In 1975 the new constitution put radio and TV under direct state supervision. Elliniki Radiophonia Tileorassi (Hellenic National Radio-Television) administers all civilian broadcasts. Ypiressia Enimerosseos Enoplon Dhynameon (YENED—Greek Armed Forces Radio and Television) administers all military broadcasts.

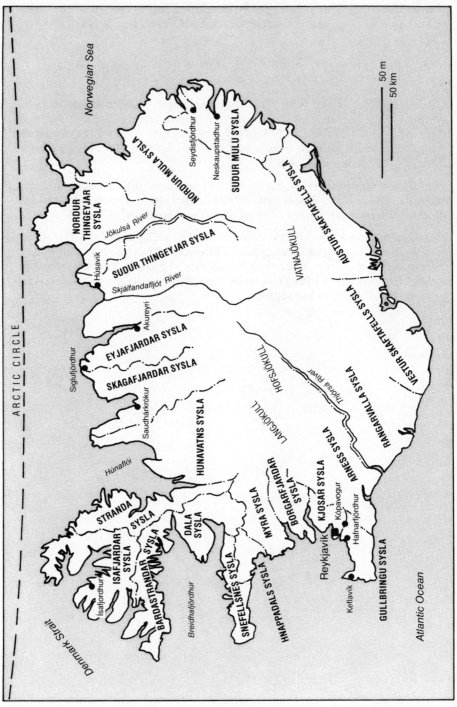

ICELAND

Features: This island consists of a mountainous, part glacier and snowfield covered, core, with much current volcanic activity; and a series of lowlands around the coast, especially on the north and southwest. Much of the central part of the island rises to over 5,000 ft/1,500 m. Fishing is the basis of most industry; the little agriculture that exists is mainly concerned with livestock farming. Minerals are few and power is obtained either from geothermal or hydroelectric sources.

Area: 39,770 sq. miles/103,000 sq. km. *Mean max. and min. temperatures:* Reykjavík (64° N, 22° W; 90 ft/27 m.) 58°F/14°C (July), 28°F/−2°C (Jan. and Feb.). *Relative humidity:* Reykjavík 78%. *Mean annual rainfall:* Reykjavík 34 in./860 mm.

POPULATION

Total population: (1984) 200,000. *Chief towns and populations:* (1982) REYKJAVÍK (83,766), Kópavogur (13,819), Akureyri (13,420), Hafnarfjördur (12,203). *Distribution:* In 1982, 84% of the population lived in towns.

Language: The official language, Icelandic, has maintained its separate identity since the 10th century. *Religion:* 93% of the population adheres to the established Evangelical-Lutheran church.

CONSTITUTIONAL SYSTEM

Constitution: Iceland is a republic. The constitution was approved by referendum in June 1944. *Head of state:* President Vigdis Finnbógadottir. *Head of government:* Prime Minister Steingrimur Hermannsson (Progressive party).

Executive: The president is elected for four years by direct vote of the people, appoints and dismisses ministers, directs the Council of State and has the power to introduce provisional legislation when the parliament (*Althing*) is not in session (this power lapses if not certified by the next session of the Althing). Presidential announcements are valid only when countersigned by a minister. The ministers, together with the president, constitute the Council of State. The ministers have a right to speak in either house of the Althing to which they are responsible, but can vote only if they are elected members.

Legislature: The Althing is composed of 60 members elected for four years. Forty-nine members are elected by proportional representation and the remaining 11 seats are allotted to the parties on a proportional basis. The Althing elects one-third of its members to form the upper house (*Efri Deild*), the remainer forming the lower house (*Nedri Deild*). Ordinary legislation may be introduced by either house, but the budget is composed each year by a united Althing. Legislation passed by the Althing but vetoed by the president becomes law if passed again by a two-thirds majority of the Althing. The Althing can declare no confidence in individual ministers as well as the government as a whole, and impeach ministers by resolution of a joint session of the Althing.

Political parties: There are six principal political parties:

Independence party. Formed in 1929 by a union of conservative and liberal groups, it has participated in most coalition governments since 1944. It represents primarily fishing and commercial interests, and stands for a liberal economic policy and a pro-NATO foreign policy. It is led by Thorsteinn Pálsson.

Progressive party. Founded in 1916, it represents agrarian interests and pursues liberal policies. It is led by Prime Minister Steingrimur Hermannsson.

People's Alliance. Formerly called the Labor Alliance, it was formed in 1956 as an electoral front for Communists and disaffected Social Democrats. It advocates a radical socialist domestic program and Iceland's withdrawal from NATO. It is led by Svavar Gestsson.

Social Democratic party. Founded in 1916, it advocates state ownership of economic resources and increased social welfare benefits. It is led by Kjartan Johannsson.

Social Democratic Alliance. Formed in 1983, with a liberal-socialist program. It is led by Gudmundur Einarsson.

Women's Alliance. Formed in 1983, it promotes the interests of women and children. It is led by Gudrun Agnarsdottir.

In 1983 the party lineup in the Althing was as follows:

> Independence party 23
> Progressive party 14
> People's Alliance 10
> Social Democratic party 6
> Social Democratic Alliance 4
> Women's Alliance 3

Local government: Iceland is divided into 16 provinces (*sýslur*) formed from more than 200 rural municipalities (*sveit*). Each province elects a council (*sýslunefnd*) headed by a government-appointed sheriff (*sýslumadur*), who is chief of police and provincial judge. The eight urban municipalities (*bæjir*) form separate administrative districts, independent of but coordinating with the provinces. Each elects an urban council (*bæjarstjórn*), which in turn appoints a chairman.

Judicial system: The common courts have two instances. The lower is the ordinary court, presided over by either a sheriff or a town judge. The higher stage is the Supreme Court (Hæstiréttur), composed of the chief justice and seven ordinary justices. In addition there are special courts, such as the maritime and commercial courts, of which the higher stage is again the Supreme Court. There is no death penalty.

RECENT HISTORY

Iceland became a republic in 1944, when the population voted in favor of severing the final links with the Danish Crown. In 1949 Iceland joined NATO and the Council of Europe, and in 1953 became a founder-member of the Nordic Council. A dispute over fishing limits with Britain (1958–64) was finally settled with Iceland maintaining 12-mile territorial waters. Fishing disputes erupted again with Britain and other countries in the 1970s and early 1980s. Icelandic politics are characterized by coalitions and consensus. The most significant political development in the postwar era was the defeat in 1971 of the 12-year-old centrist coalition of the Independence and Social Democratic parties. In 1980 Vigdis Finnbógadottir became the first popularly elected female head of state in the world when she succeeded President Kristjan Eldjárn.

Defense: Iceland, although a member of NATO, has no armed forces or defense budget of its own. American forces fulfill this function as part of NATO strategy.

ECONOMY

Background: Over 75% of Iceland's land area is unproductive; the economy depends heavily upon fish and fish products. Since the 1960s a high rate of economic growth has been maintained at the cost of inflation. In 1980 the value of GNP at current prices was estimated to be $2.62 billion; the annual average increase in GNP between 1970 and 1979 was over 2.8%, mainly owing to expansion in fishing, building and construction, and (to a lesser extent) agriculture. Expansion has been influenced by a rapid increase in the labor force. Industrial production during 1970–82 rose 3.8%. In 1980 the value of fish and fish processing production amounted to about 76.8% of visible exports at current prices. In the same year GNP per capita was $11,330, the 10th highest in Europe. Livestock farming, particularly milk and sheep products, is the most important form of agricultural activity. The major reasons for expansion in fishing and agricultural production have been mechanization and a high rate of investment.

Iceland has the highest rate of inflation among OECD countries, with consumer prices rising by more than 35% during 1972–79 and increasing by over 50% in 1980 and 1981. This is caused partly by the country's indexation system, which covers not only wages, transfers and pensions but also profits and the principal in loans, and a monetary policy that permits the krona to float against other currencies. In real terms, however, Iceland's economic growth has not lagged far behind other developed European nations. Full employment has been maintained and indexed wages have on the whole kept pace with prices.

The fishing industry employs more than 13% of the labor force, of which 5% is employed in actual fishing and 8% in fish processing. Because fishing is critical to the economy, Iceland extended its territorial waters in 1973 to 50 nautical miles thus precipitating the first and second cod wars with Great Britain, Ireland, Norway and West Germany. A third cod war erupted in 1975 when Iceland extended the limit to 200 miles; for a brief period in 1976 the country cut off diplomatic relations with Britain. Agreement was reached with Denmark and Norway on overlapping zones.

With the exception of fish-processing plants, the industrial sector is small. The major industrial plant is a Swiss-owned aluminum smelting plant, the output of which accounts for 15% of Iceland's exports.

Foreign trade: During the past decade marine exports have risen at a faster pace than the cost of imports, particularly petroleum, helping Iceland to reduce trade deficits. Small current-account surpluses were registered in 1978 and 1979, but service revenues—such as from tourism and Icelandic Air-lines—that had record surpluses in the early 1970s deteriorated with the growth of foreign debt-servicing costs, which reached 15% of exports in 1980.

Approximately four-fifths of Iceland's trade is with the OECD; the United States is the largest single market. Iceland has been a member of GATT since 1968 and EFTA since 1970, although disputes with Britain over fishing rights delayed its access to EFTA's trading arrangements with the EC until 1976. Since 1980 the EC and Iceland have conducted duty-free trade.

Employment: The working population rose rapidly from mid-1960 to a total of 118,000. In 1982 the distribution of labor was: agriculture and fishing 17%, industry and construction 37% and services 46%. Increased employment has contributed to the strong pressure of demand.

Price and wage trends: In an effort to curb inflation, the government took a series of steps in the late 1970s and early 1980s. The Economic Management Act of 1979 imposed higher taxes, increased interest rates on both savings and loans, reduced central government expenditures and revised the wage-indexation system, taking into account not only changes in prices but also the terms of trade. A new krona was introduced in 1981 and its basis of valuation was shifted from the U.S. dollar to a basket of foreign currencies. In the first quarter of 1981 all prices were frozen and wage adjustment was reduced by 7%.

Consumption: In 1981 private consumption amounted to 63% of GNP at current prices and public consumption to 12%. During 1971–82, public consumption grew by 5% and private consumption by 3.7%.

SOCIAL SECURITY

The Ministry of Health and Social Security exercises general supervision over the scheme, which is administered by the State Social Security Institute through its local offices. In the case of health insurance, the Institute supervises the various sickness funds.

Health insurance: All residents are covered by the insurance scheme. It is funded by the insured person, who contributes 2% of income subject to local income tax; and government, with the national government contributing 85% and the local government 15%. Maternity grants are financed out of pension contributions. Sickness benefits are set at a statutory minimum of IKr105 a day, plus a supplement of IKr28 for each child under age 18. These benefits are paid at half rate when the recipient is less than fully employed. The medical benefits provide that the national health service offer general practitioner services, part of the cost of specialist services, free hospital care and other services. Medical benefits for dependents are the same as for the family head.

Accident insurance: This covers all employed persons. It is funded entirely by the employer. Temporary disability benefits (work injury) are IKr132 a day, with supplements for dependents. Permanent disability pension (work injury) provides IKr2,449 a month, if the insured person is at least 75% disabled. This pension has a child's supplement provision and provides medical benefits (necessary care). Survivor pension (work injury) is basically IKr3,069 a month, payable for eight years. There is an orphan's provision in this pension scheme.

Pension insurance: This covers all residents. It is funded by employers, who contribute 2% of payroll, and by the government, which contributes the rest. Old-age pensions, available at age 67, are flat-rate pensions of IKr2,449 a month. There are special supplements. Retirement is not necessary. Disability pensions are flat-rate pensions of IKr2,449 a month. There are special supplements. (These pensions are available if the insured suffers a 75% reduction in working capacity.) A partial pension is paid for 50% to 74% disability. There are survivor benefits for widows and orphans in the form of temporary and permanent pensions.

Unemployment insurance: This covers members of trade unions. It is funded by the employer, who contributes 1% of an unskilled worker's wage per employee, and the government—with the national government contributing 2% of the above wage and the local government 1%. Minimum unemployment benefits are IKr95 a day; maximum IKr379 a day. There are dependents' supplements.

Other benefits: Family allowances are paid by the state to all residents if they have dependent eligible-age children and are in need.

EDUCATION

Primary education: Education is compulsory and free for all children until age 16. In urban areas, day schools provide elementary education. In the more remote rural districts, it is provided in state-supported boarding schools. Secondary education is then provided for three or four years. In 1974, basic schools were created from former primary and lower-secondary schools. These basic schools prepare students to take a national examination, which would allow them further education. At the end of four years of attendance at an upper secondary school or comprehensive school, the student takes the matriculation examination, which qualifies for university admission. There are three institutions of higher learning in Iceland.

Vocational education: For seamen there are one- to three-year courses at both a navigation and an engineering school. *Trade and technical schools:* These offer mainly evening classes for three- to four-year courses. *Special education:* There are schools for the visually handicapped and the deaf and hearing impaired in Reykjavík.

University education: The University of Reykjavík has faculties of theology, medicine, law and economics, philosophy and engineering and a research institute for fishing, industry and agriculture. University education is free of charge.

Educational institutions, 1982:

	Institutions	Staff	Students
Preprimary	1[1]	2[2]	4,200
Primary	1[1]	2[2]	25,000
Secondary	115	1,450	28,700
Universities and colleges	3	280	4,600

[1] 216: The same institutions may overlap here, operating on different levels.
[2] 3,220: This includes part-time teachers.
Source: Icelandic Ministry of Education and Culture.

MASS MEDIA

The press (Reykjavík) 1982:

Dailies: Morgunbladid, independent, 46,000; *Tíminn,* Progressive, 17,000; *DV (Dagbladid-Vísir),* ind., 39,000; *Thjódviljinn,* socialist, 12,000; *Altbý-dubladid,* Social Democratic, 5,000.

Periodicals: Vikan (w), illustrated, 12,000; *Uryal* (m), 4,000; *Vinnan* (m), 3,500.

Broadcasting: Radio and TV broadcasting are a monopoly of the Icelandic State Broadcasting Service (Rikisútvarpid), an independent authority. The American Armed Forces Radio and TV Service operates a 24-hour radio station. Both the U.S. Air Force and U.S. Navy operate TV services from Keflavík.

IRELAND

Features: The country consists of an extensive boulder clay and peat infilled depression, including the major bog areas, surrounded by uplands—Donegal in the northwest, Wicklow Mountains in the east, Connemara in the west and the Hercynian uplands of Kerry and Cork in the southwest. In many places these uplands rise to over 1,500 ft/450 m. and reach 3,000 ft in the Wicklow Mountains and Kerry. The central plain, drained mainly by the Shannon and Boyne, has a number of low hill ridges, especially in the northeast and southwest.

There are few mineral resources. There are substantial reserves of natural gas and discoveries of offshore oil. The Shannon provides hydroelectric power and the peat bogs provide fuel for a number of thermal power stations. Industry is concentrated mainly around Dublin Bay, Cork and Wexford. The Republic is predominantly an agricultural country with its best farmlands concentrated in the south and east where climate, soils and relief are most favorable.

Area: 27,140 sq. miles/720,280 sq. km. *Mean max. and min. temperatures:* Dublin (53° 30' N, 6° 30' W; 155 ft/47 m.) 67°F/19°C (July and Aug.), 35°F/2°C (Jan. and Feb.). *Relative humidity:* Dublin 83%. *Mean annual rainfall:* 30 in./760 mm.

Total population: (1984) 3.6 million. *Chief towns and populations:* DUBLIN (544,586), Cork (138,267), Limerick (60,665), Dún Laoghaire (54,244), Galway (36,917), Waterford (32,617). *Distribution:* In 1982 58% of the population lived in urban areas, 48% of this group in Dublin. During 1970–82 the annual rate of urban growth was 25%.

Language: Gaelic (Irish) is the official language and English the second official language. In 1984, 25% of the population was Gaelic-speaking.

Religion: About 94% of the population is Roman Catholic, 4% Church of Ireland (Anglican) and less than 1% Presbyterian. Although there is no state religion (the state, however, recognizing the special position of the Catholic church as the religion of the great majority of the population) and freedom of worship is guaranteed, the religious issue remains the fundamental basis for the continued division of Ireland from predominantly Protestant Northern Ireland.

IRELAND

CONSTITUTIONAL SYSTEM

Constitution: The constitution, adopted by referendum in 1937, describes Ireland as a sovereign independent and democratic state (nowhere as a "republic") and declares the national territory to be the whole island, but that pending reunification the jurisdiction of the Irish parliament and government shall be restricted to the 26 southern counties. *Head of state:* President Dr. Patrick J. Hillery. *Head of government:* Prime Minister (*Taoiseach*) Dr. Garrett FitzGerald (Fine Gael).

Executive: The president (*Uachtarán*) is elected by direct vote of the population for seven years and is eligible for a second term. He appoints the Taoiseach and other ministers upon the nomination of the House of Representatives (*Dáil*). He normally acts upon the advice of the government, and on the advice of the Taoiseach he dissolves parliament, although at his absolute discretion he may refuse to do so. He signs and promulgates legislation and receives and accredits ambassadors. In certain functions he is aided by a Council of State (*Comhairle Stáit*). Under certain circumstances he has the power to refer legislation to referendum or to the Supreme Court (*Cúirt Uachtarach*). The government consists of seven to 15 members, collectively responsible to the Dáil. The Taoiseach, deputy prime minister (*Tánaiste*) and minister of finance must be members of the Dáil, and only two members of the government at most may be members of the Senate (*Seanad*).

Legislature: Sole legislative power is vested in the National Parliament (*Oireachtas*), consisting of the Dáil and the Seanad. The Dáil has 166 members elected for five years by the single transferable vote system of proportional representation. The Seanad, which sits for the same period, has 60 members: 43 are elected as representatives of cultural and vocational interests; the two universities elect three each; and the remaining 11 are nominated by the Taoiseach. Legislation may originate in either house, save money bills, which must originate in the Dáil. The Seanad may delay a bill passed by the lower house for a maximum of 90 days, and may suggest amendments—except to money bills, where it has only powers of recommendation—but it has no power of permanent veto.

Referendum: On petition to the president by a majority of the Seanad and at least one-third of the Dáil, certain bills passed by both houses may be referred to the electorate.

Political parties:

The United Ireland party (Fine Gael). Formed in 1933 through the merger of the Cosgrave party, the Center party and the National Guard. Its leader is Prime Minister Dr. Garrett FitzGerald.

The Labour party (Pairti Lucht Oibre). Originally the political wing of the Trades Union Congress, the Labour party became an independent entity in 1930. Like its British counterpart, it advocates far-reaching social security programs, public ownership of essential industries and services, and participation of workers in management. Recently it has gained prominence as a coalition partner in Fine Gael-led governments.

The Republican party (Fianna Fáil). The party founded by Éamonn de Valéra in 1926, it was in power continuously from 1932 to 1948, and then four times more (1951–54, 1957–73, 1977–81 and 1982). It is currently led by Charles J. Haughey, a former prime minister.

The Workers' party. The oldest political party in Ireland, it was founded in 1905 and, until 1970, was associated with the political wing of the outlawed Irish Republican Army. It is Marxist in outlook and dedicated to the establishment of a united Ireland. It is led by Tomas MacGiolla.

Minor parties without Dáil representation include the Provisional Sinn Féin, led by Ruairi O'Bradaigh, the Democratic Socialist party and the Communist party of Ireland.

In 1982, party lineup in the Dáil Eireann was as follows:

Fianna Fáil   75
Fine Gael   70
Labour party   16
Workers' party   2
Independent Fianna Fáil   1
Independents   2

Local government: Ireland is divided into 26 counties. In addition, there are four county boroughs and seven boroughs divided into urban districts governed by elected local councils; the larger towns are governed by town commissioners. Finance is met from taxes and state grants. General supervision is exercised by the Department of Local Government, while the departments of Health and Social Welfare are responsible for health and public assistance administration.

Judicial system: The lowest courts are the district courts, which have jurisdiction over civil cases involving small amounts and conduct preliminary hearings in criminal cases. Each is presided over by a district judge who must be a lawyer of 10 years' standing. Appeal is to the circuit court, which also has civil jurisdiction and extended criminal jurisdiction. There are nine circuit court judges of whom two are assigned to Dublin. In appropriate cases the judge sits with a jury. The high court (*Ard-Cúirt*) has full jurisdiction. It consists of a president, six judges, the chief justice (*Príomh-Bhreitheamh*) and the president of the circuit court. It is normally constituted by one judge, but in exceptional circumstances a panel of three sits. It hears appeals from the circuit courts. The central criminal court is constituted by one judge sitting with jury, and appeal from its decision is to the court of criminal appeal, consisting of one judge of the Supreme Court and two high court judges appointed by the chief justice. The final court of appeal is the Supreme Court, which comprises four ordinary judges, the chief justice and the president of the high court. It sits either as a court of three or five.

Judges are appointed by the president on the advice of the government and may be dismissed only for misbehavior or incapacity, upon a resolution passed by both houses of parliament. Ireland maintains capital punishment for treason, murder of police or prison officers, political murders and certain military offences. There is no provision for divorce.

RECENT HISTORY

After an uprising against the British in 1916, proclaiming Ireland a sovereign republic, Ireland, hitherto part of the United Kingdom of Great Britain and Ireland, was reaffirmed a republic in 1919 by the independence party, Sinn Féin. Britain provided for separate subordinate parliaments for the Roman Catholic south and the six Protestant northeastern counties (Government of Ireland Act, 1920), which led to the establishment of the Government of Northern Ireland in 1921. Ireland, excluding the six counties, was accorded dominion status by Britain in 1922 as the Irish Free State. The present name of the state, Ireland (Éire), was established by the 1937 constitution. Ireland was neutral in World War II. After Ireland in 1948 described itself as a republic, Britain passed the Ireland Act (1949) declaring that Ireland had by this action placed itself outside the Commonwealth. This act also provides that no part of Northern Ireland may cease to belong to Britain without the consent of the Northern Ireland parliament. However, Ireland is not treated as a foreign state and its citizens need no passports to enter Britain.

Ireland has continually sought to end the division of the island by peaceful methods. It declined to join NATO in 1949 because of the division, but was admitted to the United Nations in 1955 and has provided forces for worldwide U.N. peacekeeping operations. In July 1961 Ireland applied for EC membership, and in 1965 signed a Free Trade Treaty with Britain.

During most of the post–World War II period, governments have tended to alternate between Fianna Fáil and Fine Gael, either with or without coalition partners. The issue of Northern Ireland is still smoldering, but Irish voters tend to be more concerned with the state of the economy at polling times.

Defense: The president is commander-in-chief of Ireland's defense forces, into which all the services are integrated, and which are composed solely of volunteers. The permanent defense force numbers over 14,012, with reserve forces of about 22,098. The 1981 defense expenditures were over £E144 million ($285 million), representing about 1.4% of GNP.

ECONOMY

Background: A shortage of natural resources, especially coal and iron, has necessitated a heavy emphasis on agriculture. However, light industry and tourism have grown over the past decades. From 1958, the year of the first national plan, the economy has expanded rapidly. In 1981, GNP at current prices was estimated to be $16.13 billion. From 1970 to 1979 GNP grew at an annual average rate of 2.3%.

Ireland joined the EC in 1973 and during the following five-year transition period received $2.2 billion in assistance as well as preferential trading arrangements. During this period the country experienced a surge in manufactured exports as well as substantial increases in farm prices that more than offset the negative effects of OPEC oil-price increases. The rate of real growth from 1974 to 1978 was among the highest in Europe, at 6%. But the economy took a turn for the worse with the second round of oil-price increases in

1979–80. Trade deficits rose by 80% because Irish exports became less competitive when the trade protection granted to Ireland as a new member lapsed in 1979, because the Irish pound's value against the British pound declined by over 14% and because wage increases averaged 19% annually. Immediately after taking office, the FitzGerald administration announced that the budget deficit would reach 18% of GNP, raising the current-account deficit to $2.2 billion. To meet the crisis, the government launched a relatively tight fiscal and monetary policy, including a freeze on public employment, addition of new taxes and social security contributions, and termination of several consumer-price subsidies.

The main industries are food and tobacco manufacturing and brewing; in recent years the output of lead, zinc and copper concentrates has grown considerably. The main agricultural products are livestock, vegetables and cereals. In 1982 the origin of GDP at factor cost was:

Sector	Percentage
Agriculture	15
Industry	31
Service	54
GDP	100

Foreign trade: Ireland's principal exports are beef, livestock and dairy products, sold mostly to Britain, Italy, Belgium and other EC countries. After a period of decline in the late 1970s, beef prices rebounded in 1980 and may benefit from revision of the EC's farm price supports. Industrial exports remain strong, led by chemicals, textiles, and machinery and transport equipment.

In 1982, merchandise exports amounted to $7.982 billion and merchandise imports to $9.618 billion, leaving a negative trade balance of $1.636 billion. The annual average growth rate during 1970–82 was 8.1% for exports and 5.9% for imports. The percentage share of merchandise exports was 3% for fuels, minerals and metals; 35% for other primary commodities; 8% for textiles and clothing; 22% for machinery and transport equipment; and 32% for other manufactures. The percentage share of merchandise imports was 13% for food, 15% for fuels, 4% for other primary commodities, 27% for machinery and transport equipment, and 41% for other manufactures. Nearly 87% of merchandise exports go to industrial economies.

Employment: The total working population numbered 1.308 million in 1982, reversing a 30-year decline. Agriculture continues to provide employment for about 18% of the working population, a share declining steadily as industrialization and mechanization in agriculture increase. In 1982 the industrial sector provided employment for 37% of the working population and services provided employment for 45%.

Price and wage trends: The labor movement is strong in Ireland; and more than 60% of the work force is unionzed. Strikes are common: during 1979 the number of workdays lost to strikes set a postwar record. Wage agreements are governed by a national understanding on social and economic development, to which the Irish Congress of Trade Unions, the Federated Union of Employers and the government are parties. The consumer price index rose by 14.5% during 1970–81, compared to 4.6% during 1960–70 and 3.8% during 1950–60.

Consumption: Private consumption was estimated to amount to 57% of GNP in 1982 (at current prices) and public consumption to about 21%. The former grew by 2.5% and the latter by 5.4% during 1970–82.

SOCIAL SECURITY

Health insurance: This scheme is under the general supervision of the Department of Social Welfare for cash benefits and the Department of Health for medical benefits. Employed persons (with certain exceptions) are covered for cash benefits. All residents are covered for medical services. The insurance is financed by the insured person, who contributes 1% of earnings; the employer, who contributes 1% of payroll on behalf of those with low and moderate incomes; and the government, which contributes to cover any deficit. Sickness benefits are basically £E31.65 a week, with supplements. Medical benefits include services furnished directly to patients by local health authorities. Medical benefits for dependents are the same as for the insured person. There are also maternity benefits and maternity grants.

Accident insurance: Employed persons, except for those in family employment, are covered under this scheme. It is funded almost solely by the employer. Temporary disability benefit (work injury) is £E47.90 a week, plus 40% to 20% (according to duration) of earnings between £E36 and £E220 a week. There are dependents' supplements. Permanent disability pension (work injury) is the same as temporary disability benefit. There are various supplements. Medical benefits (work injury) cover necessary general and specialist care, hospitalization, medicines, etc. There are survivor pensions (work injury) payable to widows, dependent disabled widowers, orphans and dependent parents.

Pensions insurance: Employed persons (with some exceptions) are covered under the scheme. It is funded by the insured person, who contributes 5.5% of earnings; the employer, who contributes 11.3% of payroll; and the government, which makes up the difference. The government funds the entire cost of means-tested allowances. Old-age pensions start at age 66. Disability pensions are available to those incapacitated for work. There are survivor pensions, deserted wife's benefits and death grants. Old-age pension is a flat-rate pension of £E45.10 a week, increased by £E3.10 a week if aged 80 or over. There are dependents' supplements of varying amounts. Means-tested allowances are up to £E38.60 a week (higher with dependents). Disability pension is £E39.75 a week. There are special allowances and supplements. Survivor pensions amount to a maximum of £E40.60 a week, plus supplements for children.

Unemployment benefits: Employed persons, with some exceptions, are covered under the scheme. It is covered by the insured, the employer and the government, each contributing basically the same as they do under the pension scheme. Unemployment benefits amount to £E34.80 a week, plus 40% to 20% (according to duration) of earnings between £E36 and £E220 a week. There are dependents' supplements.

Other benefits: Family allowances are available to qualified residents with one or more children. The government finances the whole cost. Family allowances start at £E11.25 a month for first to fifth child. There are special birth grants.

EDUCATION

Primary education: Education is compulsory between six and 15. Primary education is provided free in national schools. As far as is possible the state delegates local management of primary education to the various religious denominations, while meeting most of its costs and retaining a large degree of control over its operation. No child may be refused admission to school on religious grounds or be required to attend religious instruction against parental wishes. The Department of Education is responsible for the educational program, the approval of teacher's qualifications and payment of teaching salaries, as well as the inspection and supervision of the primary school certificate examination. There are a few private schools that receive no state assistance.

Secondary and vocational education: Secondary education begins at the age of 12 or 13 and lasts from five to six years. Admission is based on the result of the primary certificate examination or an equivalent entrance examination. Secondary schools are private institutions, which the state assists by paying grants to the school for each eligible pupil and 75% of the salaries of registered teachers. The Department of Education lays down the program for its two examinations—the intermediate certificate usually taken after three years' secondary education, and the leaving certificate taken at the end of the course at about 17 or 18 years of age. Gaelic is a compulsory subject in the leaving certificate, except for those children who have received their primary education, before 11 years of age, outside Ireland: these may substitute another language for Gaelic. Secondary education is dependent upon the ability to afford it; a few scholarships are available.

Vocational education takes the form of continuation education, supplementing primary education and providing practical training for future employment, for pupils of 13 to 14 years of age, by two- to three-year-long day courses. Since 1963, the government has introduced a system of free comprehensive schooling that combines secondary and continuation education, and has extended vocational courses so that all students take a form of intermediate certificate at all postprimary schools. After this, students may change from one system to another, and a two-year technical course leading to a technical leaving certificate has been added to the list of options. Vocational education is the function of the vocational education committees, elected by local authorities. Each committee is financed by the state (about two-thirds), by the local authority and, to a small extent, by tuition fees and miscellaneous sources.

Special education: There are special national schools for mentally and physically handicapped children, some residential and some day schools, run by both religious orders and lay organizations. In addition, there are special classes attached to ordinary national schools, mainly in Dublin.

University education: The National University of Ireland was founded in 1908 and is organized on a federal basis into constituent colleges at Dublin, Cork and Galway, and a recognized college (St. Patrick's, Maynooth). Trinity College, Dublin is mainly Protestant. Many of its students come from Britain. Both the National University and Trinity College are self-governing, but are financed through the Department of Education by annual grants-in-aid. Grants are awarded to students by the state, local authorities (with state aid) and the universities themselves.

Possession of the secondary school leaving certificate usually exempts candidates from taking the entrance examinations of the universities. Gaelic is a compulsory subject in the matriculation certificate of the National University, but not for Trinity College. The Royal College of Surgeons is in Dublin. As in Scotland, considerable numbers of students choose three-subject general degrees in preference to specialized honors degrees. Degree courses last three or four years (six for medicine). Trinity College degrees are recognized in Britain. Medical degrees awarded in Britain and Ireland are recognized on a reciprocal basis.

Educational institutions, 1982–83:

	Institutions	Teachers (full-time)	Students (full-time)
Primary schools	3,391	20,424	560,874
Secondary schools	516	12,065	206,413
Vocational schools	245	4,912	74,810
Comprehensive schools	15	541	8,668
Community schools	41	1,480	23,539
Teacher (primary) training colleges	6	*	2,511
Preparatory colleges	1	*	26
Technical colleges (third-level students only)	9	1,058	8,493
Technology colleges (third-level students only)	9	775	5,921
Universities and institutes	9	1,880	29,107

* 178 combined.
Sources: Department of Education, Dublin.

Adult education: Technical education for adults, apprentices and other persons in employment, leading in some cases to professional qualifications,

111

is given in both day and evening courses. In 1982 there were 3,400 public libraries.

MASS MEDIA

The press (1983):

Dailies: Irish Independent, Dublin, independent, 174,788; *Evening Press*, Dublin, ind., 171,707; *Evening Herald*, Dublin, ind., 132,314; *Irish Press*, Dublin, ind., 95,000; *Cork Examiner*, Cork, ind., 63,560; *Irish Times*, Dublin, liberal, 84,697; *Cork Evening Echo*, Cork, ind., 36,250.

Periodicals: The Sunday Press (S), Dublin, ind., 302,210; *The Sunday Independent* (S), Dublin, ind., 256,903; *Irish Catholic* (w), Dublin, Catholic, 35,000; *Irish Farmer's Journal* (w), Dublin, agricultural, 70,642; *Ireland of the Welcomes* (2m), Dublin, tourist, 125,000; *The Pioneer* (m), Dublin, Total Abstinence Society, 25,000; *Ireland's Own* (w), Dublin, family, 64,687; *The Kerryman* (w), Tralee, ind., 41,185.

Censorship of publications: A five-member Censorship of Publications Board, under the supervision of the Ministry of Justice, reviews books submitted by individuals or authorities (e.g. customs officials) and ocassionally stops publication. The church also exercises considerable influence both directly and indirectly on book publishers and on the press.

Broadcasting: Radio and TV broadcasting is controlled and operated by Radio Telefis Éireann, an autonomous public corporation that derives its revenue from license fees, advertising and state grants. The director-general of Radio Telefis Éireann is appointed by the government.

ITALY

Features: Italy is a peninsula protruding into the northern Mediterranéan. In the north, the Italian Alps, sometimes exceeding 12,000 ft/3,650 m. and including a number of lakes, e.g., Lake Como, provide an almost complete physical as well as political frontier; they form a broad arc from the San Remo area in the west to Trieste in the east. East and south of the Alps is the lowland drained by the east-flowing Po River (Po Valley, or Lombardy Plain). This is the most extensive area of lowland in the whole of Italy. The Apennine range rising to over 5,000 ft/1,500 m. runs the whole length of the peninsula, in places close to the Adriatic, in others closer to the western coast. In this area, lowlands are scattered and limited in extent and nearly all confined to the coastal belt. Sicily is triangular in shape with the highest region around Mount Etna, 10,741 ft/3,274 m., in the northeast. Almost the whole island is above 1,000 ft/300 m. Sardinia is also almost entirely mountainous.

Because of the hilly terrain, lack of water in summer and relatively poor soils, good agricultural land is very limited in extent. The two chief agricultural areas are the Campagna, close to Rome, and the Po Valley. Coal resources are scarce, but natural gas has been exploited on a large scale in the Po Valley and some oil has been found in Sicily. Considerable hydroelectric potential also exists in the Alps. Principal mineral ores are bauxite, mined in the central Apennines, and sulfur. Apart from the industrial development that has taken place around Rome and more particularly Naples, the main industrial region lies in the northern plain and is concentrated in particular around Milan, Turin and Genoa.

Area: 116,300 sq. miles/301,200 sq, km. *Mean max. and min. temperatures:* Rome (42° N, 12° 30' E; 380 ft/115 m.) 88°F/31°C (July and Aug.), 39°F/4°C (Jan. and Feb.); Milan (45° 30' N, 9° 30' E; 340 ft/105 m.) 84°F/29°C (July), 29°F/−2°C (Jan.); Palermo (38° N, 13° 30' E; 350 ft/105 m.) 87°F/31°C (Aug.), 47°F/8°C (Jan. and Feb.). *Relative humidity:* Rome 81%; Milan 89%; Palermo 70%. *Mean annual rainfall:* Rome 26 in./660 mm.; Milan 32 in./815 mm.; Palermo 28 in./710 mm.

Total population: (1984) 57 million. *Main towns and populations:* (1982) ROME (2,916,414), Milan (1,655,599), Naples (1,219,362), Turin (1,143,263),

113

ITALY

Genoa (774,643), Palermo (698,254), Bologna (466,593), Florence (460,924). *Distribution:* In 1982 69% of the population lived in cities; 52% of this group lived in cities with over 500,000 inhabitants, and 17% lived in Rome.

Language: Italian is the official language, but the German-speaking citizens of Trentino-Alto Adige and the French-speaking population of Val d'Aosta are guaranteed the right to use their native tongue as well as Italian. There are also Slav, Greek and Albanian minorities. *Religion:* Over 90% of the population professes Roman Catholicism. Relations between church and state are governed by the Lateran Pact.

CONSTITUTIONAL SYSTEM

Constitution: Republic. A referendum in June 1946 abolished the monarchy, and a new constitution approved by a constituent assembly came into force in January 1948 (see under *Recent History*). *Head of state:* President Francesco Cossiga (DC). *Head of government:* Prime Minister Bettino Craxi (PSI).

Executive: The president is elected for seven years by joint session of the two houses of parliament and representatives of the regions elected by the regional councils (see under *Local government*). A two-thirds majority is required, but after a third ballot a simple majority is sufficient. The president appoints the prime minister and—on the recommendation of the prime minister—the council of ministers (*Consiglio dei Ministri*); he can dissolve parliament, but not in the last six months of his office; he may request either house to reexamine legislation in more detail, but if it is passed again it must be promulgated; he promulgates laws and issues decrees with the force of law. The government wields executive power. It must present itself within 10 days of its formation to a confidence vote of both houses. It is responsible to parliament, although ministers may be nominated from outside. It can be forced to resign only by a successful censure motion. Ministers countersign presidential acts and are individually responsible for their departments as well as collectively responsible for the cabinet as a whole.

Legislature: Parliament consists of two houses. The Chamber of Deputies (*Camera dei Deputati*) has 630 members elected for five years by proportional representation. The Senate (*Senato*), which is elected for six years, has 321 members, of whom six are life senators. The remainder are elected by all Italians over 25 (the voting age for the Chamber of Deputies is 21) on a population basis, with at least seven senators per region (but only one for the Val d'Aosta). Legislation may be introduced in either house, but must be passed by both houses to become law. In exceptional circumstances, parliament may delegate legislative functions to the government.

Political parties: Italian political parties can be broadly divided into three groups: the Christian Democrats, the core of all Italian governments since the end of World War II; the Italian Communist party, the largest in Western Europe although never represented in any government since 1947; and the remaining parties of various shades and hues, whose balancing acts have kept the coalition governments alive, though usually only briefly. A descriptive listing of the parties is as follows:

Christian Democratic party, DC. The mainstay of Italian political life and heir to the pioneer Christian Democratic movement of the early 20th century (known as the Popular party and founded by Don Luigi Sturzo), DC grew to its present stature under the greatest of Italian prime ministers in the post-World War II era, Alcide de' Gasperi. Nominally centrist, DC embraces a broad spectrum of political thought from clericalism on the one hand to social reform on the other. Its left-wing element is the New Force, led by Donato Cattin, and its right wing is the Democratic Initiative. Among the party leadership are four former prime ministers, Amintore Fanfani, Arnaldo Forlani, Giulio Andreotti and Francesco Cossiga, the last of whom was elected president of the Republic in June 1985.

Italian Socialist party, PSI. The *tertium quid* of Italian politics, PSI has been the inevitable component of coalition governments in recent years. Originally founded in the 19th century, it has survived a number of factional cleavages, notably in 1947 when Pietro Nenni's faction allied with the Communists and Giuseppe Saragat's faction formed the Italian Workers' Socialist party. It is currently led by Prime Minister Bettino Craxi and Riccardo Lombardi.

Italian Social Democratic party, PSDI. Formed in 1952 through the merger of Saragat's Italian Workers' Socialist party and other anticommunist left-wing groups, PSDI has participated in all government coalitions since 1979. It is led by Giuseppe Saragat, a former president of the republic.

Italian Liberal party, PLI. The oldest of Italian political parties, founded by Count Camillo di Cavour in 1848, PLI continues the classic liberal traditions including free enterprise, laicism and economic conservatism. It is led by Aldo Bozzi.

Italian Communist party, PCI. The perennial outsider in Italian politics, the PCI on a number of occasions has come close to achieving power by parliamentary means, something no other Communist party in Western Europe has done. PCI has long maintained, especially after the death of its long-time leader, Palmiro Togliatti, in 1964, an attitude of independence from Moscow and has been a leading advocate of Eurocommunism. Its membership is not limited to workers but also includes urban intelligentsia and small owners. The PCI controls about 35% of Italian municipalities and participates in over half the nation's regional governments, particularly in central and northern Italy. It is currently led by Alessandro Natta.

Italian Republican party, PRI. Founded in 1897, PRI stands for Giuseppe Mazzini's moderate leftist ideology. Its leaders are Bruno Visentini and a former prime minister, Giovanni Spadolini.

Radical party, PR. A leftist, pro-civil rights group led by Roberto Cicciomessere.

Party of Proletarian Unity for Communism, part of the extreme left-wing Proletarian Democracy Alliance. It is led by Luciana Castellina.

Right-wing parties include the Italian Social Movement–National Right (MSI–DN), a neofascist group led by Pino Romualdi and Georgio Almirante. In 1976, over half its parliamentary delegation withdrew to form the National Democratic Assembly of the Right, DN.

Italy has a number of terrorist groups operating on the fringes of the political spectrum. The best known of these is the Red Brigades, founded in 1969, and believed to be linked with the West German Red Army Faction. Right-wing terrorist groups include the neofascist Armed Revolutionary Nuclei. More than 200 other groups are believed to be active in terrorism.

The 1983 lineup in the Italian parliament is as follows:

Senate: Christian Democratic party   120
Communist party   107
Socialist party   38
Italian Social Movement   18
Social Democratic party   8
Republican party   10
South Tyrol People's party   3
Liberal party   6
Radical party   1
Others   4

Chamber of Deputies:

Christian Democratic party   225
Communist party   198
Socialist party   73
Italian Social Movement   42
Social Democratic party   23
Radical party   11
Republican party   29
Liberal party   16
Party of Proletarian Unity for Communism   7
South Tyrol People's party   3
Others   3

Local government: Italy is divided into 20 regions (*regioni*), of which five —Sicily, Sardinia, Val d'Aosta, Trentino-Alto Adige and Friuli-Venezia Giulia—have special statutes with provisions relating to local powers and defining the extent of regional autonomy. These five regions elect regional councils (*consigli regionali*), each of which elects in turn an executive arm, the regional junta (*giunta regionale*). The other 15 regions are administrative areas only, as no regional statute has been passed by parliament. A government-appointed commissioner (*commissario*) supervises state administrative functions and coordinates them with those of the region. Italy is divided further into 92 provinces (*province*) and about 8,000 communes (*comuni*). The provincial councils (*consigli provinciali*) are elected for four years; each elects a provincial junta (*giunta provinciale*) headed by a president, as its executive arm. The central government is represented in the provinces by a prefect (*prefetto*) who may veto provincial legislation, dissolve provincial or communal councils and transfer their functions to a prefectoral commissioner pending new elections. Communal councils (*consigli comunali*) are also elected for four years, the *giunta comunale* being headed by a mayor (*sindaco*) who is also a central government official, although in the exercise of his central government powers he is subject to the prefect of the province.

Judicial system: Civil cases are dealt with in the first instance and according to their degree of seriousness by magistrates' courts (*giudici conciliatori*), district courts (*preture*) and tribunals (*tribunali*). Appeal is also consecutive and proceeds from the tribunals to the courts of appeal (*corti di appello*) and—on juridical grounds only—to the Supreme Courts of Cassation (Corte Suprema di Cassazione). Criminal cases begin at the district courts and proceed from the tribunals to the assize courts attached to the tribunals (*corti di assise presso i tribunali*). Appeal is to the courts of appeal and the parallel assize courts of appeal (*corti di assise di appello*), and from there to the Supreme Court of Cassation.

Administrative justice is separate from the ordinary system, and is composed of two judicial hierarchies, both of which have judicial as well as administrative functions. One is headed by the Council of State (*Consiglio di Stato*), composed of 87 members and divided into six sections, and the other by the Court of Accounts (*Corte dei Conti*), divided into 11 sections. Appeal from both courts may be made to the Supreme Court of Cassation and, on questions of constitutionality, to the Constitutional Court. The Constitutional Court (*Corte Costituzionale*), set up in 1955, has 15 members, of whom one-third are appointed by the president of the republic; one-third are elected by joint session of parliament; and the remainder are chosen by judges of the Supreme Court of Cassation, the Council of State and the Court of Accounts. Its main function is to pronounce upon the constitutionality of legislation passed both before and since 1948.

Judges are appointed and promoted by, and can only be removed by decision of, the Supreme Council of Magistracy (*Consiglio Superiore della Magistratura*). This body consists of 24 members, 14 of whom are elected by career judges, seven of whom are elected by joint session of parliament (elected members serve for four years and are not immediately reeligible) and three are ex-officio members (the president of the republic who presides, the chief justice and the chief prosecutor).

Trial is by jury. Divorce is legal. There is no death penalty.

RECENT HISTORY

A plebiscite held in June 1946 resulted in the abolition of the monarchy and the election of a constituent assembly, which drew up a new republican constitution that came into force in January 1948.

Under Prime Minister Alcide de' Gasperi, Italy became a founder-member of NATO and the ECSC. This policy of Atlantic and European cooperation, from which Italy has never wavered, was continued under de' Gasperi's successors, and in 1955 Italy became a member of WEU and in 1957 a founder-member of the EC.

Italy has had two long-standing disputes in the postwar period. That with Yugoslavia over Trieste was finally settled in 1954 when the town of Trieste was ceded to Italy and its hinterland to Yugoslavia. That with Austria over the South Tyrol (Alto Adige) led to terrorist activities by elements of the German-speaking population—whose main contention was that the Italian government insufficiently implemented the autonomy clauses of the regional statute (see under *Local government*)—with some aid from German and Austrian organizations. In 1960, Italian Somaliland (which became a U.N. trust territory after World War II) became independent.

Recent Italian history has been characterized by weak and uneasy coalition governments, in which the Christian Democratic party was the only constant; and by periodic scandals, waves of terrorism and economic crises. Bettino Craxi's current government is Italy's 44th since the end of World War II, and among its longest-lived.

Defense: The president of the republic is commander-in-chief of the armed forces in his capacity as president of the Supreme Defense Council. Selective military service lasts 18 months in the navy and 12 months in the other two services. Strengths of the services: army 255,000, navy 42,000, air force 69,000. The Carabinieri, an internal security force, number 110,000. The 1981 defense expenditures were L7.5 trillion ($7.2 billion), representing 1.9% of GNP.

ECONOMY

Background: The influence of the state, in terms of both initiative and control, was of paramount importance in Italy's postwar "economic miracle" —through agencies such as Ente Nazionale Idrocarburi (ENI) and Istituto per la Ricostruzione Industriale (IRI). The 1965–69 national plan diversified the economy further and eliminated structural imbalances, notably in the south. Between 1970 and 1979 the annual average increase in the growth of GNP was 2.2%. The Land Reform Agencies and the Southern Italy Development Fund (*Cassa del Mezzogiorno*), in particular, helped to initiate the development of the long-neglected south. The major growth industries since World War II have been chemicals, textiles, cars, iron and steel, metal industries and petroleum products.

The origin of GDP at factor cost in 1982 was:

Sector	Percentage
Agriculture	6
Industry	41
Services	53
GDP	100

The economic miracle of the Italian economy has been buffeted in recent years by recessions, inflation and political mismanagement. Italy remains among the poorest countries of Western Europe, only slightly above Ireland, trailing Britain by 20% and the other members of the EC by over 45%. Growth today is largely confined to the north.

Serious economic troubles began in 1969 following a series of labor strikes that cut into productivity and sharply increased production costs. The 1973 OPEC oil-price increase raised consumer prices by 20%. In 1975 the GNP fell by 4%, leading to a series of currency devaluations in 1976. Between 1975 and 1980 annual wage and consumer price increases averaged 21%

119

and 16% respectively, unemployment rose to 8% and the growth in GNP fell to between 2% and 6%. Inflation and stagflation have been the major economic issues of every Italian election since then. Efforts to cool the economy have been confined largely to the monetary policies of the Bank of Italy.

Although most businesses are small and the private sector remains vigorous, the government controls a number of industrial giants that dominate the economy. These include ENEL, the electric utility giant; ENI, the petroleum and petrochemical corporation; EGAM, the mineral processing agency; EFIM, the aerospace, aluminum processing and arms manufacturer; and IRI, the Institute for Industrial Reconstruction that controls Alitalia, Alfa Romeo, radio and television broadcasting, iron and steel, shipbuilding and several commercial banks. In addition the state runs railways and has a monopoly over the production of salt, matches and tobacco. These state enterprises employ about one-tenth of all industrial workers and have often served as models of technological innovation. At the same time they are susceptible to scandals because of political vulnerability, and to higher wage rates because of trade union pressures. Italy also has an extensive, unquantified underground economy, consisting of private firms that avoid social security contributions, taxes and minimum-wage laws by farming out work to home workers.

Foreign trade: Despite chronic trade deficits, net earnings from services, especially the lucrative tourism sector and worker remittances from abroad, help to improve current accounts. As one of the founding members of the EC, Italy enjoys free trade within the Community and adheres to its external tariff policies, including variable import levies on agricultural products coming from outside the EC. Quantitative restrictions limit imports from the Eastern bloc and Japan. Although the bulk of Italian trade is with the West, trade relations with OPEC countries are assuming critical importance. Italy retains a special trade relationship with Libya, a prewar colony.

In 1982, Italian exports amounted to $73.490 billion and imports to $86.213 billion, leaving a negative trade balance of $12.723 billion. During 1970–82, the annual average growth rate was 5.8% for exports and 3.1% for imports. The percentage share of merchandise exports in 1982 was 8% for fuels, minerals and metals; 9% for other primary commodities; 11% for textiles and clothing; 32% for machinery and transport equipment; and 40% for other manufactures. The percentage share of merchandise imports in 1982 was 12% for food, 35% for fuels, 11% for other primary commodities, 20% for machinery and transport equipment, and 22% for other manufactures.

Employment: The total labor force in 1982 was nearly 23.67 million, of whom 11% were employed in agriculture, 45% in industry and 44% in services. Unemployment in that year amounted to an above-average 8.4%. Between 1985 and 2000, the labor force is expected to grow by 0.31%.

Price and wage trends: Italian exports have been hurt by the high unit labor costs, fueled by spiraling wage rates conceded by industries through political pressures. Basic wage rates, generally negotiated on an industry-wide basis and covering a three-year period, are supplemented under the *scala mobile*, a system of quarterly cost-of-living adjustments. In 1970–74 these adjustments added an average of 25% to basic wage rates; by 1975–78 the figure had risen to 55%. As a result, Italian labor costs in manufacturing are nearly twice the EC average. In addition, unemployment benefits, 40% of which are derived from employers, are set at 90% of earnings and are payable for as long as two years. At the same time, because tax rates have not been adjusted to compensate for inflation, Italian industrial workers also bear a heavy tax burden. However, the power of the unions is being challenged; in 1980 a strike against Fiat collapsed when the majority of its workers declined to support the Communist-dominated labor confederation's wage demands.

Consumption: In 1982 private consumption accounted for 62% of GNP, and public consumption for 18%. This represented increases of 2.7% and 2.6% over 1970–82 for private and public consumption respectively.

SOCIAL SECURITY

Health insurance: Under the general supervision of the Ministry of Labor and Social Welfare and the Ministry of Health, the scheme covers all residents. It is financed by the insured person, the employer and the government. Sickness benefits (for wage earners only) are 50% of earnings for the first 20 days, and 66% thereafter. Medical benefits include services provided by doctors, pharmacists and hospitals. The medical benefits for dependents are the same as those for the insured.

Accident insurance: Under the general supervision of the Ministry of Labor and Social Welfare, the scheme covers manual workers, nonmanual workers in dangerous work and self-employed workers in agriculture. There is a special system for seamen. The temporary disability benefit (work injury) is 60% of earnings for the first 90 days of disability, 75% thereafter. The permanent disability pension (work injury) is 100% of earnings in the prior year, if the insured is totally disabled. There are various supplements. Survivor pensions (work injury) amount to 50% of earnings of the insured. There are survivor pension provisions for orphans and dependent parents.

Pensions insurance: Under the general supervision of the Ministry of Labor and Social Welfare, and the Treasury, the scheme covers most employed persons. It is financed by the insured person, the employer and the government. Old-age pensions generally begin at age 60 for men and at age 55 for women. Disability pensions are available to workers who have lost two-thirds of their earning capacity. Basically, the minimum old-age pension is L276,050 a month. There are various supplements. Disability pension benefits are the same as old-age pensions: the minimum pension basically is L276,050 a month. Survivor pension is 60% of pension paid or payable to the insured (basically, the minimum is L276,050 a month). There are pension provisions for orphans and dependent parents.

Unemployment insurance: Under the general supervision of the Ministry of Labor and Social Welfare, and the Treasury, the scheme covers employees in private employment (with some exceptions). It is financed by the employer and the government. Benefits are generous, may amount to 90% of earnings and are payable for as long as two years. There are dependents' supplements and other supplements.

Other benefits: Under the general supervision of the Ministry of Labor and Social Welfare, and the Treasurery, family allowances are available to most eligible employees with one or more children. Family allowances are L19,760 a month for each child.

EDUCATION

In 1982 5% of the population over the age of six—predominantly in the south—were illiterate (21% in 1931). Education is free and compulsory from the ages of six to 16. The sexes are taught separately where possible.

Primary education: This is the same for all children and begins at the age of six. The primary school certificate examination (*elementari*) is usually taken at 11.

Secondary and vocational education: Successful attainment of the *elementari* permits a child to continue, from the ages of 11 to 14, at the lower secondary school (*scuola media unica*), which has general and practical streams; this course terminates with the *licenza media*. Those who pass an entrance examination go on to upper secondary schools—*licei* and vocational schools. The *licei* have courses lasting for five years, divided into a lower two-year and an upper three-year section. Success in the final examination, the *licenza liceale*, is a prerequisite for university education. Other upper secondary schools are: training institutes for primary-school teachers (*istituti magistrali*), agricultural schools (*istituti tecnici agrari*), commercial schools (*istituti tecnici commerciali*), industrial training schools (*istituti tecnici industriali*), nautical training schools (*istituti tecnici nautici*) and art training schools (*istituti d'arte*). Courses last from four to five years, and after obtaining the leaving certificate the student may enter a university, university institute or fine arts academy.

Special schools: Backward children are taught in special classes attached to the elementary and intermediate schools. For the mentally and physically handicapped there are special schools, mainly private, and generally situated near hospitals or clinics.

University and higher education: Universities and university institutes are classified as state (the majority) and nonstate. The former are state-financed and state-supervized, while the latter have been set up by private organizations and are recognized by the state but depend upon the private organizations for their finance. All degrees are recognized as equal. All universities have administrative autonomy within their terms of statute. The university rector, elected by the council of professors, has virtually absolute power within the university.

There are many institutes of higher education and universities. Courses for the degree of doctor (which is a first degree) last for four years in most faculties; five years for architecture, industrial chemistry and engineering;

and six years for medicine and surgery. Higher education is not free, but grants are provided.

Universities: Bari, Bologna, Cagliari, Camerino, Catania,* Ferrara, Florence, Genoa, Lecce,* Macerata, Messina, Milan, Milan Catholic University,* Milan Commercial,* Modena, Naples, Padua, Palermo, Parma, Pavia, Perugia, Perugia Foreigners' University, Pisa, Rome, Sassari, Siena, Trieste, Turin, Urbino,* and others.

*Nonstate universities.

Educational institutions, 1982–83:

	Schools	Teachers	Students
Preschool	29,495	61,849	1,759,892
Primary	29,297	276,424	4,215,841
Secondary			
Scuola Media	10,074	272,194	2,862,639
Secondaria Superiore	7,472	209,696	2,465,903
of which:			
Technical	2,672	97,020	1,097,921
Vocational	1,671	52,881	472,252
Teacher training	879	14,019	237,657
Art Licei	247	9,493	60,562
Classical, linguistic and			
scientific Licei	2,003	36,283	597,511
Higher	755	43,961	717,368

Source: Italian Ministry of Education.

Adult education: The state-run people's schools (*scuole popolari*) provide three types of course: lower elementary education for illiterates, higher elementary courses for semiilliterates, and refresher courses of a general culture and vocational training nature. Other adult courses have been begun by private organizations, some state-assisted and others completely financed by the organizations themselves. Supplementing these schools are other facilities for adult education, such as revision courses, reading centers, music courses, family courses, itinerant courses and adult education courses proper. Since 1947, about 300,000 adults per year have passed the *elementari*. The number of public libraries is small in proportion to the population.

MASS MEDIA

The press (1981):

Dailies: Corriere della Sera, Milan, independent, 533,615; *La Stampa* and *Stampa Sera,* Turin, ind., 500,000 (morning); *Il Giorno,* Milan, ind., 180,200; *Il Messagero,* Rome, ind., 300,000; *Il Resto del Carlino,* Bologna, ind., 198,027; *Avanti!,* Rome and Milan, PSU party organ, 130,000; *La Nazione,* Florence, ind., 181,797; *Il Tempo,* Rome, right-wing, 147,700; *Paesa Sera,* Rome, Communist, 200,000; *Il Popolo,* Rome, Christian Democrat party organ, 111,000; *Il Mattino,* Naples, ind., 129,100; *La Voce*

Repubblicana, Rome, Republican party organ; *L'Unità*, Rome, Milan and Turin, PCI party organ, 300,000.

Periodicals: Domenica del Corriere (w), Milan, general, 800,000; *L'Espresso*, Rome, illustrated topical, 175,000; *Oggi* (w), Milan, ill., 743,206; *Tempo* (w), Milan, ill. top., 230,000; *Epoca* (w), Milan, ill. top., 180,000.

Broadcasting: The Italian Radio and Television Corporation (Radiotelevisione Italiana—RAI) is a joint-stock company responsible to the Ministry of Posts and Telegraphs. The autonomous governmental agency IRI holds 99.8% of the stock. A director-general appointed by the government exercises the greatest power within RAI. A committee appointed by the Ministry of Posts is responsible for program standards, and a parliamentary commission for political objectivity. There are three TV channels. Broadcasting is financed by government grants, advertising profits and the sale of licenses. Since the state monopoly on broadcasting ended in 1976, approximately 450 private TV stations have been established, as well as nearly 1,000 private radio stations. In 1983, there were approximately 13,609,000 TV receivers and 14,000,000 radio receivers in use.

LIECHTENSTEIN

Area: 61 sq. miles/158 sq. km. This little state is situated in the Alps south of Lake Constance. *Total population:* (est. 1983) 26,512, of whom about 38% are foreigners. *Capital:* VADUZ (4,896). *Language:* The official language is German. The everyday language is of Alamannic origin. *Religion:* 85% Roman Catholic.

CONSTITUTIONAL SYSTEM

Constitution: The Principality of Liechtenstein is a constitutional monarchy, and under the 1921 constitution hereditary in the male line. *Head of state:* Prince Franz Josef II. *Head of government:* Prime Minister Hans Brunhart.

Executive: The government consists of the government leader, his deputy and two government councillors. The two former are appointed for six years by the prince on the recommendation of parliament (*Landtag*), and the latter are elected for four years by the Landtag. The government is responsible to the sovereign and the Landtag. No resolution of the Landtag can be enforced as law without the sovereign's consent. In time of emergency, the sovereign can enact parliamentary law with the government leader's counter-signature without consulting the Landtag. *Legislature:* The Landtag has 15 members elected by proportional representation for four years. In 1984 women won the constitutional right to vote in Landtag elections. *Political parties:* There are three political parties: the Progressive Citizens' party, the Fatherland Union and the Christian Social party.

Judicial system: Civil and criminal cases are heard in the first instance by the county court (*Landgericht*) of one presiding judge. More serious criminal cases go to the assize court (*Schöffengericht-Vergehen*), composed of a bench of three judges, and the criminal court (*Kriminalgericht*), composed of a bench of five judges. Appeal in both civil and criminal cases is first to the superior court (*Obergericht*) and then to the Supreme Court (*Oberster Gerichtshof*), both composed of five judges.

RECENT HISTORY

Liechtenstein has closely followed the fortunes of Switzerland. A customs union was signed between the two states in 1923. In August 1984, Prince Franz Josef turned over executive authority to Prince Hans Adam. Prince

Franz Josef remained titular head of state. *Defense:* There is no army. Police are armed.

ECONOMY

Liechtenstein is one of the richest countries in the world, according to GNP. In 1977, its per capita product was $11,000, compared with $9,320 in the United States. Although less than 4% of the population is engaged in agriculture (compared to about 70% in 1923), cattle breeding is highly developed, with a main emphasis upon milk production. Other main products are potatoes, maize, fruit and wine grapes. Tourism is a major industry, with over 100,000 visitors annually. Earnings from philately amount to about one-sixth of total revenue. The main industrial sector is the metal industry, which specializes in precision goods; ceramics are also important. Industrial trades employ about 55% of the population.

Liechtenstein is a tax-haven for 30,000 holding and headquarters companies, owing to its minimal capital tax of 0.1% and the absence of 'profit, revenue or property taxes. Income from this source amounted to almost one-fifth of total revenue until 1980. Legislation enacted in 1980 tightened regulations on such companies. All commercial companies are required to submit annual, fully audited accounts. Total bank balances within the country increased twelvefold in the period 1945–63, compared to only a fourfold increase in Switzerland over the same period. The value of exports in 1980 was $480 million. About 32% of exports go to EFTA and about 42% to the EC.

SOCIAL SECURITY

The system is organized on lines similar to those of Switzerland.

EDUCATION

Public education is through the five-year *Volksschule* to the four-year *Realschule*, with an educational syllabus similar to that of a Swiss secondary school. Students may also attend the Liechtensteinisches Gymnasium (grammar school) for eight years. Although there is no university in Liechtenstein, many students attend universities in West Germany, Austria or Switzerland. There is a music school, a technical evening school, two schools for backward children and a school for mentally handicapped children.

THE PRESS (*1984*)

Dailies: Liechtensteiner Vaterland, Fatherland Union, Vaduz, 7,000; *Liechtensteiner Volksblatt*, Progressive Citizens' party, Schaan, 7,700 (5 days a week).

LUXEMBOURG

GEOGRAPHY

Features: This small, landlocked state is part of the Ardenne Massif and also of the scarplands of northern France. Mainly over 800 ft/240 m., it is dissected by a number of tributaries of the Moselle, which forms its eastern border. Farmland and woodland alternate over the area and considerable quantities of Jurassic iron ore have been worked.

Area: 1,000 sq. miles/2,590 sq. km. *Mean max. and min. temperatures:* Luxembourg (49° 30′ N, 6° E; 1,100 ft/335 m.) 74°F/23°C (July), 29°F/−2°C (Jan.). *Relative humidity:* Luxembourg 91%. *Mean annual rainfall:* 29 in./735 mm.

POPULATION

Total population: (1984 est.) 400,000. *Main towns and populations:* (1982) LUXEMBOURG (80,000), Esch-sur-Alzette (26,200), Differdange (17,300). *Distribution:* In 1982, 79% of the population lived in urban centers.

Language: The official languages are French and German, but the everyday language is a West Frankish dialect, Letzeburgesch. *Religion:* Mainly Roman Catholic, but with Jewish and Protestant communities in some centers.

CONSTITUTIONAL SYSTEM

Constitution: Luxembourg is a constitutional monarchy. The constitution dates from 1868; it was revised in 1919 and 1948. *Head of state:* Grand Duke Jean of Luxembourg. *Head of government:* Prime Minister Jacques Santer (Christian Social Party).

Executive: Executive power rests with the grand duke and a 12-strong Council of Ministers chosen by him. *Legislature:* The Chamber of Deputies numbers 64 and is elected for five years by proportional representation in four electoral districts. Legislation is first submitted to the 21-member Council of State—appointed by the sovereign—for an advisory opinion. The Council of State elects a seven-person committee (*Comité du Contentieux*) every six years, the highest administrative court in the land. Laws affecting agriculture, labor, handicrafts, private employees and commerce must first be submitted for opinion to one or more of the five professional chambers composed of representatives of these sectors of society.

Political parties: Luxembourg has a multiparty system dominated by three parties:

Christian Social party, PCS. Formed in 1914, PCS is a centrist party with strong Catholic and monarchical leanings. It was led until recently by Pierre Werner and now by Prime Minister Jacques Santer.

Democratic party, PD. The PD includes both conservatives and moderates. Sometimes called liberal because of its anticlerical stance, it is pro-free enterprise and pro-NATO. It is led by Collette Flesch.

Socialist party, POSL. Founded in 1902, the moderately Marxist POSL is the nation's strongest advocate of expanded social legislation and social insurance. It is led by Robert Krieps and Robert Goebbels.

Social Democratic party, PSDL. Formed in 1971 by a group of conservative dissident Socialist Workers' party members who objected to collaboration with communists.

Communist party, PCL. Established in 1921, the pro–Moscow PCL advocates full nationalization of the economy and opposes NATO and Eurocommunism. It is led by René Urbany.

Independent Socialist party, PSI. Founded in 1979 by a group of leftist POSL dissidents.

There are several other small parties.

In 1984, the party alignment in the Chamber of Deputies was as follows:

Christian Socialist party 25
Democratic party 14
Socialist party 21
Communist party 2
Others 2

Local government: The basic unit is the commune, administered by a council elected for six years. The executive heads of the commune are a mayor and two aldermen (*échevins*) appointed by the sovereign. The communes are grouped into 12 cantons and these in turn into *arrondissements administratifs*, each of which is administered by a government representative, the *commissaire du district*, appointed by the sovereign.

Judicial system: The lowest courts are those of the *justices de paix*—one per canton—with summary jurisdiction in minor police, civil and commercial cases. Appeal is to the two regional tribunals (*tribunaux d'arrondissements*), composed of a president and a panel of judges. These have correctional jurisdiction in all but serious crimes, and act as civil and commercial courts of the first instance. Every three months the Supreme Court (*Cour Supérieure de Justice*) appoints the Cour d'Assises as the highest criminal court; this has six judges who also act as jurors; verdict is given by majority. The Supreme Court acts as the final court of appeal and as a court of cassation. Judges and *juges de la paix* are appointed for life by the crown, and can be removed only by judicial sentence. Luxembourg abolished capital punishment in 1979.

RECENT HISTORY

Luxembourg signed a 50-year Customs Union with Belgium in 1922. After the German occupation from 1940 to 1944, the constitution was amended to rescind the former status of permanent neutrality. The same year (1948) Luxembourg joined with Belgium and the Netherlands in "Benelux" and signed the Brussels Treaty. In 1949 it became a founder-member of NATO and is also an original member of the EC (ECSC, EEC and Euratom).

In 1984, Pierre Werner, the elder statesman of Luxembourg and prime minister for a total of 17 years since 1959, stepped down in favor of Jacques Santer.

Defense: Conscription ended in 1967. The present army is a 500-man volunteer force.

ECONOMY

Background: Luxembourg's economy is closely tied to that of Belgium under the Belgium-Luxembourg Economic Union (BLEU). In the past several years Luxembourg has strained to retool its economy to changing world market conditions. Partly in response to its large hoard of gold and partly to insulate itself from Belgium's economic troubles, the 1981 extension of BLEU trade agreements includes a provision for the Grand Duchy to establish its own central monetary agency, the Luxembourg Monetary Institute, and to become an autonomous member of the European Monetary System and the International Monetary Fund.

Still dominating Luxembourg's economy is the iron and steel industry, which generates over one-third of the GDP and employs one-eighth of the labor force. The industry itself is a virtual monopoly of Luxembourg's only steelmaker, Aciéries Réunies de Burbach-Eich-Dudelange (ARBED), Western Europe's fourth-largest steel firm. Because iron ore production is only about 10% of 1968 levels, ARBED is using ore from France to maintain production levels.

Next to steel, the largest sector is banking. In 1982 there were 112 foreign banks (including 29 from West Germany) operating in the country; they accounted for four-fifths of all corporation taxes. However, the number of such banks appears to have reached a plateau. Other European governments are easing their domestic banking regulations, making Luxembourg's location less attractive. The establishment of the Luxembourg Monetary Institute and the accompanying introduction of closer monitoring of financial transactions and the institution of reserves could slow the growth of the banking sector. In addition to foreign banks, some 5,000 locally incorporated holding companies take advantage of freedom from taxation on their nondomestic dividends, although Luxembourg is not technically a tax haven and corporate taxes are by no means low compared to other European countries.

The origin of GDP at factor cost in 1982 was:

Sector	Percentage
Agriculture	3
Industry	33
Services	64
GDP	100

In 1981 the GNP at market prices was $5.2 billion and per capita GNP $14,510. The annual average growth rate during 1970–74 was 3.5%.

129

The main industries, apart from iron and steel, are chemicals, tobacco, mining, beverages and manufacturing products. The main agricultural products are vegetables, wheat, barley, livestock, dairy products and wine.

Foreign trade: See under *Belgium.*

Employment: The total labor force in 1982 was about 153,200, of whom 44% were employed in industry, 7.7% in agriculture and 48.3% in services. The population of Luxembourg is an aging one and there is a shortage of skilled labor not sufficiently compensated for by the relatively large numbers of foreign workers, estimated at 30% of the work force. In 1984 net immigration averaged over 5,000 per year. Unemployment has remained at less than 1.1%.

Price and wage trends: Between 1970 and 1979 the annual rise in the cost of living was 6.7% despite the government's price control policy. In 1977 the government and the trade unions reached an agreement to make strikes illegal. Automatic indexed cost-of-living wage increases, a wide array of tax-supported social services and worker participation in management had helped to keep Luxembourg strike-free since 1950. Luxembourg's dependence upon foreign trade, and in particular the prices of imports, is a major determining factor of all prices in the economy.

Consumption: Private consumption in 1981 accounted for 63% of GNP and public consumption for 11%.

SOCIAL SECURITY

Health insurance: Most employed and self-employed persons are covered by the scheme, which is under the general supervision of the Ministry of Labor and Social Security. The insurance is financed by the insured person, the employer and the government. Sickness benefits are 100% of earnings, payable for up to 52 weeks from the first day of absence from the job. Medical benefits comprise services provided by doctors and hospitals under contract with sickness funds, which administer contributions and benefits for wage earners. Medical benefits for dependents are the same as those for the insured.

Accident insurance: Under the general supervision of the Ministry of Labor and Social Security, this scheme covers most employed and self-employed persons. It is financed by the employer and the government. The temporary disability benefit for work-related injury is 100% of earnings. The permanent disability pension for the same kind of injury is 80% of earnings during the last year, if totally disabled. There are various supplements. Partial disability pensions pay percentages of the full pension depending on the degree of disability. Medical benefits include necessary care, including medical treatment, surgery and hospitalization. There are survivor pensions for widows, dependent disabled widowers and orphans.

Pensions insurance: Under the general supervision of the Ministry of Labor and Social Security, this scheme covers employed persons under five separate systems. There are special systems for miners, railway employees and public employees. It is financed by the insured persons, the employer and the government. Old-age pensions begin at age 65 generally. Disability pensions begin under age 65 if there is a two-thirds loss of earning capacity for wage earners or incapacity for work for salaried employees. The old-age basic pension is BF55,993 a year, plus increments. There are child's supplements and means-tested allowances. Survivors' pensions are payable to widows, dependent disabled widowers, divorced women (under certain conditions) and orphans.

Unemployment insurance: This scheme, under the general supervision of the Ministry of Labor and Social Security, covers most employed persons, self-employed persons and recent graduates of schools. The government contributes the entire cost from various tax receipts. Unemployment benefits begin at 80% of base salary during the last three months and go up to 2.5 times an unskilled worker's national minimum wage; they are reduced after 182 days. Recent graduates receive 70% of this wage, and self-employed persons receive 80% of a skilled worker's national minimum wage.

Other benefits: There are family allowances available for qualified permanent residents with one or more children. This scheme is administered by the Old-Age and Invalidity Insurance Institution.

EDUCATION

Education is free and compulsory from the ages of six to 15. All schools are run by the state except for some girls' schools—mostly convents—which are state-controlled. The Ministry of Education has complete control of the curriculum, the only duty of the local government being to nominate the staff. Teaching is in German or French, since Letzeburgesch has no written grammar or fixed spelling.

Primary education: This lasts from six to 15 years. Those who do not take or do not pass an entrance examination to the secondary or intermediate schools at the age of 12 continue at primary school. Those who successfully complete their sixth year of primary education go on to *classes complémentaires* for three-year courses. Here boys and girls are taught separately, and given a general education orientated towards later practical studies, ending with a certificate of primary studies awarded by a school commission. Those who do not successfully complete the sixth year of primary studies are prepared in special classes for practical work. Certain communes have introduced a four-year upper primary school.

Secondary education: Intermediate education consists of a three-year lower grade continuing, for some, in a two-year upper school. Secondary education proper is at three levels, two for boys and one for girls, all ending with an *examen de fin d'études secondaires.* For boys there are, first, classical lycées providing seven-year courses, divided into two-year lower and middle divisions and three-year upper divisions, with the *examen de passage* at the end of the middle grade. The classical lycées prepare their students for higher and university studies. The modern lycées offer six-year courses divided into three-year lower and upper divisions; in the upper division education is divided into industrial and commercial sections. For girls there are separate lycées with the upper division giving university entry.

Special education: Backward children are taught in special classes. There are also institutes for handicapped children, and two institutes of education and apprenticeship for juvenile delinquents.

Technical and vocational education: Apprentices in commerce, the crafts and industry attend part-time weekly education two- to four-year courses at the state centers of professional education, ending in an examination for the *certificat d'aptitude professionnelle.* Further vocational schools are the Institute of Technical Education, the Conservatory of Music and the School of Music in Luxembourg, and the State Agricultural School in Ettelbrüch.

Educational institutions (students), 1980–1983:

	1980–81	1982–83
Nursery education	7,621	7,579
Primary education	29,007	26,707
Secondary education	9,037	9,120
Middle, vocational and technical education	15,947	16,016
Teacher training	180	146
Total pupils	61,792	59,568

There were 2,718 students in university education in 1982–83.
Source: Ministère de l'Education Nationale.

Higher education: Attached to the Athénée and the Boys' Lycée in Luxembourg City, respectively, are one-year courses in arts and sciences, considered the equivalent of a year at university. Success in these courses is generally a prerequisite for admission to certain professions. In addition, there are two teacher training schools and a University of Comparative Sciences in Luxembourg. University education is obtained in France, Germany, Belgium or Switzerland. In 1969 a Centre Universitaire was created to offer one-year courses in the humanities, sciences and education, and two-year courses in law.

Adult education: The École Supérieure du Travail is an autonomous institution under the Ministry of Labor offering courses in law, finance and economics. There are also a number of private cultural organizations that have educational aims, in addition to adult education courses proper.

MASS MEDIA

The press (1983): Dailies (1982): Luxemburger Wort, Luxembourg, Christian Social party organ 79,728; *Tageblatt,* Esch-sur-Alzette, Socialist, 24,194; *Letzeburger Journal,* Luxembourg, Liberal, 14,500; *Zeitung vum Letzeburger Vollek,* Luxembourg, Communist party organ, 8,000.

Periodicals (Luxembourg): OGB-L Aktuell (m), trade union, 28,000; *Revue/ D'Letzebuerger Illustréiert* (w), illustrated, 25,947; *Soziale Fortschrett (LCGB)* (fortnightly), trade union, 17,000; *Télécran* (w), TV weekly, 26,000.

Broadcasting: The Compagnie Luxembourgeoise de Télédiffusion is a private body operating under state charter and financed solely by its own commercial activities; the state has no shares in the company, but the French state has a major holding through its company SOFIRAD. The company operates both home and overseas radio services through Radio Luxembourg, and TV services within Luxembourg through Télé Luxembourg. In 1984, there were approximately 130,000 TV receivers and 225,000 radio receivers in use.

MALTA

GEOGRAPHY

Features: This island group consists of limestone plateaus rising to over 1,500 ft/450 m. Agriculture is not very prosperous and there are no important minerals. *Area:* 122 sq. miles/315 sq. km. *Mean min. and max. temperatures:* Valetta (36° N, 14° 30' E; 230 ft/70 m.) 85°F/29°C (Aug.), 51°F/11°C; (Jan. and Feb.). *Relative humidity:* Valetta 76%. *Mean annual rainfall:* Valetta 20 in./510 mm.

POPULATION

Total population: (1984) 400,000. *Chief towns and populations:* (1982) Sliema (20,000), Birkirkara (16,000), VALETTA (14,042).

Language: Both Maltese and English are official languages. Italian is spoken widely. *Religion:* 90% to 95% of the population is Roman Catholic. The archbishop of Malta is recognized as spiritual head of Malta, and the constitution guarantees the church the right to control its own affairs.

CONSTITUTIONAL SYSTEM

Constitution: Malta is a republic. The constitution was accepted as a constitution for independence by referendum in May 1964. *Head of State:* President Agatha Barbara. *Head of government:* Prime Minister Dr. Karmenu (Carmelo) Mifsud Bonnici (Labor).

Executive: The independence constitution of 1964 established Malta as an independent parliamentary monarchy within the Commonwealth. By a constitutional amendment, the country became a republic on December 13, 1974, with an indirectly elected president replacing the British monarch. The president serves a five-year term, as does the prime minister, subject to legislative backing. The parliament consists of a unicameral House of Representatives elected on the basis of proportional representation every five years.

The major political party is the ruling Malta Labor party, led by Dom Mintoff, which espouses a socialist and anticolonialist policy. Mintoff resigned the prime ministry in December 1984 and was succeeded by Karmenu Mifsud Bonnici, leader-designate of the party. The only opposition party is the Nationalist party, which brought independence to Malta. It is prochurch, pro-NATO and pro-EC. The party's leader is Dr. Edward Fenech Adami.

Following the 1981 election, the party lineup in the House of Representatives was: Malta Labor party 34; Nationalist party 31.

Local government: There is no local government on Malta except for a civic council on the island of Gozo. *Judicial system:* Maltese civil law derives mainly from Roman law, although public law is greatly influenced by the British system. The language of the courts is Maltese. The lower courts are the criminal court and the court of magistrates, the latter acting as a juvenile court in the case of young offenders. Appeal is to the court of appeal and—in certain civil matters—further to the judicial committee of the Privy Council. The Constitutional Court hears and determines disputes over membership of the House of Representatives—in which it has final jurisdiction—and appeals from other courts on constitutional and certain other matters. Malta maintains capital punishment but no executions have taken place since the war.

RECENT HISTORY

The Crown Colony of Malta was awarded the George Cross for its resistance during World War II. In 1962 Malta became a member of the Inter-Governmental Committee for European Migration; it is also a member of the Council of Europe and GATT.

The 1971 parliamentary elections brought the Malta Labor party to power under Dom Mintoff. Under his regime Malta became a sovereign republic in 1974, but remained within the Commonwealth. Generally anti-Western in his foreign policy, Mintoff became embroiled with Great Britain over rental payments for the use of Maltese military facilities. In 1979 the last British troops withdrew from Malta. In his domestic policy, Mintoff engaged in constant skirmishes with the Roman Catholic church as well as the judiciary. His judicial reform bill of 1981—preventing courts from ruling on the validity of government actions—was branded by the International Commission of Jurists as "striking at the basic principles of the rule of law."

Defense: Malta has small local defense forces. Immediately after independence it signed a mutual defense agreement with Britain, under the terms of which British forces were to remain stationed on the island for 10 years. These troops were withdrawn in 1979. Malta is the headquarters of NATO's Allied Forces Mediterranean, with responsibility in war for convoy protection. Although not a formal member of NATO, it has the right of consultation with the NATO Council if a threat to its political security or territorial integrity is deemed to exist, with no obligation to provide armed forces or expenses to NATO. Defense expenditures for 1983 were approximately £M6.5.

ECONOMY

Background: After independence Malta remained heavily dependent for development upon loans from Britain. According to the 1964 Agreement on Financial Assistance between the two countries, Britain was to provide £18.8 million for the three years from April 1964 and £31.2 million for the next seven years.

During the early 1980s, Malta moved into the ranks of middle-income developing countries and began to experience the problems of economic maturity, especially the costs associated with the extensive social welfare system erected over the last decade. The strengths of the economy are its declining rate of unemployment, double-digit rate of per capita growth and comfortable current-account balances, as well as a relatively modest rate of inflation averaging less than 7% annually, despite the closedown of the British naval base on the main island. The nationalized drydocks—now known as the Malta Drydocks Corporation—are still the largest single employer on the island. Now run by an elected workers' council, the enterprise has been strike-free since the rise of the Labor government and has been recently expanded with help from the People's Republic of China.

In pursuit of its socialist ideology, the Mintoff administration injected a substantial state presence into the economy through nationalization of banking, broadcasting and telecommunications, as well as the drydocks; restricting certain types of imports to government departments; and participating in industrial enterprises through the Malta Development Corporation. Tourism received considerable emphasis as a revenue earner. The number of foreign visitors more than trebled between 1970 and 1979; arrivals in 1980 numbered over 726,000, while gross tourist receipts jumped to $320 million, equal to two-thirds of merchandise export earnings.

In 1981 GNP stood at $1.19 billion, with an annual per capita income of $3,470. The major production increases in recent years have been in construction, rubber, chemicals, food manufacturing, textiles and tobacco. Industry continues to center on ship repairing and building. The principal crops are onions, grapes, wheat, fodder and barley. Potatoes and fresh vegetables are the main cash crops.

Foreign trade: Although merchandise imports exceeded exports for every year during the past decade, the trade deficit was exceeded by surpluses in invisibles, including tourism. Thus, a current-account surplus has regularly contributed to the growth of Malta's foreign reserves. Reexports to and from North Africa and the Middle East account for over 10% of the export trade.

Trading is controlled for over 20 commodities, including foodstuffs, steel, cement and timber, which can be imported only by the Ministry of Trade. Foodstuffs are distributed only by the state through a rationing system. In 1980, economic cooperation agreements were concluded with Czechoslovakia, Greece and Italy. The Mintoff administration has sought to diversify trading partners and to garner aid from the East as well as the West.

Employment: In 1982 the total labor force was about 120,600. Employment in the manufacturing and other industries and in government service is increasing against a slow decline in agriculture, fishing, construction and quarrying. Malta is a country of low unemployment—less than 4%. Since the war, more than 100,000 Maltese have emigrated, over 50% to Australia.

Employment in manufacturing, which accounts for 30% of GDP, grew from 19% of the work force in 1970 to 28% in 1980. One-fifth of this number is employed in metals, machinery and transport equipment.

Malta has a high birthrate, but the labor force has grown slowly because of emigration. Unionization is high, but industrial relations have been smooth because of labor's stake in the success of the Mintoff administration.

SOCIAL SECURITY

Employees are covered against sickness, unemployment, old age, widowhood, orphanhood and industrial injuries. The Ministry of Labor, Employment and Welfare has the general supervision of these insurance schemes. They are financed by the insured person, the employer and the government. Health insurance sickness benefits are £M12 a week, plus £M7.50 for spouse. There are maternity benefits. Accident insurance benefits include a temporary disability benefit and permanent disability pension, both for work injuries. The former is £M22.50 a week for adults, and the latter is £M12.05 a week, plus £M7.65 for spouse, in the event of total disability.

There are survivor pensions for widows, dependents, aged or disabled widowers, and orphans. Old-age pensions begin generally at 61 for men and 60 for women. Disability pensions are available for people totally and permanently incapacitated for work. Old-age pensions are generally $66\frac{2}{3}\%$ of earnings, as are survivor pensions, payable to widows. There are provisions for orphans. Family allowances are available to qualified families with one or more children.

EDUCATION

Primary, secondary and special education: About 17% of the population is illiterate. Primary education is free in government schools and compulsory for all children from the ages of six to 16. Instruction is in Maltese and English. Private schools are run mainly by convents; some in receipt of government subsidies cater to both primary and (especially for girls) secondary schooling. In 1984 the Roman Catholic church operated 72 private primary and secondary schools. There are special schools for handicapped children. Some children proceed to grammar and technical schools, where they are prepared for university entrance examinations.

Technical education: The program for technical education is being expanded. Entrance to the five-year course is by examination taken at the ages of 11 to 13. The sixth form prepares pupils for A-level examinations in scientific and technical subjects. Higher technological training takes place at the Malta Polytechnic. *Vocational and adult education:* Courses in craft training and industrial apprenticeship are expanding. Evening classes offer tuition in 36 subjects. Basic education in English, Maltese and other subjects is available for adults in a large number of centers in Malta and Gozo. *Higher education:* There are two teacher training colleges with an increasing intake of students. The Royal University of Malta is the oldest institution of higher learning, having been founded in 1592. There are two other degree-granting institutions, the New University and the Malta College of Arts, Science and Technology.

Educational institutions (government and private), 1982–83:

	Institutions	Teachers	Students
Preprimary	17	363	7,645
Primary	120	1,656	33,208
Secondary:			
General	67	1,714	21,986
Vocational	22	425	5,271
Higher:			
University	1	146	1,010

Source: Europa Year Book, 1985.

MASS MEDIA

The press (1983):

Dailies: Il-Hajja, Valetta; *L-Orrizont*, Valetta, socialist; *The Times of Malta*, Valetta, 18,000; *In-...Taghna*, Pietà, 18,000.

Periodicals and weeklies: The Bulletin (w), Hamrun; *The Democrat* (w), Pietà, 10,000; *Il-Mument* (w), Pietà, 20,000; *Il-Torca* (w), Valetta, General Workers' Union, 24,000; *Lehen is-Sewwa* (w), Catholic, Pietà, 10,000; *The Sunday Times* (w), Valetta; *Weekend Chronicle* (w), Valetta, 20,000; *Givida* (w), Radio and TV guide, Gwardamanga, 14,300; *Il-Gzejjer* (quarterly), Valetta, 25,000; *Malta Review* (bimonthly), Valetta, 5,000.

Broadcasting: The Malta Broadcasting Authority is an independent public body controlling the commercial radio station Rediffusion (Malta) Ltd., and the commercial Telemalta Corporation. Broadcasting is in Maltese and English. There is also an independent radio station, Radio Mediterranean, broadcasting in English, French and Arabic.

MONACO

Features: This tiny urban state is situated on the Mediterranean coast near the French-Italian border. It is entirely surrounded by France in all directions landward. *Area:* 1 sq. mile/2.5 sq. km. *Total population:* (1982) 27,063. *Capital:* MONTE CARLO (10,000). *Language:* French (official) and Monégasque (a mixture of French and Italian). *Religion:* Roman Catholic.

CONSTITUTIONAL SYSTEM

Constitution: The Principality of Monaco is a constitutional monarchy. A new constitution was promulgated by the sovereign in 1962, and any future amendments may be made only with the approval of the National Council. *Head of state:* Prince Rainier III. *Head of government:* Minister of State Jean Herly.

Executive: Executive power is vested in the hereditary sovereign and the minister of state—seconded by the French government—who are assisted by three government councillors. *Legislature:* The sovereign and the 18 members of the National Council, elected for five years by universal suffrage, are the source of legislative power.

Local government: The four parts of the principality—Monaco-Ville, La Condamine, Fontvielle and Monte Carlo—are administered by an elected municipal council headed by the mayor of Monaco. *Judicial system:* The Code Louis of 1919 is similar to the French Code. There is a court of the *juge de paix*, a *tribunal de première instance*, a *cour d'appel* and a *cour de révision* (court of cassation). The highest court is the *Tribunal Suprême*, which is the administrative court and also safeguards fundamental liberties.

RECENT HISTORY

The constitution was suspended provisionally by Prince Rainier in 1959. The new constitution of 1962 granted more power to the elected National Council. The principality is combined in a customs union with France, but in 1962 the French government set up a customs barrier to enforce stricter control on the flow of goods between the two states. This was lifted in May 1963, and many French companies established in the principality were brought under French fiscal control. In the January 1983 elections the National and Democratic Union won all the seats on the National Council. It supports Prince Rainier.

ECONOMY

The main sources of revenue are the sale of tobacco and postage stamps and receipts from tourism (including the Monte Carlo Casino), and from the state's services as a financial center. There are a number of light industries that have a market in France and increasingly so elsewhere.

SOCIAL SECURITY

The Office of Social Assistance is directed by an administrative commission under the presidency of the mayor of Monaco.

EDUCATION

There are six primary schools, three each for boys and girls run by religious orders. There is one secondary school providing courses leading to the *baccalauréat*. The Monaco Boys School and the Condamine Girls School offer short general and vocational secondary education. In 1983–84, there were 447 preprimary, 911 primary and 2,182 secondary students in state schools. There were a total of 1,387 student in private schools.

MASS MEDIA

The press: The official weekly is the *Journal de Monaco*. A special Monaco edition of *Nice Matin* is published in Nice, France. French newspapers are widely read. There is also the *Gazette Monaco—Côte d'Azur*, published every two months.

Broadcasting: Radio Monte Carlo (RMC) is a commercial body in which the French government has large holdings; it broadcasts its official program in French. There are also programs broadcast in Italian and 12 other languages. The Société Monégasque d'Exploitation et d'Études de Radiodiffusion (SOMERA) is a subsidiary of RMC and broadcasts in French and Arabic. Trans World Radio broadcasts religious programs in French, English and 33 other languages. Television is controlled by the Société Spéciale d'Entreprises Télé Monte-Carlo. Approximately 17,200 TV receivers and 9,500 radio receivers were in use in Monaco in 1983.

THE NETHERLANDS

Features: The Netherlands is unique in Europe in that nearly 50% of its land area lies below sea level and is maintained as dry land by a complicated series of sea dikes and continual pumping. It has added considerably to its extent by the draining of the Ijsselmeer (the former Zuider Zee). More land has been reclaimed by means of the Delta Plan for the construction of dams to protect the islands between the Western Scheldt and mainland. Only in the extreme southeast, in South Limburg, does the altitude reach over 1,000 ft/300 m. This area is a dissected plateau covered with loess soil. The rest of the country can be divided into three main regions. First there are the Polder Lands, which stretch from Groningen in the north to the south and the Zeeland Islands. The part of this area fronting the North Sea is protected by sand dune ridges, in places reinforced; the rest is protected by dikes. Reclamation of this area began in the early Middle Ages and is still going on. The second area consists of the river valleys of the Maas, Lek and Waal; these valleys too are protected by dikes. Finally there are the sandy areas of the east, largely consisting of outwash sands and gravels of glacial and fluvial origin. In places, ridges of morainic material rise above the general level of the surface to about 300 ft/90 m., e.g., in Veluwe.

The reclamation of the peat and clay areas of the west and the improvement of much of the sandy areas of the east has meant that a great proportion of the country is suitable for agriculture. The most intensive cultivation is in the Polder Lands and river valleys. The chief mineral resources are deposits of coal in south Limburg and very large deposits of natural gas in the northeast. Few other minerals exist. The chief industrial centers are Amsterdam, the area around Rotterdam and stretching along the New Waterway to Europort, and the urban concentration of north Brabant and north Limburg, e.g., Tilburg, Breda and Eindhoven.

Area: Land area 14,267 sq. miles/36,948 sq. km. Total area (including low-water areas, i.e., sea-level at low tide) 18,119 sq. miles/46,924 sq. km. *Mean max. and min. temperatures:* Amsterdam (52° 30′ N, 5° E; 5 ft/1.5 m) 69°F/21°C (July), 34°F/1°C (Jan. and Feb.). *Relative humidity:* Amsterdam 83%. *Mean annual rainfall:* 26 in./660 mm.

Population: (1984) 14.4 million. *Chief towns and populations:* (1982) AMSTERDAM (712,294), Rotterdam (576,330), The Hague (seat of government) (456,726), Utrecht (236,211), Eindhoven (195,669), Groningen (162,952), Haarlem (157,556). *Distribution:* In 1982 76% of the population lived in urban centers. *Language:* The official language is Dutch. *Religion:* (1984) Protestant 30%, Roman Catholic 40%, other creeds 4%.

CONSTITUTIONAL SYSTEM

Constitution: The Netherlands is a constitutional monarchy. The constitution of 1814 has been repeatedly amended. A new constitution came into force in 1983. *Head of state:* Queen Beatrix. *Head of government:* Prime Minister Rudolph Lubbers (Christian Democratic Appeal).

Executive: Since the constitution does not acknowledge the existence of a prime minister, the sovereign appoints the ministers through the agency of a cabinet-former or *formateur*, who can usually command a majority in parliament. However, the *formateur* does not necessarily become chairman of the Council of Ministers (*Ministerraad*), i.e., prime minister, and sometimes does not even enter the government.

The sovereign gives assent to all legislation. All acts of the sovereign require the countersignature of a minister. Ministers are responsible to parliament (*Staten-Generaal*) and have the right to speak in either chamber but not to vote. They are generally members of the lower chamber, in which case they are obliged to resign their parliamentary seats within three months of their ministerial appointment. Both the Council of Ministers and the sovereign consult the Council of State (*Raad van State*) on legislative and administrative policy and the issue of decrees.

Legislature: Parliament has two houses. The Second Chamber (*Tweede Kamer*) has 150 members elected for four years by the list system of proportional representation, the whole country serving as one constituency. The 75 members of the First Chamber (*Eerste Kamer*) are elected by the provincial councils for six years, with one-half retiring every three. Legislation originates in the Second Chamber. The First Chamber has the power to accept or reject legislation, but only the Second Chamber can make amendments. Certain bills are considered by joint sessions of the two houses, with the right to make amendments.

Political parties: The Netherlands has a vigorous multiparty system, with religious parties on the one hand and secular parties on the other, the latter embracing all shades of political and economic ideologies. Because no party dominates the Staten-Generaal, coalition governments have been the rule since the end of World War II. The parties are as follows:

Christian Democratic Appeal, CDA. Formed in 1976 as an alliance of the principal religious parties, the Catholic People's party and two Protestant groups, the Calvinist-led Anti-Revolutionary party and the Christian Historical Union. CDA has been the core of most coalitions in recent times. It is led by Rudolph Lubbers, currently prime minister.

People's party for Freedom and Democracy, VVD. VVD evolved from the prewar Liberal State and Liberal Democratic parties and became a separate party in 1948. It is strongly conservative in outlook and favors

141

free enterprise, but is in favor of the separation of church and state. It is the minor partner in the current government coalition and is led by Deputy Prime Minister Gijs van Aardenne.

The principal opposition party is the Labor party, PvdA, formed in 1946 through the union of the former Socialist Democratic Workers' party with left-wing Liberals, and progressive Catholics and Protestants. It espouses democratic socialism and supports the EC. Its chairman is Max van den Berg and the parliamentary leader, Johannes M. den Uyl.

Democrats 1966, D'66. A left-of-center party led by J. Kohnstamm.

Netherlands Communist party, CPN. CPN favors the abolition of the monarchy, withdrawal from NATO and other radical measures. It is led by P. J. Izeboud.

Radical Political party, PPR. A splinter group of the former Catholic People's party, it generally represents the Catholic left. It is led by W. de Boer.

Political Reformed party, SGP. A hard-core Calvinistic party pursuing the application of Biblical principles to politics and society. It is led by the Rev. H. G. Abma.

Reformed Political Union, GPV, and Reformed Political Federation, RPF, are also Calvinistic parties with strong fundamentalist policies.

Minor parties include the Pacifist Socialist party, PSP, the Evangelical People's party, EVP, and the extreme right-wing group calling itself the Center party. The Farmers' party and the Democratic Socialists 1970 do not have parliamentary representation.

In 1983, the party lineup in the Staten-Generaal was as follows:

	First Chamber	Second Chamber
Christian Democratic Appeal	26	45
Labor party	17	47
People's party for Freedom and Democracy	17	36
Radical Political party	1	2
Democrats 1966	6	6
Political Reformed party	2	3
Netherlands Communist party	2	3
Pacifist Socialist	2	3
Reformed Political Federation	1	2
Reformed Political Union	1	1
Center party	—	1
Evangelical People's party	—	1

President of the First Chamber is Dr. P. A. J. M. Steenkamp
President of the Second Chamber is Dirk Dolman.

Local government: The Netherlands is divided into 11 provinces (*provincie*), each of which elects a provincial council (*provinciale staten*) for four years. The provincial council elects a six-member *college* to manage the everyday affairs of the province. Both college and council are under the chairmanship of a crown commissioner (*commissaris der Koningin*) appointed by the government. All cities, towns and villages in the Netherlands constitute municipalities (*gemeenten*), which elect councils for four years. Each council elects an executive college whose chairman is a burgomaster appointed by the crown for six years. The municipalities consult and cooperate through the Netherlands Union of Local Authorities, to which all belong and which the government generally consults with regard to legislation affecting municipal interests.

Judicial system: The lowest courts are the single-member magistrates' courts (*kantonrechter*), which try simpler civil cases and petty offenses. The district courts (*arrondissementsrechtbanken*) are competent in all remaining civil cases, all divorce cases and both felonies and misdemeanors; they also act as appeal courts for the magistrates' courts. The five courts of appeal (*gerechtshoven*) deal with tax matters and appeals from the district courts; they have a number of chambers, each consisting of three judges. While the courts of first instance and the appeal courts can judge facts, only the Supreme Court (*Hoge Raad*) can interpret law. Judges are appointed by the crown: they must retire at 70. There is no jury, but in some cases professional judges are assisted by skilled laymen appointed for four years. There is no death penalty.

RECENT HISTORY

The Netherlands signed a Customs Union with Belgium and Luxembourg in 1944, which very soon came to be known as Benelux. In 1954 the overseas territories of Surinam (Dutch Guiana) and the Netherlands Antilles (islands of Aruba, Bonaire, Curaçao, Saba, St. Eustatius and Dutch St. Martin) obtained political autonomy within the Kingdom of the Netherlands; defense and foreign affairs remained the responsibility of the Netherlands government. Independence was granted to Indonesia in 1949, and New Guinea was ceded to Indonesia in 1963. The Netherlands is a signatory of the Brussels Treaty (1948) and a founder-member of NATO, the ECSC, the EEC and Euratom. In 1980 Queen Juliana abdicated in favor of her daughter Beatrix.

Defense: The sovereign is commander-in-chief of the armed forces. Military service lasts 14–16 months in the army and 14–17 months in the other services. The army of 67,000 men is assigned to or earmarked for NATO service. Navy strength is 16,800, including marines, and the air force of 19,000 is also assigned to NATO. The 1982 defense estimates were Fl11.397 billion ($4.94 billion), representing 3% of GNP.

ECONOMY

Background: The Netherlands is among the most densely populated countries in the world. Intensive use is made of its limited resources, coal and natural gas. The economy relies heavily upon imports, exports and entrepot trade. Between 1970 and 1982 the annual average rate of growth at constant prices was 2.2%, causing a gradual exhaustion of the labor reserve, and consequent demand for labor has contributed to large increases in costs and prices.

The origin of GDP at factor cost in 1982 was:

Sector	Percentage
Agriculture	4
Industry	33
Services	63
GDP	100

In recent years, industrial growth has been mainly due to expansion of the metal, chemical and allied industries; the car, paper and building industries have also expanded. The major agricultural products include dairy produce and horticulture, much of which is exported. The agricultural sector continues to decline in importance.

With Western Europe's largest reserves of natural gas discovered at Groningen in 1959, the Netherlands experienced rapid industrialization and economic growth in the 1960s and early 1970s. But beginning with the first OPEC oil-price increase in 1973–74, the national economy lost its keen edge and began to slide until it reached a state of nil growth in 1980. Part of this downturn was caused by what is sometimes known as the "Dutch disease," whose symptoms were profligate consumption and the allocation of gas-generated public revenue not to industrial diversification and modernization but to the creation of a welfare state.

The nature of both output and employment has changed considerably in the past two decades. The share of agriculture and industry in both GDP and employment has dropped; there has also been a major shift in employment from private industry to the public sector. Agriculture still provides one-fifth of total exports. Manufacturing accounts for about three-fourths of total industrial output, with food processing the largest single industry. The Dutch have a strong presence in trade, banking, insurance and other financial services, a tradition dating from the 17th century.

Foreign trade: The Netherlands is a member of the EC, the European Monetary System and the OECD, and has special ties to the Belgium–Luxembourg Economic Union. It coordinates trade policies to conform to those of these organizations. Raw and semiprocessed materials constitute about 60% of Dutch imports, and finished manufactures make up over 70% of exports. About four-fifths of the trade is with other industrialized nations, some two-thirds with fellow EC countries.

In 1982, Dutch exports amounted to $66.322 billion, and imports to $62.583 billion, leaving a favorable trade surplus of $3.739 billion. The average annual growth rate during 1970–82 was 4.5% for exports (versus 9.9% during 1960–70) and 3.1% for imports (versus 9.5% during 1960–70). The percentage share of merchandise exports was 27% for fuels, minerals and metals; 24% for other primary commodities; 4% for textiles and clothing; 16% for machinery and transport equipment; and 29% for other manufactures. The percentage share of merchandise imports was 15% for food, 26% for fuels, 6% for other primary commodities, 19% for machinery and transport equipment, and 34% for other manufactures.

Employment: The total labor force in 1982 was 4.5 million—6% in agriculture, 45% in industry and 49% in services. Unemployment was 9%.

Price and wage trends: Since 1963 wages and consumer prices have risen steadily, with comparable increases in labor productivity. During 1970–75 there was an uncontrolled wage–price spiral when nominal wages increased at an average rate of 14% annually, outstripping the rise in consumer prices. Wage increases slowed considerably in the latter half of the 1970s, but real earnings declined in 1979–80 as the inflation rate reached 5.4%—still the lowest in the EC. Contributing to this development was a major income redistribution program introduced by the center-left government of Johannes M. den Uyl. Expenditures for health, unemployment, disability, retirement and family allowances—all semiannually indexed to the cost of living—rose from 14% of GNP in 1963 to 35% in 1980. In late 1978 the van Agt government announced a "Blueprint 81" plan offering a complex, interconnected set of fiscal, monetary and income policies. The goals of Blueprint 81 have largely been shelved in favor of a series of stopgap actions to prevent an economic crisis. Wage freezes were instituted in 1980, and cost of-living wage adjustments were blocked except for low income groups. In 1981 the government announced an austerity budget with spending cuts in social security and other government benefits, increased fuel taxes and higher worker contributions to benefit funds.

Consumption: Private consumption in 1982 amounted to 61% of GNP at market prices, and public consumption to 18%. This represented increases of 2.9% and 2.6% during 1970–82.

SOCIAL SECURITY

Health insurance: Under the general supervision of the Social Insurance Council and the Sick Funds Council, the scheme covers most wage earners and salaried employees. It is financed by the insured person, the employer and the government. The sickness benefit is 80% of earnings up to daily maximum earnings of Fl262. Maternity benefits are 100% of earnings, payable for a maximum of 12 weeks. Medical benefits cover services provided by doctors, hospitals and pharmacists. Medical benefits for dependents are the same as for the insured person.

Accident insurance: The provisions of the 1966 and 1968 legislation covering health insurance, sickness benefits and the disability pensions apply to all incapacities, whether work-connected or not. There has been no specific work-injury insurance since 1967.

Pensions insurance: Under the general supervision of the Social Insurance Council, the scheme covers all residents for old-age and survivor pensions and all residents over age 18 for disability pensions. It is financed by the insured person, the employer and the government. Old-age pensions are generally given at age 65: retirement is unnecessary. Disability pensions are based on percentage of loss of work capacity. Old-age pensions are Fl1,154.97 a month (full pension). The monthly supplement for a wife of any age is Fl502.68. Disability pensions are 80% of the base amount of Fl770.36 a day for a single person who is 80% disabled. There are supplements and partial disability pensions. Survivor pensions are payable to widows and orphans.

Unemployment insurance: Under the general supervision of the Social Insurance Council, the scheme covers employed persons in general. It is financed by the insured person, the employer and the government. Unemployment benefits are 80% of earnings up to daily maximum earnings of Fl262. The maximum duration is 26 weeks per benefit year.

Other benefits: Under the general supervision of the Social Insurance Council, family allowances are available to all eligible residents with one or more children. Cash benefits range from Fl146.62 per quarter for families with one child under three years of age to Fl568.67 per quarter per child for families with eight children between 12 and 17 years of age.

EDUCATION

Education is free and compulsory at private and state schools from seven to 15. Privately run schools form a large part of the educational system and are financed almost entirely out of public funds. State schools are non-sectarian but provide noncompulsory religious instruction.

Primary education: Ordinary primary education lasts six years. Public primary schools are administered by municipal authorities and private primary schools by associations and institutions.

Secondary education: There are four forms of secondary education—"general continuation," divided into lower, intermediate and higher grades, and "pre-university."

Lower general continuation education (*lager algemeen voortgezet onderwijs*) has a first transitional year and is given in either the first two years of elementary vocational schools or in two-year courses at separate elementary general continuation schools. Intermediate general continuation education (*middelbaar algemeen voortgezet onderwijs*) is replacing the previous system of extended primary education and is provided as a preparation for secondary vocational education by three- or four-year courses at separate schools. Higher general continuation education (*hoger algemeen voortgezet onderwijs*) is intended to prepare students for higher vocational education and replaces the nonuniversity preparation previously given at the secondary modern school (*hogere burgerschool*) and at the secondary school for girls. It is provided at separate five-year schools, in special departments of atheneums, lyceums and intermediate continuation schools in the form of a

146

two-year course subsequent to three years of preuniversity education or four years of intermediate continued education, and in two-year preparatory courses at primary teacher training colleges. There is a common first transitional year at intermediate and higher general continuation and at preuniversity levels.

Preuniversity education (*voorbereidend wetenschapelijk onderwijs*) is given for at least six years at gymnasiums, teaching the classical humanities; atheneums (replacing the *hogere burgerschool*), composed of literary-economic and exact science streams; and lyceums, which combine the two former.

Technical and vocational education: Schools for this form of education are mainly private; state vocational schools are maintained by municipalities. Both are subsidized by public authorities, the state providing 70% to 75% and the municipalities 25% to 30% of the public subsidy. Elementary vocational education is given at elementary technical, agricultural, domestic science, and business and administration schools providing three- to four-year courses leading to apprenticeship. From intermediate general continuation education pupils may go on for a maximum of four years to courses at secondary technical, agricultural, domestic science, and business and administration schools. There are also courses at this level for prospective social workers. For those completing higher continuation education or—generally after a one-year preparatory course—intermediate continuation education, technical, agricultural, teacher training, art, business and administration, and sociopedagogic colleges offer higher vocational education through courses lasting a maximum of four years.

Special education: Special primary education is provided for handicapped children and also for children whose parents have no settled abode. Both the types and numbers of these schools have been greatly increased.

University and higher education: Higher education is both private and public. Public institutes are fully financed by the state and private institutes are awarded state grants covering up to 95% of net costs. Leyden, Groningen, and Utrecht are state universities; the University of Amsterdam is a municipal institution; and the Free University of Amsterdam (Calvinist) and the University of Nijmegen (Catholic) are private. The state administers the technological universities at Delft, Eindhoven and Enschede, and the Agricultural University at Wageningen. The institutes of economics at Rotterdam (nondenominational) and Tilburg (Catholic) are both private. Courses generally last six years (five for law and seven or eight for medicine). Students take two examinations, the candidate's and the doctor's.

Students may be financed by scholarships, interest-free loans or a combination of both (mixed grants); the decision rests with the Ministry of Education and Science. These grants depend upon financial need and academic progress and are reviewed annually by the state. Loans are repaid over 10 years, beginning two years after the completion of studies. However, to offset the shortage of teachers, graduates entering secondary schools have their debt reduced by 10% for each year they teach.

Educational institutions, 1982–83 (full-time):

	Institutions	Students (000)
Preprimary	8,170	399
Primary*	9,735	1,297
Secondary general	1,487	836
Vocational	1,902	611
Further (nonuniversity)	363	141†
University status	22	155†

* Including special education.   † Estimates.
Source: Netherlands Bureau of Statistics.

Adult education: Most organizations are the result of private initiative and receive subsidies from the government. Generally, adult education takes the form of social and cultural work through group discussion and short courses at residential folk high schools. About 50,000 people attend such courses annually. In 1982 there were 428 public libraries.

MASS MEDIA

The press (1982):

Dailies: De Telegraaf, Amsterdam, independent, 684,300; *De Volkskrant*, Amsterdam, 255,300; *Het Parool*, Amsterdam, ind., 143,500; *Algemeen Dagblad*, Rotterdam, ind., 370,341; *Trouw*, Amsterdam, Protestant, 126,100; *Nieuwe Rotterdamse Courant*, Rotterdam, liberal, 157,234; *De Waarheid*, Amsterdam, Communist party organ.

Weeklies: Margriet, Amsterdam, women's, 615,000; *Elseviers Weekblad*, Amsterdam, independent, 142,150; *Vrij Nederland*, Amsterdam, ind. soc., 125,000; *Haagse Post*, Amsterdam, ind., 50,000; *De Groene Amsterdammer*, Amsterdam, ind., 16,000; *Story*, Haarlem, family entertainment, 560,000; *Libelle*, Haarlem, wom., 717,211.

Periodicals: Kampioen (m), The Hague, motoring, 2,000,000; *Reisblad (N.C.R.V.)* (m), The Hague, tourism, 30,000; *Economenblad* (10 a year), Rijswijk, economics, 11,790.

Broadcasting: The Netherlands Broadcasting Corporation (Nederlandse Omroep Stichting, NOS) coordinates the nearly 30 organizations broadcasting radio and TV programs in the Netherlands. It also broadcasts in its own right. The management board of the NOS consists of 33 members. The crown and cultural and social groups appoint one-quarter of the membership each. The remaining half are representatives of the main broadcasting organizations. Radio Nederland Wereldomroep broadcasts overseas in a number of languages. In 1983 there were 6,189,000 TV licenses registered and approximately 4.5 million radio receivers in use.

NORWAY

Features: Apart from the area immediately around Oslo on the Oslo Fjord and a narrow strip along the coast from Oslo to Stavanger, almost the entire country is upland. The highest part is the Jotunheimen region, rising to over 8,000 ft/2,400 m. Much of central-southern Norway is an elevated plateau tilting to the southeast; further north the land area narrows and forms a complicated ridge of mountains sloping to the sea. All along the west coast the land is indented by a series of deep, steep-sided fjords. Most of the rivers, with the exception of those draining into the Oslo area, e.g., the Glomma, are short and swift. Along the coast are numerous small islands.

Less than 5% of the land is cultivated and farming is heavily localized, the chief regions being around Oslo and along the coastal plain in the south. Elsewhere, farming is confined to favorable parts of the river valleys and the terraces bordering many of the fjords near their mouths. The only coalfield is in the Norwegian part of Spitzbergen. Iron ore is an important mineral, and there are a number of fields scattered throughout the country, of which the most important is around Sydvaranger (Kirkenes) and near Mo i Rana in Nordland. There are considerable offshore oil and natural gas deposits. Industry is highly localized, being associated either with the chief ports or the large hydroelectric plants, such as that at Rjukan.

Area: 125,000 sq. miles/324,000 sq. km. Overseas Territories: Spitzbergen, Jan Mayen, Bouvet Island, Peter I's Island. *Mean max. and min. temperatures:* Oslo (60° N, 10° 30' E; 310 ft/94 m.) 73°F/23°C (July), 20°F/−7°C (Jan. and Feb.); Bergen (60° 30' N, 5° 30' E; 140 ft/43 m.) 72°F/22°C (July), 27°F/−3°C (Jan.); Narvik (68° 30' N, 17° 30' E; 105 ft/32 m.) 76°F/24°C (July), 20°F/−7°C (Jan. and Feb.). *Relative humidity:* Oslo 80%; Bergen 82%; Narvik 79%. *Mean annual rainfall:* Oslo 27 in./685 mm.; Bergen 79 in./2,000 mm.; Narvik 29 in./735 mm.

POPULATION

Total population: (1984) 4.1 million. *Chief towns and populations: (1982)* OSLO (452,023), Bergen (207,799), Trondheim (134,976), Stavanger (90,687), Kristiansand (60,938), Drammen (49,523), Skien (45,000). *Distribution:* In 1982, 76% of the population lived in urban centers.

Language: Two Norwegian languages, "book language" (*bokmål*, formerly *riksmål*), which is strongly influenced by Danish, and "new Norwegian",

149

NORWAY

(*nynorsk*, formerly *landsmål*) based on Norwegian dialects, have equal official status. All official documents are published in both languages. Both are used equally on radio and TV and in the press and have the same educational standard. All children learn to read both languages and to write one. University entrance requires the ability to write in both languages. Nynorsk, which predominates in rural areas around the central range, is little used in business and only about 15% of all books—including virtually no translations—are published in the language. Whether the two languages should be forcibly amalgamated or permitted to fuse naturally into a common language (*samnorsk*) is a subject of dispute. The Lapps of northern Norway have their own language. *Religion:* The state religion of Norway is Evangelical-Lutheran, to which 92% of the population adheres.

CONSTITUTIONAL SYSTEM

Constitution: Norway is a constitutional monarchy. The present constitution dates from 1814 with amendments. *Head of state:* King Olav V. *Head of government:* Prime Minister Kåre Willoch (Conservative party).

Executive: Executive power is vested in the king and a Council of State (*Statsråd*), consisting of the prime minister and at least seven other ministers (of whom at least half must profess the national faith). The king's selection must be approved by parliament. He must act in accordance with the majority of the Council. Important matters of administration must bear the countersignature of the responsible minister.

Legislature: Norway has a modified form of unicameral legislature. The parliament (*Storting*) consists of 155 members elected for four years by proportional representation. It cannot be dissolved before the end of this period. The Storting elects a quarter of its members to form the upper house (*Lagting*) and the remainder make up the lower house (*Odelsting*). This division is important only for law making; all other decisions are made by a united Storting. If legislation originating in the Odelsting is twice rejected by the Lagting, it must be voted by two-thirds majority of the united Storting. The Lagting and the Supreme Court (see under *Judicial system*) together form the Constitutional Court (*Riksrett*), which tries actions against ministers, representatives and Supreme Court judges.

Political parties: The ruling party is the Conservative party, the oldest of Norwegian political parties, which favors free enterprise, strong alliance with the West, lower taxes and elimination of government control over industry. It is led by Prime Minister Kåre Willoch. Supporting the Conservative party are the Christian People's party, founded in 1933, and currently led by its chairman, Kjell Magne Bondevik, and the Center party, formed in 1920 as the Agrarian party, led by Johan Jacobsen. The principal opposition party is the Labor party, founded in 1887, which was in power continuously for 30 years until 1965. It suffered a serious reverse when it failed to bring Norway into the EC in 1972. It is led by Gro Harlem Brundtland, who was Norway's first female prime minister. Further to the left is the Socialist Left party, organized in 1975 as the Socialist Electoral Association that

151

included the Communists and the Socialist People's party. Its greatest success was in the national referendum on EC membership, to which it was strongly opposed. It is led by Theo Koritzinsky and Erik Solheim. Fringe parties include the Liberal party, formed in 1884; the Liberal People's party, formed by dissident Liberals who favored EC membership; the Progress party; the Norwegian Communist party, led by hard-line pro-Moscow faithful; and the Workers' Communist party.

In 1985, the party alignment in the Storting was as follows:

> Labor party   71
> Conservative party   50
> Christian People's party   16
> Center party   12
> Socialist Left party   6
> Liberal party   2
> Progress party   2

Local government: Norway is divided into 19 counties (*fylker*). Most are rural. The counties are further divided into rural municipalities (*herredskommuner*) and urban municipalities (*by-kommuner*). The municipalities elect councils (*kommunestyre*) of from 13 to 85 members serving for four years. Each council elects a quarter of its membership to serve as a steering committee (*formannskap*) with certain powers delegated to it. The committee elects a chairman who serves as mayor (*ordfører*) for two years. The municipalities have considerable autonomy, and certain responsibilities are statutorily imposed upon them. The state supervises the municipalities through its appointed county governor (*fylkesmann*).

Each of the rural counties forms a county municipality (*fylkeskommune*) under a county council (*fylkesting*) composed of representatives of the municipal councils within the county. The council elects a fourth of its members as a county committee (*fylkesutvalg*). A state-appointed county governor acts as the administrative head of the county.

Judicial system: With certain exceptions, no civil case can be brought before a court prior to an attempt at mediation by a conciliation council (*forliksråd*). Most municipalities elect such a council of three members for four years. It may pronounce judgment where so requested by both parties. In the town courts (*byrettene*) and county courts (*herredsrettene*), civil and criminal cases are administered by a single professional judge, assisted in appropriate cases by two lay judges (*domsmenn*). In the courts of appeal (*lagmansrettene*), three professional judges are assisted by two to four lay judges in civil cases and by a jury of 10 in criminal cases. Appeals from the lower courts are heard by the Board of Appeal of the Supreme Court (*Høyesterette Kjaeremåls-utvalg*), composed of five Supreme Court judges, and the Supreme Court (*Høyesterett*) proper, which has 18 judges including the president and sits as a court of five members.

Judges are appointed by the king upon the recommendation of the minister of justice, and must retire at 70. Otherwise they may be dismissed only by judicial sentence. There is no capital punishment for peacetime crimes.

RECENT HISTORY

After the German occupation (1940–45), Norway dropped its previous policy of neutrality and joined NATO once plans for a Scandinavian military alliance had proved abortive. In 1952 it became a member of the Nordic Council. Norway was a prime mover in the establishment of EFTA, and with Britain later negotiated for full membership of the EC. The Labor party's dominance of Norwegian politics ended in 1965 when a coalition of non-Socialists took office under Per Borten, leader of the Center party. A Labor government returned under Trygve Bratelli, but was forced out when it lost the national referendum on joining the EC. In the United Nations, Norway has played a leading peacekeeping role.

Defense: The king is commander-in-chief of the armed forces. To emphasize the defensive nature of its adherence to NATO, Norway does not permit the establishment of foreign bases upon its territory in peacetime. There are no nuclear weapons stationed on Norwegian territory. All men between 20 and 44 are liable to conscription for 12 months in the army and 15 months in the navy and air force and additional reservist training. The defense budget for 1981 was Nkr7.21 billion ($1.57 billion) representing about 2.8% of GNP. Strengths of the services: army 18,000, navy 9,000, air force 10,000, local defense and home guard 122,000.

ECONOMY

Background: Industrial expansion has been based primarily on the country's abundant water power, and to a lesser extent on natural resources such as fish, timber, ores and metals. Although economic growth in recent years has been rapid, demand has tended to rise faster than capacity and has led to pressure upon both prices and the balance of trade. The government attaches great importance to long-term planning. Annual average rate of growth of GNP between 1970 and 1982 was 3.7%.

In 1981 the value of GNP at current prices was $51.61 billion, and GNP per capita was $12,650, the sixth highest in Europe. In recent years, expansion has been strong in all sectors except forestry, fishing, agriculture and whaling. The origin of GDP in 1982 at factor cost was:

Sector	Percentage
Agriculture	4
Industry	41
Services	55
GDP	100

The main industries are iron and steel, chemicals, wood and wood processing, hydroelectric power and mining. The main agricultural products are livestock, barley and potatoes.

Norway is a welfare state committed to free enterprise. Its economy has been completely altered by the discovery of North Sea oil in the late 1960s. Oil wealth has rendered the Norwegian economy less susceptible to the recessionary oil shocks suffered by other Western nations. Norway's industrial sector contributes about one-third of GDP and employs nearly two-fifths of the labor force. The share of mining and extractive industries has risen to 10% of GDP, and this trend is likely to continue as the output of petroleum and natural gas climbs to the government-imposed ceiling of 90 million oil-equivalent tons per year. As a result of new offshore reserves discovered in 1981, proved reserves are expected to last 100 years. Drilling in Arctic water is proceeding, and Statoil, the government owned oil company, is developing in the Golden Block field in the North Sea, which may contain Western Europe's largest natural gas reserves. A $4 billion gas-gathering system is to be constructed at the Ekofisk and Statfjord fields, along with a 500-mile pipeline to West Germany.

Manufacturing accounts for about half of all industrial output and employment, led by processed food and transport equipment. Earnings from shipbuilding have declined. While its total share of the industrial sector is small, the state is the sole or major owner of the largest corporations, especially in mining and metallurgy; controls several utilities; and enjoys monopolies in grain processing and rail transportation. The government also holds the right to about four-fifths of the natural gas and oil produced in offshore fields. As a result, government expenditure as a share of GDP has risen to 55%, the third highest in Western Europe, after Netherlands and Sweden. Agriculture, forestry and fishery contribute only 5% of GDP, but Norwegian fishermen contribute about 5% of the world's fish catch.

Foreign trade: Norway is a founder member of EFTA and thus has a free-trade agreement with the EC. Norway's external tariffs are extremely low. Following 1979 GATT negotiations, the Norwegian government agreed to institute major duty concessions over an eight-year period ending in 1988. In 1981 Norway and Sweden signed a 20-year agreement to barter Norwegian oil for Swedish electricity.

In 1980, merchandise exports amounted to $17.595 billion and imports to $15.479 billion, leaving a favorable trade balance of $2.116 billion. During 1970–82 the average annual growth rate was 6.7% for exports and 4.3% for imports. The percentage share of merchandise exports was 60% for fuels, minerals and metals; 9% for other primary commodities; 1% for textiles and clothing; 13% for machinery and transport equipment; and 17% for other manufactures. The percentage share for merchandise imports was 7% for food, 15% for fuels, 7% for other primary commodities, 34% for machinery and transport equipment, and 37% for other manufactures. Nearly 88% of Norwegian exports go to industrialized free-market economies. Foreign trade now contributes half of the GNP.

Employment: The total employed population was 2,004,000 in 1982, with a decline in the relative share of primary industries and a growth in manufacturing, construction and service industries. In 1984, over 37% of the labor force was employed in industry, 7% in agriculture and 56% in services; unemployment amounted to 1.7% and was basically seasonal.

Price and wage trends: In 1980, wages rose by about 3% and the consumer price index rose by 8.8% from 1970 to 1982. The government has used price subsidies and set up machinery for coordination between employers and unions to determine wage increases.

Consumption: In 1982 private consumption amounted to about 49% GNP at current prices and public consumption to about 19%.

Health insurance: Under the general supervision of the Ministry of Social Affairs, the scheme covers for medical benefits all residents and for cash benefits most people with incomes of not less than NKr10,000 a year. It is funded by the insured person, the employer and the government. Medical benefits are cash refunds for all or part of medical expenses. Sickness benefits are 100% of covered earnings. There are also maternity benefits and maternity grants. Dependents are insured in their own right.

Accident insurance: Under the general supervision of the Ministry of Social Affairs, employees are generally covered under the scheme. It is funded by the employer and the government, with the self-employed contributing under a voluntary program. Temporary disability benefit (work injury) is the same as the sickness benefit of the health insurance scheme. Permanent disability pension (work injury) is 100% of the base amount if totally disabled. There are supplements and survivor pensions for spouses and orphans.

Pensions insurance: Under the general supervision of the Ministry of Social Affairs, universal pensions are available to all residents. Earnings-related pensions are available to all employees and self-employed persons earning over the base amount and born after 1897. The insurance is financed by the insured, the employer and the government. Old-age pensions are generally given at age 67 for both men and women. Universal old-age pensions are up to 100% of the base amount if the pensioner is single, 150% for an aged couple. There are supplements available. The earnings-related old-age pension is 45% of the difference between the average covered earnings and the base amount, based on coverage since 1967. The universal disability pension is up to 100% of the base amount if the insured person is totally disabled. There are supplements available, as well as an earnings-related disability pension. The universal survivor pension is up to 100% of the base amount if the deceased insured person was 40 years old or older; this pension is proportionately reduced for shorter coverage. The earnings-related survivor pension is 55% of the earnings-related pension of the deceased. There are provisions for orphans' pensions, and supplements are available.

Unemployment insurance: Under the general supervision of the Ministry of Labor and Municipal Affairs, the scheme covers employees (including public employees), seamen and the self-employed, aged 65 and under. It is financed by the insured person, the employer and the government. Unemployment benefit is 0.2% of annual income a day; the maximum is NKr422 daily, plus NKr6 a day for each dependent child under age 18. There are various allowances also provided.

Other benefits: Under the general supervision of the Ministry of Social Affairs, family allowances are available covering all resident children. The family allowances are entirely funded by the government.

EDUCATION

Primary education: There are few private primary schools and they receive no state aid. State education is free and compulsory from the age of seven to 16. The nine-year school is divided into a six-year junior school (*barneskole*) and a three-year youth school (*ungdomskole*), with specialization taking place only after the seventh year, entailing compulsory courses for those applying to the gymnasium and technical schools. There is a voluntary 10th year.

Secondary education: Private secondary education offering short educational courses leading to state examinations has met with considerable success. Enrollment in state secondary schools (*høgre allmenskoler*) has also greatly increased in recent years. Most schools charge no tuition fees. Secondary education includes the *gymnasium*, a three-year school. The final exam of the gymnasium is the *examen artium*, the basis for university or college education.

Special schools: All children with physical or mental disabilities are educated in special schools (*spesialskoler*) administered by the Ministry of Church and Education.

Vocational schools: A number of trades have built up their own system to suit their requirements, and each system is under the appropriate ministry. State, municipal and private technical schools take people with various entrance qualifications. They provide training at all stages of apprenticeship and opportunities for higher technical education, which is administered by the Ministry of Education. The Ministry also controls the vocational schools for commercial and clerical work (*yrkesskoler for handel og kontorarbeid*), which provide six-month or one-year courses and two-year evening courses. Secondary commercial schools (*handelsgymnasier*), run by the municipalities with state aid, provide one- to three-year courses for students having secondary school qualifications.

University and higher education: There are four universities (including the universities of Oslo and Bergen) and 10 colleges of university standing. Courses last from four to eight years. For most university courses, students decide for themselves the time that they need before taking an examination.

Adult education: People's high schools (*folkehøgskoler*) are boarding schools concentrating on general education for persons over the age of 17, the majority of whom come from country districts. All provide one-year and some two-year courses. Other adult education is largely state-aided and takes the form of lectures, direct instruction and study groups. In 1981 there were 455 public libraries.

Educational institutions, 1982–83:

	Institutions	Teachers* (Full-time)	Students
Primary	3,539	30,025	596,910
Secondary and vocational	918	15,497	188,040
Special	89	1,061	3,178
Teacher training	30	1,113	13,546
Nonuniversity	182	1,881	33,460
University	13	3,734	41,002

* Not including teachers at military colleges.
Source: Statistisk Sentralbyrå, Oslo.

MASS MEDIA

The press (1984):

Dailies: Aftenposten, Oslo, Conservative, 164,377; *Dagbladet*, Oslo, Liberal, 155,337; *Bergens Tidende*, Bergen, Lib., 94,068; *Arbeiderbladet*, Oslo, Socialist, 52,500; *Verdens Gang*, Oslo, ind., 256,747; *Stavanger Aftenblad*, Stavanger, Lib., 62,727; *Faedrelandsvennen*, Kristiansand, Lib., 44,000; *Adresseavisen*, Trondheim, Cons., 83,567.

Periodicals: Allers (w), Oslo, illustrated, 246,720; *Det Beste* (m), Norwegian edition of *Readers' Digest*, 215,600; *Blink-Kjøje* (quarterly), Haugesund, house and home, 1,650,000; *Nå* (w), Oslo, illus. news, 92,710; *Norsk Ukeblad* (w), Oslo, general, 340,087; *Det Nye* (w), Oslo, wom., 120,784; *Se og Hør* (w), Oslo, radio and TV, 202,020; *Vi fornyer oss* (annual), Høvik, do-it-yourself, 240,000; *Farmand* (w), Oslo, economic/financial, 33,700; *Motor* (m), Oslo, motoring, 463,000; *Samtiden* (m), Oslo, political/literary, 8,000.

Broadcasting: The Norwegian Broadcasting Corporation (*Norsk Rikskringkasting*) controls and operates all radio and TV as state monopolies on a noncommercial basis. Revenue is derived from annual licenses and a sales tax on receivers. In 1984, there were approximately 1,295,267 TV licenses and between 2 and 3 million radio receivers in use.

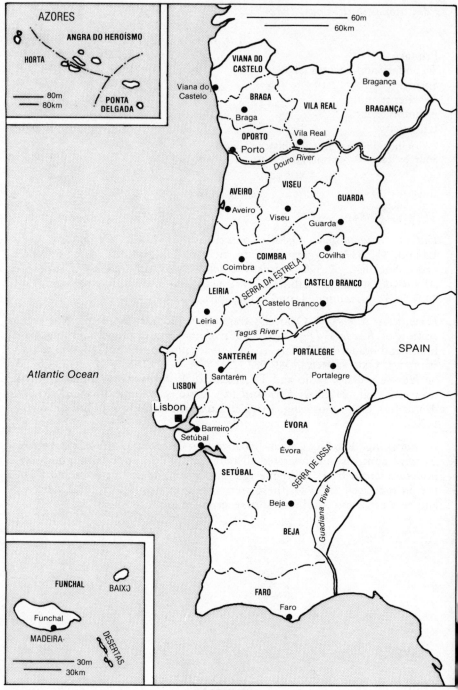

AZORES

ANGRA DO HEROÍSMO

HORTA

80m
80km

PONTA
DELGADA

60m
60km

VIANA DO
CASTELO

Viana do
Castelo

Bragança

BRAGA

VILA REAL

BRAGANÇA

Braga

OPORTO

Vila Real

Porto

Douro River

AVEIRO

VISEU

GUARDA

Aveiro

Viseu

Guarda

COIMBRA

Covilha

Coimbra

SERRA DA ESTRELA

CASTELO BRANCO

LEIRIA

Castelo Branco

Leiria

Tagus River

Atlantic Ocean

SANTERÉM

PORTALEGRE

SPAIN

Santarém

Portalegre

LISBON

Lisbon

ÉVORA

Barreiro

Setúbal

Évora

SERRA DE OSSA

SETÚBAL

Guadiana River

Beja

BEJA

FUNCHAL

BAIXO

Funchal

MADEIRA

DESERTIAS

30m
30km

FARO

Faro

PORTUGAL

GEOGRAPHY

Features: This roughly rectangular country consists of a mountainous east and north with much lower land to the west and south. The chief upland areas are the Douro uplands, which are divided in two by the west-flowing Douro; the highest parts are the Serra da Estrela, rising to over 6,000 ft/1,850 m., and the Trás os Montes, rising to over 3,000 ft/925 m. The rest of the country is divided into a series of plains and low ridges. The chief lowland areas are along the west coast and the Tagus river.

Much of the surface of Portugal is forest-covered, and scant irrigation limits agriculture; irrigation schemes have been developed along the Tagus and Sado rivers. Mineral deposits are scattered and of poor quality, only small amounts of coal, iron ore and pyrites being produced. There is some offshore oil and gas. Industry is limited both in variety and extent and is confined mainly to the Oporto and Lisbon areas.

Area: 35,500 sq. miles/92,000 sq. km. (including the Azores and the islands of Madeira and Porto Santo). Overseas Territory: Macao. *Mean max. and min. temperatures:* Lisbon (38° 30′ N, 9° W; 310 ft/95 m.) 80°F/27°C (Aug.), 46°F/8°C (Jan.); Oporto (41° N, 8° 30′ W; 330 ft/100 m.) 77°F/25°C, 40°F/4°C. *Relative humidity:* Lisbon 72%; Oporto 80%. *Mean annual rainfall:* Lisbon 27 in./685 mm.; Oporto 46 in./1,170 mm.

POPULATION

Population: (est. 1983) Continental Portugal and islands 10,099,000. *Main towns and populations:* (1981) Greater LISBON (2,069,467), Greater Oporto (1,562,287), Setúbal (77,885); Coimbra (74,616), Braga (63,033).

Language: The official language is Portuguese. *Religion:* Predominantly Roman Catholic.

CONSTITUTIONAL SYSTEM

Constitution: The constitution of April 2, 1976, defines the republic of Portugal as a democratic state based on pluralism but "committed to its own transformation into a classless society." It is a unitary state, comprising the territory on the European continent and the archipelagos of the Azores and Madeira. The present Basic Law stems from a constitutional agreement signed on February 26, 1976, by Francisco da Costa Gomes, chief of state and president of the Council of the Revolution, and representatives of the leading parties. Under this pact the Council became a consultative body with powers of absolute veto only in regard to defense. The third most important constitutional organ, the Assembly of the Republic, was empowered to override the Council in all other matters. It could also override the president by a two-thirds majority, or in the case of a presidential veto by a simple majority. A further series of constitutional reforms that came into effect in October 1982 abolished the Council of the Revolution and distributed its powers among a Supreme Council of National Defense, a 13-member Constitutional Tribunal and an advisory 16-member Council of State, with five members named by the president, five by the Assembly and six ex officio.

The constitution also guarantees fundamental political, economic, social and cultural rights, and duties of citizens. More controversial provisions call for the development of social ownership through expansion of the public and cooperative sectors and the collectivization of the principal means of production, land and natural resources. Private economic initiative is permitted in areas of activity that contribute to the progress of the community. Agrarian reform is a major directive of the constitution, empowering the government to eliminate the *latifundia*, or large estates, and redistribute expropriated property to small farmers.

Executive: The president is elected by secret and direct universal adult suffrage. There is a provision for a run-off second ballot if no candidate obtains more than half the valid vote. He serves for a five-year term and is not eligible to run for a third consecutive term. He has the right of veto over all legislation but may be overridden by a simple majority vote.

Legislature: The unicameral Assembly of the Republic (*Assembleia de Republica*) consists of a maximum of 250 members elected for four-year terms by an electoral constituency in a number proportionate to the number on the electoral register. The legislative session runs from October 15 to June 15. Between legislative sessions, the Standing Committee of the Assembly functions. The prime minister is appointed by the president from among the members of the Assembly. *Head of state:* President Gen. António dos Santos Ramalho Eanes. *Head of government:* Prime Minister Dr. Mario Lopes Soares (Portuguese Socialist Party).

Political parties: Portuguese political life since the revolution has been sharply divided between left and right, with no party enjoying clear dominance. In 1983 the Socialist party returned to power, along with the Social Democrats, to form Portugal's 15th government since the 1974 coup.

The parties are as follows:

Portuguese Socialist party, PSP. Organized in 1973 as heir to the former Portuguese Socialist Action, under the leadership of Mario Lopes Soares, the PSP won Portugal's first free election in 1975 with a plurality of 38% and formed its first government in 1976. Soares led his party into power for the third time in 1983.

160

Union of the Socialist and Democratic Left, UESD. Organized in 1978 by a number of PSP dissidents who later grouped together as the Workers' Brotherhood. It is led by António Lopes Cardoso.

Social Democrats Independent Action, ASDI. The ASDI evolved from the Association of Independent Social Democrats formed in 1979 by a group of PSD dissidents. It is led by António Sousa Franco.

United People's Alliance, APU. A coalition of the Portuguese Communist party, PCP, led by Alvaro Cunhal, and the Popular Democratic Movement, MDP, led by José Manuel Tengarrinha. The Popular Democratic Union, UDP, is also a Marxist group belonging to the Movement for Popular Unity.

United Workers' Organization, OUT, is the largest among a number of smaller leftist parties that crowd the political arena. They have short lives and frequently change labels, if not ideologies.

The right comprises at least three major parties. The Social Democratic party, PSD, is the largest and the most serious contender for power during elections. It was founded in 1974 as the Popular Democratic party. Initially espousing a number of left-of-center policies, including nationalization of key economic sectors, it steadily moved to the right under its leader, former Prime Minister Francisco Sá Carneiro. On Carneiro's death in 1980, Francisco João Pereira Pinto Balsemão became the leader of the party but yielded to Carlos Alberto Mota Pinto in 1983.

PSD's two partners in the 1980–83 government were the Socialist Democratic Center party, CDS, led by Diogo Freitas do Amaral, and the People's Monarchist party, PPM, led by Gonçalo Ribeiro Teles. CDS is a Christian Democratic party with a strong following in the north, while PPM is a right-of-center party advocating return to free enterprise and a restoration of the monarchy. On the far right are a number of neo-fascist parties, such as the Portuguese Party of the Right and the National Front.

The party lineup in the Assembly following the 1983 elections was as follows:

PSP	100	36% of the vote
PSD	75	27% of the vote
APU	44	18% of the vote
CDS	29	12% of the vote
Others	1	

Local government: The basic unit of local government is the parish (*freguesia*). Parishes are divided into three classes. In second- and some third-class parishes, the head of the family is the direct authority. In larger first-class parishes, seven-member parochial councils are nominated by the president of the local municipal chamber (in Lisbon and Oporto by the civil governor). To every parish the municipal authority attaches a delegate (*regedor*) who acts as an observer. The urban and rural districts (*concelhos*) have municipal councils composed of representatives of the parishes and corporate organizations. The councils elect two to six aldermen for three years; together with a government-appointed president they make up the municipal chamber.

The chamber has general administrative authority, but the president has certain independent duties of his or her own. In Lisbon and Oporto, the municipalities are known as quarters (*bairros*). The municipalities are grouped together into provinces. Each province has a council composed of representatives of the municipal chambers and corporative bodies. It elects a provincial board, which is headed by a state-appointed governor.

Judicial system: The lowest courts are those of the *juiz de paz* existing in each of the judicial districts (*comarcas*) into which Portugal is divided for the purposes of the separate dispensation of civil and criminal law. Appeal lies with the courts of appeal (*tribunais de relação*) in Lisbon, Oporto, Coimbra and Evora, each consisting of a president and a varying number of judges. Final decisions are given by the Supreme Court of Justice (*Supremo Tribunal de Justiça*) in Lisbon, which is composed of a president and 29 judges. Judges are appointed for life and are irremovable except in cases specified by law. There is no capital punishment except by sentence of court-martial.

RECENT HISTORY

From 1926 to 1968 Portugal was under the dictatorship of António de Oliveira Salazar. In 1932 he became president of the Council of Ministers and began to rule unopposed. Portugal remained neutral in World War II, but permitted Britain and the United States to use the Azores for surveillance of the Atlantic. The country was a founder-member of NATO in 1949, joined the United Nations in 1955 and became a founder-member of EFTA in 1960. The Portuguese Territory of Goa was annexed by India in 1961. Large Portuguese forces were committed during the 1960s against insurrections in the colonies of Angola, Mozambique and Guinea. In 1958, Gen. Delgado stood as opposition candidate in the presidential elections and was officially credited with 23% of the vote. In 1961 one of his supporters, Captain Galvão, pirated the Portuguese liner *Santa Maria*, with the aim of drawing world attention to the suppression of opposition in Portugal. In 1962 there was an abortive uprising against Salazar in Beja. Delgado was murdered (in Spain, possibly by Portuguese agents) in 1965. In early 1966 Anglo-Portuguese relations became strained over the supply of oil from Beira in Mozambique to the rebel colony of Rhodesia.

Salazar suffered a fatal stroke in 1968, marking the beginning of the end for the dictatorship. Marcello Caetano, a close associate, was named prime minister and began to initiate, very cautiously, a series of reforms without departing too radically from the policies of his predecessor. In 1969 all opposition parties were legalized, but were again outlawed in order to enable the official National Union to win all the 130 seats in the Assembly. For a while Caetano returned to the repression that characterized Salazar's dictatorship, but the winds of reform blew again with the 1971 constitutional legislation that expanded the powers of the enlarged National Assembly, granted limited autonomy to overseas territories, abolished press censorship, permitted religious freedom and mitigated some of the rigors of secret police activity. In 1973 the government party, Accão Nacional Popular (formerly the National Union), won all the 150 seats in the National Assembly.

Forty years of dictatorship ended in April 1974, when a group of military officers calling themselves Movimento das Forças Armados seized power under the leadership of a Junta of National Salvation. The leader of the junta, Gen. António Sebastião Ribeiro de Spínola, was sworn in as president, with Adelino de Palma Carlos as prime minister. Carlos stepped down after 54 days and was replaced by Gen. Vasco dos Santos Gonçalves; Gen. Spínola himself was ousted within two months, and Gen. Francisco da Costa Gomes was installed as president. Between May 1974 and November 1975, Portugal relinquished her African colonies in fulfillment of one of the main promises of the new regime.

In March 1975 right-wing military elements under Gen. Spínola led an abortive coup against the Gomes government. Upon the failure of the coup, the Junta of National Salvation was dissolved in favor of a Supreme Revolutionary Council, which was given full powers to direct and execute a revolutionary program. At the election for a Constituent Assembly, the Socialists under Mario Soares emerged as the largest party, with a plurality of 26% versus 13% for the Communists. However, increasing Communist-led agitation resulted in the resignation of Prime Minister Gonçalves and the appointment of Adm. João Baptista Pinheiro de Azevedo as prime minister. The Communists responded with a general strike followed by an uprising of left-wing military units that was crushed by loyalist troops. The failure of the coup was a major blow to Communist political ambitions and effectively blocked their plans to seize power.

The new constitution came into effect on April 25, 1976, and the first new elections under the constitution were held the same day. The Socialists came through (as they have always done since then) as the largest party, but held no absolute majority. The result has been 15 governments between 1976 and 1985, of which three have been led by Soares and one by Francisco Sá Carneiro, who managed during his brief premiership from 1979 to 1981 (when he was killed in a plane crash) to swing the country back to private enterprise and right-of-center economic policies.

Defense: Compulsory military service lasts for 16 months in the army and 24 months in the navy and the air force, with conscripts being liable for the active reserve until the age of 35 and home defense tasks until the age of 45. Compulsory military service is generally extended to three-and-a-half or four years. The strengths of the armed forces are: army 47,000; navy, including marines, 13,426; air force, including paratroopers, 10,500. The paramilitary National Republican Guard totals a further 10,000 and there are about 500,000 trained reservists. One army division stationed in Portugal is earmarked for NATO as is part of the air force. The 1981 defense estimates were E49 billion ($869 million), representing 3.6% of GNP.

ECONOMY

Background: Portugal has few natural resources and in many respects is still a developing country. The post-1974 governments inherited an economy severely debilitated from years of repression and one of the longest and

163

bloodiest colonial struggles in modern history. In trying to revive the economy, the new regime only compounded its problems through frequent shifts in direction and periodic political turmoil. The Portuguese economy has seemed to go in circles during the decade 1975–85.

The wave of nationalizations following the 1974 coup left the government in possession of a large share of the nation's industry. These seizures brought total public sector control to about 45% of the economy as measured by gross capital, compared to 10% before the revolution. With labor in power in these enterprises, wages were raised and redundant employees retained on the payroll. As a result, inflation became uncontrolled; prices of domestic goods rose 21% in 1976, 30% in 1977 and 40% in 1978. The agricultural sector became disorganized in the wake of land reform and nationalization. Output in real terms declined 5% from 1974 through 1977. By 1979 it was 11% below the 1973 level. To counter the decline, the Sá Carneiro government initiated a series of austerity programs mandating higher taxes, tighter credit, rationing and energy conservation. Despite domestic controversy over these measures, they paid off by 1984 when the current-account deficit in the balance of payments all but disappeared. But this gain in the external sector was achieved at high cost, through slower growth in the national product and high unemployment that reached $11\frac{1}{2}$%.

The annual average rate of growth of GNP in the period 1970–82 was 1.1%, and the structural change toward an industrialized economy was considerable. Growth has been concentrated mainly in the nontraditional branches of the economy, such as metals and metal products, chemicals, petroleum products, pulp, paper and hydroelectric power. There has also been substantial growth in the traditional industries of textiles and processed foods. Agriculture and the extractive sectors of the economy—mining and quarrying—have changed little in the last decade. In the 1980s the economy continued to expand, GNP at current prices increasing to $23.140 billion.

Sector contributions to GNP at factor cost in 1982 were:

Sector	Percentage
Agriculture, forestry and fishing	12
Industry	44
Services	44
GNP	100

From 1970 to 1982 industrial production increased by an annual average of 4.4%, the highest of all EFTA countries. In the same period, agricultural output declined by an annual average of 0.8%. The main Portuguese industrial and agricultural products are chemicals, pulp, paper, cork, fertilizers, hydroelectric power, cotton and other textiles, wine, sardines and other canned fish, fruit, cereals, and vegetables. The economy is heavily dependent upon foreign investment, both financial and technical.

Foreign trade: As a founding member of EFTA, Portugal enjoyed substantial trade with fellow EFTA-members until the 1970s. When Britain and Denmark left EFTA to join the EC, Portugal negotiated with the Community to receive gradual reduction in both tariffs and quantitative limits on trade in industrial products. Provisions added after the 1974 coup have extended further assistance through higher quotas for Portugal's exports, such as wines, textiles, fish and paper. In 1977, Portugal applied for admission to the EC, and became a member in 1986.

In 1982, merchandise exports amounted to $4..111 billion and imports to $9.313 billion, leaving a current-account trade deficit of $5.202 billion. In 1981 the percentage share of merchandise exports was 9% for fuels, minerals and metals; 20% for other primary commodities, 27% for textiles and clothing; 13% for machinery and transport equipment; and 31% for other manufactures. The percentage share of merchandise imports was 16% for food, 24% for fuels, 9% for other primary commodities, 27% for machinery and transport equipment, and 24% for other manufactures. Nearly 81% of merchandise exports go to industrialized economies, and 16% to developing countries.

Employment: In 1982 the total working population was 4.552 million, of whom 28% were employed in agriculture, 35% in industry and 37% in services; unemployment was 11.5%. There is still a shortage of skilled manpower; widespread seasonal unemployment; a marked reduction in the agricultural population as a result of reorganization of industry; and a decline in certain industries, such as mining.

Price and wage trends: Inflation since the 1960s has been due mainly to shortage of labor and rising demand. Largely because of recent increases in minimum wages, the general trend for wages has been to move upward faster than prices. Productivity slowed down to 5.5% in manufacturing industries in 1982. Wholesale and consumer prices during 1970–82 increased in Lisbon by 19.7% and 19.5% respectively. Since 1962 this pattern of price and wage increases has continued to contribute toward inflation.

Consumption: In 1982 private consumption accounted for 76% of GNP and public consumption for 16%. In recent years, the trend has been for private consumption to expand more rapidly than public consumption. A major item of public consumption since 1960 has been defense.

SOCIAL SECURITY

A major reform law, enacted after the revolution in 1977, guaranteed social pensions and medical services to all Portuguese, whether or not they are contributors to employment-related insurance plans. Unemployment insurance, which hardly existed under the dictatorship, was initiated in 1975 and its coverage greatly expanded under 1977 and 1979 laws. Figures given below are for 1983.

Health insurance: Under the general supervision of the Ministry of Social Affairs, through the Secretariat of State for Health, this insurance covers the entire population. The insured person contributes 8% of earnings, the employer 21% of payroll; these payments include contributions toward the medical services and social pensions of noncontributors. The state also subsidizes both systems. Sickness benefits are 60% of earnings, payable for up to three years. Maternity benefits are 100% of earnings, payable for up to 90 days before and after childbirth. Medical services are provided directly to patients in larger towns and cities by clinics operated by government-chartered medical funds. They are provided free for a year, then for up to three additional years with the patient paying half the cost (unless the patient's income is below a specified unit). Dependents' medical benefits are identical to those for the insured worker.

Accident insurance: The employer, through direct provision of benefits or insurance premiums, pays the entire cost of work-related injury. Temporary disability benefits for such injuries comprise one-third of earnings during the first three days, two-thirds thereafter. If permanently disabled, the worker receives the higher of two-thirds of the minimum wage or approximately half his or her earnings. There is a constant-attendance supplement and a minimum pension of E5,677 per month. Survivor pensions, a smaller fraction of either minimum wage or earnings, are payable to dependent widows and widowers and to orphans.

Pensions insurance: Coverage is universal, with employees, employers and the state financing noncontributors' benefits. There are special systems for fishermen and sailors, farm laborers, some liberal professions, railway and public employees, and rural workers. Old-age pensions are paid at age 65 for men and 62 for women, and require 10 years of insurance, including 60 months of continuous contributions. They comprise 2.2% of average annual earnings during the highest-paid five of the last 10 years, times years of insurance. The minimum monthly pension is 30% of earnings, or E4,500; the maximum is 80% of earnings, or E86,300. The social pension, for noncontributors, is a means-tested E3,300 a month. Disability pensions have the same benefits and restrictions as old-age pensions. There are also survivor pensions, payable to the widow, widower or dependent orphan, with a monthly minimum of E1,800. All pensioners receive a 13th month's payment each Christmas.

Unemployment insurance: This is under the general supervision of both the Ministry of Labor and the Ministry of Social Affairs, and covers all employed persons and first-time job seekers. Insured persons contribute 2.5% of earnings, or 3% if not covered by social security; the employer pays 3% of payroll; and the state contributes a balancing subsidy. Recipients must have 360 days of employment or six months of insurance, with 13 days a month or 24 hours a week of work in the last six months, or 120 days of contributions in the last 18 months. First-time job seekers are eligible if their total family income is below 60% of the national minimum wage. Benefits include 70% of the minimum wage for a single person; 80% to 100% for a person with dependents. They are payable for 180 days, or up to 365 days for persons aged 50, 540 days for those aged 55 and 720 days for those aged 60, after which they are eligible for early retirement.

Other benefits: Family allowances have been in existence since 1942 and are available to all citizens. They include E450 for each of the first two children, ranging to E600 for each additional child beyond three, with special supplements for handicapped children. There is a birth grant of E5,500, a nursing allowance of up to E1,080 per month for up to 10 months and a marriage grant of E4,800.

EDUCATION

The adult illiteracy rate declined between 1960 and 1970, from 37.2% to 29%. There are both state and private schools, but all education is geared to state examinations. The sexes are taught separately wherever feasible.

Primary education: This is compulsory, and in state schools is free from the ages of six to 14. Primary education ends with an examination and leaving certificate. *Secondary education:* This is voluntary. It is divided into two levels; a general unified course (the seventh to ninth years of schooling), which is free, and complementary courses (the 10th to 12th years of schooling). There are two sections at the last year of secondary education: preuniversity and preprofessional.

Vocational education: There are technical, commercial and industrial schools with nine-year courses, and higher commercial schools with four-year courses. *Special education:* Most special education is in the hands of private organizations.

University education: Entry to institutions of higher education is based on a quota system, fixed each year for every subject and school. Candidates must possess a secondary leaving certificate and apply to sit for a national competitive examination. Higher education is also available to adults over 25 who practice a profession and do not possess the required academic qualifications. These candidates must take and pass a special examination. There are universities in Lisbon, Coimbra, and Oporto, and also a technical university in Lisbon. Arts and science courses last five years, law and engineering six years, and medicine seven years. University fees are low and are either paid entirely by the state or reduced in the case of needy students.

Educational institutions, 1980–81*:

	Institutions	Teachers	Students
Preprimary	1,514	2,369†	39,469†
Primary	10,327	41,340	945,169
Secondary	313	18,540	492,236
Higher	79	13,013	84,173
Teacher training†	197	1,948	12,032

* Excluding private education.
† 1978–79 figures.
Source: Instituto Nacional de Estatística, Lisbon.

Adult education: In certain trades, special evening courses are free and compulsory. Other adult education is provided free by the state. A policy of making the attainment of the primary school certificate compulsory for employment was hampered by the shortage of teachers.

MASS MEDIA

The press (1982): Note: Following the 1975 coup, a number of newspapers closed down or appeared under other names.

Dailies: Lisbon—*Diário de Notícias*, state-owned, 66,500; *Diário Popular*, state-owned, 83,480; *Diário de Lisboa*, ind.-cons., 42,300. Oporto—*O Comércio do Porto*, commercial industrial, 53,220; *Jornal de Notícias*, ind., 79,840; *O Primeiro de Janeiro*, ind., 40,293. Coimbra—*Diário de Coimbra*, ind., 8,000.

Periodicals: Lisbon—*A.C.P.* (bimonthly), motoring, 80,000; *A Bola* (3 a week), sport, 150,000; *Casa & Jardim* (m), home and gardening, 35,000; *Crónica Feminina* (weekly), women's, 220,000; *Democracia 76* (f), organ of the CDS, 50,000; *Ela/Donas de Casa* (m), 40,000; *Expresso* (w), current affairs, 90,000; *Folka CDS* (w), another publication of the CDS, 200,000; *O Jornal de Letras* (w), 80,000; *O Tempo* (w), ind., 72,000.

Broadcasting: The state operates the national broadcasting service, Radiodifusão Portuguesa (RDP), into which all private radio stations were merged in 1975. A few small private radio stations are permitted to operate. TV is operated by the state-controlled Radiotelevisão Portuguesa (RTP). In 1983, Portugal had 1,488,951 licensed TV sets and 2,154,490 radio receivers.

SAN MARINO

Features: A hilly country situated on Monte Titano in the northern Apennines south of Rimini, San Marino is entirely surrounded by northeastern Italy. *Area:* 24 sq. miles/62 sq. km. *Population:* (est. 1983) 22,206. *Capital:* SAN MARINO (4,516). *Language:* Italian. *Religion:* Roman Catholic.

CONSTITUTIONAL SYSTEM

Constitution: San Marino is an independent republic whose existence as such traditionally dates back to the 4th century. *Head of state and head of government:* See under *Executive.* *Executive:* Executive power is vested in two captains-regent (*Capitani Reggenti*) who are elected every six months from and by the legislature to serve as joint heads of state; reelection may not take place until three years after a period of office. The captains-regent exercise power in conjunction with the Congress of State (*Congresso di Stato*) made up of 10 departments. *Legislature:* Legislative power is vested in the Great and General Council (*Consiglio Grande e Generale*) of 60 members elected by universal suffrage for five years. *Election results:* The major political parties are the San Marino Communist party, the San Marino Socialist party, the Socialist Unity party and the Social Democratic party; there are also the Christian Democratic party and the Committee for the Defense of the Republic. The government coalition of the San Marino Communist party, the San Marino Socialist party and the Socialist Unity party won in the 1983 election 32 seats on the·Grand and General Council. Political leaders are State Secretary for Foreign Affairs Giordano Bruno Reffi (Socialist); Secretary of State for Internal Affairs and Justice Alvaro Selva (Communist); Secretary of State for Finance and Budget Emilio della Balta (Socialist Unity party). *Judicial system:* The judicial authority is the Council of Twelve (*Consiglio dei XII*).

RECENT HISTORY

San Marino remained neutral in World War II. The Treaty of Friendship with Italy, first concluded in 1897, was renewed in 1953 and again with amendments in 1961. The country was ruled from the end of World War II until 1957 by a coalition of the Communist and Socialist parties. With the formation of a new independent Social Democratic party, it was governed until 1974 by a coalition of the Christian and Social Democratic parties.

Defense: All able-bodied citizens between 16 and 55, except students and teachers, are obliged to serve in the militia.

ECONOMY

San Marino has been united with Italy in a customs union since 1862. Its chief products are wheat, wine, textiles, cement, paper and leather. Tourism and postage stamps are also an important source of revenue. Its main exports are wine, wool products, furniture, animal hides, ceramics and building stone.

SOCIAL SECURITY

There is no social insurance system. For health treatment the San Marinesi rely upon services provided in Italy, mainly in Rimini.

EDUCATION

In 1984, there were 14 primary schools, three secondary schools, one technical school, one high school (lyceum) and vocational training schools. Diplomas from these institutions are recognized by Italian universities.

MASS MEDIA

The press (1984): Although no daily newspapers are published in San Marino, there are several periodicals. Among these are *Il nuovo Titano*, San Marino Socialist party, San Marino, 1,300; and *Ricossa Socialista*, Socialist Unity party, San Marino, 4,000. Italian newspapers are distributed.

Broadcasting: There is no San Marino broadcasting service, but Radio Televisione Italiano broadcasts a daily information bulletin for San Marino, "Notizie di San Marino."

SPAIN

GEOGRAPHY

Features: Spain is geographically compact, in spite of its size. In the north lies the east–west ridge of the Pyrenees, rising to over 11,000 ft/3,350 m. Chief north–south routes lie along the Mediterranean coast and through the relatively low-level route from San Sebastián to the Ebro Valley. This mountain region is continued westward by the lower but broader Cantabrian Mountains, which rise to 5,000–8,000 ft/1,500–2,450 m. In the southeast the Sierra Nevada and other ridges skirt the coast and, rising to over 10,000 ft/ 3,000 m., cut off most of the interior from sea influences. The isolation of the interior is further enhanced by the series of mountainous ridges bordering the very narrow coastal plain both in Catalonia and Valencia. Behind these coastal ranges is the main Spanish plateau or Meseta, which averages an altitude of some 2,200 ft/670 m. in Castile and somewhat higher in New Castile. This central plateau is divided into a large number of smaller regions, but in general terms it can be said to consist of a series of basins and intervening areas of mountainous ridges, of which the most important and highest are the central sierras, Sierra de Guadarrama and Sierra de Gredos, both rising to over 7,000 ft/2,100 m. The main areas of land below 1,000 ft/300 m., apart from narrow stretches of coastal plain, are the Guadalquivir and Ebro valleys and the areas in the vicinity of Valencia and Cartagena.

Except in the more rugged and higher part of the mountains and plateaus, farming is widely practiced, with the emphasis on cereals in the plateau. The more intensive irrigation farming is concentrated in the lower parts of the major river valleys and along the coast, e.g., Valencia. Coal and iron ore are produced mainly in the north, Oviedo being the center of the principal coalfield. Quantities of pyrites, potash and other chemicals and minerals are also produced, and the country has some hydroelectic power resources. Industry is mainly concentrated in Catalonia, especially around Barcelona, and also along the north coast.

Area: 195,000 sq. miles/504,900 sq. km. (including Balearic and Canary Islands). *Mean max. and min. temperatures:* Madrid (40° 30′ N, 3° 30′ W; 2,190 ft/665 m.) 87°F/31°C (July), 33°F/1°C (Jan.); Santander (43° 30′ N, 4° W; 200 ft/60 m.) 73°F/23°C (Aug.), 43°F/6°C (Feb.); Barcelona (41° 30′ N, 2° E; 310 ft/95 m.) 82°F/28°C (Aug.), 42°F/6°C (Jan.); Seville (37° 30′ N, 6° W; 100 ft/30 m.) 97°F/36°C (Aug.), 41°F/5°C (Jan.). *Relative humidity:* Madrid 79%; Santander 84%; Barcelona 73%; Seville 78%. *Mean*

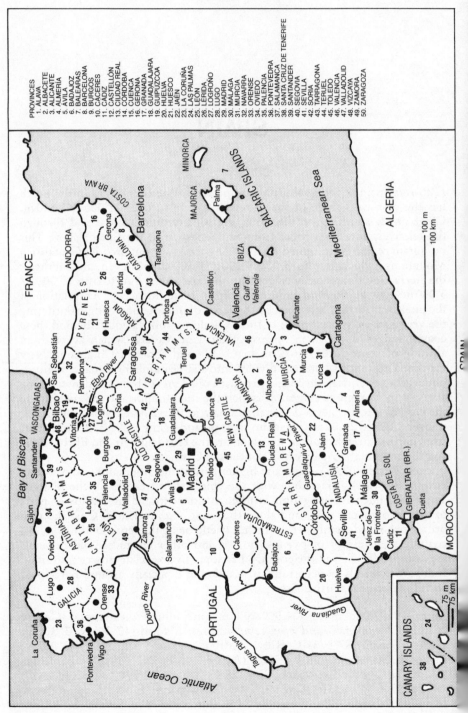

PROVINCES
1. ALAVA
2. ALBACETE
3. ALICANTE
4. ALMERIA
5. AVILA
6. BADAJOZ
7. BALEARAS
8. BARCELONA
9. BURGOS
10. CACERES
11. CADIZ
12. CASTELLON
13. CIUDAD REAL
14. CORDOBA
15. CUENCA
16. GERONA
17. GRANADA
18. GUADALAJARA
19. GUIPUZCOA
20. HUELVA
21. HUESCA
22. JAEN
23. LA CORUÑA
24. LAS PALMAS
25. LEON
26. LERIDA
27. LOGROÑO
28. LUGO
29. MADRID
30. MALAGA
31. MURCIA
32. NAVARRA
33. ORENSE
34. OVIEDO
35. PALENCIA
36. PONTEVEDRA
37. SALAMANCA
38. SANTA CRUZ DE TENERIFE
39. SANTANDER
40. SEGOVIA
41. SEVILLA
42. SORIA
43. TARRAGONA
44. TERUEL
45. TOLEDO
46. VALENCIA
47. VALLADOLID
48. VIZCAYA
49. ZAMORA
50. ZARAGOZA

annual rainfall: Madrid 17 in./430 mm.; Santander 44 in./1,120 mm.; Barcelona 24 in./610 mm.; Seville 23 in./585 mm.

POPULATION

Population: (1984) 38.4 million. *Chief towns and populations:* MADRID (3,188,297), Barcelona (1,754,900), Valencia (751,734), Seville (653,833), Zaragoza (590,750), Málaga (503,251), Bilbao (433,030). *Distribution:* In 1982, 76% lived in urban areas; 44% of this group lived in cities of over 500,000 inhabitants.

Language: The official language is Spanish. The large Catalan- and Basque-speaking minorities are permitted to use their own language for official purposes. *Religion:* The religion of the great majority is Roman Catholicism. The 1978 constitution disestablished Roman Catholicism as the official religion and provided that religious liberty for non-Catholics was to be a state-protected legal right, thereby replacing the previous limited toleration of non-Catholic activities.

CONSTITUTIONAL SYSTEM

Constitution: Spain is a monarchy. The 169-article Spanish constitution, the nation's seventh since 1812, was approved by popular referendum on December 6, 1978, promulgated on December 29. The constitution abrogated the fundamental principles and organic legislation of the Francisco Franco regime. The constitution establishes Spain as a social and democratic state and defines its political form as parliamentary monarchy. It guarantees the fundamental rights, duties and freedoms laid down in the Universal Declaration of Human Rights.

The constitution invests the king with the supreme power as head of state. His powers include naming the prime minister, who is the head of government. The Congress (*Las Cortes Generales*) comprises a Senate (upper house) and a Congress of Deputies (lower house). Congress has a maximum of 400 and a minimum of 300 deputies elected by universal, direct and secret suffrage. Each province forms one constituency and deputies are elected by proportional representation for four years. Elections must be held between 30 and 60 days after the end of each parliamentary mandate and Congress convened within 25 days of the election. The Senate is based on territorial representation. Each province elects four senators for four years. Each year there are two ordinary sessions of parliament of four and five months each; a standing committee of 21 members represents parliament between sessions.

The constitution also provides for a Council of State as the supreme consultative organ, and for a Constitutional Court.

Rights of non-Spanish ethnic groups to regional autonomy are recognized in the constitution, but must be effected by action of the Cortes. Because of the primacy of national unity, devolution is limited to such nonessential functions as health, tourism, education and police. Draft devolution statutes were presented for the Basque and Catalan areas in 1979 and were overwhelmingly approved in regional referenda. Elections for regional parliaments were held in 1980 in the Basque and Catalan provinces. Autonomy statutes have been completed for the remaining regions.

Head of state: King Juan Carlos I.

Head of government: Premier Felípe González Márquez.

Political parties: The ruling party is the Spanish Socialist Workers' party, founded in 1879 as a member of the Socialist International. Led by Felípe González Márquez, it came to office in 1982 with an absolute majority in the Cortes.

The Union of the Democratic Center, UCD, was organized in 1977 by then-prime minister Adolfo Suarez González as a liberal-centrist electoral alliance embracing the Federation of Democratic and Liberal parties, the Popular party, the Popular Democratic party, the Spanish Democratic Union, the Popular Christian Democratic party and the Social Democratic Federation. Suarez González withdrew from the party in 1982 to form the Democratic and Social Center. The Democratic Action party and the Liberal Democratic party are small splinter parties holding centrist position in politics.

The Popular Alliance Federation, AP, is a right-wing group that gained 105 seats in the Congress in 1982 and thus became the largest opposition party in the legislature. It is led by Manuel Fraga Iribarne, a former minister under Franco. One of AP's splinter parties is the Popular Democratic party.

The Spanish Communist party, PCE, is a Eurocommunist party still led by the legendary "La Pasionaria," the aging Dolores Ibarruri Gómez, who returned to Spain after 39 years of exile in the Soviet Union. Much of its popular support has been preempted by the Socialists.

Besides these major groups, there are many fringe groups, regional parties and terrorist groups of both right and left persuasions.

The lineup in the Cortes after the 1982 elections was as follows:

	Senate	Congress
Spanish Socialist Workers' party	134	202
Popular Alliance/Popular Democratic party	54	106
Convergence & Union/Catalan Left	7	12
Union of Democratic Center	4	12
Basque Nationalist party	7	8
Spanish Communist party	—	4
Democratic and Social Center	—	2
United People	—	2
Catalan Republic Left	—	1
Basque Left	—	1
Independents	2	—

Local government: The municipalities (*municipios*) are governed by a mayor (*alcalde*) and municipal council (*ayuntamiento*). One-third of the council members are chosen by heads of families and their wives; one-third are elected by the official trade unions; the remainder are coopted by those two groups.

Spain's 50 provinces (*provincias*) are composed of groups of municipalities; each is headed by a Provincial Assembly (*diputación provincial*) composed of a president and a number of elected members representing the municipalities. The provinces are governed by a state-appointed civil governor (*gobernador civil*). In 1967 the process of regional self-government was begun. In 1979 the statutes of the first of 17 autonomous communities were approved by referendum. In 1980 the first parliaments were elected; these were the Basque and the Catalan parliaments. In 1981 the Galician parliament was elected, and in 1982 the Andalusian parliament. In 1983 the remaining 13 were elected. Parliaments are elected for four years.

Judicial system: The lowest courts are those of the justices of the peace (*juzgados de paz*) whose jurisdiction is coterminous with municipal boundaries. Their civil jurisdiction ranges over out-of-court settlements and claims for small sums. They also try minor criminal offenses. Municipal and regional courts (*juzgados municipales y comarcales*), with jurisdiction over towns or regions, sit as lower courts of first instance and have criminal jurisdiction for trial of petty offenses and fraud. The courts of first instances in civil matters (*juzgados de primera instancia e instrucción*) have jurisdiction within defined judicial districts (*partidos judiciales*) over remaining civil cases, and hear appeals from the courts of the justices of the peace; in criminal cases they institute proceedings and report to higher provincial courts for judgment. They may also pronounce finally on appeals from the two lower courts in minor criminal cases.

The provincial courts (*audiencias provinciales*) act as criminal courts and also pass final judgment on cases sent up from the lower courts. The jurisdiction of the district courts of appeal (*audiencias territoriales*) extends over one or more provinces. This court functions as a plenary court for certain criminal cases, acts as a disciplinary body, and through three chambers deals with civil and criminal cases. The Supreme Court (*Tribunal Supremo*) in Madrid acts as a plenary court in criminal matters and cases covering civil responsibility of high officials; it is the highest legal body, and as the judicial council is concerned with legal appointments. As a court of justice it has six chambers which hear different types of appeals.

The judiciary is independent of the executive. Judges may be dismissed only by criminal proceedings and in cases specified in law conducted before the Supreme Court. Supreme Court judges are appointed by the minister of justice on recommendation of the Judicial Council. Divorce is permitted. Capital punishment is maintained but rarely implemented.

RECENT HISTORY

After Francisco Franco's victory in the civil war, Spain remained neutral in World War II, although "volunteer" forces (the Blue Division) fought against the Soviet Union. In 1946 the majority of states retracted recognition from the Franco regime under the terms of a U.N. resolution. This was revoked in 1950. In 1953 the United States made an agreement with Spain, by the terms of which in return for economic and financial aid the United States was allowed to establish air and naval bases in Spain. In 1955 Spain became a member of the United Nations, in 1959 of the OECD and in 1960 of GATT. A defense treaty was signed with Portugal in 1958.

Franco's death in November 1975 marked the end of the dictatorship; that end had been carefully orchestrated to ensure a trouble-free transition. The Organic Law of 1967 had named Prince Juan Carlos de Borbón y Borbón as Franco's successor. On July 1, 1976, Prime Minister Carlos Arias Navarro resigned—reportedly at the king's request—and was replaced by Adolfo Suarez González, who set in motion a series of reform measures. The National Movement was abolished by cabinet decree, and on June 15, 1977, balloting took place for a new Cortes in which Suarez's Union of the Democratic Center obtained a substantial plurality. On December 29, 1978, a new constitution came into force. Restive rightist elements in the military countered with a coup attempt that was defused only by the personal intervention of the king. The introduction of a liberal divorce bill virtually disintegrated the ruling party, setting the stage for a decisive electoral victory by the Socialists in the 1982 elections. In 1982 Felípe González Márquez was sworn in as Spain's first leftist prime minister in 46 years.

In 1982 Spain entered NATO despite opposition from within the Socialist Workers' party. In 1976 it yielded control of its North African territory of Spanish Sahara to Morocco and Mauritania. (Mauritania later relinquished its half to Morocco.)

Defense: The head of state is the commander-in-chief of the armed forces and head of the Supreme Defense Council. There is no defense minister, the service ministers being also senior service commanders. Military service is compulsory for 15 months in the army, air force and navy. Strengths of the services: army 255,000, navy 49,000, air force 38,000. Defense expenditure represented 2.02% of GNP in 1982 and the 1982 defense estimates were approximately P337.46 billion ($3.98 billion).

ECONOMY

Background: The main impetus to expansion since 1945 has come from industrial development, although nearly half the country's commodity exports are agricultural products. The high growth rate of the 1950s upset stability; prices rose considerably and there were repeated balance-of-payments deficits. The stabilization program that followed initiated a period of balanced growth between 1959 and 1963, but price inflation recurred. Between 1970 and 1979, GNP grew by an annual average of 3.0%. The main growth industries in recent years have been manufacturing (iron and steel, chemicals and construction materials) and tourism (in 1981 there were over 22 million tourists).

In terms of aggregate GNP—$199.78 billion in 1981—Spain is one of the world's dozen wealthiest states, yet its economy is still encumbered with outmoded market constraints and regional imbalances. During the 1960s and early 1970s, Spain experienced its own version of an "economic miracle" when the economy, stimulated by exports and tourism, took off at an unprecedented rate. This period of expansion came to an end when the first shock waves of OPEC petroleum price increases hit Spain in 1973–74. The real rate of growth fell from 8% in 1973 to less than 1% in 1975, and the current account from a $640 million surplus in 1973 to a $4 billion deficit in 1976. The political interregnum following Franco's death impeded the economy still further. The Suarez administration initiated an austerity regime that included wage restraints, sharp devaluation of the peseta, selective controls on prices, imposition of tight monetary policies and increased taxes. The economy responded only partially to these measures because its basic weaknesses were meanwhile aggravated by separatist violence, the return of over 225,000 guestworkers from northern European states and continuing inflation. The 1979–82 economic plan committed the government to pursue even more stringent measures.

The origin of GDP at factor cost in 1982 was:

Sector	Percentage
Agriculture	6
Industry	34
Services	60
GDP	100

During 1970–82 industrial output increased by an estimated 3.4%. The main agricultural products are grapes, cereals, fruit, vegetables, wine, olive oil and livestock products.

The most dramatic change in the structure of the Spanish economy during the past two decades has been in the decline of the agricultural sector, both in terms of employment (from 40% to 20%) and in terms of its share of GDP (from 20% to 10%). As a result, Spain now imports more food than it exports. Meanwhile, industry's share of GDP has remained fairly stable, although real output has grown rapidly as has its share of employment. Industrial stabilization and restructuring has received top priority from government planners.

Foreign trade: Spain's long-standing application for entry into the EC was accepted by the Community but took time, and ran into trouble in 1984 when Greece threatened to veto the admission unless Greek, Italian and Southern French farmers were compensated for losses resulting from competition with wine, fruit, vegetables and olive oil from Spain and Portugal. Observers generally agree that the accession of Spain and Portugal are likely to aggravate the EC's economic problems. However, EC members were anxious to strengthen the new democracies of these countries by drawing them into the Community. Meanwhile, Spain enjoyed preferential treatment from the EC based on a 1970 agreement and had liberalized its tariffs on industrial imports from the Community. A similar arrangement exists with EFTA, signed in 1980. Spain became a full member of the EC in 1986.

In 1982, merchandise exports amounted to $20.522 billion and merchandise imports to $31.535 billion, leaving a trade deficit of $11.013 billion. During 1970–82, annual average growth rate was 9.4% for exports and 4.4% for imports. In 1982, the percentage share of merchandise exports was 9% for fuels, minerals and metals; 20% for other primary commodities; 5% for textiles and clothing; 26% for machinery and transport equipment; and

40% for other manufactures. In the same year, the percentage share of merchandise imports was 12% for food, 43% for fuels, 9% for other primary commodities, 17% for machinery and transport equipment, and 19% for other manufactures. Nearly 58% of merchandise exports goes to industrial market economies and 35% to developing countries.

Employment: The total labor force in 1982 was 13.58 million, of whom 14% were employed in agriculture, 40% in industry and 46% in services; about 11.8% were unemployed. There is a general scarcity of skilled labor. Many persons have emigrated from Spain, mostly to other European countries; many of them have since returned.

Price and wage trends: In 1983, employers' groups and unions reached agreement limiting wage increases to between 9.5% and 12.5%. The pact covered about 6.5 million workers and was negotiated by CEOE (the employers' organization), CEPYME (representing small employers), the Socialists and the Communists.

Consumption: In 1982 private consumption accounted for 70% of GNP and public consumption for 12%.

SOCIAL SECURITY

All social security benefits are under the supervision of the ministries of Labor and of Health and Social Security. Most programs are administered by the National Institute of Social Security and the General Social Security Treasury. Benefits outlined below are as of 1984.

Health insurance: This is available to all employees in industry and services, and their dependents. The insured person contributes 4.8% of covered earnings, according to 12 occupational classes. The employer's contribution amounts to 25.8% of earnings, according to the same classes. The government contributes an annual balancing subsidy. Sickness benefits, available to all who have made 180 days of contributions within the last five years, amount to 60% of covered earnings up to the 21st day and 75% thereafter for up to 12 months, extendable in certain cases for up to 72 months. Maternity benefits amount to 75% of covered earnings, payable for six weeks before and eight weeks after childbirth. Medical services of all kinds are provided to patients directly through hospitals and clinics run by the Institute of Social Security. The patient usually pays 40% of the cost for medicines outside the hospital. Medical benefits are usually, except in certain cases, provided for an unlimited duration.

Accident insurance: The employer, depending on the risk category, pays from 0.9% to 18% of payroll to insure employees against work-related injury. Temporary disability benefits from such injuries include 75% of covered earnings, payable for up to 18 months, extendable for up to 72 months. If permanently disabled, a worker receives 55% of covered earnings, with a minimum of P23,565 a month. Survivor pensions, a smaller percentage of covered earnings, are payable to widows and dependent disabled

178

widowers as well as to other family dependents and to orphans. The maximum survivor pensions amount to 100% of the pension of the insured.

Pensions insurance: Coverage is available to all employees in industry and services and their dependents. Benefits are financed by workers, employers and the state under the same general scheme as for health insurance. There are special systems for agricultural workers, domestic servants, railway employees, salesmen, seamen, public employees, miners and members of some of the liberal professions. The maximum pension earnings for contribution and benefit purposes are P187,950 a month; there is a separate ceiling for each occupational class. Old-age pensions are payable at age 65, or lower for dangerous or unhealthy work, or at age 64, if the employer replaces the retiree with a youth seeking first employment. These pensions comprise 50% of covered earnings (the average of the highest-paid two of the last seven years) plus 2% per year of contribution from 11 to 35 years, up to a maximum of 100%. The minimum pension is P23,565, or, if the retiree is under 65, P20,605 per month. Payments of disability pensions range from 24 monthly payments of 75% of covered earnings for permanent partial disability up to 100% of actual earnings for permanent total disability. The minimum payment in the latter case is P33,345 a month. Survivor pensions are the same as those for accident victims.

Unemployment insurance: This has been available in Spain since 1919. Insured persons contribute 0.1% of covered earnings, according to occupational class; employers contribute 4.8% of payroll; and variable subsidies come from the state. Recipients must have made six months of contributions within the last four years. Benefits payable are 80% of average covered earnings of the last six contribution months for up to 180 days; 70%, from the seventh to the 12th month; and 60%, from the 13th to the 18th month. Benefits may in special cases be extended to 24 months, but may not exceed 220% of the minimum wage.

Other benefits: Family allowances are generally limited to eligible employees in industry and commerce and pensioners with one or more children. They include P250 a month for each child, and P375 for spouse. There are large-family grants, lump-sum payments of P3,000 for each birth and marriage grants of P6,000.

EDUCATION

The official figure for illiteracy in 1983 was 3% of those over the age of 14. Instruction is generally in Castilian Spanish. However, in 1978, the study of the Catalan language was made compulsory in Catalonia at the primary and secondary levels. The sexes are taught separately except in sparsely populated areas. In 1981 approximately 8% of the national budget was spent on education.

Primary education: Primary education is free and compulsory from the ages of six to 14. Seventy percent of children attending school go to state schools. If students do not go on to secondary school, they must enroll in first-grade vocational training from 15 to 16 years of age.

Secondary and vocational education: This is optional. Secondary education lasts from the ages of 14 to 16. Secondary schools (*institutos*) are divided into an upper and lower division and further divided into branches for sciences and letters. Courses end in the state leaving exam, the general *bachillerato.* Equivalent to the general bachillerato is the labor bachillerato, which can be obtained after seven-year courses—divided into elementary and senior grades—at agricultural, industrial and mining, maritime and fishing, and (mostly for women) "administration" schools. The majority of these schools are run by the state, but certain private centers are officially recognized.

There are over 500 state-run industrial trade schools, most of which offer courses up to the grade of master tradesman. There are also six labor universities—one private and the others supported by mutual benefit societies —which provide training in industrial trades and prepare pupils for the labor bachillerato. Technical courses last five years in the higher grades, entry being dependent upon attainment of the general bachillerato, and three years at the intermediate grade, the conditions of entry here generally being the possession of the elementary bachillerato or attainment of the master trades-man's grade.

Special education: Special education for physically and mentally handicapped children is given in schools run by both state and private organizations.

University and higher education: There are 20 state universities. In addition, a number of nonstate universities are recognized by the state. Among other higher-education institutes there are advanced education colleges and academies of art and music. University courses last five years. University education is not free, but the state provides grants for the needy.

Universities: Barcelona, Bilbao (commercial), Comillas (Pontifical),* Granada, Laguna, Madrid, Maria Christina Madrid,* Murcia, Navarre,* Oviedo, Salamanca (Pontifical),* Salamanca (literary), San Sebastián,* Santiago, Seville, Valencia, Valladolid, Zaragoza and others.

*Nonstate university.

Educational institutions, 1981–82:

	Institutions	Students	Teachers
Preschool	37,011*	1,197,897	36,846
General basic (primary)	178,846	5,629,874	214,391
Secondary	2,488†	1,124,329	67,931
Vocational	2,323†	619,090	40,190
University faculties	244	441,473	24,761

* Classes.   † Centers.
Source: Instituto Nacional de Estadística, Madrid.

Adult education: The army provides special general education for conscripts. In addition, there are evening classes run by private organizations.

MASS MEDIA

The press (1982):
Dailies: *El País*, Madrid, 348,000; *La Vanguardia Española*, Barcelona, independent, 191,804; *ABC*, Madrid, independent Catholic monarchist, 145,597; *Ya*, Madrid, ind. right-wing Cath., 109,530; *Dario 16*, Madrid, left-center, 129,816; *Levante*, Valencia, 31,316; *ABC*, Seville edition, ind., Cath. mon., 56,692; *Las Provincias*, Valencia, ind. rt., 52,316.

Periodicals: Madrid—*La Calle*, 43,590; *Diez Minutos* (weekly), 427,103; *Gaceta Ilustrada* (w), general illustrated, 125,000; *¡Hola!* (w), gen. illus., 467,673; *Muy Interesante* (m), 165,800; *Cambio 16* (w), gen. political, 168,603; *Pronto* (w), radio and TV, 822,470; *Semana* (w), gen. illus., 331,554. Barcelona—*Garbo* (w), popular illus., 337,348; *Interviú* (w), 494,347; *Sal y Pimienta* (w), 140,774.

Broadcasting: RTVE—Radiotelevisión Española—controls all sound and vision broadcasting both official and commercial. Advertising is limited. All stations broadcast the national news service of the main official station, Radio Nacional de España (RNE) (which covers all continental Spain and the Island Provinces). There is a Foreign Service of the RNE. It broadcasts in English, French, Portuguese and Arabic, as well as Spanish. The remainder of the programs on commercial stations are independent.

Atlantic Ocean

Kiruna

Gällivare

N O R R B O T T E N

Luleå

Skellefteå

VÄSTERBOTTEN

Umeå

JÄMTLAND

VÄSTERNORRLAND

Östersund   Örnsköldsvik

Härnösand

Sundsvall

GÄVLEBORG

KOPPARBERG

FINLAND

NORWAY

Falun   Gävle

Borlänge

Sandviken

UPPSALA

VÄRMLAND   VÄSTMANLAND   Uppsala

Västerås

Karlstad   ÖREBRO

STOCKHOLM

Örebro   SÖDERMANLAND

Stockholm

Mariestad   Nyköping

GÖTEBERG   Vänersborg
OCH BOHUS   SKARABORG   Norrköping

Linköping

Göteborg   ÖSTERGÖTLAND

ALVSBORG

Jönköping   KALMAR   Visby   GOTLAND

JÖNKOPING   GOTLAND

HALLAND

Växjö   Kalmar   ÖLAND

Halmstad   KRONOBERG

SOVIET UNION

KRISTIANSTAD   BLEKINGE

Helsingborg   Karlskrona   100m

MÄLMOHUS   Kristianstad   100km

DENMARK   Malmö

Gulf of Bothnia

Kattegat

Baltic Sea

SWEDEN

182

SWEDEN

Features: Sweden can be divided into four major regions. Of these the largest is Norrland, stretching from the Dal river in the south to the Finnish and Norwegian frontiers north of the Arctic Circle. The main north-south frontier with Norway consists of NE-SW range of mountains of Caledonian age, more of the belt being in Sweden than Norway. In places these mountains rise to over 5,000 ft/1,500 m. To the southeast the western edge of the Baltic Shield drops gradually to the coastal plain flanking the Gulf of Bothnia. The whole area is drained by a number of streams flowing from the mountains southeastward to the sea and providing considerable hydroelectric power potential. To the south of this region lies the Lakes Depression, a lowland area with alternating lakes, glacial ridges and lowlands. Further south is the infertile Småland plateau. Finally, in the far south is the small region of Skåne, an undulating area of fairly low relief.

The most productive agricultural areas are the Lakes Depression and Skåne and the extreme southern part of the coastal lowlands of Norrland. Sweden is poorly endowed with fuels, though there are large resources of hydroelectric power especially in the north. There are large iron-ore deposits in the Kiruna-Gällivare areas in the far north and the Bergslagen area of the east. Small amounts of other minerals are also produced. The main industrial area lies in and north and west of Stockholm, around Göteborg (Gothenburg) and on the shores of the major lakes. In the north, the chief center is Luleå.

Area: 173,400 sq. miles/449,800 sq. km. *Mean max. and min. temperatures:* Stockholm (59° 30' N, 18° E; 150 ft/45 m.) 70°F/21°C (July), 22°F/ − 6°C (Feb.); Gällivare (67° N, 20° 30' E; 1,200 ft/365 m.) 70°F/21°C, 1°F/ − 17°C. *Relative humidity:* Stockholm 80%; Gällivare 78%. *Mean annual rainfall:* Stockholm 22 in./560 mm.; Gällivare 22 in./560 mm.

POPULATION

Total population: (1984) 8.3 million. *Chief towns and populations:* (1982) STOCKHOLM (647,214), Göteborg (431,273), Malmö (233,803), Uppsala (146,192), Norrköping (119,238), Västerås (117,487). *Distribution:* In 1982, 87% of the population lived in urban centers, 35% of this group lived in Stockholm.

Language: The official language is Swedish. *Religion:* The 1951 religious freedom law considers all citizens to belong to the established Evangelical-Lutheran church unless they freely withdraw.

Constitution: Sweden is a constitutional monarchy based on a number of fundamental constitutional laws dating from 1809. A new Instrument of Government was adopted in 1973. In 1974 a new Riksdag Act was adopted. The revised constitution went into effect on January 1, 1975. *Head of state:* King Carl XVI Gustav. *Head of government:* Prime Minister Olof Palme (Social Democratic Labor party).

Executive: Executive power is vested in the Council of State of the king and his ministers (*Statsråd*). The king selects as prime minister the party leader having strongest support in parliament (*Riksdag*). No act of the king is valid unless countersigned by a minister. The prime minister selects his ministers, whose nomination like his own is not subject to formal parliamentary approval. The cabinet (*Regeringen*) consists of 15 to 16 members, of whom a maximum of five are ministers without portfolio. The government may dissolve parliament and order extraordinary elections (this happened in 1958).

Legislature: The Riksdag is unicameral. It enacts laws, levies taxes and examines government actions. At present there are 349 members of the Riksdag. There are numerous standing committees, elected on the basis of proportional representation; these include the *Utrikesnämnder* (Advisory Council on Foreign Affairs) and special committees. Members are elected for three years on the basis of proportional representation by universal adult suffrage.

Referendum: The constitution provides for a consultative referendum if government and parliament agree to it.

Political parties: Swedish political parties are conventionally grouped as socialist and bourgeois. The socialist parties are:

Social Democratic Labor party, SAP. Founded in 1880, the Social Democratic Labor party was in power uninterruptedly for 44 years until 1976, and again from 1982. Pragmatic in outlook, it appeals to a broad spectrum of Swedish voters and manages to steer a middle course in domestic and foreign policies. It is led by Prime Minister Olof Palme.

There are four wings of the Communist party, the Communist Left party, VPK, under Lars Werner, being the largest. Its Eurocommunist or "revisionist" stance provoked a breakaway of pro-Moscow hard-liners who formed the Communist Workers' party under Rolf Hagel. The pro-Peking faction is known as the Communist party of Sweden, of which a splinter faction regrouped as the Communist party of Marxist-Leninist Revolutionaries.

The non-Socialist parties together hold 171 seats in the Riksdag. The largest of them is the Moderate Coalition party, MSP, known as the Conservative party until 1968, led by Ulf Adelsohn. The Center party, CP, formerly known as the Agrarian party, was founded in 1922, and during its early years strongly supported the Socialists, even occasionally joining them as junior coalition partners. From 1979 to 1982 its leader, Thorbjörn Fälldin, was prime minister of a bourgeois coalition. The third of the non-Socialist parties is the People's party, organized in the late 1920s as the Liberal party and drawing its support from nondoctrinaire progressives. Its leader, Ola Ullsten, was prime minister in 1978–79.

In 1985, the party lineup in the Riksdag was as follows:

> Social Democratic Labor party 159
> Moderate Coalition party 76
> Center party 44
> People's party 51
> Communist party 19

Local government: There are about 1,000 rural and urban (primary) communes, which elect councils (*kommunalfullmäktige* and *stadsfullmäktige*) of 15 to 60 members each by proportional representation for four years. Each council elects an executive committee (*kommunalnämnd* or *drätselkammare*) of at least five members for a four-year period not running concurrently with that of the council. All primary communes have both autonomous and state-delegated functions, the latter being regulated by special legislation.

The province (*län*), of which there are 24, has two functions. First, all the communes in the province are grouped together into a county commune (*landsting*)—which covers the same area as the *län*—for local government purposes, primarily for health and educational matters. The landsting elects a county council for four years by proportional representation, which in turn appoints an executive committee (*förvaltningsutskott*). The larger towns are outside the authority of the landsting and conduct their own local government. The landsting has no supervisory powers over the primary communes within its area.

Secondly, the province is an area of central government administration in those issues, e.g., the police, reserved to the state. Each province has a provincial administration (*länstyrelse*) headed by a governor (*landshövding*) appointed by the state for life. Stockholm has a separate but similar status, both as an urban commune and as the 25th province under a city governor. The provincial administration has no concern with local government except that it acts in a supervisory capacity in the case of delegated functions and it is the first instance of appeal against decisions of a communal council; the second instance is the Supreme Administrative Court.

Judicial system: The courts of first instance (*underrätter*) for criminal and civil cases are the county and city courts (*häradsrätter* and *rådhusrätter*). In the more serious criminal cases the court is constituted by one professional judge sitting with seven to nine lay judges (*nämndemän*). The decision of the professional judge is decisive except where there is a contrary decision by at least seven of the lay judges, in which case their decision prevails. In minor criminal cases there are only three lay judges, and petty cases are tried by the professional judge alone. This procedure is also followed in civil cases heard in the county courts; in the city courts, civil cases are decided by a panel of three professional judges. The next instance is the court of appeal (*hovrätt*); these courts are divided into chambers each composed of a president (*lagman*) and three to four other judges. Special courts are the supreme administrative court, the law court, the labor court and the water rights court. The highest court is the Supreme Court of Justice (*Högsta Domstolen*), composed of 25 members (*justitieråd*) and divided into three chambers, each constituted by five judges. Full sessions are held for certain cases. Judges are appointed by the government and cannot be dismissed except by judicial sentence. There is no death penalty except for certain war crimes.

RECENT HISTORY

Sweden remained neutral in World War II, and has since remained free from military alliances, while seeking to further peace and reduce international tension both within and outside the United Nations. Sweden is a founder member of EFTA, the OECD, the Council for Europe and the Nordic Council, and in 1961 applied for associate membership of the EC. The country has provided both observer and combat units for U.N. forces in Korea, Gaza, Lebanon, the Congo and Cyprus, and is a member of the United Nation's Eighteen-Nation Disarmament Committee.

In 1969 Prime Minister Tage Erlander, who had led the country since 1946, stepped down in favor of Olof Palme. In 1976, the 44-year rule of the Social Democrats ended when a bourgeois coalition took office under the Center party leader, Thorbjörn Fälldin. In 1982 and 1985 the Social Democrats returned to power under Palme as the head of a minority government supported by the Communist left. In 1973 the aged King Gustav VI Adolf died and was succeeded by his grandson, Carl XVI Gustav.

Defense: Sweden aims at neutrality in the event of war, to this end maintaining very strong defense forces in relation to the size of the country. Military service ranges from $7\frac{1}{2}$ to 15 months in the army and navy and eight to 12 months in the air force. Total mobilizable strength is about 800,000 (regular forces total 64,300, over half of whom serve only 15 to 40 days per year): army 44,500, navy 10,000, air force 9,800. In 1964 a permanent force of 1,600 was placed at U.N. disposal. Sweden has no nuclear weapons. Defense expenditure represented 3.35% of GNP in 1981, when defense estimates were SKr17.312 billion ($3.79 billion).

ECONOMY

Background: Sweden is richly endowed with resources: vast forests in the north, agricultural lands in the south, large deposits of iron ore, lead and zinc, and abundant supplies of hydroelectric power. There is considerable state control of major industries and a good record of postwar employer-union relations. The period since World War II has been characterized by rapid economic development; but in 1965 the economy, fully exploited, showed signs of strain, especially in the labor market. Restrictive monetary and budgetary policies were followed between 1964 and 1966. In 1981, GNP was worth $111.9 billion at market prices. In the period 1970–79 the annual average rate of growth was 1.1%. The origin of GDP in 1982 was:

Sector	Percentage
Agriculture, forestry and fishing	3
Industry	31
Services	66
GDP	100

The main industries include metals and metal products, transport equipment and wood products. Industrial production has increased at an annual average rate of about 0.7% between 1970 and 1982. The major growth industries have been power, mining and manufacturing, especially chemical and electrical engineering, and building and construction. Many factors contributed to the slow-down of industrial production in the 1970s: a shortage of labor, the full utilization of resources, a decline in overseas demand and the government's restrictive economic policy, including restraint of credit and raising of indirect taxes. The industries most affected were woodpulp, iron and steel, and engineering products. The main agricultural products are wheat, barley, cattle, pigs and root and green crops.

Manufacturing and mining continue in the 1980s to be the main strengths of Swedish economy. The former accounts for about three-quarters of sectoral output and employment, as well as a similar share of the nation's exports. While most of the industries are in private hands, the state-owned conglomerates, such as Statsforetag, dominate manufacturing. Sweden is rich in mineral resources, which include 15% of the total known deposits of uranium. Sweden also accounts for some 5% of world iron-ore production.

Foreign trade: Sweden has signed a free-trade agreement with the EC and is a member of EFTA and the Nordic Council. Sweden grants most-favored-nation status to all countries and has one of the world's lowest tariff rates.

In 1982, merchandise exports amounted to $26.817 billion and merchandise imports to $27.591 billion, leaving a trade deficit of $218 million. The annual average growth rate was 3.2% for exports and 2.3% for imports. The percentage share of merchandise exports was 9% for fuels, minerals and metals; 12% for other primary commodities; 2% for textiles and clothing; 42% for machinery and transport equipment; and 35% for other manufactures. The percentage share of merchandise imports was 7% for food, 25% for fuels, 6% for other primary commodities, 27% for machinery and transport equipment, and 35% for other manufactures. The principal export partners are West Germany (12%), United Kingdom (10%), Norway (10%), Denmark (8%), Finland (6%), France (6%) and the United States (5%). The principal import partners are West Germany (17%), Britain (12%), the United States (7%), Finland (7%), Denmark (6%), Norway (5%) and Saudi Arabia (5%).

Employment: Of a total working population of 4.4 million in 1982, 5% were employed in agriculture, 34% in industry and 61% in services. Unemployment in the same year amounted to 1.9%; however, an acute labor

187

shortage has since developed, and labor continues to move from the north to the south.

Price and wage trends: Consumer prices increased by an annual average of 9.5% in the period 1970–82. One of the key elements in Sweden's economic prosperity has been its relatively peaceful industrial-relations climate. The tradition of industry-wide collective bargaining dates from the 1930s, when the Swedish Employers' Confederation (SAF) and the Swedish Trade Union Confederation (LO) concluded the Saltsjöbaden agreement, the first of a series of jointly formulated nonbinding wage guidelines for labor contracts. The joint SAF-LO organization, known as the National Labor Market Board, is one of the most powerful institutions in the country, administering the Investment Reserve Funds, a medium-term account in which corporations are required to deposit nearly half of the share of profits they are entitled to set aside, tax free, for future investment purposes. As a result, Sweden has one of the lowest rates among Western nations for strike days lost.

In recent years there has been a substantial growth in the relative size of the public sector. Total government outlays rose from 40% of the GDP in 1970 to 65% in 1980. Almost 30% of Sweden's GDP consists of wages for state employees, while social security benefits, subsidies and other transfers account for nearly half the public spending. Workers' social security contributions amount to one-fourth of the public revenues. Because of its welfare state commitments, Sweden's tax burden rose to 60% of GDP in 1979.

Consumption: Private consumption in 1982 amounted to 54% of GNP and public consumption to 24%. Between 1970 and 1982 public consumption grew by 3.2% and private consumption by 1.7%.

SOCIAL SECURITY

Health insurance: Under the general supervision of the National Social Insurance Board, the health scheme covers all residents for medical benefits, gainfully employed persons earning SKr6,000 a year or more, and most housewives and dependent husbands for cash benefits. It is financed by the insured person, the employer and the government. Sickness benefits are 90% of income up to 7.5 times the base amount; the maximum daily benefit is SKr359. There is a special parents' cash benefit. Medical benefits include doctor's consultation, free hospitalization (in public hospitals) and free medicine for some chronic diseases. Medical benefits for dependents are the same as for the family head.

Accident insurance: Under the general supervision of the National Social Insurance Board, the scheme covers all employed and self-employed residents. The insurance is almost entirely financed by the employer, who contributes 0.6% of payroll. Temporary disability benefit (work injury) is basically 90% of income up to 7.5 times the base amount. Permanent disability pension (work injury) is available for the totally disabled and is 100% of income.

There are partial disability pensions and medical benefits, which are the same as the ordinary sickness benefits of the health insurance program. Survivor pensions (work injury) are payable to widows, orphans and dependent parents.

Pensions insurance: Under the general supervision of the National Social Insurance Board, the scheme covers all residents, citizens and certain aliens for the universal pension, and all employees and self-employed persons earning over the base amount for earnings-related pensions. The universal pension scheme is financed by the self-employed insured, the employer and the government. The earnings-related pension scheme is financed by the self-employed insured and the employer. Old-age pensions generally are available at age 65 for both men and women. Disability pensions are available if at least 50% loss of working capacity has occurred. Universal old-age pensions are 95% of the current base amounts, or 155% for an aged couple, plus increments. There are supplements available. Earnings-related pensions are 60% of the difference between average annual covered earnings and the base amount, based on coverage since 1960. There are provisions for partial earnings-related pensions. Universal disability pensions are 95% of the current base amount, or 155% for an aged couple. There are supplements available. Earnings-related disability pensions begin at 2% of average covered earnings. The maximum is 60% of covered earnings. Universal survivor pensions are available to widows and orphans. There are supplements available. Earnings-related survivor pensions are payable to widows and orphans.

Unemployment insurance: Under the general supervision of the National Labor Market Board, the unemployment-insurance scheme covers (under union-related programs) employees belonging to approved unemployment funds established voluntarily by trade unions. Under the labor-market support program, employees and would-be employees over the age of 16 ineligible for the union-related program are covered. The union-related program is financed by the insured, the employer and the government. The labor-market support program is financed by the employer and the government. Union-related program unemployment benefits are SKr80–280 a day, according to fund and wage class of the employee. Benefits are taxed for contribution purposes. Labor-market support program unemployment benefits are SKr100 a day.

Other benefits: Under the general supervision of the National Social Insurance Board, family allowances of SKr3,300 a year for the first child and each additional eligible child, payable quarterly, are available to all eligible residents.

EDUCATION

Primary education: Education is free and compulsory from the ages of seven to 16. The school provided for by the 1962 reform is the comprehensive school (*grundskolan*) divided into lower (grades 1–3), middle (grades 4–6), and upper (grades 7–9) departments. There are no examinations and no streaming below the upper department, and generally one teacher is responsible for all subjects. In the first two grades of the upper department, pupils are offered a limited selection of subjects but no regrouping of classes. In grade 9 pupils are offered nine courses of study divided into four sections—theoretical, social, technical-mechanical and economics, all except the first having both practical and theoretical streams for further study. The teaching of individual subjects in the upper grades is by university-trained teachers. The grundskola is the responsibility of the local authorities but receives state funds for the costs of operation and construction.

Secondary schools: Entry into the upper secondary school (*gymnasieskolan*) depends upon the final marks gained in the ninth year in the primary theoretical section. In this school there are about 25 programs and 400 specialized courses, some of which are vocational. Courses last for three years, with greater specialization in the last two years, and terminate in a written and oral final examination (*studentexamen*) qualifying for university entrance. There are also technical and business high schools providing vocational education and a diploma qualifying for university entry. Parallel with the grundskola are three types of continuation school, providing two-year courses for those successfully completing the social, technical and economics section of the ninth primary grade. These courses have no examinations and pupils need not attend them directly on completion of primary education.

Special education: Slow learners are instructed in special classes at normal primary schools, and the educationally subnormal may be taught at free special day and boarding schools subsidized by county councils and government grants. Compulsory special education begins at the age of seven and may last until 23, vocational training following eight or nine years of general schooling. Children with severe mental deficiencies get training and therapy in child-care homes. Totally and near-totally deaf children are taught at compulsory, state-financed schools for 10 years, the last two being spent in vocational education. Preparatory schools for the deaf, mostly maintained by local authorities and special welfare societies with some state support, are voluntary. Children with some hearing capacity are sent to special schools and special classes attached to primary schools, where they reach almost the same levels as children in normal elementary schools. There are also special schools for the blind. State supervision is exercised over all special schools.

Vocational education: Vocational education is traditionally given on the job. Several private companies have established their own workshop schools and industry plays an important part in vocational training in the ninth primary grade. Vocational training has been much increased by the state and local authorities.

University and higher education: Sweden has five universities: Uppsala, Lund, Stockholm, Göteborg and Umeå, all with a wide range of faculties. There are professional schools, with university college status, of medicine (Caroline Institute, Stockholm), dentistry (Stockholm, Malmö), economics (Stockholm, Göteborg), technology (Stockholm, Göteborg, Lund), pharmacy (Stockholm), agriculture (Uppsala), veterinary medicine, forestry and music and art (Stockholm). Courses last from three to seven years. Almost all tuition is free. Financial aid to students is given by the state on a large scale.

Educational institutions, 1982–83:

	Institutions	Teachers[2]	Students
Primary:			
Grade 1–6			658,127
Secondary:	4,879	97,022	
Grade 7–9			340,847
Integrated upper secondary schools	520	26,779	266,352[3]
Higher:			
Teacher training Universities and specialized colleges	n.a.	n.a.	216,412
People's colleges[1]	121	2,350	14,721
Municipal adult education	329	5,339	154,483
Study circles	n.a.	n.a.	2,347,998[4]
State schools for adult education	n.a.	n.a.	n.a.

[1] Courses of at least 15 weeks.
[2] Spring term 1983. Full- and part-time teachers.
[3] Students in the four-year technical course, numbering 37,377, are excluded from study circles and counted instead in higher education.
[4] From the autumn semester 1977 those colleges and professional schools traditionally regarded as of university level were reorganized with certain other categories of state-supported institutions and restructured as common integrated schools for higher education.
Source: Statistics Sweden, Stockholm.

Adult education: There are many folk high schools offering courses of from seven to eight months. Run as boarding schools by county councils and cultural, social and religious organizations with substantial state aid, they provide certificates for entrance into general educational establishments. Adults wanting a senior high school diploma can study at senior high schools for adults or take correspondence courses. Aid for examinations is also provided by evening school. State grants are available during the final stage of studies, and also study loans. In 1982 there were 2,629 public libraries.

MASS MEDIA

The press (1982):

Dailies: Expressen, Stockholm, Liberal, 532,767; *Dagens Nyheter*, Stockholm, Lib., 408,100; *Aftonbladet*, Stockholm, Social Democrat, 423,661; *Göteborgs-Posten*, Göteborg, Lib., 294,896; *Svenska Dagbladet*, Stockholm, MSP, 186,118; *Sydsvenska Dagbladet Snällposten*, Malmö, MSP, 115,729; *Nya Wermlands-Tidningen*, Karlstad, 75,938; *Kvällsposten*,

Malmö, MSP, 117,296; *Göteborgs-Tidningen*, Göteborg, Lib., 144,061; *Arbetet*, Malmö, Soc. Dem., 103,106.

Periodicals: Året Runt (w), Stockholm, family, 393,500; *Vecko-Revyn* (w), Stockholm, Society, 131,036; *Allers Familiejournal* (w), Helsingborg, family, 271,963; *Husmodern* (w), Stockholm, wom., 181,980; *Min Värld* (w), Stockholm, wom., 153,640; *Se*, Stockholm (w), men's, 113,353; *Teknikens Värld* (f), Stockholm, technical, 34,500.

Broadcasting: The Swedish Broadcasting Corporation (Sveriges Radio) is a noncommercial limited company in which the government has no financial holdings. The only obligation to afford time to the government is in the case of important government announcements. The corporation has the sole right of decision on programs, while the government has ultimate control of the range of activities as a whole, hours of broadcasting, etc. The government influences the general administration of the corporation through its appointment of the chairman and half the board members. The director-general of the corporation—chosen by the board—has ultimate responsibility for both radio and TV programs. The government appoints a Radio Council to review programs after their transmission and submits an annual report to the government upon complaints from organizations and private individuals. Transmission is financed by license fees, radio and TV having separate budgets. In 1983, there were approximately 3,327,000 radio receivers in use and 3,235,255 licensed TV receivers.

SWITZERLAND

Features: In the northwest of the country lie the Swiss Jura Mountains, an area of NE–SW trending ridges and valleys; elevations are seldom over 3,000 ft/900 m. and the whole area is heavily wooded. To the south and east of this region lies the Swiss Plateau, some 30 miles in width and consisting in the main of numerous flat-bottomed, wide river valleys with intervening areas of higher land, rising steadily toward the Alps in the south. The region also contains a number of lakes, e.g., Geneva and Constance. Nearly two-thirds of the country is covered by the Alps. Switzerland contains part of the central Alpine mountain zone, where peaks are highest and narrowest with deep intervening valleys and lakes; altitudes in excess of 10,000 ft/3,000 m. are common.

In spite of the large proportions of mountainous land, just over half the country is farmed, though much of this area consists of Alpine summer pasture only. The areas of greatest agricultural concentration are in the valleys and in parts of the Swiss Plateau. The country possesses few minerals, the main economic resources being hydroelectric potential and tourism. Industry is largely concentrated in the plateau area, especially around Zurich, St. Gallen and Geneva.

Area: 15,940 sq. miles/41,290 sq. km. *Mean max. and min. temperatures:* Bern (47° N, 7° 30′ E; 1,880 ft/575 m.) 74°F/23°C (July), 26°F/ − 3°C (Jan.); Andermatt (46° 30′ N, 8° 30′ E; 4,730 ft/1,440 m.) 60°F/16°C, 18°F/ − 8°C; Lugano (46° N, 9° E; 900 ft/275 m.) 83°F/28°C, 29°F/ − 2°C. *Relative humidity:* Bern 87%; Andermatt 70%; Lugano 78%. *Mean annual rainfall:* Bern 39 in./990 mm.; Andermatt 53 in./1,345 mm.; Lugano 68 in./1,725 mm.

Total population: (1984) 6.5 million. *Chief towns and populations:* (1982) Zurich (707,300), Basel (363,700), Geneva (327,100), BERN (282,400), Lausanne (225,200). *Distribution:* In 1982, 58% of the population lived in urban centers.

Language: There are four national languages—German, French, Italian and Romansh—spoken by 73.5, 20.1, 4.5 and 1% of the population, respectively, in 1980. All the German-speaking population speak one of the many dialects known collectively as Schweizerdeutsch. *Religion:* In 1980, 50.4% of Swiss citizens were Protestant and 43.6% Roman Catholic.

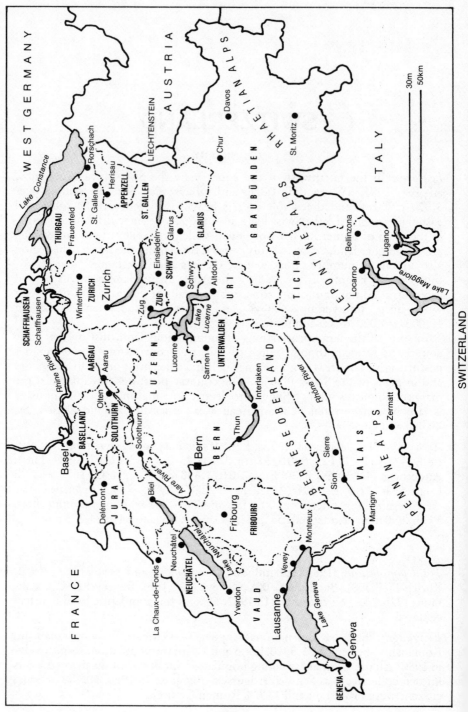

SWITZERLAND

Constitution: The Swiss Confederation is a federal republic of 23 cantons. The present constitution, with modifications, dates from 1874.

Head of state and government: The seven-man Federal Council collectively. President of the Confederation and of the Federal Council is Dr. Kurt Furgler.

Executive: The president and vice president of the Swiss Confederation are elected annually by the Federal Assembly, the vice president generally becoming the next president. The president of the Confederation is also president of the Federal Council (*Bundesrat*) on a *primus inter pares* basis. He conducts the meetings of the Council and like the six other members heads one of the seven executive departments of the government. The Council is elected by the Federal Assembly for four years following a general election, and the members are jointly responsible for government as a collegial body. Any Swiss citizen except a member of the clergy is eligible for election to the Council, with restrictions on the number of representatives from one canton. On appointment, members sever all political affiliations. The various regions, languages, religions and political parties are considered in the election. The Council is responsible to the Federal Assembly but neither a vote of censure nor a referendum can cause the resignation of the Council; councillors are generally reelected until they resign.

Legislature: The Federal Assembly (*Vereinigte Bundesversammlung*) is bicameral. The National Council (*Nationalrat*) of 200 members (previously 196) is elected for four years by proportional representation by all citizens over the age of 20. The Council of States (*Ständerat*) numbers 46. There are two representatives for each canton and they are elected for varying periods by cantonal legislation. The two Councils have equal authority. Legislation is prepared for their consideration by a committee system and must be approved by both houses before submission to the people (see under *Referendum*). Federal legislation is principally concerned with social insurance, international affairs, defense, export and import duties and internal communications. Federal revenue comes from both direct and indirect taxation.

The cantons: The cantons are sovereign states to the extent that their powers are not limited by the federal constitution. Each canton has a government (*Regierungsrat* or *Conseil d'État*) varying from five to 11 members, elected for one to five years by the population. As of 1971 women gained the right to vote in most cantons. In all but three cantons, legislation must be submitted to referendum if a sufficient number of the population so demand. In Basel every cantonal law is so submitted. In the cantons of Unterwalden, Glarus and Appenzell the people exercise their power directly at an annual convocation of the citizens (*Landsgemeinde*). The cantons derive their revenue from direct taxation.

The communes: The more than 3,000 free communes of the Swiss Confederation are the basic organs of direct democracy. In the communes, the citizen has the right—and in some the obligation—to be present at assemblies to decide on local questions.

Referendum: In addition to the cantonal referendum, there exists the national referendum to which all federal legislation must be submitted if there is a petition of 30,000 citizens against it within 90 days. The people may demand an amendment to the federal constitution with a petition of 50,000 signatures, which becomes effective if it is passed both by a majority of the electorate and a majority of the cantons; this so-called "initiative" is often exercised. The citizens within a canton may similarly propose amendments to the cantonal constitution as well as the adoption of new cantonal legislation.

Political parties: Although Switzerland has a plethora of political parties, the government and the Federal Assembly are dominated by a four-party coalition that includes the following:

Social Democratic party, a noncommunist Socialist party founded in 1888, led by Helmuth Hubacher and Dario Robbiani.

Radical Democratic party, a liberal party that led the movement culminating in the 1848 constitution. It is led by Bruno Hunziker and Jean-Jacques Cevey.

Christian Democratic People's party, formed in 1912 and formerly known as the Conservative Christian-Social party, it represents Catholic interests. It is led by Flavio Cotti and Arnold Koller.

Swiss People's party, formed in 1971, through a merger of the Farmers', Artisans' and Citizens' party and the Democratic party, it espouses a moderate agrarian and conservative course. It is led by Adolf Ogi and Hans Rudolf Nebiker.

The opposition comprises a number of minor parties, most of them receiving less than 4% each of the popular vote. The most notable among them are the Independent Alliance, Progressive Swiss Organization, Liberal party, Evangelical People's party, Green party, Autonomous Socialist party, Workers' party, National Campaign for People and Homeland and Federation of Ecology parties. Smaller parties have won representation in the Nationalrat.

The party lineup in the Federal Assembly in 1984 was as follows:

	Council of States	National Council
Christian Democratic People's party	18	42
Radical Democratic party	14	54
Social Democratic party	6	47
Swiss People's party	5	23
Liberal party	3	8
Independent Alliance		8
Workers' party		1
Evangelical People's party		3
Progressive Swiss Organization		3
National Campaign for People and Homeland		5
Green party		3
Others		3

Local government: The cantonal and communal councils are the main sources of local government. Some larger communes elect an assembly and an executive council. In smaller communes there is a council only. In most cantons a number of communes are grouped together in districts (*Amtsbezirke*) each having a prefect (*Regierungsstatthalter*) as representative of the cantonal government.

Judicial system: The system varies with the cantons, but Zurich may be taken as a model. The canton elects its own magistracy and retains its individual procedures. Civil cases are heard in the first instance in district courts (*Bezirksgerichte*) presided over by one judge. Each canton has an appeal court (*Obergericht*), and a cassation court reviews procedural questions. The Federal Court gives the final decisions in major federal civil cases. Minor criminal cases are dealt with by the district and appeal courts. More serious cases are a matter for the jury court (*Schwurgericht*) of three judges and 12 jurors, and the appeal court. The Federal Tribunal has 30 full and 11 to 13 supplementary members elected by the Federal Assembly for six years. It has seven sections and exercises jurisdiction in suits between the Confederation and cantons, and corporations and individuals, and between cantons. It tries offenses against the Confederation and is the court of appeal against decisions of certain federal authorities or cantonal authorities applying federal law. There is no capital punishment.

RECENT HISTORY

Switzerland remained neutral in both world wars. The country is the headquarters for many international organizations and has been the site of many major international conferences of the postwar period. It is a founder-member of EFTA, and joined the Council of Europe in 1963 and GATT in 1966. It is also a member of the OECD but has not applied for membership in the United Nations although it maintains an observer there. In 1961 Switzerland applied for associate membership of the EC.

After 30 years of separatist agitation in the largely Roman Catholic and French-speaking Jura, Swiss voters approved a cantonal status for the area in 1978. The creation of the 23rd canton, the first to be formed since 1815, took place on January 1, 1979. Southern Jura, predominantly German-speaking and Protestant, remained part of Bern, while the small district of Laufen will decide later whether to join Solothurn, Basel-Land or urban Basel-Stadt. In 1980 Zurich and other cities experienced an unprecedented outbreak of youth violence spearheaded by the so-called Movement of the Discontented.

Defense: The head of the Defense Department is head of the armed forces. Switzerland is alliance-free but its neutrality is based upon a high degree of military preparedness. Military service is compulsory between the ages of 20 and 50. Initial military service lasts 20 weeks, and the remaining period is spent in the reserves. In 1982 the army had 3,500 regulars and 17,000 trainees with 580,000 reservists who can be mobilized in 48 hours. The air force had 6,000 regulars and 45,000 reservists. Defense expenditure represented 1.8% of GNP in 1981 when the defense budget was SF3.49 billion ($1.84 billion).

ECONOMY

Background: Compared to other developed nations, Switzerland is disadvantaged: it has few natural resources, it is landlocked and a significant proportion of the labor force is foreign. Few countries, however, even oil-exporting ones, surpass the Confederation in GNP per capita, which is the highest in Europe. Contributing to this distinction are a number of factors: a long tradition of neutrality, peaceful industrial relations and an international reputation as a financial center surpassing even that of London. Moreover, Switzerland's nonparticipation in most international organizations, including the United Nations and the EC, as well as in internationally sanctioned embargoes, has made the country a haven for flight capital, as well as a dependable trade partner for neutral or politically isolated countries, such as Israel and South Africa. Many multinational corporations have registered offices in Switzerland, taking advantage of the country's low tax rates and discretion in financial disclosures. Swiss prominence in international banking is directly related to its secret numbered accounts, which represent about half of all foreign deposits. The banking system's total assets are double the GNP. In order to relieve the pressure on the Swiss franc, the bulk of foreign deposits is confined to noninterest-bearing trustee accounts managed by banking houses. These banks are a major contributor to the Eurodollar market, as are also the insurance and reinsurance houses. Switzerland also continues to be the world's most active gold and securities market, and the so-called gnomes of Zurich control 55% of all gold sales, including those of South Africa and the Soviet Union.

The federal government has traditionally avoided intrusion in the economy, and direct federal ownership is limited to railroads, posts and telecommunications, a minority holding in Swissair, nuclear power plants and defense industries. Consolidated general government expenditures amount to 30% of GDP as against a 40% average for the OECD. Since the early 1970s, however, the role of the federal government has increased. In the mid-1970s, as the traditional export markets were being lost and manufacturing output, employment and GDP were all declining, the government intervened to impose wage and price controls. Since then, the Confederation has experienced major alterations in the structure of industrial output and employment, and such traditional mainstays as clockmaking, construction, and the manufacture of textiles and clothing have declined by 30% to 50%.

The annual average rate of growth at constant prices from 1970 to 1981 was 6.2%. The aggregate GNP was $106.3 billion and GNP per capita $16,440 in 1981.

Agriculture throughout this period showed some fluctuation, declining since 1964. The main agricultural products are wheat, potatoes, livestock and dairy products, and wine. The origin of GDP as factor cost in 1982 was:

Sector	Percentage
Agriculture	5
Industry	50
Services	45
GDP	100

Foreign trade: Switzerland is a member of EFTA and imports and exports industrial goods on a duty-free basis within that group. It also enjoys free trade in industrial goods with the EC. In addition, the Confederation participates in GATT and pursues a liberal trade policy. Only certain agricultural and military products require import permits.

In 1982, merchandise exports amounted to $26.024 billion and merchandise imports to $28.670 billion, leaving a favorable trade balance of $2.646 billion. The annual average growth rate during 1970–82 was 3.9% for exports and 4.3% for imports. The percentage of merchandise exports was 3% for metals, minerals and fuels; 4% for other primary commodities; 7% for textiles and clothing; 34% for machinery and transport equipment; and 52% for other manufactures. The percentage share of merchandise imports was 9% for food, 12% for fuels, 6% for other primary commodities, 26% for machinery and transport equipment, and 47% for other manufactures. The principal export partners were West Germany (20%), France (9%), Italy (8%), the United States (7%), Britain (6%) and Austria (5%). The principal import partners were West Germany (28%), France (12%), Italy (10%), Britain (8%) and the United States (7%).

Employment: The total working population in 1982 was 3.09 million and unemployment—except for seasonal unemployment—was virtually nil. The large number of foreign workers has been restricted in recent years. Out of the total labor force in 1982, industry employed 43%, agriculture 7% and services 50%.

The economy has depended on foreign labor, resident aliens, seasonal workers and workers who commute from neighboring countries. In 1975, restrictions were imposed for the first time on alien workers, but Switzerland still has the highest percentage of foreign workers in Europe—over 650,000 in 1980. Unlike many other Western European countries, Switzerland has no mandatory worker participation in management. Nevertheless, labor has been cooperative in maintaining wage restraints. Only about 25% of the labor force belongs to trade unions. Firms with fewer than 500 workers employ 70% of the industrial force.

Price and wage trends: During 1970–81, the consumer price index (CPI) rose by an annual average rate of 4.8%. The average hourly wages in 1981 were $8.37 in food, beverages and tobacco; $9.82 in chemicals; $7.91 in textiles; $7.87 in wood and furniture industries; $11.0 in printing and publishing; $8.45 in iron and steel, electrical machinery and transport. In 1981, the CPI was 173.1 (with 1970 = 100), the lowest in Western Europe.

Consumption: Private consumption in 1982 amounted to 61.5% of GNP and public consumption to 12.2%. This represented increases of 1.4% and 1.8% respectively during 1970–81. This trend was expected to continue and is a measure of the government's success in restoring a balance between supply and demand.

SOCIAL SECURITY

Health insurance: Under the general supervision of the Federal Office of Social Insurance in the Department of Interior, the scheme covers members of approved sickness insurance funds (mainly providing medical benefits). Over 90% of the population belongs to a sickness fund. The insurance is principally financed by the insured person's membership fees and federal subsidies to all approved funds. The cash sickness benefit is the federal minimum of SF2 a day, applicable to all funds. There are maternity benefits and a nursing allowance (SF60). Medical benefits cover services ordinarily provided by doctors, hospitals and pharmacists under contract with and often paid directly by sickness funds. Medical benefits for dependents are the same as for the insured, and are received in their own right, only if dependents belong to a fund. Otherwise, they receive no medical benefits even if the family head is insured.

Accident insurance: Under the general supervision of the Federal Office of Social Insurance in the Department of Interior, the scheme covers all employees, with optional coverage for the self-employed. It is financed almost solely by the employer. Temporary disability benefits (work-related injury) amount to 80% of earnings. Permanent disability pensions (work injury) are 80% of earnings, if the insured person is totally disabled. Constant-attendance supplements are available. Partial disability pension is a percentage of full pension, corresponding to the degree of incapacity. Medical benefits (work injury) cover all necessary care. Survivor pensions (work injury) are payable to widows, dependent or disabled widowers and orphans, as well as to other eligible survivors.

Unemployment insurance: Under the general supervision of the Federal Office of Industry, Trade, and Labor, and the Federal Office of Social Insurance, the scheme covers employed persons, with certain exceptions. The insurance is financed by the insured person, the employer and the government. Unemployment benefits are 65% of daily earnings, or 70% if there are one or more dependents. Additional supplements are available. The maximum unemployment benefit is 85% of earnings.

Other benefits: Cantonal old-age and survivors insurance funds collect contributions and pay allowances under the family allowance program, for the federal family-allowance program. There are also cantonal family allowance programs, supervised by cantonal governments. Under the federal program, agricultural employees and self-employed owners of small farms, with one or more children are covered. Under the cantonal programs, generally, non-agricultural employees with one or more children are covered. Under the federal program, household allowances are available to agricultural employees and self-employed owners of small farms who are married.

EDUCATION

Although education is a responsibility of the cantons, each of which has its own educational authority and system, the system as a whole is fairly uniform. Children begin at the ages of six to seven and continue until 14 to 16. The federal constitution guarantees free primary and secondary education, that this education remain under the supervision of the civil authorities, and that no child be compelled to attend religious instruction against its parent's wishes. Instruction is in the language or languages of the cantons.

Primary education: From the age of seven to 13, this is the same for all children in all cantons. At the age of 13 children may take an examination.

Secondary education: Those who do not take the primary finishing examination or who fail it continue primary education until 15 or 16. The successful enter secondary schools in which the curricula are based in varying degrees on the requirements of the maturity examination. At the age of 15 or 16 secondary-school children take a cantonal examination, then either leave or go on to the age of 18 or 19, when they take the federal maturity examination, the main qualification for university entrance. Streaming permits students from both upper primary and secondary schools to embark upon technical and commercial secondary education. Children enter commercial schools at 14 and technical schools at 15, and after courses lasting three to five years may obtain diplomas or the commercial maturity certificate. Secondary technical education is supplemented by a higher stage preparing students for technical diplomas and licentiates and doctorates in economics and social sciences.

Vocational and technical education: Vocational training in industry, handicrafts, commerce, agriculture and domestic science is regulated by federal law; all professional certificates and diplomas must be valid for all of Switzerland. The federal authorities encourage vocational education by direct subsidies and other measures. The minimum age to begin apprenticeship is 15 and during the whole period of training the apprentice must attend a professional school, leading to a final examination conducted by the cantons and then to a federal certificate of proficiency. After this there are opportunities to pursue examinations for the certificate of master craftsman. The cantonal colleges of technology (*Techniken*) train engineers of nonuniversity level for engineering, chemistry and watchmaking; courses last three or three-and-a-half years.

Special education: This is provided for all severely mentally or physically handicapped children. Costs are financed partly by disability schemes. The mentally handicapped are taught separately from the maladjusted.

Higher education: There are seven universities, all maintained by the cantons—Basel, Bern, Lausanne, Geneva, Zurich, Neuchâtel and Fribourg. In addition, there is a School of Technology affiliated to the University of Lausanne; the Federal Institute of Technology in Zurich (the only school founded by the Confederation); and the School of Economics and Public Administration in St. Gallen. Geneva has several institutions affiliated to the university—a school of engineering, a school of interpreters and a graduate institute of international studies. Courses last from four to six-and-a-half years. Many students at higher educational institutions are foreign. Attendance at courses is compulsory. Grants and loans are obtainable from local authorities.

Educational institutions, selected years:

	Institutions	Staff	Students*
Primary (1970)	n.a.	14,672	398,900
Secondary (1970)	n.a.	1,758	419,000
Vocational (1970)	23	9,162	241,100
Higher (1976/77)	10	5,886*	95,600

* 1983–84 figures.
Source: Swiss Federal Office of Statistics.

Private schools: Besides private day schools, there are over 400 boarding schools in Switzerland, many of which have an international reputation. All private schools lay a greater stress on overall training than is possible at state schools. About 10% of pupils are foreign.

Adult education: Adult education is provided mainly by private organizations, in particular by the Migros Cooperative Society. These concentrate mainly on the cultural and social side of education. Courses run by cantons and communes are few.

MASS MEDIA

The press (1983):

Dailies: Tages Anzeiger Zürich, Zurich, independent, 260,000; *Basler Zeitung* Basle, liberal, 113,109; *Feuille d'Avis de Neuchâtel/L'Express*, Neuchâtel, ind., 36,828; *Neue Zürcher Zeitung*, Zurich, ind.-lib. 136,500; *Blick*, Zurich, ind., 322,098; *24 Heures*, Lausanne, ind., 100,000; *Journal de Genève*, Geneva, ind.-lib., 21,260.

Periodicals: Annabelle/Femina, Zurich, women's, 125,000; *Glücks-Post*, Zurich, 170,000; *Illustré*, Lausanne, 160,000; *Meyers Modeblatt*, Zurich, 209,358; *Orella* (m), Zurich, fashion, handiwork, 109,979; *Radio-TV-Je Vois Tout* (w), Lausanne, 117,710; *Ringiers Unterhaltungsblätter*, Zofingen, family, 268,500; *Schweizer Familie* (w), Zurich, family, 313,026; *Schweizer Illustrierte* (w), Zurich, illus., 280,000; *Der Schweizerische Beobachter* (2 a month), Glattbrugg, 471,057; *Ski* (7 a year), Derendingen, 111,000; *TCS-Revue* (m), Zurich, Zurich Touring Club, 183,179; *Tele* (w), Zurich, Radio and TV, 296,000, *Touring* (w), Bern, Touring Club Suisse, 920,096; *Trente Jours* (m), Lausanne, 444,059.

Broadcasting: The Swiss Broadcasting Corporation comprises three broadcasting societies: the Société de Radiodiffusion et de Télévision de la Suisse Romande; The Radio- und Fernsehgesellschaft der deutschen und der rätoromanischen Schweiz; and the Società cooperitiva per la radio-televisione nella Svizzera italiana. Each of these relays a service in its own language. The Swiss Broadcasting Corporation is financed by 70% of license fees and the proceeds from commercial TV, and provides program services. There is also the Swiss Radio International, which broadcasts in several foreign languages overseas. In 1983, there were 2,082,578 TV receivers and 2,364,649 radio licenses in Switzerland.

TURKEY

Features: Only a small part of Turkey, north of the Dardanelles, lies in Europe. The greater part belongs to Asia Minor and consists of a plateau area (Anatolian Plateau), generally with elevations in excess of 2,500 ft/ 760 m., divided from the Black Sea in the north by the Pontine Mountains, which rise to over 12,000 ft/3,650 m., and from the Mediterranean Șea in the south by the Toros Mountains, which rise to a similar height. The major areas of lowland border the Dardanelles and the lower parts of the major river valleys.

The main agricultural areas are along the coastal plains, in the lower river valleys and in scattered basins in the interior. A number of minerals are worked, of which the most important are coal (Zonguldak area), copper, chromium, borax, iron ore and oil. There are no large industrial regions by general European standards, but there are a number of small ones around the main towns and in the Karabuk area where the main iron and steel industry is situated.

Area: 301,400 sq. miles/780,600 sq. km. (of which 9,150 sq. miles/23,700 sq. km. lies in Europe). *Mean max. and min. temperatures:* Ankara (40° N, 33° E; 2,820 ft/860 m.) 87°F/31°C (Aug.), 24°F/−4°C (Jan.); Istanbul (41° N, 29° E; 60 ft/18 m.) 81°F/27°C (July and Aug.), 36°F/2°C (Jan.). *Relative humidity:* Ankara 72%; Istanbul 81%. *Mean annual rainfall:* Ankara 14 in./ 355 mm.; Istanbul 32 in./815 mm.

POPULATION

Total population: (1984) 50.2 million. *Main towns and populations:* (1982) Istanbul (3,034,000), ANKARA (2,316,000), Izmir (737,000), Adana (644,000), Bursa (432,000), Gaziantep (395,000). *Distribution:* In 1982, 44% of the population lived in urban centers; 42% of this group lived in cities of over 500,000 inhabitants.

Language: The official language is Turkish. Arabic and Kurdish are spoken along the frontiers with Syria and Iraq. *Religion:* Over 98% of the population adheres to Islam.

CONSTITUTIONAL SYSTEM

Constitution: Republic. The 1961 constitution was adopted by referendum after the overthrow of the Menderes government in 1960. In 1982 a new

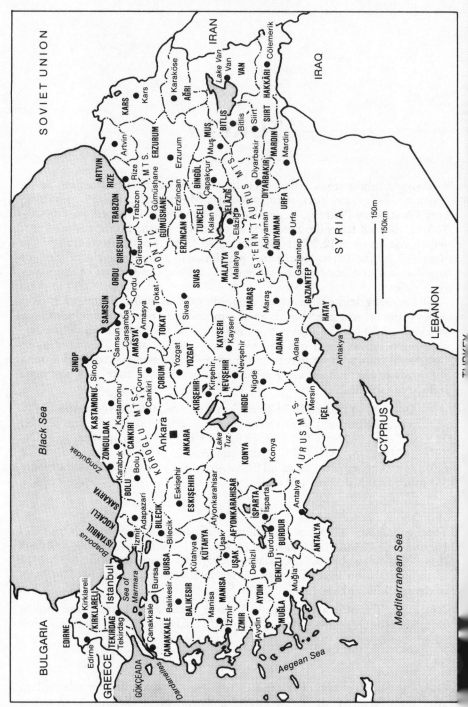

constitution was approved by referendum. *Head of state:* President Gen. Kenan Evren. *Head of government:* Prime Minister Turgut Özal.

Executive and Legislative: The 1961 constitution was suspended in 1980, following the military coup and the seizure of power by a military junta under Gen. Kenan Evren, chief of the general staff. Evren dissolved the Assembly, proclaimed martial law and set up a five-man National Security Council that designated a military–civilian cabinet under retired Adm. Bulent Ulusu.

On June 30, 1981, the National Security Council appointed a 160-member National Consultative Council, charged with drafting a new constitution. The Council produced a draft document that was approved by the electorate in a referendum in 1982. According to the new basic law:

- A unicameral 400-member Grand National Assembly was established with a five-year term.
- The president is elected by the Assembly for a nonrenewable term of seven years.
- The president is advised by a 30-member State Consultative Council, a four-member Presidential Council of senior military figures and an advisory Economic and Social Council.

Political parties: Under the terms of the new basic law, the first popular elections were held in 1983. An amendment inserted into the electoral law gave the National Security Council a veto over the candidates nominated by political parties and also the right to ban political parties that advocated divisive policies. The law also banned parliamentary representation for parties that failed to obtain at least 10% of the votes cast.

Before the polling, the National Security Council banned three of the leading parties because of their historical association with "old politics." They were the Social Democracy party, led by Erdal Inönü, son of former president Ismet Inönü; the Great Turkey party, led by Süleyman Demirel, former prime minister; and the True Path party, led by Yildrim Avci. In the event, only three parties were allowed to contest the elections, in which the Motherland party won a decisive majority with 212 seats, trailed by the Populist party with 117 seats and the military-backed Nationalist Democracy party with 71 seats. Following the elections, the National Security Council disbanded and was reconstituted as the Presidential Council. In the 1984 nationwide municipal elections, the Motherland party repeated its success by winning 41.3% of the votes. The relative percentages of the other five parties were: Social Democracy 23.4%, True Path party 13.7%, Populist party 8.8%, National Democracy party 7.1% and Independence party 1.3%.

Local government: Turkey is divided into 65 provinces (*iller*), which are subdivided into counties (*ilçe*) and communes (*bucaklar*). Each provincial governor (*vali*) is appointed by the president upon the recommendation of the minister of the interior. He appoints the officials of the province, and as chief administrative officer of the province is assisted by a staff of advisers and a provincial standing committee chosen from the provincial council, which is elected for four years and over which the governor presides.

The chief officer of the county is the *kaymakam* and of the commune the *bucak müdürü*. Each commune comprises a number of villages, each of which has a headman (*muhtar*) and a council of elders. Every provincial and county capital and town of over 2,000 inhabitants is a municipality (*belediye*) and is headed by a mayor (*belediye reisi*) assisted by an elected municipal council.

Judicial system: The lowest civil courts, the magistrates courts (*sulh hukuk*), have one judge and deal with cases concerning two parties but not the public. The civil courts of first instance (*asliye hukuk mahkemeleri*) are also single-judge courts dealing with cases that involve the public besides the two parties. The commercial courts (*ticaret mahkemeleri*) are sited in the major cities. They have a president and two assistant judges and deal with commercial cases involving larger sums; cases involving small sums are dealt with by the courts of first instance. The lowest criminal courts are the single-judge criminal peace courts (*sulh ceza mahkemeleri*). Misdemeanors are dealt with by the criminal courts of first instance (*asliye ceza mahkemeleri*), also single-judge courts. The assize courts (*ağir ceza mahkemeleri*), composed of a president and four assistant judges, have jurisdiction in all cases involving penalties of five years or more. The labor courts (*iş mahkemeleri*) deal with management-labor disputes and are composed of one judge and one representative of each of the two disputing parties. The courts of appeal (*temyiz mahkemeleri*) examine all court decisions when requested by the parties; they have several chambers, each composed of a presiding judge and several members. Members of the courts of appeal are elected by the high council of judges. Jurisdiction in military cases is exercised by the *askeri mahkemeleri*, which consist of a president and two military officers; there is a special military appeal court.

The highest administrative court is the Council of State (*Devlet Şurasi*), empowered to give its opinion upon projected legislation to the Council of Ministers. The Court of Jurisdictional Disputes (*Uyuşmazlik Mahkemesi*) gives final judgment upon jurisdictional matters between the civil, administrative and military courts. The High Council of Judges (*Yüksek Hakimler Kurulu*) of 18 regular and five alternate members is concerned with all cases relating to the character and functions of judges. The Constitutional Court (*Anayasa Mahkemesi*) has 15 members and five alternate members. It rules on the constitutionality of legislation passed by the Grand National Assembly and its judgment is final. It is also empowered to try the senior officers of the state.

The judiciary is independent of the other organs of the state. Judges serve until they are 65 unless they are incapacitated by ill-health, convicted of a crime or pronounced unsuitable to remain in office. Capital punishment is maintained.

RECENT HISTORY

Turkey was a nonbelligerent ally of Britain and France during World War II. Turkish troops fought as U.N. forces in Korea. Turkey was admitted to NATO in 1952, signed a Treaty of Alliance, Political Cooperation and Mutual Assistance with Greece and Yugoslavia in 1954, and joined Iraq,

Iran, Pakistan and Britain in the Baghdad Pact (later known as Central Treaty Organization, or CENTO) in 1955. In 1960 a military coup overthrew the government and Prime Minister Adnan Menderes and the foreign and finance ministers were executed for violations of the constitution. A new constitution was adopted in 1961 and Turkey reverted to civil government. In 1964 Turkey became an associate member of the EC.

Throughout the 1970s Turkey was beset by political, economic and social crises that its governments were helpless to overcome, and in 1980, as happened in 1960, the military stepped in and proclaimed martial law. In 1983 the military relaxed its control, at least nominally, and permitted a partial return to civilian rule. Some former political parties, however, were banned.

Renewal of strife in Cyprus in December 1963 led to Turkish aerial bombardments of Cyprus, based upon the country's rights under the Treaty of Guarantee (see CYPRUS, *Defense*). Turkey's relations with Greece have remained strained. In 1964, in accordance with its rights under the terms of the treaty, Turkey denounced the 1930 Agreement of Establishment, Commerce and Navigation, and regulated the status of Greek nationals in Turkey, on the grounds that given the Greek government's attitude over Cyprus the Agreement no longer corresponded to present circumstances. As a result, Greek nationals were expelled, but not those Greeks who were Turkish citizens.

In 1974 Turkey invaded Cyprus and occupied 35% of the island, in the north (above what is known as the Attila Line), but stopped short of annexing the territory.

Defense: The president is head of the armed forces. Military service lasts for 20 months. The army totals 470,000, the bulk of which is NATO-assigned as is most of the air force of 53,000. The navy has a total strength of 46,000. Defense expenditure in 1981 represented 6.8% of GNP at £T298 billion ($3.1 billion). American military bases are established in Turkey under NATO agreements.

ECONOMY

Background: The mainstay of the economy is agriculture, accounting for around 21% of the GDP. Crops account for about two-thirds and livestock about one-third of the farm output, with wheat and barley as the dominant cereals. The chief commercial crop is cotton, followed by opium grown under official supervision. Agricultural goods account for 60% of export earnings. Industry is largely state owned, dominated by state economic enterprises that account for 40% of industrial output and 80% of mining. Overall the industrial sector produces 31% of the GDP.

Progress toward industrialization was slow and uneven until the 1963–67 development plan, the main objectives of which were to increase the rate of industrialization, raise the proportion of investment financed by domestic savings, stabilize and improve the balance of payments situation, maintain price stability, and allow the market mechanism to play a greater role in determining prices. The plan steered the economy through a rapid growth of industry and a far greater utilization of the country's resources, including immense hydroelectric potential and considerable—largely unexploited— mineral wealth (coal, copper, manganese, chromite and antimony). In 1970–79 the annual average rate of growth at constant prices was 3.5%.

The main growth industries in recent years have been chemicals, plastics, cement, paper, rubber, metals, machinery and equipment. Other important industrial activities include food and textiles, but these have expanded at a much slower rate. The origin of GDP at factor cost in 1982 was:

Sector	Percentage
Agriculture	21
Industry	31
Services	48
GDP	100

In 1979–82 industrial production increased by 3.2%, compared with an increase of 2.5% in 1960–70. Agricultural production showed an increase of 3.2% from 1970 to 1982, compared to 2.5% during 1960–70. The main agricultural products are cereals, tobacco, hazelnuts, cotton and wool; despite the declining importance of agriculture, the government is seeking to improve it through mechanization and irrigation.

Foreign trade: Historically, Turkey's foreign trade has been small because official policy favored import substitution, and protective tariffs were erected to exclude foreign goods from the domestic market. The periodic balance-of-payment crises of recent years have forced a reversal of this policy. Since 1980 economy policy has aimed at promoting exports through tax benefits and low interest rates for exporters as well as restricting domestic demand. Since May 1981 the Central Bank has made daily quotations of exchange rates of the lira against other currencies. An export credit guarantee scheme has also been implemented for the first time in Turkish trading history. The results have been an encouraging spurt in exports, up to 45%. The strongest export potential is in agricultural products, especially to the Arab oil-producing states.

An important positive element in the balance of payments is remittances from Turkish workers in northwest Europe, which amounted to $1.6 billion in 1980. These remittances, however, are sensitive to employment levels in Western European countries and are subject to wide fluctuations.

Turkey is an associate member of the EC; full membership is tentatively envisaged for 1995. Meanwhile Turkey is committed to gradual tariff reductions on EC goods and will, in return, receive unrestricted access to EC markets in industrial goods. Some Turkish agricultural products also receive preferential access.

In 1982, merchandise exports amounted to $5.685 billion and merchandise imports to $8.812 billion, leaving a large trade deficit of $3.127 billion. During 1970–82 the annual average growth rate was 4.0% for exports and 2.0% for imports. The percentage share of merchandise exports was 7% for fuels, minerals and metals; 56% for other primary commodities; 19% for textiles and clothing; 4% for machinery and transport equipment; and 14% for other manufactures. The percentage share of merchandise imports was 3%

for food, 44% for fuels, 6% for other primary commodities, 22% for machinery and transport equipment, and 25% for other manufactures. Turkey's principal export partners are West Germany (21%), Italy (8%), France (6%), Soviet Union (6%) and Iraq (5%). The principal import partners are West Germany (11%), Iraq (15%), United States (6%), France (5%), Switzerland (5%) and Romania (5%).

Employment: In 1982 the total labor force was 18.6 million, of whom 54% were employed in agriculture, 13% in industry and 33% in services.

Turkey has one of the highest unemployment rates of middle-income countries: it reached 15% in 1979. In the 1960s and early 1970s, Turkish workers were among the country's primary exports, reaching a peak outflow in 1973, when more than 130,000 emigrated. At the end of 1977 it was estimated that more than 845,000 were abroad, the greatest number in West Germany, where Turkish neighborhoods could be found in every large city. As a result, Turkey had few serious problems with labor restiveness. The military junta that seized power in 1980 rendered labor even more powerless by outlawing strikes, banning trade unions, confiscating union funds, arresting labor leaders and doing away with collective bargaining. A 1981 labor code provided for wage increases but at a rate less than cost-of-living increases.

Consumption: Private consumption in 1982 accounted for 73% of GNP and public consumption for 11%.

SOCIAL SECURITY

Health insurance: Under the general supervision of the Ministry of Social Security, the scheme covers employees in industry and commerce. Pensioners and dependents are also covered for medical benefits. Agricultural employees are not covered. There is a special system for public employees. The insurance is financed by the insured person and the employer. Sickness benefits are 50% of earnings, or 66⅔% if the insured has one or more dependents. There are maternity benefits and a lump-sum nursing grant of £T1,000. Medical benefits cover medical services, which are ordinarily provided directly to patients through facilities of the Social Insurance Institution. Medical benefits for dependents are the same as for the insured person, except that the dependent must pay £T20 for each medical examination.

Accident insurance: Under the general supervision of the Ministry of Social Security, the scheme covers employees in industry and commerce. Agricultural and domestic employees are not covered. There is a special system for public employees. The insurance is financed by the employer. Temporary disability benefit (work injury) is 50% of earnings, or 66⅔% if the insured has one or more dependents. Permanent disability pension (work injury) is 70% of earnings during the last five years, if the insured is totally disabled. Minimum pension is £T16,424 a month. Constant-attendance supplements are available. Partial disability pension (work injury) is a percentage of the full pension proportionate to the degree of disability, if the insured person is more than 10% disabled. There are medical benefits under the program. Survivor pensions (work injury) are available for widows, dependent disabled widowers, orphans and parents. Maximum survivor pensions are 70% of earnings of the insured.

Pensions insurance: Under the general supervision of the Ministry of Social Security, the scheme covers employees in industry and commerce. Agricultural employees are not covered. There are special systems for public employees and the self-employed. The insurance is financed by the insured person and the employer. Old-age pensions are available generally at age 55 for men and age 50 for women. Disability pensions are available to insured persons who have lost two-thirds of working capacity. Old-age pensions are 60% of the average earnings during the last five years of employment. Minimum pension is £T16,424 a month; maximum, £T26,420 a month. Disability pension are 70% of average earnings during the last five years. Constant-attendance supplements are available. The minimum pension is £T16,424 a month. Survivor pensions are payable to widows, dependent disabled widowers, orphans and parents. Maximum survivor pensions are 100% of the pension of the insured.

Unemployment insurance: Under the labor code, employers are required to pay dismissal indemnities of 30 days' wages per year of service.

EDUCATION

Even though the number of schools and teachers has increased tenfold and the number of pupils by thirtyfold in the period 1923–61, Turkey's problem remains a quantitative and qualitative shortage of both schools and teachers. The national budget cannot provide the necessary additional resources; education already has second priority to defense in budget expenditure. The result is that a considerable proportion of children go without primary—and even more without postprimary—education. Although the literate population has quadrupled since 1927, Turkey still has the highest illiteracy rate in Europe—31.2% in 1980. All schools, including private schools, are under the Ministry of Education. State schools are free.

Primary education: This is compulsory for all children for five years, to be taken between the ages of six and 14. The course is divided into lower and upper cycles and ends with a certificate of primary studies.

Secondary and vocational education: Secondary education is divided into two stages: the three-year middle school and the lycée, to which there is an entrance examination. Lycée courses last for three or four years and success in the final diploma is the means of entry into the universities. Parallel to these schools are technical and commercial schools and girls' institutes offering three- to six-year courses in agriculture, engineering, building, commerce, domestic science, etc. In recent years there has been an increased emphasis on vocational education.

Universities and higher education: There are 22 universities in Turkey. Most follow German or French models, and have separate, autonomous faculties. All are financed by the state, but are constitutionally guaranteed academic and administrative autonomy. University education is free. There are, in addition, 13 institutes of advanced professional education, including the State Conservatory in Ankara, the Academy of Fine Arts in Istanbul, schools of commerce and economics in Izmir, Istanbul and Ankara, and a mining school in Zonguldak. University courses last at least four years (six years for medicine and engineering). Grants covering lodging expenses are paid mainly to students from outlying areas. Students receiving training overseas must contract to spend a number of years on their return with the government department that financed their course.

Educational institutions, 1981–82:

	Institutions	Teachers	Students
Primary	45,871	210,599	5,864,000
Secondary:			
General	5,423	80,618	1,781,000
Technical and vocational	1,900	36,327	531,000
Higher (incl. academies, teacher training and other higher technical and vocational schools, and universities)	334	22,223	241,000

Source: Türkiye İş Bankasi AS, Economic Research Dept., Ankara.

Adult education: Besides evening trade schools for adults with little primary education, there are two important forms of adult education. The people's houses (*halkevleri*), established throughout the country, provide libraries and are concerned mainly with language and literature, fine arts, drama and history. The village institutes (*köy enstitüleri*) teach with regard to the needs of the area. Children with primary education are given general and vocational education in order to make them village schoolteachers.

MASS MEDIA

The press (1983):

Dailies: Hürriyet, Istanbul, independent, 767,000; *Tercüman*, Istanbul, right-wing, 225,000; *Milliyet*, Istanbul, ind., 210,000; *Cumhuriyet*, Istanbul, left-wing, 240,675; *Son Havadis*, Istanbul, 10,000; *Günaydin*, Istanbul, 300,000; *Günes*, Istanbul, 290,000; *Yeni Asir*, Izmir, 110,000.

Periodicals: Girgir (w), Istanbul, satirical, 500,000; *Merhaba* (w), Izmir, 90,000; *Near East Briefing* (quarterly), Ankara, international business; *Türkiye Turing ve Otomobil Kurumu Beleteni* (quarterly), Istanbul, Touring and Automobile Club of Turkey.

Broadcasting: The Turkish Radio and Television Institute (Türkiye Radyo ve TV Kurumu) is an autonomous public corporation that controls all radio and TV services. Its seven-man board of governors is composed of representatives of the Institute itself, prominent cultural institutions, the universities, the minister of finance and the minister of tourism and information. The director-general of the Institute is nominated by the board of governors and must be approved by the president of the Republic, the prime minister and the minister of tourism and information. The Institute has an independent budget financed by license fees and is free to obtain foreign investment. In 1983, there were approximately 3,610,000 licensed TV receivers and 4,300,000 licensed radio receivers in use in Turkey.

UNITED KINGDOM OF GREAT BRITAIN AND NORTHERN IRELAND

GEOGRAPHY

Features: The principal lowland areas of England are the Lower Thames Basin in which London stands, the Severn Valley, the Somerset Levels, the Hampshire Basin, the Vale of York, the Fens and the area stretching from the Cheshire Plain to southwest Lancashire.

The main upland mass is the Pennine Ridge, which extends from the Cheviot Hills and Tyne Valley in the north to the Derbyshire Dome north of Derby, in the south. This region consists chiefly of millstone grit and carboniferous limestone with an overlay of glacial clay in the north; it often reaches 2,300 ft/700 m. In the northwest is the Lake District, maximum height being 3,210 ft/980 m. at Scafell. East of the Pennines lie the North Yorkshire Moors, a Jurassic upland rising to over 1,400 ft/430 m. South of the Moors are the chalk Yorkshire Wolds reaching to Lincolnshire.

South of the Pennines lie the Midlands, an area of undulating plateau with minor hill ridges. South of the Avon Valley are the Cotswold Hills (Jurassic), south and east of which lie the main chalk hill areas of England—Salisbury Plain, Chiltern Hills and North Downs and South Downs bordering, respectively, the London Basin and the Weald. Devon and Cornwall contain a number of upland areas, such as sandstone Exmoor and granitic Dartmoor and Bodmin Moor.

Scotland may be divided into three regions. In the north are the Highlands, with fjord indentations and narrow raised beaches in the west, and wider lowland areas in the east; there are a number of peaks over 4,000 ft/1,200 m. The Great Glen fault, followed by the Caledonian Canal, bisects the Highlands. To the south lie the Central Lowlands, mainly below 1,000 ft/300 m., but containing volcanic-cored uplands, e.g., Ochil and the Sidlaw Hills. This area is drained by the two principal Scottish rivers, the Forth and the Clyde. Further south still are the Southern Uplands, sometimes reaching 2,500 ft/760 m. Streams such as the Nith and Annan provide routeways from the Lowlands to England.

Wales is composed largely of land over 1,000 ft/300 m., the chief lowland areas being Anglesey, the Vale of Glamorgan and southwestern Dyfed. The southern coalfield with its narrow, deeply incised valleys and intervening

213

SHETLAND IS.
9

ORKNEY IS.
8

North Sea

80 m
80 km

OUTER HEBRIDES
LEWIS
12

SKYE
INNER HEBRIDES

6
Inverness
5
Aberdeen

SCOTLAND

MULL

Atlantic Ocean

11 Dundee
Perth
4
Glasgow
Edinburgh
10
7
1

ISLAY

32
Newcastle
Carlisle
42
13
Middlesbrough
7

North Channel

3

9

ENGLAND
33

York
Bradford
Hull
26
Leeds
22
46
Manchester
Sheffield
29 18
38
Liverpool
10
Lincoln
Stoke-on-Trent
Derby
34
28
Nottingham
Norwich
30
39
27
Leicester
36
Coventry
5
Birmingham
44
43
Cambridge
Ipswich
40
20
31
35
Colchester
15
16 Oxford
4
21
London
17
Bristol
3
41
25
47
19
37 Southampton
Portsmouth
Brighton
45
14

Londonderry 19
26
25
14
15
NORTHERN IRELAND

Belfast

17
10
22
5
4
16
20
11 23 18
1
7 24
12
12 18 9 2
3 6 13
21

ISLE OF MAN

Irish Sea

IRELAND

St. George's Channel

Cardigan Bay

WALES

Swansea
Cardiff
8
7
5
3
2
6
1

Bristol Channel

Exeter
11
Plymouth
8
12
ISLE OF WIGHT
23

English Channel

ISLES OF SCILLY
24

CHANNEL IS.
GUERNSEY
JERSEY

Strait of Dover

The Wash

FRANCE

GREAT BRITAIN

214

COUNTIES OF ENGLAND
1. AVON
2. BEDFORDSHIRE
3. BERKSHIRE
4. BUCKINGHAMSHIRE
5. CAMBRIDGESHIRE
6. CHESHIRE
7. CLEVELAND
8. CORNWALL
9. CUMBRIA
10. DERBYSHIRE
11. DEVON
12. DORSET
13. DURHAM
14. EAST SUSSEX
15. ESSEX
16. GLOUCESTERSHIRE
17. GREATER LONDON
18. GREATER MANCHESTER
19. HAMPSHIRE
20. HEREFORD AND WORCESTER
21. HERTFORDSHIRE
22. HUMBERSIDE
23. ISLE OF WIGHT
24. ISLES OF SCILLY
25. KENT
26. LANCASHIRE
27. LEICESTERSHIRE
28. LINCOLNSHIRE
29. MERSEYSIDE
30. NORFOLK
31. NORTHAMPTONSHIRE
32. NORTHUMBERLAND
33. NORTH YORKSHIRE

34. NOTTINGHAMSHIRE
35. OXFORDSHIRE
36. SALOP
37. SOMERSET
38. SOUTH YORKSHIRE
39. STAFFORDSHIRE
40. SUFFOLK
41. SURREY
42. TYNE AND WEAR
43. WARWICKSHIRE
44. WEST MIDLANDS
45. WEST SUSSEX
46. WEST YORKSHIRE
47. WILTSHIRE

DISTRICTS OF NORTHERN IRELAND
1. ANTRIM
2. ARDS
3. ARMAGH
4. BALLYMENA
5. BALLYMONEY
6. BAINBRIDGE
7. BELFAST
8. CARRICKFERGUS
9. CASTLEREAGH
10. COLERAINE
11. COOKSTOWN
12. CRAIGAVON
13. DOWN
14. DUNGANNON
15. FERMANAGH
16. LARNE
17. LIMAVADY
18. LISBURN

19. LONDONDERRY
20. MAGHERAFELT
21. MOURNE
22. MOYLE
23. NEWTOWNABBEY
24. NORTH DOWN
25. OMAGH
26. STRABANE

REGIONS OF SCOTLAND
1. BORDERS
2. CENTRAL
3. DUMFRIES AND GALLOWAY
4. FIFE
5. GRAMPIAN
6. HIGHLAND
7. LOTHIAN
8. ORKNEY ISLANDS
9. SHETLAND ISLANDS
10. STRATHCLYDE
11. TAYSIDE
12. WESTERN ISLES

COUNTIES OF WALES
1. CLWYD
2. DYFED
3. GWENT
4. GWYNEDD
5. MID GLAMORGAN
6. POWYS
7. SOUTH GLAMORGAN
8. WEST GLAMORGAN

plateau contrasts with Snowdonia in the north, with its peaks rising to over 3,000 ft/900 m.

Northern Ireland consists of a central core of lowland around Lough Neagh and extending to the coast south of Belfast, and surrounding hill areas—the Antrim Mountains rising to over 1,500 ft/450 m., the Mournes, 2,500 ft/760 m. and the Sperrins, 2,200 ft/670 m.

The chief arable areas of England are the Vale of York, East Anglia and Lincolnshire, parts of the southwest, the Cotswolds, the south and southeast and the East Midlands. Devon and Cornwall specialize in market-gardening and dairying. In Scotland, the East Central Lowlands and parts of the east coast are the chief arable areas. In Wales, livestock upland farming is characteristic except in the extreme south.

Minerals are found throughout the United Kingdom. In Northern Ireland Europe's largest deposits of lignite (low-grade, "brown" coal) were discovered in 1984. Chief local coal deposits are in Nottinghamshire, Yorkshire and Derbyshire, while there are important coalfields in the Scottish Lowlands and Lancashire and smaller ones in the Midlands, Somerset and Kent. Chief iron ore deposits are in the Jurassic belt stretching from Oxfordshire to Lincolnshire. There are important kaolin deposits in Cornwall, but the country has little nonferrous metal ore. Natural gas has been found in northeast Yorkshire and off the east coast. Considerable deposits of oil and gas have been exploited in the North Sea. Scotland possesses a number of potential hydroelectric sites.

The main industrial centers of the United Kindom are the Newcastle–Middlesbrough region, west Yorkshire and the Don Valley, southeast Lancashire, Birmingham, the Nottingham–Derby–Leicester area, London and lower Thames-side, the Central Scottish Lowlands around Glasgow, the Belfast area, and the South Wales coalfields.

Area: The total area of the United Kingdom is 94,214 sq. miles/244,956 sq. km.: England 50,327 sq. miles/130,850 sq. km., Wales 8,017 sq. miles/ 20,844 sq. km., Scotland 30,411 sq. miles/79,069 sq. km., Northern Ireland 5,459 sq. miles/14,193 sq. km., Isle of Man 227 sq. miles/690 sq. km. and Channel Islands 75 sq. miles/195 sq. km. Colonies and Protectorates: Ascension, Bermuda, British Antarctic Territory, British Indian Ocean Territory, Cayman Islands, Falkland Islands and Dependencies, Gibraltar, Hong Kong, Montserrat, Pitcairn Island, St. Helena, Tristan da Cunha, Turks and Caicos Islands, Virgin Islands. (See under *Recent History* for the independent states constituting the Commonwealth.)

Mean max. and min. temperatures: London (51° 30′ N, 0° W; 150 ft/46 m.) 73°F/23°C (July), 35°F/2°C (Jan. and Feb.); Edinburgh (56° N, 3° W; 440 ft/ 134 m.) 65°F/18°C, 35°F/2°C; Cardiff (51° 30′ N, 3° W; 200 ft/60 m.) 69°F/21°C, 36°F/2°C. *Relative humidity:* London 78%; Edinburgh 89%; Cardiff 81%. *Mean annual rainfall:* London 23in./585 mm.; Edinburgh 28 in./710 mm.; Cardiff 42 in./1,065 mm.

POPULATION

Population: (1984 est.) The United Kingdom 55,776,422, England 46,362,836, Wales 2,791,851, Scotland 5,130,735, Northern Ireland 1,491,000, Isle of Man 64,679, Channel Islands 133,000. *Chief towns and populations:* Greater LONDON (6,849,100), Birmingham (1,030,300), Glasgow (781,694), Leeds (724,200). Sheffield (543,700), Liverpool (513,500), Manchester (474,100), Bradford (462,500), Edinburgh (452,806), Bristol (405,500), Coventry (313,815), Cardiff (273,525), Belfast (297,983), Nottingham (278,600), Leicester (276,600), Newcastle-upon-Tyne (287,300), Stoke-on-Trent (257,200). *Distribution:* In 1982, 91% of the population of Great Britain lived in urban centers; of this group 55% lived in cities of over 500,000 inhabitants.

Language: English is the predominant language. In northern, central and southwest Wales, Welsh is spoken with ease by the majority of the population. The Scottish form of Gaelic is spoken in parts of northwest Scotland and the Irish form by a minority in Northern Ireland. Manx and Cornish are dead languages. In the Channel Islands a Norman-French patois is spoken in addition to English; French is still the official language of Jersey. *Religion:* The religion of most of the people is the Established Church, the (Anglican) Church of England. There are also unestablished Anglican churches in Wales, Scotland and Ireland. The established Presbyterian church of Scotland has about 2.5 million members. The "free churches" are the Methodists and Congregationalists (2,300,000), Baptists (700,000) and Unaffiliated Pentecostals (500,000). In addition, there are over 4.1 million Roman Catholics (about 500,000 in Northern Ireland), about 500,000 Jews, 830,000 Muslims and numerous minority religions.

CONSTITUTIONAL SYSTEM

Constitution: Great Britain is a constitutional monarchy. The constitution is a mixture of statutes, common law and conventions. *Head of state:* Queen Elizabeth II. *Head of government:* Prime Minister Margaret Thatcher (Conservative).

Executive: The sovereign is head of the executive in law; in fact, she acts on the advice of her ministers. She appoints the prime minister and other ministers on his or her recommendation. She summons and prorogues Parliament, and dissolves it on the prime minister's advice. She must give the Royal Assent to any legislation that has passed both Houses of Parliament before it can become law. These and other acts involve the use of the Royal Prerogative with its consequent ministerial responsibility. The sovereign is titular head of the Commonwealth, the armed forces and the judiciary.

Ministers are individually and collectively responsible to Parliament, even though some ministers sit in the House of Lords, in which case they are represented in the House of Commons by parliamentary secretaries. The prime minister is the head of the government and personally selects the ministers of the cabinet, which has supreme control over the national executive and which finally determines the policy to be submitted to Parliament and coordinates and delimits the powers of the various governmental departments. The Privy Council is composed of over 300 members appointed for life, cabinet ministers being automatically members, and the remainder being senior judges and persons of eminence in public affairs in both Britain and the Commonwealth, appointed by the sovereign on the prime minister's recommendation. The Privy Council is responsible for submitting Orders in Council for the sovereign's approval. Such orders are of two types—those made by Royal Prerogative and those authorized by parliamentary act as a form of delegated legislation; ultimate responsibility for them rests with the minister in whose department they originated.

Legislature: Parliament is bicameral. The House of Commons of 650 members (elected for England, Wales, Scotland and Northern Ireland) is elected for five years by the single-member constituency simple majority system. The House of Lords has over 1,000 members. The Lords Temporal are: hereditary peers and peeresses who have not disclaimed their titles under the 1963 Peerage Act; the several Lords of Appeal in Ordinary appointed to assist the House in its judicial function; and several hundred life peers and peeresses appointed by the crown under the 1958 Life Peerages Act. The Lords Spiritual are the archbishops of Canterbury and York, the bishops of London, Durham and Winchester, and 21 other Anglican bishops in rotation. Legislation may originate in either House, except in the case of legislation relating to financial matters, which must originate in the House of Commons. The House of Lords has no powers of revision or delay with respect to money bills, nor can it delay any other bill longer than one year. The first British ombudsman (parliamentary commissioner) was appointed in 1966, his function being to deal with complaints against the central government.

217

Northern Ireland: The 1920 Government of Ireland Act clearly distinguishes between the respective area of legislative power of the Northern Ireland and British parliaments (to which latter Northern Ireland sends 17 members). The legislative powers of the Northern Ireland parliament included law and order, local government, education, transport, agriculture, health and social welfare, and industrial development. Foreign policy, defense, customs and excise, among other matters, were reserved to Westminster.

In 1974 the Northern Ireland Act made the Secretary of State for Northern Ireland and the Northern Ireland ministers responsible to Westminster for the government of Northern Ireland. A 78-member Northern Ireland Assembly was elected in 1982. Besides the Secretary of State for Northern Ireland (who is responsible for constitutional and political affairs, security matters and operations, and other important policy issues), there are a Minister of State and a deputy to the Secretary of State (who is responsible for economic and agricultural questions) and several parliamentary under-secretaries of state (who are responsible for, among other things, education and law and order matters).

Administratively autonomous Crown Dependencies (Isle of Man and Channel Islands)

Isle of Man: The Isle of Man is governed by its own laws; it is not bound by acts of parliament unless specifically mentioned in them. The administrative body (Tynwald) is composed of the House of Keys (24 members elected for five years) and the Legislative Council composed of the lieutenant-governor of the island—appointed by the crown—the lord bishop of Soder and Man, two deemsters, the attorney-general, two members appointed by the governor and four by the House of Keys. An Executive Council of five members of the House and two of the Legislative Council, to act with the governor, was set up in 1961.

Jersey: The Lieutenant-Governor and Commander-in-Chief of Jersey is appointed by the crown as its personal representative and channel of communication. He or she may sit and speak in the Assembly of the States but not vote and has certain powers of veto over legislation. The States consist of 12 senators elected for six years, 12 constables and 28 deputies elected for three years. The bailiff, appointed by the crown, is president of the States and the Royal Court of Jersey. The dean of Jersey and the attorney- and solicitor-general may also sit and speak in the States, but not vote. Permanent laws (*projets de loi*) require the sanction of the sovereign in Council. The government is composed of committees appointed by the States.

Guernsey: The main point of difference from Jersey is in the composition of the legislature, the States of Deliberation. It is composed of the bailiff, 12 conseillers elected by the States of Election for six years, the attorney-general and solicitor-general, 33 people's deputies elected by direct vote, 10 elected representatives of the parochial douzaines and two representatives of the Isle of Alderney elected by the States of Alderney.

Political parties: The British electoral system tends to promote the two-party system. The present beneficiaries are the Labour party and the Conservative party. The Liberal party and the Social Democratic party have joined forces in an alliance.

In 1980, following the election of Michael Foot as party leader, a number of prominent Labour leaders, including Roy Jenkins, David Owen and Shirley Williams, left the party to form the Social Democratic party (SDP) and to continue the work of the Council for Social Democracy founded earlier by moderate socialists. In 1982 Jenkins defeated Owen for the party leadership, but stepped down in 1983 in favor of the latter. The Social Democratic party contested the 1983 elections as an ally of the Liberal party, but has resisted Liberal moves for a formal merger.

The Labour party itself, riven by internal dissension, has lost much of its national following in recent years. Michael Foot stepped down after the party's disastrous performance in the general election of 1983; in the ensuing leadership contest, the somewhat more moderate Neil Kinnock and Roy Hattersley were elected leader and deputy leader respectively. The party's hard-core left-wing, led by Tony Benn, suffered severe reverses both in party and national elections.

Under Margaret Thatcher, prime minister since 1979, the Conservative party has reaffirmed its dominance of British politics. Following the party's reelection victory in 1983, a rift developed between the moderates (called "wets") and those supporting Thatcher's stringent monetary and economic policies. Among the casualties of this rift were Francis Pym, foreign secretary, and William Whitelaw, home secretary.

Although the four parties—Conservative, Labour, Liberal and Social Democratic—dominate the political stage, a number of others manage to survive in the wings. These include the Ulster Unionists, Scottish National party, Welsh National party, Social Democratic and Labour party (representing Catholic interests in Northern Ireland), Scottish Labour party, National Front (heir of the interwar British Union of Fascists), National party (a splinter group of the National Front), Green party, Communist party and the (Trotskyite) Socialist Workers' party.

The party lineup in the House of Commons following the 1983 elections was as follows:

Conservative	397
Labour	209
Liberal/Social Democratic alliance	23
Ulster Unionists	11
Others	10
Total	650

The House of Lords has a Conservative majority through the hereditary peers, but in practice there is a balance between the two parties because only a minority of the hereditary peers usually attends.

Local government: The main units of local government are the counties and the county boroughs (mostly with populations of over 75,000 and separate from the counties). The counties are divided into boroughs, urban and rural districts—and the latter again into parishes. Each unit elects a council for three years by the same method as in national elections, some retiring completely at the end of the period and others electing one-third each year. The council in turn elects a chairman, and in some cases also aldermen. In England and Wales and in Northern Ireland, the chairman of most boroughs is the mayor—in the City of London and certain other important boroughs the lord mayor; in Scottish counties the convenor and in Scottish burghs the provost or lord provost. The Greater London Council and the councils of 32 London boroughs and the City of London administer the Greater London area. There are in England and Wales, in addition, 54 county councils. In Scotland there are 12 regional councils, and in Northern Ireland 26 district councils.

The powers of local authorities are defined by parliamentary act; while they maintain much independence—in the determination of their budget, freedom from ministerial inquiry, etc.—ministers have defined rights of oversight regarding certain services. Local government finance is provided about 40% by state grants, about 40% by local taxes, and the remainder from municipal rents and invested funds. The reorganization of local government is a policy of the Thatcher government.

Judicial system: The system in England and Wales differs from that in Scotland, while that in Northern Ireland is almost identical with the former. There is a clear distinction between civil and criminal law.

England and Wales. Criminal courts: The lowest criminal courts are the magistrates' courts or petty sessions. They are presided over by from two to seven unpaid laymen who obtain advice on points of law from the clerk of the court. In London and some other large cities, these courts are presided over by professional salaried lawyers (stipendiary or metropolitan magistrates) sitting alone. Magistrates' courts try all nonindictable and some less serious indictable offenses.[1] They give preliminary hearings in criminal cases and decide whether to commit the accused to quarter sessions or assizes. Appeal against conviction or sentence is generally to quarter sessions. Specially qualified magistrates sit in juvenile courts in cases involving persons under 17.

All counties and boroughs have courts of quarter sessions sitting at least four times a year. In counties, they are presided over by a bench of lay magistrates with a professional chairman sitting with a jury of 12, with unanimity necessary for conviction. In the boroughs, a recorder sits alone with jury. Quarter sessions have jurisdiction over the less serious indictable offenses, excluding among others those carrying the sentence of life imprisonment. Courts of assize are branches of the High Court presided over by a High Court judge sitting with jury and with jurisdiction over the most serious indictable offences. Assizes are generally held in county towns and certain other large towns and cities three to five times a year. Other assize courts are the Central Criminal Court (Old Bailey) in London and the crown courts of Manchester and Liverpool. The judges also deal with civil cases

---

[1] An "indictable offense" is a crime or misdemeanor.

after the criminal cases have been heard, and hear appeals on points of law from the magistrates' courts.

Appeal from quarter sessions and assizes is to the Criminal Division of the Court of Appeal, constituted by three to five judges of the Queen's Bench Division, with the Lord Chief Justice generally presiding. Final appeal is to the House of Lords; the qualified peers are the Lord Chancellor, any former Lord Chancellors, retired judges who are peers and the nine Lords of Appeal in Ordinary (see *Legislature*).

There is no capital punishment in England, Wales or Scotland. Northern Ireland retains capital punishment for certain forms of murder. A move to restore the death penalty was decisively defeated after the 1983 election.

Civil courts: The lowest courts are the county courts—of which there are about 400—presided over by a professional judge. More important cases go to the High Court of Justice, which is composed of three divisions and staffed by puisne judges (i.e., judges without any other special office), known as justices of the High Court. The Lord Chancellor is president of the whole High Court, although in practice he does not sit in any of its three divisions: Chancery—bankruptcy, patents, trust enforcement, wardship and adoption, etc.—nominally headed by the Lord Chancellor; Queen's Bench—breach of contract, actions for damages and tort—presided over by the Lord Chief Justice; Probate, Divorce and Admiralty—probate of wills, and matrimonial and shipping cases—headed by its president. In original jurisdiction judges sit alone; in appeal cases—from magistrates' courts, ministerial decisions and decisions of a judge sitting in chambers (i.e., decisions reached during proceedings that do not have to be heard in court)—a court is constituted by one to three judges of the division. Appeals from county and high courts and civil cases heard in assizes come before the Civil Division of the Court of Appeal. This is headed by the Master of the Rolls and its members are the Lord Chancellor, Lord Chief Justice, the president of the Probate, Divorce and Admiralty Division, the lords of appeal in ordinary and the lord justices of appeal. It sits in four divisions, each of three judges. Final appeal is to the House of Lords sitting as a court of three, five or seven. The Court of Appeal and the High Court of Justice together make up the Supreme Court of Judicature.

Other courts: Coroners' courts investigate violent, sudden or suspicious death. The Criminal Injuries Compensation Board compensates victims of crimes of violence. Courts martial have jurisdiction over serving members of the armed forces; appeal is to the Court Martial Appeals Court and in some cases to the House of Lords. The Judicial Committee of the Privy Council is the final court of appeal from the courts of British dependencies and certain Commonwealth members.

Judicial appointments: There is no minister of justice. The queen is the titular head of the judiciary, but the latter is entirely free from government control. The sovereign—on the prime minister's recommendation—appoints the Lord Chief Justice, the lord justices of appeal, the President of the Probate, Divorce and Admiralty Division, the Master of the Rolls and the lords of appeal in ordinary. Puisne judges, county court judges, chairmen of quarter sessions, recorders, and metropolitan and stipendiary magistrates are mostly appointed by the sovereign on the Lord Chancellor's recommendation. Justices of the peace (JPs) are appointed by the Lord Chancellor—advised by the lord lieutenants of the counties—on the sovereign's behalf. Judges hold office until the statutory retirement age of 75; inferior-court judges may be removed by the Lord Chancellor for misconduct or incapacity; judges of the Court of Session and High Court of Justice may be removed by the crown for misbehavior, or—again for misbehavior—by the sovereign on address of both Houses of Parliament.

Scotland: The lowest criminal courts are the burgh or police courts and the courts of justices of the peace. More serious cases are heard by the sheriff courts, presided over by the sheriff-principal or a sheriff-substitute, sitting in the most serious cases with jury. The highest criminal court is the High Court of Justiciary, composed of the Lord Justice General, the Lord Justice Clerk and the lords commissioner of justiciary. Cases are heard by one of these sitting with jury. Appeals in all cases are to the High Court of Justiciary and are heard by three or more judges. There is no further appeal to the House of Lords. The lowest civil courts are the sheriff courts, which have virtually unlimited jurisdiction. The Court of Session (with the same membership as the High Court) has universal jurisdiction and has two parts— the Outer House, acting as a court of first instance, and the Inner House (of two divisions of four judges each), functioning as an appeal court. Further appeal may lie with the House of Lords. The Scottish Land Court, whose chairman has rank equivalent to a judge of the Court of Session, deals with certain agricultural matters. The Lord Justice General and Lord Justice Clerk are appointed by the crown on the recommendation of the prime minister, and all other judges are appointed on the recommendation of the Secretary of State for Scotland, who is also responsible for the appointment and removal of magistrates and may (subject to annulment by either House of Parliament) remove a sheriff-principal upon report of the Lord Justice General and Lord Justice Clerk.

RECENT HISTORY

Britain's postwar history has been characterized by a withdrawal from its imperial past, an emphasis on collective security, a supposedly "special relationship" with the United States and an absence—until the 1970s—from integrated arrangements for Western European unity. In 1947 Britain signed the Treaty of Dunkirk with France, providing for mutual defense against any future attack by Germany; this arrangement was expanded in 1948 to become the Brussels Treaty by including the Benelux countries. In 1949 Britain became a founder-member of NATO. British forces fought in Korea under U.N. auspices from 1950 to 1953. After the breakdown of the proposed European Defense Community, Foreign Minister Anthony Eden played a leading role in converting the Brussels Treaty into the Western European Union (WEU) Treaty to permit German entry into NATO, and committed British forces to the Continent (BAOR). In 1954 Britain formed the South-

East Asia Treaty Organization (SEATO), together with the United States, France, the Philippines, Thailand, Pakistan, Australia and New Zealand; and in 1955 the Baghdad Pact (later the Central Treaty Organization, or CENTO), together with Turkey, Iraq, Iran and Pakistan and with the backing of the United States. The aim of both these organizations was containment of the communist world. Britain exploded its first hydrogen bomb in 1955, and negotiated a nuclear test-ban treaty with the United States and the Soviet Union in 1963; it is a member of the United Nation's 18-nation Disarmament Committee.

British forces were engaged in Malaya against communist guerrillas from the end of World War II until 1954, against indigenous terrorism in Kenya and Cyprus in the 1950s, and against Egypt in the invasion of the Suez Canal zone, following Egyptian nationalization of the canal in 1956. British forces were committed in Malaysia against Indonesian "confrontation" in 1963–66 and in Cyprus in the U.N. force in 1964.

Britain refused to join the ECSC on its formation, but was an original member of GATT, the OECD and the Council of Europe. In 1958–59, under Harold Macmillan, Britain was a prime mover in the formation of EFTA, and in 1961 began negotiations for membership of the EC, which ended unsuccessfully in January 1963 through the imposition of a French veto. British leaders renewed their efforts to obtain EC membership in 1970; a bill sanctioning entry was approved by the House of Commons in 1971 and Britain was formally admitted to the Community on January 1, 1973.

In 1947 Britain granted independence to India, separating the state into India and Pakistan. In 1948 Britain terminated its mandatory responsibilities in Palestine (out of which Israel emerged), and Ceylon and Burma became independent. In 1957 Britain granted independence to the first of its African colonies, Ghana (former Gold Coast); since then all of the other larger colonies have also become independent. In 1961 South Africa left the Commonwealth because of disagreement over its racial policies. A unilateral declaration of independence by the government of Rhodesia in November 1965 was met by the imposition of economic sanctions by the British government and by most other countries at the latter's behest. At the end of 1982 the Commonwealth consisted of the following countries:

Australia	Ghana	Malta	Sri Lanka
Bahamas	Grenada	Mauritius	Swaziland
Bangladesh	Guyana	New Zealand	Tanzania
Barbados	India	Nigeria	Tonga
Botswana	Jamaica	Papua New Guinea	Trinidad and Tobago
Canada	Kenya	St. Lucia	Uganda
Cyprus	Kiribati	Seychelles	United Kingdom
Dominica	Lesotho	Sierra Leone	Western Samoa
Fiji	Malawi	Singapore	Zambia
Gambia	Malaysia	Solomon Islands	

In 1979, a seven-year crisis over the Unilateral Declaration of Independence by the white minority in Rhodesia was resolved through British mediation. Under a new constitution agreed to by all concerned parties, the country achieved independence under black majority rule as Zimbabwe, in 1980. In 1981 British Honduras was granted independence as Belize. In 1984 the British signed a new agreement with the People's Republic of China on the return of the colony of Hong Kong to China in 1999.

The Falkland Islands, a bone of contention between Great Britain and Argentina for over a century, were the scene of a war between the two countries in 1982. On April 2 Argentina mounted an invasion of the islands, quickly overcoming the resistance of a small group of British marines. Britain responded traditionally, by dispatching a sizable armada with 5,000 troops, who succeeded in defeating the Argentine forces of occupation and retaking Stanley, the capital. The net result of the incident was to reinforce Thatcher's popularity at home and to discredit the ill-guided Argentinian generals who had launched the attack.

Closer to home, Britain was less successful. Embroiled in a virtual civil war in Northern Ireland—one of the bloodiest and longest in this century—Westminster has been unable to bring peace by either political or military means. To force Britain to withdraw, the provisional wing of the IRA (Irish Republican Army) has waged, over the years, a campaign of bombings and terrorism that sometimes reached the very doors of the House of Commons and in 1984 nearly killed the prime minister.

If the years between 1964 and 1979 could be described as the Labour era in British politics, a new Conservative era has seemed to be in the making in the 1980s. The disintegration of the Labour party and the formation of a fourth major national party—the Social Democrats—were likely to change the complexion of British politics for many decades to come.

Defense: Since 1960, Britain has no longer had compulsory military service. It possesses a nuclear deterrent based upon a bomber force at present, but for the future upon Polaris submarines. This force is to be assigned to a NATO commander, as are BAOR and some naval and air force units. There are American military bases in Britain, and Britain has a network of bases throughout the world—the main one being in Singapore—the future of which is often under review. The sizes of Britain's armed forces are: army 176,248, navy (including marines) 74,687, air force 92,701, reserves about 137,000. The 1981–82 defense budget was £12.275 billion ($27.77 billion), representing 5.7% of GNP.

ECONOMY

The British economy has great strengths and weaknesses and its performance since the end of World War II has been mixed and erratic. The home of the industrial revolution, Britain lost its political empire and economic hegemony almost at the same time and for similar reasons. The rise of newer economic powers dislodged Britain from its status as the bellwether of the industrial world, while long traditions of complacency and conservatism slowed its adaptation to changing conditions of trade and industry. The performance of British labor unions did not help either; indeed, the term "British disease" was coined in the 1960s to denote a condition of worker unrest, exaggerated wage demands and lowered productivity.

Background: Britain has few mineral or natural resources apart from large-scale coal deposits and a little iron ore. Since 1965, however, extensive deposits of natural gas and oil have been discovered in the North Sea and in eastern England. Since the pound sterling was devalued in 1949, Britain has been unable to increase production significantly without causing inflation. The economic pattern in postwar Britain has consequently been one of expansion followed by deflation; growth rate of GNP has been very slow—an annual average rate of 1.9% in 1970–79—and has been associated with constantly rising prices and incomes, and a precarious balance-of-payments position.

In 1961 the government established a National Economic Development Council (NEDC) to promote a faster and more even rate of growth, and an antiinflationary "pause" in wages, salaries and dividend payments was introduced as a temporary measure. In 1962 a further effort was made to introduce some form of incomes policy: a National Incomes Commission (NIC) was set up to report on inflationary income settlements and comment in advance on wage claims and profit levels. However, the NIC did not have the power to cancel or modify an agreement. An expansionary policy was then followed until 1964 when the economy showed signs of severe strain, with balance of payments heavily in deficit. After the general election in October, the new Labour government imposed a temporary surcharge of 15%—later reduced to 10% in response to pressure from other EFTA countries—on all imports of manufactures and semimanufactures.

In the expectation that devaluation and severe deflationary measures would be used to curb the deterioration in the balance of payments, in November 1964 a sterling crisis was precipitated by the outflow of short-term capital. In order to maintain the official exchange rate of £1 = $2.78 (minimum), the government was forced to arrange credit facilities of £330 million ($924 million) with the IMF; and the Bank of England drew heavily on the country's gold and dollar reserves to buy pounds. The crisis subsided when the leading Western European central banks made loans totaling over £1,000 million ($2,240 million).

In 1965 the balance of payments position improved and economic activity intensified, but international monetary loans continued to be necessary. Progress toward an incomes policy was made by the new government Department of Economic Affairs, which took over from the Treasury responsibility for long-term economic measures and for achieving an incomes policy. Voluntary cooperation was enlisted from unions and employers, and a National Prices and Incomes Board was set up.

By the early 1970s, Britain's GNP per capita was 10% below the European average. Attempts to achieve higher growth by stimulating demand led to repeated crises in the balance of payments and consequent squeezes on credit. The pound was again devalued in 1967 and allowed to float in 1972. The oil price shocks of 1973–74 led to a deepening of the crisis as production declined, and both unemployment and wages rose. The current deficit on balance of payments reached a peak of £3.307 billion in 1974. Although the government introduced strong antiinflation measures in 1975, unemployment reached 1.5 million in 1975 and the pound fell to a then record low of $1.57 in October 1976. In 1977 the economy showed signs of an upturn. An international safety net was announced to support Britain's reserves if they fell below $6.750 billion. Record numbers of tourists, the flow of oil royalties and a recovery of the stock market brought a current-account surplus of £293 million in 1977, allowing the government to make early repayments on the IMF debts. In 1979 the pound rose to its highest level in three years, and the Conservative government announced the abolition of exchange controls. Industry responded with increased investments except in the depressed sectors of steel and shipbuilding. The 1980–81 budget reduced income taxes, especially in the higher brackets, to provide incentives to save and invest; government optimism proved premature and the budget deficit rose to 6% of GDP. The government countered with an austerity budget in 1981–82, with a sharp increases in taxes. For the two succeeding years the government reduced real outlays by 1.6% and 2.4% respectively, in order to reduce the role of the public sector. The economy grew by 3% in 1983, an acceleration from the more modest rates of growth in the first 18 months of the recovery that started in mid-1981.

GNP grew by 1.9% in volume from 1970 to 1980. In 1982 the value of GDP at factor cost was $473.22 billion. The origin of GDP at factor cost in 1982 was:

Sector	Percentage
Agriculture	2
Industry	33
Services	65
GDP	100

Between 1970 and 1982, industrial output increased by an annual average of 0.2%. Britain's main industries are iron and steel, engineering, electronics, chemicals, textiles, transport equipment and consumer goods. The main growth industries have been chemicals, cars and fuel, especially atomic energy. The pattern of industry has gradually changed from an emphasis on textiles, machinery and coal to a more diversified range of industries, notably chemicals, transport and other engineering products. Other important contributions to Britain's economic wealth are made by British financial services and the expanding tourist industry. The country produces about half its total food supplies, the main products including cereals, vegetables and fruit.

The country's most important natural resource is energy. Offshore and natural gas deposits are sufficient to meet hydrocarbon requirements through the end of the century, while coal reserves are large enough to last another 300 years at current consumption levels. The nationalized coal mining industry supplies close to 40% of the country's energy budget. London continues to be a major financial center generating worldwide banking and insurance business, and it is also an international trading center for commodities—both traditional as well as new ones, such as petroleum and Eurodollar certificates of deposit.

Foreign trade: Although Britain's share of world trade has been steadily declining since the end of World War II, it remains a nation of merchants with a merchandise trade close to half of GNP. The trade balance has been consistently adverse, but favorable balance in the invisibles (services, return on investments and other remittances) have more than offset this deficit. The current-account patterns fluctuated widely in the late 1970s and early 1980s, responding to international market conditions.

Relations with other EC members have generally been positive, although the Thatcher government protested against being asked to pay $2.2 billion more into the EC than it recovered, despite the fact that it had the third lowest GNP per capita (after Italy and Ireland). A compromise was reached in 1981, but the issue resurfaced in 1984.

In general, trade policy is liberal with no protective tariffs against the EC or EFTA, from which Britain withdrew upon accession to the EC in 1973. Certain Japanese imports are restricted on the basis of informal understandings rather than through tariffs.

In 1982, merchandise exports amounted to $99.723 billion and merchandise imports to $97.028 billion, leaving a relatively small trade surplus of $2.695 billion. The annual average growth rate was 6% for exports and 3.5% for imports. The percentage share of merchandise exports was 23% for fuels, minerals and metals; 9% for other primary commodities; 4% for textiles and clothing; 33% for machinery and transport equipment; and 31% for other manufactures. The percentage share of merchandise imports was 14% for food, 14% for fuels, 10% for other primary commodities, 26% for machinery and transport equipment, and 36% for other manufactures. The principal export partners are West Germany (10%), United States (9%), Netherlands (8%), France (7%), Switzerland (6%), Ireland (5%) and Belgium (5%). The principal import partners are United States (12%), West Germany (11%), France (8%), Netherlands (7%), Switzerland (5%) and Belgium (5%).

Employment: In 1982 the total labor force was 26.5 million, of whom 42% were employed in industry, 2% in agriculture and 56% in services. Full employment was for a time maintained after World War II, except for regional and seasonal variations. From 1961 to 1965 the annual average for unemployment was consistently less than 2% (in 1965 the monthly average was about 1.5%, or under 400,000 persons). The picture altered radically during the 1970s. Unemployment rose by leaps and bounds, reaching a peak of 10.4% in 1981. However, the monthly increments to unemployment have been much smaller since 1982, and unemployment as a whole appears to be leveling out or even falling. Since the war there has been a drift of labor to the Midlands and the South, which the government has attempted to curb through regional planning boards, and by legislation stimulating growth in stagnant and declining areas and preventing further growth of industries in overcrowded areas. In the 1980s, the total immigrant population, exluding the Irish, was about 2.2 million, of whom about 1 million were of Asian origin and 800,000 of West Indian. They are concentrated in urban areas.

Price and wage trends: From 1970 to 1981, consumer prices rose by 14.3%. In 1983 wages rose by 9.7%.

Consumption: From 1970 to 1982, the average annual increase in private consumption was 1.4%. Public consumption increased by an annual average of 2.1% in the same period. In 1982 private consumption accounted for about 58% of GNP, and public consumption for 22%.

SOCIAL SECURITY

Health insurance: Medical care is provided to all residents, and cash sickness and maternity benefits are provided to most employed and self-employed persons. The scheme is under the general supervision of the Department of Health and Social Security. It is financed by the insured person, the employer and the government. Sickness benefits basically start at £27.50 a week, with supplements for wives, dependent husbands and children. Maternity benefits are the same as sickness benefits. Medical benefits include general practitioner care, specialist services, hospitalization and medicines. Medical benefits are administered by the National Health Service. Medical benefits for dependents are the same as for family heads.

Accident insurance: Under the general supervision of the Department of Health and Social Security, the scheme covers employed persons, but excludes the self-employed. It is financed by the insured person, the employer and the government. Temporary disability benefit (work-related injury) basically starts at £27.50 a week. The permanent disability pension (work-related injury) goes up to £53.60 a week if there is 100% disablement. Partial disability pensions (work-related injury) range from £10.72 a week for 20% disability to £48.24 a week for 90% disability. There are various supplements and survivor pensions for widows, dependent disabled widowers, orphans, and parents and other dependent relatives.

Pensions insurance: Under the general supervision of the Department of Health and Social Security, the scheme covers all residents, but is optional for employed persons earning less than the minimum weekly income level, self-employed persons whose income is below £1,690 a year and non-employed persons. It is financed by the insured person, the employer and the government. Old-age pensions are generally given at age 65 for men and age 60 for women. Old-age pensions are £32.85 a week, plus an earnings-related component. There are various supplements. Disability pensions are given for incapacity to work after the worker has received the cash sickness benefit of 28 weeks. Disability pensions are £31.45 a week, plus age-related increments. There are various supplements and survivor benefits, and pensions for widows, widowers, widowed mothers and orphans.

Unemployment insurance: Under the general supervision of the Department of Health and Social Security and the Department of Employment, the scheme covers employed persons who earn £32.50 a week or more; it excludes the self-employed and married women and widows paying reduced contributions. It is financed by the insured person, the employer and the government.

Unemployment benefit is a flat benefit of £25 a week, £15.45 for wife and £0.30 for each child.

Other benefits: Under the general administration of the Department of Health and Social Security, family allowances are available to eligible residents with one or more children. Family allowances are £5.85 a week per child, plus a £3.65 supplement for the first child of a single parent.

EDUCATION

In England, the secretary of state for education and science is responsible for all aspects of education. In the rest of the United Kingdom, education is the responsibility of the respective secretaries of state. Administration of state schools and higher education is divided among the central government departments, local education authorities and various voluntary bodies. The universities are administratively independent; their relations with the departments concerned are conducted through the University Grants Committee, and their governing bodies are appointed according to the terms of their individual charters. In England and Wales, schools supported out of public funds are of two kinds: county schools, which are wholly state-controlled, and voluntary schools, which have been provided by a voluntary body and receive state aid. In Scotland, most of the schools supported from public funds are known as public schools; there are a few grant-aided schools conducted by voluntary bodies. In Northern Ireland, county schools and voluntary schools are managed respectively by the local authorities and by voluntary managers, and the latter are grant-aided by the government.

Primary schools: State education is free and compulsory from the ages of five to 16. Primary education is divided into infant schools (five to seven years) and junior schools (seven to 11 years). The planning of the curriculum is largely in the hands of the head teacher and the staff. Primary school enrollments are very high and there is a continuing need for more teachers and school buildings. In Scotland, primary schools take children between the ages of five and 12. Curricula are similar in scope all over Britain, except in Wales, where the Welsh language is taught.

Secondary schools: Since 1944 the state educational system in England and Wales has aimed at giving all children an educational experience to suit their particular needs. Grammar schools came to be academic in orientation; secondary technical schools were general and vocation-orientated; and secondary modern schools were again general but with a practical bias. The three-tier system that evolved gave rise to differential statuses being attached to each type of secondary school and was characterized by selection. In 1964 the reorganization of secondary education was initiated in England and Wales in favor of the nonselective comprehensive school, in which a wider range of courses may be organized in a variety of ways according to local conditions and educational preferences. Basically, the three alternatives are: one tier with an 11 to 19 age-range; two tiers with a break at 13, 14, 15 or 16 years; or a three-tier system involving two breaks.

Scottish secondary education consists of two main categories, junior and senior secondary schools providing three-year courses (12–15) and four-, five- or six-year courses (12–18), respectively. Both types offer a general education with a wide choice of curriculum. In Northern Ireland, the system is similar to that in England and Wales prior to the latter's reorganization—the three corresponding types of schools being called grammar, intermediate secondary and technical intermediate.

There is no national leaving examination in England and Wales; instead, there are a variety of General Certificate of Education (GCE) examining boards and the Certificate of Secondary Education (CSE) for those not taking GCE. The GCE may be taken at ordinary (O) level, generally after five years, and at advanced (A) level after seven years. A new "16 plus" GCSE examination is to be introduced in 1988. In both Scotland and Northern Ireland there are National Certificate examinations, which may be taken at junior or senior level. A combination of O and A level certificates is the usual basis for university entrance in Britain.

Independent schools: Registration with the Department of Education and Science is compulsory to ensure maintenance of minimum standards. Independent schools, which are mainly boarding schools, may be primary (8–13; "preparatory"), secondary (13–18; "public") or primary and secondary combined. In 1980 there were over 413,000 pupils at 2,339 independent schools in England and Wales.

Special educational needs: The 1981 Education Act ensures that in England, Wales and Northern Ireland, the physically or mentally handicapped are provided for in ordinary schools. In Scotland, school-placing is decided by education authorities and parents. Where an ordinary school would not be beneficial, some 1,600 special schools throughout the United Kingdom cater for a wide range of disabilities.

Vocational education: Apart from the training of teachers, vocational education has developed independently of the state. However, in technical and art schools there are vocational courses of all kinds, generally organized by professional associations that also act as examiners. Facilities are available for both part-time day and evening studies in addition to full-time courses. The other main category of vocational education is the apprenticeship system, which aims at providing a combination of theoretical and practical instruction in a variety of trades. Day release with pay from employers is one method of training, and the government provides training centers for full-time courses to encourage industry to increase its intake of young people into skilled occupations. Technical courses last a minimum of four years, and craft courses last five years.

University and higher education: Higher education is provided by the universities (both private and state-owned), technical colleges and teacher training colleges. There are nearly 50 universities in the United Kingdom. The universities of Oxford, Cambridge, Wales and London consist of loosely federated colleges, each of which retains much independence; Oxford and Cambridge have their own entry system. The other universities are unitary institutions, each under the academic control of a senate. Courses last three or four years for bachelor degrees. Full medical courses last five to six years.

Technical colleges (including art, commercial and agricultural colleges) provide a wide range of courses. They are maintained by local education authorities and some of them have been given polytechnic status with an emphasis on degree-level studies. There are several national technical colleges linked to particular industries and administered jointly by the Department of Education and Science and the industry concerned. Teacher training colleges are called "Colleges of Education" in England and Wales; they are maintained by local education authorities and some have links with university education departments.

Universities (1982): England: Oxford, Cambridge, Durham, London, Manchester, Manchester Institute of Science and Technology, Newcastle-upon-Tyne, Birmingham, Liverpool, Leeds, Sheffield, Bristol, Reading, Nottingham, Southampton, Hull, Exeter, Leicester, Sussex, Keele, East Anglia, York, Lancaster, Essex, Warwick, Kent, Loughborough University of Technology, Aston at Birmingham, City (London), Brunel, Bath, Bradford, Surrey, Salford, Buckingham, Royal College of Art, Cranfield Institute of Technology, Open University.

Wales: Wales (Aberystwyth, Bangor, Cardiff and Swansea), St. Davids (Lampeter).

Scotland: St. Andrews, Glasgow, Aberdeen, Edinburgh, Strathyclyde, Herriot-Watt, Dundee, Stirling.

Northern Ireland: Queen's Ulster.

Educational institutions, 1980–83:

ENGLAND AND WALES

	1981	1982	1983
Number of schools (January)	32,556	32,084	31,708
Teachers (January):[1]			
Maintained primary schools[2]	194,096	186,445	180,253
Maintained secondary schools	245,368	242,622	241,357
Other schools	61,900	62,547	63,151
Total	501,364	491,614	484,761
Full-time pupils (January):			
Maintained nursery schools	15,466	14,920	14,185
Maintained primary schools[2]	4,292,940	4,099,639	3,909,198
Maintained secondary schools	4,079,499	4,035,156	3,976,569
Special schools	131,900	130,037	128,093
Independent schools[3]	528,525	522,447	514,850
Total	9,048,330	8,802,199	8,542,895
Part-time pupils (January)	216,621	230,784	252,079
Further education establishments[4]	580	567	557
Full-time students in further education[4]	508,701	560,478	603,297

[1] Full-time teachers and the full-time equivalent of part-time teachers. Figures for qualified teachers only with respect to all maintained schools, direct-grant nursery schools and special schools.
[2] Including immigrant centers.

[3] Excluding special schools. From October 1980, direct-grant schools, with the exception of special schools and three nursery schools, have been reclassified as independent schools.

[4] At autumn term of academic years, including sandwich-course students. Figures exclude universities (see below). All students in initial teacher training courses at nonuniversity establishments are included in statistics for further education colleges following the reorganization of the former colleges of education.

Source: Department of Education and Science.

SCOTLAND

	1980–81	1981–82	1982–83
Education authority and grant-aided:			
Schools:			
Nursery	519	531	541
Primary	2,543	2,520	2,509
Secondary	467	461	463
Special	319	324	330
Total	3,848	3,836	3,843
Teachers:[1]			
Nursery	711	726	742
Primary	25,846	24,616	23,289
Secondary	29,290	28,918	28,765
Special	1,736	1,681	1,641
Total	57,583	55,941	54,437
Pupils:			
Nursery	32,644	33,350	34,862
Primary	524,889	498,968	474,234
Secondary	419,373	415,763	410,048
Special	11,816	11,270	10,823
Total	988,722	959,351	929,967
Further education establishments[2]	79	78	81
Full-time teachers in further education	6,614	6,797	7,086
Full-time students in further education[3]	64,071	73,649	81,864

[1] Full-time teachers and the full-time equivalent of part-time.
[2] Vocational further education (day colleges and central institutions only).
[3] Including students in social work, etc., courses attending colleges of education.
Source: Scottish Education Department.

UNIVERSITIES* (Great Britain—academic years)

	1980–81	1981–82	1982–83
Full-time teaching and research staff	43,017	42,840	41,994
Students taking university courses:			
Full-time students	298,680	300,195	295,394
Part-time students	31,939	33,185	33,511

* 45 universities, excluding the Open University.
Source: Department of Education and Science.

UNITED KINGDOM OF GREAT BRITAIN AND NORTHERN IRELAND

NORTHERN IRELAND

(1982–83)	Institutions	Students (Full-time)	Teachers (Full-time)
Primary (incl. nursery)	1,145	191,350	8,111
Secondary	261	158,892	10,208
Special	26	2,598	297
Institutions of further education	26	15,652	2,068
Colleges of education	3	812	177
Ulster Polytechnic	1	4,839	562
Universities	2	8,621	1,082

Source: *Northern Ireland Annual Abstract of Statistics.*

Adult education: This is available in Britain through evening institutes and adult-education centers, many of which, such as extramural university courses, are assisted out of state funds. Others, such as the Workers' Educational Association, are voluntary, and some, such as correspondence and secretarial colleges, are commercial. The range of subjects varies from handicraft and vocational studies to university degree courses. In 1982 there were 13,596 public libraries, including mobile libraries.

MASS MEDIA

The press (1984):

Dailies: Daily Mirror, London, independent, 3,505,372; *The Sun*, London, ind., 4,150,191; *Daily Express*, London, ind., 1,988,339; *Daily Mail*, London, ind., 1,837,521; *Daily Telegraph*, London, ind., 1,252,847; *Financial Times*, London, ind., financial and commercial, 215,909; *The Times*, London, ind., 424,893; *Guardian*, London, ind., 410,286; *Birmingham Evening Mail*, Birmingham, ind., 284, 047; *South Wales Echo*, Cardiff, ind., 100,768; *Evening News*, Edinburgh, 123,395; *Daily Record*, Glasgow, ind., 744,605; *Evening Times*, Glasgow, ind., 982,596; *Daily Star*, Manchester, 1,501,945; *Belfast Telegraph*, Belfast, ind., 151,564.

Sundays: News of the World, London, ind., 4,535,022; *Mail on Sunday*, London, 1,574,192; *Sunday Express*, London, ind., 2,561,361; *Sunday Mirror*, London, ind., 3,598,018; *Sunday People*, London, ind., 3,367,473; *Sunday Post (Glasgow)*, Dundee and Glasgow, 1,550,154; *Sunday Times*, London, ind., 1,288,284; *Observer*, London, ind., 1,116,000.

Periodicals (London): Women (w), women's, 1,188,253; *Woman's Own* (w), wom., 1,226,218; *Woman's Weekly* (w), wom., 1,428,352; *Reader's Digest* (m), general, 1,500,000; *Encounter* (m), literature, arts, gen., 16,000; *The Listener* (w), TV, radio and lit., 29,713; *Spectator (w)*, arts, gen., *37,400; New Statesman* (w), ind. gen., 30,000; *Farmers Weekly* (published in Sutton Surrey) (w), farming, 120,593; *The Economist* (w), ind. political, business and economic, 252,863; *Country Life* (w), country living, gen., 47,048; *Harpers & Queen* (m), wom., 101,597; *Penthouse* (m), men's, 457,884; *Private Eye* (fortnightly), satirical, 200,000; *Punch* (w), humorous, 81,024; *Vogue* (m), wom., 166,432; *Radio Times* (w), radio and TV, 6,509,672; *TV Times* (w), TV, 3,107,775; *Nature* (w), scientific, 27,092; *New Scientist* (w), sci. and technology, 80,938; *The Universe* (w), Roman Catholic, illustrated, 127,452; *Jewish Chronicle* (w), Jewish religious, 50,925; *Church Times* (w), Anglican relig. news, 43,248.

Broadcasting: Public sound broadcasting is officially provided solely by the British Broadcasting Corporation (BBC), as are two TV services (BBC 1 and BBC 2). The Independent Broadcasting Authority (IBA) is a public body controlling a group of commercial companies in two channels (ITV and Channel 4). Both BBC and the IBA have independent control over such matters as programs and administration. The government has powers of final review and may issue directives to both bodies on technical and other subjects, but has no control over content of programs. The BBC's corporation under the present charter consists of nine governors responsible for the entire conduct of the organization; they are advised by a number of councils. The BBC is financed by an annual sum voted by Parliament, based on the sale of radio and TV licenses, an annual grant-in-aid also voted by Parliament and profits from the sale of BBC publications. The IBA, whose board is government-appointed, owns and operates its transmitters but studios and equipment are owned by, and programs provided by, the program companies under contract to the IBA. The Authority has wide controlling and regulatory powers regarding programs. It is financed by annual rental payments made by the program companies, which in turn derive their revenue from the sale of advertising time. There are two independent local radio organizations: Association of Independent Radio Contractors Ltd. and Independent Radio News (IRN). There are also two independent television organizations: Independent Television Companies Association Ltd. and Independent Television News (ITN). In 1984, there were 3,110,913 black-and-white TV licenses, 18,581,665 color TV licenses and approximately 18,400,000 radio receivers in Great Britain.

VATICAN CITY STATE

GEOGRAPHY AND POPULATION

Situation: Within the City of Rome on the right bank of the Tiber. *Population:* (1982) 860, of whom 566 are of Vatican nationality. *Language:* Italian. *Religion:* The Vatican is the center of the Roman Catholic church.

CONSTITUTIONAL SYSTEM

Constitution: The Vatican City State is the last remaining Papal state. The 1929 Lateran Pact between the Italian state and the Vatican (official residence of the Pope and center of the Vatican City State) gave the Holy See the full use of property rights in and exclusive power and sovereign jurisdiction over the Vatican City State. *Head of state and the Roman Catholic church:* Pope John Paul II.

Executive, legislature and judicial system: The pope is elected for life by a two-thirds majority of the Sacred College of Cardinals. He has absolute legislative, executive and judicial power. Executive power is exercised by a governor who is directly and exclusively responsible to the pope. Judicial power is delegated in the first instance to a tribunal, to the Sacra Romana Rota in appeal and ultimately to the Supreme Tribunal of the Signatura. One of the offices of the church, the Secretariat of State, represents the Holy See (and hence the Vatican City State) in international relations.

RECENT HISTORY

Vatican neutrality was respected by all combatants in World War II. The 1947 constitution of Italy reaffirmed its adherence to the Lateran Pact of 1929. In 1962 Pope John XXIII convened the Second Vatican Council to promote reconciliation and unity among Christian churches. His successor, Paul VI, visited the Holy Land and India in 1964 and addressed the U.N. General Assembly in 1965. His successor, John Paul I, died within weeks of being elected Pope in 1978. The present Pope, John Paul II, became the first non-Italian elected to the throne of St. Peter since Adrian VI in 1522. He has since traveled to over 60 countries on all the five continents.

MASS MEDIA

The press: L'Osservatore Romano is a semiofficial Italian-language daily under Vatican direction, covering both general news and the affairs of the Holy See. The official bulletin, *Acta Apostolicae Sedis,* is published monthly.

Broadcasting: Radio Vatican was founded in 1931 and is situated in Vatican City. A special treaty between Italy and the Vatican grants full extraterritorial privileges to another transmitter at Santa Maria di Galeria 12 miles northwest of the Vatican. Centrum Televisificum Vaticanum (Vatican Television Center) produces and distributes religious programs.

COMPARATIVE STATISTICS

COMPARATIVE STATISTICS

Except where otherwise stated, these tables are quoted (with permission) from *Basic Statistics of the Community. Comparison with Some European Countries, Canada, the United States of America and the Union of Soviet Socialist Republics*, published by the Statistical Office of the European Communities, Brussels and Luxembourg, 21st edition, 1982. Some figures will be found to differ slightly from those given in the Basic Information section, where other sources were used.

POPULATION AND LABOR FORCE

POPULATION, 1984

Country	Area (000 sq. km.)	Population (000)	Density (per sq. km.)	Estimated population (million), 2000
Austria	83.8	7,600	90.2	7.6
Belgium	30.5	9,900	323.2	9.8
Denmark	43.0	5,100	118.9	5.0
Finland	337.0	4,900	14.2	5.0
France	551.2	54,800	98.4	57.7
Germany	248.5	61,400	247.9	59.3
Gt. Britain	245.0	56,500	229.2	57.1
Greece	131.9	10,000	73.5	10.9
Iceland	102.8	200	2.2	0.3
Ireland	70.3	3,600	47.9	4.3
Italy	301.2	57,000	189.7	57.8
Luxembourg	2.6	400	140.6	0.4
Netherlands	33.5	14,400	418.6	14.6
Norway	323.9	4,100	12.6	4.2
Portugal	91.5	10,100	107.9	11.1
Spain	504.7	38,400	74.4	41.7
Sweden	449.8	8,300	18.5	7.9
Switzerland	41.3	6,500	153.3	6.4
Turkey	780.6	50,200	57.3	70.4
Soviet Union	22,402.2	269,000	12.0	310.2
United States	9,363.4	232,000	25.0	263.8

EMPLOYED CIVILIAN LABOR FORCE BY MAIN SECTORS, 1982
(*Percent*)

Country	Agriculture	Industry	Services	Total
Austria	9	37	54	100
Belgium	3	41	56	100
Denmark	7	35	58	100
Finland	11	35	54	100
France	8	39	53	100
Germany	4	46	50	100
Gt. Britain	2	42	56	100
Greece	37	28	35	100
Iceland	12	42	46	100
Ireland	18	37	45	100
Italy	11	45	44	100
Luxembourg	4	41	55	100
Netherlands	6	45	49	100
Norway	7	37	56	100
Portugal	28	35	37	100
Spain	14	40	46	100
Sweden	5	34	61	100
Switzerland	5	46	49	100
Turkey	54	13	33	100
Soviet Union	20	39	41	100
United States	35	28	68	100

UNEMPLOYMENT, 1976–81
(Percentage of total labor force)

Country	1976	1978	1980	1981
Austria	1.9	1.9	1.7	2.4
Belgium	6.6	8.2	9.2	9.8
Denmark	5.1	7.4	6.9	9.2
Finland	3.9	7.5	4.8	5.3
France	4.2	5.3	6.2	7.7
Germany	4.0	3.7	3.2	5.5
Gt. Britain	6.0	6.5	7.4	11.3
Greece	0.8	1.0	2.4	1.3
Iceland	0.5	0.5	0.4	0.4
Ireland	7.3	6.6	5.9	6.6
Italy	6.3	7.3	7.4	8.4
Luxembourg	0.3	0.8	0.7	1.1
Netherlands	4.2	4.0	4.7	9.0
Norway	1.1	1.1	1.2	1.7
Portugal	6.3	7.9	7.5	7.7
Spain	3.1	6.2	7.8	11.8
Sweden	0.8	1.0	1.4	1.9
Switzerland	0.7	0.3	0.2	0.2
Turkey	0.9	1.0	1.4	1.5
Soviet Union	n.a.	n.a.	n.a.	n.a.
United States	n.a.	6.0	7.0	7.5

Source: *UN Statistical Yearbook, 1981*, ILO (cited
hereafter as *UN Yearbook, 1981*).

NATIONAL PRODUCT

PER CAPITA GDP AT CONSTANT FACTOR COST, 1976–82
(1975 = 100)

Country	1976	1978	1979	1982
Austria	106	112	117	120
Belgium	105	109	112	116
Denmark	108	110	114	118
Finland	100	102	109	122
France	105	111	115	120
Germany	106	113	118	118
Gt. Britain	104	109	110	109
Greece	105	114	117	123
Iceland	104	115	113	117
Ireland	100	110	111	118
Italy	105	109	114	120
Luxembourg	103	109	111	110
Netherlands	104	108	110	111
Norway	105	113	118	126
Portugal	104	n.a.	n.a.	134
Spain	102	106	106	112
Sweden	101	99	103	107
Switzerland	100	102	105	109
Turkey	106	109	n.a.	129
Soviet Union	n.a.	n.a.	n.a.	n.a.
United States	114	116	118	119

Source: *UN Yearbook, 1981;*
Basic Statistics of the Community, 1984.

243

VOLUME INDICES OF GNP AT MARKET PRICES, 1977–81
(1975 = 100)

Country	1977	1978	1979	1980	1981
Austria	109.1	109.7	114.9	118.6	118.7
Belgium	106.5	109.7	112.3	115.7	113.6
Denmark	109.6	110.9	115.0	113.8	113.8
Finland	100.6	102.9	110.9	117.4	119.0
France	108.2	112.5	116.2	117.5	117.8
Germany	108.6	112.0	116.6	118.9	119.1
Gt. Britain	104.9	108.7	110.5	108.4	106.2
Greece	110.0	117.4	121.7	123.6	122.8
Iceland	n.a.	n.a.	n.a.	n.a.	n.a.
Ireland	108.9	115.3	118.1	121.4	122.8
Italy	107.9	110.8	116.2	120.8	120.9
Luxembourg	102.6	107.2	111.5	113.3	111.3
Netherlands	113.4	116.4	118.9	120.0	118.6
Norway	110.6	115.7	121.5	126.3	127.2
Portugal	112.9	116.7	124.4	129.5	130.1
Spain	106.4	106.3	108.3	110.2	110.5
Sweden	99.2	100.5	104.8	106.8	106.1
Switzerland	101.0	101.4	103.9	108.7	118.7
Turkey	113.4	116.6	115.6	114.7	119.8
Soviet Union	n.a.	n.a.	n.a.	n.a.	n.a.
United States	113.2	115.6	118.3	118.0	121.5

ORIGIN OF GDP AT FACTOR COST, 1982
(Percent)

Country	Agriculture, forestry and fishing	Industry (incl. construction	Services	GDP at factor cost
Austria	4	39	57	100
Belgium	2	35	63	100
Denmark	5	24	71	100
Finland	8	35	57	100
France	4	34	62	100
Germany	2	46	52	100
Gt. Britain	2	33	65	100
Greece	19	29	52	100
Iceland	n.a.	n.a.	n.a.	100
Ireland	10	38	52	100
Italy	6	41	53	100
Luxembourg	2	35	63	100
Netherlands	4	34	62	100
Norway	5	41	54	100
Portugal	8	38	54	100
Spain	7	37	56	100
Sweden	3	36	61	100
Switzerland	n.a.	n.a.	n.a.	100
Turkey	21	31	48	100
Soviet Union	n.a.	n.a.	n.a.	n.a.
United States	3	38	59	100

245

EXPENDITURE ON GDP, 1982
(Percent)

Country	Private consumption on the economic territory	Collective consumption of general government	Gross fixed capital formation	Change in stocks	Balance of exports and imports of goods and services
Austria	56.1	18.6	23.1	0.0	2.3
Belgium	65.2	18.3	17.3	−0.4	−0.5
Denmark	55.4	27.9	16.5	0.1	0.0
Finland	55.5	20.0	24.0	0.0	0.5
France	65.2	16.2	20.5	0.9	−2.7
Germany	61.6	14.0	20.5	0.5	3.5
Gt. Britain	60.8	22.0	15.4	−0.4	2.1
Greece	69.3	18.4	19.4	3.9	−13.0
Ireland	60.3	21.7	25.5	−0.1	−7.4
Italy	64.0	18.4	19.0	1.4	−2.8
Luxembourg	61.4	17.6	23.5	3.8	−6.1
Netherlands	59.3	17.8	18.3	−0.2	4.9
Norway	48.6	19.4	24.6	1.8	5.6
Portugal	70.6	14.2	31.2	4.8	−20.9
Spain	73.2	11.9	19.6	0.4	−5.0
Sweden	53.9	29.3	18.8	0.0	−0.8
Switzerland	62.4	13.2	23.1	1.0	0.4
Turkey	71.9	10.9	19.1	1.5	−3.4
Soviet Union	n.a.	n.a.	n.a.	n.a.	10
United States	65.8	18.7	16.6	−0.4	−0.7

Source: *UN Yearbook, 1981.*

FOREIGN TRADE

EXCHANGE RATES AND CURRENCIES, 1984 (April)
(National currency per U.S. dollar)

Country	Currency	
Austria	Schilling (Sch)	19.109
Belgium	Belgian Franc (BF)	55.400
Denmark	Krone (DKr)	9.972
Finland	Finnish Mark (Fmk)	5.760
France	Franc (F)	8.838
Germany	Deutsche Mark (DM)	2.717
Gt. Britain	Pound Sterling (£)	0.716
Greece	Drachma (Dr)	106.650
Iceland	Krónur (IKr)	29.500
Ireland	Punt (£)	0.880
Italy	Lira (L)	1,681.000
Luxembourg	Luxembourg Franc (LF)	55.400
Netherlands	Gulden (or Florin) (Fl)	3.041
Norway	Krone (NKr)	7.731
Portugal	Escudo (E)	137.474
Spain	Peseta (P)	151.958
Sweden	Krona (SKr)	7.997
Switzerland	Swiss Franc (SF)	2.243
Turkey	Turkish Pound (£T)	339.640

EXTERNAL TRADE, 1981

	Imports			Exports			
Country	ECU million	% of GNP	ECUs per head	ECU million	% of GNP	ECUs per head	Balance (ECU million)
Austria	18,812	31.6	2,487	14,159	23.8	1,872	−4,653
Belgium Luxembourg }	55,613	65.0	5,443	49,881	58.3	4,882	−5,732
Denmark	15,899	30.4	3,104	14,526	27.8	2,836	−1,373
Finland	12,716	28.9	2,643	12,519	28.5	2,602	−197
France	108,421	21.2	2,009	91,122	17.8	1,689	−17,299
Germany	146,855	23.9	2,381	157,881	25.7	2,560	+11,026
Gt. Britain	95,571	21.3	1,706	95,081	21.2	1,697	−490
Greece	8,017	24.3	824	3,860	11.7	397	−4,157
Ireland*	9,488	63.3	2,755	7,006	46.7	2,034	−2,482
Italy	82,108	26.0	1,436	68,170	21.6	1,192	−13,938
Netherlands	59,272	46.9	4,160	61,559	48.7	4,321	+2,287
Norway	13,991	27.3	3,412	16,058	31.4	3,917	+2,067
Portugal	8,728	41.0	891	3,710	17.4	379	−5,018
Spain	28,822	17.3	765	18,323	11.0	487	−10,499
Sweden	25,839	25.7	3,106	25,566	25.4	3,073	−273
Switzerland	27,404	32.4	4,263	24,087	28.5	2,602	−3,317
Turkey	8,011	15.5	177	4,274	8.9	94	−3,737
Soviet Union[1]	79,343	n.a.	n.a.	88,843	n.a.	n.a.	+9,500
United States[1]	249,004	8.0	1,073	216,671	7.0	983	−32,333

[1] 1982.
* Source: EEC.

TOTAL IMPORTS BY AREA OF ORIGIN, 1982
(Percent)

Importing Country	Area of origin			
	EC	Japan	U.S.	Rest of world
Austria	61.1	2.8	3.8	32.3
Belgium ⎱ Luxembourg ⎰	61.0	2.0	7.2	29.8
Denmark	48.8	2.8	7.1	41.3
Finland	33.5	4.2	6.1	56.2
France	50.6	2.4	7.0	40.0
Germany	49.1	3.2	7.1	40.6
Gt. Britain	40.8	4.7	14.5	40.0
Greece	46.2	6.9	4.2	42.7
Iceland	n.a.	n.a.	n.a.	n.a.
Ireland	73.7	2.5	11.3	12.5
Italy	41.8	1.3	6.8	50.1
Netherlands	54.0	2.1	9.4	34.5
Norway	45.4	6.1	9.2	39.3
Portugal	40.6	3.4	10.8	45.2
Spain	36.3	3.2	13.9	46.6
Sweden	50.6	3.7	8.5	37.2
Switzerland	66.2	3.7	7.2	22.9
Turkey	27.5	4.1	9.2	59.2
Soviet Union[1]	13.1	3.9	2.8	80.2
United States[1]	15.5	16.0	—	68.5

[1] 1983

TOTAL EXPORTS BY AREA OF DESTINATION, 1982
(*Percent*)

Exporting Country	Area of destination			
	EC	Japan	U.S.	Rest of world
Austria	53.1	0.9	2.9	43.1
Belgium Luxembourg	70.6	0.6	4.4	24.4
Denmark	48.6	1.6	6.2	43.6
Finland	34.9	1.1	3.2	60.8
France	48.6	1.2	5.7	44.5
Germany	48.1	1.2	6.6	44.1
Gt. Britain	41.0	1.2	13.6	44.2
Greece	46.3	0.6	8.9	44.2
Iceland	n.a.	n.a.	n.a.	n.a.
Ireland	70.6	1.3	7.1	21.0
Italy	45.8	1.1	7.1	46.0
Netherlands	72.1	0.5	3.3	24.1
Norway	71.9	0.8	2.8	24.5
Portugal	57.3	0.9	6.1	35.7
Spain	52.9	1.3	6.4	39.4
Sweden	46.6	1.2	7.1	45.1
Switzerland	48.2	2.6	7.8	41.4
Turkey	30.8	0.8	4.4	64.0
Soviet Union[1]	18.4	1.5	0.4	79.7
United States[1]	20.1	10.9	—	69.0

[1] 1983

TOTAL IMPORTS, 1975–82

(ECU million)

Country	1975	1976	1977	1978	1979	1980	1981	ECU million 1982	% of world trade 1982
Austria	7,560	10,274	12,453	12,532	14,729	17,422	18,812	18,198	1.0
Belgium Luxembourg	24,819	31,715	35,418	38,095	44,053	51,632	55,613	59,095	3.0
Denmark	8,383	11,093	11,616	11,422	13,670	14,106	15,899	17,452	0.9
Finland	6,116	6,635	6,679	6,160	8,249	11,214	12,716	13,706	0.7
France	43,682	57,647	61,784	64,215	77,705	97,102	108,421	117,882	6.0
Germany	60,442	78,912	88,863	95,406	116,310	135,243	146,855	158,445	8.1
Gt. Britain	42,905	50,122	55,522	61,638	74,746	85,653	95,571	105,986	5.4
Greece	4,301	5,429	5,999	6,150	7,028	7,634	8,017	10,189	0.5
Ireland*	3,046	3,764	4,728	5,591	7,175	7,999	9,488	9,870	0.5
Italy	31,122	39,485	42,132	44,278	56,716	71,813	82,108	87,740	4.5
Netherlands	28,389	35,832	39,970	41,532	49,053	55,369	59,272	63,934	3.3
Norway	7,793	9,912	11,282	8,963	10,015	12,178	13,991	15,772	0.8
Portugal	3,078	3,782	4,341	4,076	4,774	4,699	8,728	9,620	0.5
Spain	13,106	15,618	15,578	14,648	18,521	24,547	28,822	32,270	1.4
Sweden	14,531	17,097	17,627	16,080	20,821	23,999	25,839	28,192	1.4
Switzerland	10,699	13,193	15,681	18,565	21,382	26,097	27,404	29,189	1.4
Turkey	3,740	4,494	5,015	3,566	4,146	4,499	8,011	9,125	0.5
Soviet Union	29,812	34,123	35,770	39,668	42,169	49,524	65,280	79,343	4.3
United States	79,098	108,933	129,564	135,985	151,119	173,231	233,761	249,004	13.8

Source: UN Yearbook, 1982.

* Based on monthly averages.

251

TOTAL EXPORTS, 1975–82

(ECU million)

Country	1975	1976	1977	1978	1979	1980	1981	1982 ECU million	1982 % of world trade
Austria	6,057	7,504	8,578	9,518	11,257	12,475	14,159	15,967	0.9
Belgium Luxembourg	23,193	29,340	32,891	35,204	41,033	46,459	49,881	53,551	2.9
Denmark	7,024	8,139	8,816	9,224	10,766	12,195	14,526	15,843	0.9
Finland	4,426	5,693	6,730	6,710	8,134	10,166	12,519	13,341	0.7
France	41,981	49,915	55,667	60,118	71,510	80,150	91,122	94,379	5.1
Germany	72,666	91,155	103,316	111,340	125,243	138,787	157,881	180,026	9.7
Gt. Britain	35,288	41,458	50,276	56,090	66,042	82,063	95,081	102,698	5.5
Greece	1,855	2,295	2,411	2,645	2,841	3,728	3,860	4,381	0.2
Ireland	2,585	2,992	3,852	4,459	5,222	6,101	7,006	8,238	0.4
Italy	28,240	33,504	39,668	43,942	52,615	56,115	68,170	74,935	4.0
Netherlands	28,593	36,149	38,283	39,292	46,434	53,184	61,559	67,658	3.6
Norway	5,825	7,073	7,635	7,878	9,815	13,281	16,058	17,908	1.0
Portugal	1,556	1,618	1,772	1,905	2,543	2,503	3,710	4,264	0.2
Spain	6,192	7,806	8,942	10,250	13,276	14,956	18,323	21,000	1.1
Sweden	13,978	16,742	16,724	17,048	20,087	22,207	25,566	27,291	1.5
Switzerland	10,438	13,254	15,371	18,336	19,317	21,272	24,087	27,473	1.4
Turkey	1,129	1,737	1,526	1,789	1,804	1,974	4,274	5,885	0.3
Soviet Union	26,862	33,244	35,575	40,975	47,245	55,305	70,832	88,843	5.1
United States	86,714	102,855	105,303	112,732	132,639	158,515	209,360	216,671	11.1

Source: *UN Yearbook, 1982.*

INDUSTRY

INDICES OF INDUSTRIAL PRODUCTION, 1976–82
(*1975 = 100*)

Country	1976	1977	1978	1979	1980	1981	1982
Austria	106	111	113	122	125	123	123
Belgium	108	109	111	116	115	112	112
Denmark	109	110	113	117	117	117	120
Finland	101	102	107	118	128	132	130
France	109	111	113	118	117	114	113
Germany	107	110	113	119	118	116	113
Gt. Britain	103	108	111	116	108	104	105
Greece	110	112	121	128	129	128	123
Ireland	109	117	127	135	133	135	135
Italy	112	112	114	122	126	125	122
Luxembourg	104	104	108	111	108	100	97
Netherlands	108	108	109	112	112	110	107
Norway	106	105	116	123	132	132	131
Portugal	103	117	125	134	141	142	148
Spain	105	110	115	115	117	114	113
Sweden	99	94	92	98	99	97	96
Switzerland	101	106	106	109	114	114	109
Turkey	100	123	125	125	104	n.a.	n.a.
Soviet Union	110	111	116	120	124	129	132
United States	115	117	124	129	125	128	118

253

WAGES IN MANUFACTURING, 1973–80

(h—*hour*, w—*week*, d—*day*, mo—*month*, m—*males*, f—*females*, mf—*both*)

Country & Currency	Rate	1973	1975	1978	1979	1980
Austria Schilling	mo, mf	6665	8730	10942	11586	12495
Belgium franc	h, m	99.83	144.32	184.44	199.61	217.88
Denmark krone	h, mf	23.37	33.50	44.59	49.22	53.95
Finland markka	h, mf	7.78	11.59	15.69	17.49	19.74
France franc	h, mf	8.57	11.99	17.49	19.56	22.72
Germany Mark	h, mf	8.03	9.69	11.73	12.36	13.18
Gt. Britain pence	h, m	114.60	174.40	258.80	293.50	348.50
Greece drachma	h, mf	22.04	34.74	66.74	80.50	102.40
Ireland pence	h, mf	68.80	109.00	170.60	200.50	232.00
Italy lira	h, mf	966.00	1794.00	3244.00	3874.00	n.a.
Luxembourg franc	h, mf	121.80	164.50	215.57	227.77	244.90
Netherlands guilder	h, mf	7.36	9.95	12.49	13.05	n.a.
Norway krone	h, m	18.61	26.15	36.44	37.47	40.97
	h, f	14.18	20.41	29.24	30.15	33.55
Portugal escudo	h, mf	14.30	32.60	55.30	72.60	n.a.
Spain peseta	h, mf	n.a.	n.a.	147.20	242.23	n.a.
Sweden krona	h, mf	18.19	23.79	32.31	35.75	n.a.
Switzerland franc	h, mf	8.43	10.34	11.06	11.42	12.11
Turkey lira	d, mf	57.28	89.75	224.13	304.20	n.a.

Source: *UN Yearbook, 1982.*

HOURS WORKED IN MANUFACTURING, 1970–80

(d—*per day*, w—*per week*, m—*per month*)

Country	Period	1970	1975	1976	1978	1979	1980
Austria*	w	37.4	33.9	34.4	33.4	33.6	33.7
Belgium	w	39.9	34.8	35.8	35.2	35.4	33.4
Denmark	w	36.2	33.1	33.3	32.6	33.1	32.9
Finland	w	38.3	38.4	38.2	38.5	41.0	40.4
France	w	44.8	41.7	41.6	41.0	40.8	40.6
Germany	w	43.8	40.4	41.4	41.6	41.8	41.6
Gt. Britain	w	44.9	42.7	43.5	43.5	43.2	41.9
Greece	w	44.6	42.7	41.9	41.2	41.2	40.7
Ireland	w	42.7	41.5	42.3	42.3	42.4	41.1
Italy	d	7.80	7.68	7.67	7.72	7.65	n.a.
Luxembourg	w	44.0	40.8	40.6	39.8	40.5	40.0
Netherlands	w	44.2	41.2	41.3	41.1	41.1	n.a.
Norway	w	40.4	39.3	39.0	38.6	39.3	n.a.
Portugal	w	44.8	41.8	40.1	39.3	36.5	n.a.
Spain	w	n.a.	n.a.	n.a.	40.1	38.8	38.5
Sweden	m	151.0	136.0	133.0	n.a.	n.a.	n.a.
Switzerland*	w	n.a.	44.5	44.4	44.4	44.2	43.8
Turkey	n.a.	n.a.	n.a.	n.a.	n.a.	n.a.	n.a.

* Adult males only.

Source: *UN Yearbook, 1982.*

TOTAL PRODUCTION OF PRIMARY ENERGY, 1981

(000 tons coal equivalent)

Country	Coal and lignite	Nuclear energy	Crude petroleum	Natural gas	Primary electricity	Total primary energy
Austria	1.0	—	1.4	1.1	2.7	6.2
Belgium	4.6	3.2	—	—	0.1	7.9
Denmark	—	—	0.8	—	—	0.8
Finland	0.3	3.9	—	—	1.2	5.4
France	12.8	27.5	2.6	6.0	6.3	55.2
Germany	89.7	13.5	4.5	14.5	2.3	124.5
Gt. Britain	74.7	10.6	90.1	31.3	0.4	207.1
Greece	3.5	—	0.2	—	0.3	4.0
Ireland	1.0	—	—	1.1	0.1	2.2
Italy	0.3	0.8	1.5	11.5	4.1	18.2
Luxembourg	—	—	—	—	—	—
Netherlands	—	0.9	1.6	60.9	0.3	63.7
Norway	0.2	—	23.5	22.7	8.0	54.4
Portugal	0.1	—	—	—	0.5	0.6
Spain	11.9	2.8	1.2	—	2.0	17.9
Sweden	—	10.4	—	—	5.2	15.6
Switzerland	—	4.0	—	—	3.1	7.1
Turkey	7.4	—	2.4	—	1.0	10.8
Soviet Union[1]	340.9	24.5	613.7	408.7	15.1	1,402.9
United States[1]	429.2	75.0	479.1	413.8	26.6	1,423.7

[1] 1982

AGRICULTURE

INDICES OF AGRICULTURAL OUTPUT, 1977–81

(*1969–71 = 100*)

Country	1977	1978	1979	1980	1981
Austria	107	110	110	118	109
Belgium Luxembourg }	106	107	113	112	113
Denmark	110	109	114	115	119
Finland	99	102	107	110	103
France	107	114	121	125	123
Germany	119	122	125	125	131
Gt. Britain	113	116	119	126	122
Greece	121	132	126	134	136
Iceland	109	122	116	120	128
Ireland*	133	136	129	143	124
Italy	107	110	116	122	121
Netherlands	117	123	128	130	139
Norway	117	125	118	118	123
Portugal	80	81	93	84	70
Spain	127	139	137	143	129
Sweden	119	120	118	120	125
Switzerland	113	115	121	123	121
Turkey	130	135	140	143	144

* Source: *UN Yearbook, 1982.*

LAND UTILIZATION, 1982
(000 hectares)

Country	Agricultural area	Arable land	Land under permanent crops	Permanent meadows and pastures
Austria	3,689	1,549	99	2,041
Belgium	1,438	765	14	659
Denmark	2,897	2,638	14	246
Finland	2,540	2,379	—	161
France	31,802	17,584	1,411	12,807
Germany	12,197	7,303	179	4,714
Gt. Britain	18,795	6,930	68	11,797
Greece	9,234	—	1,000	5,271
Ireland	5,700	1,000	3	4,690
Italy	17,838	9,422	3,292	5,125
Luxembourg	128	56	2	70
Netherlands	2,018	831	35	1,152
Norway	938	830	—	108
Portugal	4,080	2,965	585	530
Spain	31,206	15,569	4,919	10,718
Sweden	3,676	2,691	—	715
Switzerland	2,020	391	20	1,609
Turkey	38,089	25,459	3,030	9,600
Soviet Union	605,466	227,400	4,866	373,200
United States	428,169	188,760	1,869	237,540

TRANSPORT

RAILWAYS, 1982

Country	Length of line operated (km.)	Passenger/km. (million)	Ton/km. (million)
Austria	5,811	7,043	10,232
Belgium	3,954	7,078	7,528
Denmark	2,461	4,003	1,551
Finland	6,092	3,274	8,214
France	34,383	55,666	62,793
Germany	28,417	39,762	60,871
Gt. Britain	17,876	30,740	17,505
Greece	2,461	1,515	693
Ireland	1,967	995	691
Italy	16,157	40,090	16,907
Luxembourg	270	252	585
Netherlands	2,956	9,230	3,319
Norway	4,242	2,425	2,813
Portugal	3,616	5,856	952
Spain	13,543	14,261	9,966
Sweden	11,340	6,851	14,296
Switzerland	3,179	9,409	7,221
Turkey	8,193	6,105	5,903
Soviet Union	143,300	347,900	3,464,500
United States	270,370	17,541	1,485,693[1]

[1] 1981

CIVIL AVIATION, 1982

Country	Number of airlines	Number of aircraft	Passenger/km. (million)	Available seat/km. (million)	Load factor (%)
Austria	1	16	1,235	2,610	47
Belgium	1	26	5,197	8,121	64
Denmark* Norway Sweden	—	—	2,970	4,816	62
Finland	1	86	10,818	17,563	62
France	1	36	2,498	4,330	58
Germany	2	121	31,876	49,138	65
Gt. Britain	2	187	44,145	68,288	65
Greece	1	44	5,184	7,871	66
Iceland	1	14	1,295	n.a.	n.a.
Ireland	1	19	2,270	3,247	70
Italy	1	61	12,044	20,348	59
Luxembourg	1	9	27	41	67
Netherlands	1	52	15,168	24,001	63
Portugal	1	31	4,008	6,245	64
Spain	1	88	15,280	24,794	62
Switzerland	1	50	11,628	17,774	65
Turkey	1	22	1,813	2,833	64
Soviet Union	1	n.a.	172,206	n.a.	82
United States	6	1,136	240,674	393,654	61

* Norway, Denmark and Sweden jointly operate SAS.

MERCHANT SHIPPING, 1981

Country	Total merchant ships: Number	000 tons gross	% world	Of which tankers: Number	000 tons gross
Austria	8	62	0.0	—	—
Belgium	312	1,917	0.5	14	287
Denmark	1,169	5,048	1.2	66	2,519
Finland	341	2,445	0.6	39	1,225
France	1,199	11,455	2.7	99	7,400
Germany	1,820	7,708	1.8	101	2,624
Gt. Britain	2,975	25,419	6.0	400	12,154
Greece	3,710	42,005	10.0	466	13,794
Ireland	156	268	0.1	7	14
Italy	1,677	10,641	2.5	257	4,361
Luxembourg	—	—	—	—	—
Netherlands	1,271	5,467	1.3	78	2,299
Norway	2,409	21,675	5.2	165	11,847
Portugal	351	1,377	0.3	17	755
Spain	2,678	8,134	1.9	108	4,920
Sweden	706	4,034	1.0	85	1,761
Switzerland	33	315	0.1	2	3
Turkey	532	1,664	0.4	59	434
Soviet Union[1]	7,713	23,789	5.6	489	4,805
United States[1]	6,133	19,111	4.5	332	8,220

[1] 1982

INLAND WATERWAYS TRANSPORT, 1981

Country	Length of inland waterways in use (km.)	Goods-carrying vessels Number	Capacity (000 metric tons)	Ton/km. (million) carried
Austria	358	218	200	7,168
Belgium	1,510	2,864	1,818	89,314
Denmark	—	—	—	—
Finland	6,057	89	n.a.	809
France	6,603	5,192	2,552	76,407
Germany	4,503	3,609	3,548	219,447
Gt. Britain	538	31	10	4,615
Greece	—	—	—	—
Ireland	—	—	—	—
Italy	2,237	572	n.a.	n.a.
Luxembourg	37	17	11	1,768
Netherlands	4,849	12,649	6,457	225,098
Norway	—	—	—	—
Portugal	—	—	—	—
Spain	—	—	—	—
Sweden	439	n.a.	n.a.	n.a.
Switzerland	21	447	645	9,261
Turkey	—	—	—	—
Soviet Union[1]	138,900	n.a.	n.a.	604,500
United States	41,403	41,941	134,451	1,761,382

[1] 1982

CONSUMPTION

COMPOSITION OF PRIVATE CONSUMPTION, 1982

Country	Food, beverages, tobacco	Clothing and footwear	Gross rent, fuel and power	Furniture, furnishings and household equipment and operation	Medical care and health expenses	Transport and communication	Recreation, entertainment, education and cultural services	Miscellaneous goods and services	Total
Austria	1,145	502	769	344	202	788	283	753	4,786
Belgium	1,221	425	1,105	612	573	711	337	748	5,732
Denmark	1,548	349	1,699	431	116	915	579	543	6,180
Finland	1,369	251	928	343	121	835	407	622	4,876
France	1,394	430	1,121	613	867	919	431	830	6,605
Germany	1,288	524	1,144	615	941	958	517	682	6,669
Gt. Britain	1,075	341	1,151	360	53	801	492	890	5,163
Greece	1,133	242	347	212	92	370	106	227	2,729
Ireland	1,199	187	321	185	73	386	292	187	2,830
Italy	1,201	351	527	281	184	539	297	598	3,978
Luxembourg	1,182	424	1,173	542	421	1,023	194	777	5,736
Netherlands	1,150	427	1,061	470	752	626	553	784	5,823
Norway	1,603	502	951	526	235	881	502	565	5,765
Portugal	577	175	91	155	68	228	73	192	1,559
Spain	1,222	397	496	333	233	479	271	463	3,894
Sweden	1,554	464	1,638	425	139	861	639	397	6,117
Switzerland	2,281	395	1,586	466	664	990	761	744	7,887
Turkey	n.a.	n.a.	n.a.	n.a.	n.a.	n.a.	n.a.	n.a.	n.a.
Soviet Union	n.a.	n.a.	n.a.	n.a.	n.a.	n.a.	n.a.	n.a.	n.a.
United States	1,171	467	1,497	438	921	1,194	584	951	7,223

CONSUMER PRICE INDEX, 1976–81
(1975 = 100)

Country	1976	1977	1978	1979	1980	1981
Austria	107.3	113.2	117.3	121.6	129.3	138.1
Belgium	109.2	116.9	122.2	127.6	136.1	146.5
Denmark	109.0	121.1	133.3	146.1	164.1	183.3
Finland	114.4	128.9	138.9	149.3	166.6	186.6
France	109.6	119.9	130.8	144.8	164.1	186.0
Germany	104.3	108.1	111.1	115.6	122.0	129.2
Gt. Britain	116.5	135.1	146.2	165.8	195.6	218.8
Greece	113.3	127.1	143.0	170.2	212.5	264.6
Iceland	132.2	172.4	248.4	361.3	592.9	863.0
Ireland	118.0	134.1	144.3	163.4	193.2	232.7
Italy	116.8	136.7	153.3	175.9	213.2	251.2
Luxembourg	109.8	117.2	120.8	126.3	134.2	145.1
Netherlands	108.8	115.8	120.5	125.6	133.8	142.8
Norway	109.2	119.2	128.7	135.0	149.5	170.0
Portugal	121.1	154.1	188.7	233.7	272.4	327.0
Spain	115.1	143.3	171.7	198.5	229.5	262.8
Sweden	110.3	122.9	135.1	144.9	164.7	184.7
Switzerland	101.7	103.3	104.1	107.8	112.2	119.5
Turkey	117.5	148.0	239.6	391.8	761.1	1,047.4
Japan	112.2	118.1	122.6	127.0	137.2	144.0
United States	110.5	112.6	121.2	134.9	153.1	168.9

Source: World Bank.

INTERNAL CONSUMPTION OF PRIMARY ENERGY
PRODUCTS AND EQUIVALENTS, 1982
(million tons coal equivalent)

Country	Coal and lignite	Crude petroleum	Natural gas	Primary electricity	Nuclear energy	Total
Austria	3.8	9.8	3.6	2.9	—	20.1
Belgium	11.2	20.6	8.2	0.1	3.2	43.3
Denmark	4.8	11.5	—	0.5	—	16.8
Finland	2.8	10.0	0.8	1.2	3.9	18.7
France	28.6	96.6	21.9	5.9	27.5	180.5
Germany	83.8	114.8	42.5	3.0	13.5	257.6
Gt. Britain	68.9	73.7	40.9	0.4	10.6	194.5
Greece	3.8	10.9	—	0.3	—	15.0
Ireland	1.7	5.1	1.1	0.1	—	8.0
Italy	12.0	90.8	21.9	4.9	0.8	130.4
Luxembourg	1.5	1.1	0.3	0.3	—	3.2
Netherlands	3.8	26.8	28.9	0.3	0.9	60.7
Norway	0.9	7.9	0.8	7.9	—	17.5
Portugal	0.4	7.5	—	0.5	—	8.4
Spain	16.7	41.8	1.9	2.0	2.8	65.2
Sweden	1.4	20.4	—	5.2	10.4	37.4
Switzerland	0.5	10.9	0.9	2.5	4.0	18.8
Turkey	7.7	14.0	—	1.0	—	22.7
Soviet Union	333.4	360.7	359.3	11.8	24.5	1,089.7
United States	361.5	659.4	429.3	28.2	75.0	1,553.4

SOCIAL STATISTICS

HEALTH SERVICES, 1981

Country	Doctors		Nurses & midwives		Hospital beds	
	Number	Population per physician	Number	Per 10,000 inhabitants	Number	Population per bed
Austria	8,888	397	30,504	40.60	85,204	88
Belgium	24,536	401	34,636	35.80	90,291	108
Denmark	10,572	482	30,698	60.50	42,535	119
Finland	9,016	n.a.	45,569	96.20	73,700	64
France	91,442	580	312,675	59.10	644,118	82
Germany	135,711	452	241,912	39.20	714,879	85
Gt. Britain	86,763	654	245,660	41.69	485,785	119
Greece	22,337	423	17,974	19.90	58,994	158
Iceland	424	518	1,341	61.00	3,775	58
Ireland	4,174	807	18,700	59.10	34,625	95
Italy	164,555	345	186,335	33.60	573,923	98
Luxembourg	505	712	1,373	38.10	4,539	79
Netherlands	24,878	560	51,976	37.50	98,933	n.a.
Norway	7,813	520	40,075	99.20	61,006	66
Portugal	18,088	n.a.	20,654	21.20	52,327	187
Spain	81,658	n.a.	44,375	12.30	192,864	186
Sweden	16,340	506	65,500	79.40	122,478	67
Switzerland	14,843	428	30,000	47.40	72,438	87
Turkey	27,241	1,648	45,405	10.80	86,526	498
Soviet Union[1]	960,500	281	—	—	3,201,000	84
United States[2]	414,900	559	—	—	719,000	322

[1] 1979
[2] 1980

HOUSING, 1981

Country	Number of occupied dwellings (000)	Average numbers	
		rooms per dwelling	persons per room
Austria	3,077	4.1	0.9
Belgium	3,811	5.0	0.6
Denmark	2,176	3.5	0.8
Finland	1,782	3.1	1.0
France	22,610	3.6	1.3
Germany	25,450	4.2	1.5
Gt. Britain	21,699	4.9	0.6
Greece	3,020	3.5	0.9
Iceland*	72.8	4.8	0.9
Ireland*	923.3	4.7	0.9
Italy	21,853	3.7	0.9
Luxembourg	138	5.3	0.6
Netherlands	4,957	5.1	0.8
Norway	1,416	4.4	0.6
Portugal	3,405	4.5	0.8
Spain	13,265	4.4	0.9
Sweden	3,852	3.8	0.7
Switzerland	2,743	4.7	0.6
Turkey	3,918	2.7	2.2
Soviet Union[1]	58,690	—	—
United States	79,000	—	—

* Sources: *UN Yearbook, 1982*; *The New Book of World Rankings.*
[1] 1970

FACILITIES IN DWELLINGS, 1982

		% of total dwelling units with:	
Country	*Electricity*	*Inside running water*	*Fixed baths/showers*
Austria	99.2	100.0	100.0
Belgium	99.7	99.3	99.9
Denmark	99.9	100.0	100.0
Finland	96.0	99.2	65.6
France	98.8	100.0	100.0
Germany	99.9	100.0	100.0
Gt. Britain	99.7	100.0	100.0
Greece	88.3	71.2	72.1
Iceland*	92.8	100.0	78.7
Ireland*	94.7	99.6	99.6
Italy	99.0	80.4	91.4
Luxembourg	99.9	98.4	98.2
Netherlands	98.1	100.0	99.4
Norway	91.7	100.0	93.9
Portugal	95.2	94.3	97.6
Spain	97.3	98.7	88.0
Sweden	99.6	100.0	91.6
Switzerland	99.9	96.1	95.9
Turkey	75.4	35.8	72.1

* Source: *UN Yearbook, 1982.*

MOTOR VEHICLES IN USE, 1982

| Country | Passenger cars | | Commercial vehicles (000) | Motorcycles (000) |
	000	per 000 of population		
Austria	2,313	308	208	91
Belgium	3,206	325	355	113
Denmark	1,367	267	282	34
Finland	1,279	266	167	43
France	18,800	349	2,571	800
Germany	23,731	385	1,617	738
Gt. Britain	15,910	283	1,919	937
Greece	911	94	880	12
Iceland	81	n.a.	9	1
Ireland	778	225	70	6
Italy	18,603	325	1,356	1,138
Luxembourg	133	365	15	3
Netherlands	4,609	323	350	93
Norway	1,279	312	164	29
Portugal	1,269	128	355	94
Spain	7,943	211	1,381	1,231
Sweden	2,893	348	194	16
Switzerland	2,394	370	180	137
Turkey	715	15	401	119
Soviet Union	9,631	36	8,304	—
United States	123,698	547	35,812	—

Source: *UN Yearbook, 1982.*

RADIO AND TV SETS AND TELEPHONES IN USE, 1982

Country	Radio receivers 000	per 000 population	TV receivers 000	per 000 population	Telephones, 1982 000	per 100 population
Austria	2,640	352	2,114	282	3,010	40.1
Belgium	4,451	452	2,885	293	3,636	36.9
Denmark	1,929	377	1,830	358	3,283	64.1
Finland	2,500	525	1,508	316	2,374	49.6
France	18,000	337	15,609	292	24,686	45.9
Germany	22,664	370	20,672	337	28,554	46.4
Gt. Britain	52,000	931	22,000	394	26,651	47.7
Greece	2,900	307	1,385	147	2,796	28.9
Iceland*	132	579	62	270	109	47.7
Ireland	1,250	371	750	223	650	18.7
Italy	13,634	240	13,170	231	19,277	33.7
Luxembourg	186	512	89	245	199	54.7
Netherlands	4,315	308	4,111	293	7,230	50.9
Norway	1,332	327	1,173	288	1,852	45.2
Portugal	1,575	160	1,203	122	1,372	13.8
Spain	9,600	258	9,424	253	11,945	31.5
Sweden	2,847	354	3,103	374	6,621	79.6
Switzerland	2,250	355	1,973	312	4,632	72.7
Turkey	4,280	97	3,099	70	1,902	4.2
Soviet Union	—	—	81,000	305	—	—
United States	—	—	142,000	624	—	—

* Source: *UN Yearbook, 1982.*

PART TWO

GENERAL

POLITICAL AFFAIRS

WESTERN EUROPE AND THE ATLANTIC WORLD

JACQUES MALLET*

FACING each other as they do on opposite sides of the Atlantic, Western Europe and the United States are linked closely and profoundly in a common civilization founded on individual freedom and respect for the principles of democracy. Two world wars have strengthened and broadened their relations in the fields of defense, foreign policy and economy. These relations now constitute one of the principal facts of world politics. They are central to European politics, the future of which is inseparable from that of the Atlantic world. European integration and the Atlantic Alliance have been weaving the same strand of history for the past 40 years.

Having been the catalyst and mainstay of the process of European integration that began after World War II, the United States has become an involuntary source of discord between European countries. The future of European unity and that of the Atlantic Alliance, which is still the basis of their common security, thus depend on whether a solution is found for this problem. While it may be true that the unity of Western Europe has an essential contribution to make to the cohesion of the West, it is impossible to imagine a united Europe if the Atlantic Alliance were irreparably divided, just as it is inconceivable that there could be a strong Alliance with a disunited Europe.

A look at the history of the relations between Europe and the United States since 1945 will provide a better understanding of today's difficulties and throw some light on the attitudes of each. It will also show why a new balance within the Atlantic world is needed, which will reflect the spectacular economic recovery of Western Europe—a recovery that the area owes to American aid, to its own efforts and to the success of the Common Market. The postwar period is over. The age of American "protection," benevolent as it was, is finished for Europe. The time has now come for the "Dialogue des Continents," a dialogue that will inevitably involve competition and occasional disagreements.

This will mean the establishment of a partnership between the United States and the European Community (EC) as first proposed by President Kennedy in 1962: that is to say, the gradual creation in all fields of a relationship between "two distinct but equally powerful entities, each bearing its

* Revised by Richard Mayne.

share of common responsibilities in the world."[1] Before examining the details of such a partnership it may be useful to review the development of Western Europe and the Atlantic world which has made it not only possible but necessary.

UNITED STATES AID

On May 8, 1945, the capitulation of the Third Reich put an end to fighting in the Old World. Western Europe came out of it victorious, thanks to 5 million U.S. soldiers and American equipment. But in fact, Europe was the great loser of the war. Hungry, ruined, uncertain of the future, the Old World watched its power and prestige melting away. Europe was confronted also by a new world balance: two giant states of continental proportions were dividing up the leadership of the world between themselves. The technical, industrial, financial and military power of the United States, strengthened already by the first world war, had been prodigiously increased by the second, while at the gates of the European West a new empire was being established, almost as menacing as Hitler's.

The United States understood that it was in its interest, as well as that of the "free world," to help and to protect Europe. The Marshall Plan and the Atlantic Alliance are the two dominant factors of this period of European history, which may be called the "American period." The Americans remained in Western Europe, where their presence was desired, and committed themselves to helping it. This was something new. In doing so, they broke with the shortsighted policy of isolationism they had pursued after the first world war. In 1945, the United States had the courage and the wisdom not to fall into this error again. Knowing that its developing industries needed new markets to match their growth, it was led, logically, to give Europe the wherewithal to feed itself and to revive its economy. One cannot be rich on one's own. In the Marshall Plan, American interest, it goes without saying, went hand in hand with an undeniable spirit of generosity.

But political motivations were still more important. Franklin D. Roosevelt had cherished the hope of organizing peace in agreement with the Soviet Union and Great Britain, within the framework of the world institutions set up in 1945. These hopes soon faded. Given the possibility of a conflict with the Soviet Union, it was necessary at all costs to ensure that Europe, and its human and industrial potential, should not fall into the opposite camp, which would have destroyed the balance of world power.

It was on June 5, 1947 that General Marshall, in his famous speech at Harvard University, announced the vast program of aid to Europe that was to bear his name. In his address he made a double appeal: to American opinion, asking it to consent to the necessary financial effort, and to the

[1] Joint declaration of the Action Committee for the United States of Europe (under the chairmanship of Jean Monnet) adopted by the representatives of the principal democratic parties and free trade unions of the Common Market countries, June 26, 1962.

countries of Europe, exhorting them to unite. The originality of the Marshall Plan lay not so much in the substitution of gifts for loans, nor in the great scale of these gifts—Marshall Plan aid to Europe between 1948 and 1952 amounted to $13,812 million[2]—as in the replacement of bilateral aid by collective aid. In other words, the Marshall Plan gave a considerable boost to European integration, for national efforts had to be coordinated if the aid were to be properly used. Some Americans at that time brought up the possibility of a customs union and of a Europe unified "on federal lines."[3] But General Marshall himself insisted that the way the Europeans were to organize the distribution of aid should be left to them.

Thus instead of keeping to the old policy of "divide and rule," the United States, which between the wars had been largely indifferent to, or suspicious of, the first attempts at European unity, this time took the initiative in support of such unity. It was in response to this American call for Europe to coordinate its plans for recovery that on April 16, 1948 the agreement setting up the Organization for European Economic Cooperation (OEEC) was signed in Paris by 17 Western European countries.[4]

The activity which had started in the economic field, and whose purpose was the rational distribution of Marshall Plan aid, the freeing of trade and payments, and the coordination of development plans, was soon to find its natural extension on the political level—the Council of Europe, constituted on May 5, 1949 by 10 countries.[5] The European Movement, which met in congress at the Hague in May 1948, had since then been calling for the election of an Assembly on the basis of universal suffrage. The Consultative Assembly of the Council which met in Strasbourg in August 1949 with Paul-Henri Spaak as its first president may have seemed a long way from this ideal, but it was a European initiative. The Americans refused to become involved, while indicating that they were disappointed by the timidity of the European negotiators.

There were also other more burning problems. The United States, having demobilized prematurely, became daily more aware of dangers presented by the Soviet Union to which Winston Churchill had already drawn President Truman's attention in 1945.

Within three years the Soviet Union, in defiance of the engagements it had undertaken toward its allies, had annexed large areas of Finnish, Polish, Ruthenian, Bessarabian and Prussian territory, and the whole of Estonia,

[2] Of which $2,753 million went to France, $3,421 million to Britain, $1,511 million to Italy and $1,389 million to Germany.
[3] Notably John Foster Dulles in a speech made on January 17, 1947.
[4] That is, almost all the countries of Western Europe except Spain. Germany was to join in 1949. Marshall Plan aid had been offered to the whole of Europe, including Eastern Europe, but the Soviet Union had refused to take part in the new organization and constrained Czechoslovakia to follow its example. (See also "The Organization for Economic Cooperation and Development (OECD)", p. 627.)
[5] Belgium, Denmark, France, Britain, Ireland, Italy, Luxembourg, the Netherlands, Norway and Sweden. Greece and Turkey joined in August 1949, Iceland in 1950, Germany in 1951, Austria in 1956, Cyprus in 1961, Switzerland in 1963 and Malta in 1965.

Lithuania and Latvia. Similarly, in three years several nations had been taken over by the Communists as a result of the presence of the Soviet army and against the peoples' wishes: Poland, East Germany, Hungary, Rumania, Albania; that is to say, a million square kilometers and 95 million people had been absorbed by a new "Eurasian" empire.

The collapse of democratic government in Czechoslovakia in February–March 1948 finally succeeded in mobilizing European public opinion. The countries of Western Europe understood then that they had to work together if they were to survive. Realization of the common peril no doubt contributed decisively to accelerating the process of European integration.

In the military field, a first attempt at European organization was made in March 1948, when Britain, France, Belgium, the Netherlands and Luxembourg signed a defensive alliance, the Brussels Treaty. But in face of the enormous strength of the Soviet Union, these countries soon realized that, alone, they were practically speaking defenseless. They had neither the men, nor the money, nor the arms to carry out their policy. So on May 4, 1948 they had to make an urgent appeal to General Marshall that the United States should provide without delay for the signatories of the treaty "what they lacked in strength." The appeal was answered immediately. This fact deserves to be underlined, for the Europeans' request came up sharply against a deep-rooted political and diplomatic tradition in the United States. It needed all the persuasion of General Marshall and President Truman to get the Senate to adopt on June 11, 1948 the Vandenberg resolution authorizing the United States to undertake a military commitment in peacetime outside the American continent. This made it possible for the North Atlantic Treaty to be signed on April 4, 1949. A few days later the Soviet Union lifted the first Berlin blockade, which had lasted for 323 days.

The aim of the Atlantic Alliance was to get a collective defense effort going around the North Atlantic in peacetime under one command. According to Article Five of the treaty, the parties agreed that "an armed attack against one of them would be considered as an attack directed against all the parties." To this legal guarantee of intervention—which is not, however, automatic[6]—a material guarantee was added: the permanent maintenance of powerfully armed American divisions on the European continent.

The guarantee of the Atlantic Alliance and the presence of American soldiers—as well as the world monopoly in atomic weapons that the United States enjoyed up to 1953—were probably instrumental in protecting Western Europe from Soviet attack, and in saving the area from the fate of Czechoslovakia. Since the signing of the treaty, the security of Western Europe has been constantly assured, and in this sense, thanks to the treaty's military organization, the North Atlantic Treaty Organization (NATO), the Atlantic Alliance has been a great success within the area it covers.

[6] Article Five of the treaty limits itself to saying that each signatory, in the event of an attack against another member country, will engage in "such action as it judges necessary." It is the "subsidiary bodies" provided for in Article Nine of the treaty, set up between 1949 and 1960 and together constituting NATO, which, by binding the United States to the defense of Europe, have given to the nonautomatic engagement of Article Five a material certainty of intervention.

The Marshall Plan also achieved its aim: the rapid reconstruction of the European economy. By 1953, in most of the recipient countries, production was 25 percent higher than in 1938.

However, United States aid did not succeed in checking the *relative* decline of Western Europe's importance.[7] Europe's dependence was manifest in the continual deficit in its balance of payments (which, in spite of the gift of $22,300 million in six years, went through three crises, in 1947, 1949 and 1951). With economic dependence went total military dependence; political dependence could not fail to ensue. In a word, the countries of Western Europe were protected and assisted countries. Economically, militarily and politically the Atlantic was dominated by the United States. This hegemony was not the result of a deliberate policy; it was the consequence of weakness on the one hand and considerable power on the other. In the long run, such a situation was to the advantage neither of the United States nor of the European countries; on both sides it created complexes—in the former, a sense of continually being the "givers" and in the latter, of continually being the "takers"—which were to have unfortunate and lasting consequences for relations between them.

BIRTH OF THE EUROPEAN COMMUNITY (EC)

To remedy this unhealthy and potentially dangerous situation, the Western Europeans needed first of all to stimulate the economic expansion of their countries, and secondly to regain their self-confidence and with it a feeling of independence. Britain had played a major role in setting up the first European organizations—a useful stage, but one of limited effect. It was followed by a new stage of European history that may be called the "French period," for this time it was France that took the initiative. Many continental statesmen felt in any case the necessity for going "faster and further."

The great merit of Robert Schuman, the French foreign minister, and of Jean Monnet, who was in charge of the French economic planning commission, was that they looked for new solutions instead of reusing the old formulas. The Schuman Declaration of May 9, 1950, the real birth of the EC, immediately transformed the relations between Germany and France. Five years almost to the day after the unconditional surrender of Germany, France proposed that the two countries' entire production of coal and steel should be placed under a common High Authority, an organization which other European countries would be able to join if they wished. In this way the economic means of war—steel and energy—would be made to serve peaceful ends. Common institutions, with limited but real powers, would supervise the running of a Common Market in a limited but basic sector of the economy. This was also to be the first stage of a European Federation.

Both Chancellor Adenauer and Dean Acheson gave this revolutionary proposal the warmest encouragement. As Britain, however, rejected the principle of supranationality, negotiations on the Schuman Plan involved only

---

[7] One example among many: in 1913 Western Europe manufactured 46 percent of the world's steel; in 1952 it manufactured 19 percent (M. G. de Carmoy, *Fortune de l'Europe*, Paris, 1953).

six countries, and the treaty setting up the European Coal and Steel Community (ECSC) was signed by them in Paris on April 18, 1951. With its coming into effect at the beginning of January 1952, economic integration had begun. The ECSC was a vast experiment; the institution of the Common Market later extended the experiment, on a more flexible basis, to the whole of the economy. The Treaty of Rome, signed on the Capitoline Hill on March 25, 1957, was a direct consequence of the Schuman Plan, and the European Economic Community (EEC) and Euratom, which it set up, fulfilled Schuman's aims of 1950.

The United States approved and supported this policy because it increased Europe's capacity for resistance to communism, and at the same time contributed to the strength of the Atlantic Alliance by giving it a more satisfactory balance. The United States had always felt the excessive disparity between itself and its partners to be a weakness in the Alliance. Furthermore, a rather oversimplified concept of the "United States of Europe" has always attracted American thought, which was even prepared to draw parallels between the efforts of the Six to work together and the creation of the United States out of 13 British colonies in 1776. From 1950 up to the beginning of 1963, the support given by the United States to the policy of European integration never failed, whether it was a question of the OEEC or the Schuman Plan or the Common Market. This support was essentially political in nature, and strong enough to make the Americans accept, from Europe, a certain degree of "trade discrimination."

The European Defense Community (EDC) project of 1952–54[8] clearly showed how far the unity of the Alliance and that of Europe were interdependent: any European crisis was of necessity an Atlantic crisis, and any Atlantic crisis became a crisis for Europe. France's European partners, and in particular, Germany, could conceive of European unity only in the framework of integration within the Atlantic Alliance, as did the United States itself. In Germany's case this was for obvious security reasons—its exposed situation on the frontier of the Soviet world, and the even more exposed position of Berlin. France, until 1958, did not conceive of it otherwise. The whole EEC rested, in fact, on this fundamental unity of foreign policy. Fidelity to the Atlantic Alliance and to its military organization NATO constituted the unwritten law of the Six; it allowed economic union to be founded on a solid political basis.

FROM COMMON MARKET TO ATLANTIC PARTNERSHIP

The European and Atlantic crisis of 1954 highlights the vitality of the EC and the irresistible attraction of the process of integration. Less than a year

[8]As the Korean war made German rearmament essential, France proposed that a European army should be formed. The treaty setting up the EDC, signed on May 27, 1952, was rejected on August 30, 1954 by the French parliament, a victim of the conjunction of Gaullist and Communist votes. In the end, the Paris agreements (October 23, 1954) gave Germany sovereignty within certain limits (notably, prohibition of the manufacture of nuclear armaments) and reconstituted a German national army integrated in the Atlantic Alliance.

after the EDC had collapsed, the Six began to move forward again. On June 2, 1955, the revival of the movement took place at the Messina Conference; negotiations for setting up a Common Market and Euratom were begun. The Treaty of Rome came into effect on January 1, 1958, and brought on to the international scene a new economic power: the principal commercial power and the second industrial power in the world, after the United States and before the Soviet Union.

The consequence of all this was a fundamental change in the respective situations of Europe and the United States. Ten years after the Marshall Plan, Common Market expansion was much more rapid than American expansion. The Common Market countries not only caught up with their balance of payments deficit, but built up their reserves to very high levels.

The success of the Common Market has had a second consequence of no lesser importance. Having begun by being suspicious, hostile and skeptical about its prospects, Britain, with its usual realism, turned to thoughts of joining the Market as soon as it achieved success and became a reality.

It was at the end of 1961 that the policy subsequently called "the Grand Design" was worked out by President Kennedy's entourage. Basically, it was a reply to a double challenge: the success of the Common Market and the rebuilding of the European economy on the one hand (coinciding with the American balance of payments crisis); and on the other hand, the prospect —somewhat alarming for Washington—of an enlarged Community, a vast preferential trade area possibly taking in the whole of the Commonwealth and covering, by virtue of this, a third of the world's commerce.

President Kennedy and his advisers understood the need for the United States to react promptly to "these challenges and opportunities." Instead of seeking to solve these new problems that Europe was posing for the United States in isolation, withdrawal and protectionism by reducing all American spending abroad; instead of replying to the European challenge with an anti-European policy—President Kennedy sought a general expansion of trade in which American exports could grow. This had indeed become a national necessity. In his famous speech of July 4, 1962 at Philadelphia he proclaimed: "I will say here and now, on this Day of Independence, that the United States will be ready for a *Declaration of Interdependence*—that we will be prepared to discuss with a united Europe the ways and means of forming a concrete Atlantic Partnership."

The first stage of this partnership was to be commercial. The American part took the form of a new piece of legislation—the Trade Expansion Act signed on October 11, 1962—giving the president unprecedentedly wide powers of negotiation for tariff reductions.

But the aims of the partnership, as President Kennedy outlined them, were even vaster. He saw in a united Europe a partner with whom the United States could deal on a basis of full equality with reference to all the huge tasks that went with the setting up and the defense of an Atlantic community, tasks that neither side could accomplish alone. The new alliance being planned between the enlarged EC and the United States would make an impressive force: 400 to 500 million people, representing twice the total production of the Sino-Soviet bloc, 90 percent of the industrial production of the free world, 90 percent of world trade in manufactured goods.

One of the keystones of this great scheme was Britain's membership in the Common Market. It is easy to understand the disappointment and anger of the United States government at the French veto of Britain's entry on January 14, 1963.[9] This crisis was a highly dangerous turning point for the European Community, in so far as from that moment the two roads—Atlantic and European—began visibly to diverge.

A NEW WORLD

The year 1963 has indeed been described as "the year the Fifties ended." In addition to the veto on Britain, it saw not only the retirement of Konrad Adenauer as first postwar Chancellor of the Federal Republic of Germany, but also the assassination of President Kennedy. 1964 saw the retirement of Nikita Khrushchev; 1965, General de Gaulle's announcement that French military integration within NATO was to end; 1966, the decision to move NATO headquarters from Paris to Brussels; 1967, a second veto on British membership of the EC; and 1968, the election of President Richard Nixon. The world had changed since the heady days of "partnership."

Deeper changes, however, had already been affecting transatlantic relations. Since 1959 and the Soviet development of ICBMs, the world had been living in a balance of terror. The United States was now in the front line. In these circumstances, the question had arisen whether the Americans would be willing to commit their whole strength to defend Europe against attack, which might involve the immediate destruction of their own cities. Furthermore, with the escalation of the Vietnam war, Europe no longer seemed to be at the center of American strategy, in so far as the center of gravity of the cold (or warm) war had moved from Europe to Asia. This sense of displacement was to be heightened with the loss of prestige suffered by America's "East Coast Establishment" and the election of a Southerner in the person of President Carter and a Westerner in that of President Reagan.

Changes in the Communist bloc were likewise affecting the European and Atlantic scene. First of all there was the de-Stalinization begun by Khrushchev and continued by his successors; second, the split between Moscow and Peking; and third, the attempts of the "peoples' democracies" to liberate themselves from Soviet supremacy (under cover of the Sino-Soviet disagreement). As a result, many Europeans became inclined to discount any threat of Soviet aggression against Western Europe; while their continuing fear of a nuclear holocaust made them mistrustful of what they perceived

[9]To save the partnership scheme from complete disaster, the president's advisers reaffirmed, at the beginning of 1963, the United States' desire to continue the Kennedy Round of tariff negotiations in the General Agreement on Tariffs and Trade, which followed on the Trade Expansion Act. They also advocated with renewed vigor the plan for a multilateral force (MLF). This plan consisted in forming a fleet of cargo vessels with international crews provided with Polaris missiles.

The Kennedy Round opened in Geneva in May 1964 and ended two years later in an agreement to cut industrial tariffs by an average of 35 to 40 percent. The MLF project hung fire, however, and was finally dropped by President Lyndon Johnson.

as "the arms race." Some even went so far as to conclude that NATO was no longer indispensable and that it was possible to envisage some form of close cooperation with the countries of Eastern Europe. These tendencies, which have some affinity with the more nationalist positions adopted by General de Gaulle, found their loudest expression in the European "peace" movements. Some of their more extreme spokesmen even gave the impression that the United States, not the Soviet Union, was the main danger to peace. These concerns and conflicts came to a head in 1984, when the European peace movements mounted a vociferous campaign against the deployment in Europe of Cruise and Pershing missiles, although these had earlier been requested by European governments as a counter to the buildup of Soviet SS-20s. A similar controversy arose over the American Strategic Defense Initiative (SDI, popularly known as "Star Wars"), which some Europeans feared might intensify American isolationist tendencies by fostering hopes that U.S. territory could be made invulnerable to Soviet missiles, thereby increasing the fears of some Europeans that a future nuclear war's chief victim would be Europe, and that deterrence would thus be undermined.

These strains within the Alliance were paralleled by difficulties in the economic sphere. In 1971, the United States felt obliged to allow the dollar to float, thereby abandoning the system of fixed but adjustable parities established at Bretton Woods. Members of the EC established their own smaller system, but France moved in and out of it, while Britain, Ireland and Italy did not join. In 1973–74, the world was rocked by the first oil crisis, when members of the Organization of Petroleum Exporting Countries (OPEC) imposed vast price increases in response to the Yom Kippur War. Inflation and recession, which had already begun to haunt the world economy, now grew apace. In search of greater stability, the Community's member states devised the European Monetary System (EMS), with a European Currency Unit, or ECU, not yet a parallel currency but a *numéraire*, based on a "basket" of national currencies. This time, all member states agreed to take part in the EMS, but Britain abstained from its exchange-rate mechanism, preferring to continue to float the pound.

BACK TO PARTNERSHIP?

One of the hopes of the founders of the EMS was that it might develop into a European Reserve System similar to the U.S. Federal Reserve. Thereby, it was thought, the EC might be able to establish a monetary partnership with the United States, with some of the beneficial stabilizing effects of Bretton Woods. Hopes of partnership had revived in 1969 with the retirement of President de Gaulle, which had opened the way to British, Danish and Irish membership of the Community, which began in 1973. A second round of tariff negotiations, the Nixon or Tokyo Round (1973–79) further reduced tariffs; and a series of Western "economic summit" meetings brought together the governments of the United States and some, but not all, of the Community countries.

But if these were hopeful signs, many tensions remained. The large quantities of "flight money" at loose in the world's capital markets, together with

American unwillingness and European inability to treat exchange rates as matters of common concern, made transatlantic parities damagingly unstable. Disputes on trade matters continued, centering on the European Common Agricultural Policy (CAP); and security problems went on plaguing governments and officials as much as public opinion. Americans were inclined to blame Europeans for "not pulling their own weight"; Europeans repaid the compliment by complaining of American "Gaullism." Essentially, the difficulties were inherent in the relationship between one superpower, with worldwide interests and responsibilities, and a group of medium-sized countries with great collective economic and commercial strength. Unless the latter can unite effectively and speak with one voice on the delicate subjects of their debate with the United States, the sheer disparity of scale will always lead to friction. A true European currency, a single European economic policy and an integrated European contribution to Alliance security—these are still, as in Kennedy's day, the key to stable partnership. Unfortunately, they are still aspirations rather than achievements.

FURTHER READING

Ball, George W. *The Discipline of Power.* Boston: Atlantic Monthly Press, Little, Brown, 1968.
————. *The Past Has Another Pattern.* New York: Norton, 1982.
Beloff, Max. *The United States and the Unity of Europe.* Washington, D.C.: Brookings Institution; London: Faber, 1963.
Birrenbach, Kurt. *The Future of the Atlantic Community: Towards European Partnership.* London: Pall Mall Press; New York: Frederick A. Praeger, 1963.
Kissinger, Henry A. *The Troubled Partnership.* London: McGraw-Hill; New York: Doubleday, 1966.
Lerner, Daniel, and Gordon, Morton. *Euratlantica: Changing Perspectives of the European Elites.* Cambridge, Mass.: MIT Press, 1969.
Lichtheim, George. *Europe and America: The Future of the Atlantic Community.* London: Thames and Hudson, 1963.
Mayne, Richard, ed. *The New Atlantic Challenge.* London: Charles Knight, 1975.
Monnet, Jean. *Memoirs.* London: Collins; New York: Doubleday, 1978.
Munk, Frank. *Atlantic Dilemma: Partnership or Community?* New York: Oceana, 1964.
Steel, Ronald. *The End of Alliance: America and the Future of Europe.* London: Deutsch; New York: Viking Press, 1964.
Taber, George M. *Patterns and Prospects of Common Market Trade.* London: Peter Owen, 1974.
van der Beugel, Ernst H. *From Marshall Aid to Atlantic Partnership.* Amsterdam: Elsevier, 1966.

WESTERN EUROPEAN SECURITY: DEFENSE AND DISARMAMENT

ANTHONY VERRIER

THE PRESENT SITUATION

WHEN "Western European Defence: NATO in Disarray" was published in the first edition of this handbook (1967), disagreements within the alliance were discussed, however much by implication, in the context of a real if not openly declared détente between the United States and the Soviet Union. Détente reflected a realization by the superpowers, stemming from the October 1962 Cuba missile crisis, the subsequent establishment of the hot line and the removal of first strike nuclear weapons from NATO's peripheral areas, that war in the nuclear age was "inadmissible." Neither superpower renounced its roles outside Europe—the United States became mired in Vietnam, the Soviet Union in the Middle East—but détente concerning each other's survival and the stability of a politically divided but economically complementary Europe was recognized as a rational compromise.

But early in 1976, President Ford dropped "détente" from his political vocabulary,[1] and it is certainly the case that thereafter, and despite President Carter's essentially pacific attitude to the Soviet Union, U.S. participants in the business of deterring nuclear war have refused to acknowledge that superpower détente is desirable, or possible, or even that it existed. All that these statesmen will acknowledge is a détente imposed by the United States on the Soviet Union because of the possession of "superiority" in nuclear weapons, whether that elusive characteristic is defined by numbers, destructive power, or accuracy.[2]

The critical characteristic, however, which all too rarely enters this argument (and which was not only notably absent from the Strategic Arms Limitation treaties, SALT-I and SALT-II, but from the Strategic Arms Reduction

---

[1] *Annual Register*, Chronology, March 1, 1976.
[2] The sources mainly relied on here are the various publications of the International Institute for Strategic Studies (IISS), which also reprint or summarize much worldwide comment and analysis.

talks and Intermediate Nuclear Forces, or INF, discussions) is *deployment*.[3] Yet it is the deployment of two U.S.-made and U.S.-controlled weapons—Cruise and Pershing-II—in the European North Atlantic Treaty Organization (NATO) countries which, since this decision was linked in December 1979 to arms control negotiations, has presented the alliance with its worst crisis since the time of its foundation in 1949. The year 1984 was NATO's 35th and the occasion for a not always convincing attempt to claim that Cruise and Pershing deployment was only a response to Soviet policies. It does seem necessary, therefore, to consider why the deployment of these two weapons should have provoked so much controversy—one that continued at the level of governmental opposition, not "peace" movements as commonly defined. *Where* a nuclear weapon is put defines what it is intended to deter. All its other characteristics must, logically, be subordinate to deployment, whether its location is known or not.

At the time of writing, the government of the Netherlands, despite—or because of—intense pressure exerted on it from various quarters, not least by Joseph Luns, the Dutch former secretary-general of NATO, remained firm in its refusal to allow Cruise to be deployed in Holland unless arms control negotiations were resumed. As a result, the Belgian government remained opposed. As a further result, 96 Cruise missiles (48 each in the Netherlands and Belgium) out of a total of 464, had for the foreseeable future to be deleted from NATO's (in reality the United States') nuclear armory. The strategic analysts, and they are legion today, who see deterrence in numerical terms—"more means better"—were made to look foolish by the actions of two minor members of NATO. The numbers in question represented in December 1979, and on paper still represent, the mathematical "matching" answer to the Soviet Union's deployment in Warsaw Pact areas in the 1970s and since of a totally different weapon, the SS-20, designed to upgrade or replace weapons of a similar mode, albeit less accurate.[4]

The SS-20 is not necessarily an INF weapon, i.e., one originally planned, like Cruise and Pershing, for a (European) theater role. The SS-20, according

---

[3] For references to SALT-I, see page 290ff. SALT-II was signed in June 1979, but the U.S. Senate has failed to ratify it. Although many categories of weapon, inspection, verification, etc., are covered by these treaties, they are essentially concerned with mutual U.S.-Soviet deterrence. The Strategic Arms Reduction Talks were begun in July 1982; the INF discussions in November 1981. Both were broken off in November 1983. European NATO was not represented at these talks, but official observers from NATO's members were given a good account of them, especially when the Soviet Union suggested, and the United States *unofficially* conceded, that the British and French "theater" nuclear systems should be considered as elements for discussion of arms reduction agreements.

[4] For a full discussion of when and why the SS-20 came into service, see Raymond L. Garthoff, "The Soviet SS-20 Decision," IISS *Survival*, May–June 1983, pp. 110–19. For the official U.S. view, see Eugene Rostow (until January 1983 director of the Arms Control and Disarmament Agency), "The Future of Soviet-American Relations" (a paper read at international seminar in London, December 14–17, 1982). Dr. Rostow argues that the Soviet INF capability greatly "outmatches" NATO's; Dr. Garthoff says that he does not believe this to be so.

to its deployment, and like varieties of submarine-launched missiles developed or upgraded in the Soviet Union for many years, can pose a threat to the United States.[5] Cruise and Pershing-II, however, *but solely as deployed in Western Europe*, pose a direct threat to the Soviet Union, and, in the latter's view, are not theater weapons at all. The deployment *reduces* threats to the United States. Indeed, to some Americans, nuclear war could be confined to Europe.[6] Thus this deployment, allegedly in response to the SS-20, placed European NATO in peril because in no sense did it enhance the nuclear deterrent balance between the superpowers. In all essentials, this balance is maintained by possession, and (at sea) relatively invulnerable deployment, of intercontinental ballistic missiles capable, whatever refinements of accuracy may be introduced, of inflicting sufficient devastation on the peoples of the United States and the USSR for superpower nuclear war to become inadmissible. Western Europe, in stark contrast, lacks this "mutual assured destruction" capacity. Cruise and Pershing-II, indeed, invite a Soviet first-strike. So, at least, ran the argument of NATO governments which opposed Cruise and Pershing-II; it is an argument to which few U.S. strategists have addressed themselves, except in *political* terms markedly lacking in reassurance.

The governments of the Netherlands and Belgium said in effect that the SS-20 would not be matched by them in numerical terms because they did not intend nuclear war, should it occur, to be fought in Europe. The SS-20 is currently targeted on Western Europe; to respond by targeting Cruise and Pershing on the Soviet Union and its satellites in the Warsaw Pact was, in the Dutch and Belgian view, to invite a nuclear war *in* Europe, decoupling the United States from its commitment to defend its NATO allies by risking its own nuclear destruction. Spain, a member of NATO since 1982, has said that nuclear weapons will not be placed on its soil. Norway and Denmark have expressed similar reservations, but would, in principle, allow nuclear weapons to be deployed if war broke out. France, continuing to pursue its solitary "independent nuclear deterrent" path, remains outside NATO's planning and command structures, although much contemporary French strategic thought favors a hostile attitude to the Soviet Union and thus supports the deployment of Cruise and Pershing-II.[7]

Britain, the German Federal Republic and Italy, whose governments accepted the deployment of the two weapons on their countries' soil, are nevertheless still faced with varieties of opposition to this assertion of U.S. power in the alliance. Opposition ranges from pacifism at one extreme to critical strategic analysis (based on the twin arguments that Cruise and

[5] The development, over many years, of the Soviet seaborne Cruise systems, is discussed by Joel Wit in "Soviet Cruise Missiles," IISS *Survival*, November-December 1983, pp. 249–60.

[6] For a balanced discussion of these issues see Christopher Coker, *U.S. Military Power in the 1980's*, London: Macmillan for the Royal United Services Institute (RUSI) for Defence Studies, 1983. The RUSI can hardly be considered as either "soft" on the Soviet Union or hostile to the United States.

[7] For a useful analysis of contemporary French strategic thought, see the *Times Literary Supplement* for June 1, 1984, pp. 603–04.

Pershing-II are provocations rather than deterrents and that NATO, as always, should improve its "conventional" forces) at the other. The public in European NATO countries remains, as usual, bemused, although opinion polls suggest that a majority of people are opposed to Cruise and Pershing. It is widely believed that a president of the United States might sacrifice Europe to save America by ordering the weapons to be used, in extremis no doubt, but as a preferred choice to invoking the intercontinental ballistic missile (ICBM) arsenal.

IMPLICATIONS OF CRUISE AND PERSHING-II

This deliberately concentrated and encapsulated summary of the 1984 strategic dispute within NATO (the arguments are elaborated below) masks the really fundamental issues which not only divide the alliance but have a genuinely international dimension, transcending the security of the superpowers and their allies and satellites. An explanation for the steady, alarming, destabilizing decline in U.S-Soviet relations since the late 1970s might well—despite the 1979 Soviet invasion of Afghanistan, the SS-20 and similar shocks to the U.S. nervous system—be found in a psychological rather than a political, let alone a strategic, context; the same can be said of various Russian reactions to President Reagan's anticommunist rhetoric. The fact remains that the international community, not merely NATO's members, enters the last 15 years of the 20th century with rather less chance of nuclear war being avoided than was the case during the years of détente. It is no comfort to be told that nuclear war, if it comes, will be accidental rather than deliberate, the result of fear supplanting calculation.

In consequence, prospects for *disarmament* as such must be dismissed. *Arms control* is in truth the only form of disarmament it is rational to expect, because it provides for the removal of obsolescent nuclear weapons, not only for limitations on the numbers of launchers and/or missiles and/or warheads of modern types. But prospects for arms control have taken a savage knock, although it is probably true to say that even the most bellicose American or Russian spokesman genuinely desires to return to the negotiating table. Whatever American or Russian perception of each other's objectives and methods may be in vogue, 40 years of the nuclear age have taught that deterrence, however maintained, is preferable to nuclear war, whether "winnable" or not. A crumb or two of comfort may be proffered readers by reminding them that Americans and Russians do talk to each other sub rosa, even and especially when formal arms negotiations have broken down or have been broken off. What they talk about can be stated simply: nuclear war is inadmissible even by accident. In consequence, *communication* between Washington and Moscow by more secure and rapid means than the presidential hot line must be continuously improved.

THE UNITED STATES AND EUROPEAN NATO

In a reference book devoted to Western Europe and in a chapter concerned with NATO it is necessary to concentrate on the, as it were, parochial issue which so divides members, and which was summarized above in its ostensibly strategic terms. The issue, in its real political terms, can also be stated simply or, preferably, posed as a crude, enduring, 35-year-old question: Why should the United States risk its own destruction by nuclear fire in order to deter or contain war in Western Europe? It is a question—*the* question—which has dominated all NATO's internal disputes since 1949, whatever diplomatic verbiage is used to pretend •otherwise and whatever expedients have been suggested or produced to make issues seem academic rather than cumulatively divisive.

This unanswered question—or, perhaps, unanswered until December 1979—explains the British and French independent nuclear deterrents, demonstrations of a profound skepticism that any U.S. president would sacrifice his country to save his allies.[8] (Curiously, another question has rarely been asked since the Soviet Union acquired an effective retaliatory nuclear capacity in the early 1960s: Would any declaratory U.S. readiness to make the sacrifice deter Moscow from attacking Western Europe?) But the crude question, whether answered or not, explains why, in 35 years, NATO collectively and European NATO in particular have failed to establish and keep in the field "conventional forces," whose overall capacities (métier and technological superiority matching the Russian mass conscription) would, arguably, deter the kind of limited war which, if unconfined, would be the prelude to a probably uncontrollable nuclear exchange.

To treat the question subtly rather than crudely, NATO is faced with a seemingly permanent and insoluble paradox. Nuclear weapons, on the record of more than 35 years, do deter, whatever the probability that Western Europe is ipso facto more at risk than the United States, and however implausible it may seem which mutual superpower nuclear deterrence can be extended to countries which lack their own credible deterrents—credible in relation to the Soviet Union. Therefore, say some—and all the apologists for Cruise and Pershing-II: Rely on the deterrent; in fact, improve it. Improve conventional forces also, at least on paper, but believe, above all, in the capacity *and* the determination of a U.S. president to deter the Soviet Union from making war on, or in, Western Europe.

Unfortunately for this comforting thesis, or bland assumption, influential Americans have not only thrown doubts on its credibility but, since at least the autumn of 1979, have stated in relatively plain words that it is no longer admissible. The clearest statement was as follows: "Don't you Europeans keep asking us to multiply assurances we cannot possibly mean, and which if we do mean we should not want to execute, and which if we did execute would destroy our civilization."[9] Thus Henry Kissinger, speaking in Brussels on September 3, 1979. In doing so, he cut through much of the complicated, highly technical (and frequently unintelligible or just plain meaningless) theories about which nuclear weapons achieve what purposes

---

[8] For an uncharacteristically candid official analysis of British skepticism, see "Britain's Strategic Nuclear Force; The Choice of a System to Succeed Polaris," made available by the Ministry of Defence in July 1980.

[9] Reported in the *International Herald Tribune*, September 4, 1979.

and on whose behalf. Such theories have been the curse rather than the blessing of strategic debate for much of the nuclear age.

Kissinger immediately regretted that "the interpretation of my remarks has been that the United States is no longer prepared to defend Europe."[10] One could also say, in treating his disclaimer with reserve, that in September 1979, Kissinger was no longer the U.S. Secretary of State but merely a private citizen with the awkward habit of saying what many thought—or knew—but preferred to conceal, especially if they knew. To which naïveté the only answer can be, "Not so." Kissinger, even before his revived support for the Republican party and Ronald Reagan, and his subsequent employment by the latter on missions here and there, was as potent a figure in 1979 as he had been when he was one of those who kept détente in being. Changing his assessment of Soviet policies, speaking his mind without the inhibitions of office and using language that the general public could understand, Kissinger went to the heart of the matter.

But, apologists for the United States will say, it was Helmut Schmidt, a figure as potent as Kissinger, who asserted two years earlier, on October 28, 1977, that Western Europe was at risk because of Soviet superiority in theater nuclear forces; that the risk should be lessened if not entirely removed by matching these forces if U.S.-Soviet negotiations on their deployment failed; and that, in the process, Western Europe's security would not be markedly lessened. If negotiations succeeded (on theater forces none were even in train in 1977), it might even be possible to reduce the number of nuclear weapons in Europe. If negotiations failed, the United States would, in effect, be coupled still more closely to its NATO allies by virtue of the fact that Cruise and Pershing-II (or any similar weapon) would extend America's deterrent capacities vis-à-vis the Soviet Union by forcing the latter to weigh the risks of a limited nuclear war that might get out of hand.

Again, one must say, "Not so." We can at this point set aside the strategic complexities, tactfully refraining from stressing that a sea-launched Cruise, technically possible and much propagated in some quarters at the time, might well have matched Soviet missiles *and* reduced the risks of nuclear war in Europe. It is the case that Chancellor Schmidt, in an on-the-record lecture prepared with his customary care and imbued with the knowledge acquired in nearly a decade of office, was concerned to "extend" SALT-I and II to the European theater.[11] At no point did Schmidt even mention, let alone plead for, more nuclear weapons in NATO's armory. Apart from the fact that his lecture was mainly devoted to economic, social and security (antiterrorist) issues, what he actually said on nuclear deterrence was almost completely different from what those who in any case wanted Cruise and Pershing-II deployed alleged that he said, or all but demanded.

[10] Reported in the *Daily Telegraph*, September 4, 1979.
[11] Schmidt was delivering, in London, the 1977 annual IISS Alastair Buchan Memorial Lecture. For a detailed analysis of Schmidt's words, which he later came to regret as having had the opposite effect to the one intended, see Richard J. Barnet, *Allies; America, Europe, Japan Since the War*, New York: Simon and Schuster, 1983, p. 372. Note that since June 1984, a small number of Cruise missiles have been supplied to the U.S. submarines, although their roles have not been stated.

THE "THEATER" DEBATE

Because so much misunderstanding, deliberate or otherwise, has stemmed from the October 28, 1977 speech, it seems important to repeat Schmidt's key passages, followed by a summary of NATO deliberations up to December 1979. Schmidt in effect said: SALT [I and II] codifies the nuclear strategic balance between the Soviet Union and the United States. To put it another way: SALT neutralizes their strategic nuclear capabilities. In Europe this magnifies the significance of the disparities between East and West in nuclear tactical and conventional weapons. Schmidt knew perfectly well, as did the U.S. administration, that the Soviet Union, especially when reassured by SALT provisions relating to ICBMs (and thus by the stability of "mutual assured destruction" deterrence), had been upgrading shorter range (although not necessarily theater) nuclear weapons. Although much play was made later with the real or supposed advantages thus given to the Soviet Union vis-à-vis NATO in terms of *numbers*, there was, in fact, no secret to discover and reveal about *disparity*. What Schmidt therefore went on to say was that

> We [in European NATO] are not unaware that both the United States and the Soviet Union must be anxious to remove threatening strategic developments from their relationship. But strategic arms limitations confined to the United States and the Soviet Union will inevitably impair the security of the members of the alliance vis-à-vis Soviet military superiority in Europe if we don't succeed in removing the disparities of military power in Europe parallel to the SALT negotiations. *So long as this is not the case we must maintain the balance of the full range of deterrence strategy* [italics added].

It can be argued, of course, that if negotiations fail to remove disparities, only additional weapons will do so. Schmidt supported the December 1979 NATO twin-track decision (to deploy Cruise and Pershing-II if INF negotiations failed), and has disagreed with his own Social Democratic party in its belated opposition to placing these weapons on German soil. But the key italicized sentence must surely be read as it stands. The only rational interpretation of the words is that NATO's collective armory should be utilized to neutralize the possibility of nuclear war anywhere in the alliance. The armory should not be used to create new threats to stability, above all by the deployment of U.S.-made, U.S.-owned and U.S.-controlled weapons which, in effect, decouple the alliance.

There were in 1977, and there are today, many ways to maintain the balance, above all by the further deployment of seaborne missiles, both submarine- and surface-carried, whose varying location (and hence variable range) would pose a challenge to the Soviet Union comparable to the U.S. Navy's original deployment of the Polaris weapons systems in the early 1960s. What does *not* maintain the balance is the deployment of weapons which positively invite a preemptive attack. For example, to put Cruise into Greenham Common, a thickly populated area in England, where secrecy and security are alike at risk, is to make a mockery of deterrence based on maximum invulnerability and hence minimum provocation.

That NATO's European members thought along these lines between October 1977 and December 1979 is sufficiently illustrated by study of the alliance's deliberations and recommendations, and, in particular, of the high level and special consultative groups that were set up to consider the issues. Between June and October 1978, NATO's Nuclear Planning Group (NPG) also studied the issues posed by Schmidt, and its deliberations led the December ministerial meeting to state: "They [NATO Ministers] discussed in broad terms possible approaches for theater nuclear forces' modernization both with regard to the medium- and long-term programs."[12] It is important to note that by October 1978 the Soviet modernization program was not only all but openly acknowledged, but *complete*. Thus subsequent Soviet actions regarding the SS-20 and other weapons have been almost entirely confined to *forward* deployment in Warsaw Pact countries, presenting the Cruise and Pershing-II policymakers with an almost insoluble problem in terms of U.S.-European NATO relations. The Soviet move *followed* the announced Cruise and Pershing-II deployment—in fixed site locations—and thus illustrated perfectly the "hostage to fortune" dilemma of the recipient countries. When SS-20s are targeted on Greenham Common and similar locations, any notion of "extended deterrence" or Schmidt's "full range of deterrence strategy" can be dismissed. There is, of course, a case to be made not merely for improving NATO's theater nuclear capabilities, but for matching Soviet numbers. But the case is gravely weakened, looked at strategically, if the compensatory weapons are deployed in vulnerable locations. Schmidt's refusal, in October 1977, to define which weapons best "extended" deterrence, and where, must constantly be borne in mind.

Possibly aware of latent dangers, the December 1978 NATO ministerial meeting concentrated on improved, not different, weapons for theater deterrence, and did so within the context of long-range planning. The formal lapse of the May 1972 U.S.-Soviet SALT-I agreement (although it remained in force informally) doubtless concentrated Western European ministerial minds on the likelihood that Washington and Moscow would continue to seek accord on "mutual assured destruction" deterrence but might not pay sufficient attention to varieties of weapons which from about this time, and in recognition of the variable deployment factor, became known as long-range theater nuclear forces (LRTNFs). The definition, or designation, does, of course, reveal the near futility of trying to extend deterrence by categorizing weapons in terms of their technical characteristics and not by their function and deployment.

There is little doubt that in these years, in sharp contrast to the late 1960s and early 1970s, European NATO governments observed with increasing dismay the correlation in much U.S. strategic thought between maintaining the superpower strategic balance and lessening the possible dangers to the United States arising from commitments to its NATO allies. The rapid increase in Soviet LRTNF capabilities—greater accuracy and mobility, deployment of independently targeted (MIRVed) warheads—and the fact that the United States had not engaged in a comparable *land-based* modernization program (because superpower relations transcended all other considerations)

---

[12] NATO communiqués etc., are taken from the relevant volumes of *Keesing's Contemporary Archives*.

forced European NATO to wrestle with the issue posed by Schmidt in October 1977. But neither in that year nor later did NATO's Western European governments support or recommend the deployment of *additional* weapons, let alone those whose characteristics and functions were likely to cause dispute within the alliance. In fact, until the Soviet invasion of Afghanistan in December 1979, the United States and its allies followed separate paths. The former concentrated on SALT-II and hence superpower deterrence in the context of MIRVed missiles; the latter became increasingly anxious over Washington's seeming indifference to Schmidt's arguments *except* in the terms so brusquely summarized by Henry Kissinger.

THE LAST YEARS OF DÉTENTE

In the critical years 1978 and 1979, no responsible politician or official in European NATO revived the idea of the region's establishing its own nuclear deterrent force. This idea had enjoyed something of a vogue in the early 1960s, although largely for reasons peculiar to the domestic politics of the German Federal Republic at the time rather than as a revival of French hopes of the early 1950s for a European Defense Community. The idea has of course, perhaps inevitably, begun to resurface in the wake of the initial deployment of Cruise and Pershing-II. What had allayed, if not disposed of, West European concern during the years of Jimmy Carter's presidency (1977–81) was his apparent willingness to heed the NATO allies' reactions to the drift of U.S. policy in the aftermath of Vietnam and the October 1973 Arab-Israeli war. But the more recent revival of interest in the Western European Union by its seven members (Britain, France, Italy, the German Federal Republic, Belgium, the Netherlands and Luxembourg) may turn out to be something other than a straw in the wind.

The drift of U.S. policy was undoubtedly toward "America first" on the basis of détente and both explicit and tacit agreement, indeed cooperation, with the Soviet Union on a whole range of issues capable of involving both superpowers in accidental war. The high-water mark of this policy was the Kissinger-Gromyko cooperation during and after the October 1973 Arab-Israeli war. Despite American concern over some Soviet actions in the Middle East and Africa thereafter, this cooperation sufficiently sustained a relationship for Carter to hope for the continuation of détente. But he was not prepared—or his advisers were not anxious—for European NATO to be sacrificed in the process. The neutron bomb concept, which if executed would have established a nonfallout nuclear zone in Western Europe and thus, in theory, validated the idea of a limited nuclear war confined to the Continent, was attacked so harshly by America's allies that on April 7, 1978 Carter abandoned it. When President Brezhnev visited Bonn between May 4 and 7 of that year, Schmidt was able to reassure him that both détente and *Ostpolitik* were in good shape. Schmidt's continued concern over "disparities" had not blinded him to the bigger issue of sustaining good relations with the Soviet Union.

By the early months of 1979, however, Carter was widely seen in U.S. politics as a feeble president, unable to "stand up to" the Soviets. Yet the

May NATO ministerial meeting confined Schmidt's concern to the bottom of the agenda. The communiqué, after dealing with many other matters, merely said: "Theater nuclear modernization: measures are being developed, both in the short and in the long term, to ensure that NATO's theater nuclear forces *continue to play* [italics added] an essential role in NATO's deterrence and defense posture." But by September, virtually on the eve of the presidential election year, it was clear to perceptive observers of the strategic scene that former President Ford's doubts about the value of détente were about to be echoed by every Republican and would be put in militant language by those American strategic analysts who had been frustrated during détente but sustained by hopes of a red-blooded politician succeeding an ineffective one.

The September 1979 conference of the International Institute for Strategic Studies (IISS) at Vilars, Switzerland, coinciding with Kissinger's appearance in Brussels as a critic of entangling alliances (or troubled partnerships), was notable for a sustained and occasionally savage attack on the strategies of both détente and mutual assured destruction by the academic Young Turks who hoped to advise a Republican president-elect after November 1980. McGeorge Bundy, perhaps the most distinguished American participant at the conference (as a former special assistant for national security affairs to presidents Kennedy and Johnson and a senior member of the East Coast strategic establishment), was subjected to much intemperate criticism after his eloquent, passionate defense of détente and the concomitant notion of an indivisible NATO. The Young Turks declared that a hostile Soviet Union, whose nuclear armory now exceeded that of the United States, must be confronted by a policy that would force the nuclear issue in Europe. Little attention was paid to ICBMs, much to LRTNFs. The latter, however, were seen not in Schmidt's terms but in terms of an extended deterrence that would put the Soviet Union on notice to consider the consequences of a new generation of Western European-based missiles. Such missiles would be not only targeted on the Soviet Union, as the *existing* NATO theater armory was, but would be designed in characteristics and deployment to "limit" nuclear war to Europe.

The Vilars conference, although ostensibly a private affair, was an important milestone in deteriorating U.S.-Western European relations because of the way the criticisms were made. There was nothing new about nuclear weapons in Western Europe, and although U.S.-controlled LRTNFs and variants thereof *once redeployed* posed a new kind of challenge to Moscow, it could be argued that because modernization was a continuous process it was not surprising that it should lead to the production of weapons of the same type but with longer range and greater accuracy. But these arguments, although heard at Vilars, were subordinated to the prevailing mood. On the U.S. side, the Bundy generation excepted, this was one of fear that an undoubted disparity reflected a Soviet determination to wring assorted benefits and advantages from it. There is some irony in the contrast between an American obsession with weaponry and a concomitant assertion that the Soviet Union intended to pursue a policy of diplomatic hostility toward Western Europe as a result.

Of course, in a sense, these U.S. fears have been justified. Deployment of Cruise and Pershing-II has enabled the Soviet Union to put diplomatic pressure on European NATO by virtue of a simple fact: there is an unavoidable strategic and geographical disparity between the full range of nuclear weapons unambiguously under Soviet control, located at (if not always identifiable at) various and varying sites in the Soviet Union and its Warsaw Pact satellites, and what are ostensibly NATO's theater nuclear weapons, subject to a not very clearly defined form of U.S. control and located at sites known to the world at large. It is this disparity, which geography to some extent unavoidably sustains, that Schmidt sought to lessen by emphasizing not just the full range of nuclear deterrence, but above all the full scope of America's commitment to its allies' security. The point must be made again that U.S.-controlled nuclear weapons at sea pose a strategic challenge to the Soviet Union. Cruise and Pershing-II, in stark contrast, pose a temptation to the Soviet Union *unless* a preemptive strike on them is to be deterred by the threat of a retaliatory strike from missiles in the United States or at sea. But President Reagan and his advisers have been conspicuously silent on this version of "extended deterrence"—in truth, Schmidt's version of it. Silence reflects the uncomfortable fact that seaborne deterrence raises the specter in American minds of a Soviet preemptive strike at the U.S. heartland.

NATO: DECEMBER 1979

It is in the context of these preliminaries to the advent of the Reagan administration that one must consider three events: the NATO ministerial conference of December 1979; the rifts that subsequently widened within the alliance (not all of them due to strategic issues as such); and the Strategic Arms Reduction Talks and INF negotiations that came later. The December 1979 decisions were arrived at only after protracted debate—in fact, at a specially convened additional conference which concluded on December 12, 1979. Its communiqué said:

1. The May 1978 [Western nations] summit in Washington dealt with the political resolve to meet the challenge posed by the continuing momentum of the Warsaw Pact military buildup. This situation has been aggravated over the past few years by the Soviet decision to implement programs modernizing and expanding their *long-range* [italics added] nuclear capacity. In particular they have deployed the SS-20 missile, which offers significant improvements over previous systems in providing greater accuracy, more mobility and greater range, as well as having multiple warheads; and the Backfire bomber, which has a much better performance than other Soviet aircraft deployed hitherto in a theater role.

2. Western LRTNF capabilities have remained static. Indeed these forces are increasing in age and vulnerability and do not include long-range land based and theater nuclear missile systems.

3. These trends have prompted serious concern within the alliance, because, if they were to continue, Soviet superiority in theater nuclear

294

systems could undermine the stability achieved in international systems and cast doubt on the credibility of the alliance's deterrent strategy by highlighting the gap in the spectrum of NATO's available nuclear response to aggression.

4. After intensive consideration, including the merits of alternative approaches, and after taking note of the positions of certain members, ministers concluded that the overall interests of the alliance would best be served by pursuing two parallel and complementary approaches of TNF [theater nuclear force] modernization and arms control.

5. Accordingly, ministers have decided to modernize LRTNF by the deployment in Europe of U.S. ground-launched systems comprising 108 Pershing I-A [Pershing-II] and 464 ground-launched Cruise missiles, all with single warheads. All the nations currently participating in the integrated defense structure will participate in the program.

Many comments could be made on this communiqué, but aside from caveats and much ambiguous language, such as the reference to Soviet long-range weapons and to nations participating in the integrated defense program, two statements must be dismissed as inaccurate. Western LRTNF capabilities had *not* remained static, as is revealed by even a cursory reference to the IISS's widely respected annual *Strategic Survey* and *Military Balance*. In particular, U.S. submarine-launched missile systems had been modernized by 1979, including the independent British Polaris, whose original purpose was to support European NATO in precisely the LRTNF role which the communiqué declared had suffered a reverse. Secondly, the complementary approaches—to TNF modernization and arms control—were disingenuous in two respects.

Pershing-II, as its designation implies, is a modernized replacement for Pershing-I, a weapon with essentially the same tactical short-range functions as its predecessor. But Cruise, although in fact merely a more sophisticated version of the World War II flying bombs, is a new weapon in NATO's armory. (Not, to be sure, in Russia's—the USSR's equivalent weapon was mostly deployed at sea by 1979, a process that has subsequently been accentuated.) U.S. Cruise, after much debate and interservice rivalry was developed primarily as a land-based weapon. Deploying Cruise in NATO's remote areas might have made sense in purely operational terms, but to do so in areas where its mobility can be destroyed by civil strife makes no kind of sense at all. This is not the argument of those who oppose Cruise's deployment for ideological or nationalistic reasons, but of those who believe that the more invulnerable a nuclear weapon is the less likely it is to cause accidental war.

More fundamentally still, the complementary, or twin-track, approach was not one toward arms *control*, but was aimed at the removal of the SS-20 in its entirety. The Americans' so-called zero option, whereby there would be no deployment of Cruise and Pershing-II if *all* SS-20s were removed from the firing line, was one which it is hard to believe any member of the Reagan administration expected the Soviet government to take seriously. The Soviet nuclear armory, under such an option, would have been substantially reduced, but NATO's would have been impaired only by denying refinements to existing weapons. This was not zero option but zero sum. It can of course also be argued that under the option, removing 464 Cruise missiles from European NATO would show that the United States was not pursuing a strategy of deploying provocative weapons in order to protect the American heartland. But, per contra, one must repeat that at no time has the Soviet government accepted the option, although it has been willing to consider permuting the numbers of INF weapons on both sides in order to strike and maintain a rough balance.

SUMMARY

Enough has been said in this cursory analysis of fundamental differences within NATO to indicate that the issue of Cruise and Pershing-II has little to do with modernization or a renewed Soviet nuclear threat, but much to do with two overriding—and paradoxically complementary—preoccupations of the Reagan administration: to stand up to the Soviets *and* to avoid nuclear war affecting the United States during the process of talking tough. It is much easier for one to stand up and talk tough if others are exposed to the danger of a riposte. This comment may seem extreme, but both superpowers have conducted a slanging match during the past five years with scant regard for European security.

Most Western analyses of strategic issues still emanate from the United States. The power and emphasis there has in these five years shifted away from the Atlanticist, East Coast establishment, which in the years following NATO's foundation sought to establish not only that nuclear war was inadmissible but that its deterrence must be a seamless garment. Throughout the 1950s, the West Coast strategic establishment was arguing an "America first" policy, reflecting both geographical perceptions and psychological factors. During the years of détente this establishment was silent. Now it is once more in full cry. Whatever one's perceptions of Soviet policy—to the author, it is a policy composed of fear, suspicion and aggression, very much in that order—NATO is divided when the superpower which inevitably dominates it appears to have preoccupations other than the security of its allies.

Perhaps the final word should be with the London *Financial Times*, a journal with a high reputation for objectivity. In an article on December 23, 1983, shortly after the Geneva negotiations had broken down, the European editor wrote:

Under Ronald Reagan, Washington has come to mirror the militarism and ideological rigidity of Moscow. To suppose that Reagan's Washington will find a way out of the present crisis requires a heroic effort of optimism, and it is perhaps an effort we should not repose any faith in. It is all the more striking, therefore, that the recent NATO meeting issued a strongly conciliatory declaration underlining its desire for détente and co-operation. That has long been the aspiration of most West European countries; and if anything can be done to improve the international climate, the odds are that it can only be done by the concerted efforts of the Europeans.

Nothing that has happened since those words were written has lessened their validity.

FURTHER READING

International Institute for Strategic Studies. Various publications, especially *Survival; Military Balance; Strategic Survey.*
Royal United Services Institute. *Journal.*

GERMAN DISUNITY

PHILIP WINDSOR

THE deep-seated hostility between the two superpowers that has dominated the diplomacy of the 1980s is frequently called the new cold war. That phrase implies a reversion to an older pattern of historical antagonism, but in doing so it is more misleading than suggestive. The new cold war is not particularly about issues but rather about mistrust itself—a mistrust that deepens into the most intense suspicion when it comes to the question of nuclear armaments and nuclear strategy. But the old cold war, although it developed under the looming shadow of nuclear weaponry, was not really concerned with strategic confrontation. Intercontinental missiles had not even been developed when it was at its height. It was very much concerned with interests and issues, and at the center of these was Germany. The "German question" and its offspring, the "Berlin problem," were the two issues in international politics which for many years were permanently capable of touching off a third world war or defining the conditions for an enduring peace. Germany was, and still is, the one area where the armed forces of the world's two dominant powers have stood facing each other, ready to fight at a moment's notice or at the slightest infraction of their territorial position.

The cold war between the Soviet Union and the Western powers spread over many parts of the world and covered a wide range of ideological and political questions. But it originated in a conflict about what to do with Germany. It may be argued, indeed, that it began before World War II, when, from Munich to the Nazi-Soviet Pact, the major European powers were maneuvering to avoid a war with Germany or ensure that if it came it would be directed away from themselves. Thereafter, the major powers were united only against Germany; they were never able to agree on a policy toward Germany. Germany's industrial power and military potential ensured this; each side in the cold war required the country as an ally against the other, and both hoped at different times to gain control over the whole of Germany. The Soviet Union offered reunification on terms that would have made Soviet domination virtually certain; the Western powers insisted that the only acceptable basis for reunification was one that would have allowed the whole country to join NATO. But, equally, both sides recognized that the division of Germany was an adequate basis for the security of Europe—so long as it kept East and West apart. A clear frontier was safer than an ill-defined area of competition. So the cold war oscillated between these two positions. It was either a competition for the alliance of a reunified Germany, or else an agreement not to go to war but to stay put on the basis of a divided Germany.

The "division of Germany," therefore, has never been a straightforward historical phenomenon; on the contrary, it has meant different things to different people at different times. In West Germany itself, it took a long time for a general national attitude to emerge toward relations with East Germany, the Soviet Union or the country's Western allies. For a few years there was a national consensus on the management of these three sets of relations, but this again degenerated into conflict in 1983. West German *policy* has, however, generally been more coherent than the conflicts within the country might have suggested; and if it was largely shaped in the early years by the nature of the relations among the victorious powers of 1945, it also did much to influence their relations in subsequent years.

West German policy falls into four main historical phases. The first was a period of major decision which lasted for some 10 years after World War II. The second was a period of immobilization and gradually growing frustration that led to demands for a change. The third began in 1966 and led to a fundamental reappraisal of West Germany's foreign policy, culminating in the successes of *Ostpolitik* in the 1970s. The fourth phase, beginning in 1979 and lasting until the present, has been marked by a growing sense of the tensions between West Germany's role in the Western alliance, its place in East-West relations and its own relations with East Germany. These periods will be considered in detail later. The changes in West German foreign policy themselves reflect the inconsistent, even contradictory, nature of the policies of the external powers; and in discussing the West German position it is necessary to remember that this was to a high degree and for a long time more dependent on the interests and relations of the other countries involved in the situation than the policy of any other important power.

The Western allies—to use a term that glosses over differences of opinion and interest which have at times been fundamental—insisted over many years that they did not accept the division of Germany, and that the objective of their policies was reunification "in security and freedom." But after 1955, the basis of their relations with the Soviet Union was a tacit acceptance of the fact that Germany would not be reunified in the foreseeable future. Other agreements would have to come first, so long as these were not based upon an explicit acceptance of the two Germanies. That remained the Western position until 1972, when in fact the allies of the Federal Republic established embassies in East Berlin. At first glance this might appear to have been a success for Soviet policy, though in reality it was more of a success for West Germany's own *Ostpolitik*. The Soviet Union after 1955 was reconciled to the division of the country and to stabilizing the cold war along those lines. The trouble was that it attempted to force an explicit recognition of this division on the Western powers—to make them recognize East Germany. It was in attempting to do this that the Soviet Union precipitated the crises over Berlin which brought the world very near that war which neither side, once it had accepted the division of the country, had any cause to fight. Both sides risked war to establish a position which already existed, and found it impossible to reach any agreement to alleviate the situation because of a clash of priorities. The Western powers refused to admit that agreement with the Soviet Union implied the recognition of East Germany; the Soviet Union insisted that recognition in one form or another was an essential condition of any agreement in Europe.

Throughout these years, West Germany was bound to be at once the most conservative and the most radical of the Western powers. It was conservative because it held out more obdurately than any other country against agreements with the Soviet Union that implied even the most attenuated recognition of East Germany. It also refused to recognize that the lands beyond the Oder-Neisse Line, which have formed a part of Poland since 1945, were Polish; they were merely "under Polish administration." In deference to Western German feelings, and because the cession to Poland of these lands in 1945 was officially an interim measure, the other Western powers also took this view, though President Charles de Gaulle on occasion made it clear that he accepted the Oder-Neisse Line as the eastern frontier of Germany. But West Germany was also the most radical of the Western allies because it continuously attempted to identify any progress toward a settlement of the cold war in Europe with progress toward reunification. This all-or-nothing position, although based on the reasonable premise that German reunification was the prime objective of West German foreign policy, also did much to perpetuate the cold war and ensure that reunification could not come about.

This is the pattern of relations which developed around the division of Germany. The Soviet Union insisted that any European settlement must be based on the recognition of East Germany, and was prepared to start dangerous crises to secure this end. The Western powers, though they tacitly recognized the division of the country, were not prepared to recognize East Germany—if for no other reason than that this would have been fatal to their alliance with West Germany. Every Soviet demand only strengthened their formal commitment to the eventual reunification of the country. The relations between the two power blocs alternated between a grudging rapprochement based on the status quo (which was the pattern of 1955) and sharp periods of crisis which heightened their outward determination to change the status quo (as for example the Berlin crises between 1959 and 1961). In all this, West Germany played an essential part, insisting that the actual position was intolerable, but ensuring that it could not be changed. At the same time, East Germany exploited its position within the Soviet system to pursue a policy of unremitting hostility to the Federal Republic while continuously pleading for the "normalization" of relations between the two German states. This might almost have been designed to ensure that no West German politician could contemplate concessions or demand anything less than full reunification. The pattern was one of a total impasse, and at times it looked as if it could go on for ever. But in 1966 it began to break up with the advent of new forces in West German politics. Ten years of deadlock were coming to an end, and the history of Germany was entering a new phase, which would now be defined by the changing relations between West Germany and the Soviet Union and by the creation of a relationship between the two Germanies themselves.

THE WARTIME AGREEMENTS

The origins of the historical phases in West German policy lie in the wartime agreements between the allies. At the end of the war, all three of the major allied leaders were playing for time. None of them was anxious to reach a quick settlement of the German problem. As the end of the war approached, Stalin was preparing a number of Communists in the Soviet Union to take over the Soviet zone during the period of occupation and turn it into a springboard for a reunified Germany under Communist domination. In part, his calculations were certainly influenced by the apparent intention of the U.S. government to limit the occupation of Germany to a very short period—a couple of years in Roosevelt's view. For the same reason, Churchill was anxious to keep the United States committed to Europe for as long as possible, and avoid commitment to any plans that could mean a quick withdrawal—and a renewed struggle for the control of Europe. Roosevelt, torn between a desire to ensure the permanent subjugation of Germany, an anxiety to co-operate with the Soviet Union to secure the future peace of the world, and the immediate necessity of mediating between those two suspicious and unequal powers, the Soviet Union and Great Britain, had no clear policy at all. There is no evidence that the United States had drawn up any plans other than cooperation with the Soviet Union.

In these circumstances, the history of the wartime conferences and agreements is easier to understand. Their enormous oscillations between plans for the total pastoralization of Germany and plans for industrial reparations over the foreseeable future, their almost arbitrary and certainly outrageously careless drawing of different zonal boundaries and/or different successor states, their total lack of appreciation of the importance of Berlin and the access rights of the occupying powers are now of no more than academic interest. The fundamental truth seems to be that as the end of the war drew nearer, the major allies became increasingly conscious of their own divergencies and correspondingly anxious to avoid a definitive settlement which would drag their conflicts into the open. Hence the astonishing transition from the Yalta agreement of February 1945, which envisaged "the complete . . . dismemberment" of Germany, to the attempts at Potsdam a few months later to create a unified administration in which all the allies would participate in running a single country. Hence, too, the fact that when agreement on these lines was found impossible to reach, the zonal boundaries degenerated into partition lines between East and West Germany. But the agreement that the allies drew up at Potsdam in the summer of 1945 is still the only guiding principle that they have in common for their future policy toward Germany. They are still officially bound to work for the creation of a unified German government, and in official theory no peace treaty can be signed between Germany and the victors of World War II until the country has been reunified; the relations between the allies and the two German states are officially only provisional relations with provisional states until such time as a reunited country replaces both of them. Officially, of course, the United States, the Soviet Union and Great Britain are still allies.

The blatant unreality of the Potsdam agreement does not mean that it is unimportant. It is the only official document which recognizes that the three countries (France was not invited to Potsdam, which meant a further element of confusion and unreality) have a common interest in the future of Germany or a common obligation not to come to arbitrary decisions on their future policies toward the whole country without consulting each other. It means that any threat of a separate peace treaty between one of the powers and one part of Germany is, and will be seen to be, a hostile act to the others—as when Khrushchev threatened to conclude a separate peace treaty with East Germany during the Berlin crisis of 1958–59; and this in turn meant that no one side in the cold war could do very much to change the status quo without running immediate risks of a third world war. In effect, the Potsdam agreement was a guarantee of conflict that prevented any gradual series of changes from taking place to the detriment of either side or its own part of Germany. It was one of the supports on which the whole structure of international relations during the cold war depended. And it ensured that what Dean Rusk called the "truce lines" of 1945 became the boundaries of two separate German states. This paradox is understandable in the light of subsequent developments.

THE STRUGGLE FOR GERMANY

Development of the East–West Split

Churchill and Truman met Stalin at Potsdam, just outside Berlin, in July 1945 at about the time that the Western occupying forces were entering Berlin for the first time. The war in Europe had been over for two months, and during this period the Russians had had ample time to organize Berlin, as the future capital of Germany, in their own interests. In Berlin, and in the Soviet zone of Germany, they had created an "Anti-Fascist Coalition" of all political bodies that were prepared to cooperate with the new authority, and had already promulgated certain social reforms as well as set up a new and, in the circumstances of the time, extremely efficient administrative organization. There is plenty of evidence that this was intended as a trial run for eventual takeover of the whole of Germany, and that the Soviet zone was to be a model of social reform and of German participation in the administration which would attract the inhabitants of the other zones. This was the shape that Stalin's dual policy toward Germany finally took. But at the beginning it depended on the simple stratagem of keeping the Communist Party in the background; the Anti-Fascist Coalition was to be an amorphous grouping of all political parties in which none had a distinct identity. A month before Potsdam, however, there was a change of line that is still hard to understand. Out of the blue, Marshal Zhukov, the Soviet military governor, ordered the formation of "free political parties and trade unions," and the German Communist Party, the KPD, which had hitherto been managing the Anti-Fascist Coalition in the background, emerged along with other political parties as a separate force. The discreet extension of Communist power that was originally expected had turned into an open struggle for the control of Germany between Communist and anti-Communist forces.

This struggle was to take two forms: on an official level, between the allies, it centered on the economic administration of the country and turned into a sharp dispute, primarily between Britain and the Soviet Union, about reparations deliveries (since the British zone contained the Ruhr); on a half-acknowledged level it was an attempt by the Communist party to win control of the German population by forcing a merger with the Social Democratic party (SPD), traditionally the largest and most powerful party in the country, and this struggle centered on Berlin. For the Soviet zone rapidly came under almost complete Communist control, and the merger was pushed through there without any trouble.

But Berlin was the one part of Germany that was administered by all the allies (though even here the city was divided into national sectors) and if the KPD, with Soviet backing, could gain control of the capital city while it was under the control of all four allies, they could demonstrate to the rest of the country that Western occupation did not mean protection and at the same time could take the biggest single step toward extending their control. Between 1945 and 1946, therefore, two simultaneous conflicts were going on: the one fought out in the Allied Control Council and at the foreign ministers' conferences, and the other, the political struggle in Berlin. This is a vital period because much of the subsequent course of German history was then determined. On the political level, the final result was a decisive defeat for the Communists. The Social Democrats, from an almost hopeless political position and without any real support from the Western allies until the last moment, and faced with the threat of kidnapping and intimidation organized from East Berlin, resisted a Communist attempt to force a merger of "the two proletarian parties," and finally managed to have elections held in the capital in which—in the three western sectors—they won an overwhelming victory. The Communists found themselves in a minority in the new city government of Berlin.

This defeat followed a decisive demarche by Molotov at the Paris foreign ministers' conference in July 1946. At that moment, confident of electoral victory, he had rejected a series of French proposals for what amounted to the economic dismemberment of Germany and had insisted on an all-German government and a peace treaty. In so doing, Molotov put an end to the half-alliance between France and the Soviet Union that had hitherto immobilized the development of Western policy toward Germany; France was now to find itself increasingly drawn to the Anglo-American development of a separate West German economy, while the Soviet Union had been deprived by the election results in Berlin of the one alternative to separate development on which it had placed its hopes: all-German elections resulting in an all-German government.

The result of these events was the enduring division of the country, and the beginnings of a split in Berlin itself into its Eastern and Western halves. The creation of a separate West German economy, based first on the Anglo-American bizone, and later on the three Western zones, was not intended as an attempt to divide the country, any more than the Anti-Fascist Coalition was intended to divide the Soviet zone from the rest. But the effect in both cases was the same; what began as an attempt to set up a working model for the whole of the country ended by making it impossible for the occupying powers to agree on an overall policy. And what looked like a secondary effect at the time turned out to be just as important: the French determination that if dismemberment was not a feasible policy then Germany must be integrated into a Western European economic structure that would make it impossible for the country to enjoy unfettered control of its enormous economic resources. Such integration was the alternative to dismemberment, and there is no doubt that it was originally intended to be restrictive, though it was also coupled with a conscious determination on the part of some French statesmen to create the kind of Western European union that is associated with the names of Monnet and Schuman. But the division of Germany went hand in hand with European integration, and this did much to ensure that the division was permanent.

Equally, the split in Berlin ensured that conflicts of policy among the allied powers would be intensified by a struggle for the control of the capital, and that local conflicts in the political life of Berlin itself would be magnified into interallied disputes. For the next few years—until *after* the Berlin blockade of 1948–49 at least—the Western allies continued to regard Berlin as the last hope of allied cooperation, and to do everything in their power to avoid a division of the city; but this very concern, coupled with the military weakness of their isolated position in Berlin, ensured that the Soviet government would be able to apply pressure to Berlin as a means of furthering its own policies, and generally treat it as a hostage to allied agreement.

The Marshall Plan, Currency Reform and the Berlin Blockade
Neither of these developments was very clear in 1946. A unified government continued in the city until 1948; the Anglo-American bizone did not begin to function effectively until 1947; the French zone did not join it until 1948; the real battle for the future of Germany was not joined until the Berlin blockade. But in fact, the next two or three years saw the playing out of the fundamental decisions which had been taken by the end of 1946. Two closely connected events were of decisive importance in this development; currency reform and the Marshall Plan.

A major factor in British, and subsequently French, support for the unification of the Western zones was the growing belief that the Soviet Union was determined to ruin Western Europe economically. General Marshall's speech in June 1947 offered them a guarantee against this; it offered indeed the prospect of economic salvation along with a solution, for the time at least, to the problem of what to do with Germany. And, equally, it removed a major cause of French obstruction—the fact that hitherto German resources had offered practically the only source from which France could hope to rebuild its own economic strength. American help was surer, and would be to the political advantage of France as well, in marked contrast to its own German policy. But the success of the Marshall Plan, and of the whole European Recovery Program, depended on restoring the strength of the West German economy. Germany was perhaps the biggest single cause of

Britain's economic weakness after the war, and the compromises in the reparations agreements that had been reached at Potsdam had meant for a time that both Britain and the United States were subsidizing German reparations to the Soviet Union. Reparations payments from the American and British zones had been suspended in 1946, but the drain on U.S. as well as British resources that West Germany represented in 1947 could have led to the total economic breakdown of Western Europe, while the bizone itself could not hope to recover while it suffered from an outdated currency system that had survived the war. There is in fact evidence that the decision to substitute a new and realistic currency in the bizone had already been taken in 1947, but it was not until the United States and Britain had had a final confrontation with the Soviet Union at the end of the year, and won the support of France at the London Conference in February 1948, that they went on to consolidate the economic division of the country and introduce the new currency.

The results were spectacular; an overnight boom in West Germany, as the currency reform suddenly restored internal confidence, produced a stable price structure and enabled the country to take part in the export and investment program of Western Europe. But the currency reform also led directly to the Berlin blockade. By now the Western powers had set up a de facto German government in their zones, and Berlin was the one place where the original nature of the occupation still persisted. But the blockade was not really a trial of strength between the two sides in the cold war, fought out on the one remaining battleground. Soviet purposes seem, in retrospect, to have been far vaguer than that, and there are some indications that the Soviet leaders were surprised to find a full-scale crisis developing out of a bit of vengeful obstruction. As the crisis developed, there is no doubt that they set out to exploit it—but rather by trying to reverse the electoral decision of 1946 and win the population of West Berlin over to their support, by alternating threats and promises, than by making any deliberate effort to force the Western allies out of Berlin. But the blockade is also of the greatest interest psychologically. It enabled the inhabitants of West Berlin to stand up to Communist intimidation; it forged their political cohesion under the leadership of an ex-Communist mayor, Ernst Reuter; and it forced the Western allies into a demonstrative commitment that they had not made before. After the years of Nazi rule and the comparative helplessness of the occupation, it gave West Berlin, and through it West Germany, a chance to reassert itself, to throw a psychological bridge back to the Germany that had existed before 1933. In these respects it did for Germany something of what the Battle of Britain did for Britain after the years of appeasement in the 1930s.

The blockade had, however, very little effect on the division of Germany. It completed the isolation of Berlin and helped indirectly to establish an East German constitution at about the same time in 1948 that the West German Basic Law was being drawn up. Apart from that, the struggle for Germany had virtually finished before the blockade began, and the negotiations that put an end to the siege did little more than consolidate the status quo. Both sides acknowledged stalemate. Berlin was not incorporated into

East Germany, but West Berlin was specifically prevented from becoming a part of West Germany too. The two German states had come into existence, and neither the Soviet Union nor the United States was willing to risk a new conflict by trying to force further changes.

The Policy of "Peaceful Coexistence"

But though the struggle was over, the conflicts of policy were not. After his defeat in 1949, Stalin reconsidered his foreign policy. He gave up all attempts to drive the Western powers out of Germany, but he still hoped to secure the reunification of the country—on terms, of course, that would bring it within the Soviet sphere of influence. In 1952, he proposed a new attempt at reunification, even making Germany an offer of military sovereignty that was left carefully undefined. The offer was rejected out of hand by the Western powers; whereas Stalinist foreign policy never abandoned the hope of reunifying Germany, the Western powers had by now reconciled themselves to its indefinite partition. The real change came after Stalin's death. After two years of confused maneuvers and delays, his successors also made up their minds to accept the division of Germany—and this was what was really meant by "peaceful coexistence." In effect, Khrushchev was telling the Western leaders that he was satisfied with status quo in Europe.

But the Western powers had also progressed during this time. In 1952, they were determined to harness the military potential of Germany to their own alliance system through the restrictive mechanism of the European Defense Community (EDC), just as they had already begun to harness its economic potential through the process of European integration. By 1955, when the plans for the EDC had finally been rejected in France, they were ready to incorporate West Germany into NATO. The Soviet Union, though it did everything it could to oppose this, still showed subsequently that it was willing to settle for an acknowledged partition. This was the essence of Soviet policy after 1955—and along with the integration of the Federal Republic into NATO it makes 1955 a crucial year. But it was asking too much of the Western powers to expect them to acknowledge the division of Germany—to recognize, that is, the East German regime. In any case, their commitments to the Federal Republic, the terms of the treaties under which Germany entered NATO, prevented this. The result was that after 1955 there was a neat reversal of positions. The Soviet government, which had hitherto made German reunification an important aim of its foreign policy, now insisted that the final division of Germany should be a basic condition of "peaceful coexistence"; while the Western powers, which had been content to accept the division of Germany in the early years after the war as part of the price of Western European recovery, were now adamant in their insistence that Germany must some day be reunified. Meanwhile, they refused to countenance any form of recognition of the East German government. It was in this context that Khrushchev tried to force his views on the West by putting renewed pressure on Berlin.

The crises that developed over Berlin between 1958, when Khrushchev sent his ultimatum to the West, and 1961, when the Berlin Wall was built, did not, however, mark a return to the old cold war. The struggle over

Berlin arose from the Soviet attempt to dictate the conditions of peaceful coexistence to the Western allies. In Soviet eyes, at least, it was an attempt to divide Europe into clear spheres of influence and have done with the cold war; and the Western powers' insistence that this division was not final, and that some day Germany would be reunified, looked to the Eastern European leaders remarkably like an affirmation of their will to carry on with the cold war. The fact that West Germany fully shared and supported the Western view, and was indeed its chief protagonist, only exposed the Federal government to the constant suspicion (voiced openly in the Soviet Union and Eastern Europe but shared by a great proportion of the Social Democratic parties in Western Europe) that it had an active interest in the cold war, and that its only hope for the reunification of Germany lay in prosecuting the struggle with undiminished zest.

GERMANY'S CHOICE

The process of integration into the Western system had not gone without question in West Germany. Even before the Federal Republic was established in 1949, the two leading parties had taken up opposing positions. From the beginning, Adenauer, who had established a dominating position in the Christian Democratic Union (CDU), was determined to identify the new republic with the Western world as closely as possible. Recognizing that it could achieve its own independence and ultimate sovereignty as a grant from the allies, he sought to make it in effect a part of the Western alliance—even though there was no prospect that Germany would be allowed to join NATO, and that in 1949 very few politicians were prepared to consider seriously the possibility of German rearmament. But after the outbreak of the Korean war in 1950, Adenauer offered the United States a German contingent in the defense of Europe, and it was thereafter only a matter of time. The sense of inevitability of German rearmament was no doubt one reason why France, the original proponent of the EDC, dragged its feet on the issue and finally rejected it, only to see Germany join NATO in a far more independent form in 1955. It was also no doubt a primary consideration in Stalin's offer of reunification in 1952; but the choice of integration into Western Europe, combined with the long-term prospect of rearmament, had long been made by then. Adenauer was building up to a position of negotiation from strength, relying on the alliance of the United States and on partnership with the countries of Western Europe to create a base from which reunification might eventually be achieved. All the events of the next few years seemed to confirm that only "strength" paid off.

To the SPD opposition, these years seemed crowded with missed opportunities. Their early leaders, Kurt Schumacher, and Ernst Reuter in Berlin, both deplored the rigidity of Adenauer's foreign policy. Reuter was much more insistent than Schumacher on the need for Western protection—it is scarcely an exaggeration to say that Schumacher regarded all the allies with equal suspicion—but he also insisted that West Germany must be prepared to renounce the advantages of "living in the West" for the sake of the East Germans, particularly after the East German rising of 1953. He repeatedly denounced the pursuit of prosperity for its own sake, which rapidly became a characteristic of West Germany's restricted international position, and called on the inhabitants of the West to "sacrifice their last shirt" for the chance of reunification of the country. All Social Democrats were in the beginning distrustful not only of German rearmament (to which they stayed uncompromisingly hostile until Khrushchev's Berlin crises helped them change their minds) but also of Germany's integration into Western Europe. This, they argued, prevented any chance of reunification and condemned the inhabitants of East Germany to the harsh and miserable existence that the Ulbricht regime had imposed on them.

After the East German rising, Reuter was particularly bitter in his criticism not only of the Bonn government but also of the passivity of the Western allies. In his analysis, 1953, if not 1952, provided the chance of a fresh approach to the Soviet Union, which at that time might have been glad to wash its hands of its East German colony. It is hard to judge how excessive a hope this was, since no approach was made, and since much has been made known since 1953 of the confusion and uncertainties of the new Soviet leadership at the time. But in fact, the rising of 1953 did no more than confirm that both sides had accepted the division of the country; and though the Soviet Union was to engage in some frantic diplomatic activity in the next two years to prevent Germany from joining NATO, the Geneva conferences of 1953 only confirmed in the end that all the major powers were content with the existing situation—and that the West Germans were too.

In fact, during these years, West Germany was choosing between security under a Western guarantee and the doubtful hope of reunification through Soviet goodwill, and made a very definite choice. But the implications of this choice were not always seen clearly, except by the very few men who helped to frame Adenauer's foreign policy. The year 1955 was a turning point in the history of postwar Germany, not only because it marked the Federal Republic's final integration into the Western world and the abandonment by the wartime allies of all discussion of reunification, but also because Adenauer drew from these circumstances the conclusion that the time had come to open diplomatic relations with the Soviet Union. One of the guiding principles of German foreign policy, from the time the Federal Republic was free to have one in 1955, was the Hallstein Doctrine—West Germany's insistence that any state that established relations with East Germany would be committing an unfriendly act. In 1957, Bonn broke off relations with Yugoslavia because the latter had recognized East Germany, and thereafter it was generally assumed that no country could have relations with both Germanies at the same time. And yet, in 1955, the Federal Republic had opened relations with the Soviet Union, the country that not only created East Germany but that in the same year made a ponderous declaration of its full sovereignty. This might seem to have been a flagrant breach of the doctrine. In fact, it was at the basis of it. West Germany, which claimed to be the custodian of the sovereignty of the whole of Germany—a claim recognized by the Western allies—was bound for this very reason to safeguard the future interests of the reunified country, to assume the onus of negotiating

Germany's position and to mediate as far as possible on behalf of Berlin and the East Germans by maintaining close relations with the Soviet Union.

In other words, the implications of Adenauer's foreign policy were not only that reunification was ruled out, that West Germany should be able to obstruct any Western move that seemed to imply recognition of East Germany (such as President Kennedy's proposal for an international access authority to safeguard Western rights in Berlin), but also that the Federal Republic should renounce all direct influence over East Germany even while assuming a kind of responsibility for its future in its relations with both the Soviet Union and the Western world. The result was that West German foreign policy was for long periods condemned to a purely passive and negative role, and that "negotiation from strength" became practically a self-defeating slogan. Its final failure was demonstrated in August 1961 by the Berlin Wall, which was built to keep East Germans inside East Germany, but also divided the whole country more completely than ever before.

REAPPRAISAL OF GERMAN FOREIGN POLICY

Adenauer's foreign policy was brilliantly successful in the short term and in the limited field of ensuring the prosperity and security of West Germany. As a step to the long-term objective of reunification it was a complete failure; indeed, every short-term success ensured more completely the long-term failure. By 1955, Adenauer had achieved everything that could have been hoped for 10 years previously; 10 years later, nothing had changed apart from the deterioration in the position of Berlin. Meanwhile, the pressure for an active policy toward East Germany had been growing in the country. There was a general assumption in the Western world in this period that the pressure for reunification inside West Germany was bound to die away as regional pressure groups began to disappear and the hopelessness of the cause became more obvious. Rather, the reverse was the case. In the early 1950s, most Germans were too busy, or too anxious, to care deeply about reunification. Thereafter, the course of the Berlin crises and the growth of a new and articulate generation unburdened by association with Nazism combined to produce a growing demand that something be done. There was little active expectation that reunification itself would be achieved, but there was a growing pressure for a new attempt to improve the conditions of life in the other half of the country—if necessary at the expense of the Hallstein Doctrine.

The building of the Wall stimulated the growth of this pressure and indeed did much to legitimate it. The Berlin crises between 1958 and 1961 had seemed to threaten fundamental changes in the whole of Europe; in the end they changed practically nothing. What they did do was help to change German foreign policy. The Soviet government had tried to force the Western powers to recognize East Germany; they refused. West Germany was made for a time to feel insecure, and seemed to question the U.S. commitment. East Germany was brought to the verge of collapse by the loss of many thousands of refugees, whose determination to leave while there was still time was stimulated by the Berlin crises themselves. Then the Wall was built to prevent them getting out and things looked very much the same as before. But this was not how it was seen in Germany, where the building of the Wall had an enormous psychological effect. The East Germans were now in a worse condition than ever before, or so it was believed; in fact, there is little doubt that conditions in the East improved very considerably after the building of the Wall, and even that a relative and intermittent freedom of expression began to develop. But West Germany had condemned itself to impotence by a doctrinaire refusal to develop a realistic policy in Eastern Europe. The pressure for change came from different quarters—from Arnold Beitz, the managing director of Krupps, who had established his own forms of semidiplomatic contact with the Polish government; from Willy Brandt, the mayor of West Berlin, leader of the Social Democrats and from 1966 foreign minister, who argued for a form of "Berlin initiative" in contacts with East Germany; from Erich Mende, the leader of the hitherto rightist Free Democrats and sometimes a powerful influence on the government, who demanded a much more wide-ranging series of contacts with East Germany; from some influential figures in the Protestant church and in some universities; and eventually from some members of the Christian Democratic cabinet itself. When Adenauer was eventually persuaded to resign, the Erhard government responded to these pressures by announcing a "policy of movement" in Eastern Europe. It seemed a new departure in German foreign policy.

But West Germany had not escaped the choice between integration into the Western system and an independent foreign policy that had dogged it for so long. This was the period of U.S. attempts to create an Atlantic Community on the basis of an integrated NATO, attempts that Germany supported and that inevitably circumscribed its freedom of maneuver in other spheres. The policy of movement did not, in fact, amount to very much. It was in essence an attempt to isolate East Germany from the other Eastern European countries by cultivating economic and cultural relations with them, and by attempting to persuade them to recognize the links between Bonn and West Berlin, since draft trade agreements with these countries specifically include Berlin as part of West German "territory." In other words, it was an attempt to concentrate the cold war against East Germany, not an attempt to unfreeze the general German situation. It was a continuation of Adenauer's foreign policy carried out by a partial reversal of the Hallstein Doctrine. Given the Soviet Union's overall control of Eastern Europe, and the concerted hostility of the Warsaw Pact countries to West Germany at a time when it looked as if Bonn might be given some sort of share in nuclear planning as part of the process of Atlantic integration, this kind of policy could not get very far. It laid the basis for improved relations with some Eastern European countries, notably Czechoslovakia and Hungary, but it did not affect the position of East Germany within the Eastern system, and it increased, as it was designed to, the gulf between East and West Germany.

FROM THE POLICY OF MOVEMENT TO OSTPOLITIK

During 1966, astonishing changes took place in the West German approach to the question of how to deal with East Germany—precisely because the policy of movement, while achieving a limited success in changing relations with Eastern Europe, had only emphasized that East Germany was not included. At the same time, the high and general expectations of a new period of détente in Europe encouraged governments in both Bonn and East Berlin to be a little more adventurous in their relations with each other, while also allowing them greater freedom of movement. The changes in West German opinion itself were shown by the electorate's new mood of concrete realism—a readiness to accept the Oder-Neisse Line for example—as opposed to the older long-term aspirations for a complete and united Germany. A new criterion seemed to have arisen, one which was later summarized by Willy Brandt in his call for *Wandel durch Annäherung*, the nearest English approximation to which is "transformation through rapprochement." Its object was to make the East German regime less repressive towards its own people by giving it a vested interest in good relations with the Federal Republic. That also implies the means: the Federal Republic's great potential economic leverage. Under Willy Brandt, first as foreign minister and then as chancellor, the earlier limited approach of the policy of movement was transformed into a much more comprehensive design for creating a pattern of good relations between the Federal Republic and the Soviet Union, Eastern Europe as a whole and East Germany in particular. There were powerful obstacles. At a meeting of Eastern European Communist parties held at Karlovy Vary, Czechoslovakia, in April 1967, East Germany and the Soviet Union managed between them to prevent any other Communist state from following the example of Rumania and opening relations with the Federal Republic. It was a kind of Hallstein Doctrine in reverse. Yet in the end Brandt succeeded, with the support not only of his own Social Democratic party but also of the Free Democrats. It is no slight on him to recall that he was greatly helped in this by the Soviet invasion of Czechoslovakia in August 1968. Having reasserted its mastery in Eastern Europe and promulgated the Brezhnev Doctrine—by which it sought to impose rules of behavior on states that were becoming, in Soviet eyes, far too assertive and independent—the Soviet Union now felt much freer to engage in closer relations with the Federal Republic and to allow similar relations to develop with other members of the Warsaw Pact. Only a little while before, it would have regarded such relations as dangerous evidence of West German "penetration." But now it needed these relations for economic reasons, and it also had a political prize to gain: West German recognition of East Germany. Soviet and West German motives were clearly very different; Bonn wanted to transform the East German system, Moscow to shore it up. But they had a temporary convergence of interest, and this dominated the negotiations of 1969–72.

Their outcome was a compromise whereby the two German states recognized each other—but, on the insistence of West Germany, only as two member states of a single German nation. This is not a meaningless legalistic formula. It signifies that the two are not actually foreign states; it maintains the right of East Germans to become West German citizens; and it allows each country to express views (sometimes even with practical results) which, if expressed between two foreign states, would be construed as unwarranted interference in each other's internal affairs. For obvious reasons, the East German government was reluctant to accede to this deal. It was forced to do so by the Kremlin, which removed Ulbricht from power and installed Erich Honecker as his successor in order to clinch the pact. Other elements of the bargain were that the Federal Republic recognized all frontiers in Europe as inviolable (meaning that they could not be changed by force) but not as immutable (thereby holding out the ultimate hope of German reunification). Finally, a separate but related agreement over Berlin elicited a Soviet recognition of Western rights in Berlin and of the legitimacy of a West German presence and certain representative functions.

Since then, Berlin—which on so many occasions in the past had nearly precipitated a third world war—has virtually disappeared from the newspapers. Along with the normalization of relations between the Federal Republic and Eastern Europe, this fact represents one of the great achievements of *Ostpolitik*. In the internal context of West German politics, it also created a renewed domestic consensus. In spite of initial misgivings on the part of the CDU, all parties supported *Ostpolitik* once it was tied to the Berlin agreements. It looked as if West Germany had now found a new internal political coherence to match its growing economic power and its new and pivotal role in East-West relations. This certainly remained true as Helmut Schmidt succeeded Willy Brandt in the post of chancellor, and as the 1970s continued. In many respects Germany proved invaluable to the Western alliance in its dealings with the Soviet Union and Eastern Europe. But as détente came under strain, as negotiations over arms control foundered and the new cold war began, the tensions in West German society revealed themselves anew.

THE NEW UNCERTAINTIES

The fourth phase in West German politics started in 1979. This occurred not because of the Soviet invasion of Afghanistan at the end of the year but because, a few weeks earlier, the Federal Republic had succeeded in persuading its NATO allies that new U.S. missiles should be deployed in Western Europe unless a radical arms control agreement had been reached with the USSR by the end of 1983. The agreement was not reached, and the missiles were deployed. But in the intervening years, the new cold war had really set in, and the question that West Germany had to face was whether it should try to preserve what Germans refer to as the "fruits of détente" in Europe, and whether, if it did so, it would still be regarded as a loyal ally by the United States. The dilemma was not one that the West German political system found it easy to cope with—the more so as many years of uninterrupted economic success began to give way to gloomy prognostications and evidence of certain structural weaknesses. Germany's central role in East-West relations became in itself less important, but at the same time produced deep political divisions, leading to a change of government. When the missiles were introduced, the SPD, which had originally called for them, now opposed them, while the CDU government insisted that they were a test case for alliance solidarity. The consensus which had emerged in response to the Berlin crisis in 1959, and which was so powerfully strengthened by the development of *Ostpolitik*, had now broken down. Germany today is a confused and divided country.

Yet the legacy of the earlier years remains. Brandt did not succeed in his fundamental aim of transforming East Germany. Indeed, that country has been remarkably successful in maintaining the policy of *Abgrenzung*—literally "demarcation," but meaning in this context a distinction between areas in which it cultivates good and even friendly relations with the Federal Republic and those in which it will have no truck with the Republic. Nonetheless, relations between the two Germanies are in many respects very close indeed. This sometimes worries Washington and certainly angers Moscow at a time when relations between the superpowers are bad. It also opens many questions for the future. These can be summarized by saying that "the German question" is now taking a new form—one in which the criterion is not, for the foreseeable future, that of German reunification but that of an autonomous relationship between two German states independent of what else is happening in East-West relations.

FURTHER READING

Bell, Coral. *Negotiation from Strength*. London: Chatto and Windus, 1962; New York: Alfred A. Knopf, 1963.

Brentano, Heinrich von. *Germany and Europe*. London: André Deutsch; New York: Frederick A. Praeger, 1964.

Freund, Gerald. *Germany Between Two Worlds*. New York: Harcourt, Brace, 1961.

Grosser, Alfred. *The Federal Republic of Germany*. London: Pall Mall; New York: Frederick A. Praeger, 1964.

Jakobsen, H. A., and Stenzl, Otto, eds. *Deutschland und die Welt*. Munich: Deutscher Taschenbuch Verlag, 1964.

Midgley, John. *Germany*. London: Oxford University Press, 1968.

Moch, Jules. *Histoire du réarmement allemand depuis 1950*. Paris: Robert Laffont, 1965.

Nettl, J. P. *The Eastern Zone and Soviet Policy in Germany 1945–50*. London and New York: Oxford University Press, 1951.

Sharp, Tony. *The Wartime Alliance and the Zonal Division of Germany*. London: Oxford University Press, 1975.

Speier, Hans. *Divided Berlin*. London: Thames and Hudson; New York: Frederick A. Praeger, 1961.

Strauss, Franz Joseph. *The Grand Design*. New York: Frederick A. Praeger, 1965; London: Weidenfeld and Nicolson, 1966.

Windsor, Philip. *City on Leave: A History of Berlin 1945–62*. London: Chatto and Windus; New York: Frederick A. Praeger, 1963.

Yergin, Daniel. *Shattered Peace*. London: Deutsch, 1977.

PARLIAMENTARIANISM IN WESTERN EUROPE

RICHARD MOORE*

THE natural—and to some extent proper—pride of Britons in their parliamentary institutions has made them reluctant to admit the merits of Continental constitutional systems. They believe that under the Fourth and Third Republics, French politics were little more than a series of scene changes punctuated by brawls between the stage hands. They are hardly aware of the parliamentary politics of any other Continental state and indeed British newspapers make little enough effort to keep them informed. If they are rather more aware than most of the facts of political life they may concede that parliamentary democracy works well enough in Northern Europe, where however it is dull, but cannot be successfully imported into the states of Central and Southern Europe. They fortify their conviction that the British system is best with the belief that it has no rivals, only inferior imitators in distant places where the Speaker's wig has been more faithfully copied than the Speaker's authority.

As the only European power of the first rank that has remained faithful to parliamentary government throughout the present century, Britain has something to boast of. But it should recognize that if its parliamentary liberties have been an inspiration to its neighbors in times of crisis, this is largely because the spirit of its political institutions is basically similar to the ideals that they also have sought to establish over several hundreds of years.

The parliamentary tradition has its classical origins in Athens and Rome. Here and there in the Middle Ages it had a local form that flourished, as in the Venetian Republic, the Icelandic Althing and the Swiss Confederation. The States General in the Netherlands proved the stamina of parliamentary institutions in the struggle with Spain, and the English revolution of the 17th century made the House of Commons a center of power. It was left to France to turn the particular into the general and to proclaim a doctrine of government by assembly as an idea of universal application.

It is to 1789 more than to any other date that the democrats of Europe look. The convenient, if misleading, shorthand of Left and Right originated then, and the assertion of popular representation, not as a practical convenience but as a moral imperative, was made by the revolutionaries. The

*Revised by Richard Mayne.

corruption of democracy—popular dictatorship based on a totalitarian theory —made its terrifying appearance soon after, in the Committee of Public Safety.

British politics are to this day influenced by that tremendous convulsion in which the most powerful and glittering despotism in the world fell before the assault of democracy. From the fall of the Bastille onward no European revolution, however hostile to liberty, has not had to use some of the language of democracy, and no clique or junta clinging to power has long been able to deny all the aspirations of the great revolution. It can be claimed with some confidence that in Western Europe today those aspirations are nearer to being fulfilled than ever before. The spread of the suffrage to all classes and both sexes, the spread of prosperity in the years immediately following the war, a greater sense of community among some European nations, better communications and a higher standard of education—all these have been accompanied by the continuation or the establishment of parliamentary government throughout Western Europe. The most notable confirmation of this trend has been the restoration of democracy in Greece, Portugal and Spain.

VARIETY OF EUROPEAN DEMOCRACIES

The American dream of making the world safe for democracy has not yet been fulfilled, however, even in some of the European states where it is the official foundation of government and the established principle of the great majority of politicians. There is a fascinating variety in the parliamentary methods of Europe, but as regards the power and security of parliamentary democracy, each country may be placed in one of three main categories.

The first can be described as those fortunate countries where the principles of parliamentary democracy and the constitutional order are not seriously challenged by any significant section of opinion. In this category come Britain and the Irish Republic, all the Scandinavian countries except Finland, the Netherlands, Belgium, Luxembourg and Switzerland.

The second category consists of those countries where there is no immediate threat to the constitutional order and little overt hostility to parliamentary democracy, but where its reestablishment followed a period of dictatorship, sometimes very recent, and where it is still sometimes challenged, notably by factions of both Left and Right. Earlier examples are Germany and Austria; the most recent, Portugal and Spain.

The third group consists of those countries where part of public opinion organized in political parties or in other institutions is hostile to the principles of liberal democracy and may be suspected of exploiting its parliamentary forms only to encompass their destruction. France, Finland, Italy, Malta, Cyprus, Greece and Turkey are so placed.

Within each category there are differences of degree. In Britain and Ireland, among the countries of the first category, the shadow of the IRA is still not entirely banished from politics. The practices of the Ulster Unionists do not bear a close scrutiny. The linguistic fanaticism and racial prejudice of the Volksunie in Flanders are incompatible with parliamentarianism. There is a large Communist party in Iceland. In several countries there is widespread skepticism about the pretensions of political parties and the efficiency of parliaments. But nobody expects a coup to be attempted, much less to be successful, in any of these countries, and that is a rare enough phenomenon in the modern world to allow them to claim the title of unchallenged democracies.

FRANCE

The perennial fascination of French politics was for a time reduced by the consensus government of de Gaulle. Aghast at Algeria and irritated by the exaggerated evils charged to the Fourth Republic, the French public asked for a father figure and got him. The General's impeccable style made the surrender to his authority seem less abject. His careful use of words—unlike the far Right with which he was unfairly compared, he always spoke in the name of the Republic—and his undeniable electoral victories made it difficult to make moral objections to his claims.

The mood soon passed. The 1967 edition of this Handbook recorded that "by the end of 1965 France was moving back to government not by consensus but by conflict and horse-trading." The retirement of President de Gaulle and his replacement in 1969 by Georges Pompidou, next by Valéry Giscard d'Estaing and then, in 1981, by the Socialist leader François Mitterrand have intensified this trend. There is a fierce fondness for political life in France that is occasionally silenced but easily reawakened. The Palais Bourbon was often dismissed as a comedy and sometimes passionately loathed but it seldom failed to draw an interested audience and its virtues were as real as its vices. Walter Bagehot thought the French parliament of his day was full of Disraelis. Certainly the standard of debate, if not always of behavior, remained high to the end of the Fourth Republic. The instability of which de Gaulle and the Anglo-Saxons made mock was more apparent than real. In the first 10 years of the Fourth Republic there was a much higher turnover of ministers in London than in Paris, with the admittedly important exception of the office of prime minister. Under the French system, able ministers could spend years in the same post while in England they were reshuffled with alacrity.

If in 1967 the deep ideological divisions in France could be described as "almost benign" in appearance, the victory of the Left in 1981 greatly sharpened the virulence of the opposition. Right-wing extremism once more emerged as a political specter; but its almost universal condemnation, and President Mitterrand's success in reducing the Communist vote, are both hopeful auguries in a period of economic difficulty and hence political tension.

ITALY

In Italy, ideological conflict still holds a central place in political life. Outside the country's political institutions, extremist groups have resorted to terrorism, as in West Germany—partly in reaction against a parliamentary system they accuse of immobility. Within the system, ideology remains important. With the largest, and for the most part the most intelligently led Communist party in Western Europe, and as the home of the Roman Catholic Church, which has learned to refine its ideas and its political methods to the point of the exquisite, Italy could hardly be otherwise. There, as in Britain before 1914, politics are meant to be passionate and expected to be intricate. Ideas matter and eloquence tells. The time of the technocrat—in politics it should not be dignified as an age—is not yet.

It is a very important fact that the ravaged economies and shattered societies of Western Europe in 1945 were rebuilt by parliamentary governments. The *Wirtschaftswunder*, the Italian boom, the French escape from stagnation, owed much to Marshall Plan aid and purely technical factors, but one of the underlying strengths of liberal democracy in Europe is that it presided over the success stories of recovery. With recession replacing boom in the wake of two oil price "shocks," it was understandable that the establishment, in Italy as elsewhere, should come under fire. The Italian response began with an "opening to the Left" by the ruling Christian Democrats, followed by the election of a Socialist prime minister, Bettino Craxi. But the coexistence of the two great blocs in Italian politics—Communist and Christian Democrat—has so far always led to minority or coalition governments whose freedom of action is thereby limited. This may cause immobility, but it can also act as a brake on extremist policies. Prophecy is difficult and dangerous; but the Italian government's continued resistance to terrorism by "extraparliamentary" fanatics suggests that the democratic system implanted after the war by Alcide de' Gasperi has grown tenacious roots.

COMMON PROBLEMS

Since 1948, no European country has seen its parliamentary liberties destroyed by Communism. Perplexing problems rather than imminent perils are now the dominant features of European politics. The dangers of passionate conviction are being replaced by the difficulties of debilitating doubt. How far and in what ways can parliamentary institutions be said to be undermined by these problems and doubts?

Purely technical difficulties are more noticeable but probably less important than a failure of nerve and loss of confidence. It is true that the scale of modern government, the ramifications of a modern economy and the fluidity of a modern society make the day-to-day work of running a nation much more difficult than before 1914. So, most notably, has the post-1974 recession. How can governments tackle economic problems the causes of which are outside their control? How can central banks control an international market dominated by "flight money"? What relevance has an annual budget in the era of five-year plans? How can a minister supervise a bureaucracy running into hundreds of thousands? What sure foundations for educational policy or penal law are there when moral values and social status are as mobile as they are today? Such problems are common to all the Western European states; it may further be asked whether the technical aspects of these problems or those of morale present the greater difficulty.

SCANDINAVIA

If mere scale or a top-heavy administration were the central weakness the Scandinavian countries might be expected to have come near to solving their problems. Their populations are small and in the economic sphere especially have a well-established practice of cooperation. There are no great political tensions—only a general dissatisfaction. Democracy is an unchallenged sovereign but not a very inspiring one. The design is brought up to date: ombudsmen are introduced; the Storting (Norway) and the Folketing (Sweden) televise their most important debates; the Danish second chamber has been abolished and the Swedish one is on the way out; Swedish parties are granted substantial subsidies to propagate their ideas; in Denmark a sophisticated version of the referendum designed to give a parliamentary minority the right of appeal to the country has been tried out. Political youth movements are enormous. The press in both the capitals and the provinces probably reaches a higher average standard than anywhere else in the world. All this is impressive, but unsatisfying.

Some of the dissatisfaction in the Scandinavian countries may spring from their relative isolationism and ineffectiveness on the European stage—even now that Denmark has joined the European Community (EC). Successful in many ways, "as nowhere else in the world" as Hugh Gaitskell once said, they still make little impact and are aware of it. There is a touching but slightly absurd interest in the debates of the General Assembly of the United Nations, since there in the lobbies with Dahomey and Panama, Denmark may seem to matter and Sweden to sway decisions; but most politically minded Scandinavians sense, if they do not recognize, that for model democracies to play so small a part in extending democracy through the European mechanism to the supranational stage is an unfortunate reflection on their values.

There are excuses: professional neutrality in the case of Sweden; fear of losing their cultural identity; traditional distrust of Catholic Europe and recent dread of West Germany. But excuses are not reasons and to the most self-consciously rational people on earth the situation is deeply disturbing. Sweden remains neutral; Norway decided by referendum to reject the chance to join the EC; Denmark, although a Community member for more than a decade, shows little enthusiasm for making the Community more effective, more united and more political. If Scandinavian democracy is to become much more than a well-oiled mechanism it must be willing to help to power future European democracy.

IRELAND AND BENELUX

If the Nordic countries suffer from too quiet a life, some of the other small states have been unquiet too recently and for too long not to relish some repose. Such is Ireland's case, where more pragmatic policies seem to be replacing ancient heroic stands. But Dublin has long understood that the destiny of Ireland lies in the European Community; and since becoming a member the country has been in the forefront of those concerned to develop

318

political and constitutional strength. The Netherlands shows the same spirit. The resistance of the Dutch government and Dutch opinion to Gaullism was as notable as, in Belgium, Paul-Henri Spaak's determination to force the European idea forward and not just to concentrate on the commercial side of the Common Market. What the Low Countries are trying to do is to develop, on a European level, the parliamentary institutions that, for all their defects, have so much helped their own countries.

The Dutch parliamentary tradition is an old and proud one. It proved its value first in bringing the cities and towns together to defend their liberties and then in reconciling the religious communities to one another. Voting follows the sectarian line to a very large extent in the Netherlands, but the necessities of parliamentary life have compelled the Protestant lion to lie down with the rapidly growing Catholic lamb. The Netherlands is historically biased toward the Protestant north. Its parliament, by allowing Catholic citizens a full share in public life while permitting only slow change by consent, has preserved the country's unity as no other system could.

The parliamentary system is inevitably superior to one of personal or presidential rule in any seriously divided country. A citizen must be Protestant or Catholic, atheist or Marxist, a Fleming or a Walloon. Parliament must be a mixture and therefore less menacing to minority and majority alike. The collapse of the Belgian state would seem to be inevitable if its parliamentary system were to go. Under this system it pays the parties to straddle the linguistic gap, although the bulk of Belgian Socialists are Walloons and the mass of Catholic voters are Flemings. The incipient violence of a factious state that feels itself to be two nations is thus restrained.

The Benelux leaders, made aware by World War II of the helplessness of small powers in modern circumstances, see in the building of Community Europe a chance to bring the spirit of compromise into international relations, not in temporary phases of good feeling but as a permanent characteristic of European civilization. They learned their political lessons in a harsh school, but of all the European governments they have been the aptest pupils. From the foundation of the Council of Europe there has been hardly any wavering. A simple thesis has been argued: Europe must be built and to be true to itself and its interests the building must have democratic foundations.

GERMANY

If the politicians of some of the smaller states of Europe are seeking to enlarge the role of democracy, in some of the larger ones they are only just beginning to make it work. West Germany gives some grounds for optimism. The Federal Republic provides by far the most civilized government Germany has had since it became a unified state. The competition may not be great but the achievement is considerable. The physical devastation and moral ruin of 1933–45 make as unpromising a background as could be imagined to the attempt to develop a German democracy, but successive general elections have witnessed the elimination of extremism from parliamentary life.

"Extraparliamentary activity" and terrorism, or intemperate reactions against them, could conceivably reverse all these gains, but it does not seem likely. In spite of the recession, there is still great prosperity in West Germany; and in spite of the recession's political repercussions, there is a real and deep sensitivity to liberal values, cultivating not only the forms but the spirit of democracy. Few countries have shown themselves more aware of some of the new dangers to constitutional government. Reversing the general trend toward decentralization, West Germany has given great powers to its *Länder*. It is helped by the memory of the princely states of old Germany, but it was a bold decision all the same. It is significant that the antidemocrats have made the federal system one of the main targets of their abuse. An attempt has also been made to protect the interests of the opposition and to put checks on the government's handling of spy cases.

The greatest weakness of West German democracy is that it has not captured the imagination. It is pedestrian. The debates in the Bundestag are duller than those in most British county councils. Ministers sit on a platform and lecture the deputies. There is little humor and less wit. It is no answer to say that the best work is done in committee. No doubt it is, but as the committee meetings, although they publish a record, are not open to the press and public, they have small chance of enlivening public discussion. The Bonn system has many virtues, but it cannot provide that sense of participation, or of public drama, which is the strength of the British and French systems at their best. The challenges in Germany are still so concealed from the public in internal party conflicts that they do not necessarily reflect public opinion. Only when the Bundestag is seen to provide the "grand inquest of the nation" will it have met the essential requirements of a parliamentary system.

Still, in many respects Bonn can demonstrate its superiority to Westminster. The political education provided may be less stimulating but the administrative powers of parliamentarians over ministers are much greater. In Germany, as nearly everywhere else in Western Europe, the age of specialization is recognized by giving opportunity to specialists. Deputies work through a permanent committee system, not merely examining legislative proposals, but scrutinizing general policy and the actual facts—not always related—in their own spheres.

BRITAIN

In Westminster there is an obstinate resistance to providing the structure and means by which MPs could really exercise some control over governmental administration. It is not enough to boast of question time and motions on the adjournment, when the opportunities for MPs to discover the really important questions to ask are so painfully restricted. The mother of parliaments is still regarded with respect on the Continent but also with a growing awareness of her arthritic condition.

Popular superstition still accords to the Commons a much more powerful role than it in fact enjoys. While the beginnings of a committee system have now been established, it is by no means as elaborate as the German model, and far less powerful than the American. The lack of proportional representation still hampers the smaller parties, including the Liberal-Social Democrat alliance, which can command up to 30 percent of the popular vote. The result is that a minority of the electorate can still elect a government with a very large majority in the House of Commons. Short of revolt on the Government back benches, it is then impossible for MPs to make much serious impact on policies decided by the Treasury front bench.

So long as MPs deny themselves the means that would allow them to examine effectively the administration and general policy of the government, as well as its legislative proposals, they will have little independent power. The interests will lobby in Whitehall rather than Westminster; and no argument, however powerful, will shake the prime minister from office while party discipline is as solid as it is today. The decline in the authority of the House, a matter of informed comment for over half a century, is masked by the dramatic confrontations across the floor. The pride of elected persons, against which Lincoln warned more than a hundred years ago, provides a cushion of conceit against reality.

Just how ineffective the House has now become in many of its most fundamental functions is revealed by the fact that not since 1921 has a single government estimate been rejected. The control of taxation, in classical parliamentary theory the keystone of the power of the representatives, has almost completely evaporated. This gradual degradation of parliament in Britain is the more painful in that the Commons remains capable of checking its own decline. There has been no shock to the constitutional system which has left British politics nervelessly twitching. Throughout the last war Churchill never failed to remind the House that he was its servant, and indeed there was a notable revival of parliamentary influence during the war. The defeat of the proposed tax on books, the agitation on the rights of aliens in 1940, deservedly raised the good opinion of the House in itself.

Conceivably, the emergence of a three-party (or, more strictly, four-party) system may make for change. So may the longer-term effects of radio broadcasting of debates, whether or not television is admitted to the Commons in its wake. What is clear is that the Conservative and Labour parties will accept proportional representation only as a very last resort, and that this will long delay any really forceful reassertion of the House's will against the government. Likewise, the broadcasting of parliamentary debates, while it heightens the gladiatorial spectacle, has so far done little to publicize and in consequence strengthen Parliament's scrutinizing role.

CONCLUSIONS

Because the parliamentary tradition is so strong in Britain, the weaknesses of the House of Commons suggest that they are the result of the age rather than the place. The inadequacy of parliaments is in fact as common a characteristic of modern Europe as their theoretical power, and cannot be corrected, as the Scandinavian examples show, by mere changes in the mechanism, valuable though these can be.

Parliamentary government depends for its vitality on belief in the power of words to alter facts. Darwin and Freud as much as Marx have made us doubt this possibility. The scientific age has little faith in the reality of reasoning as a means of arriving at value-judgments. Now politics are a matter of values. They are concerned with preferences much more than with probabilities, and the more democratic a society is the more this is true. But if at the same time the people believe that their motives and understanding are crude and limited, the values propounded by politicians will be mediocre. A parliament concerned always with opinion polls, which collate the superficial judgments of the mass, will seldom rise to heights. It is the growing belief that parliamentary government is necessarily, as opposed to usually, unheroic that undermines its authority. This may seem to be unlikely in the consumer age; but the general response to the late President Kennedy (more to the legend than to the achievement) and the success—with their supporters—of Ronald Reagan and Margaret Thatcher prove the deep-seated longing for courage and style in democratic leaders.

If modern parliamentarians seem petty it is often because they are concerned with petty problems. Matters that should be settled at a local level are drawn by the processes of administration to the center and there, if not decided, at least debated. The preference for technicalities over ideals frightens parliamentarians away from the discussion of questions of principle. It is striking that of all the assemblies that have shown most deliberative vigor in recent decades, the Vatican Council must claim a high place. St. Peter's may seem an odd place for the practice of the parliamentary arts, but practiced they most certainly have been.

This has been possible because, although divided on many issues, prelates live within a common frame. Strong feelings can be expressed and tough wrangles on profound matters sustained because of this. It is no accident that at the time when party feeling was far stronger than it is today, when personal rancor and division on deep questions were on almost daily display, the Commons was called "the best club in London." The characteristic of a club is not that the members like one another but that they agree to abide by certain rules. It is the absence of common rules which makes the parliamentary arena so often seem a sham and empty show.

Does the remedy lie in parliamentary development at the European level? The European Parliament is a meeting place for parliamentary democrats from all over the Community, left, right and center. It even includes the Communists. Directly elected since 1979 by universal adult suffrage, it is the only forum large enough to grapple with the scale of modern economic, social and—yes—political problems.

Of course there will remain, especially in the larger countries, much to be done on a national scale. But it is becoming increasingly apparent that if parliamentary government is to be the pattern of the future it must develop—as it is developing—at Community level too. The Community's battles, over the budget, over farm prices, over countless humdrum details and sometimes, it would seem, over mere words, may often appear petty or even pointless. But as the House of Commons understood so well when it defeated the monarchy in the 17th century, the words, and the forms they clothe, are vital.

FURTHER READING

Bibes, Geneviève, et al. *Europe Elects Its Parliament*. London: PSI, 1980.

Borella, François. *Les Partis politiques en Europe*. Paris: Editions du Seuil, 1984.

Cocks, Barnett. *The European Parliament*. London: HMSO, 1973.

Coombes, David. *The Future of the European Parliament*. London: PSI, 1979.

————, et al. *European Integration, Regional Devolution and National Parliaments*. London: PSI, 1979.

Henig, Stanley, and Pinder, John, eds. *European Political Parties*. London: George Allen & Unwin, 1969.

Holt, Stephen. *Six European States*. London: Hamish Hamilton, 1970.

Pridham, Geoffrey, and Pridham, Pippa. *Towards Transnational Parties in the European Community*. London: PSI, 1979.

Sidjanski, Dusan. *Europe: Élections et la démocratie européenne*. Paris: Stanke, 1979.

COMMUNIST PARTIES IN WESTERN EUROPE

CAROLE WEBB

INTRODUCTION AND OVERVIEW

For Communist parties in Western Europe, the period since 1945 has witnessed a significant ebb and flow in political and electoral expectations. Most commentators would identify the "flow" with the two or three years immediately following the end of World War II and again with the middle 1970s. The ebb tide is most commonly associated with the duration of the Cold War and, more recently, with the electoral setbacks of the leading Communist parties in Western Europe and the international politico-military uncertainties experienced during the period from 1979 to the present day.

This is the case with the postwar development of Communist parties in Western Europe, if demonstrable political success (as measured by the acquisition of power and the fulfillment of overt political objectives) is taken as an acceptable and ideologically neutral criterion. In 1945, Communist parties surfaced in the newly liberated political arenas in Western Europe to claim a stake in political reconstruction that would be worthy of their contribution to the defeat of Nazism and their perception of the political and economic ramifications of "reconstruction." There were, briefly, governments with communist ministers in France, Italy, Belgium, Austria, Denmark and Norway. There were mass party organizations rapidly taking shape through the Partito Comunista Italiana (PCI) in Italy and the Parti Communiste Français (PCF) in France. Even outside the four Communist parties of France, Italy, Spain and Portugal, whose subsequent political development gave them a significance throughout Western Europe that the other parties could not aspire to, Communist party membership elsewhere in Western Europe amounted to some 750,000. It was not unknown in the postwar years for some of these parties to win more than 10 percent of the votes in national elections. Communist hopes in the postwar years proved, nonetheless, to be an illusion.

By the beginning of the 1950s there were no Communist ministers in France, Italy, Austria, Belgium, Denmark and Norway, and electoral support had fallen away significantly. The postwar years provided an instructive, if ultimately unproductive, apprenticeship in the politics of balancing domestic political strategies with the choices and tactics forced on the parties by the freezing of relationships between the USSR and the United States.

In fact, it was open to question how much political initiative had lain with the Communist parties in the wake of the Resistance, its political and psychological inheritance, and the domestic political and economic uncertainty following the end of the war in Western Europe. The Communist parties' espousal of political action, in collaboration with non-Communist parties, in support of new democratic regimes in Western Europe had partly depended on the tolerance of their domestic allies. But the parties' acute sense of domestic political opportunism had also been favored at least as much by the temporary suppression of doubts and suspicions internationally—and especially between Eastern and Western Europe—about the durability of the bond of mutual interest linking the United States with the USSR.

By 1947, doubts and suspicions had turned into visible realities and the enforcing of stark choices. The suspicion with which the United States and its Western European allies viewed the USSR's interests in Eastern Europe, and especially in Germany, created a hostile political climate. Communist parties, expressing doctrinal and international loyalty to the Communist party of the Soviet Union (CPSU), were thrust into opposition, indeed into political ghettoes outside what became the mainstream of the public political arena. In France and Italy particularly, but also elsewhere, the Communist parties' political base was frozen by the national and international postures adopted in the Cold War.

Not for the first time in their 20th-century search for national political success, the Communist parties' historical, ideological and organizational bonds with the CPSU assumed greater importance as the parties failed to register significant gains in the national electoral, parliamentary and governmental arenas during the 1950s. Their domestic political strategies were only partly influenced by the dominant preoccupations and political relationships within their own countries. But the articulation of such a close and imperfectly controlled link with the USSR and international communism was nevertheless problematic.

For some, the international political community of Communist parties continued to be a vital source of support and ideological reinforcement. This was particularly true for those parties that were small and isolated, and whose political currency had been undermined by the success of the liberal democracies in anchoring economic and political reconstruction to the framework of the Atlantic Alliance. For the minor Communist parties, the kinks that began to appear in the solidarity of the international Communist movement after 1956 were unlikely to make a sufficiently resounding impact on their national political arenas to enable them to move to reestablish a realistic foothold in the political debate in their countries.

For the Italian and the French parties, on the other hand, the relationship with the CPSU and, through it and because of it, with the USSR and *its* particular political objectives, was central to the parties' domestic political fate. Burdened by their ideological commitment to the USSR, the parties proved unable to prevent that commitment being used to further the

USSR's own external interests. The Italian and French Communist parties were not free agents, at liberty to determine, for example, the conditions under which alliances might be forged with socialists and with other opposition groups. They were political handmaidens rather than initiators of political action. As the 1950s drew on, Communist parties throughout Western Europe found themselves bystanders in a political and economic spectacle of recovery and political consolidation that did not conform with the script as they had seen it drafted at the end of the war. They had anticipated prolonged economic chaos and political vulnerabilty and, as a result, conditions ripe for the eventual socialization of Western Europe.

In Italy, the political dominance of the Christian Democratic party, and the successful identification of its own domestic and foreign policy with loyalty to the new Italian Republic, cast the Italian Communist party as the untrustworthy outsider. In France, the political sea change from the Fourth to the Fifth Republic in 1958 was traumatic for the French Communist party. It moved from being a party at least able to retained a visible presence in the National Assembly (it had 150 out of 596 seats in 1957), to a party scarcely able to maintain any kind of position in the country's new political institutions. The French Communist party had been drastically affected by the Fifth Republic's new electoral laws. In the 1958 election, these produced 1.7 percent of the seats in the National Assembly (10 out of 578) for the French Communist party in return for 20.5 percent of the total votes cast in the final ballot.[1]

During the following 20 years, Western European politics in their national, regional and international settings afforded opportunities and created awkward political and ideological dilemmas for those Communist parties forced to debate the nature of their relationship with the Soviet Union. It would be foolhardy to attempt any kind of brief summary of the complex evolution of positions that brought a number of Western European parties from the slow realization, following Khrushchev's revelations at the 20th Congress of the CPSU in 1956, that de-Stalinization might cast doubts on some features of Soviet socialism, to the openly critical and questioning postures adopted as a result of the Warsaw Pact's invasion of Czechoslovakia in 1968, the Soviet Union's invasion of Afghanistan in 1980 and the Polish coup d'état in 1982. The extent and depth of the changes in the parties still trigger controversy and continue to pose questions for lively political debate and scholarly analysis. This has been particularly marked in Italy and France, where the last decade of political initiatives by the Communist parties has left the Italian party without influence in government (though with almost 30 percent of the vote) and the French party with its lowest percentage of the vote since the war, as a result of the party's performance in the direct elections to the European Parliament in 1984.

Nor, of course, do the Communist parties in Western Europe conform

---

[1] See D. Blackmer and S. Tarrow, eds., *Communism in Italy and France*, Princeton, Princeton University Press, 1975, for interpretations of the strategies adopted by the PCF and PCI during this period.

to a single pattern. The basic ideological and historical ties that bind them to the Soviet Union must be set against persistent evidence of national diversity. The variation in political style, pattern of leadership and preferred or tolerated political allies has provided much grist to the mill of attempts to establish whether "national roads to socialism" *outside* the USSR and in the shadow of the Soviet Union can be conceived, let alone successfully undertaken. It is precisely the theme of national (or rather, Western European) roads to socialism that in the 1970s came to preoccupy the largest and most well-placed of the parties (as judged by levels of domestic support and the visible changes in their relationships with the Soviet Union) as they contemplated their political options.

By comparison with the 1950s and 1960s, Communist parties in Italy, France, Spain and Portugal found themselves in the 1970s closer to the mainstream of political debate. Many of their preoccupations and public stances appeared to be more in tune with those of their political competitors. In France, Spain and Italy, Communist parties pressed for a variety of alliances to secure further electoral gain or, in the case of the Spanish party, to strengthen its credentials as a prosystem party in the period after the death of General Franco). They avowedly took advantage of, and even partly justified their strategy by reference to, the establishment of détente and a military standoff between the two superpowers in Europe. Moreover, they sought to take advantage of their own, albeit muted, debates on freedom of expression in socialist societies, to advocate a pluralist, peaceful and parliamentary road to political change. It was also significant that they were able—not so much through a reformulation of their own programs and ideas but as a result of exogenous factors—to contribute more postively than they had for two decades to the foreign policy debate in Western Europe, including European integration, in ways that could not be readily dismissed as purely Soviet propaganda.[2]

The "high point" of political success for the Italian and the French Communist parties came with their attempts to achieve significant electoral advances. These, however, ultimately fell short of the targets considered necessary for the exercise of political influence. The Italian Communist party, having achieved its highest percentage of the vote in the 1976 general election (34.4 percent), failed to translate this support into direct participation in government. Between 1976 and 1979 it maintained an uneasy position within the parliamentary majority, but without ministerial representation in the largely Christian Democrat government, supporting the government's program but unable to take full credit for the policies on which it had negotiated its support. The PCF went further, in 1981, following the victory of the Left Alliance in the French general election, by accepting four ministerial posts in the largely Socialist cabinet. The party's first ministerial experience since 1947 lasted until 1984 when the growing rift between the Communists and the Socialists convinced the Communist party that it had nothing more to gain by clinging to its foothold in government.

[2] These points are made at greater length in Carole Webb, *Eurocommunism and Foreign Policy*, Policy Studies Institute, Studies in European Politics No. 4, London, 1979.

Even so, Communist parties throughout Western Europe still have not advanced significantly toward their political goals. In spite of their drives to escape political isolation and to acknowledge at least some of the political and economic currency deployed in Western European politics, they have failed to make the political impact they anticipated at the national or, indeed, the European level. Of the largest parties, the French communists are, arguably, even more beleaguered in the 1980s as a result of their experiment with the union of the Left, which has left their party as the "poor relation" of the rejuvenated Socialist party in terms of votes and political influence. The Spanish Communists failed to outbid the Socialists for mass support in the restoration of democratic political activity after 1974 and in the parliamentary and national political contests since that time. The Italian Communist party has witnessed not the "historic compromise" between itself and the dominant Christian Democratic party but rather, in recent years, a modified multiparty coalition led neither by the Christian Democrats nor by the Communists, but by the representatives of the much smaller Republican and Socialist parties.

THE PURSUIT OF "EUROCOMMUNISM"

It was in the 1970s that the largest of the Communist parties in Western Europe came to be identified with the "Eurocommunist" movement. This affected both the evolution of the Communist parties themselves and the accentuation of particular trends in European politics at national and regional levels.

At one step removed from the electoral and political contests and debates, it is the Communist parties' perceptions of the political context that have shaped party strategies and tactics. These perceptions appear to have been influenced by an interplay of domestic and international factors that in themselves reflect significant changes in Western European politics since 1945. Such influence has, of course, been partial. It cannot be said, for example, that the process of Western European integration contributed directly to the decision of any Communist party in Western Europe (even of the French, Italian and Spanish parties most involved with European Community issues) to adopt different tactics in the search for greater domestic political influence. Nonetheless, it is clear that the network of political and economic ties associated with membership in the EC has made it more difficult for Communist parties to win domestic support and achieve credibility by adhering to positions formulated under a different set of political and economic conditions in the 1950s. The economic and perceived political consequences of the survival and expansion of the EC has undoubtedly been influential, especially when taken together with the tantalizing, but still distant objective of realizing the fruits of détente by achieving a more independent role for Europe in world affairs. These factors have played some part in the campaign by Communist parties to enage in political debate in Western Europe in ways less likely to be self-defeating than in the past. These external considerations are not all important; however, external awareness has been more enduring than the interparty jousting and squabbles that have dominated discussions on the current and future state of the parties, particularly in France and Italy.

Political activists and scholars have long debated, sometimes fiercely, the existence of Eurocommunism itself. The concrete and visible indices of a concerted attempt by Western European Communist parties to establish a new and collective identity for themselves have been few and increasingly difficult to find in the less heady political climate of the 1980s. In the 1970s, commentators pointed to three main developments: (1) the electoral advance of Communist parties in France and Italy and the potential political opportunities afforded to the Portuguese and Spanish parties by the regime changes in those two countries; (2) the gestures of defiance made against the USSR as the cornerstone of the international Communist movement, culminating in the disagreements that surfaced at the East Berlin summit meeting of European Communist parties in June 1976; and (3) the Madrid "summit" of March 1977, which brought the French, Italian and Spanish party leaders together in an apparent affirmation of Western European solidarity. Undoubtedly, the public gestures during that period masked more fundamental differences separating the mass parties, like the French and the Italian, from the small, more marginal and more hardline parties elsewhere in Western Europe. The public gestures also concealed significant differences in the tenor, rationale and enthusiasm among the French, Italian and Spanish parties in their adherence to a Eurocommunist platform. Skeptical observers of Communist politics were unconvinced by the parties' avowed conversion to political pluralism. They preferred, instead, to emphasize the continuity of the parties' ideological commitment, including the survival of their belief in the "conquest of power," the paucity of changes in party organization and the continuing reservoir of loyalty for the CPSU and the USSR among the parties' rank and file.

Believers in change—and, indeed, the political elites who responded to overtures from the Communist parties in the 1970s—have been more inclined to take note of what they have seen as significant signs of political adaptation. These have included the refusal (as in the case of the Spanish and Italian parties) to defer to the absolute solidarity of the international Communist movement and the absolute authority of the Soviet model of socialist society. More obliquely, a few commentators have linked the changes in the positions of some Communist parties in Western Europe to the economic and political requirements of advanced industrialized societies.

The inconclusiveness of the scholarly debate on Eurocommunism was, by the early 1980s, overtaken by the steady erosion of the electoral position of the French and, to a lesser extent, the Italian parties. In addition, the loss of political impetus by the Spanish and Portuguese parties, as they ceded ground to more broadly based and, in the eyes of the electorate, more convincing Socialist parties, appeared to confirm the erosion. On one level, the political "gains" for the Communist parties following this period of political reflection, and occasional internal rancor and confusion among the rank and file, accompanied by renewed attempts at political overtures toward erstwhile sworn enemies on both the Right and the Left, have been very few.

While it may not be counted as a "gain" by the party, the Spanish Communist party's publicly expressed and debated dissatisfaction with its strategy under Santiago Carrillo in the post-Franco period, and the disputed inheritance of a Eurocommunist path, have nevertheless begun to open up the party's internal channels of dissent and caused the party to reflect further on its internal operation and its future campaign strategy. By contrast, the French Communist party's electoral losses in national, local and European elections and its inability to gain leverage from its participation in government with the Socialist party have not, so far, led to any comparable internal party scrutiny.

COMMUNIST PARTIES IN WESTERN EUROPEAN POLITICS

On another level, the Communist parties' adoption of Eurocommunist platforms for electoral and domestic political alliance purposes has undoubtedly opened up some political debates in Western Europe. These had either been artificially closed or narrowed by the Cold War, or have only recently come into prominence with the prospect of radical political change at the national level, coinciding with doubts about the scope for national maneuver at the international level. In effect, Eurocommunism has exposed some of the possibilities implicit in the adherence to détente as the overriding principle of international relations in Europe and the dilemmas for potentially vulnerable economies, set to change ideological course, in an increasingly interdependent and partially integrated Western Europe. Although these debates were undoubtedly distorted by preoccupations (particularly U.S. preoccupations) with the security risks implied by Communist participation in government in Italy, or even in France, they have nevertheless revealed some common preoccupations across Western Europe. These have included the exposure of differences in focus and priorities between U.S. and Western European interests in NATO and the broader Atlantic Community, and, within Western Europe, the balance to be struck between autonomy and interdependence under the umbrella of the EC.

It is still difficult to identify, on the one hand, the Communist parties' preferred alternatives to existing relationships and historic ties, and, on the other, the extent of their agreement on major issues that would test their relationship with the USSR if they were ever to come to power. The differences exposed in the 1970s, for example, between the PCI and the PCF on NATO membership and attitudes toward the EC were pressed the more sharply, not because the two parties felt compelled by their own convictions to take up different positions, but rather because the dynamics of their respective domestic debates and party competition made them play different roles in foreign policy.

In Italy, postwar perceptions of the interrelationship between that country's regime, its internal stability and its participation in the Western Alliance and European institutions, were particularly sharpened. The interrelationship was strongly articulated by the Christian Democrats, partly to secure their party's own position after World War II, and was taken up by the Italian Socialist party in an effort to demonstrate its credentials as a governing party in the 1960s. The Italian Communist party partially softened its earlier rejection of such an interrelationship in the light of its own assessment of Italy's continuing economic and political vulnerability. Thus, under the leadership of Enrico Berlinguer in the mid-1970s, the party condoned Italy's involvement in the framework of Western cooperation, in recognition of the irreversible features of Italy's postwar economic development and also out of concern for the need to protect a future Left government in Italy from the consequences of too sharp a break with the past. The PCI's accommodation of continued Italian membership of the EC and NATO has been tempered by its advocacy of institutional and policy reform of the former and of a minimal formal defense commitment to the latter.

In France, in contrast, the domestic context and the political debate on the Left have failed to exert comparable pressures on the PCF to modify its international stance. The party has not been induced to come to terms in anything but the most uneasy way with what it sees as a hostile international environment that would have to be held at arm's length in the event of a Communist government's taking power in France. The Gaullist tradition of aggressive resistance to external constraints, where these implied French subordination or the insensitive treatment of national pride, created a quite different context for the articulation of external interests and opportunities compared with the Christian Democrat tradition in Italy. In this sense, the PCF's ideological commitment was in close conformity, at least outwardly, with French national preoccupations. Furthermore, the Socialist party, as the PCF's main target in its domestic strategy in the 1970s, was moving further in the direction of the PCF itself in terms of its own internal debate on the impact of disruptive external influences on the French economy. In addition, and in remarkable contrast to the cautious attitude of the PCI, the PCF in 1977 appeared to abandon its opposition to the French nuclear force on the grounds that a future Left government in France might need to resort to extreme measures to defend itself against attempts to engineer its downfall.

In Spain, the awareness of external constraints on domestic choices had been partly obscured by the sense of isolation induced by the Franco regime's restricted involvement in Western Europe. Nevertheless, the Spanish Communist party has been as acutely aware as other parties that the absence of formal political and military constraints has not prevented the Spanish economy from becoming dependent on a range of international economic relationships over which it can exert little control. The Spanish Communist party has declared itself in favor of Spanish membership of the EC and appears to support the extension of the Community's economic and political aspirations as essential for the underpinning of democracy and economic development in Spain.

The Communist parties' changing views on the EC can be taken as a substantial indicator of the future relations that the parties envisage between socialist economies and external economic interests and pressures. Many would argue that the rhythm and interlocking nature of economic and continued industrial growth in Western Europe, together with the increasing difficulty for governments of managing domestic economies so as to achieve declared objectives, have combined to raise the cost of, or even to prohibit, radical changes in national economic policies. Such changes may still be seen by Communist parties as imperative for the fulfillment of their political and economic objectives—in spite of the experience of the Mitterrand government in France after 1981, which undermined confidence in its ability to sustain, by Communist party standards, a fairly modest shift in economic policy. For Italy and France, in particular, the pursuit of history left-wing strategies poses difficult choices for the Communist parties and their voters. The choice lies between accepting, on the one hand, the existing framework of economic interdependence and its implied requirements of predictability and orderly economic management and, on the other, searching for a more controllable, but possibly less prosperous, national economic strategy.

A continuing feature of the Communist parties' quest for greater political influence in Western Europe from the early 1970s onward has, therefore, been the parties' varying awareness of the opportunities and constraints produced by the changes in the foreign policy environment in Western Europe. Détente itself (notwithstanding the bitterness and recriminations triggered by the debate on the modernization of nuclear weapons throughout Europe) and the anticipated decline in the significance of the two politico-military blocs have undoubtedly created a more fruitful context for consideration of particular national interests. Within this context, the parties have had an opportunity to examine future options, while not overlooking the interests of the USSR and the primacy of Soviet perceptions of opportunities in Western Europe. As the PCF has learned to its cost, Soviet perceptions do not necessarily coincide with those of a Communist party in opposition and unable to divert the USSR from its concern to woo successive French governments as part of its own wholly national strategy in Western Europe.

The juxtaposition of opportunity and constraint in the foreign policy environment of Western Europe neatly mirrors the underlying tension in the position of the major Communist parties. They had made their bids for serious political consideration across a broad front in the 1970s, only to find themselves still without access to power nearly a decade later. For states in Western Europe, the financial, economic and strategic costs of striking out independently seem to have become too great to contemplate seriously, even though national preoccupations and priorities often diverge significantly from one another. For the largest of the Communist parties, their bid for more influence in the national debate and in government has been made in domestic and international conditions that have greatly constrained any change in the direction of their countries' external ties and therefore the fulfillment of their own domestic goals.

The parties' experiences of attempts to seize the political initiative in the 1970s will take some time to digest as the party leaders and the rank and file come to terms with both the domestic and the external changes that have forced a reconsideration of their own positions. One point is clear. The Communist parties will not find it easy to dissociate Western European states from the increasingly dense political and economic network of ties that have been woven in the aftermath of postwar reconstruction. Western European "regional solidary," affirmed but imperfectly achieved in the 1970s, might well become an exploitable political asset for Communist parties as they contemplate their tactical and strategic postures for the future.

FURTHER READING

Albright, D. E. *Communism and Political Systems in Western Europe*. London: Westview Press, 1979.

Machin, H., ed. *National Communism in Western Europe*. New York: Methuen, 1983.

McInnes, N. *Eurocommunism*. London: Sage, Washington Papers, 1977.

Middlemas, K. *Power and the Party: Changing Faces of Communism in Western Europe*. London: André Deutsch, 1980.

Mujal-Leon, E. *Communism and Political Change in Spain*. Bloomington, Indiana: Indiana University Press, 1983.

Yearbook of International Communist Affairs. Stanford, California: Stanford University Press, annual.

ECONOMIC AFFAIRS

THE ECONOMIC CHARACTER
OF
WESTERN EUROPE

MARIANNE GELLNER

THE countries of Western Europe share certain common features that are rooted in geographical proximity and historical experience, and which have been strengthened in the last four decades by political as well as economic pressures, exerted both from without and from within. These common features of Western European countries have been reflected in a remarkable similarity in their domestic economic policy objectives; widespread recognition of a community of interest, both in relations with each other and with the rest of the world; and the new common problems and opportunities presented by a rapid and accelerating rate of technological change.

EUROPEAN NEOCAPITALISM

The common point of departure underlying domestic policy objectives in Western Europe is the existence of capitalist systems based predominantly on private ownership and private enterprise in all but a few basic sectors. Within this framework, and with the lessons of the 1930s vividly in mind, Western European governments set out after World War II to evolve policy instruments to supplement and guide the market mechanism in pursuit of certain broad objectives. These objectives may be defined as the fullest utilization of national growth potential, full employment, stability of prices, balance of payments equilibrium and the raising of living standards on a broad base. In other words, the general goal was to achieve sustained growth without inflation, and consistent with external balance and the demands of social justice.

From the start, the emphasis and expression given to each of these policy objectives differed, sometimes quite radically, from country to country. For instance, the collective memory of prewar experience weighed heavily and lent special significance to the objective of full employment in Britain, but to the maintenance of price stability in West Germany, and to improved infrastructure and industrial efficiency in France, whereas in Scandinavia social justice ranked particularly high. Necessarily, rather different considerations applied to the less developed countries—Greece, Turkey, Spain, Portugal and Ireland—where the primary economic problem was fundamental structural change.

The basic driving forces behind government action after World War II stemmed from social pressures for secure and general prosperity. The postwar "Keynesian revolution," pioneered by Britain, recognized that governments could and should act toward ensuring economic stability. The emphasis was on avoiding mass unemployment; the main concern was for controlling the trade cycle, chiefly by countercyclical fiscal policies and other measures for adjusting aggregate demand to the available supply. Later, attention spread beyond the shorter-term concern over trade cycles to factors concerning longer-term economic growth, structural imbalances and the control of inflationary pressures under full-employment conditions. These factors raised policy issues related to the supply and allocation of labor and capital. Fiscal policies were extended to serve other major subsidiary aims, some directed toward supplementing or stimulating private investment and generally fostering productive efficiency, others toward equalization of incomes and social security.

The welfare aspect of government policy was, indeed, outstandingly prominent in several Western European countries (France, West Germany, Austria), and has exceeded the United States' effort by a good margin in all nations except Switzerland, Ireland and the less developed Mediterranean countries. Thus the traditional juxtaposition of centralized government direction of the economy on the one hand, and the free sway of private initiative disciplined only by market forces with the minimum of safeguards on the other, began to be superseded. Instead, the view gained ground that there was room for government intervention on quite a broad front as a normal and essential supplement to the working of the price mechanism; and the search was generally for the widening of public participation in economic policy determination through reinforced parliamentary control and three-cornered consultation and cooperation between government, management and labor, with the proviso that the principle of free wage bargaining be maintained. The move was away from reliance on the autonomous and automatic functioning of the market, and became accepted in principle, whatever the political color of governments at any given time. Efforts were made toward better command of the economic and social environment in advanced industrial mixed economies, i.e., economies that rely primarily on market forces but where the state plays a significant role.

A notable expression of this evolution in attitudes was experimentation in national planning, pioneered by France, the Netherlands and Norway during the period of reconstruction and widely taken up in differing forms and with varying degrees of success. It was not part of the West German "social market" concept, which stressed only the social-security aspect of government intervention. But in fact, West German economic practice (including certain aspects of indicative planning) was not far removed from the general trend even before the Social Democrats came to power for the period 1969–82.

Most of the publicly owned sectors in Western European countries are highly capital-intensive and their extent, though varying widely, has become almost everywhere far greater than in the United States and in Japan. In most Western European countries, public utilities, rail, air and urban transport, and telecommunications are government-owned or municipally owned. France and Britain have nationalized coal industries, and government ownership extends beyond the basic infrastructure into manufacturing (iron and steel, motor vehicles, chemicals, oil refining, shipbuilding) and banking and commerce. This situation obtains in Italy, Austria, West Germany and the Scandinavian countries as well. In other countries, for example Belgium, public ownership is strictly limited.

The historical origins of nationalized sectors in Western European countries vary profoundly. In Germany and Italy, for instance, they were a legacy of the financial collapse in the Great Depression and the subsequent Hitler and Mussolini regimes. In France and Britain, large-scale nationalization came after World War II—in France as an aftermath of the German occupation and in both countries out of a desire to improve the economic performance of, or to rescue, failing private enterprises. Latterly, in Britain, under the Conservative government of Prime Minister Thatcher, the pendulum swung back toward private control and the disposal of public assets (as in the cases of Britoil, Jaguar, British Telecom).

Arising partly through historical accident, and often extending over a wide range of activities in individual countries, the management and policies of publicly owned enterprises—and the method of their control—have taken very different forms, including near-autonomous nationalized enterprises run on commercial lines, as Renault in France or the IRI and the ENI in Italy.

THE TURNING OF THE TIDE IN THE 1970s

For the first two postwar decades domestic economic policies appeared eminently successful and allowed rising output, rising living standards, the attainment and maintenance of full employment, relatively shallow cyclical movements and the extension of social welfare—although some countries lagged in certain of these respects. During the 1960s, however, cost-push inflation, fueled by incomes rising faster than productivity, became an issue and prompted many Western European countries to experiment with various forms of price-incomes restraint, ranging from consultative procedures and the establishment of "guidelines" to outright temporary price and/or wage freezes. More than one attempt at coherent incomes policies was made in some major countries, but beyond short-term alleviation of inflation, their lasting tenability and efficacy remained in question.

In the meantime, general government expenditure had been growing rapidly and at a faster rate than national income; its share of gross domestic product (GDP) in Western Europe increased from some 30 percent in the mid-1950s to around 45 percent in the mid-1970s, in a range from 48 percent (Sweden) to less than 30 percent (Spain, Greece, Switzerland)—national differences that have been widening. Retrenchment after 1973, when oil prices quadrupled, could not prevent public spending taking an ever rising share of GDP, since economic growth had slowed down even more and the weight of transfer payments to the unemployed was increasing in most countries.

By 1980, the public expenditure share of GDP had grown to over 60 percent in Sweden, about 50 percent in West Germany and around 45 percent in France, Britain and Italy, compared with about a one-third share in the United States and Japan. As a result, constraints on the public purse became a matter of urgency in some countries faced by mounting national indebtedness and governmental inability or unwillingness to impose higher taxes. Even in France, where a Socialist government came to power in 1981, resort to fiscal restriction became unavoidable by 1983.

The objectives of government policies, as set out at the beginning of this chapter, have remained valid. However, the slowdown in economic growth in the 1970s, accompanied by apparently inexorable inflationary pressure, called for reappraisal of the means for achieving these objectives. At the end of the troubled 1970s, and in the wake of the second oil shock of 1979, preference for maintaining restrictive monetary and fiscal policies in the face of flagging demand had come to predominate in Western Europe; this trend was sustained by the ascendancy of monetarist economics, which held that control of the money supply was not only necessary for price stability but would also ensure growth without inflation in the long run. Stimulating demand by deficit budget spending came to be seen by the majority of policy-makers as impractical, inflationary and self-defeating. Other ways, on the microeconomic level, were sought to encourage private initiative and promote a more efficient responsiveness on the part of the economies. The result so far has been reasonable control of inflation in most European countries by 1982–83, but at the price of prolonged recession, tardy recovery and mounting mass unemployment on a scale not seen since the 1930s.

THE INTERNATIONAL DIMENSION

Little mention has been made so far of the impact on the economy of Western Europe of the world environment, and none of the international institutional framework, which was partly formative and partly the result of domestic developments.

In the immediate aftermath of World War II, a rapid readjustment to the polarization of world power between the United States and the Soviet Union was necessary. Further, the need was felt for an effective answer to the economic challenge of the Communist system, which hardly threatened the economic might and social fabric of the United States but which pushed uncomfortably against the door of Western Europe. An acceptable framework had to be found for the reentry of West Germany into the family of nations. Traditional relations with the primary producing countries were being thrown out of gear by the loss of empires and the emergence of the North–South confrontation between the world's rich nations and the poor ones.

On the economic side, the philosophy on which the postwar international trade and monetary system was founded—that of multilateralism and anti-restrictionism—exerted an important influence. So did the historic Marshall Plan aid offer of the United States. There ensued, on the one hand, the flow of capital from the United States to Western Europe. Marshall Plan aid proper amounted to U.S.$13 billion over four years, but the total transfer of official capital in the first postwar decade, including military expenditure, was nearly twice as large. This, and the accompanying flow of technical know-how, helped to give Western Europe some leeway and the confidence to attain the initial impetus for economic expansion.

At the same time, the Marshall Plan provided the incentive for Western Europe to get together in the Organization for European Economic Co-operation (the OEEC), which was important primarily during the first post-war decade of acute dollar shortage. The OEEC's main significance undoubtedly lay in opening the way—through the European Payments Union and trade liberalization measures—to a dramatic revival in trade within the region, but it probably helped to establish new habits of thought in a much wider sense.

The international monetary system—the gold exchange standard—set up at the Bretton Woods conference in 1944 was brought fully to the test only after the de facto attainment of convertibility of the major European currencies at the end of 1958. It provided for a fixed exchange-rate system, adjustable only in the exceptional circumstances of a "fundamental disequilibrium."

Another agency set up as a result of Bretton Woods and designed to constrain national policies in the interest of international community was the General Agreement on Tariffs and Trade (GATT). This upheld the principle of nondiscrimination (no new preferences except for the formation of customs unions and free-trade areas); forbade unilateral or exclusionary policies; excluded increased tariff protection as a policy weapon in all but exceptional circumstances; and decreed transparency, eliminating import quotas except in agriculture and on a few specific commodities.

Such was the broad setting against which the six original European Community (EC) countries—France, Germany, Italy, Belgium, Luxembourg and the Netherlands—set out on their experiment in European economic integration. This integration was first initiated in the creation of the European Coal and Steel Community in 1952 and was fully institutionalized with the coming into operation of the Treaty of Rome on January 1, 1958, which established the European Economic Community (EEC). The failure of Britain to negotiate association with or membership of the EEC led to temporary economic division in Western Europe, with the formation in 1959 of a second trading group, the European Free Trade Association (EFTA), whose more limited aim was to establish free trade in industrial goods among Britain, Scandinavia, Austria, Switzerland and Portugal. The customs union of the six nations was completed in 1968 and their jointly managed market in agriculture was established product by product.

Part Three of this book is devoted to the history, significance and consequences of the moves toward European integration—a momentous and difficult new departure in European affairs. These moves reinforced existing expansionary forces of the 1960s, not least by capturing the imagination of the business communities within the six EC countries themselves, and also in Britain, the United States and Japan, thus incidentally bringing an unprecedented influx of foreign investment capital. The EC countries have also gained by being able to speak with one voice in trade negotiations.

This was tested in the Kennedy Round of multilateral negotiations (1964–67), which represented a significant step forward in trade liberalization on the global level, effecting a 50 percent across-the-board tariff reduction (except for certain sensitive items) to an average of seven percent for the United States, 8.3 percent for the EC and 10 percent for Japan. By that time, the OEEC had been reconstituted as the Organization for Economic Co-operation and Development (the OECD) with the accession of the United States and Canada as full members, later to be joined by Japan, Australia and New Zealand, thus providing a platform for the examination of problems common to the world's industrial nations. The EC itself was eventually enlarged with the accession of Britain, Denmark and Ireland (1973), Greece (1981), and Spain and Portugal (1986).

In the meantime, a changing world environment was first highlighted in 1971 by the abrupt suspension of the convertibility of the U.S. dollar into gold, which spelled the collapse of the Bretton Woods fixed-exchange-rate system and its replacement by floating exchange rates under the Smithsonian Agreement. Bretton Woods had allowed more freedom than the old-style gold standard, but this freedom had rarely been put into practice and it had been criticized for some years for inhibiting national policies when domestic and balance-of-payments requirements came into conflict. Floating exchange rates brought a new set of problems, however, in the form of increased risks of instability, uncertainty and disruptive speculative capital movements. Indeed, exchange rates proved unexpectedly volatile, although within the EC alignment of currencies, first in "the snake" and from 1979 under the European Monetary Agreement, cooperation prevailed in the quest of greater cohesion and stability.

Secondly, the era of trade liberalization was grinding to a halt under new pressures that had built up. Their gravity was not fully appreciated at first under conditions of booming world production and trade immediately preceding the oil-price-induced slump of 1975, the deepest since World War II. The Tokyo Round of negotiations for further tariff reductions, initiated in 1973, did come to a successful conclusion in 1979, but this could not allay fears that the spirit of GATT might soon be surviving in name only. Nontariff barriers were increasingly resorted to in an effort to insulate domestic economies and to protect jobs in the United States, Europe and elsewhere. These barriers operated against imports from a particular country (such as Japan) or a group of countries (such as the newly industrializing countries of the Third World). They were applied bilaterally or multilaterally and included common EC measures (notably, orderly marketing of steel), but also persisted in trade within the EC itself. They included import licensing, restrictive application of standards, export subsidies, voluntary export restraint, import quotas, and antidumping and countervailing measures. Besides iron and steel, the most notable industrial products involved included textiles and clothing, ships, automobiles, domestic appliances and electronic and communications equipment.

In the 1970s a new obstacle to economic progress came into startling prominence: the need to ease structural and institutional readjustments demanded by the changing competitive balance between the developing and the industrial countries, between the world's major oil producers and consumers, among the three major Western industrial regions (the United States, Western Europe, Japan), and not least within Western Europe itself, where the very success of industrial and social advance created new problems of imbalance of seemingly paralyzing dimensions. The open trading system laboriously extended over three decades is in jeopardy, unless new ways are found to resolve the national policy dilemmas posed by the growing interdependence of nations.

STRUCTURAL ASPECTS

Western Europe occupies some three percent of the world's land surface, contains around eight percent of the world's population, and accounts for almost 30 percent of the world's income. Living standards rank high, and they increased rapidly in the first three postwar decades. By the mid-1970s, per capita income in Western Europe had reached on average about three-quarters that of the United States. Japan, in turn, had by then caught up with Western Europe and attained an income level comparable with the European average.

Table 1 illustrates some key features that characterize Western Europe in comparison with other world regions. It will be seen that Western Europe's manufacturing output was roughly equivalent to that of North America and slightly over three times as much as Japan's. The three regions together accounted for no less than 85 percent of the free world total, indicating that the developing countries, despite their recent progress, still lagged far behind. The value of goods traded across frontiers by Western European countries greatly exceeds that of any other world region. Partly this is due to the greater interdependence of the numerous relatively small and diverse nations within the region, now largely free of tariffs in trade among themselves. But even when the substantial trade among Western European countries is discounted, the region's trade with countries outside it exceeds in value the total trade of the United States. More particularly—and in common with Japan but in contrast to the United States—Western Europe is highly dependent on imports of raw materials and energy. Moreover, Western Europe predominates among world regions as a market for manufactures, a fact perhaps not always appreciated; at the same time, it supplies manufactured exports to Third World countries at an annual value which exceeds that of the United States and Japan combined. As far as temperate zone food production is concerned, the common agricultural policy and rapid productivity gains have moved the EC from deficit to self-sufficiency and even to an overproduction that is accumulated in stockpiles.

Although by world standards the differences in economic structure and income levels among the individual Western European countries are relatively narrow, they are nevertheless substantial. The range of per capita income encompasses some of the world's most prosperous countries, Switzerland and Sweden at one end of the scale, and Ireland, Greece, Portugal and Turkey at the other. Among the EC countries, a comparison of per capita GDP in real values for 1980 placed West Germany, Denmark and France as

Table 1
STRUCTURE OF WORLD ECONOMY, 1980
(percent of world total)

	Western Europe	North America	Japan	Soviet bloc	Rest of World
Population	8.4	5.6	2.6	8.6	74.8
Real GDP	29.8	24.2	8.8	14.4	22.8
Average per capita income as % of world average	352.0	430.0	331.0	166.0	30.0
Exports	40.4	14.2	6.5	7.9	31.0
Imports	44.3	15.4	6.8	7.8	25.7
Value added in manufacturing (1975)*	36.4	37.0	11.9	—	14.7

EXTERNAL IMPORTS AS % OF CONSUMPTION, 1978

	Western Europe	U.S.	Japan
Primary products	37.3	14.1	41.3
Energy	59.8	19.7	94.9
Agriculture	20.3	7.3	19.0
Manufactures	9.2	6.3	3.9

* Percent of world, excluding Communist countries.
Sources: U.N. Conference on Trade and Development (UNCTAD), *Handbook of International Trade and Development Statistics*, 1981 and 1983; World Bank, *World Development Report*, 1979.

the most prosperous; they had reached over four-fifths of the U.S. level. Great Britain, once the leader, had fallen somewhat below the European average and stood only five percent above Italy and some 20 percent below West Germany and 15 percent below France.

An outstanding characteristic of the last 20 years has been very rapid structural change. Many continental countries of Western Europe emerged from World War II with partially backward economic structures and agricultural sectors rooted in ancient tradition, fragmented and at low productivity levels. In the less developed Mediterranean countries and Ireland, reserves of underemployed farm labor still exist, and the share of agriculture in total GDP amounts to around 15 percent in Ireland, Greece and Portugal. In Spain, however, this proportion has been sharply reduced from an estimated 22 percent in 1960 to six percent in 1982. As the first two columns of Table 2 indicate, this was the most dramatic example of a general trend away from the land.

But industry, too, has declined in relative importance in most of the countries listed. Only Norway and Finland have increased the share of industry in their economies, and Italy, whose national figures embrace the dichotomy of the industrial north and the developing south, shows, on balance, no change over the period. In all the other countries, the relative size of the industrial sector has declined by a factor ranging from five percentage points in France to 13 in the Netherlands. When manufacturing is singled out within the industrial sector, even more striking contrasts are obtained. The decline is steepest in Britain, where the share of manufacturing in total GDP fell by over 40 percent in the period, to 19 percent, against 35 percent in Germany, 25 percent in France, 22 percent in the United States and 30 percent in Japan. It was the services sector that gained in relative importance, by no less than 10 to 13 percentage points in most Western European countries, to account for between 55 and 65 percent of total output in 1982. This was a recession year, and industrial activity may have been relatively somewhat more depressed than that of other sectors. But the general direction of change toward deindustrialization in the major countries indicated in the table remains valid.

Table 2
DISTRIBUTION OF GDP
(percent)

	Agriculture		Industry		Services	
	1960	1982	1960	1982	1960	1982
Great Britain	3	2	43	33	54	64
West Germany	6	2	53	46	41	52
France	11	4	39	34	50	62
Italy	12	6	41	41	47	53
Belgium	6	2	41	35	53	63
Netherlands	9	4	46	33	45	63
Denmark	11	5	31	24	58	71
Sweden	7	3	40	31	53	66
Norway	9	4	33	41	58	55
Finland	17	8	35	55	48	57
Austria	11	4	47	39	42	57
Spain	22	6		34		60
United States	4	3	38	33	58	64
Japan	13	4	45	42	42	54

Sources: World Bank, *World Development Report*, 1984, and UNCTAD for Spain.

Another aspect of rapid structural change relates to regional disparities. This can best be illustrated by specific instances. There has been a trend in the iron and steel industry away from indigenous sources of iron ore and coking coal to coastal sites within easy access of deep-sea harbors for the supply of imported high-grade raw materials. This trend has led to a greater dispersal of production centers—away from the traditional continental heartland of the Ruhr–Lorraine–Luxembourg–eastern Belgium triangle, for instance—and the associated rise of new major steel producers in the Netherlands, Italy and Spain. At the same time, the closure of obsolete steel mills has met with strong resistance and has demanded special assistance measures, especially where the livelihood of whole communities was at stake. Shipbuilding—although significant in the economies of only a few countries, such as Norway—is another traditional industry of overwhelming importance to the local populations concerned. Like steel, it suffers from worldwide overcapacity since the collapse of world demand in the 1970s. Japan has become a major shipbuilding nation as Western Europe's share of world output of merchant vessels fell from two-thirds to one-third between 1960 and 1979. At the same time, Spain arose as the world's third-largest shipbuilding nation.

The European automotive industry played a very different role. It experienced dynamic growth during the period of economic expansion and came to account for five to eight percent of manufacturing output, employment and investment in the major European car-producing countries and to over 10 percent of manufactured exports. But technological change brought economies of scale and mass production in a highly competitive world environment. This, in turn, brought mergers, multinational control, corporate strategies reaching across national frontiers and a trend for car assembly plants to be moved from traditional production centers to Southern Europe and developing countries. These examples illustrate the measure of dislocation of traditional centers of manufacturing.

POSTWAR ECONOMIC GROWTH

The rate of economic progress in Western Europe since World War II has been remarkable by world standards and in very striking contrast to the relative stagnation of the interwar years. It has brought structural changes and an almost uninterrupted rise in output and productivity. However, three phases need to be distinguished: reconstruction and recovery stretching into the 1950s; the unprecedented continued economic expansion throughout the 1960s that was cut short by the worldwide deep recession of 1975; and the failure since then to regain sufficient growth momentum for the full utilization of productive capacity.

This is clearly reflected in Table 3, which shows the growth rates of GDP for Western Europe in three postwar decades:

Table 3
GROWTH OF GDP, 1950–80
(average annual compound rates, percent)

	1950–60	1960–70	1970–80
Western Europe	4.8	4.8	2.9
% of which EC members	5.8*	4.6	2.9
North America	3.0	4.6	3.3
Japan	8.0	12.4	4.6
Soviet bloc	9.3	6.7	5.3
Developing countries	4.8	5.6	6.0

* The Six only.
Sources: UNCTAD Handbook, 1983, and U.N. National Accounts Yearbooks.

North America, Japan and the Soviet bloc shared in the slowdown between the 1960s and the 1970s. The developing countries started, of course, from a much lower level and managed to sustain a slowly accelerating growth rate throughout the three decades. Within Western Europe, Britain has lagged conspicuously, whereas the fastest growing European countries (in terms

345

of per capita output) were Germany, France, Italy, Austria and the Mediterranean countries of Greece, Spain and Portugal. Japan has exceeded by a good margin the growth record of the fastest growing Western European countries, advancing at the peak period more than twice as fast.

In historical perspective, too, the Western European growth record of the 1950s and 1960s stands out as quite exceptional. It has been shown[1] that over the century from 1870 to 1976 (which included two world wars and the interwar depression), the average annual growth rate of 11 Western countries ranged between a low of 1.8 percent for Britain and a high of around three percent for Scandinavia—the rate for the six original EC countries ranging between 2.1 and 2.7 percent. What, then, lay behind the rate of accelerated growth so abruptly ended during the 1970s?

THE CONTRIBUTION OF SPECIAL FACTORS

One set of special factors concerns elements of recovery, readjustment and catching up after prewar stagnation and wartime disruption. Parallel with this runs the thesis that much of the great expansion in European and world trade acted as a stimulus to growth and was due to the progressive liberalization of trade.

The aftermath of the war had a significant impact on every aspect of European economic life in the late 1940s and well into the 1950s. The effect of war was not so much physical destruction (in West Germany, industrial investment during the war is estimated to have exceeded war damage plus the value of obsolescent plant), as the existence of pent-up demand, not least for housing, and of other profound dislocations. Once resources were successfully harnessed, postwar recovery and readjustment contributed to the requirements of the respective peacetime economies. Recovery in European trade lagged somewhat behind that of production, and in some industrial sectors—for example, energy and steel and above all housing—supply tended to be slow in catching up with demand. Postwar recovery is usually discounted as an economic element after about the mid-1950s, but West Germany did not attain a "normal" peacetime footing until some years later.

The expansionary influence of trade liberalization operated not only in the first but also in the second phase of the unexpectedly consistent economic buoyancy of the 1960s. From the mid-1950s to the mid-1960s, trade liberalization is estimated to have contributed about one-half of the increase in trade among the world's industrial countries, the other half deriving from growing incomes. Liberalization policies had gone further in Western Europe and played an important part in shaping the two outstanding characteristics of world trade in that period; trade in manufactures expanded more rapidly than world industrial production, and trade among industrial countries expanded more rapidly than trade between these countries and the developing world.

Moreover, machinery and transport equipment were the most expansive among the manufactured goods entering world trade. Also, contrary to

[1]See A. Maddison, "Phases of Capitalist Development," Rome: Banca Nazionale del Lavoro, *Quarterly Review*, June 1977.

prewar experience, the advanced countries (Western Europe, North America, Japan) provided a faster growing import market for capital goods than the developing primary producing countries. It cannot be doubted that this expansionary world environment stimulated economic activity. West Germany is the outstanding example of a country that benefited from export-led growth.

DEMAND AND SUPPLY

The stimulus exercised on Western European economies by buoyant export markets was transmitted by boosting total demand. Yet in the light of subsequent experience, it seems clear that trade liberalization would not have progressed had it not been for generally buoyant and stable demand at home and abroad. It was evidently helpful to Western European exporters that the United States entered a period of accelerated growth in the 1960s which helped to sustain growth impetus in Western Europe once the postwar catching-up phase had lost momentum. Similarly helpful in sustaining demand was the fact that cyclical swings in Western economies—though steeper in the United States and Japan than in Western Europe—were nevertheless relatively shallow and dispersed, so that recession in one country tended to be offset by rising demand in others. Anticyclical demand management held problems, it is true, of correct timing, and the hazards of "overshooting" and of operating within the balance-of-payments constraint. But recession in European domestic markets was typically marked merely by a slowdown, often quite a mild one. A rising trend in real incomes was ultimately decisive in sustaining demand, as was the availability of, and the desire for, an increasingly sophisticated range of goods for greater material comfort.

Postwar structural changes in the European economies indirectly stimulated demand, but their primary impact was on the supply side. The most direct way in which this made itself felt was through increased industrial employment—a trend reversed even in the 1960s in several important countries, including West Germany and Britain, and replaced by expanding service employment. Initially, there was an ample reservoir of displaced workers on the continent, anxious to rebuild their lives. The influx from Eastern Europe of some 10 million refugees into West Germany—which continued until the erection of the Berlin Wall in 1961—added to the labor force and augmented the large numbers of the unemployed yet to be absorbed there. In West Germany, the average rate of unemployment was over seven percent in 1950 and still over five percent in 1954, but had fallen below one percent in 1960. In Britain, on the other hand, full-employment conditions were rapidly attained and maintained within the cyclical range of 1.5–2.5 percent until the early 1970s. The absorption of postwar unemployment took rather longer in other countries, notably Italy, Belgium and Denmark, and at varying rates, until about the mid-1960s.

Then there was the surplus labor available in low-productivity agriculture for release into other occupations in several countries, including Italy, Austria and Finland but excluding Britain. The drift from the land, accompanied by impressive productivity gains alongside an increase in the average size of farms, continued through the 1960s and 1970s after full-employment conditions had been established in one country after another. In the 1960s, overfull employment began to be a problem. One symptom of the tight labor situation was the appearance of temporary immigrant workers, mainly from Italy, Spain and Greece, but also from Turkey, Yugoslavia and elsewhere. They were employed in France, Germany, Switzerland, Sweden and Belgium, to name the most important host countries. In the 1970s, when jobs began to be scarce, immigration was sharply curtailed, and by the early 1980s— significantly, in the light of what has already been said about the relocation of industry—Spain had changed from being a source of emigrant labor to being a net receiver of immigration.

Finally, perhaps the most important ingredient in the period of accelerated growth was the remarkably high rate of capital investment, accompanied by high returns on investment in terms of output. Technological change brought changes in production techniques, accelerated by the catching-up element (applying also to Japan) in bridging the technological and productivity gap vis-à-vis the United States, a gap that had widened conspicuously during the war. Production costs were lowered, often through economies of scale, and scope was offered for new product ranges alongside rapidly developing sales and marketing techniques. The growth rate in the volume of nonresidential fixed investment for the period 1955–73 was highest in France among the major European countries—7.9 percent per year—and was the longest and most consistently sustained right up to the end of the period. Comparable rates for West Germany, Britain and Italy were 6.5, 5.8 and 5.3 percent per year. In the case of West Germany and Britain, a leveling out process began somewhat sooner than in France, and growth remained conspicuously flagging there, and in the rest of Western Europe, through and beyond the following decade.

As a result, the rate of increase of gross fixed investment for 13 West European countries fell very dramatically when the 10 years to 1970 and the succeeding 12 years to 1982 are compared—from an annual average of 5.8 percent to merely 0.1 percent. In the 1960s France, Spain and the Netherlands had invested at above average rates; in the succeeding period, there was an absolute decline in the annual rate of investment in the Netherlands, Scandinavia and Switzerland, and a slowdown to between 0.6 percent and 1.3 percent in France, Germany, Italy, Spain and Britain.[2]

CAUSES AND CONSEQUENCES OF THE SLOWDOWN

In the simplest terms, rising output is generated in market economies by demand or demand expectations, and the ability to supply at competitive cost and at a price acceptable to the customer. The rate of output, in turn, both determines and can be affected by available labor and capacity-utilization rates. In the favorable postwar environment, the upward curves of demand and supply in Western Europe proved mutually reinforcing. Accelerated

[2] World Bank, *World Development Report*, 1984.

growth, in turn, not only facilitated the pursuit of desired social objectives but also provided opportunities, unfortunately not always seized, for ensuring greater flexibility in the economies and for overcoming inherent resistance to change.

In the course of the 1960s, the special factors which had favored growth were beginning to lose their force. Business confidence was riding high, however, despite the appearance of bottlenecks on the supply side (labor shortages, lead times in capacity expansion, booming raw material prices) and despite the partly consequent acceleration in domestic inflation rates. Indeed, inflation itself served to feed growth in certain important respects. Real interest rates (adjusted for inflation) attained historically low levels and borrowing risks were reduced: it was more advantageous to hold assets than liquid reserves. On the part of the workers, bargaining power increased and pressure was on for ensuring that real incomes would continue to rise. Inflation expectations in decision making at all levels tended to become self-fulfilling. Internationally, there were latent causes of instability, notably differential inflation rates between countries, causing payments problems and eroding competitiveness for some countries under fixed exchange rates. Latent imbalance was discernible in other respects, too: it arose principally from a failure to adapt domestic production capabilities quickly enough to the changing demand patterns, both at home and abroad, created by the great expansion in international competition opened up by trade liberalization and the freeing of capital movements.

The introduction of a flexible exchange-rate system in the early 1970s became, on balance, a destabilizing factor in the conditions that ensued. The two oil shocks, added to an already destabilizing situation, telescoped impending issues by their sheer abruptness, and seriously undermined the confidence of governments, financiers and business people in the possibilities of future growth without inflation. Moreover, new adjustments became imperative as an era of cheap energy, sustained by cheap and plentiful oil supplies, changed to one where energy conservation, exploration and substitution for oil became issues; and an era of expanding world markets and of capacity expansion programs developed into one of uncertainty, in which payment imbalances began to affect numerous countries and the seeds were sown for the severe debt problems of the Third World.

In this new setting, the economic cycles within Western Europe, as in the rest of the industrial world, became unusually closely synchronized. They proceeded from a steep upsurge in 1972–73 to deep recession in 1975, and the subsequent period of recovery was cut short in 1979 by the second oil shock. Western European productivity in terms of GDP per person employed fell from an annual average of 4.5 percent in the 20 years up to 1973 to about two percent in the succeeding 10 years. Peak inflation rates in Western European countries generally occurred from about 1979 to 1981. Inflation, more serious and in double figures in some countries (Britain, Italy, France) and exceptionally well contained in others (West Germany, the Netherlands), subsided in almost all of them by the spring of 1984 to rates ranging from three percent in West Germany, five percent in Britain, to 8.5 percent in France.

Thus inflation was down but production was only very hesitantly edging up. The GDP growth rate for Western Europe was 1.3 percent in 1983 and increased to an estimated 2.2 percent in 1984, with little improvement expected for 1985. At least 2.5 percent GDP growth was required just to keep unemployment steady in the EC of the Ten. But in the meantime, the number of unemployed in Western Europe had grown from 5 million in 1970 to 11.5 million in 1980 and to 18.5 million in 1983, or to about 10.5 percent of the labor force, with a further rise to 20 million estimated by the end of 1985.[3] These increases occurred over and above reduced working hours, part-time working and withdrawals from the labor market, including early retirements. They were compounded, on the other hand, by a temporary acceleration in the growth rate of the population of working age to a record 1.1 percent per year in the period 1979–82, owing to the postwar baby boom, which in Western Europe had peaked about the mid-1960s. The population of working age is expected to stabilize at zero growth after 1986. Just as the exceptional inflow of school-leavers created its own problems, so may the greater outflow for retirement of the generation born after World War I, which is about to begin. This implies a greater social burden, since the population of pensionable age is already relatively high and life expectancy is lengthening. Those at work in Western Europe to supply the rest of the population with goods and services represented only 59 percent of the total number of Western Europeans in 1983. At the same time, the number of those registered as unemployed for 12 months or more rose, after three years of recession, from 27 percent in 1979 to 40 percent of the total number unemployed. For governments, the main dilemma became one of squaring the circle between lagging tax revenues, the desire to reduce taxes as an incentive to growth, and public expenditure for emergency programs and the visibly mounting social demands. Deficit financing was held to be taboo, in principle, as being inflationary, according to the current conventional economic wisdom.

The immediate outlook appears bleak, indeed, for attaining a path of sustained balanced growth which could eliminate the waste of human resources that has been generated. The remedies are elusive and controversial. The myriad microeconomic measures proposed or already implemented are directed toward structural readjustment on the one hand, and the alleviation of the human problems (high youth unemployment, for example) on the other. They do contain essential ingredients for a remedy but, on the whole, appear to treat the symptoms rather than the cause. World trade has been languishing for five years—not helped by the previously noted spread of protectionism—and such revival as has occurred in Western European export opportunities has owed much to cyclical recovery in the United States. The Japanese, most severely affected by the first oil shock, appear to have weathered the second better than most, with an inflation rate below three percent in March 1984 and GDP growth for that year estimated at five percent. Their economy, rooted in their own traditions and attitudes, has proved more adaptable in radically changed circumstances. The North Americans

[3]OECD, *Employment Outlook*, September 1984.

increased the numbers at work by nearly 18 million in the 10 years ended in 1983 (against a net loss of 1.5 million jobs in Western Europe). The unemployment rate in the United States was reduced, during recovery, from 10.5 percent at the end of 1982 to 7.5 percent in the spring of 1984; during the presidential election year of 1984, it approached the historically "normal" level for that country. A large budget deficit, "inadvertently" accumulated and judged unsustainable, played its part in stimulating demand, while the inflation rate was held down to about five percent by means of high interest rates that, in turn, impeded the easing of monetary policies in Western Europe.

The recent better performance in staging a cyclical recovery outside Western Europe does not appear to have a particularly secure basis in the longer term, and offers only limited hope. A lasting solution, when it comes, will have to incorporate a more imaginative and less dogmatic and nationalistic approach than has been evident so far. It will need to combine a rediscovery of confidence in a secure and hopeful future with an agreed, measured constraint on everyone's part—governments, investors, management and wage earners—all those whose individual decisions and actions can so easily be self-defeating if not mutually consistent. Such a change of heart is not likely to be achieved in a hurry.

FURTHER READING

Cox, A., ed. *Politics, Policy and the European Recession*. London: Macmillan, 1982.

Maddison, A. *Economic Growth in the West: Comparative Experience in Europe and North America*. London: Allen and Unwin; New York: Twentieth Century Fund, 1964.

Organization for Economic Cooperation and Development. *Economic Outlook* (Biannual) and *Employment Outlook* (Annual).

Pierre, A. J., ed. *Unemployment and Growth in the Western Economies*. New York: Council on Foreign Relations, Inc., 1984.

Pinder, J., ed. *National Industrial Strategies and the World Economy*. London: Croom Helm, 1982.

Saunders, C., ed. *The Political Economy of the New and Old Industrial Countries*. London: Butterworth, 1981.

Shanks, M., ed. *Lessons of Public Enterprise: A Fabian Society Study* (esp. Chapter XVII, "Lessons from Abroad" by Peter Lowell). London: Jonathan Cape, 1963.

Shonfield, A. *In Defence of the Mixed Economy*. Oxford: Oxford University Press, 1984.

———— *Modern Capitalism: The Changing Balance of Public and Private Power*. London and New York: Oxford University Press for the Royal Institute of International Affairs, 1965.

Tew, B. *International Monetary Cooperation 1945–65*. 10th rev. ed. London: Hutchinson University Library; New York: Hillary House, 1965.

THE EUROPEAN CAPITAL MARKET

WILLIAM M. CLARKE

AN ILLUSTRIOUS HISTORY

"The lamps are going out all over Europe; we shall not see them lit again in our lifetime." Sir Edward Grey's deep forebodings on August 3, 1914, might, with a little adjustment, have been applied with just as much truth to the European capital markets in 1930. One by one they were closing their doors to foreign issues. Not for another 30 years would they be re-opened.

Even now, more than five decades after the Great Depression, the capital markets of Europe remain a shadow of what they once were. London's Stock Exchange can still boast a turnover (in equities and fixed interest) equal to the rest of the bourses of the European Community (EC) put together, but it still lags behind New York and Tokyo. Parts of Western Europe are as prosperous as Japan and the United States, yet the savings and wealth of Europe are still not being mobilized for investment, either internally or externally, on anything like the old scale. The stock markets of Europe—Paris, Milan, Frankfurt, Brussels, Amsterdam, even London—remain isolated from each other at a time when Eurocurrency loans are spanning the globe. Why?

To discover the answers it is necessary to reach deep into the past, and to assess the recent course of politics and economics, as well as finance. Two world wars, a major world slump and the subsequent appearance of two economic superpowers, the United States and Japan, all form part of the explanation. But it is within Europe itself that the final answer, and the only hope for a European financial renaissance, still lie.

It is not necessary to go back to the origins of the Amsterdam Stock Exchange in 1613 or of the London Stock Exchange in the 1670s to get the full flavor of what the European capital market once was. In fact, it was not until the middle of the 19th century that both exchanges really came to fruition and that others, particularly in Paris and Berlin, followed suit. Holland led the field in the 18th century, Britain in the 19th. But only after the Napoleonic wars were both countries beginning to benefit from the major shift in economic wealth resulting from the industrial revolution. For the first time, money had started to accumulate in commercial hands. The wealthy princes of Florence, Lucca, Venice and Genoa were being joined by manufacturers from the north of England. Joint stock companies had been established. Soon the savings accumulating in the hands of this new industrial class were being invested in shares in a variety of enterprises finding their way to the Amsterdam and London stock markets. By the middle of the 19th century, the volume of foreign shares available in both centers had begun to expand significantly. Foreign government issues were soon a normal part of the London scene. Foreign bonds were available in Amsterdam, Paris and Berlin.

During the second half of the 19th century, this process blossomed to a remarkable degree. Between 1850 and 1914, it is estimated that British investment abroad rose from £500 million to close on £3.7 billion, and that of this the bulk was made up of bonds issued on the London capital market. This overseas investment had gone to help build railways, harbors, plantations and other developments all around the world. Paris had done the same, financing (to its later regret) the major share of the Russian state railways. In contrast to common practice since 1945, the underdeveloped countries of that time raised funds directly in London, Paris or Berlin, received cash and immediately spent it on the developments they needed. European manufacturers were paid in cash and everyone was happy, or reasonably so. Now these capital markets are no longer operating on the old scale. The poorer countries' needs are greater, their debts already astronomical and their fixed-interest borrowing—provided for so long by individual governments, international agencies and, more recently, by international banks—needs to be buttressed once more by international equities. Unfortunately, the 19th-century source has run relatively dry and has hardly recovered from a half-century of political shocks and economic change.

There was a recovery of sorts throughout the 1920s, after the interruption of World War I, though the lending by some of the European markets became somewhat feverish toward 1929. Money was eventually being lent on ridiculous terms and occasionally to borrowers who, at other times, would not have merited attention. But this did not last. By the early 1930s, foreign lending was virtually a thing of the past. Confidence had been shattered by the 1929 crash. Britain imposed a rigid exchange control over foreign lending in 1932 and extended the regulations four years later. Other centers did the same. Tariff barriers were raised and exchange controls introduced. Things continued in this way until World War II broke out in 1939.

POSTWAR REVIVAL

During the early postwar period, Europe had much to contend with in reconstruction at home and did not take much heed of the needs of others abroad. From 1948 onward, vast amounts of U.S. dollars flowed to Western Europe, and Europe's own savings were put to the same purpose. Cities were rebuilt and industries reformed. Trade recovered within Europe. But it was not until 1956 and later that it could be said that prosperity had finally returned.

The first financial center to behave in the old way was Zurich. Switzerland had escaped not only wartime destruction but also the postwar erosion of money values. The cost of living remained remarkably stable; Swiss banks were as discreet as ever; and it was not long before the natural inflow of capital from outside, coupled with Switzerland's own savings, allowed the Swiss authorities to reintroduce foreign issues on the Swiss capital market. The market was strictly controlled, but it was a beginning. Not until the major Western European currencies regained convertibility at the end of 1958 did other capital markets follow Switzerland's lead. Amsterdam eventually allowed a significant volume of foreign borrowing in 1961, though none in 1959 and 1960, and hardly any in 1962 and 1963. The London market was active throughout this period, and particularly during the 1950s, but most overseas issues were for Commonwealth borrowers. For virtually the first 15 years after the war, only four basically foreign loans were arranged: for Iceland, Norway, and twice for the World Bank.

It is now clear that 1958 was a turning point for Western Europe and for the European capital market too. It was the year of General de Gaulle's return to power in France. The subsequent prosperity and stability in France inevitably led to the convertibility of the Western European currencies on December 29 and, a few days later, to the launching of the Common Market. Soon, "economic miracles" were occurring all over Western Europe. West Germany's was the first, soon to be followed by those of Italy and France. Output rose steadily, gold flowed in and payments moved into surplus. What caused this economic upsurge is less significant to the subject of this chapter than the consequences, which were almost immediate. Given the confidence provided by convertibility, traders, manufacturers and investors all began to move money across frontiers with an ease and assurance not seen in Europe for over 25 years. Both short-term and long-term money was involved. Big firms began to leave surplus funds in different centers depending on the rate of interest offered. Some borrowed money in Amsterdam. Several British companies raised funds in Zurich; the World Bank borrowed in Milan; Japan raised money all around Europe; several European groups raised dollar funds in London; Copenhagen made a Swiss franc issue in London. The world was getting smaller again, and money was on the move.

What was moving, however, was not predominantly the old-style flow of capital through the issue of bonds or equities on individual capital markets in domestic currencies, readily convertible into other currencies. It is true that Zurich, Frankfurt, Amsterdam and London began to raise such money for foreign governments and enterprises in the late 1950s and 1960s; such issues have increased since. But the major transformation, and what was ultimately to be regarded as the major source of international funds for the world boom of the 1960s and early 1970s, was seen in the so-called Eurodollar market.

EUROCURRENCY

Its place of origin may remain in dispute (whether Paris or London), but the place of its development does not. London-based banks were quick to attract surplus dollars held in Europe, and just as quick to lend them for productive purposes. The Eurodollar was born, probably in 1956. But it was not until four years later that it was referred to for the first time in print.[1] Thereafter, its growth was phenomenal. Eurodollars were neither confined to Europe nor were they entirely made up of dollars. Yet the short-hand term had a point: most of the deposits happened to be dollars, and most of them happened to be in Western European hands. The whole process was a return to the type of operation common throughout the 1920s. It can take place only when currencies can be freely held and transferred from one foreign holder to another. Although the U.S. dollar was in this position earlier, it was not until the major Western European currencies were made fully convertible that this deposit business could develop fully. Holders of surplus currencies who knew they would need the use of them at a certain specified time found that London banks, for example, were willing to accept them and pay attractive rates of interest.

This business mainly began with dollars held in Western Europe. German traders, for example, who had earned dollars, instead of at once switching their earnings into marks and getting dollars again when they needed them at a later stage, decided to place them with a London bank and earn interest into the bargain. Why did they not place their dollars with U.S. banks? Because, under Regulation Q of U.S. banking legislation, the rate of interest American banks could offer on such deposits was limited. This gave ample scope for enterprising foreign banks to offer rates that American banks could not match. Since this situation arose just as the United States began to run an extremely large deficit with the rest of the world, there was a growing supply of dollars being earned abroad, particularly in Western Europe. International banks in London were in the forefront of these Eurodollar developments—or Eurocurrency, as it was soon to become, with the extension of the market to other currencies used externally. Even before the end of the 1950s, total Eurocurrency credits outstanding had reached $1 billion. They are now close to $2,000 billion.

Most of the dollars deposited with the London banks were invested for the appropriate period in ways that brought the banks concerned a useful profit margin after taking account of the interest rate they themselves were paying. Short-term funds went into short-term projects. Quite soon, however, these short-term funds were being rolled over (that is, renewed) so that longer-term financing needs could be met. And the number of foreign banks attracted to London by the development of such a new and exciting source of international funds began to mushroom. From 80 in the late 1950s, the total reached over 300 thirty years later and it is now well over 400.

For the next two decades, the Eurocurrency market acted as the world's major source of short- and medium-term financing. It developed new techniques to meet special situations and extended its lendings from corporate

[1] In *The Times* (London) financial review for October 24, 1960.

firms and governments in the developed world to those in the more needy developing world. It even spawned a capital market of its own—the Euro-bond market—once the New York capital market was restricted by internal fiscal measures in the early 1960s. The finance for such issues, essentially bonds in accepted convertible currencies, came from individuals, private corporations and other international investors. They were handled by one or two "lead" banks, underwritten by many more, and were often issued in two centers.

Between them, the Eurocurrency and Eurobond markets offered loans ranging from six months to 15 years and had, to a great extent, taken over the medium- and long-term lending formerly undertaken by a combination of bank loans and capital market issues in domestic currencies. The replacement was far more evident in Europe than in the United States. Although domestic dollar issues were restricted in New York from 1963 onward (first by the introduction of an interest equalization tax and later by controls on overseas investment), such issues continued and eventually revived, acting as an alternative source of funds to the Eurobond market. The same could hardly be said of Europe, and it is important to know why, for the same reasons apply today as 20 years ago. What, in essence, had transformed the remarkable financing power of London, Berlin, Paris and Amsterdam, capable of supporting railway, harbor and mine finance on a colossal scale in the early 20th century, to a handful of almost provincial financial centers by the 1970s and 1980s? The answer is partly historical, partly political and largely economic.

The two world wars and the slump between them had thrown parts of European industry into the hands of the banks, restricted some of the former capital markets to dealings in domestic debt, and disrupted the financial links between them. The result was a marked contrast between such centers as Zurich, London and New York, still capable of mobilizing savings through a wide range of institutions to firms in need of long-term capital, and those like Paris, Milan and Brussels, where bank finance dominated and capital issues were a relative rarity.

This capital market imbalance, both within Europe and between Europe and the United States, was the challenge faced by the EC from the outset. If it was to mean anything, and particularly if it was to live up to the Treaty of Rome, the Community had to contemplate the free movement of capital within its borders and to stress the need for both liberalization and harmonization in relation to capital flows between its member states. But the translation of hopes and intentions into action was slow and disappointing.

Two early Council directives (1960 and 1962) abolished restrictions on credits tied to commercial transactions, on direct investments and on purchases of stock exchange securities. A third directive was intended to complete the liberalization, but was delayed, shelved and, in 1977, finally withdrawn. By that time, restrictions were creeping in again and the initiative had been lost.

Harmonization was also pursued in the narrower area of the bourses themselves, in efforts to protect investors and to bring stock exchange practices more closely into line throughout the EC. A common minimum level of conditions to be met by companies seeking a listing on a recognized EC stock exchange was agreed upon. Prospectuses and half-yearly accounts were treated similarly, and a program of harmonization of company law was pursued. These led to harmonization directives, often laying down minimum requirements, the contents of which are gradually being adopted by individual member countries. Here again, progress has been slow and capital market developments, it has now been realized, are unlikely to be stimulated solely by generalized agreements of this kind. While the EC was trying to harmonize itself, the Eurocurrency market had developed from $1 billion to close on $2,000 billion, and the New York and Tokyo stock markets had begun to form dynamic structures for the 1990s. A new European assessment, and initiative, were urgently needed. They came, appropriately, from both the Commission and the European bourses themselves.

AN INTEGRATED EUROPEAN CAPITAL MARKET

The Commission's recent reassessments have included two important conclusions: that the expansion of the Eurocurrency market is no substitute for the development of an integrated European capital market, and that the Commission itself is hardly the best agent of change, being rather a catalyst for prodding appropriate initiatives from the private sector. On the first point, the Commission put its views quite succinctly: "The Euromarkets' contribution to connecting up national markets is indirect and imperfect, because of the wide variety of national exchange rules governing the conditions in which residents have access to Euromarkets. In particular, communication via the Euromarkets usually involves nonmember currencies and conditions beyond the control of the authorities of the member countries." On the question of the role of the Commission itself, and the need for new initiatives, the then Commissioner Christopher Tugendhat put the matter equally plainly: "I do not believe that viable markets can be created by the issue of a decree from the authorities . . . what we need is not a Community directive, but supply and demand." He added that the Commission "attached great importance to close and frank collaboration with stock exchange circles."

The European bourses were not slow to respond. The chief executive of the London Stock Exchange, Jeffrey Knight, welcomed the change of accent, commenting:

> It takes a very long time to bring a Directive into law, while security markets are constantly changing and adapting to new circumstances; a regulator needs to be flexible in order to keep up. Similarly, it has become clear that the markets could not, indeed, should not, be forced to become uniform and integrated. The Community Stock Exchanges work in different ways for historic, political and social reasons. In some member states they play a far greater part in the financial system than in others. In some the equity markets are strong; while in others banks and debt finance are dominant. The markets have established themselves over many years and have proved themselves in different ways. It would clearly not be appropriate to seek a formula to "harmonize" the stock exchanges.

His conclusion was a simple one: any initiatives "should be spear-headed by the exchanges themselves."

The fruits of this are beginning to be seen. The European bourses had already set up a Committee of Stock Exchanges in the EC in 1972 and, given the new approach and encouragement by the Commission in Brussels, jointly appointed consultants to "undertake detailed studies with a view to developing a European Securities Market on a progressive basis." Attention was focused on what already existed and on the future role of equities. The subsequent recommendations covered practical stock exchange matters as well as the financial climate needed for the development of an integrated capital market.

Individual governments and stock exchanges are beginning to respond too. Part of the reason for this has been the growing debt crisis of the developing countries. From the autumn of 1982 onward it became clear that Mexico was not the only country close to bankruptcy or, more accurately, to repudiating its outstanding debts. Poland, Argentina, Brazil, Zaire, Venezuela and other nations have all since added to the anxieties of the international banks and governments who lent them fixed-interest credit on too lavish a scale. It was only a step from this crisis to the conclusion that the banks involved would for some time be far less inclined to lend on so large a scale, and that equity issues through the world's stock markets might be a better alternative. Other factors have also played a part, but the result has been a growing emphasis on private equity finance and on the conditions and incentives that might encourage it.

In France and Belgium, fiscal incentives have been offered to encourage stock market investors: the new Monory and De Clercq laws. The emphasis has also shifted toward support of small businesses, particularly those needing the facilities of a stock exchange. Hence the encouragement of the Unlisted Securities Market in London and similar "parallel" security markets in Holland, France, Denmark and Belgium, and corresponding plans in West Germany. Major structural changes in the stock exchanges of London, Paris and Amsterdam are also in train. The switch from London's traditional dealing system (in which a jobber acted as a wholesaler, while a broker acted on behalf of individual investors) to a more unified system has probably been the most radical of all. It reflects, in part, the new competitive spirit introduced by the Thatcher government. The abolition of dealing rules is already leading to new groupings of banks and brokers, and to the possibility of larger, more securely financed units, better able to compete with the existing security-house giants of New York and Tokyo.

Creating a European dimension, however, requires more than just progress in individual European centers. Cooperative initiatives will be needed too, especially in the area of market information and in the methods of settling outstanding business. It is here, above all, that new technology can provide exciting new opportunities (as well as, perhaps, crippling expenditure). Compatible information systems need to be introduced at the outset—a proviso that hardly needs contemplation in New York or Tokyo. Such a thought has already led to a major feasibility study and to the subsequent introduction of the IDIS (Interbourse Data Information System) project. Its object was to link the European bourses to each other electronically by the end of 1985, enabling share prices of the same stock on different European bourses to be shown on the same screen. The next step might be the most exciting: the introduction of bid and offer prices and the direct linking of information to actual deals. If shares are able to be traded more easily, the settlement of the ensuing debts (including payments, transfers of certificates, registrations, and so on) are bound to need similar treatment. This is another matter for the combined resources of the bourses, the central securities depositories and the Commission.

Thus, belatedly, Europe's stock markets have begun to put their individual houses in order and to cooperate more closely with their neighbors. Unless the climate in which these bourses have to operate also improves, however, their efforts will have been useless. The major obstacles to progress remain individual exchange controls, taxation imbalances, fiscal constraints and government controls over the movement of funds across frontiers and over their precise investment. Both the Commission and individual member governments, therefore, still have a crucial role to play in reducing restrictions and improving the financial climate.

The Commission has put forward its own ideas of what should be done on an EC basis, with the emphasis on flexibility, practicality, the human factor and, above all, an outward-looking approach to the future. It is being encouraged by its own Committee on Economic and Monetary Affairs to remain pragmatic and even more aggressive in its liberalization approach; to embrace the banking and insurance sectors as integral parts of any viable capital market; and to reemphasize the crucial role played by the European Monetary System.

Whether these combined actions will restore Europe's capital market to its former status remains to be seen. But the opportunity is at last being recognized. As the chief executive of the London Stock Exchange recently summed it up:

> Deregulation is spreading world-wide having started in the United States and spread to Canada and Australia, and now to London. Our philosophy in Europe must surely be that attack is the best form of defense. We in Europe have an ideal opportunity to find a niche in world-wide 24-hour trading of securities, being ideally placed in the time zone between the closing of the Far East markets and the opening of the North American ones: we must work to exploit that for, if we do not, our capital markets will become increasingly irrelevant as trading, even in our own domestic stocks, migrates across the Atlantic or to the East.

The opportunity is there, and the risk is too. It would be truly ironic if Western Europe, which managed to supply private risk capital for the development of North America in the 18th and 19th centuries, out of remarkably low income levels, failed to turn its present prosperity to similar use on a global scale in the last quarter of the 20th century.

FURTHER READING

Cairncross, A. K. *Home and Foreign Investment 1870–1913*. London and New York: Cambridge University Press, 1953.
Clarke, W. M. *The City in the World Economy*. Harmondsworth: Penguin, 1966.
———. *Inside the City*. London: Allen and Unwin, 1979 and 1983.

Einzig, Paul. *The Euro-Dollar System.* London: Macmillan; New York: St. Martin's Press, 1964.

———. *Foreign Dollar Loans in Europe.* London: Macmillan; New York: St. Martin's Press, 1965.

European Commission. *Intégration Financière.* Brussels, 1983.

Macrae, Hamish, and Cairncross, Frances. *Capital City.* London: Methuen, 1973 and 1984.

Report of the Committee on Finance and Industry. Cmd 3897. London: HMSO, 1931.

Report of the Committee on the Working of the Monetary System. Cmd 827. London: HMSO, 1959.

Segre report: *The Development of the European Capital Markets*, Brussels: Commission of the European Communities, 1966.

Stonham, Paul. *Major Stock Markets of Europe.* London: Gower, 1982.

TECHNOLOGY IN
WESTERN EUROPE

KEITH PAVITT

THE capacity to commercialize innovations based on advanced technology is fundamental to Western Europe's well-being. High-wage industrialized countries have their main competitive advantage in sectors intensive in innovations and in the use of technology and skill.

SPURS TO INNOVATION

The past achievements of the German chemical industry, and the present ambitions of the French nuclear energy industry, illustrate that a lack of natural resources has been an important stimulus to innovation. But so has an abundance of natural resources, as in the case of mining machinery and metal-using industries in Sweden, agricultural-machinery and food-processing industries in Denmark and the production of coal-mining equipment in Britain. Defense procurement has also spurred innovation in aerospace and engineering in Britain, France and (mainly before World War II) Germany. So have large, technology-based firms. Swiss chemical firms, for example, have moved from dyestuffs into pharmaceuticals and then into pesticides; Philips, in the Netherlands, has diversified from electric light bulbs into a wide range of light electrical and electronic products.

European Integration

The postwar political drive for closer European integration has also been associated with innovation in the so-called big technology sectors—aircraft, space, nuclear energy and sections of the electronics industry—all of which have required heavy government funding for research and development, and have often involved intergovernmental and interfirm cooperation across national boundaries.

These sectors and programs have maintained their hold on the public imagination over the past 25 years. In 1957, the establishment of Euratom got more publicity than the prosaic beginnings of the Common Market. In the 1960s, President de Gaulle in France and Prime Minister Wilson in Britain stressed the importance of European technological cooperation in resisting what was then considered to be the "American Challenge." When Britain eventually joined the EEC in the early 1970s, Prime Minister Heath reaffirmed this conviction, as did President Mitterrand's government, elected in France in 1981. Its earliest and, perhaps, most influential expression was in Jean-Jacques Servan-Schreiber's book *The American Challenge*, originally published in 1967 as *Le Défi américain*.

The "big technologies" are the key ones for defense equipment, in particular, and for transport, communications and energy supplies. They are therefore fundamental to a modern industrial economy. Large-scale programs of research, development, testing and production engineering are necessary for commercial success. Countries outside Europe—particularly the United States—have considerable monopoly power over these technologies' development and use, growing out of the large-scale federal expenditures in the 1950s and 1960s on research and development activities and public procurement. Given these conditions, it was argued that similar subsidies should be given to European firms to ensure Europe's control over those technologies critical to its industrial future.

Such reasoning has been used to justify either national or European government subsidies. Advocates of closer European integration have gone further, suggesting that "the imperatives of modern technology" inevitably require closer European collaboration. In the emerging, promising areas of technology, they argue, it would be opportune to begin developments on a European scale, before nationally-based interest groups emerge. European programs would ensure a larger scale of resources, thereby increasing efficiency; access to more than one national market, making possible longer production runs; and the sharing of investment costs and financial risks.

There are also similar arguments for large-scale European enterprise in a competitive market on the U.S. model. A large Common Market, it was argued, would allow the pressure of competition to coexist with firms large enough to be able to exploit economies of scale. It would also encourage Europe to assimilate the modern management techniques associated with large-scale U.S. enterprise. Without these changes, Western Europe would become an underdeveloped satellite of the United States.

Such was the essence of the arguments first advanced in the 1950s and 1960s. At the time, skeptics pointed out that, from the mid-1950s to the mid-1960s, European-based firms had grown more rapidly than U.S.-based ones, while other schools of thought maintained that U.S. technology was increasingly available in Western Europe through trade in goods, licensing agreements and the European operations of U.S. multinational firms.

Before considering this debate in greater detail, it may be useful to recapitulate the history of European efforts to meet the "American Challenge."

Euratom

Euratom's purpose was ambitious, its formal powers extensive. It was intended to facilitate the growth of a peaceful European nuclear energy industry by developing a common market for nuclear goods, ensuring access to nuclear fuels and controlling their civilian uses, and promoting nuclear research and development on a European basis. Its future looked promising. The Suez Crisis had exposed Western Europe's vulnerable dependence on Middle Eastern oil supplies. The commercial application of nuclear energy had begun in Britain. Here was a new technology of promise, and its needs apparently dictated programs on a European scale.

Yet by the late 1960s, just 10 years later, Euratom had failed. With the exception of the Joint European Taurus (JET) fusion project, Europe's nuclear effort had become both national and derivative. By the early 1970s, every country in Western Europe, except Britain, was developing thermal nuclear reactors based on technology originating in the United States. By the end of the 1970s, Britain was also exploring the possibilities of adopting the American technology because of technical and economic difficulties with reactors of its own design.

Three lessons emerge from this experience. First, it is very difficult to predict or to plan the development and commercialization of a technology that is radically new. By the early 1960s, the prospects of nuclear energy looked less promising than in the late 1950s. At least until 1973, oil became increasingly plentiful and cheap, as did coal. At the same time, greater experience in designing, building and operating nuclear plants revealed technical difficulties, the resolution of which increased costs. And political opposition to nuclear power was growing.

Secondly, it is difficult to establish supranational European programs in new technological fields perceived as promising, because national groups will also be eager to develop and control them. President de Gaulle and the Commissariat à l'Energie Atomique believed nuclear technology had to be developed nationally; those who wrote Euratom's obituary tended to blame Gaullist France for its death. If France had not clipped Euratom's wings, however, groups in West Germany might well have done so. West German nuclear-equipment suppliers and electrical utilities did not allow the German government to dictate the development of their thermal nuclear-energy technology, and were even less inclined to allow European institutions to do so.

The third lesson from Euratom's failure is that European nations were not only unwilling to give more power and initiative to European institutions, but were sometimes unwilling to cooperate among themselves in major technological developments. When President Pompidou abandoned the French gas-graphite reactor technology in the early 1970s, he turned to the United States to license light-water technology, in spite of an offer of the same technology from West Germany.

European Launcher Development Organization (ELDO)
In the early 1960s, when the space race was developing between the Soviet Union and the United States, a promising future was foreseen for a European space effort. A European launcher was considered necessary in order to eliminate the U.S. monopoly. France, West Germany, Italy and the Benelux countries, therefore, took up the British offer of the Blue Streak rocket, originally conceived for military use, and agreed to finance the development of further stages of the rocket and to provide ground-base tracking facilities.

This program was another failure. Despite considerable expenditure and many tests, the Europa rocket never worked. As in the case of nuclear energy, initial expectations about space technology's immediate commercial prospects were naively optimistic. But ELDO's failure illustrates other problems.

The first is that a country may propose a program of European action not because a sector is considered promising, but because the country has a technology, program or product that it is unwilling to continue to finance by itself. Europe, in such cases, may find itself sharing the costs of failed or disappointing national programs. This was Britain's real motive for offering the Blue Streak to Europe. It also hoped—wrongly—that the rocket would help persuade President de Gaulle to allow Britain to join the EC. Similar national offers of European cooperation have been made since: a large computer system was offered by France in the late 1960s; Rolls-Royce was offered to Europe by the British just before it went bankrupt in the early 1970s; in the early 1980s, France was interested in international money for the continuing development of its sodium-cooled fast breeder reactor.

The second problem is that national priorities differ. In the case of space technology and ELDO, the differences between France and Britain turned out to be considerable. For the former, a European launcher was a necessary condition for independence, and Europe should be prepared to pay for it. For the latter, launcher services should be bought from the lowest-cost supplier, which was the United States. Behind these differing national positions were different degrees of trust in the United States. In the area of space technology, this translated into France's independent development of military missiles and Britain's purchase of the U.S. Polaris missiles and, later, of Trident.

A third problem illustrated by ELDO's failure was the difficulty of managing multilateral development projects on a merely cooperative basis. Integrated design, development, testing and production never existed for the Europa rocket. Each country produced its part of it, which was then assembled at the testing site. Many of the technical shortcomings and cost overruns grew out of this lack of integrated design and organization. On the other hand, the European Space Research Organization (ESRO), which had been set up at the same time as ELDO to develop a European program of basic research in space, was more successful, partly for the very reason that program management was better integrated. ESRO became the basis for the existing European space organization—the European Space Agency (ESA).

Concorde and Tornado
Management problems also arose in European aircraft programs, two of which ran into difficulties. The Anglo-French development of the Concorde, the supersonic airliner, was a technical success but a costly commercial failure, since no airline other than British Airways and Air France bought it. Cooperation among Germany, Italy and Britain to develop a military aircraft —the Tornado, formerly called the MRCA, or Multi-Role Combat Aircraft —resulted in cost overruns large enough to compromise the plans of the military in the three participating countries for equipment purchase over the next ten years.

The countries involved in both these projects were unwilling to accept the technological division of labor and interdependence that would have made possible a unified management structure, the specialization of technical tasks and the delegation of authority, permitting flexible, rapid decision making. Instead there was management by committees, and joint or duplicate development projects, which inevitably decreased efficiency. There were also duplicate production lines, which decreased the possibility of dynamic learning economies.

In both projects, misplaced emphasis was given to technological ambition. Concorde was the world's first supersonic jet transport, and Tornado the world's second swing-wing fighter (the first was the relatively unsuccessful American F-111). In the case of Concorde, this technical ambition originated in government laboratories; the plane's developers failed to realize that it was cost per passenger seat mile that sold civilian aircraft, not speed. For Tornado, technical virtuosity was necessary to enable the aircraft to meet the different, partially conflicting operational requirements of the three European air forces involved; separate aircraft, meeting each of the national requirements, might have been simpler and cheaper.

Concorde's example also demonstrates the great difficulty in stopping large-scale European technological projects once they have been started. The British Labour government tried to halt Concorde in 1964, but the French government refused. From 1966, it was clear to many that Concorde would be a commercial failure; nonetheless, it continued. Powerful lobbies in politics, government departments and agencies, and management and trade unions in both countries were able to perpetuate its existence well beyond what made commercial sense.

LEARNING FROM FAILURE

Thus, instead of bringing economies of scale, European programs have sometimes involved heavy coordination costs, unjustified technological optimism and ambiguity in higher objectives, coupled with rigidity in lower-level procedures and tactics. Some of the problems have been the same as those experienced by national governments in supporting big technology programs. They include the difficulties of distinguishing the real national or collective interest from special pleading by lobbies and interest groups, and of coping with inevitable uncertainties, whether technological, commercial or political. Other problems are specific to European programs—in particular, conflicts between Community-wide powers and national interests, conflicts between member states over priorities, interdependence and trust. There have been some successes, however, and the lessons of past disappointments have been learned by governments, industries and policy analysts.

European governments have learned, individually and collectively, to deal more carefully with newly emerging technologies. Instead of committing themselves to full-scale development at a very early stage, they have learned to take an incremental, step-by-step approach allowing continuous review and adjustment. Thus, the inevitably expensive European JET project, which seeks to demonstrate the feasibility of controlled thermonuclear fusion, is not seen as the first step in an inexorable European march over the next 30 to 50 years toward reactors generating energy from this radically new course. It is seen, instead, as the sort of risky, long-term technological bet

365

that a group of industrially advanced countries should be taking in an area of such global importance as energy.

The EC institutions have also begun to finance smaller-scale programs of research and development related to unconventional energy sources. Although not necessary on grounds of scale, this European initiative can be justified by the efficiency of pluralism when uncertainty is high. In such circumstances, flexibility and speed in decision making are particularly important, but are often lacking in the existing programs because of a complex and heavy structure of committees, all with national representatives defending what they consider to be national interests.

There are some bigger obstacles to the joint development of energy technology, namely the disparity in energy resources among Community member states. Now that increasing independence and diversification of sources have become major objectives of national energy policies, priorities for technological development are bound to differ between those countries having their own oil and/or gas (the Netherlands and Britain), those having coal (West Germany and Britain) and those having little in the way of indigenous energy resources (Belgium, France and Italy).

France, West Germany and Italy, for example, are collaborating on the development of the sodium-cooled fast breeder reactor, with the main focus at present on the construction of the French-designed Super-Phénix. While many of the organizational difficulties of previous European efforts have been overcome, there remain two problems. First, Britain plays only a minor part, despite its considerable expenditure on fast breeder development at Dounreay, Scotland. Second, the program aims at a full-scale demonstration plant as the basis for subsequent commercial development. It has been argued that, given the technical and economic uncertainties surrounding breeder reactors in general and the sodium-cooled fast breeder in particular, an exploratory and incremental development program of more modest proportions might have been more appropriate.

There have also been difficulties in promoting European work on coal technology. While West Germany and Britain have a clear interest in technology related to the development and use of their deep-mined coal (automated mining, on-site burning, fluidized heat combustion, and coal gasification and liquefaction), France gives much higher priority to nuclear energy than to coal technology, preferring to buy cheap coal from Australia, Poland, South Africa and the United States.

In the European Space Agency (ESA) differences in national priorities have been explicitly recognized for some time, with member countries able to choose to participate to varying degrees in a number of programs. West Germany has played a large role in the European contribution to the U.S. Spacelab program, as has France in the development of the European rocket Ariane and Britain in the development of a maritime communications satellite. France and West Germany have also cooperated in the development of communications satellites. Important areas for the future include the next phase of the Ariane rocket program, which, given the difficulties facing the U.S. space shuttle program, has had some success in obtaining orders for European launcher services. ESA is also developing satellites for the direct beaming of television programs.

In general, European governments and industrial firms appear to have learned that interdependence is essential for efficient management of technological programs. The most strikingly successful example of this is the European Airbus, in which France has the design leadership and where there is a clear division of labor among the participating countries in research and development and production. A company has now been established to develop a family of such aircraft on a European scale. In the program of the ESA, European aerospace firms have developed procedures to enable them to work together more efficiently as consortia.

At the same time, the European institutions appear to have concluded from Euratom's failure that they should aim to complement national programs rather than compete with them. Perhaps they have become too modest: in Community research and development programs that relate to the external costs of technological advance in such areas as pollution or nuclear safety, it would be valuable to have their unfettered professional advice and analysis.

It has also been increasingly recognized that technology spectaculars are not necessarily the most appropriate vehicles for European action. Successful Anglo-French cooperation has existed for years in the development of helicopters. Compared to Concorde, the Airbus is a dull, prosaic aircraft, and the Ariane rocket has proved technically and commercially rather more successful than the earlier Europa. Technically dull projects often have the advantage of being less risky and less likely to attract misplaced enthusiasm.

In addition to these changes, there has been better analytical understanding of the nature and limitations of government's role in technological development in a mixed economy, with more emphasis on fundamental research and exploratory development across a broad technological front. There has also been a clearer appreciation of the difficulties experienced by European countries and companies in catching up in such technologies as aircraft and electronic components, where early developments in the United States were stimulated by defense and space markets, and where there are great potential economies in design, development and production. Successful programs for imitation have all depended on the capacity of government to analyze and understand the industry's dynamics and, together with the firms, to formulate and execute a realistic strategy. Sometimes success has needed luck: the fortunes of both the Airbus and Ariane depended, to some extent, on mistakes and gaps in U.S. programs. In most cases, the short-term costs of entering an industry have had to be weighed against the longer-term benefits of gaining a foothold in a sector with good market prospects.

AMERICAN CHALLENGE—OR JAPANESE?

Perhaps this more relaxed and deliberate attitude toward European technology over the past 10 years also reflects Europe's growing technological and industrial strength and confidence when compared with the United States. Some of the fears expressed by Servan-Schreiber and others have turned out to be unfounded. On the whole, Western Europe has continued to improve its industrial productivity and exports relative to America, partly reflecting the successful transfer of U.S. technology to Western Europe. More recently, it has been shown that the vigor with which countries closed the technology and productivity gaps with America during the 1950s and the 1960s depended on the rate of investment (reflecting the rate of embodiment of world best-practice technology), and on the distance from the U.S. level of technology (reflecting the technical possibilities for improving productivity).

Moreover, this technology transfer does not appear to have depended mainly on the very rapid expansion of European production by U.S. firms, nor on the technological depletion of European firms, which is what Servan-Schreiber had feared. The world sales of large European (and Japanese) firms continued to increase faster than those of U.S. firms in the 1970s, just as they had in the 1950s and 1960s. Table 1 shows that the U.S. share of large firms' sales decreased from 71 to 56 percent between 1962 and 1981, while that of the EC countries increased from 25 to 34 percent and that of Japan from four to 10 percent.

Table 1 also shows that industrial research and development activities in Europe increased in relation to those in the United States. The U.S. share of total industrial research and development dropped from 76 to 52 percent between 1964 and 1981, while that of the EC increased from 20 to 31 percent and that of Japan from four to 17 percent. The U.S. position is even less flattering in terms of industry-financed research and development (i.e., excluding government-funded industrial research and development as part of military and defense programs); the U.S. share declined from 65 to 48 percent, while those of the EC and Japan increased from 28 to 30, and from seven to 22 percent respectively.

Finally, Table 1 shows that statistics on patenting activity in the U.S. also reflect the decline over time of the relative importance of American innovative activities compared to those of the EC, as well as the rapid growth of those of Japan. In percentage terms, U.S. patenting statistics overestimate the relative importance of U.S. patenting activities, since firms tend to patent more intensively in their home markets. However, taken together with research and development statistics, those on patenting enable us to identify in greater detail the relative strengths and weaknesses of firms, countries and groups of countries in different technologies and industrial sectors.

Broad sectoral comparisons of research and development expenditure show that sectors of relative innovative strength in the United States include aerospace, those of Japan include metals and metal products, and those of the EC include chemicals. More detailed statistics on U.S. patenting confirm these results, and in addition show U.S. strength in a range of technologies linked to abundant natural resources, as well as Japanese strength in motor vehicles and engines and in bioengineering. They also show the relative strength of both Japan and the United States in major electronics-based technologies.

These patterns are mirrored in Table 2, which shows the relative technical strengths and weaknesses of the EC as reflected in relative shares of patenting in the United States in 27 sectors. Sectors of relative EC weakness include metallurgy, natural resource-based technologies and major electronics-based

Table 1
PERCENTAGE DISTRIBUTION OF MULTINATIONAL FIRMS AND INNOVATIVE ACTIVITIES AMONG THE EC COUNTRIES, UNITED STATES AND JAPAN

	World sales of largest firms, according to country of origin		Expenditure on research and development activities in business enterprises (current prices and exchange rates)		Privately financed research and development activities in business enterprises (current prices and exchange rates)		Number of patents granted in the United States, according to country of origin	
	1962	1981	1964	1981	1964	1981	1963	1982
EC	25	34	20	31	28	30	14	21
United States	71	56	76	52	65	48	85	64
Japan	4	10	4	17	7	22	1	15

Sources: J. Stopford and J. Dunning, *Multinationals: Company Performance and Global Trends*, London, 1983; OECD, *Research and Development in the Business Enterprise Sector, 1963–1979*, Paris, 1983; OECD, *Selected Science and Technology Indicators, 1979–1983: Recent Results*, Paris, 1984; U.S. Commerce Department, Office of Technology Assessment and Forecast, *7th Report, 1977* and *Industrial Patent Activity in the United States: Part 1*, 1983.

technologies (calculators, computers, office equipment; image and sound equipment; electronic components and devices; telecommunications). On the other hand, the EC is relatively strong in chemicals, nuclear energy and road vehicles, and in sectors strongly influenced by electronic technology, such as specialized and general industrial equipment.

In the light of these statistical comparisons, the current political and industrial concern about the state of technology in the EC, compared to the United States and Japan, needs careful definition. The EC has been progressively closing the gap compared to the United States in terms of research and development expenditure and patenting activity, and it has a strong position by world standards in many sophisticated technologies, including electronics-based production equipment. However, there are three causes for concern. First, as is evident from Table 2, there is the relative EC weakness in three sectors of electronics technology that are expected to offer enormous growth prospects in future: telecommunications, office equipment and consumer products. Second, in spite of a closing of the gap compared to the United States, per capita research and development expenditures by business enterprises are still higher in the United States than the average for the EC countries, and have now been overtaken by Japan. Third, the EC average hides very considerable technological gaps among the member countries. The discussion of the technology gap will be continued further on.

Two sets of beliefs are held much less firmly now than they were in the 1960s. First, size is no longer seen as a sufficient condition for industrial innovativeness; in large firms, coordination costs are considerable, as are the problems of motivation, and mergers may remain cosmetic without internal rationalization or change. Secondly, there is less faith in American management techniques and the appropriateness of business school education for managing innovation and change. In the United States, it has been argued that excessively short-term performance criteria are often used by management specialists, so stifling innovation. In West Germany, engineers still tend to dominate management, and this may not be a bad thing.

Finally, the relative U.S. decline in industrial research and development since the 1960s is reflected in a similar decline in government-financed research and development. Table 3 shows that the U.S. share of total government-financed research and development decreased between 1965 and 1981 from 77 to 53 percent of the total, while that of the EC increased from 21 to 39 percent and that of Japan from two to eight percent. The American lead in defense and space research and development is still great, but not so overwhelming as it was in the 1960s; and the relative importance of defense and space research and development has declined from 72 to 47 percent of total government expenditure. On the other hand, government expenditure on research and development in energy and manufacturing (mainly in civil aviation and electronics), basic research and agriculture increased from 21 to 38 percent of the governmental total, and the EC share in all these categories of research and development expenditure remains high.

Table 2
TECHNICAL SECTORS OF RELATIVE STRENGTH AND
WEAKNESS OF THE EC, ACCORDING TO SHARE OF
PATENTS IN THE UNITED STATES IN 1981

Sector	*Percentage Share of U.S. Patenting*
Total	19.5
Nuclear reactors	32.8
Pharmaceuticals	32.6
Plastic and rubber products	25.7
Road vehicles and engines	24.5
Metal apparatus and machine tools	22.6
Chemicals and petrochemicals	22.0
Process equipment	21.8
Specialized industrial equipment	20.5
General industrial equipment	20.2
Power plants	19.9
Bioengineering	19.5
Materials handling	19.2
Telecommunications	18.5
Agricultural and construction machinery	18.4
Other transport	18.0
Instruments, controls, photographic equipment	17.9
Electronic components and devices	17.8
Electrical industrial equipment	17.8
Building materials	17.6
Metallurgical and other processes	16.4
Aircraft	16.3
Image and sound equipment	15.5
Textiles, clothing, leather, wood	15.4
Food and tobacco	15.1
Calculators, computers, office equipment	14.4
Metal products	14.0
Mining and wells equipment	13.5

Source: Information provided to the U.K. Science Policy Research Unit
by U.S. Commerce Department, Office of Technology Assessment and
Forecast.

OTHER CHALLENGES

The 1970s saw the emergence of newly industrialized countries competing
on the basis of price in an increasingly wide range of standard industrial
goods. Along with higher energy prices, such competition has increased
the pressure on European industry for technical innovation.

No less disquieting has been the emergence at the same time of clear differences among the EC countries in their capacity to adapt, innovate and increase
productivity. The belief that the liberalizing trade and investment would
lead to a uniform closing of the technology and productivity gap between
Europe and the United States turned out to be partly wrong. The productivity
gap among the EC countries began to grow in the late 1960s, with Italy

Table 3

PERCENTAGE SHARES OF GOVERNMENT-FINANCED RESEARCH AND DEVELOPMENT IN THE EC, UNITED STATES AND JAPAN, 1965 AND 1981

	Total		Defense		Space		Energy		Manufacturing industry		Agriculture		Advance of knowledge	
	1965	1981	1965	1981	1965	1981	1965	1981	1965	1981	1965	1981	1965	1981
EC-9	21	39	18	27	3	16	46	40	46	86	23	40	68	65
United States	77	53	82	72	97	79	53	50	47	4	61	32	17	11
Japan	2	8	0	1	0	5	1	10	7	10	16	28	15	24
Percentage of all government research and development expenditure in the three regions	100	100	43	38	29	9	8	10	3	5	2	4	8	19

Sources: OECD, *Changing Priorities for Government Research and Development*, Paris, 1975, and *The Objectives of Government Research and Development Funding, 1974–1985*, Paris, 1983.

and Britain having ever-lower productivity compared to the other member countries. A particular feature of the British problem is a lower level of productivity in manufacturing than in services or agriculture. An EC report[1] also concluded that member countries differed considerably in their adaptation to the shocks and changes of the 1970s. Once again, Italy and Britain were at the bottom of the pile, with West Germany at the top. One of the report's measures of adaptive capacity was trends in the structure of exports. Contrary to the trend in all the other industrially advanced countries, Britain's manufacturing exports have been moving out of skill-intensive and technology-intensive sectors. Previous analysis had already shown that within most manufacturing-equipment product groups, Britain was exporting standard price-sensitive goods, while Germany and other countries of northwest Europe were exporting technically more sophisticated and quality-sensitive goods. The only marked exception to this general rule was the area of military equipment, where British exports were technically sophisticated and successful.

Today, Britain's "technological dowry" to Europe looks less ample than it did in the 1960s. Table 4 shows that, together with France, Britain's share of the EC governments' expenditures on research and development shrank between 1965 and 1981. Britain's research and development expenditures have remained sizeable in relation to defense, where they continue to account for nearly half the EC total, and they have increased their share in agriculture. But the British share declined in space, energy, manufacturing industry (mainly civil aviation and electronics) and the advance of knowledge (mainly basic research).

In two areas, the reduction of the British share reflected periods of financial stringency and commercial rigor following expensive technological failures. After its experience with Concorde, the British government did not put up money at the beginning of the Airbus project, although a British company, Hawker-Siddeley, put up its own money and designed and built the wings. Similarly, after the failure of ELDO's Europa rocket, successive British governments gave relatively low priority to research and development, although British companies continued to play leading roles in the European consortia of space companies.

In one sense, this financial stringency was misplaced. The main justification for government intervention was to overcome short-term barriers to get long-term benefits. Financial constraints did not stop the British government from rejoining a successful Airbus program, or from increasing its expenditures on space research and development in the light of improving commercial prospects. This policy of increased research and development expenditures in areas of emerging commercial promise was in marked contrast to the British practice of the 1950s and 1960s, when the country tried to be among the first to develop large-scale technological programs, but was relatively slow and unsuccessful with engineering and commercial follow-through.

[1] The Maldague Report, consisting of two parts: *Sectoral Change in the European Economies from 1960 to the Recession* (1978) and *Changes in the Industrial Structure in the European Economies Since the Oil Crisis, 1973–78* (1979), published by the Commission of the European Communities.

Table 4

NATIONAL PERCENTAGE SHARES OF GOVERNMENT-FINANCED RESEARCH AND DEVELOPMENT IN THE EC

	Total		Defense		Space		Energy		Manu-facturing industry		Agriculture		Advance of knowledge	
	1965	1981	1965	1981	1965	1981	1965	1981	1965	1981	1965	1981	1965	1981
Belgium	2	2	1	0	2	3	2	2	4	3	7	3	2	2
Britain	30	25	46	48	19	14	18	15	39	20	17	29	20	18
France	33	28	36	39	36	32	40	19	31	25	33	32	25	22
West Germany*	27	31	16	10	35	33	29	42	21	32	28	17	38	40
Italy	4	9	1	2	4	14	9	20	0	16	2	8	8	9
Netherlands	4	5	0	1	4	4	2	2	5	4	13	11	7	9
Percentage of all EC governments' research and development expenditures	100	100	37	27	5	4	17	11	6	10	2	4	28	32

Source: See Table 3.
* Expenditures for West Germany are for 1967 and 1981.

Thus, in relation to government programs in space and civil aircraft, Europe has offered a framework for Britain to convert its programs from those of a world power to those of a medium-sized, European power. The same conversion has not occurred, however, in the field of energy. The British government's largest program, the sodium-cooled fast breeder reactor at Dounreay, is still largely independent of European developments, as are Britain's research and development defense programs. And the country's biggest joint program, the Tornado combat aircraft, still has not surmounted conflicting national interests and pressures for technological embellishment.

While European policies related to the big technologies obviously remain important, they are now overshadowed by the more general need for a strong European capacity for technology, innovation and adaptation. The subject matter is more prosaic than the big technologies. It includes, for example, movements in the textile industry toward industrial markets and quality, in mechanical engineering toward the integration of electronics and new materials, and in chemicals towards more high-value products and less energy- and scale-intensive production processes. This presents difficulties to the policy maker, since it encompasses a wider range of sectors with different characteristics and the need for decentralized decision making.

This context helps explain the apparent failure of British industry, on the whole, to take advantage of the dynamic economies of scale that were expected after Britain's entry into the EC. Some problems had been predicted: the redirection of British industry's trade, production and commercial activities away from Commonwealth markets toward Europe was bound to take time. Other problems were not predictable; the slowdown in world trade, investment, productivity and employment began precisely when Britain joined the EC, and made major initiatives in production methods and entering new markets more costly and risky. Other problems are still the subject of endless disputes: in particular, the effects of the policies and behavior of management, workers and the government of the day.

One long-standing problem is the level and pattern of technology and skills in British industry. Dynamic economies of scale can be exploited only when the demand for the product being made is buoyant and increasing; demand depends, in large part, on product design and development, and on related marketing. Furthermore, the rate of learning—in terms of increases in productivity following increases in production—is neither automatic nor preordained. It depends on the skill and flexibility of management and workers; and "learning by using" often requires continuing feedback between the production process and research and development activities. Yet British industry's research and development expenditures have shrunk relative to those of other EC countries.

Table 5 compares Britain's share of EC total industrial research and development, industry-financed research and development, and patenting in the United States. All three shares show a decline between the 1960s and the early 1980s. Over the same period, West Germany increased its shares considerably, and France slightly. EC countries' relative sectoral strengths in industrial research and development activities in the early 1980s are

Table 5
INTERNATIONAL DISTRIBUTION OF INNOVATIVE ACTIVITIES IN THE EC (*Percentages*)

	Research and development in business enterprises		Privately financed research and development in busines enterprises		Patents granted in the United States	
	1964	*1981*	*1964*	*1981*	*1963*	*1982*
Belgium/Luxembourg	2.9	3.1	3.8	3.9	1.5	2.2
Britain	37.5	24.7	34.4	20.3	31.3	18.9
Denmark	n.a.	1.0	n.a.	1.2	1.3	1.1
France	22.5	22.1	16.4	20.2	14.6	17.5
West Germany	26.3	37.7	30.7	41.3	39.7	47.9
Greece	n.a.	0.1	n.a.	negl.	0.1	n.a.
Ireland	0.1	0.2	0.1	0.2	0.0	0.2
Italy	5.6	6.5	7.9	7.6	5.9	6.7
Netherlands	5.1	4.6	6.7	5.2	5.6	5.5

Source: See Table 1.

correlated with relative sectoral sales of large firms. Britain has its largest sectoral share of both in aerospace, followed by the chemical-linked sector (food, drink and tobacco; textiles, clothing, footwear and leather; rubber and plastic products), and then by machinery (electronic, electrical and non-electrical). Transport comes out at the bottom by both measures. In West Germany, the pattern of relative strength by both measures is the reverse —weakness in aerospace and the chemical-linked sectors, but strength in nonelectrical machinery, chemicals, transport, metals, and electrical and electronic machinery. France is relatively strong, by both measures, in aerospace, metals and metal products, the chemical-linked sectors and transport.

In absolute terms, Britain had more large firms' sales and research and development activities than West Germany in the aerospace and chemical-linked sectors; West Germany had more than twice Britain's large firms' sales and research and development activities in chemicals, transport and machinery. Britain had more large firms' sales and research and development activities than France in electrical and electronics, chemicals, machinery and instruments, and the chemical-linked sectors. France had more than Britain in transport and in metal and metal products. In aerospace both countries were about even.

Such comparisons are inevitably broad. A more detailed breakdown of innovative activities would give a more precise picture of each country's relative technological strengths. For example, within the chemical industry, one sector of increasing British technological strength is in fine chemicals. This is reflected in both increasing absolute expenditures on research and development in pharmaceuticals and an increasing share of patenting in the United States between 1963 and 1981; the American patenting measure also shows improving British technological performance in mining and wells, and in food and tobacco. Similarly improving sectors in France have been nuclear energy, aircraft and telecommunications; in West Germany, they have been process equipment, nuclear energy, aircraft, and mining and wells; and in Italy, pharmaceuticals, specialized industrial equipment, telecommunications, office machinery and textiles.

THE FUTURE

So far, membership of the EC has not led to any noticeable increase in the innovative dynamism of British industry. If anything, it has served only to highlight the problems more clearly, although such problems would certainly have occurred if Britain had stayed outside the EC. Withdrawal now, and protection, would only make matters worse. What, then, can be done at the European level to improve the innovative resources in Europe in general, and of Britain in particular?

European institutions, procedures and practices have evolved to cope fairly well with the problems of big technology programs in aircraft, space and— to some extent—energy. Some of the programs concerned are within EC institutions, some outside. Further initiatives are envisaged within the EC framework. There are efforts to liberalize public markets in such high-technology sectors as telecommunications and energy generation. These efforts could be extended to consider the effects of deregulation of public utilities on the development of new technologies related to energy and communications. In addition, the EC is now fostering cooperation among European firms to develop fundamentally important technology, a program similar to the one instituted in Japan by the Ministry of International Trade and Industry to develop the technology of very-large-scale integration for computers. Such initiatives are all the more welcome within the EC framework, given the present concentration on protecting such uncompetitive sectors as steel, textiles and shipbuilding, instead of encouraging innovative industrial activities.

Experience has shown, however, that it would be illusory to expect any EC program to result in a rapid change in European technological competitiveness in electronics compared to the United States and Japan. Such competitiveness in production equipment is already strong, and is increasing in telecommunications. In office machinery and consumer electronics, improved competitiveness ultimately depends on the long-term commitment, resources and strategies of individual European firms. European governments have yet to demonstrate, either individually or collectively, that they can influence productively these aspects of firms' behavior.

In addition to advancing frontier technologies, an overriding long-term objective of European technological policy should be to bring all member countries up to the West German level of skill, technology and capacity for innovation and adaptation. Innovation and adaptation are among the main determinants of manufacturing productivity; together with wages, they are the main determinants of competitiveness, relative exchange rates and levels of industrial employment. They are therefore fundamental to both the welfare and the relative power of the EC member countries. Continuing differences are likely to create pressures for protection and to hinder agreement on common policies.

The Community offers a favorable framework for diffusing West German industrial skills and technologies to other countries. Part of this diffusion will be through normal commercial channels: trade in capital goods, licensing agreements, direct foreign investment, and the international movement and training of skilled people. Other ways can be positively encouraged by national and Community policies: exchanges of experience, information and people involved in training and retraining engineers, managers and skilled workers; the spread of West German industrial-banking competence to all regions of the EC; and the spread of those managerial and technical support systems that are now available to small firms in West Germany. Some of these activities could be encouraged through the European social and regional funds and by the European Investment Bank.

Finally, historical perspective can help clarify this solution. Joining the EC made Britain face a challenge that had been with it, and with France, since the beginning of the 20th century—namely, how to respond to the innovative dynamism of West German industry. World War II taught France the cruel lesson that it had to take up the challenge, and it did so reasonably successfully, while Britain felt able to avoid it. Whether the challenge is finally recognized and met in Britain will determine the country's future. If it is not taken up, continuing decline (certainly relative, and perhaps absolute) will follow, whether the country is inside or outside the EC. This course is not inevitable. Some firms and industries have shown that the challenge can be met. If others can be encouraged to emulate them, regeneration could replace decline. And what is true of Britain is true of Europe too.

FURTHER READING

Carter, C., ed. *Industrial Policy and Innovation.* London: Heinemann, 1981.

Cornwall, J. *Modern Capitalism: Its Growth and Transformation.* London: Martin Robertson, 1977.

Costello, J., and Hughes, T. *The Battle for Concorde.* London: Compton Press, 1971.

Cruickshank, A., and Walker, W. "Energy Research, Development and Demonstration in the European Communities." *Journal of Common Market Studies,* Vol. 20 (1981), pp. 61–90.

Davidson, W. "Patterns of Factor-saving Innovation in the Industrialised World," *European Economic Review,* Vol. 8 (1976), pp. 207–17.

Dosi, G. "Institutions and Markets in High Technology Industries: An Assessment of Government Interaction in European Micro-Electronics," in C. Carter, ed., *Industrial Policy and Innovation.* London: Heinemann, 1981.

Duchêne, F., and Shepherd, G. "Industrial Adjustment and Government Intervention in Western Europe." Sussex European Research Centre, 1980. (Mimeograph)

Dunning, J., and Pearce, R. *The World's Largest Industrial Enterprises.* London: Gower, 1981.

Foch, R. *Europe and Technology.* The Atlantic Papers 2. London: Atlantic Institute, 1970.

Franko, L. *The European Multinationals.* New York: Harper and Row, 1976.

Freeman, C., et al. *Unemployment and Technical Innovation: A Study of Long Waves and Economic Development.* London: Frances Pinter, 1982.

Gardner, N. "Economics of Launching Aid," in A. Whiting, ed., *The Economics of Industrial Subsidies.* London: HMSO, 1976.

Hartley, K. *A Market for Aircraft,* Institute for Economic Affairs, Hobart Paper no. 57, 1974.

Jewkes, J. *Government and High Technology.* London: Institute for Economic Affairs, Occasional Paper No. 37.

Kaldor, M. *The Baroque Arsenal.* New York: Hill and Wang, 1981.

———. "Technical Change in the Defence Industry," in K. Pavitt, ed., *Technical Innovation and British Economic Performance.* London: Macmillan, 1980.

Layton, C. *European Advanced Technology: A Programme for Integration.* London: Allen and Unwin, 1969.

Nau, H. *National Politics and International Technology: Nuclear Reactor Development in Western Europe.* Baltimore: Johns Hopkins University Press, 1974.

Pavitt, K., ed. *Technical Innovation and British Economic Performance.* London: Macmillan, 1980.

———. "High Technology," in C. Cohen, ed., *The Common Market: Ten Years After.* London: Philip Allan, 1983.

Plowden Report, *Committee of Enquiry into the Aircraft Industry.* London: HMSO, 1965.

Stopford, J., and Dunning, J. *Multinationals: Company Performance and Global Trends.* London: Macmillan, 1983.
Williams, R. *European Technology: The Politics of Collaboration.* London: Croom Helm, 1973.

COMMUNICATIONS IN
WESTERN EUROPE

RICHARD MAYNE

THE railways were the first "fathers of Europe" in modern times; they removed geographical barriers to trade. Bismarck, uniting Germany by force, proclaimed the virtues of *Blut und Eisen* (blood and iron) in 1886; but German unity had begun fifty years earlier, with the *Eisenbahn* (railway) itself.

Western Europe, likewise, owes much of its recent unity not only to the statesmen and bureaucrats who have worked for it, but to the meteoric growth of communications in every sense of the word. The process is so familiar, so much part of daily experience, that Europeans tend to ignore it. They take on board each decade's innovations, then take them for granted, as successive generations have accepted central heating, frozen vegetables, digital watches, pocket calculators or home computers. The appetite for novelty is matched by the ability to forget it.

This chapter will attempt to show how the three Ts—transport, tourism and telecommunications—have transformed Western Europe since World War II; how they are still transforming it; and how that transformation will continue in ways that are difficult to predict. Every change, as it comes, has political implications. And because history abhors the obvious, the results of change are seldom symmetrical or straightforward. What could unite Europeans may well divide them: what could ideally strengthen Europe may expose it to undue influence from outside. The only lesson from past change that remains constant is the need to look ahead and act.

TRANSPORT

Postwar

Forty years have witnessed a revolution in European transport. Only part of it was due to recovery from the war.

When World War II ended, Europe's roads were in a nightmarish state. In West Germany, 740 out of 958 major river bridges were impassable. In Sicily, there were no permanent bridges between Catania and Palermo. All the Rhine bridges, and many across the Seine and the Loire, had been destroyed. The highways themselves were pitted with craters; streets in towns were blocked with tons of rubble.

The railways were worse hit still. Long stretches of track were out of commission—12,000 kilometers (7,500 miles) in Germany, 4,000 (2,500 miles) in France, two-thirds of the entire network in Greece. In the Netherlands, only 25 percent of locomotives were in working order; in Belgium, only 40 percent. In Germany, fewer than half the railway cars were usable, and in France fewer than one-quarter.

Even the waterways were paralyzed. In France, out of 8,460 kilometers (5,288 miles) of traffic-carrying canals and rivers, only 509 kilometers (318 miles) were navigable at the time of the Liberation. Thirty-five percent of the Rhine's barge fleet had been destroyed, and 90 percent of that on the river Oder.

For civilians, flying was still a novelty. In 1938, when Neville Chamberlain had flown to Munich to meet Adolf Hitler, it had been his first journey by air. Cordell Hull, the U.S. secretary of state, first flew in 1943; and in 1945, when President Harry Truman wanted to fly home from Europe after the Potsdam Conference, his advisers prudently forbade it. "They all yell their heads off," he characteristically complained.

Reconstruction
The ravages of war were surprisingly quickly remedied. In Berlin, choked with more than 400 million cubic meters (520 million cubic yards) of rubble, it was estimated than 10 trains a day, with 50 wagons each, would take 16 years to clear it away. In the event, the task took months, not years. Roads were patched, torn tracks relaid, sunken barges recovered from canals, locks repaired, bridges rebuilt. Within a decade, much of Europe's physical surface had been restored—and, in transport, the first signs of exponential growth had appeared.

Roads
By the mid-1950s, one in 25 of all Western Europeans possessed an automobile, and every year two million new cars were being driven on to the roads. Motorcycles and motor scooters, too, were becoming popular: by 1958, some 17.5 million of them were snarling across Western Europe, competing for road space with 21.5 million trucks, buses and private cars.

At first, Europe's roads were ill-adapted to this sudden invasion. As of 1960, only just over 3,000 kilometers (1,875 miles) of highway had been built in Western Europe. The first of them, in Italy, dated from 1926; but by later standards this was little more than a rather straight main road. In Germany, the first highway projects had predated Hitler: one of them, between Cologne and Bonn, had been planned by Cologne's then mayor, Konrad Adenauer.

But although here and there—in the Netherlands and France especially —there had been pioneer initiatives in the 1930s, the war had put a stop to new highway projects. When peace returned, many countries were reluctant to embark on ambitious new plans. Capital, raw materials and even labor were all in short supply. When the French government presented the bill that eventually became its first Motorways Construction Act, it struck a note of caution typical of the time: "France possesses a remarkably well-developed and well-situated network of *Routes nationales*, which with suitable modernization can meet every need. There is therefore no call to launch

382

into a vast program of long-distance motorways, as has been done in certain other countries where the existing road systems were much less adequate." The government proposed, in fact, only one such link road, between Paris and Lille.

But if France made a slow start, the sextupling of traffic in 20 years gave every incentive to accelerate the road-building program. In 1961, the government undertook to start building 110 kilometers (69 miles) of highway every year. Seven years later, this figure had almost doubled. By 1970, the entire north–south axis from Lille to Marseille had been completed. Between then and 1980, thanks largely to the introduction of the controversial toll system to attract private capital, France put 4,019 kilometers (2,512 miles) of highway into full operation. By that time the network covered the country, save for the Massif Central.

Second in the highway-building race during the 1970s came the Federal Republic of Germany, with 2,867 kilometers (1,792 miles); then Spain, with 1,590 kilometers (994 miles); next Italy, with 1,559 kilometers (974 miles); and then Britain, with 1,392 kilometers (870 miles). By 1983, in absolute figures, West Germany had by far the most extensive highway system, covering 7,919 kilometers (4,949 miles). France came second, with 5,907 (3,692 miles); Italy was third, with 5,900 (3,688 miles); Britain fourth, with 2,666 (1,666 miles); then Spain, the Netherlands, Belgium, Austria, Switzerland, Sweden and Denmark. Even tiny Luxembourg had 58 kilometers (36 miles) of highway to itself.

Like most innovations, the growing highway network was a mixed blessing. It greatly reduced journey times, by comparison with traditional roads. The new international routes made Europe feel more united as one drove at high speed from one country to another—sometimes not even being stopped at a frontier post. There were fewer accidents per mile and per passenger than on many normal trunk roads; and the highways funneled traffic away from villages and parts of towns.

At the same time, however, highway driving tended to dull the senses. There was little time to enjoy the countryside; and if highway Europe felt more united, its unity was often depressingly and uniformly ugly. Those accidents that did occur, especially in fog, were often very serious. In order to bypass human habitation, the road builders had sometimes despoiled the scenery; while in the towns themselves they had erected eyesores. Hasty construction meant in some cases rapid obsolescence. Worst of all, at the very time when some of Europe's long-planned roads were being built, a combination of rises in oil prices and new concern for the environment led many more people to question their raison d'être. Roads attract traffic—not only away from the railways, but far in excess of planners' calculations. Europe's highways were no exception. They certainly helped to link European countries and reduce the effects of distance, but these advantages were bought at considerable price.

Railways
Partly in response to the competition from road freight and passenger networks, Europe's railways were also undergoing modernization. By the

mid-1950s, rail traffic was still growing, but markedly more slowly than just after the war. The roads were taking the railways' customers, offering convenience, door-to-door travel, flexibility, cheapness and only slightly slower speed. The railways began to lose money: by 1957, only those in the Netherlands and Switzerland were able to break even without state subsidies. Experts blamed not only the competition, but also management, rate policies and, especially, run-down capital equipment.

So the railways began to fight back. In their very early days they had led the battle against Europe's national barriers. From 1886 onward, through the International Standards Convention, they had achieved "technical unity" —compatibility of track and rolling stock—throughout Europe. The Bern Convention of 1890 had long facilitated the cross-frontier transport of both passengers and goods. In 1953, the EUROP agreement made it possible to use rolling stock jointly, rather than promptly sending every railway car back to its country of origin whether or not it could be filled for the return journey—as is still the practice with aircraft on scheduled flights. In 1954, most notably, a Dutch railway official, Dr. Den Hollander, conceived the idea that culminated in the Trans-Europ-Express—a luxury passenger train that sped across frontiers at 100 miles per hour. With air-conditioning, reclining seats and a public-address system, it closely resembled an aircraft, and it was intended to. Later, the Trans-Europ-Express example was followed by such further refinements as the British "125" trains, running in normal service at speeds up to 125 miles per hour; the TGV (*train à grande vitesse*/high-speed train) in France; and the Advanced Passenger Train in Britain. They were fast and comfortable, and they went to and from city centers; for many continental journeys, especially in uncertain weather, they presented tough competition to the airlines.

But all these trains were supplying mainline services. Away from such showcases, Europe's railways could be much less glamorous: ancient rolling stock, dirty upholstery, unpredictable delays. Britain's minor branch lines were a case in point; but they were not unique. Suburban services around Paris were primitive and overcrowded, with high, hard, upright, plastic-covered seats. Even in West Germany, local trains could offer austere accommodation. Freight customers complained of delays and bureaucracy; and even where diesel and electric trains had long since replaced steam, many of the railways' trappings recalled the 19th century.

On the whole, however, since they were ecologically sound, safe, reliable, and a good place to work (although not yet equipped with telephones), trains had much to recommend them. Most Western European governments recognized this and were generous with subsidies. Yet without an integrated transport policy to encourage freight and passengers back to the railways, there seemed little doubt that the long-term trend was the other way.

Waterways

Europe's waterways, likewise, made an impressive recovery in the early years after World War II. Between 1949 and 1957, traffic on them more than doubled. On the Rhine, the Seine and the other major continental arteries, the sight of fast power barges, sometimes in pairs, one often pushing the other, became as familiar as it had ever been. Deep in the water with loads of coal, sand, cement, scrap or other heavy cargoes, the barges flew many national flags—sometimes obscured by houseplants or the family washing. Swift, cheap and reliable, canal and river transport was, nevertheless, dwindling in Britain. Here, on a waterway network dating mainly from the first Industrial Revolution, the growing trend was instead toward providing floating vacation trips—some in handsome new fiberglass motor launches, some in lovingly restored wooden barges. Meanwhile, on continental rivers, growing numbers of dinghy sailors were braving the industrial traffic in pursuit of their sport.

Airways
It was Europe's airways, however, that most spectacularly symbolized and embodied the postwar transport revolution. In this, for once, Britain was at first in the lead. British European Airways came into being less than a year after the war had ended in Europe: it was formally established on August 1, 1946. In its first month's operation it carried 9,300 passengers. Ten years later, it flew as many people on any single summer's day.

Similar, if slightly later and slower growth was shown by the British airline's continental counterparts: Air France, the Dutch KLM, the Belgian Sabena, the German Lufthansa and the Italian Alitalia. Only the Scandinavian countries decided to share a joint airline, SAS. By the mid-1950s, London, Paris, Frankfurt, Rome, Copenhagen and Berlin were among the world's busiest airports, each handling about a million passengers a year. By 1984, annual flights within Western Europe were totaling 170 billion passenger-kilometers (106 billion passenger-miles). The skies seemed to be full of sitting travelers.

Many were business passengers, able now to pack into a day trip what otherwise might have taken half a working week. Many, too, were civil servants and government ministers. By contrast with Chamberlain's rare and fateful trips abroad, face-to-face meetings with foreign counterparts had become a matter of routine. In 1983, Prime Minister Margaret Thatcher made six separate visits to other Western European countries, including three two-day meetings of the European Council—the European Community's (EC's) Heads of State and Government—as well as bilateral summit meetings in Bonn, Paris and Rome. In London, meanwhile, Thatcher received the heads of government of West Germany (twice), France, Italy (twice), the Netherlands, Ireland and Greece.

Before World War II, such frequent high-level contacts would never have occurred. Their effect on mutual understanding is literally incalculable: even when they involve argument and continuing disagreement, they expose each party to the other's views. At a less exalted level, it is now commonplace for specialist ministers and officials to be traveling "abroad" constantly for collective or bilateral meetings. Whereas previously they had to consider only what colleagues and opponents in their own countries might think of a proposed course of action, their horizons and their professional "constituency" now unavoidably include "foreigners." Some national civil servants —from the foreign ministries, but also from other major departments—may well spend one or two days a week away from their desks and their countries. They may even come to know their foreign counterparts better than they know some of their fellow officials back home.

"Culture-contact" of this sort is indispensable for the effective uniting of Europe. Personal relations between officials and ministers of different countries can often solve problems where the exchange of written minutes cannot. All this would be impossible without air travel.

Nevertheless, if the tally of airborne movements seems impressive, this is not to say that Europe is exploiting the potential of air travel to the full. An airline for every country is an expensive luxury, maintained in part by restricting free competition and jointly keeping prices high. In March 1985, the price charged per mile for a one-way trip from London to Brussels on a scheduled flight was 38.38 pence. This compared with 5.6 pence per mile for a one-way flight from London to Los Angeles. Long-haul flying may benefit from economies of scale, but hardly to this extent. On a round-trip charter flight between London and Athens, moreover, the price was only 4.19 pence per mile. Business travelers, ministers and civil servants taking these infrequent, crowded and costly flights to Brussels were evidently paying —and reclaiming from the taxpayer—"whatever the [artificially restricted] traffic would bear."

The EC Commission, hampered by a mandate that excludes air and sea transport until the governments specify otherwise, has only cautiously criticized the airlines' price-fixing cartel. In a first memorandum on airfares, it has suggested allowing price competition within a 25-percent margin—but only after long negotiations between the parties concerned. Critics of the present regime, long upheld by the International Air Transport Association on supposed grounds of safety, have urged the Commission to go much further and propose the deregulation of European airfares by applying to them the Community's normal antitrust laws. The governments' stakes in the present system make them seem unlikely to accept such a step, although a very limited Anglo-Dutch agreement has made a small, carefully publicized dent in current overpricing.

TOURISM

The past

The public to whom airfares really matter are those without expense accounts: principally, the tourists. The spread of tourism in Western Europe has been at least as spectacular as the growth of transport itself.

In past centuries and in the early decades of this one, traveling in Europe was for the adventurous and/or the rich. The Grand Tour attracted young scions of wealthy families, usually accompanied by tutors. Scholars, journalists and fortune-hunters made less stately progress; the journalists wrote up their vicissitudes when they returned. Early editions of European guidebooks gravely discussed the dangers of banditry. In certain inns, the guest was taking his life in his hands.

As travel grew safer, it became a family pastime. Large parties, complete with children and servants, would descend with voluminous baggage on spas and watering places. Genteel foreign colonies sprang up in cities like

Rome or Florence or Aix-les-Bains; there were tea shops and libraries for the homesick; there were continental editions of newspapers and books.

Postwar

Something of this atmosphere still lingered for the first tourists in continental Western Europe after World War II. Many still traveled on their own or with a few friends. Trains were slow; they stopped at frontiers for customs and immigration control; in third-class compartments there were still wooden seats. Accommodation was scarce, cheap and chancy. But within a decade, everything had changed.

Package tours

First in coaches, then by plane, finally in jumbo jets, the package tourists arrived. Travel agents found that by booking ahead in bulk they could offer travel and inclusive accommodation for less than the cost of a normal round-trip journey. The beneficiaries found safety (and economy) in numbers —rather as novice investors on Europe's stock exchanges were relying on mutual funds or unit trusts.

Before long, a vast industry had developed. Its foundations were threefold: the tour operators, with their tempting four-color brochures; the charter flight companies, with their cheery atmosphere and attractive fares; and the hotel proprietors, with their modern palaces of mass-produced luxury, white concrete pleasure-and-leisure complexes springing up around Europe's coasts.

By 1957, when jet air travel was still at an early stage, some 35 million Europeans were traveling abroad every year. By 1983, the total had leapt to some 150 million—nearly as many as the combined populations of Britain, Italy and France. In cash terms, tourism was very big business. European tourists alone, in 1983, accounted for a turnover of more than U.S.$51 *billion*; by another reckoning, tourism made up nearly two percent of Western Europe's gross domestic product (GDP). For some poor and/or popular countries, the tourists' contribution to the GDP was as much as four—and in one case eight—percent.

The biggest tourist earner in 1983, and by far the most popular destination, was Italy, closely followed by Spain and Austria. Ireland came next in popularity, then Belgium, perhaps accounted for by official and business trips. Britain followed; then came Switzerland, Portugal, West Germany, France, Greece and the Netherlands. Strictly comparable figures for Denmark and Sweden are not available, since both nations ignore tourist arrivals and count only the number of tourist nights spent in the country. Norway, which does record arrivals, seems the least frequented of all. Preferences differ very little, in the choice of countries to visit, between European tourists and those from the rest of the world. Very broadly speaking, there is an annual southward pilgrimage in search of soft currencies and the sun.

A melting pot?

It would be pleasant to believe that these huge annual flows of people and money help to create a sense of solidarity in Europe. The evidence is patchy and subjective.

Some have claimed, very plausibly, that travel narrows the mind. People notice those facts that confirm their existing beliefs, and tend to ignore others; even Charles Darwin confessed this weakness. Travelers already prejudiced —against British food, French plumbing, German plumpness or Italian flexibility as regards time—may return with further evidence; they seldom change their minds. European literature, on every level, confirms that even travel writers inhabit a mirror maze of distorted reflections.

Package tours, moreover, tend to insulate travelers from all but contacts with waiters in the country of their choice. A good guide may remedy matters; but not all guides are competent. Individual travelers, without guides, may make more varied contacts; but much will depend on their linguistic skill. On package tours or otherwise, children and the elderly may be especially disconcerted by foreign food, smells, customs and noise. Ubiquitous souvenir sellers and tourist trap restaurants will reinforce the worst of stereotyped views.

And yet, despite all such disadvantages, the tourist migrations are gradually eroding ancient animosities. Small things will linger in the memory: unexpected kindness to a bewildered stranger; the skill of a foreign sportsman; the friendliness of children; a minor drama shared. More superficially but far more pervasively, the growing availability of foreign goods—especially food and drink—is slowly turning the alien into the familiar. Does the exoticism disappear too? Hardly, it would seem, when last summer's tourists resort to sympathetic magic, as if almost believing that a meal of lasagne, eggplant and Chianti will conjure southern sunshine into a wintry northern evening with rain beating at the windows.

It takes an effort of memory or imagination to realize the scale of the change. For years after World War II, it was impossible to buy Dutch pipe tobacco in Rome, British chocolate in Paris or German wine in a London self-service store. Clothes, shoes, kitchen utensils all differed from country to country far more than they do now. So did Europeans. One small sign of change was noted in the 1950s by an American reporter. German women, he delightedly discovered, were no longer flaxen-haired Gretchens or Brünnhildes: they had acquired Italian glamor. Today, that observation seems both sexist and archaic; young Europeans everywhere share a common style. And their true vernacular is their music.

TELECOMMUNICATIONS

Travel only partly accounts for such cross-frontier similarities, superficial as they sometimes are. The mass media are its obvious auxiliaries.

Radio
Broadcasting is a further instance of postwar change. Forty years ago, a radio was still a "wireless set"—an often imposing piece of wooden furniture, placed at a fixed point in the room. With the adoption of transistors, radios have become as portable as paperbacks—personal, informal, increasingly equipped with lightweight headphones: a private, individual line to . . . what?

Twist the dial for an answer. On long and medium wavelengths, very similar sounds are being transmitted all over Europe: mostly, the hypnotic beat and melodic arabesques of variegated rock music. With lyrics often in English, like the names of many groups, British or American listeners may feel both flattered and diffident, uneasy at a cosmopolitanism whose basis seems so artificial. Why, they may wonder, are these Swedes or Luxembourgers imitating U.S. blacks or Liverpudlian teenagers of more than 20 years ago? The explanation would involve complex cultural history; the fact is that they are.

Telephones

Nor is electronic frontier-crossing confined to radio. It was in 1963 that Subscriber Trunk Dialing became possible on the London–Paris telephone line—seven years before a London subscriber was able to dial New York. Today, with direct dialing or button-pushing extended over most of Europe and much of the world, many find it hard to remember life without it—calling the international operator; spelling out the country, the city, the exchange and the number; waiting while clicks and buzzes echoed down the line; sometimes totally failing and having to book another call in advance. Now, friends, business contacts and national or European civil servants can pick up the telephone and converse across frontiers as quickly as if they were near neighbors in the same town. It would be astonishing if such ease of contact had not brought political dividends. The most notable instance, in recent years, was the odd and awkward intimacy with which the West German chancellor, Helmut Schmidt, and the French president, Valéry Giscard d'Estaing, chatted together by telephone—in English.

Already, the increasing ease of international telephoning has somewhat reduced the need for business travel. In real terms, the costs of telecommunications have been falling, while those of transportation have tended to rise. In 1970, for example, 40 liters (10 gallons) of motor fuel in France cost the same as 140 basic telephone charging units; by 1980, the same amount of fuel, measured in telephone units, cost 260, or nearly twice as much. True, not all face-to-face contacts can be dispensed with; but surveys suggest that many can. The increasing possibilities of teleconferences and, in a lesser degree, the videophone have also extended the telephone's appeal. Provided that some degree of trust exists already, telephoning rather than traveling can save the individual's time, money and trouble, while also husbanding society's energy resources.

Further developments are at present more advanced in the United States than in Europe. One is facsimile transmission as a substitute for ordinary mail. In 1979, the United States had 120,000 facsimile transmitters in operation against only 6,000 in France. The Eighth French Plan called for 300,000 by 1985; but the quality and speed of transmission do not always compare well with alternative methods such as videotex, using a TV screen with an alphanumeric keyboard, or teletex, linking two word processors. While all such innovations hold the promise of more immediate and informal cross-frontier contacts, they also very obviously pose the problem of compatibility between rival systems. Too often in the past, European countries have made their choices on largely technical grounds without considering what their

389

neighbors are planning. Finding their systems mutually incompatible, they have then been obliged to devise complex and costly bridging machinery.

FAST, DIANE, ESPRIT and RACE

To try to prevent such ill-coordinated development, the EC Commission has combined research, exhortation and the offer of financial incentives, notably in the field of information technology. The acronyms above refer to four of its successive efforts.

FAST, an experimental program in *F*orecasting and *A*ssessment in *S*cience and *T*echnology, was launched in 1978 to identify long-term priorities for joint research and development. Among other things, it found that while information and communications in the broadest sense provide more than a third of the Community's jobs, the new markets in information technology were dominated by the United States and Japan.

DIANE, inaugurated two years later, in February 1980, stands for *D*irect *I*nformation *A*ccess *N*etwork for *E*urope. Within a further two years, it had grouped together more than 300 data bases throughout Europe, some, such as the Community's own CRONOS statistical data base, providing factual information, others containing bibliographies. All these are linked via Euronet, a Commission-sponsored network for the dissemination of information, set up and managed by the national postal and telecommunications authorities. Its control and management center is in London, with five switching nodes at Frankfurt, London, Paris, Rome and Zurich, all equipped with European-made computers and linked by high-speed lines. Concentrator terminals in Amsterdam, Brussels, Copenhagen, Dublin, Luxembourg and Athens connect the user terminals with the nearest switching node, thus providing a service throughout the Community and Switzerland, with further links to come.

ESPRIT, the *E*uropean *S*trategic *P*rogramme for *R*esearch and development in *I*nformation *T*echnology, began in pilot form at the end of 1982, linking 200 research projects and 638 businesses and universities in all the member states. A larger-scale ESPRIT program, with 1,500 European currency units (ECUs) to spend over the first five years of its 10-year term, was launched in 1984. Its main areas of action are: advanced microelectronics, advanced information processing, software technology, office automation and computer control in manufacturing. While none of these is directly involved with telecommunications, many depend on them for their full exploitation.

RACE is the Commission's most recent attempt to work toward Community-wide standards for telecommunications equipment. The acronym, standing for *R*esearch in *A*dvanced *C*ommunity in *E*urope, is significant. "The Europeans," the London *Economist* wrote on October 6, 1984, "seem determined to handicap themselves in the technology race. . . . On October 2nd, the French government confirmed that it was going no further with the joint development of a cellular radio system with West Germany. There will probably now be four incompatible systems in operation in the EEC." RACE is an effort to prevent such incoherence in telecommunications, where Community firms still have respectable shares of the market. With a 500-million-ECU budget, it plans to promote European research and development by firms from different Community countries, partly in order to side-step governments' reluctance to open their procurements markets to any but national firms.

Overall, the Commission's objectives seem so sensible that it is hard to believe that they need such vigorous pursuit. With Europe's distances already so much shrunk by technology—and with European industries already so much threatened by U.S. and Japanese competition—is it not obvious that joint research and development, joint manufacture and joint procurements are essential? It may be obvious; but experience proves the relevance of the *Economist*'s warning, and of the reflection with which this chapter began. Technology that could unite Europeans all too often divides them. Television has been—and could again be—a case in point.

TELEVISION

Until now, television within Europe has been profoundly national. The only citizens of the Community who enjoy anything like a TV common market are those of the Benelux countries—merely because their areas are small enough to receive the overspill from each other's programs.

National regimes

Throughout the Community, television is run on different models from one country to another. In Belgium, it is a public service within the three linguistic communities: Flemish, French and German; there is no advertising, although cable companies may transmit whatever they receive from neighboring countries. In West Germany, the *Länder* are responsible for broadcasting, using funds from both license fees and advertising. In Denmark, state television enjoys a monopoly and is financed by license fees and government subsidy. In Greece, the state controls broadcasting and collects a fee from each individual resident, although television also receives advertising revenue. In France, the government has majority shareholdings in the national, regional and other companies set up when broadcasting was reformed in 1982; the funding comes from advertising, from the companies and from a TV license fee.

In Ireland, broadcasting is under government license, and is financed partly by advertising and partly by grant. In Italy, save for certain exceptions including cable TV, broadcasting is a state monopoly, financed by advertising, publications and "subscription fees." In Luxembourg, although the government controls the guidelines on advertising time, broadcasting is in the hands of a profit-making public limited company. In the Netherlands, authorized (and sizable) political, church and other groups enjoy allocations of airtime, and are financed partly by license fees, partly by advertisements and partly by subscription. In Britain, the BBC is an independent public corporation financed by a license fee, while commercial television relies on advertisements.

What all these systems have in common is that each is designed to reach only the inhabitants of the country concerned, and they are for the most part unable to receive other countries' television broadcasts. The technical reason for this is that television carrier waves pass through the atmospheric layers from which radio waves bounce back to earth. So while governments have been largely powerless to prevent their citizens eavesdropping on each others' sound radio broadcasts, television has remained national.

This has led to anomalies. In Britain, undertakers are forbidden to advertise on television; in Italy, makers of boats and pet food; in France, there can be no advertisements for margarine. More seriously from the point of view of international communications, when color television began to be adopted in Europe, France chose the SECAM system (*Sequential Color with Memory*), used elsewhere only in the Soviet Union and parts of Africa and Asia, while all other Western European countries opted for the Anglo-German PAL system (*Phase Alternation Line*). As well as raising the question of compatibility, this clearly divided the would-be common market in television sets.

Television without frontiers?

Two developments now making rapid headway have opened the prospect of removing the cosy partitions that at present divide the national TV audiences. One is cable, already in operation in parts of Europe at the time of going to press. The other is *Direct Broadcasting by Satellite* (DBS). Both are expensive, and both are potentially interlinked. Both have been hailed as potentially revolutionizing Europe's television habits. Both will have major battles to fight if they do. Both, finally, risk making Europe not stronger but more vulnerable, unless governments are prepared to plan ahead and act together.

Cable was the first to capture the public imagination. Already used extensively for pay-TV systems in the United States, it has begun in Europe, partly to service close-knit or remote communities, partly as a vehicle for further advertising. Several governments are studying or have studied the problems it poses; Britain, for example, established a Cable Authority in 1984. Part of its intention was to control the broad lines of what may be transmitted, no doubt with a view to avoiding some of the excesses current in the United States. But, theoretically, it would be possible by means of cable to wire up the whole EC so as to achieve "television without frontiers." Cost and government reluctance, however, make this seem unlikely.

Satellites seem a far more plausible vehicle for pan-European TV. Already used routinely for transatlantic transmissions, mostly for news items, in recent years satellites have been launched in some numbers on behalf of European broadcasting organizations. Conceivably, they could offer a choice of as many as 20 programs at a time. Equipped with a suitable receiving dish, a family or a community (perhaps linked by cable) could gain access to programs from all over Europe, if not from further afield.

The prospect may seem tempting; but, as the EC Commission has pointed out in a discussion paper, it remains fraught with practical difficulties. In the first place, not all European governments seem likely to authorize the use of private dishes. Some, at least, will want to retain their monopoly as long as they can. Second, to regularize the position of European-wide television would mean tackling some of the discrepancies caused by purely national policies in the past. PAL and SECAM are one example; another is Europe's jungle of conflicting laws about advertising on TV. A further cognate problem is that of copyright; others include conflicting laws on the protection of children, on libel and on the right to reply.

Battles ahead

All these considerations suggest that it will be some time before European governments come together to establish truly European television. This seems a pity, to say the least. All surveys confirm that television is most people's main source of news and even commentary; and at present both remain as national in viewpoint as the broadcasting systems that put them out. If European solidarity is desirable, European television should be a priority goal.

It need not mean a monolithic, colorless, stateless service. With ample scope for brilliant dubbing or subtitling, it could simply mean the ability to tune in to whichever programs, from whichever country, took the viewer's fancy at a particular time. Some programs, no doubt, would prove more popular than others; some viewers would be adventurous, others might not. But at least everyone would have the right to travel electronically—as they can, indeed, by telephone or by turning the radio dial.

Two kinds of pressure would appear to be working in this direction. One is the desire of advertisers to have television access to more than their national markets. In the smaller countries, especially, this is a tempting goal. The other pressure is human nature. When citizen's band radio became available in Europe, it was illegal in several countries: but this hardly prevented its being used, and eventually legitimized. The same applies to videocassette recording—legally questionable, but universally popular. Once private dishes begin to be more readily available—or kits or instructions for making them—no law on earth is going to stop some eager "breakers" from using them, like smugglers in the sky. In the long run, no doubt, governments will come to terms with them. Why not in the short run, now?

One final consideration underlines that question. In the past, U.S. banks and businesmen have been quicker than some Europeans to exploit the common market in the making. Already, American series break into even the most chauvinist schedules of European TV. With DBS increasingly available, and with European governments standing by inactive, or merely trying to cling to their national monopolies, Europe risks being flooded with yet more series like *Dallas*. Or, perhaps even more disturbingly, if the Soviet Union knew its propaganda business, with similar compulsive trash from the USSR.

FURTHER READING

Bakis, Henry. *Géographie des télécommunications*. Paris: Presses Universitaires de France, 1984.
Dewhurst, J. Frederic, et al. *Europe's Needs and Resources*. New York: Twentieth Century Fund; London: Macmillan, 1961.
Dunkley, Chrustopher. *Television Today and Tomorrow*. Harmondsworth: Penguin, 1985.
Mathelot, Pierre. *La Télématique*. Paris: Presses Universitaires de France, 1982.

Moynahan, Brian. *Airport International*. London: Macmillan, 1978.
OECD. *Information in 1985*. Paris, 1973.
———. *Telecommunications: Pressures and Policies for Change*. Paris, 1983.
———. *Tourism Policy and International Tourism*. Paris, 1984.
———. *Transport and Telecommunications*. Paris, 1983.
Priou, Jules-Marie. *Les Transportes en Europe*. Paris: Presses Universitaires de France, 1971.
Rickard, Charles. *Les Autoroutes*. Paris: Presses Universitaires de France, 1984.
Smith, Anthony. *The Politics of Information*. London: Macmillan, 1978.
United Kingdom. Home Office. *Report of the Inquiry into Cable Expansion and Broadcasting Policy*. London: HMSO, 1982.
Wallace, William. *Britain's Bilateral Links Within Western Europe*. London: Routledge and Kegan Paul, 1984.
Wallstein, René. *Le Téléphone*. Paris: Presses Universitaires de France, 1984.
Wheen, Francis. *Television*. London: Century Publishing, 1985.

ENERGY IN WESTERN EUROPE

RICHARD BAILEY

A CONFUSED SITUATION

ON first consideration, the working out of a strategy for energy production and use appears to be reasonably straightforward. Nations need energy for heat, light, transportation and powering industrial machinery. Abundant supplies of fuel at low cost are a condition of economic expansion and industrial growth. If energy has to be imported, foreign currency must be earned to pay for it. The higher the proportion of indigenous fuel available, the less the strain on the balance of payments. So far so good. In practice, the position is complicated by the peculiar characteristics of the fossil fuels—coal, oil and natural gas. Each requires considerable investment before production can begin, so that although reserves may be proved to exist, their development will take place only if supplies are sufficient in quantity and quality to justify production at costs covering the heavy outlay involved. Fuels are only partly interchangeable. Each has certain prime uses to which it is suited at maximum efficiency. Oil is exceptional as being the only fuel able to power aircraft, and much the most convenient fuel for road transport vehicles. Nuclear energy, the sole use of which is to produce electricity, represents an important but highly controversial additional source of energy. All the fossil fuels and nuclear energy make characteristic contributions to the pollution of the atmosphere and the environment.

Energy forecasting is a notoriously difficult operation, depending as it does on successfully calculating what will happen to a number of variables on both the supply and the demand sides. The starting point is the equally daunting task of determining the level of economic activity, which in turn decides the demand for energy. At any given time, energy policy involves a choice between available fuels on the basis of long- and short-term factors. Market forces come into account, but fuel prices are never determined solely by direct competition. There are different costs of production for the same fuel in different countries and in different parts of the same country. For energy more than for other commodities, price is only one of the factors taken into account by the consumer. More important is the capital cost of the equipment required for its use, and the running costs, reliability and convenience of individual fuels. Coal, oil, gas and nuclear energy are all used to produce electricity, which is a secondary fuel. The capital cost of an electric power station, which takes 10 or more years to construct, has to be recouped over a working life of 20 to 30 years. A switch from coal to oil or gas, or vice versa, is an expensive operation, so that unless power stations are built for dual firing, they are generally committed to burning the same fuel throughout their working lives. The experience of the past three decades has underlined the difficulty of balancing the long-term energy situation, which may be one of scarcity, with the fact that current demand may be met from abundantly available fuels, most of which may have to be imported. The concentration of effort on increasing indigenous coal production in the 1950s gave way to dependence on imports of cheap Middle East oil, followed—after the 1973 Organization of Petroleum Exporting Countries (OPEC) oil price increases—by a period of uncertainty. This coincided with the development of North Sea oil and gas, increased investment in the British coal industry under the 1974 *Plan for Coal*, ambitious nuclear programs and a hasty consideration of alternative energy sources utilizing the power of the sun, wind, tides, and so on. In the 1980s, for a variety of reasons, demand for energy has fallen, the anticipated scarcity of oil supplies has not materialized and oil prices have stabilized. At the same time, abundant cheap coal has come on to the international market from Australia, the United States, South Africa and a number of Third World countries. Nuclear energy, which had been hailed as the great stabilizing factor, faded after the Three Mile Island accident which gave rise to endless debates about safety, security and environmental pollution.

Although the energy problem has been on its agenda throughout the life of the European Community (EC) it has not so far proved possible to formulate and implement a comprehensive common energy policy. In the early days, progress was hampered by the separation of responsibilities among the European Coal and Steel Community (ECSC, dealing with coal), Euratom (nuclear energy) and the EEC (oil). The merging of the three communities and the creation of a single executive in 1967 brought the major fuels under the responsibility of one new commission. The main concern at that time was the rapid run-down of the uneconomic part of the coal industries of the six original member nations and the extent to which the social costs involved should be met from national or EC funds. In Britain, following the publication of the 1965 Fuel Policy White Paper,[1] worked-out and uneconomical pits were closed at the rate of around 40 a year, with the majority of closures in the older coalfields. The number of collieries fell from 698 in 1960 to 292 in 1970, and subsequently dropped to around 200 by the end of 1982. In the same period in West Germany, the number of pits was halved; in France and Belgium also, coal production fell to a very modest level.

Immediately after World War II, more than 80 percent of the total energy requirements of the countries that now form the EC were met by coal, while oil accounted for only 10 percent. By 1973, solid fuels covered only 23 percent of requirements; oil accounted for 59 percent; natural gas, a relatively new fuel, 12 percent; and the other six percent was divided between

[1]Ministry of Power Cmnd 2798, *Fuel Policy*, London, HMSO, October 1965.

hydroelectric and nuclear energy.[2] The rise in demand for oil, which coincides with the period of full employment of the 1950s and early 1960s, was due to the fuel's increasing use in electric power stations, in generating steam in industrial plants, domestic heating and as a raw material for the petrochemical industry, in addition to its traditional role as an aviation and motor vehicle fuel.

THE RISE OF OPEC

Compared with coal, the development of the oil industry took place in an atmosphere of high drama mixed with intrigue.[3] Oil (including the offshore oilfields of the North Sea) is often found in remote places and must be exploited by high technology, using capital-intensive methods devised by some of the world's largest multinational corporations. Over the years, these corporations have discovered the oil, brought it out of the ground, fixed its price and taken control of its distribution. In the Middle East, politics inevitably became a major factor in the relationship between the national governments and the oil corporations, notably in the Suez crisis of 1956 and the Six-Day War of 1967. The oil corporations generally negotiated separately with each government on the development of its resources, but controlled pricing arrangements among themselves. This arrangement was gradually upset as some of the producing governments began to ask what would happen when their oil reserves were exhausted through too rapid exploitation. Venezuela, which had become the world's leading oil exporter by 1945, complained with justification that its reserves were being run down in order to conserve U.S. domestic resources. This led to the first fifty–fifty arrangement for sharing oil profits between a host government and the oil corporations, a system that was quickly followed elsewhere. A further development was the introduction of the system of "posted prices," which fixed the host government's revenue according to a formula that took account of the royalty per barrel, the income tax paid by the corporations and the realized price of crude oil. The importance of this change was that it gave the host governments a simple market by which to gauge their share of the proceeds. If posted prices were going up, government revenues were rising, and vice versa. Armed with this indicator, the oil producing nations took steps to form themselves into an association to secure better terms from the oil corporations. In 1960, OPEC was formed with Iran, Iraq, Saudi Arabia and Kuwait as founder members. These four states were later joined by Algeria, Libya, Qatar, Indonesia, Nigeria, Ecuador, Gabon, Venezuela and the United Arab Emirates.

What the members of this far from homogeneous group had in common was dependence on oil revenues to finance their development and balance their budgets. All resented the fluctuations in their incomes brought about by changes in posted prices not under their control. There the similarities ended. OPEC countries with small populations were able to build up massive

[2] "The European Community and the Energy Problem," *European Documentation Periodical*, January 1983, p. 7.
[3] Anthony Sampson, *The Seven Sisters*, London, Coronet Books 1977.

reserves of foreign currency, far in excess of the needs of their own development plans. The more heavily populated countries, such as Iran, Iraq and Nigeria, introduced ambitious plans for industrial development, the cost of which soon outstripped their oil revenues. For most of the 1960s, OPEC did not succeed in raising posted prices above their pre-1960 levels. However, its members were learning not only how to fix prices and control production, but also which actions were politically possible and which self-defeating. On June 4, 1967, the Six-Day War broke out with the invasion of Egypt by Israel. The Arab states agreed to shut down the oil wells and imposed a boycott on trade with the United States and Britain because of their support of Israel. This upset, however, lasted little longer than the war itself, as the oil producing states found they were damaging themselves far more than anyone else. The most lasting outcome of the Six-Day War was the closure of the Suez Canal, which continued for the next eight years. One effect of this blockade was the introduction of supertankers to carry huge cargoes of oil around the Cape of Good Hope to Europe and America.

The next move by the OPEC states was to raise the question of participation in the ownership of the oil concessions. In 1971, Algeria nationalized 51 percent of all French interests in its oil, and Libya took over all the assets of British Petroleum and other corporations operating concessions in its territory. The other oil states were more circumspect, and started off by taking a smaller share of the established concessions. The oil corporations hoped that participation would bring better relations with the host governments, and argued that what mattered was not the ownership of the oil but the ability to buy and distribute it. They had no sooner accustomed themselves to the fact of participation than the Yom Kippur War of October 1973 broke out. Hostilities began just as the delegates from OPEC and the oil corporations were gathering in Vienna to renegotiate posted prices for 1974. With inflation above 15 percent and a general shortage of oil, prices could only move upward. The OPEC delegates, led by Sheikh Zaqui al-Yamani of Saudi Arabia, demanded various amendments that would have raised the posted price to around U.S.$5 a barrel. This the corporations refused and negotiations broke down. The Arab members, left to themselves, agreed on a cutback in oil production varying from 5 to 20 percent, and imposed an embargo on oil exports to West Germany and Holland. The Israelis signed a cease-fire on October 21, but the oil price negotiations remained deadlocked and the embargoes continued in force. Oil prices were virtually out of control, fluctuating according to what the industrial countries, anxious to maintain supplies, were prepared to pay. Eventually a price of U.S.$11.65 a barrel was agreed on by the OPEC states as the minimum acceptable posted price.

By the beginning of 1974, oil prices had quadrupled in comparison with their level 12 months before. The era of cheap oil had ended, and the oil corporations had lost control of the industry.

The rise in oil prices had serious effects on the level of economic activity not only in the industrialized countries but, more especially, in those countries of the Third World that do not produce oil. In Western Europe, governments attempted to restrict energy consumption by economizing on fuel use and reducing oil imports. The rise in the inflation rate and the depreciation of the dollar cushioned the impact of the oil price increase, bringing it to a level equivalent to that of January 1974 at constant prices. The price rise in Middle East oil made it possible to develop the oilfields of the North Sea; in Britain, the National Coal Board (NCB) was even able to push up coal prices in line with oil prices. The crisis in Iran early in 1979 led to a fall in supplies followed by some panic buying. The OPEC states decided to raise crude oil prices, which increased during 1980 to double their 1978 level. As it became clear that stockpiling was not necessary, the supply situation became easier. The outbreak of the Iran–Iraq War in 1982, though raising anxieties for the safety of supplies from the Arabian Gulf in the event of the closure of the Straits of Hormuz, did not lead to further price increases.

EC REACTIONS

The oil price increases of 1973 and 1979–80 completely changed the energy balance of the EC and other Western European states. When the energy crisis broke in October 1973, the EC was still without a common energy policy. The adjustments in attitudes that have taken place since then have all centered on the new situation in which the supply and price of oil are determined by the OPEC countries. The immediate reaction was not, as might have been expected, to close ranks and agree on steps to help the Federal Republic and the Netherlands to overcome the difficulties of the embargo on their oil imports. Instead, ministers from Britain, France, and other countries hurried off to the Middle East in an attempt to strike the best deals they could to protect their own national interests. The first coordinated action took place not within the Community but in the framework of the Organization for Economic Cooperation and Development. A new organization, the International Energy Agency (IEA), was set up by the United States, Canada, Japan and Norway, together with all the EC member states except France. The EC is not a member as such, but it has participated in the work of the IEA since the end of 1974 in the dual role of coordinator of the views of EC member states and of the actions of the IEA and the Community.[4] The IEA has to some extent diverted attention from the formulation of a common energy policy by securing agreement on a framework of general principles and cooperation among its members. The major advance has been the agreement reached at the summit meeting in Tokyo in June 1979 by the governments of the United States, Canada, Japan and the EC to restrict oil consumption and accelerate the development of other energy sources. In practical terms, these commitments involved doing things that would have been included in any common energy policy; practicing a realistic oil pricing policy, promoting energy savings, encouraging the production and use of coal and coordinating measures to develop alternative energy sources.

[4]"The European Community and the Energy Problem," p. 19.

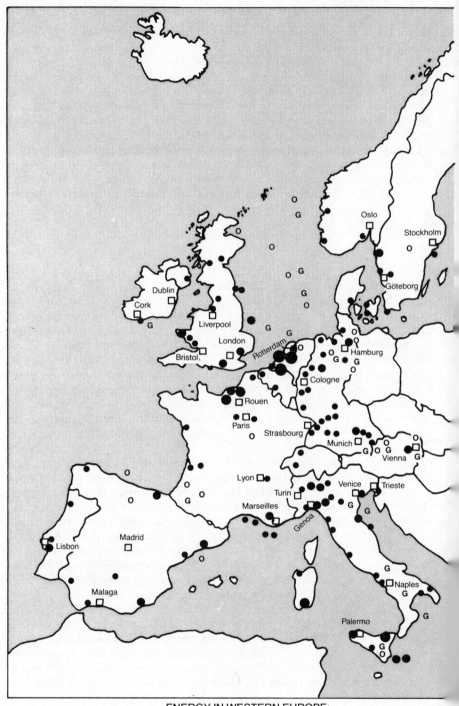

ENERGY IN WESTERN EUROPE:

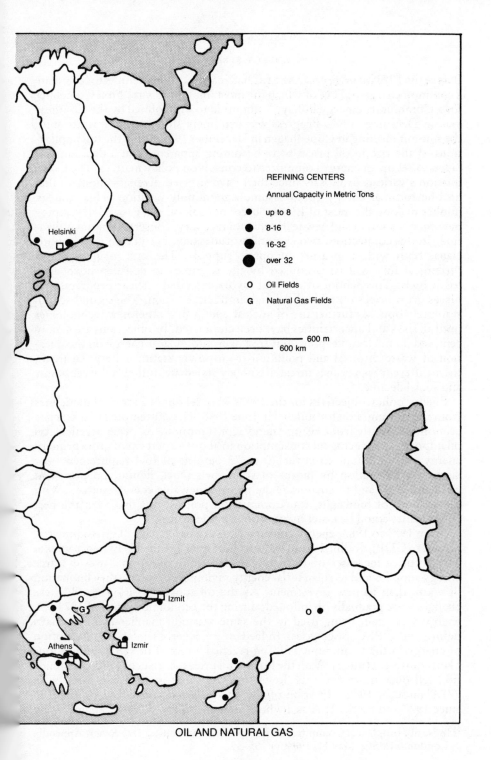

REFINING CENTERS

Annual Capacity in Metric Tons

● up to 8

● 8-16

● 16-32

● over 32

O Oil Fields

G Natural Gas Fields

Helsinki

Izmit

Izmir

Athens

OIL AND NATURAL GAS

EC ENERGY STRATEGY

Before the 1973 oil price crisis, the EC had made various attempts to formulate a common energy policy, of which the most important was "First Guidelines for a Community Energy Policy," submitted to the Council by the Commission in December 1968. Progress was extremely slow, and it was not until the summit meeting in Copenhagen in December 1973, when the full implications of the rise in oil prices were becoming apparent, that a decision was taken to set up an energy committee to consult on policy matters. The Commission's various proposals since then have stressed diversification, so that no one form of energy could assume a monopoly position. This strategy implies making the most of EC resources of coal, oil and gas and developing new energy sources and new techniques of recovery, conservation and utilization. In this connection, two extreme attitudes have been taken up by politicians, both with a measure of public support. The first assumes that a "technical fix" will be produced by the scientists to end dependence on fossil fuels. This school of thought favors extended nuclear programs and places great hopes on a breakthrough in nuclear fusion. The second school resolutely opposes further use of nuclear energy and other new technologies until all risks and uncertainties have been eliminated. Its objections are mainly centered on nuclear weapons, but spill over into nuclear energy on the question of waste disposal and pollution from power stations. Between them, these different approaches threaten a policy stalemate, followed by economic and social decline.

Energy policy objectives for the 1990s were set out in a series of guidelines from the Commission formulated in June 1980. These attempted to dissociate economic growth from rising energy consumption, to place a ceiling on oil imports by reducing oil consumption to about 40 percent of gross primary energy consumption, to cover 70 to 75 percent of fuel requirements for electricity generation by means of solid fuels (coal, lignite and peat) and nuclear energy and to encourage the use of renewable energy sources. With the wisdom of hindsight, the Commission pointed out that even the best laid schemes could be upset by variations in fuel prices.

From 1973 to 1983, energy consumption as a percentage of gross domestic product (GDP) declined from 83.4 to 67.5 percent in the EC as a whole. The oil price increases of 1973 initially led to more rational use of scarce energy supplies and to substantial energy savings due more to the elimination of waste than to new investment. As the oil supply position eased, these changes were gradually abandoned; during the economic upturn of 1978–79, energy was again being used in the same wasteful manner as in the days before the OPEC price rises. Indeed in 1979, gross inland consumption of energy in the Community of Ten reached a record of 986.3 million tons of oil equivalent (mtoe). With the further oil price increases of 1980, consumption fell once more and was down to 893.2 mtoe in 1983 compared with 871.9 mtoe in 1972.[5] In spite of the energy savings achieved by the Ten since 1973 and by the IEA as a whole, experience has shown that any easing

[5]House of Lords Select Committee on European Communities, *17th Report* Appendix 1, London, HMSO, May 11, 1984, pp. 55–59.

of the oil supply situation is liable to give rise to a mood of complacency, encouraging governments, corporations and householders to lose interest in conservation and further diversification of the energy mix. At the same time, there are doubts about the extent to which the fall in energy use was due to prudent behavior (and is therefore structural and permanent) and how much was due to the decline in activity in the old smokestack industries and steel owing to the recession. It is also a matter of concern that although dependence on imports of OPEC oil had fallen, energy imports in 1984 still cost the Community 3.8 percent of GDP, exactly the same figure as in 1974. A significant fall in oil prices could undermine the economic basis of long-term projections in the use of alternative fuels and greatly reduce production of high-cost North Sea oil. Any significant economic recovery in Western Europe would probably see oil used extensively once more in industry, and in some cases cause electric power stations, despite the pious resolutions of 1974, to switch to coal.

INDIVIDUAL FUELS

Coal

In 1952, when the ECSC was created, the main policy objectives were to maintain competition within the Community and ensure free choice for the consumer. West Germany was then, as now, the main coal producer among the Six, and the other members were all importers with supplies coming from West Germany, Poland and the United States. With the enlargement of the Community in 1973, total EC coal production was broadly doubled by the joining of Britain, the principal Western European coal producer. In the 1960s there was a steady decrease in coal production in the EC as oil imports rose; total production capacity by 1974 was 270 million tons a year. In 1982, the Commission published an energy strategy paper, *The Role for Coal*,[6] which analyzed the position to the end of the century and identified four basic problems. These were: how to secure increased use of coal; the agenda for research, development and demonstration; security of supplies; and social questions associated with the restructuring of the industry. The estimated demand for coal in the EC by the end of the 20th century is 500 million tons, of which about half will have to be imported. Production in the Community in 1983 was around 240 million tons, with half of that from Britain, 90 million tons from West Germany, 18 million tons from France and six million tons from Belgium.[7]

The prospect of importing some 250 million tons of coal a year raises formidable logistic problems. Port facilities need improvement to take large bulk carriers of coal, and rail and road networks will need increased capacity for coal distribution. The main sources of imported coal at present are the United States and Poland, but Australia, South Africa and a number of Third World countries are now involved in the international coal trade on an increasing scale and could be major suppliers in the 1990s. Such a high level

[6]*The Role of Coal in the Community Energy Strategy.* European Commission COM(82)31.
[7]*Memorandum on the Financial Aid Awarded by the Member States to the Coal Industry in 1982.* COM(82)817, p. 2.

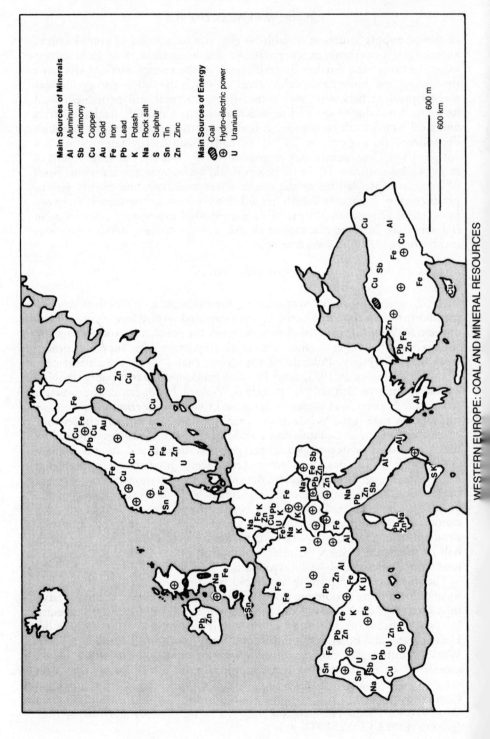

Main Sources of Minerals

Al	Aluminum
Sb	Antimony
Cu	Copper
Au	Gold
Fe	Iron
Pb	Lead
K	Potash
Na	Rock salt
S	Sulphur
Sn	Tin
Zn	Zinc

Main Sources of Energy

Coal
⊕ Hydro-electric power
U Uranium

600 m
600 km

WESTERN EUROPE: COAL AND MINERAL RESOURCES

of imports has given rise to fears that suppliers might form a cartel on the lines of OPEC and force up prices. The number and variety of coal exporting countries, however, and the fact that, except for the United States and Poland, they combine low labor costs with low-cost opencut mining, should maintain competition. In mid-1984, the price of a ton of Australian coal unloaded in Rotterdam was £16–£19 and from the American Appalachian fields, £23–£27, compared with the average price of British deep-mined coal of £45 a ton.[8]

The other half of Community strategy is to maintain indigenous production at as high a level as possible at competitive prices. In its 1984 budget, the Commission proposed granting subsidies from Community funds to raise productivity through modernization and restructuring, and sums were allocated for this purpose. National governments also provide subsidies, the size and scale of which are monitored by the Commission to prevent unfair competition. In the British coal industry the situation is complicated by the need to restructure and relocate an aging industry. The old coalfields of South Wales, central Scotland and northern England have become uneconomic because of the exhaustion of their main seams. These old pits are very costly to operate and production cannot cover costs. In 1983, it was estimated that 12 percent of the annual output of British coal was being produced at a loss of £250 million to the NCB. Coalfields in the East Midlands and parts of South Yorkshire operate profitably, but in the industry as a whole progress is held back by the burden of the loss-making pits.

The coal strike of 1984 centered on the question of pit closures. The NCB argued for a smaller, high-productivity industry based on developing newly discovered deposits at Selby in East Yorkshire, Belvoir in the East Midlands and in other areas in the Midlands. The NCB objective was to produce 120–140 million tons a year. The National Union of Mineworkers protested that the existing *Plan for Coal*,[9] negotiated with the NCB and the Labour government of 1974, had set a target of 170 million tons. Yet there was no market for British coal unless the price was competitive with other countries' exported coal, and the cost of subsidies to reduce export prices would be prohibitive. Furthermore British industry would have to pay more for its electricity than the rest of the Community because of the high cost of domestic coal. The political factors involved made the prospects for British coal uncertain; the advantages to the country of large indigenous resources of coal may prove illusory.

Natural gas
Natural gas is a relatively new fuel in Western Europe. Deposits were discovered in the Po Valley in northern Italy and at Lacq in southwestern France in the early 1950s, but it was not until the discovery of the vast Dutch Groningen gas field in 1959, followed by the finds in the southern basin of the North Sea, that gas use really began to expand. In 1971, the

[8]G. L. MacGregor, Chairman, NCB, quoted in "MacGregor Rebuffs Union" by David Young, *The Times* (London), April 11, 1984.
[9]*The Plan for Coal*, London, NCB, 1974.

certain and probable reserves of natural gas in the Community of Ten were 4.2 trillion cubic meters, with production expected to last for 40 years. Both figures have now fallen as production has increased and no new major fields have been discovered. The continental gas grid, to which all continental Community members except Denmark and Greece are connected, distributes supplies by pipeline or through terminals receiving liquefied gas from the natural gas resources of Western Europe (mainly Norway), the Soviet Union, the Middle East and North Africa. Production of gas in the southern basin of the North Sea passed its peak in the late 1970s, and future production will come from both the Brent field in the northern basin and the Frigg field, which overlaps the British and Norwegian sectors. Britain is connected to the Norwegian Frigg field by pipeline to St. Fergus, near Aberdeen, which carries gas purchased on long-term contract. The more southerly Norwegian Ekofisk field is connected to Emden and thence to the continental gas grid. There are strong arguments for connecting the British gas grid to the Community system by means of a pipeline to France.

The most important development for the future supply of gas was the agreement signed by Ruhrgas in November 1981, on behalf of a consortium of West German gas corporations, for the purchase of gas from the western Siberian gas fields. This provided for the construction of a pipeline with an annual capacity of 50 billion cubic meters a year. These supplies were in addition to the 22 billion cubic meters received annually under existing contracts by West Germany, France and Italy. As a result of the new and current contracts, by 1990 West Germany will be dependent on the Soviet Union for 34 percent of its natural gas supplies. France, Italy, Belgium and possibly the Netherlands will all participate in separate agreements. Austria and Switzerland also receive Soviet gas. These arrangements were undertaken independently of the EC on the responsibility of the organizations concerned.

The Commission has reacted to the increase in gas imports (which, when those from Algeria and Norway are included, may be as much as 45 percent of consumption by 1990) by advocating increased exploration for indigenous reserves and the diversification of sources of imports. Provision has also been made for more storage, greater reserve production capacity, expansion of the capacity of the Community gas grid and increased research into substitute natural gas and coal liquefaction.

Oil

The development of the international oil market and its effects on the countries of Western Europe has already been described. Production of oil within the Community is confined to those countries with territorial waters in the North Sea—Britain, Denmark, West Germany, the Netherlands, Belgium and France—and outside the Community, Norway. Of these states, only Britain and Norway have become significant oil producers. Output from the 31 offshore fields in the British sector should maintain self-sufficiency until the mid-1990s; and if a significant part of the resources not yet under development, and possible new discoveries, can be proved commercially viable, Britain could remain self-sufficient well beyond the end of the century.[10]

[10] "United Kingdom Energy Outlook," *Esso Magazine*, Supplement, Winter 1983–84.

If OPEC had not pushed up oil prices, North Sea reserves could never have been profitably developed.

Nuclear Energy

The important role that nuclear energy could play in providing the Community's energy needs was recognized back in 1957 in a report settling the objectives for Euratom. In the 1960s, the first large nuclear plants, which could compete with coal-fired power stations, were completed in the United States. Britain took the Western European lead in the development of a nuclear industry, based on its wartime research experience. The development of nuclear energy has been frustrated, first by problems in deciding on the most efficient type of reactor, and more recently by organized opposition to the building of nuclear power stations.

There is a strong case for diversity in nuclear power plant design. Britain built a number of Magnox gas-cooled reactors in the 1960s that are still operating cheaply and reliably. These were followed by the advanced gas-cooled reactors (AGRs), some of which encountered considerable design and technical problems during construction. Experience has overcome many major problems, however, and the AGR station at Hinckley Point has proved to be a model of efficiency; this has enabled the national AGR program to be implemented. The British program of the 1970s was based on gas-cooled technology, while U.S. and Community authorities have adopted the pressured water reactor (PWR). The British Central Electricity Generating Board's plans for a PWR station at Sizewell on the Suffolk coast has been the subject of a most intensive public inquiry. If it is decided not to continue with gas-cooled technology, most, if not all, future nuclear reactors in Europe could be PWRs. In the event of a nuclear accident as serious as that at the PWR reactor at Three Mile Island, there could be a major swing of public opinion against nuclear energy in general—even though there are design differences between PWRs in use in different countries. At Community level, more than one type of reactor should be included in the nuclear progams of the member states.

In considering competition between fuels, the balance between coal and nuclear power is critical. Oil and gas reserves, both worldwide and on the North Sea continental shelf, will be exhausted more quickly than coal reserves. Coal used for electricity generation is unlikely to fall much below present levels before the end of the century. Beyond that, developments in the technology of coal utilization, including gasification and liquefaction, will decide whether any but the least expensive imported coal will be competitive with nuclear power in the generation of electricity. The Community's nuclear plans include supplying nuclear fuels, funding research on the fast breeder reactor in France and Britain, developing nuclear fusion technology, and drawing up various programs on nuclear safety and waste disposal. The official objective is for nuclear power to supply 14 percent of total Community energy requirements by 1990.

In the Community, only France has succeeded in coming anywhere near to implementing its nuclear program. Eighty percent of its energy will be produced from nuclear power stations by the year 2000. Projections have had to be reduced constantly in the light of events, and the decline in expectations for nuclear power in the Community is matched by a similar trend in other OECD countries.

PROSPECTS FOR THE FUTURE

The pursuit of policies of energy self-sufficiency for the EC has been increasingly recognized as unrealistic. For Britain it is agreed that reserves are sufficient to sustain coal use long after oil and natural gas reserves, used at present rates, have been exhausted. Even so, British coal production, assuming the restructuring of the industry to eliminate unprofitable pits, could only supply about a quarter of total Community requirements by the end of the century. Experience in the past decade has shown that in spite of anxiety about the security of oil supplies there has been a reluctance to switch to coal because it is less convenient to transport and handle than oil or natural gas. The 1984 coal strike in Britain also raised the question of security of supplies. The level of economic activity, especially in the demand for electricity and steel, may further dampen demand for coal. The fall in oil prices after 1982 and the general glut in supplies provided further, possibly short-term, reasons for not making rapid changes in energy patterns. Western Europe will continue to rely on imports of oil, coal and natural gas to supplement inadequate or high-cost indigenous resources. Britain, unless the coal industry is modernized, faces the unique prospect of being self-sufficient in high-cost coal and producing high-cost electricity while its industrial competitors on the Continent have the benefit of low industrial costs based on cheap imported coal.

The replacement of fossil fuels by nuclear energy and alternative fuels—wind, wave, geothermal and solar energy, and use of the biomass—has made less progress than anticipated in all the policy-making exercises of the OPEC era. The building of new nuclear capacity has been slowed down. The scientists' dreams of a sudden breakthrough in nuclear technology have become part of a public nightmare about the dangers of radiation and pollution. This does not mean that a breakthrough in fast breeder reactor technology or nuclear fusion might not take place; but the possibility of its occurrence should not be included on the positive side of energy forecasts just yet. For the countries of Western Europe, national energy policies will continue to foster the development of indigenous reserves of oil, gas and coal, with shortfalls made good by imports. The EC can usefully undertake the important role of coordinating research programs, assisting investment in new and established energy sources and helping finance the restructuring of the coal industry. Finally, it is important to remember that most past predictions of energy supply and demand for 10 years or more ahead have been proved wrong. The best insurance against a future energy crisis is the diversification of fuels used and of supply sources and, given the long lead times involved, flexible arrangements for keeping the energy position constantly under review. The very last thing that is required is an energy version of the EC's common agricultural policy—with levies on fuel imports, annual price reviews, subsidies galore and surpluses sold off at knockdown prices to the Eastern bloc.

FURTHER READING

Burn, Duncan. *Nuclear Power and the Energy Crisis: Politics and the Atomic Industry.* London: Macmillan for the Trade Policy Research Council, 1978.

Coal: Bridge for the Future. Report of the World Coal Study (WOCOL). Cambridge, Massachusetts: Ballinger, 1980.

Ezra, Derek. *Coal and Energy.* London: Ernest Benn, 1978.

Kohl, Wilfred L. *After the Second Oil Crisis: Energy Policy in Europe, America and Japan.* Lexington, Massachusetts: D. C. Heath/Gower, 1982.

Parker, Geoffrey. *A Political Geography of Community Europe.* Sevenoaks, Kent: Butterworth, 1984.

Seymour, Ian. *OPEC: Instrument of Change.* London: Macmillan, 1980.

Shepherd, Geoffrey, et al., eds. *Europe's Industries: Public and Private Strategies for Change.* London: Pinter, 1983.

Twitchett, Carol, and Twitchett, Kenneth J., eds. *Building Europe: Britain's Partners in the EEC.* London: Europa, 1983.

AGRICULTURE IN WESTERN EUROPE

JOHN MARSH

DURING the late 1940s, Western Europe suffered from food shortages. Consumer choice was limited by rationing as well as by price. By the 1980s, agricultural surpluses seemed intractable and consumers were at risk through excessive consumption of foods rich in fat and sugar.

This transformation is counted a success by both the industry and the policy maker. It is also frequently perceived as a cause for concern, threatening the livelihoods of many who work in farming, and inducing ever-growing public expenditure in support of agriculture. From an atmosphere of "produce more food," discussion has swung to "supply control and budgetary constraint." This chapter attempts to explain how this situation has come about and to explore some of the resulting policy issues.

CHARACTERISTICS OF WESTERN EUROPEAN AGRICULTURE

Within Western Europe, physical conditions create a diversity of production opportunities. Differences in climate, terrain and soil type range from Arctic conditions in parts of Scandinavia, through the mountains of the Alps and the fertile plains of the Low countries to Mediterranean heat. Economic conditions, too, vary greatly: between 1973 and 1980, for example, the average gross domestic product per capita in Sweden was almost 10 times the level in Turkey. Political differences and agricultural policies impose additional constraints. Since the 1960s, a growing proportion of Europe's agriculture has been subject to the common agricultural policy (CAP) of the European Community (EC). Even within the EC however, important differences in the way farming is perceived, in the development of policies outside the CAP, and in the national economic environments have allowed great variety to persist.

This diversity makes any generalized description of agriculture difficult, if not dangerous. There are, however, some common tendencies influencing agriculture in Western Europe, and these form a background helpful for understanding policy issues.

First, agricultural production has been growing more rapidly than food consumption. During the 1970s, agricultural output grew by almost a quarter. Only in one country, Portugal, did it actually decline. Population grew, too, but only by some five percent. Although per capita income rose, expenditure on food did not keep pace. Most Europeans are already well fed. Given more money, they tend to increase their diet's diversity, convenience or quality. They do not buy larger quantities. In richer countries it is likely that the volume of food bought will decline, as people adjust to a more sedentary life and a centrally heated environment.

Second, this growth of production has been made possible by improved technology and increased capital investment. One indication of this is sustained improvement in crop yields and livestock performance. During the 1970s, for example, average wheat yields rose by some 36 percent, average milk yields per cow by 16 percent. Another symptom has been the growing use of machinery and chemicals. Between 1969–71 and 1980, tractor numbers rose by 36 percent. In the Europe of the Organization for Economic Cooperation and Development (OECD), which covers all of Western Europe, fertilizer consumption grew at a compound rate of some 5.5 percent per year between 1961 and 1970, and by 2.1 per cent between 1971 and 1980.

Third, this production increase has occurred despite a sustained decline in the number of people engaged in agriculture. During the 1970s, although jobs elsewhere in the economy were scarce, the population engaged in agriculture continued to fall. By 1983, one-third fewer people were involved in farming than in 1970, a decline of 7.6 million people. This reduction occurred in all Western European countries, even Britain, where only 2.8 percent of the working population remained in agriculture as of 1970. One result is that throughout Europe labor productivity has risen substantially. In several countries, such as Belgium, France and West Germany, agricultural labor productivity has risen only slightly more rapidly than productivity in manufacturing; in Austria, Finland and Britain, it has risen decidedly faster.

Fourth, the reduction in the number of people engaged in farming has permitted some increase in farm size. Measured in area terms, the smallest group still accounts for the largest number of farm households, although for a very small proportion of the land area. Among the 10 members of the EC, 46.4 percent of farms were below 12.4 acres/five hectares but they were responsible for only 7.2 percent of the land farmed. In contrast, larger farms, though small in number, were tending to increase in size, and controlled a larger fraction of the total agricultural area. In France, for example, the largest group (123.5 acres/50 hectares and over) accounted for only 5.5 percent of households in 1960, but 13.3 percent in 1980. In Germany, where farm sizes are generally smaller, the increase in the same group was from 1.1 percent to 3.9 percent, while the middle-sized units (20–50 hectares) grew from 8.8 percent to 22.3 percent. There remain important differences among European countries: in Britain, one-third of farm households are above 50 hectares and account for 82 percent of the land area. Comparisons in terms of land area alone can be misleading. Small areas intensively cultivated may generate higher levels of output than wide expanses of hillside; thus, although farm sizes in the Netherlands remain modest in area terms, many farms there produce more than larger units elsewhere in Europe. Despite the tendency to increased farm size, agriculture in Europe remains overwhelmingly a family business. In a growing number of cases, farming accounts for only part of the household income. In Germany, part-time farming has become a principal type of farm organization.

Fifth, European governments have continued to protect their agricultural sectors from international competition. The most important example of this is the CAP, but non-EC members also intervene to protect farming. They do so in a variety of ways, giving different weights to commonly shared objectives. These include providing a secure food supply, maintaining stable price levels, improving farm incomes, maintaining rural communities, improving national trade balances and promoting economic growth. This insulation from the vagaries of the international market has contributed to the general expansion of production. It has also exacerbated the adjustment problems faced by the rest of the world as a result of fluctuations in output.

Sixth, the growth of output at a rate exceeding growth in consumption makes Europe increasingly self-sufficient in foodstuffs. Once self-sufficiency is exceeded, extra output can only be sold at prevailing world prices. Since these are well below the levels paid to most farmers in Western Europe, the result will be growing subsidies to bridge the gap, reduced prices to farmers, some measure of supply control or a mixture of all three. Unless transfers from taxpayers or consumers are allowed to increase, adjustments that will make farming less profitable seem inevitable. Already, falling real prices and declining real incomes for most farmers in Western Europe are one effect of surpluses. Another is the growing recognition among many Western European governments that a reappraisal of their attitude to international trade in agricultural products is needed.

Seventh, the existence of abundant food supplies, the introduction of new methods of crop production and animal husbandry, and the decline in the agricultural labor force has increased the importance of ecology in political debate. The new so-called green politics are not proagriculture. They are concerned with pollution and the rapid consumption of finite natural resources. They are critical of farming methods that rely on chemicals to remove pests and weeds and result in a loss of wildlife. They resist the extension of the arable land area through drainage and mechanized cultivation, which further erodes wildlife habitats and leads to greater uniformity in the appearance of the countryside. Some critics claim that food produced by modern methods tastes less pleasant or is actually damaging to human health. Such attitudes may well be a luxury affordable in a densely populated affluent society. They are nonetheless a matter for serious political concern in the formation of agricultural policy.

Eighth, agriculture in Western Europe is affected by common tendencies in the food manufacturing and distribution industries. A growing proportion of all food is processed. The EC estimated in 1981 that some three-quarters of the total agricultural production went through some form of processing, and this share is expected to grow.[1] Very different degrees of processing are involved, from the pasteurization and bottling of whole milk right through to the manufacturing of "oven-ready TV dinners." The processing industry

[1] EC Commission, *The Agricultural Situation in the Community, 1982.*

includes a wide variety of sizes and types of firm, but in some product areas and in some commodities, such as milk and bread, there is a tendency for economies of scale to lead to concentration of processing and manufacture among a small number of firms. In some countries, such as Holland and Denmark, farmer cooperatives play a major role in first-stage processing.

Throughout Europe, retail food trading has tended to change from small family businesses to large, multiple-outlet supermarkets and hypermarkets. These organizations exercise substantial market power in relation to food manufacturers and farmers. Products of inadequate quality or excessive price may cease to find an outlet. Own-brand production may impose rigorous conditions on farmers and processors. Within large retail organizations, highly processed products can be economically transported over large distances. Hence, the area within which farmers have to compete in "home" markets has tended to expand.

Ninth, the process of agricultural change has profound regional implications for most Western European countries. While farming accounts for only a minority of jobs, its influence on the level of employment in the rural community is much greater. The supply of farm requisites, the marketing of farm products, and the provision of advisory services all create jobs. The existence of a "critical mass" of such employment justifies the existence of village shops, schools and social facilities. Many of these activities already face increased urban competition, as personal transport has become more widely available. The decline of farming employment adds to these pressures and can encourage the withdrawal of business from rural areas. In regions remote from major centers of population, such trends can lead to the depopulation of the countryside and the neglect of agricultural land. At the same time, urban unemployment and inadequate urban housing make the flow of people from rural areas unwelcome. Such tendencies have given rise to attempts to discriminate, within agricultural policy, in favor of the disadvantaged region. More substantially, they have focused attention on the inadequacy of policies confined to agriculture alone, and the need to seek solutions to farm problems within a more comprehensive regional policy.

Tenth, just as the dynamics of agricultural change tend to make the policy maker look more closely at the role of agriculture within the economy and the region, so the growing flood of farm output in Western Europe is forcing fresh thought about international trade. For traditional agricultural exporters, a conflict of interest is evident and inevitable. Both North American and Australian exporters see the EC as a major threat and criticize its subsidized sale of farm products. Many Europeans argue that the enormous overproduction should be used to feed hungry people in the Third World. Food aid is often seen as both morally desirable and politically convenient. Past attempts to achieve a more rational pattern of agricultural trade have foundered on the rocks of national interest and agricultural pressure groups. The history of negotiations over the General Agreement on Tariffs and Trade (GATT), as well as over the several international commodity agreements that have sought to regulate agricultural trade, suggests that countries are unlikely to reconcile conflicting interests through agreements providing a more stable environment for trade in farm goods. Agriculture as a focus of international dispute thus increasingly raises for Europe the question of how far it should (or indeed must) expose its farmers to a more stringent economic climate in order to secure broader strategic and economic goals.

THE COMMON AGRICULTURAL POLICY

The six countries that established the EC were determined to include agriculture within its framework. They recognized that agriculture presented special problems and agreed that the form of its inclusion within the EC should be by a common agricultural policy, now widely called the CAP. The details of this policy were to be worked out after the EC came into existence. Its objectives were, however, spelled out in the Treaty of Rome, Article 39.1:

The common agricultural policy shall have as its objectives:
a. to increase agricultural productivity by developing technical progress and by ensuring the rational development of agricultural production, and the optimum utilization of the factors of production, particularly labor;
b. to ensure thereby a fair standard of living for the agricultural population, particularly by the increasing of the individual earnings of persons engaged in agriculture;
c. to stabilize markets;
d. to guarantee regular supplies; and
e. to ensure reasonable prices in supplies to consumers.

So stated, these objectives were unexceptional and unexceptionable. They were typical, indeed, of the agricultural policy objectives of most developed countries. What mattered was how they could be translated into policy decisions.

After considerable debate, the Six chose to employ two types of policy. The first would support and regulate the market for key products; the second would promote the structural development of agriculture. From the outset, however, the CAP has been dominated by market policy, with structural proposals receiving relatively little financial support. The reasons for this are straightforward enough. Since agricultural goods had to be allowed to cross EC frontiers to achieve EC free trade, prices throughout the EC would inevitably respond to the overall balance of supply and demand within the market as a whole. Traditionally, prices to farmers had been supported above world levels, though in differing degrees. Internal competition, if not moderated through a common administered price policy, would have forced many high-cost producers out of farming. Again, the Common Market needed both to give effect to preference for EC production and to shield internal markets from disruption by price fluctuations in the world market. Some form of price policy was essential to achieve these ends. Finally, by the relatively simple administative device of controls at EC frontiers, price levels could be regulated throughout the Community. Policies to improve farm structure required a much more detailed, administratively costly and interventionist approach. Neither in terms of its political maturity nor of its bureaucratic resources was the EC ready for this in the early 1960s.

414

The consequences of this emphasis on regulating prices have been far-reaching. For most products, a common market regime relied upon the imposition of variable levies (and in some cases, tariffs) on imports and the operation of an intervention system which could remove from the internal market goods produced within the EC that could not be sold there at the administered price. To permit exports from the EC, export subsidies (known as restitutions) were needed to bridge the gap between the higher internal and the lower external prices.

This system of market regulation, along with the reliance on price support to achieve income goals, created an environment in which it was easier to compromise on high rather than low administered prices. Such a compromise occurred in the initial setting of cereal prices. Because cereals enter into the costs of livestock production and compete for land with other arable and grazing enterprises, prices for these products too had to be high. Given the continuing improvements in productivity realized by new technology, the result was a sustained stimulus to increased output. In time, the effects of this trend included growing budget costs to remove unwanted products from the market; growing distortion of world trade, as the EC first reduced its own imports and then became a net exporter of some products; and growing anomalies, as substitute products not subject to CAP import levies invaded markets within the EC.

The determination of high price levels implied a substantial transfer from EC consumers to producers. In effect, this amounted to the difference between the price they actually paid for food and the price they would have paid had markets been unrestricted and open to imports. The level of the implicit transfer varied with movements in world prices, but since the gap between EC prices and actual world prices has normally been considerable, the total cost may safely be assumed to be substantially greater than the more visible budget payments needed to finance intervention and exports. Such transfers gave rise to surprisingly little opposition from consumers. In part this was due to history. Food had been scarce, past real prices had been even higher; the level of prices fixed under the CAP did not seem excessive to most citizens of the Six. Again, during the 1960s and early 1970s, real incomes rose strongly and the share of food in private expenditure fell. The sense of burden represented by agricultural support thus probably diminished. Another factor in consumer quiescence was the absence of well-organized pressure groups to counter the substantial efforts of agricultural lobbyists in national capitals and in Brussels. Britain's admission to the EC in 1973 gave fresh weight to consumer interests, since British agricultural policy had traditionally encouraged lower food prices. This was not enough, however, to upset the convenient EC compromise in favor of high prices.

A third consequence of the price level and the CAP system proved more disruptive. It was clear that member countries which were net importers of agricultural products were effectively underwriting the agriculture of net exporters. They paid higher prices for imported food; the budget derived extra revenue from their imports from third countries, but required additional expenditure to subsidize exports from, and intervene in, member countries which were more than self-sufficient. So they found themselves at a double disadvantage. In political terms, the debate focused on budgetary transfers rather than the total flow of resources. The main net loser from this system of farm support was Britain, and its government resolutely sought relief. In effect, the agricultural system was an important progenitor of the so-called British problem.

A fourth result of this emphasis on price policy has been that agricultural problems are seen as commodity problems, rather than as questions of how best to use resources and how most effectively to help agricultural workers adjust to changes in their industry. The debate has not been concerned with how to promote "the optimum utilization" of resources as the Treaty of Rome stipulated, but rather with how to cope with an excess flow of milk or cereals reaching the EC market, or how to arrange commodity prices to achieve improved levels of farm income. As the EC has become self-sufficient in a growing number of products, the consequences of raising commodity prices have been constrained by budgetary implications. The outcome is a failure to achieve income levels regarded as satisfactory, despite an expenditure on agriculture that threatens to outstrip EC budgetary resources.

This fundamental weakness of a dependence on price policy was diagnosed early in the life of the EC. In 1968, the "Memorandum on the Reform of Agriculture in the Community" put forward a radical view of changes in resource use, land and labor that were required within the EC by 1980. It also suggested various structural policies to help the EC's agriculture to adapt. This diagnosis and proposals became known as the Mansholt Plan after the commissioner then responsible for agriculture. It formed the ground-work for later discussions on structural policy within the CAP.

Three distinct types of structural policy can be identified. In the wake of the Mansholt Plan, policies were favored easing the exit of people from farming and promoting the improvement and enlargement of farms capable of generating an income equivalent to others in their area. These policies were administered through directives requiring each member state to imple-ment the policy, but leaving them some degree of freedom as to how this was done. A second type of policy sought to improve the marketing of farm products through grants encouraging the formation of farm coopera-tives. A third approach emphasized the regional dimensions of agricultural-resource use. Various directives addressed the problems of hill and mountain agriculture (1975); special aids for agriculture in the Mediterranean region (1977); and the creation of integrated development programs (1979) for speci-fic areas in which farming, although central to the survival of the rural com-munity, could not alone generate sufficient income. More recent policy initiatives concentrate on providing extra protection for the less-competitive regions, rather than promoting change, and this reflects an important shift in opinion within the EC. In the 1960s and early 1970s, resources released from farming could expect to be reemployed elsewhere in a growing eco-nomy. By the late 1970s, this sanguine assumption had vanished in the face of rising unemployment in all member countries. So, far from pursuing the Mansholt vision of an efficient, modern and moderately large-scale agriculture that could compete in world markets, contemporary policy is more concerned to conserve rural communities and preserve farm jobs.

Despite the growing interest in structural policies, the proportion of the EC budget spent in this direction remains small (three percent in 1983). Price policy is much more costly (64 percent in 1983), and as output grows beyond the capacity of EC markets, its call on resources threatens to accelerate. If it does so, it will put at risk the EC's financial stability and political cohesion. Substantial changes are therefore implied for agricultural policy and agriculture within the EC.

THE FUTURE OF AGRICULTURAL POLICY

Agricultural policies have traditionally been somewhat separate from the more general issues of social and economic policy. The very existence of the CAP testifies to this attitude among EC members. Such isolation is increasingly being challenged, as forces outside the agricultural sector demand a say in public policy toward it. Many of the issues perplexing farm policy makers in Europe during the 1980s have this characteristic.

Markets for farm produce seem destined to impose a growing constraint on agricultural policy makers. In terms of the total volume of production, supply control seems bound to play an increasing role. Within the EC, the imposition of a "superlevy" on milk production—in effect a quota—demonstrates one approach. For other sectors, the emphasis may be on price cuts to limit both the level of output and the cost of dealing with surpluses. More generally, support for investments that increase output seems likely to be reduced if not removed. The need to limit supply implies that the traditional means by which farmers have sought to increase income—by producing more at a protected price—will be blocked.

Market forces not only dictate a cut in the volume of output but also seem likely to play a growing role in the mix of products and their quality. European consumers buy an increased share of their food through large-scale retailers exercising substantial market power. Such organizations, in competition with each other, seek consistency in supply, products of good appearance and storage characteristics, and responsive prices. Products failing to meet these standards may have to be disposed of at very much lower prices. Already a considerable proportion of food is subject to processing, and some to considerable manufacturing activity. Processors find themselves under pressure from large retailers to discount prices, and in turn must buy competitively from farmers. In part this is a matter of price, but it may extend much further into the variety of crops grown, the conditions of husbandry and the timing of activities on the farm. Agricultural policy is likely to be concerned with the balance of power between several parts of the food industry. The promotion of farmer marketing organizations and the monitoring of monopolistic pressures will surely play a growing role in debate.

In the longer term, the need for Western Europe's agricultural policies to become better integrated into world markets will tend to preoccupy policy makers. First, as a substantial exporter—its exports amount to half the world total for dairy products and a substantial proportion of cereals and sugar—the

EC is forced to be aware of the effects of its actions on world markets. Increased sales may depress prices, and so disproportionately increase the cost of restitutions needed to enable it to clear its own market. Attempts to share markets with other exporters offer one possible route to diminishing this problem. Second, the political odium of dumping Western European produce on world markets could provoke retaliatory actions by other countries who resent the damage to their own farm sectors. As the largest importer and exporter in the world, the EC is vulnerable. Some accommodation with other countries seems essential. Third, although EC prices have traditionally been well above world market levels, this need not be so in the future. World demand for food imports may be expected to grow as more developing countries become newly industrialized countries. EC supply costs can even fall, if new technology is exploited to promote greater efficiency instead of simply greater production. In a number of commodity areas, the EC could become a commercial exporter rather than a reluctant dumper of food products. If it is to do so, it must immediately seek to control supply, and in the long run to lower production costs.

Pressures from outside agriculture, which make themselves felt through the market, are reinforced by a number of other external forces. Agricultural policy seems likely to be influenced by these new considerations.

Within a society generally well fed and much more urban and mobile than its predecessors, new farming methods have given rise to a growing chorus of disapproval from those seeking to defend the environment. In some EC countries this has already resulted in the election of "green" candidates to assemblies and parliaments. All major parties have grown anxious to demonstrate their sensitivity to these issues. In practice this is difficult, partly because the various environmental groups are not agreed on what they want, and partly because implementing some of their ideas would impose substantial costs on consumers, taxpayers or the existing occupiers of agricultural land. For the agricultural policy maker, environmental pressure groups create a dilemma. Public concern about the countryside can create a new market for agricultural resources, unrelated to the market for agricultural commodities. In the process it may contribute to supply-control policies. Unfortunately, while the attraction to the public of environmental "goods" is not disputed, there are few ways in which it can be measured: can the "consumers" of, for example, a beautiful view or the sight of a rare bird be made to pay for the privilege? So the revenues resulting from an environmental use of agricultural resources may not prove sufficient for their owners. Indeed, policies designed to achieve environmental goals while retaining agricultural resources tend to raise farm production costs. At a regional level, this conflicts with the need to compete in world markets. At the level of the individual farm, it implies lower incomes unless prices to consumers are raised or taxpayers foot a larger bill.

A possible solution to this dilemma is to recognize the diversity of farming and amenity values of Western European land and to seek to give priority to environmental objectives and poorer land, while encouraging the development of agriculture on the best acreage available. Such an approach would be difficult to administer and would give rise to many anomalies, where boundaries appeared to conflict with common sense. It would also reverse the policy that has sought to protect farming in less-favored areas, through investment aids designed to make farms more viable. It may, however, come to be accepted as the most practical compromise available.

A further pressure on Western Europe's agriculture arises from the changing perception about the effects of animal fat on human health. In several countries, government-sponsored reports have advocated substantial cuts in the consumption of meat and dairy products. If consumers respond, this would imply far-reaching consequences for agriculture. More than half of the value of final output of EC agriculture is derived from livestock products. The markets for many of these, especially milk, are already overloaded and tend to be price-inelastic. Reduced consumption would intensify the problems of oversupply and budgetary cost. Although there would be some growth in demand for "healthy" products to replace those now causing concern, this is unlikely to generate the same level of revenue or to lead to increases of activity in the same places where livestock production would be likely to contract. Consumers may prove unresponsive to medical advice, or the food industry may find ways of removing undesirable constituents from traditional products, but the longer-term implication of contemporary nutritional advice seems to be that agricultural policy makers will have less rather than more freedom of action in adjusting EC policy to the needs of this century's final decades.

CONCLUSION

If many of the pressures upon agriculture within Western Europe now arise outside the industry, it is increasingly clear that responses to them and to traditional agricultural problems demand policy actions lying beyond the conventional limits of agricultural policy. The industry has to become more competitive; it cannot support incomes through product-price manipulation alone. Pressures to conserve the environment threaten to raise costs, while the implication of dietary advice is that demand is likely to fall. The long-standing problem of low farm incomes seems likely to become more acute as a result of these pressures. In many parts of the Western Europe, rural communities will disintegrate and rural services become too costly to retain. Action within agriculture cannot contain these forces or avoid these tendencies. Instead, the industry's problems have to be visualized within a broader framework of alternative uses for resources within the Western European economy as a whole. To do so puts agriculture in a position close to that of many other established European industries confronted by rapid technical change. None can survive by increasing production of unwanted goods or retaining obsolete methods. The challenge to the policy maker is not to find ways of making such traditional activities financially feasible, but to promote flexibility both within the agricultural industry and beyond it, so that it can confront the opportunities of the next century.

WESTERN EUROPEAN
INCOMES POLICIES

CHARLES FORD

A just wage, which is sufficient to establish and maintain security for a family, is the concrete means of verifying the justice of the whole economic system.

Pope John Paul II, *On Human Work*

INTRODUCTION

There has been a gradual progression of European governments' wages policies from the crude wage restrictions of the early 1960s to incomes policies embracing nonwage incomes (i.e., profits and directors' emoluments of all kinds) and then to policies that began to include prices. This was largely a reflection of collective discussion within the Organization for Economic Cooperation and Development (OECD), in which the Trade Union Advisory Committee (TUAC) plays an influential role.

Since the early 1970s, the wheel has come full circle. OECD turned its back upon the discussion of prices policies and nonwage incomes, and came increasingly to embrace crude wage policies once more. Some of its member governments, such as the United States and Britain, placed all the onus for inflation upon the trade unions and sought to undermine the unions' very existence by pressing policies for wage "flexibility," by which was meant real and nominal wage restraint and even cuts. Europe moved from full employment in the 1960s to a situation marked by inflation in the 1970s, and on to a period of mass unemployment in the 1980s. Governments now put policy emphasis upon improving profit levels. There has indeed been recent evidence of improved profits in the European manufacturing sector, but few signs of increased investment. Thus European governments' efforts to shift incomes from employees to entrepreneurs, in order to improve profits and investment levels, have so far proved abortive. In the meantime, concepts of equality in the distribution of the social product have been thrown overboard.

It is pertinent to observe the change in the vocabulary of economic analysis over the last decade or so. The notion of nonwage incomes adopted by OECD in its 1966 report on "Policies for Prices, Profits, and Other Nonwage Incomes" was a response to TUAC arguments that if there were to be an

420

incomes policy, equity required that it should embrace all incomes, not only wages.

The views of TUAC were cogently expressed in the following much-quoted statement:

> An argument can be made out for planning or guiding incomes; an argument can also be made out for leaving them unplanned or unguided; but there is nothing at all to be said for planning or guiding half the incomes and leaving the other half unguided or unplanned and subject to market forces or varying degrees of monopoly control.

The phrase "nonwage incomes," however, has been slyly transmogrified into "nonwage *costs*." Currently, right-wing economists are not only focusing upon the need to limit nominal and real wages, but urging reductions in the social wage—social security benefits—saying that these, too, are contributing to inflation. Thus any discussion about profits and other nonwage incomes has been avoided by a single-minded focus upon a simplistic equation: inflation equals rising wages and other labor costs. This obscures the essential fact that rising social charges are mainly caused by the social costs of the economic policies adopted in the 1970s and 1980s by many OECD member governments. Their essential characteristic was adopt restrictive fiscal and monetary policies to limit demand and thereby to increase unemployment. It was this policy of abandoning full employment that was the principal cause of falling profits, falling investment and drooping economic expectations.

A further significant change in economic vocabulary can be seen by tracing the origin of the current buzzword among right-wing economists, politicians and publicists: flexibility. When Gösta Rehn, the Swedish economist, then director of OECD's manpower and social affairs division, first expounded the idea of flexibility in the 1960s, he saw it as flexibility throughout working life. Workers should have the opportunity of publicly financed periods of education through sabbatical leave. Instead of retiring at a fixed age, they should have the option of early retirement or of continuing to work after the normal retirement age. Today, however, flexibility has come increasingly to apply to job arrangements, and the word is used especially as a synonym for wage cuts.

FLEXIBILITY

The British model

In Britain, the call for wage flexibility is more and more often directed at young workers and even those on minimum wages. In an open letter to Prime Minister Thatcher printed in *The Times*, on December 20, 1984, a group of peers, Tory members of Parliament, business people and academics called for the abolition of Britain's 26 wages councils. These councils existed for the benefit of workers whose precarious position, it was accepted by all previous governments, needed special protection against exploitation. These miscellaneous spokespeople for private business interests brushed aside Britain's obligations to the International Labor Organization (ILO), which require member countries to maintain machinery to enforce minimum rates of pay where wages are exceptionally low. In their view, social security benefits set an effective floor to wages in Britain. They then reduced their own argument to nonsense by next urging reduction in the employers' social security contributions as well. Unemployment, they asserted, is determined not only by labor costs, but also by the monetary advantage of working as compared to not working.

This argument was effectively disposed of in *The Causes of Unemployment* (1984), a book published by the Institute of Fiscal Studies, which demonstrates that the Conservative government's abolition of earnings-related supplements to unemployment benefits greatly reduced the income of the unemployed. It also shows that the average income of the unemployed in 1983 was only 60 percent of previous earnings at work, compared with 73 percent in 1980. A mere three percent of the unemployed could expect to receive 90 percent of their previous earnings. It is paradoxical that the most powerful de facto wages policy exists in Britain, whose present government purports not to have one.

The most exhaustive presentation of the case for *not* having an incomes policy in Britain is to be found in *The Delusions of Incomes Policies* (1977), jointly written by Samuel Brittan and Peter Tilley. The former also published during 1984, in the *Financial Times*, several articles advocating wage flexibility—in other words, a low-wage policy.

The fallacy of flexibility has by now been powerfully demonstrated by authoritative sources that cannot be suspected of being, in Thatcherite terms, "wet" (insufficiently loyal to hard-line policies). The first was by Grieveson Grant, the British stockbrokerage firm whose latest *Economic Review* forecasts 3.8 million unemployed by 1987. It suggests that it is misleading for Nigel Lawson, Chancellor of the Exchequer, to suggest that high real wages are the source of unemployment. According to the report, the present unemployment rate probably has little to do with recent wage increases, which have lagged behind productivity. Lawson, adds the report, needs to do a great deal of empirical work to back his claim that wage cuts would help.

The second blow to the flexibility school of economics was delivered by, of all people, an economic adviser to the Bank of England, Sir Bryan Hopkin, former chief adviser to the Treasury. He rejected the idea that high wages can provide a general explanation of unemployment. "Since 1972," he wrote "profits have never been low enough as a result of high wages to deter producers from supplying at the then current rates of wages and prices."[1]

A further shock to the flexibility theory came unexpectedly from the OECD's *Economic Outlook* for December 1984, which stated quite unambiguously that real labor costs in the member countries have, in recent years, been rising more slowly than productivity. There had been a fall in labor's share of total value added, which is now less than in 1973. OECD foresees a further fall to have occurred in 1985. The study goes on:

> The link between real compensation and unemployment, though clearly indicated by economic theory, has been difficult to verify; it is uncertain how strongly, and with what lags, wage moderation will by itself create new jobs. Simple correlations have been interpreted by some as providing evidence that the increases in

[1]Bank of England, December 1984, *Quarterly Bulletin*, Vol. 24, no. 4, p. 512.

unemployment over the second half of the 1970s were accounted for by "unwarranted" increases in real labour costs. But the further sharp rise of European unemployment since 1979 is difficult to explain in this matter, because labour cost gaps narrowed at the same time.

Finally, if further testimonial is needed, we may add the evidence of Wilfred Beckerman, fellow of Balliol College, Oxford, who was for many years a leading economist at the OECD. Writing in the *Lloyds Bank Review* of January 1985, he argued that there is inadequate evidence that unemployment results from workers pricing themselves out of the market. Moreover, international differences in wage flexibility are of no significance and cannot, therefore, account for the degree of unemployment. In a brilliant analysis based upon the latest economic and computing techniques, he demonstrates that it is the flexibility of commodity prices, and not wages, that has made the key contribution to the recent conquest of inflation in advanced industrialized countries. Commodity price changes reflect the rate of economic expansion of contraction in the industrialized world. He showed also, that there was a highly significant relationship between proportionate changes in wages and import prices, in that a 10 percent increase in import prices would result in a 2.5 percent increase in wages in the representative OECD country. There was also a "highly significant" relationship between wages and productivity.

International aspects
Wage-flexibility arguments concentrate upon wages as the key factor in costs and usually exclude such international influences as imports, exports, and changes in the value of currencies. A 1982 OECD study, *International Aspects of Inflation*, also shows that "import price changes have been a key—and highly volatile—determinant of domestic inflation rates." This was mainly due to swings in raw material prices which, in turn, reflected the world business cycle. But what determines the world business cycle? It is obviously government decisions about the rate of economic expansion. The conclusion is that as international trade comes to represent a larger and larger share in gross domestic product, import prices, especially those of raw materials, will have an increasing impact upon domestic price levels, irrespective of what happens to wages. These raw-material prices will reflect the world economic business cycle and will be independent of wage levels, certainly in less-developed exporting countries, where wages of workers concerned are below subsistence levels. The key policy issue would thus appear to be how to stabilize the price of raw materials and not how to cut wages in developed or developing countries.

In 1976, an integrated program for commodities was adopted at the fourth U.N. Conference on Trade and Development (UNCTAD), along with a timetable for the negotiation of a Common Fund and International Commodity Agreements (ICAs) for 18 commodities of export interest to developing countries. A $6 billion Common Fund was envisaged to finance buffer stocks and other price stabilization measures. In June 1980, agreement was finally reached on setting up the Common Fund with two windows. The first would finance buffer stocks, the second, investments in product diversification, research, processing and marketing. A total of 90 countries, representing two-thirds of the paid-in capital, had to ratify the fund before it could enter into force. Although a ratification deadline of March 31, 1982 was set, by June 1982 only 29 countries out of the 85 original signatories had also ratified the agreement. Enthusiasm was thought to have waned because of problems faced by the ICAs, and because of the voting structure of the fund, which is heavily weighted in favor of the major contributors. Key rules relating to the fund's borrowing and lending operations have still to be settled.

UNCTAD is also considering proposals for a compensatory facility for export-earnings stabilization, with a subscribed capital of $10 billion. The facility would contribute toward the foreign exchange cost of the balance of payments support necessitated by shortfalls in export earnings. Loans would be made to developing countries at concessional rates to cover up to 10 percent of these shortfalls.[2] Changes in the exchange value of currencies also affect costs. The 1969 revaluation of the West German mark, for example, and its later strength, increased West German relative unit labor costs very sharply indeed between 1969 and 1975 and reduced the gross profit rate in manufacturing from about 23 to 13 percent. Thus a government's decision about the value of its national currency can reduce the rate of profits substantially—in this case by over 40 percent at a stroke.

Advocates of flexibility hold that wages should be reduced in order to compensate for this decline in profits. Of course, we are never told that wages should go up when profits go up: flexibility always works one way.

Governments and international organizations advocating flexibility should be asked:

1. If low wages mean more employment, how is it that some countries, such as Sweden, with the highest wages have the lowest levels of unemployment?
2. How much downward flexibility of age and nonwage costs in developed countries will be necessary in order to compete with the wages and conditions obtaining in less-developed countries (LDCs)?
3. What advantages will accrue to workers in developing countries as a result of increasing access to markets in developed countries for the exports they produce? To date, increasing access to developed countries' markets does not appear to have reduced unemployment greatly in LDCs or to have improved the miserable conditions under which these workers live.
4. Real wages in LDCs are already flexible in a downward direction, and in most of them social security is virtually nonexistent. How has this helped to solve unemployment in these countries?
5. What steps can be taken to ensure that trade expansion is accompanied by parallel improvements in the incomes and living standards of workers in LDCs?

[2] See International Confederation of Free Trade Unions, *1983 World Economic Review.*

6. How far will real wages have to be cut in both developed and developing countries in order to secure the desired "adjustment" to the new international division of labor?

CONSENSUS POLICIES: TWO COUNTRIES' EXPERIENCE

If we accept that social and economic consensus is a desirable objective of state policy, we can only deplore that many European countries seem further from such general agreement than at any time in the last quarter century. To what extent did governments' adoption of restrictive economic policies reflect the failure of the trade union movement to come up with acceptable policy alternatives? Was it inevitable that the decision about which section of the community in the importing countries should bear the burden of increased oil prices after 1973 would lead to a heightening of social and economic tensions and the imposition by European governments of more or less draconian solutions? Such questions will probably remain unanswerable.

However, such social democratic countries as Sweden and Austria have shown that income distribution favoring capital through policies of real wage cuts and social security deregularization is not the only way of conducting economic affairs. The former has achieved one of the world's highest standards of living as a result of social-consensus policies guided by social democratic governments in power for half a century, apart from a recent six-year interregnum. Unemployment in Sweden is now running at three percent compared with a total European average of over 13 percent. Despite this low level of unemployment, inflation is only currently seven percent a year. Swedish labor organizations have agreed to restrict pay rises to five percent (including wage drift) in 1985, with a guarantee of a real wage increase. As a result of social consensus, the Swedes have maintained full employment in recent years without causing excessive inflation. At the same time, government-imposed solutions in some other countries have failed.

Austria has also been successful in maintaining a climate of cooperation and concertation, avoiding the confrontation prevalent elsewhere.

> The social partners . . . agree on a broad framework of the socio-economic policies which can, in turn, be the subject of discussion and consultation with government, so that there emerges a broad consensus which receives wide support at least for its main outlines. The social partners themselves modify to some extent their own behaviour in the light of the requirements of government.[3]

The key institution in Austrian incomes policy is the Joint Commission for Prices and Incomes. This is made up of eight representatives from trade unions, business and agriculture, and four from government. There is a subcommittee on incomes in which trade unions and employers sit, which has the power to approve or reject negotiations on new collective agreements on wages and salaries. There is also a subcommittee on prices that reviews all price increases. An agreement with employers ensures that only price increases approved by the subcommittee will be applied. Two-thirds of all consumer goods are covered by this by direct government price fixing. The

[3] H. Suppanz and D. Robinson, *Prices and Incomes Policy: the Austrian Experience*, Paris, OECD, 1972.

Commission for Prices and Incomes has the task of settling any issues that cannot be resolved in the two subcommittees. The system facilitates control over the level of productivity, costs and profits, and is thus able to limit prices to levels justified by cost increases. The system enabled consumer price increases to be limited to an average of 5.1 percent per year between 1978 and 1983, one of the lowest rates in Europe.

WAGE INDEXATION

Among the principal targets of those advocating flexibility are schemes indexing wages to increases in retail prices. Such schemes have been adopted in the postwar period in several European countries, including Italy, Belgium and Denmark.

In February 1984, the Italian government tabled two decree-laws containing a series of measures aiming to bring inflation below 10 percent and to promote employment. This move came after the main Communist-controlled union refused to endorse the government's proposals for a renewal of the 1983 social pact on labor costs, thereby creating a serious crisis within the ranks of the unified trade union confederation, which is composed of the three main union groups, CISL, UIL and CGIL. When the new decrees failed to pass in February, then lapsed because of parliamentary filibusters, they were reintroduced in April. The first, dealing with Italy's pay indexation system, the *scala mobile*, and family allowances, became law on June 14, 1984. This decree cuts by four percentage points the automatic cost-of-living increases for a period of six months. In return, it increases family allowances. The indexation system returned to normal in August 1984. The government also agreed to hold down rises in government-controlled prices and charges to below 10 percent, and to freeze scheduled rent increases until the end of 1984.

The second decree, concerning job creation, deals with the introduction of "solidarity contracts" to promote job sharing, employment-training contracts and part-time work. This decree has been operative since February 1984. The Italian Communist party subsequently initiated the constitutional procedure of a national referendum to repeal the decree-law's effects on the wage-indexation system.

Belgium was the only country in which wage indexation previously almost entirely compensated for price increases. However, it is frequently forgotten that wage indexation affects gross pay, and that after tax and social security deductions some wages and salaries lagged behind price increases. But with the coalition government's[4] austerity measures, which in February 1982 introduced a wage freeze for workers earning above the minimum wage (27,357 francs a month), wage indexation was suspended for three months. For the second half of 1982, it was allowed only up to the minimum wage level. Under the previous wage-indexation system, total pay rose by a certain percentage, varying from industry to industry, whenever the index of retail

[4] Social Christians and Liberals. The Socialists, who had participated in the previous government, withdrew in March 1980 because of their opposition to tampering with the indexation system.

426

prices rose by a given percentage. In 1983, it was planned to return to this original indexation system. The government subsequently decided, however, that in 1983 and 1984 there would be no pay increases above those resulting from a new system of wage indexation. This modified system ensured that compensation for price increased would no longer be paid in the month that the consumer index reached a certain level, but workers would have to wait four months before they were compensated. It goes without saying that this greatly increased the loss in real wages.

On February 17, 1984, the Belgian parliament approved a new austerity program, designed to reduce the budget deficit from 500 to 300 billion francs over three years without increasing unemployment which, at the end of February 1984, stood at 12.5 percent of the working population. One of the essential elements of this program is to impose new "wage moderation" measures on all Belgian workers. Between 1984 and 1987, they will lose two percent of any pay increase linked to the retail price index. This measure affects all workers, including those in the public sector and the self-employed. In addition to this general two percent reduction, the government also decided on a general 3.5 percent reduction in the public service payroll. This will be done by introducing new forms of part-time work, with a corresponding reduction in wages, and by cutting jobs. Part-time work and job sharing will be encouraged in all sectors. Social security benefits will also be partially deindexed, pending a complete revision of the system in 1985. To stimulate employment, tax concessions will be given to companies modernizing or converting plant. At the same time, companies making exceptionally large profits, especially as a result of wage cutbacks, will have to reinvest in Belgium or even make the money available to the treasury without interest. The industry-level collective agreements that were concluded in 1983–84 under the government's austerity measures were extended for 1985–86. All wage and salary increases outside the indexation system are forbidden for a further period of two years. The generalization of the 38-hour week will be subject to collective bargaining between the parties.

In Denmark, the government suspended the wage-indexation system for the duration of the 1983–85 collective agreements. Indexation of sickness and unemployment benefits was also suspended. A provisional central agreement was signed in February 1983 between the unions and the employers' organizations to cover the period following the government's pay freeze (October 1982–March 1983) until February 1985.[5]

FORMAL OBJECTIONS TO INDEXATION

In November 1983, the ILO Committee on Freedom of Association examined trade union complaints concerning Australia, Canada (Quebec) and Belgium. The three cases involved wage freeze measures taken by the governments concerned. First was a simple wage freeze law passed in Australia; then a Canadian law extending collective wage agreements by three years, thereby maintaining wages at their previous level; lastly, there were the

[5]*Pay Developments in Western Europe, 1982–83*, European Trade Union Institute (ETUI), June 1983.

Belgian wage moderation decrees referred to above. The complaining trade unions considered that this type of legislation constitutes an infringement of freedom of association, since it suspends the right of recognized organizations of employees to put forward claims regarding their conditions of employment, and it introduces state interference in the machinery for voluntary negotiation between employers' and workers' organizations.

The ILO committee, while agreeing that in a period of financial and economic crisis a government had to take action, emphasized how important it was for the state authorities to refrain from changing the content of freely negotiated collective agreements. Parties to collective bargaining negotiations, for their part, should take into account the major economic and social policy considerations invoked by the government. If, for compelling national economic reasons, a government considers that wages can no longer be fixed by collective bargaining, any restrictions should be introduced as exceptional measures and only to the extent necessary. They should not apply for more than a reasonable period, and they should be accompanied by guarantees protecting the standard of living of workers.

It is precisely these guarantees, in fact, that are lacking at the present time. The only real guarantee of the workers' standard of living is the trade union movement, but this has been weakened by rising unemployment and by governments in many countries enthusiastically redistributing income in favor of the well-to-do. While real wages have declined, therefore, profits and company directors' emoluments have risen sharply.

A study of international wage indexation made by the French Ministry of Finance[6] demonstrated with the exception of Italy and the United States an almost perfect indexation of wages to consumer prices, irrespective of whether there was formal indexation in the countries concerned. In another study on indexation for the Council of Europe, Jacques Lecaillon commented:

> The relaxation or abolition of statutory or contractual provisions may not be sufficient to attenuate or remove what are seen as the undesirable effects of the adjustment of wages to the cost of living; in many instances it is the behavior of employer and trade unions themselves that ought to change.[7]

This study would have been even more valuable had it shown how much wages rose above the levels established by the system of formal indexation, in order to indicate the part due to collective bargaining at industrial or firm level. In Belgium, for instance, that figure is very small indeed—about one percent a year. This may be taken as an indication that where effective systems of price indexation exist, they have a tendency to replace collective bargaining for all intents and purposes. Lecaillon points out, however, that indexation contributes to social harmony. "It reduces the number of disputes, for it is easier to negotiate the mechanisms of indexation, once the principle has been accepted, than the level of wages."[8] A further advantage of indexation is that it establishes an agreed basis for wage increases—*past* price

[6]*Mécanismes et enjeux de l'indexation*, June 1981.
[7]*Effects of Mechanisms for Adjusting Wages to the Cost of Living During a Recession and in Times of Economic Growth*, Strasbourg, 1983, p. 7.
[8]Ibid.

increases. Thus indexation will tend to reduce that part of wage claims that is based upon *future* price increases, although it is debatable to what extent this element is in fact embodied in wage claims.

History

The principal defect of incomes policies is that only rarely do they adequately cover nonwage incomes. Restraint in wages, therefore, usually leads to a burst in profits and dividend distribution to shareholders, accompanied by appreciable increases in share values. While workers' incomes are circumscribed, those of shareholders—a minority in all countries—tend to increase. Not only do their incomes increase, but so do their assets through increases in share prices. Thus the longer a period of wage restraint lasts, the greater is the redistribution of incomes and assets in favor of the well-off. Any equitable system must ensure that workers' sacrifices under an incomes policy are not automatically converted into gains for capital holders.

In the great international debate about incomes policies during the 1960s, TUAC sought to develop a reasoned analysis of how workers might share in asset formation. A trade union seminar under OECD auspices was held in May 1967 in Florence. Its analysis, by Derek Robinson and Solomon Barkin, rather optimistically concluded that the trade unions, "having accepted, often painfully and with considerable disillusionment, that they cannot secure the degree of economic equity they believe desirable through orthodox collective bargaining over money wages, are seeking to attain it through a combination of bargaining over money wages and wealth assets."[9]

Unions had hoped to change the distribution of capital assets and other wealth through collective bargaining, but had come to accept that this was impossible. Unions had also put faith in social security schemes and taxation, but recognized the limits of these and, in the case of taxation, the possibilities of evasion and avoidance. The unions also regarded social security systems as an inalienable acquired social right and certainly did not foresee systematic governmental attempts during the 1980s to cut back benefits, which were portrayed as an onerous burden on entrepreneurs. The worst, perhaps, is yet to come.

The only country with experience of capital-sharing plans at the time of the 1967 OECD seminar, was West Germany. Under its Capital Formation Act of 1961, individual savings up to 312 marks per year were made tax deductible. These funds were to be made available for loans to the employing company, for the purchase of shares, or for housing. A change in the law was later sought by the unions, so they could negotiate about capital savings schemes. The Capital Savings Act of 1965 gave West German unions this right. The scheme remained, until recently, of limited effect, since it enabled West German workers to deduct only relatively small annual savings. Under the latest Capital Savings Act, however, operative from January 1,

[9] See its final report, *Workers' Negotiated Plans for Capital Formation*, Florence, OECD, 1970, p. 152.

1984, a worker may acquire, over six years, a capital of over 11,000 marks, to which he or she has contributed only 6,000. Over 10 years, as much as 24,460 marks may be accumulated.

At the 1967 OECD seminar, only two other countries' trade union movements supported capital savings schemes: Italy's CISL and the Netherlands'. But the idea made little headway in these two countries, nor was it successful in Denmark. To support reindustrialization and reduce unemployment, the Danish Social Democratic government proposed in 1981 that the constraints on supplementary pension funds be relaxed and that a substantial portion of these funds be directed to industrial investment. The proposed plan was defeated in parliament in November 1981, then became the focus of general elections held in December, which resulted in the fall of the government.

The Swedish example
Sweden was, in the event, the only country to succeed in emulating West Germany, although its scheme took a different form. Despite Sweden's success in maintaining full employment and controlling inflation, as well as in securing a more just society based upon a fairer income distribution, it has signally failed to deal with the problem of the concentration of wealth in a few hands. "One percent of all Swedish households hold 75 percent of all corporate shares owned by households, and another 10 percent hold all the rest, leaving 89 percent of the population with no shares at all."[10] Swedish trade unions set three goals for wage earner funds: they should increase capital formation, increase wage earners' influence on corporate decisions and prevent the distribution of wealth from becoming more unequal. Proposals for wage earners' funds were first put to the union congress in 1976, and were subsequently discussed in a book by the union economist Rudolf Meidner. They were taken up by the union congress and the Social Democratic government, but the Swedish electorate was not ready for such changes, and the proposals were thought to be a contributory factor in the defeat of the government in 1976.

Five regional funds, however, have since been established, each of which will receive a maximum of 400 million kronor a year derived from profit sharing and a levy on the total wages bill. Thus 2 billion kronor in all will be paid into the funds each year. They will be linked to the present pension funds, through which they will receive funds for investment. The five regional funds are managed by boards of nine government-appointed members, including five from trade unions. These boards will constitute five new management boards within the National Insurance Pension Fund. Twenty percent of surplus profits will be paid into the fund. Between 1.5 and 2 billion kronor will be transferred to the regional funds each year from this profit sharing. For companies with profits up to 500,000 kronor, six percent of their total payments for wages and salaries are exempt from profit sharing. The financing is then topped up by a 0.2 percent levy on the total wage bill within the norms of the pension system. This levy provides 0.6 billion kronor per year. Workers in the public sector help finance the funds by

[10]R. Spant, *Investment of Unions' Pension Funds: The Case of Sweden*, AFL-CIO Pension Fund Seminar, January 19, 1981.

means of the wage-bill levy. The regional boards are not restricted to investing the money in their own region. The funds cannot, however, own more than 49 percent of a company, together with the pension fund. Up to 1990, the five regional funds will have around 14 to 17 billion kronor to invest in companies, a sum representing approximately five to six percent of the total value of shares on the Swedish stock exchange. Real interest of at least three percent will be paid back to the pension fund system, as will income from the funds' investments. A link is thus created between the funds and each individual worker.[11]

The Wage Earner Fund Law was passed by the Swedish parliament in December 1983. It should be emphasized that the new Swedish scheme is not a company-level, but a nationwide profit sharing scheme. Some existing company profit sharing schemes, however, have enabled employees to own a significant part of the shares. The employees of the Handelsbank, for example, are its biggest shareholder. It should also be pointed out that the Swedish national supplementary pension fund already has substantial investments in industry. The fact that there are no company-level pension schemes in Sweden promotes job mobility. This aim is also served by the new employees' savings scheme.

It is, of course, too early to assess the effects of all this. According to the *Financial Times* (September 4, 1984), however, as the stock market began to mark time at the beginning of 1984, brokers began to see the scheme as "a major potential source of new capital." The Swedish press announced at the end of January 1985 that Swedish business people were eager to secure loans from the employee investment funds. Four out of the five regional funds announced profits at the beginning of 1985 for the previous six-month period. They will thus be able to contribute 10 million kronor to the supplementary pension scheme. The parliamentary opposition to the present Social Democratic government, however, threatened to end the scheme if it had obtained power in the general election of September 1985.

The Swedish government, nevertheless, takes the view that international developments over the past decade—especially concerning unemployment—have reflected the gradual abandonment of the increasingly difficult task of economic stabilization. The government feels that European governments have capitulated before the difficulty of the task, and have acted generally in the following way:

1. Policy is made to concentrate more and more on raising profits and restraining wage costs.
2. Subsequently, employment and income distribution aims are abandoned.
3. Finally, high unemployment is actively used as a means of gaining acceptance for high profits and low wage costs.

Employee investment funds can, in the view of the Swedish government,

1. reduce conflicts about income distribution, inflation and wage drift, and promote acceptance of high profits;
2. increase the flow of risk capital; and

[11] See *Trade Unions and Collective Capital Formation*, ETUI publication, 1983.

3. make possible a greater share of profits for workers and an influence over how they are used.

Lost opportunities

What would have been the benefit of such plans had they been put into operation in several countries over the last couple of decades? One of the prime weaknesses of our current economies is that workers have no savings to fall back on. In all developed countries—with the exception of Japan— workers have derisory amounts put aside in savings. Moreover, shareholding is limited to a small percentage of the population. The advantage of workers' savings schemes is that purchasing power is withdrawn from the economy, but instead of being converted into increased assets for a minority of share-holders, it is changed into increased assets for the majority of the population (wage earners). This cannot but have a stabilizing effect upon social and industrial relations, since in the absence of full employment it provides a source of income to supplement unemployment pay and redundancy allow-ances (if any) or a nest egg to be used for house purchase or other expenses. Moreover, it may be seen as a means of securing a source of income for retirement, since in many European countries retirement pensions are still inadequate and are currently under attack by governments. In view of the growing percentage of retired people in European countries as we reach the end of the 20th century, it is recognized almost everywhere that it will be increasingly difficult to finance old-age pensions—especially since short-term employment prospects may be increasingly gloomy because technologi-cal change is cutting manpower requirements.

In the past it was sometimes argued by employers that workers' savings schemes were disguised wage increases, and by some trade unions that they were a means of reducing workers' incomes. In fact, if workers' saving schemes were subject to collective bargaining procedures, it is more than likely that because such schemes would increase the volume of investment capital, employers would be willing to devote a greater total amount (wages + profits allocation) to wage savings schemes than would otherwise be the case. Such an outcome would clearly depend upon the collective bargaining strength of the union as well as upon the goodwill of employers. The existence of workers' savings funds generally would probably lead to greater capital investment, economic growth and therefore full employment.

The principal reason for the restrictive economic, fiscal and monetary policies of governments in recent years has been a desire to restore lagging profits. The disastrous consequences are well known. By early 1985, un-employment in the European Community was running at 11 percent, or double that of four years previously. As well as increasing human misery and social tensions, government policies in Europe have led to economic havoc. Vast sums have been lost in sacrificed production, in payments to maintain the unemployed and in reduced world trade. Workers have suffered substantial reductions in real wages and real incomes, because of the com-bined impact of reduced wage increases, continued inflation, and income tax and social security payment increases. The unions' collective bargaining strength has undoubtedly been greatly weakened. It is at least arguable that workers' savings plans, had they been adopted in a number of key European countries, might have made possible a recovery of investment that would so have changed the economic outlook as to enable governments to avoid the drastic and damaging economic remedies they adopted. Moreover, workers' savings plans would most probably have secured a substantial shift in the distribution of wealth.

Some readers will undoubtedly say that workers' savings plans are mere reforms—tinkering with the system, and so on. Yet do they honestly believe that many European electorates are ready to adopt radical socialist or other solutions at the present time? All the evidence is to the contrary. Even if a particular government succeeds in holding back real wage increases in one country in order to compete with lower export prices in international markets, other countries will do likewise. Thus we shall be faced with a downward spiral of wages and purchasing power. Indeed, it might be argued that this has already begun.

CONCLUSION

Contemporary political, social and economic policies have not yet begun seriously to reflect, and grapple with, the convergence of a whole group of serious new problems that impinge upon employment and incomes: rapid technological change; expansion in international trade; increasing international mobility of fixed and liquid capital; increasing international mobility of manpower; increasing concentration and rationalization of firms. This theoretical and policy void has been filled by simplistic and outmoded recipes to cut wages and social security benefits and, in the United States and Britain and to a lesser extent in some other countries, to hamstring the trade unions. Rapid technological change and export drives by developing countries and the newly industrialized countries, with whose price levels European countries are unable at present to compete, lead to increases in unemployment. Sooner or later we shall be obliged to adopt modern European policies to preserve, as well as to create, jobs. This will require coordinated industrial, technological and trade policies, without which extremist political groups, on the Right and Left, will probably become much stronger. In the meantime, the income-distributive effects of workers' savings plans would be a way of making the present anarchic economic system more tolerable.

FURTHER READING

Barkin, Solomon, ed. *Worker Militancy and its Consequences: The Changing Climate of Western Industrial Relations.* New York: Praeger, 1983.

Blackaby, Frank. *An Incomes Policy for Britain.* London: Heinemann, 1972.

Boltho, Andrea. *The European Economy Growth and Crisis.* Oxford: Oxford University Press, 1982.

Commission of the European Communities. *Annual Economic Review 1984–85.* Brussels, 1984.

———. *Employee Participation in Asset Formation.* Brussels, 1979.

Edgren, Gösta, et al. *Wage Formation and the Economy.* London: Allen and Unwin, 1973.

Emerson, Michael. *Europe's Stagflation*. Oxford: Carendon Press, 1984.

Harbridge, Raymond J. *Challenge or Disaster? Industrial Relations in the 1980s*. Oxford: Clarendon Press, 1981.

Keynes, John Maynard. *The General Theory of Employment, Interest and Money*. 1936.

Meidner, Rudolf. *Employee Investment Funds: An approach to Collective Capital Formation*. London: Allen and Unwin, 1978.

OECD. *Collective Bargaining and Government Policies in Ten OECD Countries*. Paris, 1979.

———. *Economic Growth 1960–1970*. Paris, 1966.

———. *Wages and Labour Mobility*. Paris, 1965.

Thurow, Lester C. *Macro-Economics, Prices and Quantities*. Englewood Cliffs, New Jersey: Prentice-Hall, 1983.

Winton, J. R. *Lloyds Bank Review*, No. 145, October 1976.

WESTERN EUROPE'S ROLE IN WORLD TRADE

JOHN PINDER

WESTERN Europe has been the prime mover in shifting the basis of the world economic system from the traditional self-sufficient village to the interdependent global village. Since international trade is a principal product of this shift, it is not surprising that Western Europe still has a larger share of world trade than any other region. Europeans had already established a global trading network during the age of discovery; and with the industrial revolution, they converted this network into a world economic system in which industrial nations, most of them European, bought materials from, and sold manufactures to, the rest of the world. But the ability to develop industries is not a European monopoly. First the United States, then Japan and now many other countries have become strong exporters of industrial products. The world is in transition from the imperial system, in which manufactures were exchanged for materials, toward a more equal interdependence based mainly on the exchange of manufactures. This is the economic context in which Western Europe's role in world trade must be understood.

The political context is also of European origin: the modern state. The very term *international trade* presupposes a nation-state, with an interest in the trade that crosses its frontiers. The imperial system was organized mainly by European nation-states and gave them the economic space for their industrial development. But in the first half of the 20th century the disaster of national autarky, sandwiched between two world wars, showed that the nation-state was no longer a viable basis for organizing Western Europe's economy. Europeans therefore created the European Community (EC), through which the greater part of trade within Western Europe is conducted without encountering traditional trade barriers, and which regulates, through its common commercial policy, the greater part of Western Europe's trade with the rest of the world. As far as trade is concerned, the functions which elsewhere are performed by nation-states are in Western Europe predominantly the responsibility of the EC.

About one-quarter of the world total of international trade is trade among the various Western European countries, and this is usually included in statistical tables of world trade. But the trade within Western Europe is not directly relevant to the subject of this chapter. A table has therefore

435

Table 1
INTERREGIONAL WORLD TRADE 1982 (as % of total)

Destination / Origin	Advanced Market Economies				Third World				Soviet Group	Unspecified	World Total
	Western Europe	North America	Japan	Australia, New Zealand, South Africa	West Asia	South and Southeast Asia	Latin America	Africa			
Advanced Market Economies											
Western Europe	...	5	1	1	5	2	2	4	3	1	23
North America	6	...	2	1	1	2	3	1	1	—	17
Japan	2	3	...	1	1	3	1	—	1	—	12
Australia, New Zealand, South Africa	1	1	1	...	—	—	—	—	—	—	3
Third World											
Western Asia	5	1	2	—	...	2	1	—	1	—	13
South and Southeast Asia	2	3	2	—	1	...	—	—	1	—	10
Latin America	2	4	—	—	—	—	...	—	1	—	7
Africa	4	1	1	—	—	—	—	...	—	—	6
Soviet Group	4	—	1	—	1	1	1	—	...	1	9
World Total	26	18	10	4	10	11	8	5	6	2	100

Source: Calculated from GATT, *International Trade 1982/83*, Geneva, 1983, Table A23.
Note: Intra-regional trade has been excluded.
... not applicable; — less than 0.5 percent.

436

been constructed (Table 1) which excludes Western Europe's internal trade and, likewise, the trade within other regional groups.

More than three-quarters of Western Europe's trade with every other region is accounted for by the EC, with the sole exception of the Soviet group, in relation to which the EC's imports are two-thirds and the EC's exports nearly three-fifths of Western Europe's total. The EC's share of interregional trade will become yet more preponderant now that the Community has been enlarged to 12 members. In considering Western European trade policies toward other parts of the world the EC's policies will be used as a proxy for Western European policies as a whole; this will show how far one of the aims of the EC has been fulfilled, in that a common policy based on common institutions and instruments has created in Western Europe one of the world's two great trading powers.

TRADE WITH THE UNITED STATES

Nine-tenths of the world's interregional trade is shown in the first four rows and the first four left-hand columns of Table 1, which report the trade of the advanced market economies represented in the Organization for Economic Cooperation and Development (OECD). While Japan has rapidly increased its share to about one-tenth of interregional imports and exports, Western Europe's share is still around one-quarter and North America's is not far short of one-fifth; the United States is of course the dominant trader in North America as the EC is in Western Europe.

It appears that the world trading system, over the last two decades, has been led by a diarchy of the United States and the EC. In the earlier years after World War II it was far from evident that this would be the case. The United States towered over the world economy in those years, partly because the European economies had been shattered by the war but partly also because the several states of Western Europe, not yet bound by common institutions and policies, could offer no political counterweight to the United States. The international monetary and trading system, based on Bretton Woods and the General Agreement on Tariffs and Trade (GATT), were therefore established under firm American leadership.

These institutions, created by the Americans for the international system, served Western Europe well, as the revival of the Western European economy demonstrates. But it was the EC, an institution the Europeans themselves established, which enabled them to counterbalance the Americans in terms of trading policy. This was first clearly demonstrated by the Kennedy Round of tariff negotiations in GATT. Following the establishment of the EC by Belgium, France, Italy, Luxembourg, the Netherlands and West Germany in 1958, the United States, whose partners in GATT had previously all been greatly inferior in strength, was now confronted by a trading unit of equal size and, with the EC's common external tariff, equal bargaining power. President John F. Kennedy's reaction was the Trade Expansion Act of 1962, which enabled the United States and the EC, followed by their international trading partners, to negotiate cuts of about one-third in their import duties. The Tokyo Round, which achieved similar results in the 1970s after the

EC had been enlarged to include Britain, Denmark and Ireland, confirmed the EC's status as joint leader with the United States of international trade negotiations.

With tariffs roughly halved since the 1950s, the diarchy has evidently guided world trading policy in a liberal direction. But the series of recessions that started in the 1970s has placed the liberal system under serious strain. There has been constant friction between the EC and the United States over trading issues. The United States has been irked by the EC's common agricultural policy (even if the EC remains the largest export market for American farmers) as well as by some aspects of the common commercial policy; and the EC has protested against U.S. restrictions on imports of steel and some other manufactures. But restrictions have proliferated on the imports of both the EC and the United States from other countries rather than on the trade between them, which has remained largely open. It is the dollar rather than U.S. trading policy that has caused the major problem for European trade.

Whereas the EC has become a trading superpower by creating the common tariff as a powerful instrument of its common commercial policy, its common instruments of monetary policy remain relatively weak. Western European exchange rates and interest rates therefore remain heavily dependent on U.S. economic policy, transmitted through the international currency and capital markets. A strong dollar has been helpful to European trade, although protectionist pressures in the United States are the other side of that particular coin. But the high interest rates that have accompanied the high U.S. budget deficit may have a more profound effect on Europe's place in the world trading system.

One motive for establishing the EC was a desire to match the size of the U.S. market and hence, it was hoped, the power of American industry in sectors where scale is important. Although Europeans managed to become competitive with Americans in many industrial sectors, the fear of being overpowered by American high technology has persisted from the 1960s, when Jean-Jacques Servan-Schreiber wrote *Le Défi américain*, to the 1980s, when the European Parliament's report on the competitiveness of Community industry gave expression to a widespread concern. Europeans fear that their hard-won success in competition with U.S. industry will be vitiated by a failure to compete with the Americans and the Japanese in the key industries of the future, those based in particular on microelectronic technologies. The weakness of European industrial investment is one of the disquieting signs that Europe is not reducing the American or Japanese lead; and the high interest rates are a most significant cause of inadequate investment. Fears about the future health of Euro-American trade relations stem more from a relative weakness in the new technologies, and hence from the effects of economic and monetary policy on general economic development, than from frictions and quarrels between the EC and the United States over trade policy as such.

TRADE WITH JAPAN

Europeans have been given a salutary shock by their trade with Japan. It is less than two decades since the Japanese were regarded as makers of inferior manufactures produced by cheap labor and sold at cut prices. Japan has now established itself as number one in a series of sectors ranging from cameras through motorcycles, consumer electronics, steel and automobiles to such products as numerically controlled machine tools and robots that are on the leading edge of production technology. The consequence has been continued pressure on European industry in one sector after another, and surpluses of over U.S.$10 billion a year in Japan's trade with Western Europe—and with the EC, for that matter.

The yen has been undervalued in relation to European currencies, and a logical European reaction to the Japanese trade surplus would be to seek to rectify this. But in the absence of powerful common instruments of monetary policy, the EC has relied instead on getting the Japanese to impose voluntary export restrictions (VERs) on those products which hit European manufacturers hardest in their home markets. The formula of VERs circumvents GATT's injunction against import restrictions aimed at a particular trading partner. But the VERs are trade restrictions nevertheless; and Europeans must ask themselves why they have had such frequent recourse to measures that are a confession of competitive weakness as well as a threat to the open trading system.

The answer must be that Japanese companies and Japanese management are superior in the growing number of sectors in which Europeans fear Japanese competition. Japan's success is due not to cheap labor or facile imitation but to greater skill in applying new technology efficiently to make new products that people want to buy. This answer raises the further question whether Europeans can learn from Japan in the future, just as the Japanese learned from Europe in the past; and this leads on to a consideration of differing national attitudes toward Japanese direct investment, which has been welcomed in Britain but criticized in France. It also raises the question of how far other countries that are following Japan in the development of industry may also be able to convert an advantage of cheap labor into a superiority of technology and management.

TRADE WITH CANADA, AUSTRALIA AND NEW ZEALAND

The problem of trade between Western Europe and the countries of European settlement in the Commonwealth is quite different, however. Traditionally, these countries sold food and raw materials to Western Europe and bought manufactures; their major European trading partner was Britain. After Britain joined the EC, the sales of raw materials continued largely undisturbed because the EC, like Britain, offers an open market for most such materials. But the sales of agricultural products immediately became a bone of contention. The EC's common agricultural policy, with its tendency to self-sufficiency in the produce of temperate-zone agriculture, clashed with the traditional exports of such foodstuffs from Canada, Australia and New Zealand to Britain. The consequent loss of markets had no great impact on the trade of Canada and Australia as a whole, because this trade had come to account for a minor share of their total exports, however significant this might be for particular areas or for individual producers. But New Zealand has depended heavily on its sales to Britain of butter and lamb in particular. Special arrangements were negotiated, when Britain joined the Community, for a continuation of part of this trade. But the trade has nevertheless declined, with consequent damage to New Zealand's economy. With the EC's butter surplus a perennial problem, the special arrangements are always under threat when they periodically come up for renewal.

Given the complementarity between those countries with their natural resources and the EC with its economic strength, and given the cultural affinity between them, there is scope to develop a very strong economic relationship over the longer term. But in the first decade of British membership of the Community, this potential has been largely obscured by friction over agricultural policy.

TRADE WITH ASIA AND LATIN AMERICA

Western Europe's trade with the Third World is spread widely throughout Africa, Asia and Latin America. As Table 1 shows, Western Europe is nearly twice as big a trading partner for the Third World as is North America; and the EC is, by the same token, a much bigger trading partner for the developing countries than for the United States.

The spread of Western Europe's trade with the South has its roots in mercantile and imperial history; and the pattern of exchange between strong industrial Europeans and weak colonial producers of primary products persisted into the second half of this century. But in recent years two new factors have at least gone some way to redress the balance: the formation of the Organization of Petroleum Exporting Countries (OPEC); and the emergence of the newly industrializing countries (NICs) as powerful exporters of a growing range of industrial products.

The impact of the oil exporters' cartel comes out clearly in Table 1, which shows trade in each direction between Western Europe and West Asia at five percent of total interregional world trade—exceeded only, and only by a small margin, by the trade between Western Europe and North America. The exports from West Asia to Western Europe are predominantly oil, while West Asian countries' imports are industrial products that they buy with their export earnings. Until 1973 the price of oil was heavily influenced by the U.S. and European oil companies. But the governments of oil-producing countries were securing increasing control over their national resources, and in 1973 OPEC seized the opportunity of a tight market to raise the price of oil fourfold, with further big increases in subsequent years.

Higher prices would, in any market system, have followed the pressure of growing demand on higher-cost marginal resources. But it was the shift of market power from an oligopsony of oil companies more sensitive to consumers' interests, to a cartel of exporters dedicated to producers' interests, that caused the oil price explosion. The consequent wave of cost-push inflation, demand deflation, trade deficits and international debts have caused great turbulence in the world economy since 1974.

Some of the EC countries initially reacted to this unprecedented show of strength on the part of Third World trading partners by seeking separate arrangements to secure their oil supplies in the new market conditions. They soon made efforts to form a common EC policy; but those efforts have not been very effective. The most significant aim is to reduce dependence on imports of oil, and oil consumption has indeed been restrained; but little of this restraint has been due to the common policy. The EC has also tried to stabilize its relations with leading oil exporters. through a Euro–Arab dialogue; but this seems to have had scant influence on trade. The EC continues to be highly dependent on Middle East oil supplies and exposed to damage by supply cuts or sharp price rises, even if a weaker market has since 1983 caused financial problems for the less richly endowed OPEC members (see Table 2).

While the producers of no other commodity have been able to turn the tables on the industrialized North in the way OPEC has done, another group of countries has shown that Northern hegemony need not be a permanent feature of the world economy. Just as Japan rose to supply one-tenth of total world exports of manufactures, so since the 1970s a group of NICs has emerged to export manufactures on a similar scale. Most of these NICs are Asian or Latin American: Brazil, Mexico, India, Hong Kong, Singapore, South Korea and Taiwan are among the most important ones; and the EC is a very important market for them. By 1982, the EC imported $19.8 billion of manufactures from developing countries other than the oil exporters —more than one-third of total EC imports from that group. The labor-intensive sectors of clothing and footwear still provide the bulk of this trade. But the element which, following the example of Japan, has given Europeans cause for disquiet is the success of a number of NICs in mainstream capital-intensive industries such as steel, shipbuilding, machine tools and some branches of electronics. Many Europeans have come to fear an ineluctable process of deindustrialization as low-wage producers, acquiring up-to-date technology and modern skills, compete the Europeans out of European and international markets.

The days when industrial Europeans could dominate Asian and Latin American producers of primary products are not likely to return. But it is far from certain that the Asians and Latin Americans will sweep all before them as the Japanese have done. The new industrial revolution, based on microelectronic technologies, requires not just the application of mature technologies that can be bought off the shelf, let alone cheap and plentiful labor, but rather the managerial and technological skills to devise constant improvements for new production systems. Some East Asian countries may follow the Japanese in doing this better than the Europeans. But it seems probable that Europeans will sustain an advantage in these skills for many years to come, offsetting the low wages of South Asians and Latin Americans. The EC, which pioneered the generalized system of preferences for imports from developing countries and has adopted more liberal policies than the United States toward development and Third World debts, will probably hold its own in relation to the NICs. But so long as Europeans continue to lack confidence in their economic future, restrictions will remain more important than preferences and liberal attitudes in the EC's treatment of imports from the NICs.

Table 2
PROPORTION OF OTHER REGIONS' TRADE WITH WESTERN EUROPE IN 1982
(Percentages of each region's interregional exports and imports)

	North America	Japan	Australia, New Zealand, South Africa	West Africa	South and Southeast Asia	Latin America	Africa	Soviet Group	World Total
Exports to Western Europe	33.4	15.7	24.8	37.7	19.4	29.3	60.8	49.0	25.2
Imports from Western Europe	26.5	6.7	36.4	49.3	19.1	23.1	59.4	45.6	22.5

TRADE WITH AFRICA

There are few NICs in Africa south of the Sahara. It was, moreover, in Africa that the founding members of the EC had their strongest imperial connections. So it was here that the EC established a special link with EC member countries' former colonies, first in Part IV of the Treaty of Rome, then in the Yaoundé Convention, both of which offered free entry into the Community for the bulk of the African signatories' exports as well as aid from a European development fund. When Britain joined the Community, this arrangement was renegotiated and widened to include almost the whole of Africa as well as Commonwealth countries in the Caribbean and the Pacific, and it was given the new name of the Lomé Convention.

The African, Caribbean and Pacific (ACP) signatories to the Lomé Convention have, then, preferential access to the EC market compared with other Third World countries in Asia and Latin America. But the paucity of NICs among them shows that they have not yet been able to use this advantage in the interests of modern economic development. Africa remains, moreover, more dependent than any other region on its trade with Western Europe, which accounts for three-fifths of both its exports and imports. The Lomé Convention certainly offers some benefits for the Africans, but it has neither helped to reduce their dependence on Europe nor, despite provisions relating to industrial cooperation, has it had much impact on their industrial growth. The Convention has, perhaps, reflected a backward-looking attitude on the part of Europeans, more concerned to conserve certain past relationships than to build their relationships with the growth points in the international economy.

TRADE WITH THE SOVIET UNION AND EASTERN EUROPE

The trade of the Soviet group is, after that of Africa, the most oriented to Western Europe, which accounts for nearly half the group's exports and imports. The Soviet group looms much less large, however, in Western Europe's trade, accounting for only 13 percent of Western Europe's exports to other regions in 1982 and providing only 17 percent of Western European imports. Three-quarters of Soviet exports to Western Europe are oil and gas, and this gave rise in the early 1980s to a dispute between some EC member countries and the United States. The Americans expressed hostility to the construction of a gas pipeline from Siberia to Western Europe, on the grounds that West Germany and some other countries would become too dependent on Soviet supplies of energy. The Europeans' response was that they could weather any reduction of those supplies and that the trade, so far from being a cause of destabilization, would help to stabilize East–West relations (see Table 3).

Apart from Soviet oil and gas, the EC is indeed very little dependent on its imports from the Soviet group, which could for the most part be readily replaced by competing products from industrialized countries or the Third World. The fact that the EC imports more from Sweden or from Switzerland than from the whole Soviet group shows, indeed, how far East–West trade remains below the level that would be natural among market

Table 3
PROPORTION OF WESTERN EUROPE'S TRADE WITH OTHER REGIONS IN 1982
(Percentages of total Western European exports and imports)

	North America	Japan	Australia, New Zealand, South Africa	West Asia	South and Southeast Asia	Latin America	Africa	Soviet Group	Unspecified	World Total
Western European exports	21.4	3.1	5.3	20.0	9.2	7.9	17.0	13.1	2.4	100.0
Western European imports	23.0	7.5	3.1	19.2	8.0	8.6	13.5	17.0	—	100.0

economies. The economies based on centrally directed industries have not been successful in producing competitive manufactures; and this is a more fundamental obstacle to trade than the difference between the systems, with state-trading bureaucracies on the Eastern side confronting many trade restrictions in the West. Less important still has been the much-publicized failure to conclude a trade agreement between the EC and the Soviet group's Council for Mutual Economic Assistance (COMECON). Soviet reluctance to accord juridical recognition to the EC and the Community's suspicion that such an agreement could enhance Soviet influence over the trade of the smaller Eastern European countries have stood in the way of a formal trade pact. It is questionable, however, how far formal agreements would influence the actual level of trade. A major increase in the Eastern Europeans' earnings of hard currencies with which to increase their purchases of Western capital equipment must wait, rather, on the spread of reforms to make the Soviet-bloc economies more market-oriented.

CONCLUSIONS

The EC is a giant in world trade. This survey of its trade relations with each region of the world shows that the European commissioners, the national ministers and those officials, both European and national, who are responsible for the EC's external economic relations lead a far from idle life. On the whole, the EC has remained a stabilizing element in the world trading system, but its stance has been more reactive than creative. The United States has been less ready than it was in earlier postwar years to perform the principal constructive role in an increasingly interdependent international economy, yet the Europeans have been unable to fill the gap. This is partly a matter of ideas and partly of institutions.

Any discussion of the choice of ideas has to be somewhat subjective, so the reader should regard what follows as illustrative rather than authoritative. With imperfect markets typical of the modern economy, pure laisser-faire liberalism is not enough. The market system has to be supplemented by industrial policies to ease adjustment and promote technological development. Free trade must, accordingly, be accompanied by coordinated or common industrial policies. The alternative of a reversion to more insulated national markets is not viable, because that would suffocate the new industrial revolution. If the EC is to prosper in the future, it must not only develop its own common industrial policies but also seek to coordinate them with the industrial policies of other countries.

This is much easier said than done. Coordination of policies is hard enough among the similar economies of the EC members themselves. It is harder between the EC and the United States, where a negative ideological view of industrial policy is more prevalent than in Europe. It is harder still with the Japanese, whose satisfaction with the unique social system that shapes its industrial policies may well be justified. It is remote in relation to most Third World countries, although some, such as Brazil and Mexico, may be heading for a greater compatibility with the European economies. To conceive of policy coordination in relation to the Soviet group, short of far-reaching economic reforms, requires a leap of the imagination. But if it is indeed true that wider markets and coordination of industrial policies will be a condition of future economic progress, the EC needs to be studying the obstacles and developing the concepts that will be needed to overcome them.

One reason for its failure to do so up to now, and for its mainly passive or reactive posture in the world system, is the weakness of its institutions. The will to generate ideas for policy may be lacking if the means to take them up and implement them are felt to be inadequate. The EC's institutions may be strong enough to enable it to react to outside pressures—if often too little and too late; but they have seldom shown themselves strong enough to take decisive initiatives and to sustain strategies in order to accomplish long-term aims. Yet for the EC, with its deep involvement in the world trading system, the development of that system to meet the needs of the future world economy will become increasingly necessary. If the EC fails to produce initiatives and strategies to that end, it is far from sure that others will.

FURTHER READING

Commission of the European Communities. *The Competitiveness of European Community Industry.* Document of the Commission's Services III/387/82. Brussels, March 5, 1982.

Coombes, David. *Politics and Bureaucracy in the European Community.* London: Allen and Unwin, 1970. (Especially chap. 8, "The Kennedy Round Negotiations.")

Economic Commission for Europe. *The European Economy from the 1950s to the 1970s.* New York: United Nations, 1972.

Feld, Werner. *The European Community in World Affairs.* New York: Alfred, 1976.

Freedman, Lawrence, ed. *The Troubled Alliance: Atlantic Relations in the 1980s,* Part II, "The Economic Dimension." London: Heinemann Educational Books for NIESR, PSI and RIIA, 1983.

GATT. *International Trade.* (Annual.)

Pinder, John. "Europe in the World Economy 1920–1970," in Carlo M. Cipolla, ed. *The Fontana Economic History of Europe: Contemporary Economies, Part One.* London: Collins, 1976.

———. "Western Europe and the South: A Question of Political Economy," *Third World Quarterly,* Vol. 6, no. 1, January 1984.

———, and Pinder, Pauline. *The European Community's Policy Towards Eastern Europe.* European Series No. 25. London: Chatham House and PEP, 1975.

Servan-Schreiber, Jean-Jacques. *Le Défi américain.* Paris: Denoel, 1967.

Stevens, Christopher, ed. *The EEC and the Third World: A Survey.* London: Hodder and Stoughton for ODI and IDS. (Annual since 1981.)

Svennilson, I. *Growth and Stagnation in the European Economy.* Geneva: Economic Commission for Europe, 1954.

WESTERN EUROPEAN ECONOMIC AID TO DEVELOPING COUNTRIES

CHRISTOPHER STEVENS

An important feature of European aid to developing nations over the past decade has been the emergence of the EC as a substantial donor. By the early 1980s, for example, over 20 percent of British aid was channeled through EC institutions. This proportion may grow even larger.

Such a change would have important implications for less-developed countries (LDCs). EC aid is more narrowly focused geographically than are the combined programs of the member states, and questions have been raised concerning its efficiency. This chapter examines recent trends in Western European aid and explains the convoluted division of responsibilities among the various participants. It concludes by assessing the case for and against EC aid.

TRENDS IN EC AID

All of the principal Western European aid donors increased their aid between 1970 and the early 1980s (see Table 1). Aid increased on three levels: in terms of the total volume of resources made available; as a proportion of the donors' gross national product (GNP); and as a share of the total given by the industrialized countries.

In 1970, the seven principal Western European aid donors made commitments of some $2.5 billion. This was equivalent to 37 percent of the total aid commitments of the main industrialized countries. By 1981–82, the average annual commitments of the Western European donors had increased to $12.4 billion, and their share of the total had risen to 46 percent. Over the same period, the Western European donors increased their aid as a share of GNP by a greater amount than the industrialized countries as a whole. Nonetheless, only three countries, the Netherlands, Denmark and France, achieved the target set in 1970 by the U.N. General Assembly for donors to give at least 0.7 percent of their GNP as aid. Moreover, in the case of France, the target was only reached if aid to overseas territories and *départements* is included.

The two largest European donors are France (including overseas territories

447

and *départements*) and West Germany, followed at some distance by Britain and the Netherlands. In terms of aid as a percentage of GNP, however, the list is rather different, being headed by the Netherlands, followed by Denmark, France, Belgium and West Germany. The United States has been the largest single donor throughout the period, but the EC as a group is even more important. In 1981–82, the United States provided some 19 percent of world aid, but the EC countries as a group provided 33 per cent. Moreover, while U.S. aid was equivalent to only 0.24 percent of its GNP, the proportionate share of the EC was over twice as great, at 0.53 percent.

The figures in Table 1 may paint too rosy a picture of the aid scene. While the general trend during the 1970s was an increase in aid, this has been reversed during the recession of the 1980s. Changes in policy in Western Europe are only just beginning to make their effect felt on actual commitments of aid. Hence the figures for 1981–82 rather overstate the current volume of European aid, and its share of GNP.

Table 1

WESTERN EUROPEAN OFFICIAL DEVELOPMENT ASSISTANCE (ODA)

	Total ODA ($ million)		ODA as share of GNP	
	1970	1981–82 average	1970	1981–82 average
1. Principal EC donors:				
Belgium	120	540	0.46	0.59
Britain	447	1,990	0.36	0.41
Denmark	59	410	0.38	0.75
France (a)	971	4,060	0.66	0.73
Germany	599	3,170	0.32	0.47
Italy	147	740	0.16	0.22
Netherlands	196	1,490	0.61	1.08
2. DAC total (b)	6,807	26,810	0.34	0.37
3. (1) as a % of (2)	37	46	—	—

Notes:
(a) including overseas departments and territories.
(b) Members of the Organization for Economic Cooperation and Development (OECD) Development Assistance Committee (DAC), which comprises the principal industrialized-country aid donors.
Source: OECD

The large figures in Table 1 may also mislead by giving a false impression of the importance of the flows for LDCs. For most developing countries, official aid remains a small, if potentially useful, contribution to total earnings. India, for example, receives more British bilateral aid than any other country, and in 1983 received £128 million. This was equivalent, however, only to £0.18 per capita (see Table 2). Of course, this partly reflects India's large population, but even Kenya, another favored recipient of British aid, received only £1.83 per head. Only in a small group of countries with tiny populations and, often, special features does aid represent a major income source. Examples are the Falkland Islands and St. Helena.

Table 2

PER CAPITA RECEIPTS OF BRITISH GROSS BILATERAL AID, 1983

Country	Per capita aid (£)	Aid volume (£ million)
Major recipients by volume		
India	0.18	128
Sudan	1.67	32
Kenya	1.83	32
Tanzania	1.59	30
Sri Lanka	1.97	20
Bangladesh	0.28	25
Major recipients per capita		
Falkland Islands	4,526.65	9
St. Helena and Depts.	1,306.68	6.5
Turks and Caicos Islands	602.45	4.2
Anguilla	203.68	1.4

Note: Per capita figures are based on 1981 population.
Source: "The UK Aid Programme," ODI *Briefing Paper*, No. 5. London, December 1984.

Over the years there have been significant shifts in aid policies. Generalization is risky, because there are many differences in detail between the approaches of the various donors, not least those that are members of the EC. However, in broad terms there were changes during the 1970s in the financial terms of aid, its geographical direction and its sectoral allocation.

During the 1970s, the provision of loans tended to give way to grants, and there was increased emphasis on channeling aid to the poorest countries and to the poorest people within those countries. This change of geographical focus went hand in hand with a sectoral focus that favored aid to agricultural and rural development.

During the early 1980s, policies changed once again, this time as a result of pressures created by the recession and by an environment less sympathetic to aid. In particular, there has been a growing emphasis on the use of aid to facilitate trade. A favored vehicle for this is to use aid to "soften" a financial package for projects to be undertaken in developing countries.

Another feature of the changed emphasis of the 1980s is a growing preference for bilateral over multilateral aid. During the 1970s, the share of aid being channeled through such multilateral agencies as the World Bank and the U.N. agencies increased. The trend is now in the opposite direction, although because of the lead times noted above, this has not yet translated itself into a fall in the level of commitments. In 1983, for example, Britain channeled 41 percent of its aid through multilateral agencies (see Table 3).

The one multilateral agency that may avoid this trend is the EC. In 1983 the Community absorbed 39 percent of British multilateral aid, and this

Table 3
DISTRIBUTION OF BRITISH GROSS AID EXPENDITURE, 1983
(£ million)

	£ million	%
Gross bilateral aid	693	59
Gross multilateral aid	477	41
BILATERAL AID		
Financial	428	36
Project	237	20
Aid and trade provision	33	3
Program aid	51	4
Debt cancellation	23	2
Other	84	7
Technical Cooperation	232	20
Personnel	78	7
Students	45	4
Consultancies	22	2
British Council	33	3
Research	19	2
British Volunteer Program	5	–
Other	30	3
Administrative Costs	33	3
MULTILATERAL AID		
U.N. Agencies	54	4
Contributions to development agencies	40	3
Contributions to other technical cooperation activities	14	1
World Bank Group	205	18
International Development Association (IDA)	193	17
Other	12	1
Regional Development Banks	15	1
European Community	185	16
European Development Fund	75	6
Food aid	51	4
Disaster relief	3	–
Mediterranean associates	17	2
Nonassociated countries	18	2
Social and Regional Funds	12	1
Other	9	1
Other International Organizations	17	2

Source: "UK Aid Programme," ODI *Briefing Paper*, No. 5, London, December 1984.

proportion is likely to grow during the rest of the 1980s. The reason for this is that the largest EC aid program—the Lomé Convention—operates on a five-year basis. The aid package agreed to in 1984 for the second half of the 1980s is relatively generous. Since the total aid budgets of the European member states are under pressure, it is likely that this fixed Lomé commitment will take an increasing share of a declining total. Hence the EC aid program, which is already of major importance for both donors and recipients, is likely to become increasingly prominent in Western European efforts.

FOUNDATIONS OF EC DEVELOPMENT POLICY

The EC's aid program is just one element in a broad set of economic relations with developing countries. Three principal elements shape Community-level policy toward the Third World. They are the common external tariff (CET), the common agricultural policy (CAP) and the partially common aid policy.

The existence of the CET means that the foundations of Europe's foreign trade regime are established at the EC level. Thus the member states adopt a common position at meetings of the General Agreement on Tariffs and Trade (GATT) and of the U.N. Conference on Trade and Development (UNCTAD), and have negotiated at EC level a host of bilateral and multilateral trade agreements with Third World states. The CET's purity is reduced in practice as member states adopt to a greater or lesser extent national policies that influence trade flows. Most important are the growing number of nontariff barriers (NTBs) to imports. Whereas the EC institutions have an unambiguous responsibility for setting tariff policy, their position on NTBs is much less secure. The member states have negotiated bilaterally numerous "voluntary export restraints" with developing countries. Nonetheless, the most important NTB for the Third World, the Multifiber Arrangement (MFA), which limits LDCs' exports of clothing and textiles, is still negotiated at Community level, even though the EC's internal solidarity was heavily strained during the negotiations for the third MFA in 1981.

Agricultural trade policy is particularly significant, both because of the importance of agriculture for many LDCs and because of the extensive protection applied under the CAP. This tends to limit Third World agricultural exports to the EC of two kinds of commodities. The most important are those that compete directly with European produce (often unprocessed tropical products). There are also a small number of competitive products for which special agreements have been negotiated in the face of strong opposition from the EC farming lobby, which keeps them under continuing pressure.

Aid is the third main element of the EC's Third World policy. Unlike trade and agriculture, it is only partially common. There are three main strings to Europe's aid bow: multiannual Community-level programs, annual EC programs and member-state national programs.

The largest of the multiannual Community-level programs is financed outside the EC budget: the European Development Fund (EDF). This fund finances the aid provisions of the Lomé Convention, which links the EC to 65 countries in Africa, the Caribbean and the Pacific (the ACP). The EC also has financial protocols to its commercial agreements with a number of other Third World states, most notably those in North Africa and the

Middle East. These provide multiannual commitment, although the funds are drawn from the normal annual budget.

Second, there are annually agreed aid programs financed out of the EC budget. These include the food aid program and the nonassociates' aid program that covers all countries lacking a specially negotiated, multiannual aid agreement. This substantial group includes India, China, the Association of Southeast Asian Nations (ASEAN) and the whole of Latin America.

Finally, there are the member states' bilateral aid programs. Some of these tend to reinforce the geographical and political bias of the EC's efforts, but with some member states the reverse is true. The French and Italian bilateral programs, for example, have a geographical focus similar to that of the EC, but Britain has used its aid to offset the EC's geographical emphasis on Africa and its neglect of South Asia. The proportion of aid channeled through EC and bilateral programs varies widely between the member states, from 59 percent of Italian official aid disbursements in 1979 to six to nine percent of those from Denmark, France and the Netherlands (see Table 4). Overall, about 10 percent of the Ten's official aid is channeled through EC aid programs. The Commission would like this proportion doubled.

The picture is made yet more complicated by the fact that part of the member states' own aid programs are channeled through other organizations. Of these, the most important are such multilateral agencies as the World Bank, the Asian Development Bank, the U.N. Food and Agricultural Organization and the World Food Program. In addition, an increasing share of national and EC aid is channeled through nongovernmental organizations (NGOs). In 1981, some 600 EC NGOs were active in the development field, and between them they disbursed over $900 million in aid.

ORGANIZATION OF EC AID

As in the national administrations of most member states, there is a section of the EC Commission with titular responsibility for "development"—the Directorate-General for Development (DG VIII). But, again as in the member states, this section deals with only one corner of the wide range of policies affecting the Third World. The Directorate-General for External Relations (DG I) has responsibility for many trade issues; it led the renegotiation of the MFA. Since 1985, it has also been responsible for relations with Asian, Latin American and North African developing countries. The Directorate-General for Agriculture (DG VI) is the all-powerful guardian of the CAP, in charge of negotiations on: the international wheat agreement; implementing the ACP sugar protocol, under which the EC imports cane sugar; and mobilizing food aid, once DG VIII has negotiated a program. Despite these limitations, DG VIII has a wider portfolio than do most if not all of the member states' aid ministries. As custodian of the Lomé Convention, it has direct responsibilities for trade as well as aid.

This three-way split in responsibilities within the Commission is illustrative of the diffuse system of decision making on Third World issues. Multiplicity of authority causes both confusion—not least to the outside observer—and delay. The Commission, the Council, and a host of their

Table 4
AID PROGRAMS OF THE MAIN EC DONORS, BY MEMBER STATE, 1979
(Percentages)

	Belgium	Denmark	France	West Germany	Italy	Netherlands	U.K.
Bilateral programs	69	55	83	65	8	69	72
Contributions to multilateral agencies other than EC	18	39	10	26	32	23	16
Contributions to EC programs (EDF plus payments from EC budget)	13	6	8	10	59	9	12

Note: National percentages do not all total 100 because of rounding of figures.
Source: Great Britain, House of Lords, London: Select Committee on the European Communities, *Development Aid Policy.*

joint committees, the European Parliament, and even the Economic and Social Committee have fingers in the pie. In addition, these bodies are paralleled by a range of Third World and joint EC–LDC forums.

As in other areas of EC policy making, the Commission is responsible for proposing policies within the areas where decisions are made at Community level, and for the implementation of agreed policy. But it is the Council of Ministers that makes the decision whether or not to accept a Commission proposal. Difficult decisions are often delayed, sometimes for years, either because the Commission is pushing a policy that is unacceptable to some member states or because the member states are at loggerheads so that no Commission proposal is acceptable to all. Food aid has been particularly badly affected. Much-needed reforms in its administration have been held up for several years. Since food aid financed from the EC budget must be agreed on annually, it can be delayed by broader budgetary arguments. It also involves all three Commission directorates-general with a Third World interest (DGs I, VI and VIII). Not surprisingly, the Court of Auditors' annual reports frequently carry criticisms of lengthy delays in food-aid deliveries and of other program shortcomings.

The foundation of the European Parliament's involvement is its power over the EC budget, and its right to be consulted on all new Commission proposals. Hence it has greater formal responsibilities for Third World policies that are financed out of the budget (e.g., food aid, aid to nonassociates and CAP farm prices, which have a major impact on LDCs) than for extrabudgetary policies (e.g., Lomé) or those without direct budgetary implications (e.g., aspects of trade policy). For this reason, the Parliament has urged that Lomé be "budgetized"—financed out of the ordinary EC budget. Much of its work since 1979 has been devoted to producing capacious reports and resolutions designed both to influence the Commission and, perhaps more importantly, to contribute to the debate on development policy. Some initiatives of this kind can attract significant political attention, such as its probe into food aid to Ethiopia.

Alongside these bodies is a set of joint EC–Third World institutions. Those relating to the Lomé Convention are the most extensive. The ACP are represented in Brussels by the Committee of ACP ambassadors, which is serviced by an ACP Secretariat. These are matched by a joint EC–ACP committee of ambassadors (and various specialized and ad hoc subcommittees thereof), which deal with many of the detailed issues arising from implementation of the Convention. The highest joint institution is the ACP–EC Council of Ministers, which meets annually (preceded by a meeting of the ACP Council of Ministers). It is supposed to undertake the joint decision making promised by the Convention, but since this has never lived up to expectation, neither has the Council. To complicate the picture further, there is the EC–ACP Consultative Assembly. The Assembly is supposed to represent parliamentarians, but because some ACP states do not have parliaments, the 126 members of the European Parliament on the Assembly often sit opposite ACP ambassadors. Indeed, there is a considerable overlap of the people who attend all these joint forums, which only adds to the outside observer's confusion. The Consultative Assembly has no formal powers, but like the European Parliament is a forum for speculative discussion and is the only body that discusses such political issues as Southern Africa.

There are similar joint organizations for some other LDCs. There is an annual EC–ASEAN Council of Ministers which, because of the commercial importance of ASEAN states, tends to attract higher-level European political representation than does the ACP–EC Ministerial Council. The Commission and the South Asian countries have set up joint committees, which meet at intervals to forward the implementation of the commercial cooperation agreements between them.

THE LOMÉ CONVENTION

On the basis of its three foundations—CET, CAP and aid—the EC has negotiated over 20 bilateral and multilateral agreements with the Third World. All of the agreements are different, and some are distinctly more favorable than others. In broad terms, there are three main groups of beneficiaries: Africa, the Caribbean and the Pacific, which benefit from the Lomé Convention; North African and some Middle Eastern countries, which have individually arranged trade and aid agreements; and the rest of the Third World (including China, India and Latin America), which have a variety of trade regimes, all less generous than those in the first two groups, and a small aid budget.

The Lomé conventions are the most generous and fully developed of the agreements. The first Convention was signed in 1975 for five years, following the enlargement of the EC. Lomé II covered the period 1980–85, and Lomé III will run until the end of the decade. The EC's partners are the 65 ACP states. Despite the inclusion of the Caribbean and the Pacific, it is Africa that is the principal focus of interest.

The Lomé conventions are an outgrowth of the former colonial relations of the EC member states, modified by two factors. The first is the desire of some states for Europe to have its own "sphere of influence," extending through the Mediterranean to Africa. The second is the difference in economic structure between the former colonies in Asia and those in Africa. Under the Lomé conventions, the EC accords the signatories a more preferential trade regime than is available to any other group of countries, including free entry of industrial exports to the EC market. It has been possible to combine such apparent generosity with Europe's self-interest, since the African states—unlike those in Asia—are able to take only limited advantage of it.

The relationship suffered initially from being grossly oversold and then, when it failed to live up to unrealistic expectations, from understating its actual achievements. At the time of its signature, Lomé I was hailed as a major innovation in North–South relations. A point of particular interest was its claim to be an equal partnership. It was signed in the aftermath of OPEC's 1973 oil shock, with ringing talk of "commodity power" providing an LDC charter. But it failed to live up to the promise of equal partnership, as the world recession deepened and the industrialized countries no longer felt threatened by commodity power.

Both sides agree that there have been failures during Lomé I and II. The EC has tended to see the causes of the failure in terms of aid applied inefficiently by the recipients. For the ACP, donor-aid restrictions and the limiting "small print" of trade preferences are the source of the problem. The criticisms of aid fall into two groups, which are given different weights according to the critic. One is that the aid has been poorly used, too often financing projects that are either badly designed or nullified by a hostile policy environment. The other is that aid has been badly administered by the donor, with lengthy delays in spending. Not surprisingly, the EC has tended to emphasize the former and the ACP the latter.

The task of assessing the validity of the criticism that Lomé aid has been misapplied is made difficult by the absence of any systematic, comprehensive and rigorous evaluation of aid projects. While a little economic and a lot of financial evaluation does occur, the EC has no adequate counterpart to the World Bank's Operations Evaluation Department, with its independent power for in-depth examination of any project and its annual audit of project performance. A prima facie case, however, exists that EC aid has been poorly applied, if only because there has been a generally low success rate with aid in Africa.

The hallmark of Lomé aid has been to give the recipients an unusual degree of freedom in setting spending priorities. Not surprisingly, the few good, independent evaluations that have been made show that its impact has varied according to the characteristics of the recipient government. Where the recipient has a well-prepared, effectively implemented plan of action, Lomé's flexibility has made it particularly valuable; when governments have been self-serving or simply disorganized, the results have been less impressive.[1]

Critics of the EC's performance as an aid donor argue that it is slow and cumbersome. This, they argue, is due to the duplication of project appraisal procedures, over-centralization and the meddling of the member states. Lomé aid projects have to surmount three separate, and usually sequential, approval procedures: first by the EC's quasi-diplomatic delegation in the field; then by the Commission (DG VIII); and finally by a body representing the member states, the EDF committee.

Each Lomé Convention contains a figure specifying the total allocation of aid. Although the conventions are of a specific duration, there is no requirement that the aid identified be disbursed or even committed during this period. Once agreed, the bulk of the aid is technically channeled through the European Development Fund (EDF). In addition, the European Investment Bank (EIB) provides loans both inside and outside the Convention framework.

Responsibility for administering aid is split between the Commission and the EIB on a sectoral basis. Immediately after the Convention is signed,

---

[1]Compare, for example, Adrian Hewitt, "Malawi and the EEC: the First Seven Years" with Trevor Parfitt, "EEC Aid in Practice: Sierra Leone" in Christopher Stevens, ed. *EEC and the Third World: A Survey 4—Renegotiating Lomé.* London: Hodder and Stoughton, 1984.

the EDF (excluding the allocation for Stabex and Sysmin)[2] is divided into allocations for each ACP state and for regional projects involving two or more states. This done, the EC sends programming missions to each state to agree an indicative aid program that functions as the framework for implementation. After that, the selection and submission of projects can begin.

The ACP submit their proposals to the EC delegation on the spot, which makes an appraisal and then forwards it to Brussels. The staff in DG VIII makes its own appraisal, and then puts the project to the EDF committee. In theory, this is only an advisory body, since the Commission has final responsibility for approval, but in practice the committee's opinions are never ignored by DG VIII. The net result is delay: by the end of 1983 (four years after its signature), only 44 percent of Lomé II aid had been committed, and a mere 18 percent had been disbursed. The rate of spending, moreover, has slowed: Lomé II commitments were lower in 1983 than in 1982.

What virtues does Community aid possess to set against such disadvantages? The principal one is that the aid program is part of a broader economic relationship between the EC and its favored partners. Aid is only a small part of the North–South relationship. One statistic may illustrate this fact. The Lomé III aid budget has been set at $6 billion for five years; this compares with a debt-service burden for sub-Saharan Africa alone of some $11.6 billion per year over 1985–87.[3]

There have been various attempts within Western European states to take account of this discrepancy between aid and other economic flows by creating governmental agencies with responsibilities for all aspects of the relationship —ministries of North–South relations. None have succeeded. When the Ministry of Overseas Development was being planned in Britain during the 1960s, it was hoped that it would play a very broad role. The new ministry had been promised in the Labour Party's election manifesto, and its shape and structure had been the subject of a Fabian working group. The Fabian proposal contained some elements of great significance: the ministry should formulate, develop and execute all aspects of Britain's Third World policy; and it was to have a planning staff of economists with significant influence over policy—a somewhat daring innovation at the time. The battle for responsibility over all aspects of Third World policy was lost immediately. Although it has had a voice on trade and financial issues for most of its existence, the ministry has largely been concerned with formulating, administering and executing the aid program. In the short-term, the aim of making it independent of the Foreign Office had more success. The first minister, Barbara Castle, had a seat in the Cabinet and in consequence a significant degree of political leverage. In 1967, however, the Cabinet seat was lost, and in 1970 the new Conservative government downgraded the ministry to a department of the Foreign Office. Ministerial status was retrieved under the 1974 Labour government, but in retrospect, the period since 1967 can

[2] Stabex provides partial compensation for shortfalls of export revenue on a range of ACP primary commodities. Sysmin provides special aid to some mineral-exporting ACPs to partially offset the effects of major price falls.

[3] See World Bank, *Towards Self-Sustained Development in Sub-Saharan Africa*, Washington, D.C., August 1984.

be seen as a downward trend in the department's prestige and influence, masked only by the personal standing of individual ministers.

The interaction in the Commission is potentially very different. The Commissioner for Development Cooperation has a much higher profile than do any of the aid ministers in the member states, being a fully fledged member of the Commission, equal in status to other commissioners; in contrast, most national aid ministers are of noncabinet rank. Because of the Lomé Convention, the Commissioner for Development Cooperation has responsibilities for trade as well as aid. Moreover, on trade matters, the directorate-general shares the field not with a department, as in most member states, representing the interests of domestic industry, but with DG I. The combination of this wide range of bona fide interests (however tenuous some of them may be in practice) and the Commissioner's "cabinet" status gives the potential of investigating the whole range of North–South policies.

The essential word in all of this is *potential*. There is nothing automatic about the Commissioner's breadth of responsibilities. At a time when the proportion of Western European aid channeled through the EC is increasing, this needs to be borne clearly in mind. The EC is neither as efficient nor as effective as some other donors. If it operates within narrow horizons, therefore, the trend to increase its aid may, paradoxically, be to the detriment of the Third World. If, on the other hand, it starts to broaden understanding of North–South economic links, and to influence European trade and financial policies, the Third World would benefit substantially.

FURTHER READING

Casson, Robert, et al., eds. *Rich Country Interests and Third World Development.* London: Croom Helm, 1982.

House of Lords Select Committee on the European Communities. *Development Aid Policy.* London: HMSO, 1981.

———. *A Successor to the Second Lomé Convention.* London: HMSO, 1984.

OECD Development Assistance Committee. *Development Co-operation.* Paris: OECD, annual.

Stevens, Christopher, ed. *Hunger for the World.* London: Hodder and Stoughton, 1982.

———. *The Atlantic Rift.* London: Hodder and Stoughton, 1983.

———. *Renegotiating Lomé.* London: Hodder and Stoughton, 1984.

SOCIAL AFFAIRS

THE ENVIRONMENT HAS ARRIVED

TONY ALDOUS

PERHAPS the most significant point about a chapter on the environment is that it appears at all. The last edition of this Handbook had no such chapter. Its inclusion is a recognition that in recent years public awareness of "the environment" has become much keener. Partly as a result, governments and other institutions—in Europe as well as in other parts of the world, but especially the developed world—have increasingly felt the need to intervene, and to be seen to be intervening, on the side of "the environment," or to invoke it in pursuing their policies.

The buildup of public concern about the environment over the last decade or two can be traced in a number of international declarations, conferences and campaigns. These have included European Conservation Year, 1970 (initiated by the Council of Europe and concerned primarily with the natural environment); the U.N. Environment Conference in Stockholm in 1972 (pollution; energy, resource and ecological conservation); European Architectural Heritage Year, 1975 (historic buildings and towns); the "Water's Edge" campaign, initiated by the Council of Europe in 1984; the European Campaign for Urban Renaissance Year, launched in 1980, again by the Council of Europe; and the World Conservation Strategy, set forth in 1980 by the International Union for Conservation of Nature and Natural Resources, the U.N. Environment Program and the World Wildlife Fund.

WHAT IS "THE ENVIRONMENT"?

Now at first sight, at least, this appears a motley collection of programs and associations; and it prompts us to define our terms. "Environment" and "conservation" are slippery words. To some people they evoke the field of wildlife conservation, to others the protection and enhancement of the urban environment, to still others pollution control, resource conservation or population control. In Britain, for example, an "environmental health officer" is what used to be called a public health inspector: someone concerned with hygiene and localized pollution in homes and workplaces; "environmental engineering" concerns itself with air conditioning and heating in buildings; and to an engineer or architect, "environmental works" may sometimes mean no more than the landscaping of space left over after

460

building. But the appropriation of "the environment" to activities that previously carried more humdrum labels at least suggests that "the environment" is now perceived by a wider public as "a good thing."

For present purposes, "environment" is taken to include both natural and constructed habitats, and this chapter concerns itself with efforts to protect and enhance them. Thus the crucial aspects to be covered include pollution control; land-use planning, conservation of historic buildings and settlements and the revitalization of the inner area of large cities; wildlife protection and landscape conservation; and waste disposal and the prudent use of resources. Energy conservation falls within this ambit not only because it is part of resource conservation but because virtually every means of producing energy has an important impact on the environment; transport is included because transport policies can either damage the environment or provide the means of conserving and enhancing it.

The selection of topics is to some extent arbitrary. "Environment" is, in a sense, everything around us—a proposition underlined by Barbara Ward and René Dubos in the official U.N. Stockholm conference publication *Only One Earth*: our environments are both vulnerable and interconnected.[1] But for practical purposes, limits must be set. So if a common thread runs through all these topics, it is a concern that people's power to change their environment has outstripped their awareness of the consequences and ability to regulate that change.

NO FRONTIERS TO POLLUTION

A further justification for considering "environment" from a wider-than-national viewpoint is that in the last decade or so threats to a safe, wholesome and agreeable environment have increasingly been perceived as being of more than local concern. There are a number of reasons for this. One is the scale of impact resulting from modern technology. If an oil tanker is wrecked on, say, the coast of Spain or Ireland, every European country with an Atlantic or North Sea coastline is potentially affected. And whatever the causes of the acid rain that has been attacking forests in Scandinavia and Germany (and more recently fish breeding grounds in Scotland), one point is now abundantly clear: frontiers are irrelevant, individual governments and pollution control agencies powerless to control this type of pollution.

A second factor is the increasing economic interdependence of the nations of Western Europe, especially those belonging to or associated with the European Community (EC). The Community's policies have increasingly removed or lowered tariff barriers and are seeking to abate administrative and nontariff obstacles to trade. As this process continues, other disparities loom larger. But cost differentials in the production and transport of goods frequently have an environmental dimension. Use of fertilizers and herbicides on farms; the maximum permitted size and weight of heavy trucks; the level and cost of treatment required for discharges from industrial plant into the

---

[1] Barbara Ward and René Dubos, *Only One Earth: The Care and Maintenance of a Small Planet*. London: Penguin, 1972.

neighboring water and air—all these now powerfully interact with international market factors.

Europe's common heritage
A third factor follows from the way in which new technologies are applied first in one country, then in others, and from the speed of media coverage of any mishap. What happened when a cloud of chemicals escaped from a factory making herbicides in Seveso in Lombardy in 1976 was very relevant to people in other countries, not only because toxic materials and their effects may cross frontiers, but because it is the kind of hazard that needs to be guarded against in Düsseldorf and Lyon, Barcelona and Piraeus, Stockholm and Teesside. Public opinion will no longer let governments pigeonhole these things tidily into narrow national compartments.

A fourth factor has to do with people's perception of "property." Europe's assets in natural landscape and wildlife as well as its man-made heritage are now seen not just as the affair of the individuals or nations controlling them, but as international assets. Venice in Peril was accepted as a challenge not just to Italy but to the world; the wetlands of Western Europe are regarded as a wildlife habitat whose importance goes beyond the nation-state, since migratory wading birds are not the most punctilious respecters of national frontiers. As these words were being written, the 13th-century south transept of York Minster was ravaged by fire. It would have been surprising if offers of help and contributions to the £1 million cost of repairs had not come from all over Europe as well as beyond.

The EC: supranational dimension
What distinguishes Western Europe from other parts of the world is the existence in the EC of a supranational body with law-making powers to some extent independent of its member states. Part of the thrust behind the 1972 Stockholm conference was a strong belief by many leaders of opinion that conservation in a broader sense implies a degree of self-denial, that unbridled economic growth is a luxury the world can no longer afford. Economic imperatives need to be modified by an international regime of environmental good housekeeping.

But as Nigel Haigh has pointed out in his *EEC Environmental Policy and Britain*,[2] international law only sticks so far as the nations affected by it agree to be bound. It is basically a process of horse-trading and political pressure. The Stockholm conference ended up asserting the sovereign right of nation-states "to exploit their own resources pursuant to their own environmental policies,"[3] qualified only by a moral duty not to cause damage to others. As Haigh remarks, in international law "the actors can only be the governments of the nation-states and enforcement is left to them individually."

[2] Nigel Haigh, *EEC Environmental Policy and Britain: An Essay and a Handbook*. London: Environmental Data Services, 1984.
[3] See OECD, *Economic Measurement of Environmental Damage*. Paris, 1976; OECD, *Environmental Damage Costs*. Paris, 1974; and OECD, *The Environment: Challenge for the '80s*. Paris, 1981.

In the EC it is otherwise. Community institutions have the power to make legislation—regulations, directives and decisions—that bind member states or their citizens. That power has given a new dimension and a new impetus to the management of the environment in Europe.

POLLUTION

Acid rain

One rough-and-ready approach to discussion of pollution in the past has been to deal with it under the headings of Air Pollution, Water Pollution and Pollution of Soils and Solid Waste. This approach has always clearly had its limitations, but growing awareness of the complexity and interrelationship of chemical and biological reactions has made it palpably untenable. This is demonstrated graphically by the current debate on so-called acid rain.

Concern about the effects of deposition of acid pollutants in rainfall—and dew and "fog-drip"—first became widespread in the early 1970s. The acid rain syndrome has been particularly acute in Scandinavia and West Germany, with forest trees and fish in lakes and rivers dying on a large scale. One estimate puts the annual damage in the EC and Scandinavia at between U.S. $500 million and U.S. $3.5 billion. In the Black Forest in West Germany, more than one-third of the trees are reported to be affected—some of them dead, others with thinning of crowns, premature aging and accelerated needle fall.

Further damage has been discovered in the Netherlands, France, Belgium and Austria; while in Southern Sweden one tree in 10 is said to be affected to some extent. One Swedish estimate suggests that even if only one tree in every 100 has been destroyed by acidification, the annual loss to the economy is around 500 million Swedish kronor (about U.S. $55 million). Other effects include damage to fish of the Salmonidae family. In some Scandinavian lakes no fish have survived, in others the trout population has been wiped out. Acid rain also has an effect on the yield and quality of farm crops.

Causes disputed: The damage is not, however, the point in dispute. At first it was widely believed that the sole culprit was airborne pollution from factory and power station chimneys emitting sulfur dioxide and nitrogen oxides, which then oxidize in the atmosphere to the more toxic nitrogen dioxide. Domestic pollution control had conventionally dealt with this problem by requiring the installation of tall chimneys, in the belief that the toxic gases would then be dispersed and diluted. But now, it seemed, the cumulative total of pollutants from the power stations and factories of Europe negated this assumption. Tall chimneys simply meant that the ill effects came to roost further afield and were harder to trace back to the source. The problem could only be dealt with internationally.

But against the political demand for industrial nations, including West Germany and Britain, to spend large sums on scrubbing devices in chimneys, came an increasing plea for caution. Scientists, not only in Britain but in

Uppsala in Sweden, stressed that the chemical reactions were much more complex than at first supposed; complicating factors include release of acidity by snowmelt and the character of soils and of the underlying rock formations. One school of thought suggests, for instance, that treating "target" waters with lime may be a more effective answer to acidification of lakes.

Britain's power stations "the main culprits": Sweden's National Fisheries Board has been empowered to make grants toward the liming of lakes and watercourses for just this purpose since 1976; however, Naturvardsverket (the National Environmental Protection Board) argues that the spreading of lime is not a permanent solution but only a partial, stopgap measure—a means of temporarily alleviating its injurious effects. The board asserts that sulfur and nitrogen compounds from the burning of coal and oil are the main culprit behind acidification, and points a finger at Great Britain as the largest identified source of sulfur emissions. The nature of bedrock in Sweden and Norway means that the effects of acidification are felt sooner, but, the argument runs, other countries should not assume that their apparent immunity from acid rain's dire effects will continue for ever.

The political pressure, in North America as well as in Europe, for measures to combat acidification culminated in a 30-nation conference in Munich in June 1984. While everyone present subscribed to Chancellor Kohl's remark in his speech of welcome that countries today face serious environmental problems "which do not stop at frontiers and can only be solved in unison," agreement on what remedies to take was harder to achieve. While a number of countries were ready to go along the lines of an earlier agreement in Ottawa to reduce sulfur dioxide emissions by 30 percent by 1993, the British steadfastly declined to spend the estimated £1.7 billion over 10 years that this required, arguing that more research was needed to clarify the nature of acidification damage and the best ways of dealing with it.

Economic motives: A number of factors affect the varying attitudes of governments on this issue. One, obviously, is the differing nature of the advice given by scientists, which reflects genuine uncertainty about the nature of acidification and the extent to which acid rain is its cause. But many observers see economic factors as dominant. In times of recession, a government in charge of an ailing economy may understandably drag its feet in following an expensive course of action that, through even marginally higher electricity and other production costs, may make its products less competitive. The principle widely applied in national policies, "make the polluter pay," has very different implications when superimposed on the free competition policies of a common market.

It seems improbable, however, that Britain will long be able to resist the pressure of opinion, at home as well as abroad, in favor of a cutback on power station emissions. The logic of the argument, expressed in its 1984 report by Britain's Royal Commission on Environmental Pollution, that acid rain is only part of a complex pattern of interacting pollution, may be double-edged. If pollutants interact in a way that baffles expert analysis, then surely there is a case for trying to make reductions in all significant areas, whether or not scientists have been able to establish precise links or quantification.

Another mitigating factor, at least when judged by standards of gross national product, is that pollution control itself creates economic activity. In fact, there may be a net gain in terms of employment. In West Germany, for instance, it has been estimated that in the period 1978–80 the environmental protection industry created *or protected* some 145 jobs.

Lead in motor fuel

In another area of great public concern, the shoe is on the other foot. Britain, partly as a result of some skillful campaigning by the ad hoc pressure group CLEAR (Campaign for Lead-free Air), has been, with West Germany, among the European nations pushing for the compulsory use of lead-free fuel in cars by an early date. Others, including Italy and France, have urged delay. Their refining industries, it is observed, are less geared to the changes required.

In May 1984 the EC Commission produced a compromise, two-speed proposal allowing those states wishing to do so to introduce lead-free motor fuel from 1986, but with the date for compulsory lead-free car engines set only at 1989. The extra cost per car is expected to range between five percent and 19 percent, but two factors have helped to overcome what might have been serious consumer resistance. One is growing concern about the effects of lead—including brain damage in young children. The other is the fact that the United States and Japan are ahead of Europe on this issue. Working to common standards for EC and North American markets offers some advantages of economy, and at the very least EC automobile makers will not be competing against others working to lower standards.

Wider than Europe

Probably one reason why the Community has not made more progress in the matter of air pollution is that this kind of pollution—and its commercial implications—go further than EC boundaries and further than Europe itself. Solutions depend on wider international agreement and in no small measure on commercial pressures, such as those generated by tougher standards in North America and Japan. The Organization for Economic Cooperation and Development, representing these countries as well as Western Europe, has been an important influence here. Water pollution and the control of polluting wastes are, by contrast, generally more susceptible to EC regulation. Even accepting that these different forms of pollution are often inextricably linked, it is here that most progress has been made.

The basis of EC environment policy

The EC's environment activities rest, not on any explicit power in the EC's constitution, the Treaty of Rome, but on an implied power in its objects. Article 2 of the treaty calls for the harmonious development of economic activities, and its preamble lays down the aim of "constant improvement of the living and working conditions of their [the member nations'] people." From this has been inferred the need and the authority to create within the EC Commission an Environment and Consumer Protection Service, which is charged with carrying out the Community's environment program. Furthermore the close connection, already noted, between commercial competitiveness and the costs of pollution and pollution control make an EC policy desirable; and so does the international nature of many threats to the environment.

EC environment goals: The EC's Environment and Consumer Protection Service came into being in 1972. The primary objectives of EC environment policy were:[4]

1. to prevent, reduce and as far as possible eliminate pollution and nuisances;
2. to maintain a satisfactory ecological balance and protect the biosphere;
3. to avoid damage to the ecological balance;
4. to improve working conditions and settings of life;
5. to ensure that more account is taken of environmental aspects in town planning and land use;
6. to work for those ends with other countries.

Pollution the priority: In practice, the EC's first two Action Programs for the Environment, covering the years 1973–77 and 1977–81, were more limited in scope. The scale of the environmental problems affecting the Community and the environment program's own shortage of resources led it to concentrate on pollution.

Shortage of resources and the nature of the EC Commission's powers have, indeed, significantly shaped its approach to the environment. Having, as it were, got in on the coattails of economic programs and goals, the environment has not enjoyed over-generous funding. Though the EC funds devoted to environment have risen from an initial 0.5 million units of account in 1973 to some 10 million European currency units (ECUs) in 1983 and 12 million ECUs in 1984, these still represent only about four to five percent of the total Commission budget (26,952 million ECUs in 1984) as against 62 percent for agriculture. More to the point, applied to the range and scale of the EC's environmental problems, they do not go very far.

Reliance on legislation: Moreover, unlike national governments, which have control of the administration of their laws and programs, the Community must depend largely on national governments for administration on the ground. The result, as Nigel Haigh has pointed out,[5] is that in shaping its environment policy the EC has tended to rely on the one instrument it could control: legislation. The first two action programs resulted in the passing by the Community of more than 70 separate pieces of legislation—directives, regulations and decisions—the bulk of which attacked the problems of pollution.

[4] Paraphrased from *The European Community's Environmental Policy.* Office for Official Publications of the European Community, 1984, p. 26.
[5] Haigh, op cit, p. 21.

The EC and water pollution

The action programs here operated in three priority areas: definition of quality objectives; protection of the aquatic environment from pollution by dangerous substances; and protection of the sea against oil pollution. Directives (which are binding on EC member states) have prescribed minimum quality levels for fresh and sea water related to what they are used for, e.g., drinking, bathing, supporting fish and shellfish; and monitoring systems are in operation.

The first measure to be taken to prevent release of dangerous chemicals into water was a so-called framework directive of 1976 aimed at preventing pollution by chemicals whose toxicity, persistence and bioaccumulation posed a serious, permanent threat to the environment. A directive to limit discharge of mercury into Community waters from the chloralkali-electrolysis industry followed, and the Commission has since put forward other directives dealing with specific hazards such as cadmium, aldrin, endrin, dieldrin and mercury used in other industries.

Slow process

The process of framing and passing legislation is not rapid. Sluggishness should not, however, be attributed simply to foot-dragging by those states whose short-term economic interests stand to be adversely affected. Different approaches to pollution measurement and control exist in different member countries. To be effective, Community directives must entail uniform standards and have a rigorous technical basis. Quality levels apparently designed for the sluggish and heavily used bathing water of Mediterranean resorts have appeared to some ludicrously inappropriate to the storm-tossed and tide-scoured beaches of the Atlantic and the North Sea; and the EC has to tread a delicate path between evenhandedness and taking account of disparate conditions and traditions. In the final analysis, its standards must be sufficiently clear, uniform and unambiguous to stand up as a test of pollution control performance.

The EC's attempts to deal with hazards created by chemicals fall into three categories: manufacturing standards; control of use; and preventive testing and notification. It has issued directives setting out Community standards for certain types of chemical product, covering, for instance, the biodegradability of detergents and the classification, packaging and labeling of pesticides, solvents and paints. A second set of directives seeks to regulate the use of certain harmful substances, including pharmaceuticals with harmful active ingredients and chlorofluorocarbons—the gas propellants widely used in aerosols and thought by some experts to have a damaging effect on the earth's protective ozone layer.

Uniform testing: The Community's preventive measures in this field include the establishment in 1979 of a uniform system for the testing of chemicals, and notification of their makeup to member governments before marketing. Backed by mandatory tests for health and environmental effects, this system enables EC governments to monitor dangerous chemicals and exercise control before the effects become serious. The so-called "Seveso" or "post-

Seveso" directive requires for the first time that member states consult each other and the citizens of neighboring Community countries where they could be affected by a major industrial accident.

EC action on noise
Noise pollution has also been the subject of a series of directives establishing maximum noise levels for everything from heavy trucks and buses to motorcycles, agricultural tractors and subsonic aircraft. A further series of drafts submitted to the Council of Ministers for approval seeks to set maximum levels for certain types of equipment used in the construction industry, including air compressors and pneumatic drills, and even for domestic lawn mowers. The approach is two-pronged: reducing maximum permitted levels; and requiring manufacturers to provide details of noise levels, both for the benefit of users and to make official inspection easier. A new front in the fight against unnecessary noise opens up with the Commission turning its attention to domestic appliances. Here the approach is to oblige manufacturers to give details of noise levels on their product labels. The Commission and member states are working on a project for measurement of present and future noise levels around airports, providing comparability between different national measures of airport noise.

THIRD ACTION PROGRAM

Already in the second (1977–81) action program, the thrust of EC environment policies was changing, with more emphasis on prevention rather than cure. The third environmental action program, instead of containing a detailed list of individual measures, extends this positive approach, calling for environmental factors to be taken into account fully and early enough to influence the planning of all major development activities. These are specifically stated to include not only extraction of raw materials and industrial and urban development, but also agriculture, energy, transport and tourism.[6]

The EC started its life in a world whose underlying philosophy was still one of unquestioned growth and exploitation. But in the face of unlimited power to exploit, human beings must be much more self-disciplined if the resources and environment on which they continue to depend are not to be prodigally devoured.

Limits to Growth
A group of scientists and industrialists, alive to this danger, founded the Club of Rome, which set out the nature and extent of this danger in a 1972 report, *Limits to Growth*.[7] The EC's third action program reflects that Club of Rome warning in a more thoroughgoing way than the two earlier

[6] *Ten Years of Community Environment Policy*. Brussels: Commission of the European Community, 1983, p. 59, par. 163.
[7] Meadows, D. H., et al. *The Limits to Growth*. London: Earth Island Ltd., 1972.

programs. The Community is now less concerned to play the role of environmental fire brigade; it is concerning itself increasingly with environmental good housekeeping.

What are the instruments of this new and broader phase of Community policy? One underlying philosophy seems to be that better information on the cost and damage caused by various forms of pollution and environmental impact will of itself bring about improvements. The decision makers at every level, becoming aware of the extent of the damage, will modify their plans in order to avoid or lessen it. Thus it is argued that, if the damage to health and loss of productivity caused by excessive factory noise is properly quantified and presented, it will become evident to the firms concerned that in their own interests they ought to spend money on reducing noise levels. Some research sponsored by the Commission has also investigated the correlation between excessive noise and unnecessary consumption of energy.

Environmental impact assessment

In this campaign of information, one potentially very useful tool is "ecomapping"—more accurately called environmental mapping—on which considerable work has been done in member countries. The ultimate aim is to produce a computerized data base, much of it on a one-kilometer grid, which would allow Community decision makers rapid access to information on such factors as terrain, ecological value, mineral resources and recreational potential for every area of the EC. But the key tool at present is environmental impact assessment (EIA). Whether the project under review is a new road or reservoir, urban development in the countryside, exploitation of mineral reserves, an industrial plant or process, or the marketing of a new chemical product, the overall and objective assessment of the impact it will make on the environment is a salutary antidote to the tendency of developers (public as well as private) to judge schemes by narrow commercial or other inward-looking criteria. The EC's 1976 *Sixth Directive on Dangerous Substances* to all intents and purposes requires an EIA to be carried out before new chemical substances are marketed; but a wider draft directive requiring impact studies in advance of a range of large-scale public and private development projects has been under consideration by the Council of Ministers since 1980 and has not yet won agreement.

From this, it is plain that the new thrust of EC environmental policy is no soft option. It provokes a different, but no less formidable, kind of opposition than that occasioned by more specific regulations. For instance, some developers are inclined to oppose impact assessment because of its cost and the possible delay factor. Some governments—Britain's included—while accepting that EIA is a useful tool, are chary of superimposing it on already lengthy consultation and inquiry procedures. Yet the logic of the Community's competition policies in the long run requires that developers in different countries should be subject to similar constraints.

ENVIRONMENT AND AGRICULTURE

The authors of *Ten Years of Community Environment Policy*[8] concede that the third action program, with its broad aim of ensuring good environmental housekeeping at every level of decision, will be no walkover. They see one of the potential battlegrounds as the point where the EC's Common Agricultural Policy (in any case contentious) and its Environment Policy meet. This leads to the consideration of another sphere of the European environment: its countryside.

The countryside environment

Conservation of the countryside has three separate but interconnected aspects: landscape, wildlife and communities. They are involved—sometimes not so smoothly—with a fourth aspect, agriculture. A few decades ago the farmer was seen as the natural ally of conservation, but in many places today certain kinds of agriculture and agricultural economics are regarded as the main enemy, if not of rural communities then certainly of traditional landscape quality and of wildlife.

What has brought about this change? Four factors may be mentioned: the power and availability of chemical fertilizers and herbicides; mechanization; the opening up of wide markets by improved transport and the removal of tariffs; and some systems of subsidies. One needs to be cautious in pointing the accusing finger at the last of these. A recent letter to *The Times* of London[9] serves to make points about both subsidies and pesticides. The correspondents warned against the new but increasing practice in Corfu of spraying the flora under the island's venerable and abundant olive trees in order to clear undergrowth and make harvesting easier. Those responsible, warned the *Times* letter, should beware of the ecological effects, not only on the island's wildlife generally but on the olive trees themselves, which might well be bound by an ecological chain to the species sprayed. But what of subsidies? Well, those olive trees were planted when Corfu was under the rule of Venice, and the Venetians gave a bounty for every tree planted. That seems to have been an example of the thoroughly beneficent use of subsidies!

Landscape conservation: Of the three kinds of countryside conservation mentioned above, landscape conservation probably has the longest organized tradition in Western Europe. Most nations of the region have protective designations including national parks, although in some countries these have at least as much to do with protection of flora and fauna as with landscape. This is particularly so when protection is concerned not with the wild uplands, but with gentler, vulnerable lowland landscape, which new buildings and significant changes in husbandry alike can transform quite drastically almost overnight. Recent awareness of this threat has been the motivation behind such initiatives as the new regime of management for the protected landscapes of Central Sjaelland in Denmark. These are seen not just as landscape but as a complex network of villages, individual houses and farms,

[8]*Ten Years of Community Environment Policy*, p. 61, par. 169.
[9]*The Times*, London, July 14, 1984.

manor houses, mills and small harbors, forming an integral part of the ecology of the area.

What makes this Lejre–Ledreborg–Selsø region particularly vulnerable is its proximity to Copenhagen. While Denmark has tough laws restricting urban development to zones containing only five percent of its land area, the impact of recreation cannot be thus circumscribed. It can only be managed. The answers adopted neatly combine landscape and ecological conservation, conservation of historic buildings and provision for recreation. They included restoring the 16th-century manor house at Selso—empty for 150 years—and turning it into a museum; and the conversion of the Ledreborg estate—4,500 acres (1,800 hectares) of woodland, ploughland, lake and park—into a nature park. At one stroke this solution provides for visitor management and landscape preservation.

Conservation and public access: Traditionally, voluntary organizations concerned with countryside preservation, like Britain's National Trust (founded 1895, now numbering one million members), Switzerland's *Ligue Suisse pour la Protection de la Nature* (100,000 members) and the Netherlands' 250,000-member Society for Nature Conservation have seen conservation and public access as complementary goals. Weight of numbers and the new mobility have required some adjustment of that assumption, with such tools as countryside education and interpretation called in as aids to cushion the developing friction. So-called informal recreation now often requires formal management regimes. Ancient forests like the New Forest in England and the Forest of Crécy in Picardy now have quite elaborate management plans; and new ways are being developed to minimize conflicts among farmers, recreationists and conservationists.

The economics of countryside conservation: The economic context of countryside conservation, touched on earlier, has profound importance. On the one hand, the most fertile and best managed lowland farms are often most profitably exploited—at least in the short term—by the creation of a new "open-plan" landscape of large fields. This is ecologically and, many would argue, visually poorer than, say, the complex patterns of fields and hedges created in lowland England by 18th-century and earlier enclosures. Certainly the tendency, found throughout Europe, to dig up trees and hedges and fill in ponds and marshes severely reduces wildlife habitats.

On the other hand, small peasant or hill farmers may find it difficult to survive and make an acceptable living unless they receive national or international subsidies to cushion competition from producers more favorably placed. And it is belatedly becoming plain to a wider public that the rural landscapes they unthinkingly regarded as "natural" are in fact not only man-made but man-maintained. A French peasant farmer in the Auvergne dies: his children decline to take over the holding because they see it as yielding too little reward for too much toil; and so in a matter of two or three years, pasture, arable land, vineyard and garden become overgrown. Impenetrable scrub takes over where for centuries husbandry held sway. A similar pattern can be found in upland areas from mid-Wales to Crete, where tourism's rich pickings tempt a more demanding generation away from the land.

Draining the marshes: At the other end of the scale, the effects of the drive to "improve" potentially fertile land to the detriment of a landscape and wildlife habitat increasingly valued by conservationists, is well illustrated by the case of Halvergate Marshes in England's Norfolk Broads. Here, there has been a long tug-of-war between farmers who wished to drain the marshes because—with subsidies offered by the Ministry of Agriculture—they could farm profitably, and official and unofficial conservationists, including the Broads Authority and the national agencies charged with protection of landscape and wildlife, the Countryside Commission and the Nature Conservancy Council.

Because of the power of the farming lobby, and the Ministry of Agriculture's until now narrow criterion of agricultural productivity, British farmers have for years been encouraged by generous grants to clear hedges, fill ditches and drain ponds and marshes in order to achieve marginal increases in productivity. As government began to take account of conservation, this aspect of countryside policy—for which a different department, Environment, is ultimately responsible—was never integrated into agricultural policy; and Britain has now arrived at the ludicrous position where one ministry offers farmers grants to undertake improvements while another ministry or its agents then try to dissuade them, with a different set of payments, from making.

Flora and fauna reduced: Behind such controversy lies a growing concern about three underlying issues. First, there is the cumulative effect of new methods of farming on the rural environment. Already, in some intensively farmed areas, the variety and numbers of flora and fauna have been much impoverished, so that survival of species may depend not on the farmed countryside at all but on nature reserves and, by an odd twist of events, on the gardens and public open spaces of nearby towns. The use of pesticides and fertilizers also causes concern, both because of their incalculable effect on ecological chains and because of the residual pollutants that find their way into watercourses. A series of accidents in which aerial crop spraying has injured or caused illness to human beings serves to underline the fact that farming is no longer a private, self-contained business, and that people are among the species of fauna directly at risk.

The second underlying issue is whether European agriculture is, indeed, making sensible use of scarce resources. Why should the Community or national governments be pouring in generally indiscriminate subsidies that encourage farmers to indulge in yet more energy- and resource-consuming agricultural methods, when in a number of areas there are large surpluses which the EC finds it difficult to dispose of? This is clearly not good environmental housekeeping.

Changing rural economies: To many of the individual governments, of course, the systems of subsidies that produce these surpluses have become inseparable from support for rural communities and their votes in elections. But in fact, throughout Europe the numbers of people working on the land has fallen markedly in recent years, both as a proportion of population and absolutely—in France, for example, from 2.3 million (11.9 percent) in 1973 to 1.8 million (8.6 percent) in 1981. The equivalent fall in Italy is from 3.4 million (18.3 percent) to 2.7 million (13.3 percent) and in Greece—the most "peasant" of the Ten—from 1.1 million (36.1 percent) to 1.0 million (30 percent).

The inference that can be drawn from these figures is that if rural communities are surviving, or are to survive, it must be by diversifying their economic base. Tourism is an important factor almost everywhere; so are certain kinds of small business. The word processor on which this chapter was written operates with a program supplied by a computer software firm in the tiny Yorkshire village of Pateley Bridge (population less than 2,000). Entrepreneurs in the field of electronic communications have been quick to perceive that, provided they have telephone wires for data transmission, they need not be in large towns to do their business. They are often now choosing to set up in the countryside.

"Numbers bias" against the countryside: But rural communities frequently suffer from what may be called a "numbers bias" on the part of both government and commercial accountants. They are considered too small to rank for certain services and facilities, and these can be provided only if support is given in the form of subsidies and special treatment. Concern that the villages of Europe should not languish and die recently led to the establishment, at a conference in Marburg in the German Federal Republic, of a new body: the Council for the Conservation and Reanimation of Europe's Villages and Small Towns—mercifully shortened to "Europe's Village Council." Its chief instigator was Francis Noel-Baker, former British member of parliament and owner of rural property in Greece. He makes the point that there have been campaigns for saving historic towns and outstanding stretches of countryside, and preserving the inner city; but the most ancient, and for many people most agreeable, unit of human habitation, the village, has been neglected.

One reason for this is a confusion between the interests of rural communities and those of agriculture. Governments, and to some extent the EC, have concentrated their rural aid on farmers. And despite clear declarations from the Commission that at least some of the funds provided under the Common Agricultural Policy can be used for related social and economic underpinning, there has been a reluctance—especially in the British Ministry of Agriculture—to take advantage of this. Yet relatively small sums spent on encouraging new rural enterprises and supporting essential rural services would seem to yield better value than the much larger amounts that go to produce wine lakes and butter mountains.

HISTORIC BUILDINGS AND TOWNS

The preservation, care and use of historic buildings and towns is another area in which great changes have taken place over the past decade or two. At the beginning of the 1970s, the general approach throughout Western Europe concentrated on the protection and care of individual monuments and buildings. Preservation, rather than conservation, was the name of the game. But there were already signs of a change. Two movements in particular can be identified: area conservation rather than preservation of individual structures; and pressure for conservation to have a social and economic dimension.

In Britain, local authorities were by this time making increasing use of the right to designate conservation areas, a power given them by Parliament in 1967 as a result of a bill promoted by Duncan Sandys, founder and president of the Civic Trust. The essence of the conservation-area approach is that it takes account of the value not just of individual buildings but of groups of buildings and their setting, of total "townscape." A main street or a square and the streets that lead into it may not contain even a single building of the highest architectural quality, yet the composite picture may be outstandingly attractive and command the affection and loyalty of both local people and visitors.

Good looks not enough
In France, architects had carried out exemplary schemes of restoration in old towns like Colmar in Alsace and Sarlat in the Dordogne, previously threatened by dereliction. It had been demonstrated that, working through agencies using a mixture of public and private funds and with substantial pump priming from the state, architects, planners and entrepreneurs could convert neglected buildings into sought-after homes and workplaces that would thereafter be cared for by owners with sufficient interest and resources. But, increasingly, those responsible found themselves, to their surprise, under attack. They had, they were told, been guilty of abetting "gentrification"; they had achieved physical repair at the expense of destroying the traditional population and economy.

European Architectural Heritage Year
These two themes—the need for conservation of buildings to take account of groups and townscape, and the need for such conservation to have a social and economic dimension—came through very strongly at the launching in Zurich in 1973 of a two-year program culminating in European Architectural Heritage Year (EAHY), 1975. EAHY was the creation of the Council of Europe and intended to do for the built environment broadly what European Conservation Year had done for the natural environment. Much of the impetus for it came from Duncan Sandys, founder president of Europa Nostra and a founder of the European Movement.

EAHY proceeded by way of a series of pilot projects, selected by the participating nations as models of conservation at its best and exemplars to others in Europe. These ranged widely in scale, but there was a refreshing emphasis on conserving whole neighborhoods and on social benefit. Examples of this are found at Krems an der Donau, Austria, where low-cost rental housing has been created in renovated courtyard buildings; at Helsingør, Denmark, where younger people were encouraged and helped to undertake the renovation of houses in the historic heart of the town; and Bologna, Italy, where the Communist city administration set great store by its determination to combine high-quality restoration, low-cost public housing and a thriving local economy in the historic center.

INDUSTRIAL HERITAGE

Other themes ran through the Heritage Year pilot schemes, including making historic streets and squares exclusive to pedestrians, and the curbing of obtrusive and out-of-character advertising. One significant trend was toward a keener appreciation of 19th-century buildings and of the industrial heritage generally. The first was dramatically demonstrated by the restoration and improvement of late 19th-century apartment blocks in the Charlottenburg district of Berlin, with their characteristic *Berliner Zimmer* overlooking newly improved and landscaped courtyards; the second by the conservation of the Egelsberg Ironworks in Sweden, restored at a cost of some 4 million kronor—in scale and historical importance a project comparable to the remarkably successful Ironbridge Gorge Museum in Britain.

The way in which what may start as conservation of industrial heritage comes to include conservation of social heritage is well illustrated by another of the Swedish EAHY pilot projects, in the mining area of Falun, where the object was to conserve a large area of 18th- and 19th-century miners' wooden houses. The Falun project illustrates a characteristic of many mid-1970s conservation schemes in various countries: the need to explain, consult and go forward on the basis of cooperation where owner-occupation is common. Some 70 to 80 percent of the Falun wooden houses were in private ownership.

CONSERVATION AND TOURISM

Ironbridge's phenomenally successful open-air industrial heritage museum—backed by the state-appointed development corporation of Telford New Town—shows how conservation, starting from a view of the historical importance of heritage, can yet provide the catalyst for the social and economic revitalization of a whole community previously in decline. It underlines the link with two other trends in Western Europe: away from manufacturing and toward service industry, which in time of recession makes tourism a staple of more and more national economies; and toward shorter working hours and weeks and longer holidays. Historic towns and open-air museums, as well as historic houses, castles and cathedrals, are seen as having an increasing role in tourism, especially "second-break" tourism—which, the more northerly European countries like to stress, is not as dependent as main holiday tourism on an assured supply of sun and warm seas.

In many locations, tourism is conservation's best chance of generating the funds it needs. It also requires a certain discipline. To succeed, conservation must explain itself and its objectives to a wider lay public. A graphic example of this is the British government's creation in 1984 of a new public agency, English Heritage (officially, the Commission for Historic Buildings and Monuments), to combine the functions of safeguarding and providing repair grants (which government departments have on the whole managed well) with that of presenting and interpreting the state-owned monuments (where standards have sometimes fallen abysmally low).

Tourism needs firm management

A partnership between tourism and historic buildings conservation is not, of course, new. The use of historic castles, abbeys and manor houses as hotels and restaurants, run by a public agency and helping to cover the costs of their maintenance, is well demonstrated in Spain (*paradores* and *hosterias*) and Portugal (*pousadas*), quite apart from the thousands of historic buildings whose owners open them to the public at least partly as a means of generating the funds to maintain them. In some cases, the weight of tourism is seen as threatening the quality of the visitor's experience: Mont St. Michel in Normandy is but one example. At this point, the developing skills of "visitor management" must be added to the conservation armory. Another example is Stonehenge, a prehistoric monument whose magic has been spoiled by heavy visitor pressures and poor management. Significantly, in his first public pronouncement as chairman of the English Heritage commission, Lord Montagu of Beaulieu (himself proprietor of a historic estate) set management solutions for Stonehenge as a priority task.

The Council of Europe followed up Heritage Year with a more broadly based campaign—the European Campaign for Urban Renaissance, aimed at revitalizing life in cities and especially in their inner areas. (This is discussed below in the context of urban planning and development.)

POSTWAR CITY PLANNING

In the decades immediately after World War II, the pattern of urban change in most countries of Western Europe mainly took the form of large-scale redevelopment and new development.

Architects, planners and politicians saw the physical damage done by war as presenting opportunities to create improved conditions for people to live and work in. They were ambitious and confident. Planning laws in varying degrees gave local and national governments power to control development, but in general "new" was seen as "good" and development and redevelopment as the necessary vehicles of economic growth.

Development took different forms in different places. In Britain, for example, the 1950s and 1960s saw the building of new towns; edge-of-town low-rise housing estates; office blocks and shopping centers often built in partnership with local authorities; and industrialized high-rise housing in the inner city. In France, it took the form of a different, in some ways more ambitious, style of new town; city center redevelopment, often with more panache but not necessarily more successful than in Britain; the first out-of-town shopping centers or hypermarkets, built to cater to a car-owning suburban population; and high-rise moderate rent public housing, the HLMs (*habitations à loyer modéré*). In Sweden, a large-scale program for the building of low-cost municipal housing produced blocks of flats whose monotony of appearance and inconvenience of location made them by the 1970s unpopular and in many cases unlettable—the same reaction, incidentally, as in some British conurbations, notably Merseyside.

The inner city devitalized

In these and other countries—especially in the more prosperous north—the overall effect of these various kinds of development was to undermine the viability and appeal of much of the inner city. Official attitudes may also be seen as reflecting the 1960s faith in big solutions, with small firms elbowed out, in the name of separation of housing and industry, by officials who did not then appreciate the importance of a multitude of small enterprises to the economic health of a city. But in the 1970s the worm began to turn. Local populations rebelled against the sacrifice of their livelihood and local environments to some generalized and often very distant public gain; they rebelled, too, against what they saw as a certain arrogance in architects and planners.

Finland: losses regretted

In Finland, a country with a well-developed planning system, the expansion of Helsinki into new suburbs and satellite towns like Tapiola appears the epitome of rationality and good taste. But critics increasingly complain that the new neighborhoods all too often lack the character and convenience to be found in older quarters officially regarded as too densely populated. In the boom years of the 1960s, large numbers of characteristic wooden and stone buildings were demolished in Helsinki and other Finnish towns to make room for what are now seen as new buildings in an alien tradition. Popular regret in Helsinki at the loss of a familiar and distinctive townscape echoes a complaint to be heard from Dublin and Birmingham to Zurich and Athens—that redevelopment in a debased and anonymous "international" style of architecture has made one town look like any other.

But the shortcomings of the buildings that did go up in city centers were nothing compared to the blighted rings of the inner city that in some instances surrounded them. In the 1970s, governments began to see that something had gone badly wrong. As economic boom tailed off into recession, ambitious plans for the rebuilding of inner-city areas began to look increasingly unattainable. And local populations began to express themselves more vociferously, demanding that their needs and interests should command official attention. At the same time, a new generation of town planners, molded by such trans-Atlantic influences as the writings of Jane Jacobs and the concept of "defensible space," rediscovered the attractions of a gradual, incremental approach to the revitalization of the languishing inner city.

Campaign for Urban Renaissance: Dutch projects

This was part of the reason, then, for the Council of Europe's Campaign for Urban Renaissance—for "A Better Life in Towns." Different countries, of course, interpreted the theme differently and pursued their goals by varying mechanisms. The Dutch, for instance, devised machinery in which the Ministry of Welfare, Health and Cultural Amenities and the Ministry of Housing, Planning and the Environment jointly funded programs of renewal and improvement in selected urban areas—including better educational and recreational facilities. Essential to the Dutch strategy is the boosting of population and employment. The right of the local population to have their say is specifically recognized in the latest renewal projects. In physical terms, the approach implies less violent and smaller-scale change, a commitment to keep the character even of run-down working-class neighborhoods by rehabilitating the better buildings and filling in with new buildings of harmonious design. Amsterdam's Jordaan neighborhood is a good example of this.

Sweden: changing development goals

In Sweden, the program of building large estates of low-cost but ultimately unpopular multistory flats had assumed the continuance of both economic boom and migration to the cities. Neither, in fact, continued on the scale expected. Instead, two kinds of development became popular in turn: first, single-family houses on the outskirts of towns and cities, encouraged by fiscal incentives to home ownership; then, and increasingly toward the end of the 1970s, renovation and improvement of inner-city tenement blocks by their conversion into new apartments owned by the tenants as a cooperative but retaining an equity in rising values. In the late 1970s and 1980s, Sweden's approach to its housing stock and to life in towns and cities has been to make the most of what exists—in several ways.

Botkyrka: polyglot problem town: Botkyrka, a suburban municipality of Greater Stockholm, had to bear heavier strains than almost any other area in Europe during the 1960s. Its population rose from 10,000 to 80,000 in 10 years, as immigrants found it a likely area of the city in which to settle. It has 100 nationalities speaking 60 languages and, presumably, living in less spacious conditions than are usual in Scandinavia. The results: social unrest, alienation, violence, vandalism. The social remedies employed to try to counter these problems include the Folk Opera—a municipally sponsored project in which 400 Botkyrka residents of many different nationalities produce a musical drama about the town based on melodic and dramatic ingredients that everyone understands and responds to; a scheme for pupils to paint their own school buildings, in the belief that they are more likely to respect and care for what they have achieved themselves; and a "nursery" estate for small businesses alongside the largest housing area.

Ostra Nibble: repairing a 1960s failure: Swedish efforts have also been aimed at improving the unpopular housing developments of the 1960s. At Ostra Nibble, a housing estate on the outskirts of the recession-hit industrial city of Hallstahammar, the local authority, helped by a special central government agency, has put much money and effort into improving both social and physical conditions.

Its version of the formula "A Better Life in Towns" includes play groups, story hours for children, dances and study groups; the upgrading of the flat grassed areas between buildings into a real park, with residents involved in planning and planting; and, for the blocks of apartments themselves, better insulation, refacing of facades to give more variety and individuality to buildings, entrances with forecourts, new laundries and do-it-yourself workshops. Tenants, under the auspices of a tenants' association, took part in every stage of the work, which helped to keep down costs. But, say Elisabet and Jan Viklund in the Swedish Institute's *Current Sweden*, "The most important

478

thing is that Ostra Nibble has been relieved of its social stigma. Today it is an area which people choose to live in."[10]

Getting rid of the stigma: Cantril Farm

There is a further parallel with Britain's Merseyside. Cantril Farm in the Knowsley area north of Liverpool was a housing development that had become a byword for poor conditions and vandalism. It suffered from bad planning, some poor construction, an inconvenient location and lack of social and recreational facilities, as well as a high incidence of unemployment and social deprivation. An experiment now taking place rests on the transfer of ownership and management from a hard-pressed local authority to an independent trust on whose board serve leading members of the building and development industries. The trust, in partnership with Knowsley Council and with considerable government funding, is upgrading Cantril Farm— now renamed Stockbridge Village—and working to create a more balanced social mix by changing the tenure of some of the dwellings from rental to owner-occupation. Again, removal of stigma is the aim. Stockbridge Village, like Ostra Nibble, is to become a place where people choose to live.

Environment's "social dynamic"

These two cases make the point that, certainly in the restless, mobile Western Europe of the 1970s and 1980s, "good" and "bad" environments depend on factors other than the quality of bricks and mortar, grass and trees, and even on more than the skill and imagination of architects and town planners. Behind the tangible facts of the urban environment lies a social dynamic that colors how people see these facts and profoundly affects their success or failure. Especially in public housing projects, this can be a sensitive ingredient of success or failure. The perception that some aspect of a building or its surroundings is unfriendly or badly designed can touch off a wave of hostility and trigger teenage vandalism and lack of tenant care and respect, so that a housing scheme acclaimed by architectural critics becomes a byword for design failure and social breakdown.

In discussing "urban renaissance" it is necessary, however, to distinguish between two different situations: run-down and unpopular districts (typically inner city but also including places like Cantril Farm that may actually be on the edge of the built-up area), which need help from government or public agencies if their environment is to be improved and their viability as attractive places to live and work restored; and run-down central sites such as the Les Halles area of Paris and Covent Garden in London, which are nevertheless attractive to the public and developers because of their central position.

Central areas: no residents' veto: One must also distinguish between areas where the interests of the local population can broadly be accepted as paramount, and those that have a citywide, or even national or international role. In the latter circumstances, local opinion clearly has the right to be

[10] Svenska Institutet, Stockholm, *Current Sweden* No. 303, June 1983.

consulted—and consulted in such a way that it may influence decisions crucial to it—but it does not necessarily have the right of veto.

In British cities, several devices have been employed: special funding for inner-city projects administered by "partnership" committees of local authority representatives and central government departments, led by the Department of the Environment; urban development grants on the U.S. model, providing "topping up" finance to make desirable but commercially unremunerative developments viable; and, in two areas of specially acute decay, the establishment of urban development corporations charged with stimulating and overseeing redevelopment. Modeled on the earlier limited-life, limited-remit new town development corporations, these two urban development agencies—one for London's and one for Liverpool's redundant docklands—are run by appointed boards rather than elected councils. They have had fair success in "selling" what had been regarded as no-hope areas as zones of opportunity.

Garden festivals: It fell to one of these agencies, the Merseyside Development Corporation, to preside over the 1984 International Garden Festival. The British government, after years of lobbying by the landscaping profession, adopted a device well tried in several other European countries, notably Germany and Holland. The garden festival formula rests on the notion that reclamation of suitable areas of derelict land can be linked to a one-season garden festival, revenues from which help to pay for permanent new landscaping of high quality. After the festival in Liverpool, the city was left with new riverside park as well as campus sites for factories and offices and attractive landscaped sites for new housing.

German garden festivals have built up their attendances from 1.5 million at Hannover in 1951 to 11 million at Munich in 1983. Liverpool's festival is estimated to have attracted something over 3 million, and the second British garden festival, to be held at Stoke-on-Trent in 1986—though only national, not international—may well exceed that figure. Apart from the tangible gains, garden festivals have two crucial functions in times and places of recession: to boost the morale of a city and its people; and to give a glimpse of the kind of environmental standards that can be achieved if landscaping is regarded not as an afterthought, a cosmetic to be dispensed with if budgets need to be cut, but as an essential part of urban design, as crucial to its success as service roads or interior decor.

A new breed of planners: The entrepreneurial approach adopted by the two British urban development corporations and the organizers of the garden festivals underscores a change of approach on the part of the planning profession, which may also be seen in varying degrees in other Western European countries. The land-use planning system created by Britain's 1947 Town and Country Planning Act has often been held up as the most developed town-planning system in the world, giving local and national authorities power to guide development for the benefit of the community at large. And, for all its faults of sluggishness and inflexibility, it can be said to have worked reasonably well in a buoyant economy. In recession, the need is otherwise. Planners must be stimulators and enablers rather than merely regulators.

They can no longer stand aloof from the fray. This has clear advantages, but it also worries conservationist groups. They fear that, if the choice is between environmentally bad development and no development at all, planning authorities may opt for the bad.

TRANSPORT AND THE ENVIRONMENT

Transport, both of freight and of passengers, has its impact on the environment. Large-scale transport development, of roads, bridges and airports, has an obvious effect; and some forms of transport, such as movement of freight by canal and movement of people by rail, are more benign to the environment than others. The scale and ramifications of airports in particular, have caused widespread worry and controversy. At both London and Frankfurt, the busiest points in the European air network, plans for providing extra capacity have led to protracted battles—with the Frankfurt protesters, like those in Japan some years back, carrying their opposition to the point of being prepared to obstruct newly built runways.

The impact of a large airport

The arguments about the location of—and indeed the necessity for—a third London airport illustrate the point. The proposed site at Stansted, 36 miles (58 kilometers) northeast of central London, would take an additional 1,400 acres (570 hectares) with a further 1,900 acres (770 hectares) earmarked for further expansion. It would mean, according to noise consultants retained by Essex County Council, the local planning authority, that more than 24,000 people at present living in rural or semirural tranquility would find themselves within the 30-NNI (noise and number index) noise disturbance zone and would "experience a highly significant and noticeable deterioration in their environment."[11] Moreover, a large modern airport brings with it the impact of large-scale urbanization. It would create or lead to the creation of an additional 25,000 jobs, and would call for the building of an additional 18,500 homes. A stretch of peaceful and attractive countryside would become Third Airport City. At the time of writing, the result of the third inquiry into an airport proposal for this site (two other lengthy inquiries had already led to such a development being turned down) was still awaited.

Aircraft noise controls: Efforts to achieve control of aircraft noise present a mixed picture in the mid-1980s, with international agreements and pressures leading to quieter civil aircraft, and local restrictions (for instance, on nighttime operations) bringing about some improvement in the conditions suffered by people living and working near airports, but with traffic still increasing, albeit less rapidly than had been forecast. The ability of the aviation industry to get its own way has certainly been reduced as it has been transformed in public perception from something glamorous and novel to a workaday, unromantic necessity of life.

[11] Evidence given by J. D. Charles of Bickerdyke Allen Partners to the Stansted Airport public inquiry, on behalf of Essex and Hertfordshire County Councils and East Hertfordshire and Uttlesford District Councils. (Document ref. HE231)

At present, aviation exhibits an obsessive concern with "economies of scale." Its future may well lie in diversification of routes and types of aircraft, with more and smaller regional airports providing a wider range of direct services, often using smaller, quieter, short-take-off planes, and with energy costs perhaps even giving a boost to efforts to promote freight transport by airship.

Roads and traffic

As far as road transport and roads are concerned, numbers again seem to pose the main long-term threat. Even with pollution-free electric traction, the private automobile in compact European towns and cities would remain a powerful threat to the environment, and heavy trucks even more of a threat. All European countries accept in varying degrees the need to subsidize public transport, but whereas the French and West German governments appear to have decided to spend enough to make it attractive, Britain's attitude all too often appears to have been to spend the minimum to get by. Proposals for congestion taxes—for instance, using meters in cars, activated by buried cables sending signals related to the degree of congestion to be expected at any given time and place—have lain unimplemented and untested.

"Highwaymen" tamed: Although in some countries major roads continue to trigger off major environmental battles, the procedure everywhere is closer now to the concept of environmental impact assessment than would have seemed possible 10 years ago. This is particularly so with urban roads. All over Europe, the road engineers have left monuments to their earlier environmental barbarism: the *Sopraelevata* in Genoa, ploughing its way through the urban fabric between the waterside and the heart of the city; the right bank riverside highways in Paris; London's elevated Westway, running horrifyingly close to second-floor windows of Victorian terrace houses. But the elaborate Ringway system of which Westway was to have been an early installment was axed because it proved politically disastrous to whichever party proposed to carry it through; most of the *quais* on the left bank of the Seine were left tranquil and untrafficked because they formed an environment that French public opinion was ultimately not prepared to sacrifice.

In the cities, certainly, the road planners have learned that the environmental price of high-capacity roads is not acceptable. In the countryside, the arguments are less clearcut; integration into the landscape is now often very skillful, and though major roads still destroy some habitats, it may be noted that they create or safeguard others precisely because people do not generally explore the shoulders of highways on foot.

Goods transshipment depots: In this area some European countries have made progress. Holland has long banned heavy freight vehicles from certain historic towns, making traders and haulers transship goods at edge-of-town depots into smaller, feeder vehicles. Greece has lately adopted a perhaps desperate but nonetheless effective short-term solution to traffic congestion and pollution in Athens. You can drive into the city center only on alternate days, according to your car's registration number. EC funds can and do help to finance public transport projects that would otherwise not have been carried through. Examples include the remarkably successful Tyne and Wear Metro (which has sharply reduced the level of car commuting into Newcastle); the electrification and upgrading of Dublin's suburban rail system; and the widening of England's South Yorkshire Canal to make it a viable means of transport for minerals, solid waste and other bulk cargoes.

Transport and energy

As well as its relative impact on the environment, transport also affects energy consumption; indeed, energy conservation is involved at every turn with other kinds of environmental impact. But what serves the needs of one kind of conservation does not always help another. For instance, from the point of view of impact on landscape, a nuclear power station may be preferred to a coal mine; but other aspects of nuclear energy, not least the disposal of radioactive waste, make it the bête noire of a large section of conservationist opinion, as demonstrations in Brittany and at sites in West Germany show.

To take a less contentious example, the Dinorwic pumped storage power station near Snowdon in Wales is benign to the environment from an energy point of view. It uses surplus off-peak electricity to pump water to an artificial lake near the top of a small mountain, so that at times of peak energy demand it can be released to power turbogenerators. The operation of the power station requires, even indirectly, the consumption of relatively small quantities of nonrenewable fossil fuels, and it obviates the need to build additional conventional generating capacity. But in terms of impact on the landscape, it was—with its lake dams, roads and other artifacts—very contentious; and despite the considerable achievements of the Generating Board's consultant landscape architects, it remains so.

The death of a forest: Hydroelectric power schemes can cause much more extensive damage to the environment, as a proposal to build a dam across the Danube at Hainburg in Austria shows. The Hainburg dam's purpose would be twofold: to produce cheap electricity, and to regulate the flow of the river so as to allow navigation at all seasons. But it would also mean, say ecologists aided by the World Wildlife Fund and the Franz Weber Foundation, the "almost certain death" of the Auwald, one of Europe's last remaining alluvial forests, which provides a habitat for 30 species of fish, otters, 40 kinds of tree and thousands of birds, among them black storks and cormorants.

The other side to the energy coin is the way Western European society wastes it. The logic of an overall "good housekeeping" approach to the environment would imply not only restraint in the use of private cars where energy-conserving public transport can supply people's needs, but much higher standards of insulation in buildings, incentives for "total energy" package schemes, use of waste incineration to produce power, and much more urgent and large-scale experimentation in use of wind and wave power.

Conflicting conservation goals: It must be conceded, however, that the notion of a global scheme of things in which various conservationist policies work together in harmony is a myth. The demands of different aspects of conservation frequently conflict. The scale and number of aerogenerators (the giant

483

modern equivalent of windmills) needed to make a sizable contribution to present-day power demands is calculated to send landscape conservationists into paroxysms of fury; schemes for damming North Sea and Irish Sea estuaries to harness wave power have already caused concern among conservationists worried about the shrinking habitats of wading birds. The use of wave power to generate electricity, though expensive in capital terms, may be the least objectionable answer. The sea is big enough to take the visual impact; the energy is there in plenty.

THE ENVIRONMENT LOBBY

Finally, a word about the harnessing of public opinion to environmental goals, and about pressure groups—local, national and international; ad hoc, single topic and multitopic. Some, like Switzerland's *Schweizerheimatschutz*, founded in 1905, are long-established and almost part of "the establishment"; others like Britain's Friends of the Earth and the Greens in West Germany, are new, restless and uninhibited.

The contrast may be noted between the West German Greens—a single national movement, represented in parliament, devoted to conservation of the environment in all its aspects—and the (in its way) equally powerful, but highly fragmented and deliberately apolitical environmental lobby in Britain. Why are the approaches so different? Of course, an Ecology Party exists in Britain, but even with a more favorable electoral system it would scarcely be a serious political force. The British approach has been pragmatic, ad hoc. But organizations like the 30,000-strong Council for the Protection of Rural England and individual civic societies do wield political power and do change the course of events. The all-embracing environmental pressure group, though it has a certain appeal and strength because of its breadth, can the more easily trigger off opposition.

A complete change of climate
As the author of *Ten Years of Community Environment Policy* says in his preface, "If, 26 years ago when the European Community was founded, one had spoken of the environment, people would no doubt have thought that one was referring either to the climate or the state of business confidence."[12] Now, virtually every government in Western Europe has a Minister of the Environment or its equivalent, and every large national and multinational company has staff charged with demonstrating that it is doing the right thing by the environment, even when it is intent on despoiling some section of it.

Where will this universal concern lead in the next decade or so? In a curious way, economic recession, though it makes some of the tasks of environmental control harder to achieve, gives us pause to absorb the lessons so far. The lessons of E. F. Schumacher's *Small Is Beautiful* are still being learned. In Europe as in the developing world there are often surprising economic and environmental savings to be achieved from smallness of scale.

[12] *Ten Years of Community Environment Policy*, p. 3, par. 1.

Public opinion, increasingly vociferous in the defense of its habitat, is more inclined to accept gradual, incremental change.

Toward more positive policies

At the same time, industry increasingly sees the need for uniform constraints to be placed on competitors in different countries. It is also learning that measures to control pollution, planned in good time, are easier to cope with than public opinion reacting against unexpected environmental damage and demanding expensive remedial action.

In the Community as in individual countries, we may be moving into a period when regulation to prevent abuse of the environment gives way, to some extent, to increasing use of inducements to positive conservation and enhancement of environments. But for that, there has to be a change of heart in departments of state in many countries, and in the EC a greater willingness to provide effective funding for the Commission's positive environmental work.

FURTHER READING

Aldous, Tony. *Battle for the Environment*. London: Collins Fontana, 1972.
———. *Goodbye, Britain?* London: Sidgwick & Jackson, 1975.
Arvill, Robert. *Man and Environment*. Harmondsworth: Penguin, 1967.
Fairbrother, N. *New Lives, New Landscapes*. Harmondsworth: Penguin, 1972.
Haigh, Nigel. *EEC Environmental Policy and Britain*. London: Environmental Data Services, 1984.
Mabey, Richard. *The Pollution Handbook*. Harmondsworth: Penguin, 1974.
Meadows, D. H., et al. *The Limits to Growth*. London: Earth Island Ltd., 1972.
Schumacher, E. F. *Small Is Beautiful*. London: Blond and Briggs, 1973.
Ward, Barbara, and Dubos, René. *Only One Earth: The Care and Maintenance of a Small Planet*. Harmondsworth: Penguin, 1972.

FOREIGN LABOR IN WESTERN EUROPE

MALCOLM J. MACMILLEN

SEVERAL categories of foreign labor in Western Europe can be identified. There is, first, migrant labor of the guestworker type, recruited for a specified and usually short period. The second category includes immigrant workers who stay longer or settle permanently. This category includes those whose initial intention or hiring agreement was for a short stay, but who have remained, together with their economically active spouses, for a longer period, and those who came with the intention of settling for long periods or permanently. The third category consists of children of the first two groups, children either born in the host country or who accompanied, or later joined their parents there. Frontier and seasonal workers, another category, are not always regarded as a part of the foreign labor force; but in Switzerland, for example, they constitute nearly one-third of the foreigners working in the country.

For any particular host country,[1] the size of the foreign labor force and its breakdown into the above categories is the result of a wide range of political, economic and sociocultural factors in the host country and in the countries of emigration.

In the years since World War II, the number of foreign workers has grown rapidly, and in the nine countries with which this chapter is concerned—Austria, Belgium, France, West Germany, Great Britain, Luxembourg, the Netherlands, Sweden and Switzerland—it totals over 6 million (Table 1). Considerable numbers of the self-employed are not included in this figure, and in addition it is estimated that the number of illegal foreign workers is equivalent to about 10 percent of legal workers. The combined foreign population of the nine countries is over 13.6 million (Table 2), about one million less than the population of the Netherlands, the sixth most populous state in Western Europe. These statistics do not include all the labor force, or population of foreign origin or all ethnic minorities, because of naturalization in the past and automatic nationality on entry. For example, compare

---

[1] This term, which usually implies that the foreigner is a temporary guest, is used here as an equivalent for "country of immigration," "labor importing country" and "receiving country." Similarly, "home," "sending" or "labor exporting" country, "country of emigration" and "country of origin" are synonymous.

Table 1
FOREIGN LABOR IN NINE WESTERN EUROPE COUNTRIES, 1982[a]

	Stock		Employed (Working)		Employees (Working for others)	
	Number (000s)	Share of Total Labor Force (percent)	Number (000s)	Share of Total Employment (percent)	Number (000s)	Share of Total Employees (percent)
Austria	166.0	5.0	156.0	4.9	154.4	5.6
Belgium[b]	332.2	8.0	277.2	7.5	—	—
Britain[b]	—	—	—	—	779.4	3.6
France	1,503.0	6.4	1,250.0	5.9	—	—
Germany	2,037.6	7.4	—	—	1,709.5	7.7
Luxembourg	—	—	66.0	41.5	—	—
Netherlands	241.0	4.3	200.8	4.1	185.0	4.3
Sweden	227.7	5.3	214.4	5.1	—	—
Switzerland	—	—	749.4	24.8	—	—

[a] The criterion for country selection was a foreign labor share of at least 3.5 percent. Definitions of foreign labor vary among countries.
[b] Data for 1981.

Sources: OECD, *SOPEMI (Continuous Reporting System on Migration)*, Paris, 1981 and 1983.
Eurostat, *Employment and Unemployment*, Luxembourg, Statistical Office of the European Communities, 1984.
OECD, *Economic Surveys*, various countries and years, Paris.
International Labour office, *Year Book of Labour Statistics*, Geneva, various years.

Table 2
FOREIGN RESIDENTS IN EIGHT WESTERN EUROPEAN COUNTRIES OF LABOR IMMIGRATION, 1981–82* (000s)

	Belgium 1982	France 1982	West Germany 1982	Great Britain 1981	Luxembourg 1981	Netherlands 1982	Sweden 1982	Switzerland 1982	Total (000s)	Proportion of Total (percent)	Proportion of Population of Emigrant Countries, 1982 (percent)
EC countries	525.3	491.6	1,214.0	673.0	57.2	140.2	57.5	582.9	3,741.7	28.1	1.4
Greece	21.4	7.9	300.8	20.0	0.2	4.1	13.1	9.2	376.7	2.8	3.8
Italy	276.5	333.7	601.6	94.0	22.3	21.0	4.4	412.0	1,765.5	13.2	3.1
Other	227.4	150.0	310.2	559.0	34.7	115.1	40.0	157.3	1,593.7	12.0	3.1
Other European countries	159.1	1,385.1			35.2	206.7					
Austria			175.0				3.2	30.6	208.8	1.6	2.8
Finland			10.0				160.0	1.5	171.5	1.3	3.6
Portugal	10.5	764.9	106.0	12.0	29.3	9.4	1.6	16.7	950.4	7.1	9.5
Spain	57.8	321.4	173.5	23.0	2.1	22.7	3.2	102.6	706.3	5.3	1.9
Turkey	66.1	123.5	1,580.7	16.0	0.1	148.0	20.3	46.8	2,001.5	15.0	4.3
Yugoslavia	5.9	64.4	631.7	6.0	1.5	14.1	38.5	54.8	816.9	6.1	3.6
Africa	143.7	1,573.8		78.0	0.6	102.5					
Algeria	10.9	795.9	5.1				0.8	1.8	814.5	6.1	4.1
Morocco	110.2	431.1	42.6			93.1	1.3	1.2	679.5	5.1	3.4
Tunisia	6.9	189.4	25.2				0.9	1.8	224.2	1.7	3.4
Other or not specified	57.6	229.6	703.1	1,329.0	2.8	88.2	118.2	85.1	2,382.1		
Total	885.7	3,680.1	4,666.9	2,137.0	95.8	537.6	405.5	925.8	13,334.4	100.0	
Proportion of population of immigrant countries (percent)	9.0	6.8	7.6	3.8	26.2	3.8	4.9	14.5			

* The definition of foreign residents varies among countries; see text.
Adding the foreign population of 291,000 in Austria (1981, for which there is no country breakdown) raises the total for the nine immigration countries to 13,625.4 million.

Sources: OECD, SOPEMI (Continuous Reporting System on Migration), Paris, 1983.
Eurostat, Demographic Statistics, Luxembourg, Statistical Office of the European Communities, 1984.
World Bank, World Development Report, New York, Oxford University Press, 1984.
OECD, Economic Surveys, various countries, Paris, 1983 and 1984.

the figure for Great Britain in Table 2 with 3.2 million in Great Britain born outside the country and 4.5 million in Great Britain living in households with a non-British-born head of household (1981).

The foreign labor and population phenomena have generated considerable discussion of their short- and long-term effects on both host and home countries. They have also influenced official relationships between the two groups of countries, and have led indirectly to the dropping of a question on ethnic origin from the 1981 British population census. However, for some European host countries, foreign labor and the problems identified with it are not phenomena confined to the postwar period. In 1914, 17 percent of the labor force and over 15 percent of the population of Switzerland were foreign; immigration controls reduced the latter to nine percent in 1930. Foreigners accounted for 6.6 percent of the population of France in 1931, and in response to rising unemployment immigration restrictions were instituted the following year.

What distinguishes the period after World War II is that migration has been more sustained and of longer term or more permanent nature, resulting in proportionately higher foreign populations. It has also involved more countries, with home countries geographically more distant from and culturally less similar to the host nations; and more of the home countries have been sovereign states. In addition, the postwar period has been one of greater commitment in the host countries to full employment (at least until the 1980s) and to greater equality and concern for human rights.

IMMIGRATION COUNTRIES

From optimism to disillusionment

The majority of people who migrate do so primarily for economic reasons—for better employment opportunities and higher wages. With the exception of mild recessions of short duration, the demand for labor in Western Europe grew steadily until the recession of the 1970s. Effective labor supply to these activities grew as employment in primary sectors contracted, as the female activity rate rose and as labor productivity increased at historically unprecedented rates. However, male activity rates fell, and labor shortages were met by resorting to foreign manpower.

On the other hand, countries in the Mediterranean basin and distant former colonies of European states were experiencing historically high rates of growth of population and potential labor force, which were not matched by a growth in domestic employment. In the absence of migration controls, this meant that Western Europe, with its higher wage levels, faced an almost perfectly elastic supply of foreign manpower. The developing nations expected considerable economic benefits from labor emigration: the export of surplus manpower, the receipt of foreign exchange from remittances and the eventual return of migrants with new skills. Furthermore, the reductions in unemployment and poverty might also have domestic political advantages.

In this scenario, migrants and their host and home countries all stood to gain economically. France, which was officially concerned about its prospective population size as well as about labor shortages, concluded recruiting agreements through its Office National d'Immigration (ONI), founded in 1945. London Transport and the British hotel and catering trades started recruitment in Barbados in 1956. The supply of Eastern European refugee labor to West Germany declined, and the Federal Labor Office opened recruitment offices in Mediterranean countries, concluding its first bilateral agreement with Italy in 1955. The member states of the European Community (EC) were able to recruit workers from other EC countries under the free movement of labor provisions of the Treaty of Rome, which had become fully effective by mid-1968; but the narrowing of differentials in unemployment and wage rates between member states resulted in insufficient intra-EC migration to satisfy the demand for labor.

By the end of the 1960s, both West Germany and the Netherlands had official bilateral recruitment agreements with eight countries. Under these agreements and the permit policies of some other countries (Switzerland, for example), the option not to renew temporary work and residence permits led employers, trade unions and governments in host countries to believe that, whenever recession threatened indigenous employment, the stock of foreign labor could be reduced. In addition, single migrant workers would not be expected to, or were not permitted to, impose heavy demands on social overhead capital and the welfare state.

Reality has diverged from the expectations held by the authorities in both host and home countries. The reason for this is the change in parameters affecting and affected by migration, which had been considered either constant or amenable to official intervention. Western Europe has experienced intercultural and racial tension, intolerance, and violence. In some quarters it was recognized that their incidence—and their avoidance—was partly determined by the relationship between foreign population growth and the pace of cultural assimilation and attitudinal change. However, even in some countries that considered themselves to be places of permanent settlement, lax immigration and work permit formalities resulted in the entry and employment of more foreigners, especially from countries culturally dissimilar to the host, than had been anticipated or considered socially desirable or politically acceptable. For example, the ONI did not have total control over entry and employment in France, and the proportion of clandestine to total migrants increased from 26 percent in 1948 to over 90 percent in the early 1970s.

More important in explaining the growth of foreign labor and a more permanent foreign population was the fact that migrant labor ceased to perform its intended role of a temporary and highly variable supplement to indigenous labor. It became complementary, and hence an integral part of the total labor force. A number of sectors were highly dependent upon foreigners. For example, in 1973, more than 30 percent of employment in the French building and construction trades was foreign; in 1974, more than 18 percent of employment in the textiles and clothing industries in Austria was foreign. This high dependence on foreign labor was the result of the behavior of indigenous workers and employers. With employment growth, indigenous labor moved into higher paid and higher status jobs, and employers filled the resultant vacancies with foreigners. Nationals increasingly shunned low-status occupations as the proportion of foreigners in them rose. The alternative to foreign recruitment was for employers to raise wage rates in order to retain and attract indigenous workers; but if this had been done while maintaining traditional wage hierarchies and relativities, the marginal cost of extra labor would have been raised considerably.[2]

Dependence on foreigners became so significant that some employers opposed the entry restrictions that were widely introduced in 1973–75. Also, employers increasingly preferred not to rotate foreign labor on short-term contracts because of the cost of recruitment, training and workplace adaptation that would be involved. The integration of foreigners into the labor force became such that mass repatriation in times of recession became inconceivable. A French government study in 1977 concluded that this action would cause indigenous unemployment to rise rather than fall.

As migrants stayed longer, pressure grew, on social grounds, for the admission of their dependents. Because the activity rate of spouses was high, their entry also increased the labor supply. Changes in the age and sex distributions of the foreign population raised the demand for social overhead capital and public services. Foreign labor was recruited to fill the low-status occupations in the public services. In 1973, more than 30 percent of employment in the French health sector was foreign. As a result of these self-feeding processes, migrant labor became immigrant labor and the total foreign population increased beyond expectations.

Although there were warnings (in France and Switzerland, for example) that dependence upon foreign labor was distorting the domestic production structure and preserving low labor productivity rather than promoting long-run comparative advantage, most of the problems associated with foreigners that began to emerge were not those of their contribution to production. On the one hand, immigrants demanded improvements in their political rights, working conditions, housing, education and access to vocational training; on the other, the indigenous population began to claim that migrants were competing for jobs and housing and were in general imposing a burden on the social economy. There is no doubt that immigrants were subjected to extensive discrimination and to living and working conditions inferior to those of the native population. However, there is no evidence that the relationship between the taxation or social security contributions of the immigrants and their receipt of state benefits made them any more or less of a burden on the state than the indigenous population of comparable socioeconomic status. In Switzerland, the highly selective immigration system resulted in the ratio of foreigners' pension contributions to payments being as high as 5:1. A 1977 French government analysis of public expenditures and receipts concluded that immigrants had a beneficial effect on the public finances.

The immigrants' demands for improved conditions and the growing apprehension of the indigenous populations, fanned in some countries by overt racism (in Great Britain, for example) and in others by government statements

[2]Another alternative would have been direct investment by the labor-short sectors in labor-surplus countries, but these countries would not necessarily have been those that exported labor to Western Europe.

that the host country was not a country of permanent immigration (as in West Germany), did little for the cause of social integration. The Commonwealth Immigrants Act (1962) that restricted entry to Great Britain from the New (that is, nonwhite) Commonwealth had been preceded for several years by sporadic racial violence. By the early 1960s, Switzerland, having experienced a trebling of its foreign labor force between 1955 and 1964, recognized that its delicate cultural, ethnic and religious balances were threatened; in 1963 it imposed entry restrictions. In Switzerland, however, physical hostility to foreigners was rare, and host-immigrant relations were highly politicized at the central level. The national population frequently used its legal option of public referenda to voice its opinion on the subject and to influence public policy.

The countries of emigration also became more officially concerned with the conditions and status of their nationals in Western Europe and with what they viewed as failures on the part of host governments to fulfill the terms of bilateral agreements in areas such as housing, education and labor training. As an example, after a series of anti-immigrant demonstrations, murders and bombings contributed to a rapid deterioration in Franco-Algerian relations, in December 1973 Algeria imposed a ban on further labor migration into France.

By the early 1970s, foreign workers and their dependents were believed to be the cause of a wide range of economic, social and political problems in many host countries. The official reason for the widely imposed immigration restrictions of 1973–75[3] was the economic recession, but there are clear indications that this only provided a convenient excuse.

Economic effects of foreign labor
Have foreigners conferred a net economic benefit on host countries? The basis for any empirical analysis is a theoretical model, and the one typically used in this area is the standard aggregate neoclassical model. Adopting the normal assumptions, this predicts that employment of foreigners increases domestic output in the short run—the benefits accruing both to domestic capitalists and to the foreign workers themselves—and that the total and per capita wages bill of indigenous labor declines. Empirical analysis confirms the aggregate output effect. For example, between 1967 and 1971, the contribution of foreign workers to the French GDP was estimated to be 4.6–5.0 percent; it was also calculated that the employment of 460,000 immigrants in Britain in 1974 would have raised national income by 1.33 percent. Sectoral studies give support to the relative direction of the expected functional income effects. In the short run, the increase in returns to capital outweighs the fall in returns to indigenous labor; if capitalists are indigenous, the income of the indigenous population increases. Aggregate studies for France and Britain confirm this welfare effect.

Investigation of longer-run effects on output and economic welfare is conceptually and empirically more difficult because the dynamic impact of

[3] Neither intra-EC worker migration nor that between members of the Nordic Common Labor Market, which includes Finland and Sweden, was affected by these restrictions.

immigration has to be considered. This includes the effects of foreign workers and their dependents upon domestic capital formation and the rate of productivity growth. These factors in turn are influenced by nonstatic variables such as migrants' skills, their ages and activity rates, and their propensity to save money and remit funds abroad. These variables are also partly determined by factors in host and home countries that affect family immigration and return to the country of origin. Even for a single effect—for example, that of foreign employment on labor productivity and its growth—several opposing mechanisms may operate, and the overall impact remains elusive. The Swiss work permit system enabled employers to retain only the most productive foreigners; but between 1960 and 1973 the GDP per person employed grew more slowly than in the majority of the nine immigration countries here considered.

Given that some determinants vary among host countries and that others, demographically related, had not been completely worked through, it is not surprising that a decade ago it was impossible to reach firm conclusions on the likely long-run output and economic welfare effects. A similar conclusion emerges from rather limited studies of the effects on inflation, balance of payments and indigenous unemployment. The concentration of migrants in more developed regions may have discouraged employers from locating in high-unemployment regions, and thereby contributed to continuing regional imbalance.

In the last decade, however, the view that immigrant populations are not so economically advantageous has gained ground. The restrictions on labor immigration slowed down worker entries; but the average length of stay had increased, and with it a higher proportion of foreign labor had become eligible for unemployment and other state benefits. A lower propensity to return home was also the result of family unification policies in host countries, the lack of improvement in or the deterioration of employment opportunities in home countries and, in Turkey, an unfavorable political climate. The restrictions themselves also contributed because migrants could not be assured of reentry.

In contrast to earlier postwar recessions—in which unemployment in host countries could be alleviated by migrant returns, resulting in similar recorded unemployment rates for indigenous and foreign workers—in the last decade migrants' unemployment rates have risen above national averages. For example, in the West German recession of 1967, when total employment fell by 3.2 percent, one-quarter of previously employed foreigners returned home; in 1975, when total employment fell by 3.4 percent, only 15 percent of previously employed foreigners departed. Across Western Europe, the foreign unemployment rates in the 1980s have been typically 40 to 60 percent higher than the overall national averages.[4]

Some countries that severely curtailed labor entry in the 1970s significantly reduced their foreign worker stocks. For example, between 1974 and 1978,

[4]Official statistics probably underrecord foreign unemployment because some migrants do not register, even if they are entitled to various benefits, for fear of losing their work or residence permits.

the stock in West Germany fell by 17.8 percent and the number of annual and established foreign work permits in Switzerland fell by 17.5 percent; but the decreases in the foreign populations were 3.5 and 15.6 percent respectively. Rates of both immigration and emigration/return have been lower in the past decade; and the net effect of migration flows, of the foreign population's natural increase and, in some countries, of changes in nationality status, has been an increase in the total foreign population. Of our nine countries, only Switzerland had a smaller resident foreign population in 1982 than in 1974, although it has been increasing since 1979.

Thus, even those countries that officially did not (and currently do not) regard themselves as countries of immigration and permanent settlement have become such. By the time employment growth ceased (total civilian employment in the EC being lower in 1981 than in 1974) migrant labor had become immigrant labor and migrants' children were entering the labor force of host countries in unprecedentedly high numbers.

In addition to higher unemployment benefits, an immigrant population with dependents and a high rate of natural increase requires more social overhead capital and has more claims on welfare state provisions than one that consists of short-stay workers. Some of these claims on the public sector—for example the special educational needs of migrants' children—are proportionately higher than for an indigenous population of the same size and age distribution. Even countries that do not regard immigration as permanent have felt obliged to allocate real resources to these welfare benefits and other measures (social work and counseling, for example) in order to facilitate the integration of foreigners into the host society. For EC countries, the European Social Fund (ESF) is able financially to assist these measures; the ratio of applications for migrant operations to budgeted resources was the highest of all ESF areas of intervention between 1978 and 1983 (except in 1982).

The recognition of these originally unanticipated claims on real resources, the difficulties (foreseen and experienced) of integrating the foreign population, especially where it is highly concentrated in urban areas, and the continuation of anti-immigrant attitudes, have led to attempts to stabilize, and in some countries reduce, the size of the foreign population. In the last decade, measures adopted have included higher penalties for illegal entry and employment (several countries), limiting the entry of dependents—in some cases (Belgium, Germany) by lowering the age limit up to which migrants' children can join their parents—and tighter control of residence permits (Sweden). There have also been official host initiatives to increase employment in high-emigration regions of particular home countries (Sweden, in Yugoslavia). The range of policies to increase outflows and assist returning migrants includes financial assistance for repatriation (France,[5] Germany), vocational training for returning migrants (France, Germany, the Netherlands, Switzerland), refund of social security contributions

[5] Under the French government scheme, 94,000 foreigners returned between August 1977 and the end of 1981; 50 percent of these were employed, 14 percent were unemployed and 36 percent were nonactive dependents.

(Germany) and financial assistance for setting up enterprises in the emigration countries (France, Germany, the Netherlands).

The extent of this list should not be interpreted as an indication of a large-scale official attack by host governments on their foreign populations. Positive measures for the benefit of foreigners living in host countries have included improvements in their legal and residence status, legislation to reduce discrimination and a range of policies to improve education, housing and social integration. Nevertheless, it can be concluded that economic considerations have, in the last decade, joined sociopolitical factors as reasons for official disquiet about foreign labor and its dependents. In a period of slow economic growth, social integration has a better chance of succeeding if foreign population growth is also slow.

Socioeconomic position of immigrants
Entry conditions, immigrants' legal and political status, and naturalization policies are so complex, varying among host countries and among immigrants from different countries in the same host country,[6] that these aspects of immigrant welfare cannot be discussed satisfactorily here. Space limitations also preclude a discussion of differences among the socioeconomic positions of migrants from different countries within particular host countries. However, some observers claim that European guestworker policies do not conform to the provisions of the Universal Declaration of Human Rights, and that the existence of large foreign populations without full political rights has been detrimental to Western European democracies because of the gap between their official stance and actual practice on human rights.

With some notable exceptions, for example medical workers in Britain, foreign labor is typically employed in manual, low-skill jobs. In France (1975), the percentage of the unskilled and semiskilled in the foreign labor force (nearly 50 percent) was over twice that for nationals, whereas the proportion in managerial and professional occupations was less than half that for nationals. In West Germany (1978), over 80 percent of foreign workers were in manual occupations, compared to under 40 percent of Germans.

The skill distribution of foreigners has not been static. Between 1971 and 1979, the proportion of foreigners in supervisory and technician occupations in France increased from 2.8 percent to 4.7 percent, while the unskilled and semiskilled proportion fell from 66.8 percent to 47.9 percent.[7] Such changes have occurred in several countries and are due to higher skill levels on entry (party resulting from changes in the distribution of new workers by country of origin) as well as to skill improvement during the employment period in the host country. In West Germany in 1966, the skill distribution of previously unskilled workers from four recruitment countries was: skilled, three percent; semiskilled, 51 percent; unskilled, 46 percent. A study in West Berlin (1976) revealed that between their first and last jobs, the proportion of Turkish workers classified as unskilled had fallen by 13 percent, whereas the proportions of skilled workers and foremen had risen by 48

[6] Current rules governing Swiss work permits include over 200 pages of directives. Compare also Britain's Immigration and Nationality Acts.
[7] In establishments with 10 or more employees.

495

percent and 87 percent, respectively. A 1977 investigation of migrants returning to Greece showed that between their first and last jobs in West Germany, the skilled proportion had risen from four percent to 16 percent. Given that those less skilled tend to have a higher propensity to return, the skilled proportion of those remaining in West Germany was probably higher than this.

French data for 1970 indicate that, standardizing for skills and occupations, legally employed foreigners are paid wage rates comparable to those of indigenous labor. This may not be typical, but trade unions in host countries have come to insist on comparability in order to protect the wage rates of their indigenous members. However, as indicated earlier, it is to be expected that foreigners, by increasing the supply of labor, depress wage rates, other things being equal. Clandestine workers do not receive comparable wage rates, nor do their employers pay social security contributions. In Sweden (1975), the proportion of foreigners performing repeated and monotonous work and subjected to higher noise levels at work was twice that for Swedes. (These data and much of those that show higher rates of work accidents among foreigners in other countries are not standardized for sector or occupation.)

Comparable statistics on the sectoral distribution of foreign employment are not available, but manufacturing dominates, typically ranging, in continental host countries, from 37.5 percent in Sweden (1982) to 57.1 percent in Germany (1981). Other significant concentrations are found in building and construction in France (29.2 percent in 1979); in public administration in Sweden (30.2 percent, including 23.7 percent in hospitals and social welfare, 1982); and in hotel work and catering in Austria (12.8 percent, 1981). The degree of sectoral concentration is much lower in Switzerland and Britain.

The high dependence on foreign labor in some sectors and the higher than average unemployment rates for foreigners have already been mentioned. Not all of the unemployment is explained by sectoral, occupational and skill differences between foreign and indigenous workers. A quarter of the decrease in foreign employment in Austria in 1974 and 1975 was due to the replacement of foreigners by nationals.

Immigrants are highly concentrated in urban areas and in particular districts within cities. In Great Britain, over 50 percent of the nonwhite population live in the conurbations of Greater London and the West Midlands; these two regions account for 17 percent of the country's total population. About one-quarter of the populations of Brussels, inner London and Frankfurt am Main is foreign, and in some districts of Frankfurt am Main the proportion is 70 to 80 percent. West German local authorities can use residence controls to limit inflows if the proportion of foreigners rises above 12 percent, and in the late 1970s 45 cities had such bans, although not all of them had reached the 12 percent criterion. On the other hand, because of employer pressure, restrictions had not been imposed in some cities that were above the 12 percent threshold. The high birthrate of immigrants and the exodus of nationals has caused public services, especially education, to be dominated by foreigners in some inner-city areas.

The quantity and quality of foreigners' housing is typically below national averages. In France, several hundred thousand immigrants used to live in shanty towns; in Germany foreigners pay higher rents than do nationals for comparable private accommodation.

The opportunities and channels for immigrants to change their legal and political status and other conditions not related to work (housing, education, etc.) are limited, and they vary among countries. Only in Sweden do foreigners have full voting rights in local elections. West German societies and organizations (including the churches) that are an integral part of the welfare-state system and have been active in immigrant welfare have used their official position to influence government policy regarding foreigners. In contrast, the Italian immigrant-related societies in Switzerland were founded by the immigrants themselves, and Italian consulates are also active in immigrant welfare issues. Consequently, improvements in the legal position of Italians in Switzerland, codified in bilateral agreements, have been the result of Italian state efforts.

The operation of some immigrant associations, especially those aiming to preserve cultural identity with the home countries, may distance foreigners from nationals, and thereby weaken efforts toward social integration in the host countries. Migrants' children may be especially divided between seeking to retain strong links with the home country and achieving social integration in Europe.

The second generation

There are now over 4.5 million foreigners under the age of 25 in the eight continental host countries; and the number of migrants' children up to the age of 16 remaining in nine main emigration countries was estimated at over 2 million in 1977. Migrants' children now account for 40 to 50 percent of the total foreign population in some host countries, and over half of the 4.5 million foreigners under 25 were born there. The vast majority of these have received or are receiving all their education in the host countries and have had little or no experience of their parents' country.

Of the current and anticipated problems of immigration, those relating to migrants' children are probably the cause of greatest concern. The dilemma facing host and emigration countries and each migrant family is that while it is desirable for the second generation to be integrated to some degree in the host country, at the same time there are advantages in retaining cultural identity with the parents' country of origin. Integration into the host country's economic and social framework is required for upward social mobility; and adequate social provision for children is necessary on humanitarian grounds. Inadequate social provisions or opportunities for the second generation lead to frustration and ill feeling on the part of immigrants, and raise tensions between foreign and host communities. The retention of cultural identity by young foreigners helps them to reintegrate in their parents' country should they return, and several host and emigration countries hope that they eventually will.

The second-generation immigrant population appears to be retaining, not improving, its parents' socioeconomic status. Young foreigners, compared to young nationals, tend to be overrepresented in certain types of vocational training and in the shortest educational cycles—both of which lead only to low-skill manual occupations, in which the proportion of foreign labor is already higher than that of nationals. Young foreigners currently experience higher unemployment rates than do young nationals—for example, 1.8 times higher for those under 25 in France, and 1.7 times higher for the 20–24 age-group in Sweden. The outcome—low-status jobs and high unemployment—contrasts strongly with the second generation's aspirations. Young foreigners regard their parents' occupations and associated social status as inferior and hope that their own education and training in the host country will enable them to experience upward socioeconomic mobility.

It is widely agreed that the foundation for successful integration in the host country is education, and competence in the host language is considered to be the most important element of education. Inadequate linguistic ability is closely related to nonattendence and dropping out in the earlier years of formal schooling; this in turn leads to underachievement in education and in vocational training. There are a variety of pre-school, curricular and extracurricular arrangements for host-language instruction.

Immigrants are often unaware of the range of vocational training programs, in which frequently there are inadequate places, and young foreigners tend to be overrepresented in inappropriate training schemes. Although there are numerous statistics that purport to confirm migrants' educational and training failures and missed opportunities in these areas, the statistics are rarely standardized to take other factors into account. One study found that migrants' school performance in France (1981) was not very different from that of indigenous children with similar socio-occupational backgrounds.

Emigration countries wish their young nationals to participate fully in the host economy. Some countries of emigration, however, do not favor a high degree of social integration because this would separate the second generation even further from the culture and society of their parents' country. Some immigrant nationalities prefer their children to attend their own national schools in the host country. Instruction in the parents' mother tongue is regarded as the key to the maintenance of cultural links with the country of emigration. Division of the financial and organizational responsibility for this, between host education authorities and emigration countries, varies from one host country to another.

Young foreigners in many host countries are in a unique position in that neither the host nor the emigration country is fully responsible for their welfare. They show little propensity to return to a country with which they are not really familiar; at the same time, their socioeconomic position in the host country is marginal. The term "home country" has been deliberately avoided in this section; young foreigners do not know where their "home" is or where they belong culturally. Some observers see them as culturally torn between two societies; others regard them as part of a new and unique culture of migration.

EMIGRATION COUNTRIES

In the early postwar years, most of the foreign labor in the nine immigration countries taken as a group was from other countries in Western and Southern Europe. With the continual increase in the demand for labor, the host countries that organized worker migration were forced to seek workers from more distant countries. By the early 1980s, Italy remained the chief source of foreign labor for Western Europe, but as a major supplier it had been joined by Turkey, Portugal and Yugoslavia. These four countries account for nearly half of the foreign worker stock in the nine host countries (Table 3).

Table 3
STOCKS OF FOREIGN LABOR IN NINE WESTERN EUROPEAN
COUNTRIES OF LABOR IMMIGRATION, BY MAIN LABOR
EMIGRATION COUNTRIES, 1981–82[a]

| | Emigrant Labor in Western Europe | | |
| | Number (000s) | Share (percent) | Proportion of Domestic Labor Force (percent) |
	(1)	(2)	(3)
Algeria	290.1	4.8	8.6[b]
Finland	98.3	1.6	4.1
Greece	159.3	2.6	4.3
Italy	857.3	14.2	3.8
Morocco	213.1	3.5	2.1[c]
Portugal	505.9	8.4	11.9
Spain	386.3	6.4	3.0
Tunisia	77.1	1.3	4.3[d]
Turkey	810.2	13.4	4.5
Yugoslavia	585.7	9.7	5.9
Other	2,043.3	33.9	

[a] Data from immigration countries is for 1982, except for Belgium and Britain (1981). Definitions of foreign labor vary among countries.

[b] Proportion of labor force in 1977; immigrant labor as a proportion of the 1982 population of working age was 3.0 percent.

[c] Proportion of the population of working age.

[d] Proportion of the labor force in 1980.

Sources: OECD, *SOPEMI (Continuous Reporting System on Migration)*, Paris, 1983.

Eurostat, *Employment and Unemployment*, Luxembourg, Statistical Office of the European Communities, 1984.

OECD, *Economic Surveys*, various countries, Paris, 1983 and 1984.

International Labour Office, *Year Book of Labour Statistics*, Geneva, various years.

The three main economic benefits expected from short-term labor emigration to Western Europe were fuller employment at home, the availability

499

of skills acquired abroad and the receipt of foreign exchange. The extent of these advantages depends on a wide variety of factors, including the number of migrants; their employment, occupation and skills prior to departure; the reuniting of families in the host countries; the propensity to save and remit foreign exchange; the propensity to return; the nature of employment on return; and the types of outlay financed by remittances and accumulated savings. For example, the higher the proportion of low-productivity (or unemployed) emigrants, the smaller will be the short-run output loss; the higher the propensity to return and the lower the rate of family unification in the host country, then the higher will be remittance flows.

The economic impact of labor emigration and return has been studied at the micro level (village and regional) and at the national level. As in the case of immigration countries, the quantification of the net aggregate effect of migration requires a sophisticated model to accommodate complex inter-relationships. For example, the loss of skilled labor that is complementary to unskilled labor reduces the production and potential export of goods requiring unskilled labor, thus partially offsetting the foreign exchange gains from labor remittances. Another trade-off concerns skills and returns. The longer the period abroad, the greater is the degree of skill acquisition and the consequent upward socioeconomic mobility and integration in the host country. This lowers the propensity to return. Thus a choice exists between encouraging early return with low skills, and encouraging longer stays with more skill acquisition but a lower propensity to return. Many of the relevant response coefficients necessary to perform a satisfactory empirical investigation of the economic effects of emigration have not been formally quantified, but there is evidence that they vary among immigrant nationalities and among host countries.

Emigrant labor
Data in Table 3 (col. 3) show that the stock of emigrant labor in Western Europe is significant compared to the size of the domestic labor force of the emigration countries. In order to relieve the pressure on domestic employment opportunities, the emigration countries would lose less output if their unemployed, low-skill and low-productivity workers migrated. More than half of the Turks, Yugoslavs and Greeks who entered West Germany as workers were skilled in their country of origin; this represented a serious loss of potentially productive manpower. In 1972, the Turkish State Planning Organization estimated a domestic shortage of 384,000 skilled workers, while about half this number of skilled workers was abroad. Even if the emigrants' skills did not match the domestic skill requirements, this too represents a failure in manpower planning. In three of the five years from 1976 to 1980, over 70 percent of Turkish emigrants (most of them going to non-European destinations) were skilled. High expectations of skilled emigration will discourage domestic firms from training labor—a lower rate of human capital formation.

It is also known that many migrants have higher standards of education and vocational training than the national averages for several countries of origin, and that many of these migrants do not come from those countries' least developed regions. The nature of organized labor recruitment is such that emigration countries do not have a great deal of control over the composition (skill, education, rural/urban origin) of the migrant population. Agricultural output has fallen in some areas, not only because of manpower losses but also as a result of the substitution of remittance receipts for work.[8]

These observations suggest that although employment abroad has probably reduced domestic unemployment and underemployment, at least in the short run it cannot be regarded as a simple, innocuous safety valve in the labor market. Unemployment did rise in the labor exporting countries after the imposition of entry restrictions in Western Europe in the 1970s, but not all of this was due to lower volumes of emigration. Other contributory factors were a reduction in employment opportunities in other traditional regions of immigration (North America and Australia) and slower domestic employment growth; for example, total employment in Spain fell during 1973–80. Portugal had the additional problem of absorbing over half a million people from its former African territories in the mid-1970s.

Contemporaneous with the fall in employment opportunities in Western Europe was an increase in the demand for labor in the oil exporting countries of North Africa and the Middle East. India and Pakistan, traditional sources of emigrants to Britain, became increasingly important suppliers of labor to this region. For several years, Libya and Saudi Arabia have been the main destinations of Turkish workers, so that by 1981 there were more Turkish workers in Libya than in any European country except West Germany. Fewer than half of the Yugoslavs employed abroad by Yugoslav enterprises now work in Western Europe: in 1982, nearly half of these workers were in Iraq. However, it is unlikely that this new host region will be able to provide employment opportunities on the previous Western European scale, and some reports of adverse working and living conditions faced by migrant labor in this region are reminiscent of those in the earlier phases of employment in Europe.

Return migration
It has not yet been possible to identify with any precision the factors that determine the propensity to return. One study of workers arriving in and departing from West Germany between the years 1961 and 1976 investigated a wide range of possible variables. Nationality itself appeared to be the most important, the tendency to return ranging from 90 percent for Italians to seven percent for Greeks, five percent for Yugoslavs and three percent for Turks. A survey (1977) of Greeks returning from West Germany revealed that the main motives for return were related to children, the most common single reason being the problem of educating the children in Germany.

It will be recalled that a high proportion of immigrants in Western Europe are in manual work and semiskilled or unskilled jobs, and that there is less

[8] Between 1960 and 1965, more than 50 percent of men aged 15–46 emigrated from Drama province in Greece. In one area of Anatolia (Turkey), remittances were 1.4 times the value of the main marketed cash crop. Employment in the area was adversely affected by migrants granting use of their land to mechanized farmers, the latter's profits being used for more mechanization.

tendency for those in other occupations to return. Skilled returnees do not invariably use their skills on return, whether because they had little intention of doing so (a reluctance to perform the tasks that were considered of low status in the host country), or because of insufficient demand for their particular skills in the return locality or because of the nonrecognition of vocational qualifications acquired abroad.

It is appropriate to discuss here the microeconomic aspects of remittance of current income and accumulated savings. It would be possible to combine these funds, in the form of foreign exchange, with the labor and entrepreneurial services of returning imigrants, so as to promote local economic development by financing socially productive, job-creating investment.[9]

Survey data from several countries show that the vast majority of funds are not used for such purposes. Purchases of and improvements to housing and other real estate (sometimes causing property speculation) feature prominently,[10] as do purchases of consumer durables (usually of a high import content) and expenditure on children's education. Relatively small proportions are allocated to entrepreneurial investment, although a higher proportion of migrants are self-employed upon return than before emigration. Returning migrants aspire to occupations that they regard as superior both to their preemigration jobs (especially if they were in agriculture) and their host-country employment.

Compared to other emigration countries, Turkey has made more effort to associate returning migrants and remittances, with a view to local development and the reintegration of the returning migrants in the economy. The Village Development Cooperatives, instituted and financed by workers abroad, have not been successful because of inadequate organization, planning, supervision and access to credit. Similar problems have been experienced by the Workers' Companies that are aided by the Turkish and West German governments. By the early 1980s, there were 226 companies (128 of them in production and employing over 17,000 people), in which 230,000 Turkish workers had invested more than DM700 million. However, this figure of 226 companies represents only 56 percent of the 400 companies created since 1963–64. Other host countries have schemes designed to facilitate the reintegration of returning migrants in order to encourage their return.

The general conclusion from a number of studies of the local economic impact of migration, return and the use of remittances is one of growth in income and demand but no improvement in the supply side of the economy. This result has been called "static expansion"—more of the same.

Some returning migrants experience social and economic adjustment problems as a result of unemployment (although the unemployment may be

[9]At the individual level, the size of these funds is not insignificant. A survey of over 500 emigrants returning to Greece in 1977 recorded average accumulated savings of U.S. $35,000 from an average period abroad of 11.4 years; and a local Spanish study (1976) recorded total remittances of up to U.S. $40,000 for married couples who had been abroad for about 10 years.

[10]An interesting case is a fishing village in Leiria, Portugal. Emigration freed accommodations that were let to tourists, and remittances were used to purchase more holiday accommodations.

by choice, as part of a rational job-search strategy), and frustration if their occupational aspirations are not fulfilled. Migrants' children may have an inadequate knowledge of the language and find it more difficult than their parents to adjust to a society with which they do not completely identify. Although attempts are being made in emigration countries to facilitate children's integration by training programs and language instruction, some children prefer to return to the host country.

A survey of adults returning to Puglia, Italy, found that they had experienced more justice and equality abroad than in Italy, and more than half expressed a favorable verdict on social conditions in the host country, being impressed by the honesty of social relations and respect for rights. Ninety percent of emigrants returning to Greece (1977 survey) thought that emigration had been beneficial, and 40 percent viewed their return as not beneficial (perhaps explained by the fact that 75 percent of the sample had experienced unemployment on their return). More than half preferred to reemigrate if they were able to enter host countries, and more than 20 percent had reemigrated at least once before. Notwithstanding the problems experienced by foreigners in Western Europe, the lower propensity in the last decade to return home and the opinions of returning migrants suggest that emigration retains its attractiveness at the individual level.

Remittances
The potential macroeconomic impact of remittances would appear to be extremely beneficial. In 1981–82, their value was equivalent to 4.5–5.5 percent of the GDP for Morocco, Turkey and Tunisia, over seven percent for Yugoslavia and over 13 percent for Portugal. The external debt situation of many developing countries has brought into sharp focus the foreign exchange constraint on economic growth. The capacity utilization rate in Turkish manufacturing is as low as about 50 percent as a result of material shortages. Countries for which remittances have been regularly equivalent to over one-fifth of their merchandise imports are listed in Table 4.[11] Remittances can also be used to relieve a domestic savings constraint on economic growth. Receipts by Morocco, Yugoslavia and Turkey were equivalent to over 20 percent of gross domestic investment in 1981–82; for Portugal, the figure was about 40 percent.

Labor exporting countries aim to attract their emigrants' savings by a variety of incentives, such as preferential interest rates on foreign currency deposits, tax concessions and preferential treatment of imports of machinery

[11]Countries in Table 3 but excluded from Table 4 include:
Algeria: the remittances-imports rate was about 12 percent in 1980–81.
Greece: the remittances-import rate fell from more than 20 percent in 1972–73 to 11 percent in 1980–82.
Italy: remittances in 1982 were U.S. $1.2 billion, the fourth largest flow, and the remittances-imports rate was about three percent throughout 1972–82.
Spain: the remittances-imports rate fell from over 13 percent in 1972–73 to about three percent in 1980–82.
Tunisia: the remittances-imports rate was about 12 percent in 1981–82.

Table 4
MIGRANT REMITTANCES AND MERCHANDISE IMPORTS: SELECTED COUNTRIES OF LABOR EMIGRATION*, 1972–82

(Column 1: Migrant remittances, U.S.$ millions, current prices;
Column 2: Column 1 as percentage of merchandise imports, f.o.b.)

| | Morocco | | Portugal | | Turkey | | Yugoslavia | |
	(1)	(2)	(1)	(2)	(1)	(2)	(1)	(2)
1972	152	21.4	882	43.2	740	52.6	963	32.4
1973	243	23.4	1,025	37.2	1,183	62.9	1,398	33.9
1974	372	22.0	1,059	24.7	1,425	42.4	1,621	23.4
1975	516	22.8	1,097	31.0	1,300	30.7	2,004	28.4
1976	671	29.1	1,014	25.6	983	21.5	2,269	33.6
1977	—	—	1,226	27.1	982	19.3	2,430	27.1
1978	—	—	1,695	35.5	983	24.4	3,240	33.9
1979	—	—	2,455	39.7	1,694	38.1	3,773	29.4
1980	—	—	2,931	34.0	2,071	29.9	4,450	31.9
1981	1,013	26.4	2,845	31.2	2,490	31.9	4,928	36.4
1982	849	22.3	2,599	28.9	2,187	28.3	4,350	34.8

* For selection criteria, see text. For Turkey and Yugoslavia, nearly all the recorded remittances were from European countries, whereas in recent years two-thirds of Portugal's inflow was from non-European countries. No data on Morocco's sources.
Sources: OECD, SOPEMI (Continuous Reporting System on Migration), Paris, various years.
World Bank, World Development Report, New York, Oxford University Press, 1983 and 1984.
International Monetary Fund, International Financial Statistics, Washington, D.C., various issues.

and consumer goods. More attention has been paid by policy makers to maximizing the inflow of remittances than to attracting them into socially productive uses. The high propensity of migrants to allocate remittances to current consumption and property investment has been mentioned previously. There are reasons for this: some of the incentives encourage such expenditures; migrants perceive nonresidential investment opportunities to be limited; typically they have had little or no entrepreneurial experience; in rural areas especially they have a high liquidity preference, which is partly the result of a lack of appropriate financial institutions.

In the longer term, dependence on remittances as a major source of foreign exchange and investable funds may be disadvantageous. First, remittance receipts cannot be guaranteed on a year-to-year basis (as Table 4 shows) because they are influenced by variables such as the number and the disposable incomes of emigrants and their propensity to save and to remit; the latter variable is influenced by incentives to attract remittances and the propensity to return to the country of origin. Some of these factors are unstable and not easy to predict. Instability in receipts introduces more uncertainty in the management of short-run demand and foreign exchange. In the longer term, fluctuations make investment and development planning in general more difficult.

Second, substantial inflows of labor income will raise the parity of the recipient's currency above the equilibrium rate as determined by the supply of and demand for tradables. The exchange-rate overvaluation reduces the competitiveness of domestic products in both home and export markets and encourages the import of capital goods. In Greece, this raised the capital-intensity of manufacturing above that which would have been determined by relative availability of domestic capital and labor.

A third potentially adverse effect of remittances is that, in so far as they have replaced domestic savings and trade-generated foreign exchange, they may have delayed the adoption of domestic policies that would have raised the domestic savings ratio and encouraged the growth of foreign exchange earning activities. Similarly, by relieving the pressure of labor supply on employment opportunities, labor emigration may have delayed policies that would have increased domestic employment.

CONCLUSIONS

The employment of foreign labor in the period after World War II helped several Western European countries to achieve the highest and most sustained rates of economic growth they have ever experienced. The postwar boom conditions lasted longer than anticipated, and foreign workers became more permanent and more fully integrated in the host economies. The entry of workers' dependents changed the structure of the foreign population from one that mainly comprised working males to one that increasingly resembled the structure of the host population. The unanticipated growth and changing structure of the foreign population gave rise to a number of political, social, and economic problems.

Countries that actively recruited foreign manpower as a policy choice failed to understand that labor as a factor of production cannot be separated from its human, political, cultural and social attributes. Hence they failed to anticipate many of the effects of labor immigration. Countries that were more accustomed to the immigration of family units appear to have permitted entries, especially those from countries with less similar cultures, at a rate that proved too great for the pace of social integration and attitudinal change on the part of the indigenous population.

The "golden age" of postwar economic growth came to an end in the recession of 1974–75. By then, the countries of immigration had a larger foreign population and more immigrant-related problems than they had anticipated. These problems, now exacerbated by a decade of virtually no employment growth, have encouraged host governments to continue to restrict inflows and to encourage repatriation. However, unless such efforts are more successful than in the past, the foreign population will become a larger proportion of the total population because of its higher rate of natural increase. Furthermore, the marginal socioeconomic status of the foreign population is being perpetuated as young foreigners enter a slack labor market with fewer, or less appropriate, educational and training qualifications than young nationals—who themselves are experiencing, in contrast to previous decades, unemployment rates higher than the national average.

505

In such circumstances, and in the absence of sustained employment growth, the pace of future socioeconomic integration will have to depend on more positive efforts, especially with respect to the second generation. Equally desirable are improvements in the politico-legal status of foreigners. The continued existence of a large and increasingly permanent immigrant population with politico-legal rights inferior to those of the rest of the population is likely to threaten the democratic basis of Western European states.

Whereas the experience of Western Europe with immigration may be characterized as one of unanticipated developments, that of the labor emigration countries may be characterized as one of missed opportunities; and it is by no means certain that their economies will have benefited in the long run. Not only have these countries lost (permanently in some cases) skilled, educated and productive manpower, but returning migrants and remittances have not been used in the most socially productive manner. Had emigration been of low-productivity workers, their absence could have provided a breathing space in which policies designed to create more employment might have been formulated and implemented. Similarly, remittances could have been regarded as a windfall foreign exchange gain and used for investment in activities in which the particular country had a comparative advantage. But migrants' freedom to choose the allocation of their own savings and their type of employment on return must be respected. This being so, increasing the social benefits of migration depends on appropriate relative prices, on an appropriate and wide-ranging system of incentives (not just those relating to remittances) and on appropriate social and governmental institutions. The fact that such institutions have not been wholly appropriate in the past is, of course, a reflection of the emigration countries' relative economic status.

Although it is now too late to influence labor emigration to Western Europe, it would appear that there is still opportunity for the implementation of policies which would result in greater social benefits from returning immigrants and remittances.

FURTHER READING

Böhning, W. R. "Estimating the Propensity of Guestworkers to Leave," *Monthly Labour Review*, Vol. 104 (May 1981), pp. 37–40.

Castles, S., et al. *Here for Good: Western Europe's New Ethnic Minorities*. London and Sydney: Pluto Press, 1984.

Clark, M. G. "The Swiss Experience with Foreign Workers: Lessons for the United States," *Industrial and Labour Relations Review*, Vol. 36 (July 1983), pp. 606–23.

Macmillen, M. J. "The Economic Effects of International Migration: A Survey," *Journal of Common Market Studies*, Vol. XX (March 1982), pp. 245–67.

Martin, P. L. and Miller, M. J. "Guestworkers: Lessons from Western Europe," *Industrial and Labour Relations Review*, Vol. 33 (April 1980), pp. 315–30.

OECD. *Migrants' Children and Employment: The European Experience*. Paris, 1983.

———. *SOPEMI (Continuous Reporting System on Migration)*. Paris, from 1973. Annual.

Penninx, R. "A Critical Review of Theory and Practice: The Case of Turkey," *International Migration Review*, Vol. 16 (Special Issue, 1982), pp. 781–815.

Rist, R. C. *Guestworkers in Germany: The Prospects for Pluralism.* New York: Praeger, 1978.

Sapir, A. "Economic Reform and Migration in Yugoslavia: An Econometric Model," *Journal of Development Economics*, Vol. 9 (1981), pp. 149–81.

Stahl, C. W. "Labour Emigration and Economic Development," *International Migration Review*, Vol. 16 (Special Issue, 1982), pp. 869–99.

Swamy, G. *International Migrant Workers' Remittances: Issues and Prospects.* World Bank Staff Working Paper No. 481. Washington, D.C.: World Bank, August 1981.

INDUSTRIAL RELATIONS IN WESTERN EUROPE

COLIN BEEVER

GENERAL statements about industrial relations in Western Europe are not easy, because a number of exceptions can always be made. The structures, systems, laws and practices are as different from country to country as are cultures and languages—perhaps more so. To describe these facets of industrial relations country by country would make for superficiality and tedium. There are, however, general pressures and tendencies, arising from common economic, industrial and social trends, which are having a common impact and which can be analyzed in terms of Western Europe as a whole.

The European Community (EC) with its membership of 12 countries, is the heart of Western Europe. Only two professionally neutral countries of any size, Austria and Switzerland, and part of Scandinavia are excepted from this grouping. It is the Community that has therefore taken the initiatives in studying and making proposals about the three main problems of industrial relations affecting Europe in the 1980s: high unemployment; pressures for wider employee representation and information; and, finally, the problems associated with multinational companies will be examined in turn.

UNEMPLOYMENT: CAUSES AND RELIEF

In the 1960s and early 1970s, Western Europe was riding high in terms of ability to keep its people employed. Subsequent world recession eroded this ability, and the impact of an even higher rate of technological advance also bit hard into employment, with the result that the unemployment rate took off and was still climbing in 1984. The trend was further intensified by a new determination among some European governments to pursue what is generally known as a monetarist policy. This may be currently described as a priority concern to keep the rate of money supply and public expenditure in the economy down, while restricting any improvements in per capita social benefits to something below the rate of inflation.

The average unemployment rates (male and female) rose in the Community from 2.4 percent to 10.6 percent of the employed population over the years 1971–83. There was no deviation from this upward trend in any country, and by 1984 the unemployed totaled about 13 million. For the individual countries, the average unemployment rates in 1983 were:

Belgium	14.4%	Ireland	15.2%
Britain	11.7%	Italy	11.9%
Denmark	9.7%	Luxembourg	1.5%
France	8.9%	Netherlands	14.3%
Greece	1.7%	West Germany	8.4%

The other main factor in the sharp rise in unemployment, in addition to the recession and the new monetarism, is the increasingly rapid introduction of high technology in industry and commerce. During the 1950s and 1960s, this process, which was then called automation, was felt mainly in productive industry, typically in the replacement of people by transfer machines on production flow lines. In the late 1970s and the 1980s its effects were much more on sophisticated control mechanisms for machinery, especially through use of the microchip, and in the burgeoning field of information technology, through ever cheaper, physically smaller, but continually more powerful computer systems.

These developments do not necessarily lead, wherever they are applied, to there being fewer jobs available, because in some cases they give a boost to the competitiveness and therefore the market share of the company making the innovations. In general, however, there is at least a short-term job loss as the available work is partly taken over by machine.

The issue of unemployment increasingly dominated industrial relations in Western Europe during the late 1970s and the 1980s. Union demands for job retention and more job creation have been parallel to the demands of political opposition parties in various countries. The huge and prolonged mining strike in Britain in 1984 was about the future number of jobs and working mines in the industry, not about pay or hours. The 1984 national strike in the West German metalworking industries was about the reduction of weekly hours. It would be untrue to say that the jobs and work sharing issue has taken over from the pay issue as the first union priority in industry generally, but it has come to run it a close second at local and national levels. At the international level it has become the dominant issue, because this is the level at which it is difficult to separate industrial issues from broader economic and political ones.

Collective bargaining over pay and conditions plays relatively little part in the work of officials of international trade unions or employer organizations—they are coordinators, lobbyists, and social and economic strategists who must rise above domestic industrial and industrial-relations battles. Such people must have the broadest of views. The unions seem to function fairly well at this level, and have heard empathetic echoes of their views from the European Parliament.

Employer representatives often tend to plough the same furrow as their government spokespeople when it comes to expounding a philosophy on international industrial and economic trends. Unions believe that their industrial strength comes through solidarity, one with another. Employers believe this about themselves too; but under the Community's anticartel and antimonopoly regulations, particular employers also know that their strength

509

comes through acting individually and aggressively within a competitive market. Employer instincts in general are therefore to resist any union demand that would apparently face them with an overhead cost eroding immediate competitiveness.

The main body responsible for putting the trade union case at EC level is the European Trade Union Confederation, or ETUC (see the separate chapter, p. 638, on the trade unions and integration). ETUC speaks for most union national centers in the Community countries, with the exception of the large Communist-oriented center in France and some of the minority Christian Democrat-oriented centers in West Germany, France and the Netherlands. The main body responsible for putting the employer viewpoint is the Union of Industries of the European Community (UNICE). This comprises the central industrial federations of each of the 12 Community countries—the Confederation of British Industries, for instance, and its equivalents elsewhere.

UNICE's ultimate authority derives from its council of presidents, consisting of the presidents of each of the national federations affiliated with it. It has many specialized committees to deal expertly with particular problems and policy issues. UNICE is frequently consulted by the Commission of the EC, and it has close links with the Community's Economic and Social Committee, for whom it provides the employers' section secretariat. In other words, it has roles, functions and contacts for employers similar to those of ETUC for trade unions.

Not surprisingly, ETUC and UNICE have totally different policies with regard to unemployment and how it might be reduced. ETUC and its research and information offshoot, the European Trade Union Institute (ETUI) have produced detailed and consistent policy statements favoring a better sharing and distribution of the available work through shorter hours, longer holidays, earlier retirement, and other means. They also want greater stimulation of the European economy by higher public investment, which would then work through and have its effect on the private sector. ETUC has proposed a public investment program by governments and the Community amounting to an additional one percent of gross domestic product. The investment would go to the sectors of transport, housing, energy, health, education, telecommunications, urban renewal and environmental protection. On the issue of hours, ETUC has said that to create new jobs, "the reduction of working time must be sufficiently large and must be introduced in a short period of time so that it will not entirely be absorbed by productivity gains or reorganizations of work and production."

UNICE, on the other hand, is broadly against intervention in the economy by government and the Community, with some exceptions—planning for the introduction of new technology, for example. On the reduction of working time, UNICE, together with the wider Employers' Liaison Committee of which it is a member, takes the firm view that unemployment cannot generally be alleviated by a reduction in working time. Neither group, however, is opposed to discussions on the reorganization of working time in line with industrial restructuring.

Disagreements between unions and employers over these and other matters led to a deterioration in the climate of industrial relations in the early 1980s at Community level, reflecting a deterioration in a number of member countries at national and local level, often for similar reasons.

The EC Commission, and in particular its previous social affairs commissioner, Ivor Richard, stepped into this breach and made their own positive recommendations to help alleviate the situation. These recommendations followed a number of detailed studies made by the Commission.

Among other objectives, the Commission has been particularly keen to reduce the levels of youth unemployment, which have been up to 40 percent of total unemployment for those aged under 25.

The Community has long had means of alleviating unemployment at regional or local level through its Regional Fund and its Social Fund; these, however, have never been thought of as tools for tackling structural unemployment in Europe, but only for localized and regional relief. But in the early 1980s, partly because of the constant prodding of ETUC, measures to combat unemployment in general began to be formulated, including consideration of the management and reduction of working time as a significant contribution.

In spite of a total lack of agreement between the unions and the employers' organizations, which were consulted at every stage, the Commission came up with a series of conclusions and recommendations that in most ways reflected what ETUC had consistently said, but qualified it somewhat in the light of employer reservations. A Commission study at plant level revealed that "A reduction in working time is generally accompanied, at least in the short run, by an increase in labour productivity per hour. There tends to be an intensification of work, a reduction of idle time, and less absenteeism. In order to maintain the same level of production, therefore, the workforce needs to be increased less proportionately than hours are reduced."[1]

The Commission concluded that there should be not just a reduction but also a reorganization of working time as an instrument of economic and social policy. The reduction should be a target, set perhaps in percentage terms by the Community; but the responsibility for implementing reduced and reorganized working time should be left for settlement between the parties, at sector or enterprise level. The Commission made it clear that a reduction in individual working time, by itself, could not solve the Community's employment problems. Such reductions as were made would be more likely to create jobs if they were fairly large, although in that case the risk might also be larger.

The Commission also held that a reduction and reorganization of working time could help toward sustained economic growth through reduced public expenditure on social benefits, which would release more resources for public investment. This, again, echoed ETUC arguments.

In June 1984, the Commission eventually submitted a somewhat watered-down recommendation to the Council of Ministers for adoption as official Community policy. The text invited member states to include reduced

[1] European Community, *Social Europe*, July 1983.

working time in their consideration of ways to deal with unemployment. It did not, however, set targets, deadlines or methods.

The European Parliament was in favor of this initiative. The Council, with one exception—Britain—voted to accept it. The French president of the Council refused to accept Britain's vote as a veto and referred the matter to a meeting of the European Council—the summit meeting—for further consideration and, perhaps, approval. Even the West German representative was in favor of the recommendation, although the employers in the huge West German metalworking industry had been holding out against a national strike backing the union's attempt to reduce hours to 35 per week. Britain's lone arguments against the recommendation were that the competitiveness of Europe in relation to the rest of the world had declined, and that this was the cause of major job losses. Shorter hours would further decrease competitiveness; if they created any further jobs at all, it would be for Europe's competitors, not for Europe.

It remains to be seen whether other member states can overcome or ignore British resistance so that the Community can press ahead with this major initiative. If it could, this might significantly modify the adverse climate of industrial relations in Europe.

EMPLOYEE REPRESENTATION AND INFORMATION

There have been two other important industrial relations initiatives within the Community in the last decade or so, and these have generated even more dissension than proposals to reduce working time. It is a measure of their controversial nature that they have taken many years to process through the Community machinery, and that no positive conclusion on them had been reached by mid-1984. One is the draft Fifth Directive on company law, providing among other things for direct employee representation on the boards of certain large companies. This is one of a series of measures designed to harmonize company law in the Community. The other initiative is generally called the "Vredeling proposal" after the Dutch former social affairs commissioner who initially sponsored it. It would provide for detailed information about company affairs to be made available to all employees.

Each initiative has gone through many drafts by the Commission, each is strongly supported by unions and equally strongly opposed by employers, and each has the broad sympathy of the European Parliament; yet each has eventually been pulled up short by the Council of Ministers or seems likely to be. Broadly the same alliances emerge on these subjects as on the unemployment question: the unions, the Commission and the European Parliament want to move; the employers and the individual representatives of governments are very cautious about any change in the status quo.

The Fifth Directive

The draft Fifth Directive had its origins in the West German system of

512

Mitbestimmung, or codetermination, whereby employees are represented on the higher tier of the two-tier board system that operates the larger companies in that country. A related system operates in the Netherlands and another in Denmark. The unions concerned like it; the employers do not, but have learned to live with it. The unions have brought pressure within the Community to extend by law the system of employee representation on boards throughout the Community countries, but strong employer views have been expressed against successive drafts. The British Trades Union Congress also has reservations, based on its belief that these matters are more appropriately dealt with by individual unions in particular circumstances rather than by international law, and that it is wrong in principle to provide for representation of all employees, irrespectiveof whether they are union members. The Commission, however, had its own reasons for wanting this initiative because it would help to bring about a harmonization of differing national company laws.

The first draft of the Fifth Directive was produced in 1972, but various objections were made; in 1975, a discussion paper was produced proposing a much greater degree of flexibility to take account of varying national laws and positions. The question has since received intermittent consideration, but progress has been very slow, partly because of the desire to take account of the position of future new members of the Community. It was long and hotly debated in the Economic and Social Committee and in the European Parliament in 1982, and as a consequence new drafts were prepared and put to the Council in 1984.

These proposed that the Fifth Directive would be obligatory only for public limited companies employing over 1,000 people within the Community, whether or not through subsidiaries. Employee representatives would be elected by secret ballot under a proportional representation system, with all employees having a vote. Representatives would be guaranteed freedom of expression. There would be equal rights for workers and shareholders to nominate between one-third and one-half of the board members, either to the supervisory board of a company with a two-tier structure or to a unitary administrative board.

Three other options, however, would be allowable to meet different circumstances. The first would be to have a co-opted supervisory board with similar and equal proportions of employees and shareholders on it, but with final decision of co-optation left to an independent tribunal if either side objects to a nomination. The second option would be to create a separate body at company level, composed entirely of employees' representatives and with functions limited to information and consultative rights identical to those of a supervisory board. Finally, some other form of employee participation might be agreed upon by collective bargaining corresponding to the principles of the other models. If such an agreement were not concluded within a year, one of the other options would apply automatically.

Ultimately, the draft Fifth Directive would provide the right to opt out for employees who decided by majority vote that they did not want any participation procedures at all.

The Vredeling proposal

Perhaps the most heated controversy on social and industrial relations policy has occurred over this draft directive, originally introduced in 1980. Its purpose was to provide procedures for informing and consulting employees in large undertakings with complex structures, including multinational firms.

It would provide that the management of a parent company should, on the same date each year, forward a clear picture of the parent undertaking and its subsidiaries as a whole to each of its subsidiaries. Local management would then provide this information without delay to its employee representatives. The information would outline the company structure, the company's economic and financial situation, probable business developments, production and sales, employment situation and probable trends and investment prospects. Oral explanations would also be provided on request. Consultation with employees would be required where the parent management was proposing major changes affecting employees. These would include transfers, closures, major modifications in production and similar decisions. Subsidiaries would have to be informed in good time before a final decision was taken so that employees could themselves be informed and allowed 30 days to consult and give their opinion on the proposed changes.

The Community's Economic and Social Committee and the European Parliament were both consulted about this draft directive, and it received a mauling from both bodies. In October 1982, the Parliament proposed a number of radical amendments that the Commission later accepted in producing a further draft. That draft was modified in July 1983 and submitted for Council approval again.

The amendments were indeed radical. The original draft would have made the directive applicable to national corporations and multinationals with subsidiaries employing at least 100 people in the Community. The later text changed the minimum to 1,000 employees. The original draft had also proposed the passing on of information by the parent company at semiannual rather than annual intervals, and it would have given employees an automatic right to open consultations with the parent company if their subsidiary management did not communicate or consult. This latter provision was amended to allow employees the opportunity only to put a complaint in writing to the parent firm. The amended draft also tightened up on the subject of secret and confidential information; it would allow a company to withhold information which if disclosed could substantially damage its interests or lead to the failure of its plans. Where there is a dispute over confidentiality, the matter is to be referred to a tribunal or other competent national authority for settlement.

The reason the Vredeling proposal generated so much heat and the most intensive (and successful) lobbying that the European Parliament has seen was that it would directly affect the rights of multinational companies and limit their field of action. ETUC had long pressed the view that multinational companies had supranational powers not matched by any other institution, and that the European Community, as the only body that could regulate them, should therefore create supranational law laying down binding norms on their conduct. The Commission had also taken the view that all employees in the Community should be entitled to information in line with Organization for Economic Cooperation and Development and International Labor Organization voluntary guidelines, and with the best practices already adopted in member states such as Germany, Belgium and the Netherlands. At present, the information and consultation rights of most workers are limited to the local level and do not correspond to the reality of decision making on the management side, which is usually at a higher or group level. In the case of multinationals, decisions may be made in another country altogether, often outside the Community.

UNICE has taken the view that the mandatory procedures originally advocated by the Commission would have been untenable in practice and would have put a heavy burden on all enterprises, particularly small and medium-sized ones. Great problems would have occurred about confidential information, and the authority of local managements would have been undermined. Hence the intensive lobbying—particularly noticeable among U.S.-owned multinationals—and the Commission's consequently amended draft.

This is an outstanding example of how control over the conduct of industrial relations in the Community is moving gradually to Community level. It is an inevitable consequence of the Community's social action program—of which the Vredeling proposal was a part—under the terms of which, social policy has come to be regarded as separate in many ways from economic policy. Making international law on social matters cannot but affect the climate of industrial relations.

MULTINATIONAL COMPANIES

Many unions regard multinational companies as their biggest problem in Europe, not just on the basis of the flow of information and the possibilities of consultation, as has been discussed above, but because in a number of respects these companies are difficult to pin down. Unions need not only information to do their job properly; they need also to carry on a dialogue with the ultimate bosses, to bargain collectively with them and, in the last resort, to put effective sanctions on them if bargaining gets nowhere. The unions' problem is that they lack power and authority within their own international structure to do these things, while national unions have not been willing to give up that authority.

ETUC is not a collective bargaining body, except in some strictly limited senses vis-à-vis the European Commission. It has no direct contact with multinational company representatives, although it may have some incidental contacts. The International Confederation of Free Trade Unions (ICFTU) has, however, 16 international trade secretariats (ITSs) covering the main industrial sectors on an international basis. Because they are international industry specialists, they are potentially the only union organizations that could effectively negotiate with multinationals. They can theoretically tackle multinational companies at their international headquarters, including those companies that operate in Community countries but whose top management is in the United States.

In fact, the ITSs usually cannot negotiate effectively because they do not have final authority to impose sanctions on companies proving intransigent. They can only recommend certain actions to their affiliates, leaving it to those national organizations to make the decisions. Some affiliates may be willing to help impose sanctions; others will not, either because the issue does not appear to affect members in their country directly or because of fear that the multinational might retaliate by moving operations to another country. The multinationals know and understand this union weakness well, and in consequence are not usually inclined to bargain meaningfully with ITSs.

Under these circumstances, it is not surprising that unions increasingly look for multinationals to be constrained by legally enforceable international regulations. The Community, for its part, must either move in that direction or admit the existence of a major sector of the economy and social system where it cannot achieve harmonization between member countries. This would allow distortion of the competitive process and undermine the free market between member states.

Pursuing the objective of constraining the multinationals, the Commission has produced, in addition to the Fifth Directive and the Vredeling proposal, a key draft regulation. Known as the European Company Statute, it would establish a legal basis for setting up European limited companies, which would operate in more than one Community country, have head offices in the Community and own a certain minimum operating capital. Such companies would have to maintain a two-tier board structure, with the supervisory board consisting of one-third employees and one-third shareholders, the other third being co-opted as independent members by these two groups. This draft, however, seems to have lain fairly dormant since 1975, when it was amended.

More limited but nonetheless significant pieces of Community legislation have actually been adopted, harmonizing national legislation on collective redundancies, for example, and laying down an information and consultation procedure for them. Another example concerns the transfer of business or parts of businesses. Employees' rights are guaranteed when, as a result of a closure or a merger, they find themselves working for a new owner. In the case of an employer's bankruptcy, another directive guarantees the payment of wages and other outstanding claims on the part of employees. All these pieces of legislation apply, of course, to all companies, not just to multinationals; but they potentially affect multinationals more than others. Multinationals would be inclined to move their operations to another country if a growing burden of purely national constraining legislation seemed to be adversely affecting their financial position or freedom of action. Where legislation is Community-wide, however, they cannot do that except by pulling out of Community operations altogether and forfeiting their tariff-free sales within a huge European market.

There are many other pieces of pending draft legislation that could affect multinationals directly or indirectly on such matters as employment conditions, taxes, protection of shareholders, takeover bids, oligopoly situations, provision of accounts information, and so on. This does not mean that the Commission and the Community are unaware of the benefits arising from multinational companies in terms of employment, technical advancement and efficiency of operations. Multinationals are accepted as a welcome and inevitable presence in any modern industrial society. The Community's purpose is to ensure that all great concentrations of industrial power recognize their minimum social and economic responsibilities to society. National governments have often been unwilling to enforce such behavior, and trade unions, so far, have been unable to do so.

CONCLUSION

The climate of industrial relations in Western Europe is being influenced to an ever greater degree by arrangements made at the international level. Although trade unions and employers' organizations have only limited authority to act at this level, they each influence the European Community, which is probably now the main force in bringing about changes in employment conditions throughout Europe. Meanwhile, the main collective bargaining, especially on pay issues, is still conducted at traditional levels —national, sectoral or local—by unions and employers organized at these levels. This pattern seems to be set for some years ahead, although international collective bargaining in Europe between unions and employers is a development that seems certain to come about in due course.

FURTHER READING

Annual Reports on the Development of the Social Situation, 1980–82.

ETUC. Congress reports, press releases and ETUI studies. Brussels, 1981–84.

European Communities, Brussels. Monographs from the European File series, especially Nos. 11/81 and 9/84.

European Parliament. "Report on the Harmonisation of Social Legislation in the Member States, 2 April 1984." Working document of Committee on Social Affairs and Employment No. 1-66/84/B. Luxembourg, 1984.

Eurostat. Statistical series, especially *Social Statistics 1982–84.*

Jacobs, Eric. *European Trade Unionism.* London: Croom Helm, 1973.

Macbeath, Innis. *The European Approach to Worker Management Relationships.* British–North American Committee, U.S.A., 1973.

Official Journal. Numerous dates for official texts of Community documents, both final and draft.

Peel, Jack. *The Real Power Game: A Guide to European Industrial Relations.* London: McGraw-Hill, 1979.

Social Europe, July 1983. Memorandum on the reduction and reorganization of working time.

THE SCANDINAVIAN
WELFARE STATE

VIC GEORGE

DESPITE their many differences, the Scandinavian countries appear to outside observers a fairly homogeneous group. They are countries with stable parliamentary democracies, high standards of living, common cultural backgrounds and well-developed social-welfare programs. This homogeneity has grown out of their joint historical past as well as out of deliberate political efforts by the Nordic Council, established after World War II. This chapter is concerned with the general trends of the social-welfare program of the Scandinavian countries and therefore will emphasize the similarities between these programs.

American and European social scientists showed a keen interest in Scandinavian social-welfare programs beginning in the late 1930s as a result of Sweden's "Middle Way" approach to these issues. Some saw this approach as the ideal political compromise and the best way toward improved social conditions; others viewed it with suspicion, fearing that it would gradually undermine democratic institutions and lead to dictatorship. Both these expectations have proved false, and Scandinavian countries today remain advanced welfare capitalist societies, very similar to the affluent countries of Western Europe.

All Scandinavian countries are advanced welfare states in the sense that they spend a substantial proportion of their wealth on social services, employ a large part of their labor force in public services and have enacted a complex body of government rules and regulations in an attempt to influence social and economic affairs. They spend about one-quarter of their gross national product on social security cash benefits, health services, education, housing and the personal social services—Sweden being the highest and Iceland the lowest spender. Public employees constitute 37 percent of the total economically active population in Sweden and 23 percent in Finland. In both social security and public employment, the Scandinavian countries are in the top section of the international league of advanced capitalist societies, with the United States and Japan tied for bottom place.

SOCIAL SECURITY

The Scandinavian countries have social security systems that are fairly comprehensive in terms both of the risks for which benefits are paid and the number of people covered by the various schemes. These systems have developed gradually over the last hundred years but, as in many other European countries, the main strides forward have been made since the end of World War II. They have their origins in the workers' clubs and the benefit societies that sprang up in the wake of industrialization to protect workers against the loss or interruption of income. Bismarck's social-insurance legislation in Germany in the 1880s prompted similar legislative measures in Scandinavia. Once government intervention started, it was bound to grow and develop as part of the demands by organized labor for a better deal.

As in all other advanced industrial societies, whether capitalist or centrally planned, social security systems in Scandinavia are dominated by expenditures on the elderly. Retirement pensions are by far the most expensive of all social security benefit schemes. Formerly, the needy elderly had to rely on poor relief, but by the mid-1930s all the Scandinavian countries had means-tested state pension schemes. It was not until after the end of World War II that universal retirement pensions without means testing were introduced, first in Sweden in 1946 and finally in Iceland in 1965. These pension schemes provided flat-rate amounts, irrespective of the retired person's previous standard of living. The next step was the introduction of an earnings-related retirement pension on top of the basic flat-rate pension. The argument for this was the same as that voiced in many other countries: people become accustomed to a certain standard of living while at work, and it is right that when they are not earning they should receive benefits that enable them as far as possible to maintain their positions. Thus today all Scandinavian countries, with the exception of Iceland, have retirement pensions that consist of a basic flat-rate amount and an earnings-related supplement reflecting the retired person's previous income history. In addition to these state pensions, there are the company pensions provided by some employers, as well as the private pensions arranged by individuals with private insurance companies. In other words, while the state ensures that all the elderly have a minimum income, it allows the income inequalities experienced during working life to continue almost unabated during retirement from work.

Benefits for the sick and the disabled have developed along lines similar to those of retirement pensions. Provided on a voluntary basis at first, and administered by voluntary sickness funds, these benefits have gradually been made almost universal. Their administration varies, and they can be the responsibility either of a government department or a private, nonprofit organization. The important point, however, is that everyone is, in principle, covered.

Unemployment insurance benefits were the last to be introduced, not only in Scandinavia but in many other countries. This form of benefit had to wait until it was generally recognized that unemployment was not the fault of the individual but the result of economic forces beyond his or her control. Interestingly enough, however, only Norway and Iceland have made insurance against unemployment compulsory; in the other three countries it is still voluntary in theory, though in practice trade unions with unemployment funds insist that their members join their fund. All Scandinavian countries place a great deal of emphasis on positive labor-market policies—promoting full employment, labor mobility programs, and training and retraining schemes. The payment of unemployment benefits, important though this is, should not detract from the government's more important responsibility of helping to create employment opportunities for all its citizens.

However comprehensive insurance schemes may be in principle, there will always be individuals who, for a variety of reasons, fall through the insurance net; for these, a means-tested public assistance scheme is necessary. In Scandinavia this is the responsibility of the local government, unlike Britain and other countries where it has become a responsibility of the central government. The combined provision of various insurance benefits and of public assistance should ensure that no one has an income that is below a certain level set by governments—that no one is in officially defined poverty. In all countries, however, including the Scandinavian ones, there are people who are in official poverty for a variety of reasons. They may be unwilling to apply for means-tested benefits; they may be ignorant of how to apply; or their benefits may be reduced in order to protect work incentives. Poverty, therefore, has been substantially reduced but not eliminated in any advanced welfare state inside or outside Scandinavia.

Social security is the single most expensive service in all advanced European countries, and its costs are constantly rising as the numbers of the elderly, the unemployed and one-parent families grow. Thus the index for social security expenditure per capita has more than doubled in all Scandinavian countries since 1970. For this reason, if for no other, the cost of social security is spread among the central government, the local authorities, the employers and the employees in different degrees varying from one country to another. In addition to the problem of cost, there is also the question of how to keep the whole system responsive to changes in the social structure. For example, there is no universal benefit for one-parent families, despite the fact that in Sweden in 1979, 27 percent of all families with dependent children were one-parent families. It is no surprise that one study found that 20 percent of one-parent families had received public assistance over a number of years—a proportion that was three to six times higher than that of two-parent families with children.

HEALTH CARE

The health standards of any nation are affected by many factors other than its provision of health services: working conditions, housing, diet, leisure, and so on. This is not to deny the importance of health services, but to put them within the wider societal framework that enhances or hampers their effectiveness. Whatever indicator of health one uses, it is apparent that standards have risen substantially throughout Scandinavia. Taking all the Nordic countries as a group, deaths under one year of age per thousand live births (the infant mortality rate) declined from 71 in the years 1921–30 to 23 during 1951–60 and to eight in 1980, with slight variations among the countries. Life expectancy at birth in Denmark has risen from 61 years in 1921–30 to 71 years for men and from 62 to 77 years for women in 1980. For Finland, the corresponding figures are 51 to 69 for men, 55 to 77 for women; for Iceland, 56 to 74 for men, 61 to 80 for women; for Norway, 61 to 72 for men, 64 to 79 for women; and for Sweden, 61 to 73 for men, 63 to 79 for women. As one would expect, however, the rise in life expectancy has been less spectacular at age 65; it has increased by about one year for men and by about four years for women. By international comparisons, both infant mortality and life expectancy rates are very favorable indeed. The sharper rise in life expectancy among women, however, has meant that as in most advanced industrial societies, problems of inadequate income, care and companionship among the elderly are primarily problems of elderly women.

Health and medical services have a long history in all Scandinavian countries, dating back to public health legislation during the second half of the 19th century. This type of legislation, common to all nations during the early stages of industrialization and urbanization, was designed to reduce the risks of epidemics arising from unsanitary conditions. It was only during the 20th century that health insurance legislation was introduced to make the provision of all types of health care—doctors, dentists and hospitals —either free or almost free of charge at the point of consumption. As the table below shows, health service is provided free in Sweden and Denmark, but involves some direct charge to the individual consumer in the other countries. Equally clear from the table are the different degrees of financial responsibility borne by the central government. In most Scandinavian nations, however, local authorities have been made responsible for the administration of health services in an effort to make these agencies more responsive to local needs and demands. This has produced a system of finance and administration described by some as "decentralized centralization."

Financing of Health Services, 1979
(% contributions)

	Denmark	Finland	Iceland	Norway	Sweden
Central government	21	39	73	12	15
Local authorities	66	27	8	29	47
Employers	13	27	18	43	38
The insured	—	7	1	16	—

Source: Nordic Council, *Yearbook of Nordic Statistics*, 1981, table 196, p. 281.

Like all other advanced industrial states, Scandinavian countries are experiencing a rise in the cost of health care as well as shortages in the supply of those types of medical services that involve complex technological forms of treatment. The number of doctors, nurses, midwives and dentists has grown so much in Scandinavia that today health personnel rates there are among the highest in Western Europe.

Advanced industrial societies, including those in Scandinavia, have developed comprehensive medical service systems but have not created positive health policies. Not enough attention has been given to health education and preventive services. Alcohol consumption remains high in all Scandinavian countries, despite efforts by some of them to reduce it. Only sporadic campaigns have been mounted with regard to smoking, diet and exercise. While there is good reasons for such campaigns, it is equally true that excessive government control offends against individual liberty. Improvement in health attitudes can only come about gradually, and mainly through health education programs involving not only the government agencies concerned but the mass media as well. The medical profession, too, can play a more positive role than it has done so far.

The general improvement in the provision of health services and the general rise in health standards have not reduced inequalities between the top and bottom of the social structure. The working class does not have as good access to health services as middle- or upper-class groups, and the gap in mortality rates between social classes has not narrowed very much in recent years.

EDUCATION

State education has a long history in Scandinavia, where it developed, as it did in other countries, out of church schools. During the Middle Ages, the church established grammar schools, closely connected with cathedrals and monasteries, with the aim of educating the higher clergy. These schools thrived over the centuries and were the main source of candidates for the emerging universities and holders of the most important positions in church and government. It was not until the 17th and 18th centuries that the church began to establish elementary schools to teach religion and the three R's—reading, writing and arithmetic—mainly to children who were not destined for the grammar schools. The state took over responsibility for elementary education during the 19th century, and by the beginning of the 20th century compulsory elementary education was established throughout Scandinavia. Thus there came into existence the well-known two-track school system: the grammar school for the children of the middle class, and the elementary school for the children of the working class. The first led to university education and white-collar positions; the latter usually led only to jobs in the labor market.

The weaknesses of this form of schooling were apparent, and after the end of World War II political pressures mounted in all countries for a new school system that was less wasteful of individual ability and less obviously class-ridden in its provisions. By the mid-1970s all the Scandinavian countries had reformed their school systems. What emerged was a nine-year compulsory and comprehensive system for all children from the ages of seven to 16. In some of the countries this nine-year school is divided into stages, but the important point is that children move from one stage to the next by age and not on the basis of socioeconomic background. Attempts have recently been made to integrate into the nine-year comprehensive school children with different types of mild handicaps. Schools enroll children in their immediate neighborhoods and efforts are being made to integrate the schools with their communities as far as possible. The starting age of seven is late by European standards; it probably had its origin in the climate and geography of the region, with the long dark winters and the long journeys that children had to make to school in the countryside. Today this starting age creates problems because of the high proportion of working mothers. The need to provide more preschool facilities is therefore pressing. At present such provision is far from adequate, existing for only 39 percent of children below the age of six in Denmark and down to a low of 14 percent in Iceland.

The creation of the nine-year comprehensive school meant that many more young people than before were being prepared for the next stage of schooling, which was the stepping stone to the university and other forms of full-time higher education. It was therefore not unexpected that the mid-1960s witnessed an expansion of university education to cope with the potential demand. This was also the period when social scientists from many countries were providing evidence of the positive effects of higher education on economic growth. Thus political and economic considerations combined to bring about a threefold increase in university students during the 1960s—a phenomenon that was seen to a greater or lesser extent in other advanced industrial societies.

This increase in the number of university places did not, however, mean that university entry was any easier than a couple of decades ago, because it was paralleled by a similar increase in the number of qualified applicants. For this reason, entry to university has remained biased in favor of young people from professional and other middle-class family backgrounds. Some progress has been made toward the reduction of educational inequalities, but not enough to change the structural disadvantage from which working-class young people have always suffered. More progress has been made in narrowing the differences in access to university education by sex.

Education has, of course, an important influence on people's income, housing and health. Those with university education have average incomes between two and three times greater than those with elementary education only. Income, in turn, affects both the quality of housing as well as health standards. These statistical correlations involve several mutually reinforcing processes, all of which point to a simple but important point. Education largely reflects family background, and it cannot therefore be seen as a vehicle for substantially reducing, let alone abolishing, class inequalities. Without the existing educational policies of loans and grants to university students, however, these inequalities would be even greater. In other words, while education policies in Scandinavia and in other advanced welfare states do not reduce income inequalities in any significant way, they do prevent them from becoming wider.

HOUSING

With the exception of Denmark, industrialization and urbanization came later to Scandinavia than to other industrial European countries. As late as 1930, more than half of the population of Sweden lived in rural areas; today, four-fifths of the Swedes live in urban areas. This has meant that

Scandinavian countries escaped the worse excesses of unplanned urban growth, a common feature in industrialized nations of Western Europe during the 19th century. By the 1930s, however, it was generally accepted that government and local authorities had a duty to impose some controls on both the quality and the geographical location of newly constructed housing. On the other hand, since the end of World War II, most Scandinavian countries have had to spend a high proportion of their national income on housing in order to cope with rapid urbanization during this period.

Housing construction statistics bear out the effects of this late urbanization. In Denmark, 55 percent of the dwellings existing in 1975 were constructed before 1950; the corresponding percentages for Finland, Sweden and Norway were 37 percent, 44 percent and 47 percent respectively. Sweden has pursued the most active housing policy of all Scandinavian countries since the war, with the result that today it has one of the most progressive housing standards in the world. Initially, most emphasis was given to building large blocks of apartments to satisfy the general need for housing. Currently, an increasing proportion of new dwellings are family houses for owner-occupation. Indeed, in all Scandinavian countries, there has recently been a decline in the number of new dwellings constructed every year and a corresponding increase in the quality of new housing. As a result of these postwar housing policies, Scandinavian housing standards are high when judged by such physical criteria as the provision of piped water, bathrooms and toilets, and central heating. When judged, however, by such social criteria as play facilities for children, special housing arrangements for the elderly and disabled, and so on, standards are much lower than in other countries. As industrial countries become more affluent, housing standards must more and more be judged by social as well as physical criteria. Moreover, all Scandinavian countries exhibit the usual problems of overcrowding and unsatisfactory housing conditions in those parts of their larger cities where large concentrations of immigrants and students live.

Government aid for housing takes various and complex forms, but can be divided into two kinds: government aid to private builders, housing associations and cooperatives for the construction and modernization of dwellings; and government subsidies to help individuals buy their houses or pay their rents. Over the years, governments have given preferential treatment, mainly in the form of larger grants, to dwelling construction by associations and cooperatives. Financial assistance to individuals can take the form either of loans at low interest rates or weekly rent allowances to low-income groups, the elderly and the handicapped. Over the years, government policy, particularly in Sweden, has shifted away from subsidizing housing construction toward subsidizing people to buy or rent their housing. Housing remains, however, a commodity produced and purchased largely on a private basis.

CONCLUSION

Some social scientists believe that what determines the range and standard of social policies is the level of a country's economic growth rather than its political system. An examination of welfare provision in Scandinavian

524

countries suggests, however, that political factors are an important variable. Clearly, the state of the economy sets certain limits to social welfare, but political factors and social values are important in shaping social services in advanced industrial societies where the material wealth exists to support such services. The political commitment to, and the public support for, social services is higher in Scandinavia than in such other affluent countries as the United States or Japan. Evidence of this commitment is that the backlashes against welfare that have occurred during recent years in some advanced industrial countries have had only a passing and minor influence in Scandinavia. There are many reasons for this political and public commitment to welfare, but one of them is the universal provision of social services, with the result that all sections of the community are benefited rather than merely the needy and the deprived. Indeed, a close examination of welfare provision shows that the middle classes benefit, on the whole, as much as the working-class sections of society. It is this feature of the welfare state that has helped to make it such a relatively stable political system during the last 40 years in Scandinavia and elsewhere.

FURTHER READING

Castles, F. G. *The Social Democratic Image of Society.* London: Routledge and Kegan Paul, 1978.

Childs, M. W. *The Middle Way.* New Haven, Conn.: Yale University Press, 1947.

Dixon, C. W. *Society, Schools and Progress in Scandinavia.* New York: Pergamon Press, 1965.

Friis, E. J., ed. *Det Danske Selskab*, Nordic Democracy, 1981.

———. "The Nordic Welfare States," *Acta Sociologica*, Vol. 2 (supplement), 1978.

Korpi, W. *The Working Class in Welfare Capitalism.* London: Routledge and Kegan Paul, 1978.

Kuusi, P. *Social Policy for the Sixties: A Plan for Finland.* Finnish Social Policy Association, 1964.

Nelson, G., ed. *Freedom and Welfare.* Ministries of Social Affairs of Denmark, Finland, Iceland, Norway and Sweden, 1953.

Nordic Council. *Yearbook of Nordic Statistics.* 1981.

Wilson, D. *The Welfare State in Sweden.* London: Heinemann, 1979.

EDUCATION IN
WESTERN EUROPE

BRIAN HOLMES

HISTORY OF COMMON EDUCATIONAL INSTITUTIONS

The most powerful educational institutions in Western Europe since the Middle Ages have been the universities. Academic institutions known as grammar schools, catering to a small minority of children, were established to prepare young people for these universities and the learned professions. Many of the grammar schools, such as the *lycées* of France, were set up in the 19th century and run by the state; Britain, depending largely on private endeavor until 1902, was an exception. The teachers in these academic secondary schools and the professors in the universities formed a community of scholars. In many countries, the links between members of these two groups still remain close, principally because all of them are university graduates. The most usual name for the traditional university preparatory school is *Gymnasium* (as in Austria, Cyprus, Denmark, Germany, the Netherlands, Norway, Sweden and Switzerland). In France it is the *lycée*, in Belgium the *athénée* (for boys) and *lycée* (for girls) and in Italy the *liceo-classico*. In England, grammar and independent public schools functioned exclusively as university preparatory schools. Now, everywhere, the trend is for newer forms of university preparatory school to develop.

Schools that provided education for everyone were not firmly established in Europe until the 19th century. The points of contact between these schools and the academic secondary schools were slight, since the former made no attempt to prepare pupils for university entrance. Gradually, during the 20th century, the schools preparing young children for the academic secondary schools and those providing education for the mass of children in the elementary system were brought together to form a unified pattern of primary schools. By the end of World War II, most national systems included primary schools to which children went, irrespective of ability, until the age of 10 or 12. Pupils were then transferred to one of a number of postprimary schools or remained in the senior classes of the same elementary schools. A distinction was made between "secondary schools," which prepared pupils for university entrance, and other types of postprimary schools.

Among the latter were special vocational schools, where children were trained for particular occupations. In many countries, an extensive system of such schools was established; the age at which children entered them varied, as did the range of occupations for which they were prepared. England and Wales were exceptions; neither technical nor commercial schools developed to any extent until after 1902.

Teacher training institutions in Europe developed along similar lines. Normal schools were established in the 19th century to train elementary school teachers. Initially, and even as late as 1980 in many countries, trainee teachers were recruited from the elementary schools. In the training colleges, a continuation of general education and professional training was provided. In England and Wales, by 1940, the vast majority of would-be teachers had attended a secondary school. In general, the two systems, elementary and secondary (including teacher training), were separate.

Since 1945, moves have been made to bring the two very different systems of teacher education and training together. The McNair Report in Britain in 1944 proposed that all teacher education should be linked with universities through area training organizations. One of the proposals made by the Robbins Committee in the 1960s was that all teachers should be graduates, and as a result bachelor of education (B.Ed.) degrees were introduced.

A somewhat similar duality grew up in higher education. During the 19th century, special technological institutions were established to train engineers and commercial personnel. In France, the *grandes écoles*, set up to prepare top-level civil servants and military personnel, achieved the highest prestige; elsewhere, though, the technological institutions were regarded with less favor than the universities. In England, most of the 19th-century civic universities evolved from technical colleges and included engineering faculties.

Postwar reform movements in Europe have generally attempted to break down the traditional distinction between schools for members of a small elite and those for the masses, and between liberal education and vocational or manual training.

NATIONAL AIMS IN EDUCATION

The U.N. Declaration of Human Rights, signed in 1948, undoubtedly had a major influence on educational aims in Western Europe. Article 26 proclaimed: "Everyone has the right to education. Education shall be free, at least in the elementary stages. Elementary education shall be compulsory." The declaration went further: secondary and higher education should be made available to all those who could benefit from it. By 1945, most Western European countries possessed compulsory systems of elementary education. Their higher aims today reflect U.N. ambitions. Yet establishing aims that make lifelong education a human right did not lead immediately to its realization in practice. The generalized destruction after World War II, plus long-established, resilient European educational traditions and institutions delayed reform, despite reform proposals and national legislation.

Three changes created postwar problems in the highly selective Western European educational systems. First was an explosion of aspirations and expectations, which found expression in demands for an extension of compulsory school attendance and for greater equality of opportunity to enter secondary schools and universities. Second, the postwar baby boom meant that thousands more children crowded into the primary schools in the early 1950s, increased the problems of secondary school selection in the middle and late 1950s and created unprecedented pressures on the universities to expand during the early 1960s. Third, all the nations participating in the war had suffered great material damage. The Allied ministers of education in exile formulated plans during the war that led to the rapid reestablishment of educational systems throughout Western Europe after 1945. The 1960s became a decade of economic growth, while the 1970s were a period of economic crisis. It is against such a background of economic changes, fluctuations in the size of school-age population and persisting high demand for education that reforms in Western European education should be viewed.

In spite of legislation in most Western European nations, until recently there remained two parallel forms of second-level education. Long secondary education prepared young people for the universities and teaching; short second-level education was provided in either technical-commercial schools or terminal general nonvocational schools. At least three models persisted. Structure 1, consisting of three types of school—university preparation, teacher training and technical-commercial—provided parallel postprimary courses of instruction. Structure 2 was made up of two types of school providing for university preparation and general nonvocational education. Structure 3, one type of school, offered, at least up to the age of 15, a common program for all children.

While the general tendency has been to move from Structure 1 to Structure 3 (Structure 2 being largely restricted to Britain), much still remained to be changed. Educational reformers throughout Western Europe had as their objective the transformation of differentiated systems of second-level schooling, either by postponing selection and differentiation by school type or by creating a common or comprehensive school for all children up to the maximum age for compulsory attendance. During the 1960s, determined efforts were made to move away from Structure 1 toward Structure 3. These efforts met with varied success. This general tendency may be illustrated by describing some of the main features of reform legislation in selected countries, and then outlining the national systems as they existed in 1984.

England and Wales
Perhaps the most significant aspect of the 1944 English Education Act was the manner in which it abolished the old dual system in terms of control, finance and objectives between secondary and elementary schools. Education was reorganized in all three stages—primary, secondary and further. Local education authorities (LEAs) were made responsible to the minister of education for providing services at each level. The reforms abolished fees, proposed raising the school-leaving age and advocated part-time education in county colleges up to the age of 18. In 1965, the school-leaving age was raised to 16 effective as of 1970. According to the 1944 Act, secondary education was to be provided according to the "age, aptitude, and ability" of individual

children; beyond this, LEAs were free to organize secondary schools as they wished.

Since about 1946, the Labour party and Labour-controlled LEAs have favored Structure 3, while the Conservative party has preferred Structure 1. Between 1945 and 1965, educational debate centered on the fairness of the 11-plus procedures, while social scientists tried to show the extent to which the class origins of parents determined the educational opportunities of their children. Opposition to change weakened over the years, and in 1965 a Labour minister of education and science was in a position to ask all LEAs to submit their proposals for moving toward a comprehensive secondary school system. Local authorities were invited to select one of six models. The choices offered have given rise to very considerable variety in the ways in which second-level education is organized in England and Wales. In the Inner London Education Authority (the largest LEA in Britain), for example, comprehensive schools enroll pupils at the age of about 11 and retain them through the sixth form prior to admission to an institution of higher education or to the world of work. Leicestershire County Council LEA has middle schools for students from the age of 10 to 16, and upper secondary schools. Several authorities have sixth-form colleges, while a few LEAs retain selective grammar schools.

Sweden

In Sweden, the connection between the elementary and the secondary school turned out to be the most crucial problem for the 1940 School Committee. Since 1927, transfer from the primary schools has been possible after either four or six years. The 1946 Parliamentary School Commission, appointed by a Socialist government, proposed to resolve this dilemma by introducing a "unitary," or "comprehensive," school organization for the entire period of compulsory education. The report was fiercely debated, and experiments based on its recommendations were tried out in 14 districts. By 1959, about one-third of the school districts had started comprehensive schools. Experimentation and research had provided evidence that such schools offered an appropriate solution to the problem of differentiation. In 1963, the Swedish parliament resolved that nine years' compulsory attendance at school was to be required for all children.

The new comprehensive school (*grundskolan*) system was to be introduced gradually and completed during the school year 1972–73. The new type of school was divided into three departments. In the lower (grades 1–3) and middle (grades 4–6) departments, all the pupils of an age-group take the same subjects, and pupils in one grade are taught by the same teacher. As far as possible, these practices continue in the upper department (grades 7–8), but in addition to the common nucleus of subjects, a number of optional subjects are offered so that for the first time pupils are divided into groups according to their option. The principle accepted is that parents choose the subjects their children are to study in the upper department. In the ninth grade there are nine streams and five sections, two of which are practical and two theoretical.

After the comprehensive school, children may transfer to one of two kinds of shorter education (a two-year continuation school or a three-year vocational school) or to one of two kinds of longer education: an academic grammar school (*gymnasium*) or a vocational *gymnasium* (technical or commercial), lasting three years. So, in principle, the Swedish reform delays selection and differentiation until the ninth year of school, but even then, choice is based upon parents' wishes in consultation with the pupil after information has been provided them by the school.

France

The object of the French educational reforms has been to delay selection and differentiation. The reforms are, in principle, based on the recommendations of the Langevin-Wallon Committee, established in 1944, for an undifferentiated postprimary school (*école unique*) for children from the ages of 11 to 15. Only under the presidency of Charles de Gaulle, however, was it possible to issue a number of decrees and ordinances designed radically to reform the structure of French education at the secondary stage. A decree of January 6, 1959, covered all the important aspects of education. Compulsory schooling had three levels: an elementary cycle from the age of six, lasting five years; an observation cycle, lasting two years, provided in various types of postprimary school; and a terminal cycle of varying length provided in one of a variety of institutions. The object of the observation cycle was to assess the abilities of children in order to advise parents on the most appropriate form of subsequent education. Orientation councils were responsible for advising which course a child should follow. If parents preferred another course, the child took an examination to establish his or her ability to follow it. There were to be possibilities of transfer from one stream to another, as well as opportunities for children who had not been admitted earlier to a regular orientation class to take an examination at about the age of 13 to enter special classes preparing them for the course of studies they had chosen.

The 1959 decree also provided for shorter education courses after the period of orientation in either general secondary or technical schools. Longer education was provided in general or technical *lycées*—courses leading to the higher school examination (*baccalauréat*). There were three sections in the first two years of the five-year course, seven sections in the third and fourth years, and five in the fifth year. By extending observation and orientation to four years, the distinction between long and short education was retained; except for the classical language option, the integration of study programs continued. Long general education in classical and modern *lycées* led to the universities. Long technical education led to higher technical education for those who were successful. The tendency since 1962 has been to move toward Structure 2, providing a variety of courses in general secondary schools. In these schools there was also a two-year transitional stream from the age of 12 (largely for rural children), followed by terminal practical education taught by general secondary school and specialized teachers. The intention, thus, was virtually to postpone selection (except for very able children who select the classical language option) until the end of nine years of schooling.

The Haby Reform of 1975 was in many ways true to the spirit of earlier reforms. Under this law, the primary-secondary program was to remain as before: 12 years in a five-year elementary school (*école élémentaire*). The law assumed that children would spend one or more years in a preschool establishment (*école maternelle*). After the five-year elementary school, pupils enter a four-year *collège*. The first two years constitute a common cycle of studies; the third and fourth years are the guidance cycle (*cycle d'orientation*). At the end of the guidance cycle, pupils decide whether to go to a *lycée* or to enter directly into the work force as apprentices. The academic-technological *lycées* lead, in three-year courses, to the university entrance examination (*baccalauréat*) or to a technician's certificate. Vocational *lycées* lead, in one year, to a certificate of professional education or, in two years, to a certificate of professional competency or to a certificate of professional studies.

COMMON FEATURES OF NATIONAL SYSTEMS IN THE 1980s

Most Western European countries are extending their preschool provision by means of nursery schools or kindergartens. France provides preschool education for children between the ages of two and six on a voluntary basis. Most kindergarten children between four and six are maintained privately in West Germany. State nursery schools accept children between three and six in Italy on a voluntary and free basis. In Luxembourg, all children over four are entitled to admission to a *jardin d'enfants*. Children may be admitted to nursery schools in the Netherlands at the age of four. Day-care institutions cater to children up to the age of three, and full-day institutions for children up to six in Norway. Local authorities in Sweden must provide places for six-year-old children. Preschool education is optional in Turkey.

Compulsory education starts at seven in the northern countries—Iceland, Norway and Sweden. Elsewhere, compulsory education normally starts at the age of six. England, Wales and Luxembourg are exceptional in that compulsory attendance is from the age of five. Transfer from the first level of education takes place between the ages of 10 (Germany) and 12 (Austria, Netherlands, Belgium, Cyprus, Greece, Luxembourg and Switzerland). Transfer is at 11 in Denmark, France, England and Wales, Italy, Spain and Turkey. For some children, the primary or second primary stage is prolonged: in Austria and Norway to 14; in Iceland and Sweden to 13. Selection or transfer procedures have traditionally been based upon examination and other test results. Entrance examinations to secondary schools have been abolished in many countries, including England and Wales, Austria, Denmark, Finland, Spain and Sweden. The Netherlands, some *Länder* in Germany and Belgium have followed France in introducing an orientation cycle for pupils who have completed first-level education. These trends are part of the movement to make secondary education open to all in comprehensive schools. Reform movements have generally made the age of transfer less precise than formerly.

The age of compulsory school attendance varies too. By 1965, legislation had been passed raising the leaving age to 16 in France (effective 1967), Britain (effective 1970), Sweden (under the 1962 reforms) and some cantons of Switzerland. Fifteen was the age in some of the *Länder* of Germany, in Austria, Iceland, most areas of Norway and in the Netherlands. Fourteen was still the leaving age in Belgium, Denmark, Ireland, Italy, Luxembourg and Turkey. In Cyprus, Spain and Greece it was still 12. Encouragement to stay beyond the statutory age on a voluntary basis was given in 1963 in Belgium, Spain, Ireland, Italy, the Netherlands, Denmark and Turkey.

The period of compulsory attendance has thus been lengthened in most Western European countries. The age at which compulsory attendance ceases, and the actual years of compulsory attendance, nevertheless vary. In Britain, the leaving age of 16 ensures 11 years of compulsory attendance. France and the Netherlands, where pupils start school at six, and Luxembourg, where the starting age is five, have a 10-year period of compulsory education; in Denmark, Finland and West Germany, the period is nine years; in Belgium, Italy, Spain and Sweden, it is eight years; and in Greece, compulsory attendance lasts six years. In most countries, many pupils stay on after the maximum age they are compelled to attend school.

EFFECTS OF POPULATION PRESSURES

In practice, the good intentions of the reformers were often thwarted, modified or abandoned as a result of political and professional opposition and hard economic facts. Perhaps of greatest importance, however, were the forces of expansion arising from the postwar population explosion.

The bulge in crude birthrates during 1945–49, taking figures for the 1930s as a base, was around 30 percent. In Denmark, the crude birthrate rose from about 18 per thousand of population in 1935–39 to about 22 per thousand during the period 1945–49; in France, in the same period, from 15 to about 20; in the Netherlands, from 20 to 26; and in England and Wales, from about 15 to 18. Only in a few countries, such as Germany, Italy and Spain, did the crude birthrates in the late 1940s remain steady or drop compared with the rates during the late 1930s.

The resulting increases in births in the postwar period were impressive. In France in 1940, some 559,000 babies were born; in 1945, the figure was 643,000, and by 1950, it had reached 862,000. In England and Wales in 1940, births numbered approximately 540,000; in 1945, they were 680,000; and by 1950, the figure was 698,000. These increases were of the order of three to six percent per year. Furthermore, infant mortality rates dropped everywhere between 1945 and 1960. The rates in Scandinavia, the Netherlands and England and Wales were always less than in France, Italy and Spain. But in France, the rates dropped from some 72 per thousand live births during 1945–49 to 46 in 1950–54 and 21 in 1960. In Sweden the corresponding figures were 26 in 1945–49, 20 in 1950–54 and 17 in 1960. In England and Wales, the drop was from 39 in 1945–49 to 28 in 1950–54 and 22 in 1960.

These trends account for the increases in the number of school-age children. Statistics are not readily available, but throughout Western Europe

UNESCO population figures show that between 1955 and 1960, the size of the five to nine age-group remained fairly constant at around 36 million. There was an increase of some two million in the size of the 10–14 age-group over the same period, and a rise of four million in the 15–19 age-group. These crude statistics show how the postwar population explosion affected the different stages of education between 1945 and 1965.

UNESCO statistics (see Table 1) show how the increases in primary school-age populations were reflected in school enrollments in the early 1950s. By the second half of this decade, the rate of increase had slowed down and in some countries had declined. Approximate figures give some idea of trends, but it should be noted that comparative educational statistics need to be used with care, because of changes in systems of classification and because of the difficulties of establishing categories that apply equally to all countries.

Table 1
PRIMARY SCHOOL ENROLLMENTS (000)

	1950	1955	1960	Percentage increase 1950–60
Austria	856	747	722	Fall
Belgium	804	839	919	14
Britain (England and Wales)	4,066	4,714	4,302	5.7
Denmark	434	526	559	29
France	4,063	5,171	5,822	45
Greece	900	948	921	2.3
Iceland	15	17	23	53
Ireland	468	501	501	29
Italy	4,640	4,741	4,494	Fall
Netherlands	1,241	1,452	1,416	14
Norway	343	447	430	Reclassification
Spain	2,793	3,117	3,777	32
Sweden	707	844	808	14
Turkey	1,617	1,982	2,866	77
West Germany	6,377	4,865	5,081	Fall

Increased secondary school enrollments reflect not only school-age population increases but changes in government policy. Raising the school-leaving age obviously made a considerable difference, but many campaigns to encourage pupils to remain at school on a voluntary basis have also had an effect. Changes in terminology, and hence in the classification of school types, also influence figures. As stated, opportunities exist to enroll in general, technical or teacher training secondary schools. Some indication of policies of expansion at the second stage can be gained from enrollment figures in general secondary and technical secondary schools. Turkey provides an example of a phenomenal expansion of secondary education. The growth in enrollments in Norway reflects reorganization under the reform laws. The approximate figures in Table 2 are derived from UNESCO sources.

Table 2
GENERAL SECONDARY SCHOOL ENROLLMENTS (000)

	1950	1955	1960	Percentage rise 1950–60
Austria	54	79	81	50
Belgium	123	237	292	137
Britain (England and Wales)	1,975	2,395	3,261	66
Denmark	98	128	130	32
France	818	1,027	1,701	106
Greece	185	200	273	47
Iceland	5	6	10	96
Ireland	54	65	83	56
Italy	533	697	1,624	Reclassification
Netherlands	216	317	483	120
Norway	33	49	129	Reclassification
Spain	222	328	476	114
Sweden	135	177	222	75
Turkey	90	165	373	314
West Germany	829	1,169	1,239	50

Enrollments in vocational education should be treated with care, because in West Germany and Austria vast numbers take part-time vocational instruction. The age range of such students is very considerable. It should also be noted that there are usually at least two levels at which technical education is provided at the second stage. One level prepares technicians and other highly skilled personnel who might expect to become foremen in industry or commerce. Very approximate statistics, nevertheless, give some indication of the extent to which, as a result of expansion, technical education has been relatively neglected, or has received a proportion of the increase in students similar to that of the general schools or has gained on them proportionally (see Table 3).

With a few exceptions, a general tendency to expand general secondary rather than vocational secondary education is apparent from Tables 1–3. This suggests that Structure 2 represents an intermediate phase of development between Structure 1 and Structure 3 in the evolution of the second stage of education in Western Europe during the early postwar period.

By the mid-1970s, demographic trends continued to push school enrollments up in line with the rise in total populations. Table 4 illustrates how populations and school enrollments grew in selected Western European countries.

Population increases were not the same everywhere, and the rise in enrollments was far greater in some countries than in others. Between 1960 and 1970, school enrollments in Turkey almost doubled, although the population increased by only 28 percent. Over the same decade, school enrollments in Italy rose by 34 percent, while the population grew by not more than 6.7 percent. These variations indicate the extent to which nations were attempting to catch up, under conditions of population expansion, with those

Table 3
VOCATIONAL SECONDARY SCHOOL ENROLLMENTS (000)

	1950	1955	1960	*Percentage rise* 1950–60
Austria	111	189	210*	90
Belgium	228	238	339	49
Denmark	112	121	145	30
France	242	292	550	128
Iceland	3	2.6	2.8	Fall
Ireland	518	743	460	Fall
Italy	518	743	460	Fall
Netherlands	282	347	488	75
Norway	46	48	50	Fall
Spain	154	167	209	26
Sweden	95	120	171	80
West Germany	1,832	2,482	1,866*	1.8

* Includes part-time enrollments.

Table 4

GROWTH OF POPULATION AND SCHOOL ENROLLMENTS

		Population (000)	*School enrollments* (000)
Netherlands	1960	11,480	2,271
	1970	11,790	2,699
	1974	11,960	3,025
Belgium	1960	9,153	1,497
	1970	9,637	1,832
	1974	9,846	1,833
Denmark	1960	4,581	868
	1970	4,928	916
	1974	5,025	969
Finland	1960	4,430	925
	1970	4,606	955
	1974	4,651	950
France	1960	45,684	8,384
	1970	50,669	10,022
	1974	52,913	10,514
Italy	1960	50,223	6,958
	1970	53,565	9,352
	1974	55,023	10,685
West Germany	1960	55,433	6,862
	1970	60,700	9,553
	1974	61,259	10,910

European countries that had virtually established compulsory education for all.

During this period, the composition of populations in Western Europe was changed by influxes of foreign workers. The presence in schools of pupils from diverse home backgrounds—in terms of language, religion and ethnicity—created problems of policy in all those nations committed to the provision of education as a human right regardless of gender, race, religion, language, social class or place of residence. By the 1980s, the problems of providing education in multicultural societies were preoccupying the attention of educators throughout the European Community (EC) as a consequence of the free movement of labor stipulated in the Treaty of Rome. Other difficulties were caused by the economic crisis, the long recession and the growth of unemployment. The general decline in the number of pupils enrolled in schools is shown in Table 5. Declines occurred first, naturally, at the first level of education. Later, second-level enrollments dropped. The pressure to strengthen or reintroduce vocational education and thereby to return to Structure 1 became stronger. A notable example of this was the creation of the Manpower Services Commission in Britain. Considerable attention was paid to relationships between school and work. The Sixth Educational Plan in France (1971–75) took into account repetition rates in first-level schools and premature dropout rates at the second level. It proposed that no pupils should leave school without having obtained an education that would prepare them for a job, and that all education courses should provide basic knowledge in technology and the natural sciences. The simple extension of compulsory schooling as a way of meeting the uncertainties of the labor market was not regarded as an adequate response to rising youth unemployment. Indeed, the policy in West Germany was to retain vocational and technical training courses in schools, even though well-qualified skilled workers were not immediately able to obtain appropriate jobs.

Table 5
ENROLLMENTS, 1981 (000)

	Total First stage	Total Second stage	Vocational Second stage
Belgium	821	835	300
Britain	4,911	5,342	255
Denmark	426	499	126
France	4,507	3,936	1,114
Italy	4,336	5,229	1,597
Netherlands	1,270	1,413	576
Sweden	662	606	163
West Germany	4,776	4,301	610

EXAMINATIONS AND UNIVERSITY EXPANSION

All three structures in the highly selective educational systems of Western Europe prior to the 1960s were maintained by examinations that served the functions of selection, testing acquired knowledge and providing acceptable vocational qualifications. Children faced major examinations at three main points in their school career: on transfer from primary school, at the end of shorter secondary education, and at the end of longer secondary education. In practice, the examinations taken at the end of shorter secondary education covered general, technical and vocational subjects in countries with highly differentiated second-level schooling. The system in England and Wales was less diversified, and examinations leading to technical qualifications were not taken at the end of the first stage or the second stage of second-level education.

In France, the examination system was highly organized. Each stage of education was completed by a certificate or diploma that qualified the student either to proceed to the next stage of education or to enter a particular occupation or profession. Thus there was a certificate at the end of primary education, certificates for various levels of technical competence and a certificate for those who left at the end of the short general education. The final *baccalauréat* was prepared for by students in the *lycées* or technical *lycées* and colleges in classical, modern or technical studies. To enter one of the higher institutes (*grandes écoles*), special competitive examinations were taken. Possession of a *baccalauréat* gave automatic right of entry to any French university.

Between 1962 and 1965, the *baccalauréat* was the subject of considerable debate regarding the desirability of making it the final school examination instead of the first university examination. The tradition of a two-part examination (the first part was to be abolished in favor of a qualifying test or, alternatively, school records) and the desirability of adding some conditions to the requirement that entrants to the university should have a *baccalauréat* were also discussed. During 1960–65, further attempts were made to use the *baccalauréat* as a link between the two separate systems of teacher education: that for elementary school teachers and that for academic secondary school teachers. The fact that diplomas in technical education were considered equivalent to parts of the *baccalauréat* helped to break down the distinction between university preparation and other forms of long secondary education.

The Haby Reform proposals, which became law in 1975, modified the *baccalauréat* examination. The new award was first conferred in 1979. At the end of the 11th grade (*classe de première*), students are tested on a core curriculum—French, philosophy, mathematics, economic and social studies, and physical and natural sciences. On the results of these examinations and their cumulative record, students enter the final form or grade, where they are examined in the specialized subjects they have chosen to study. Students passing the 11th-form examinations are awarded a diploma of general secondary studies. Success at the end of the 12th year earns a *baccalauréat*. For this, students must pass in four subjects, at least three at advanced level. The Haby Reform reduced the highly differentiated system of second stage, second-level schools and the multiplicity of examinations.

Throughout continental Europe, the final examination at the end of the classical option in the university preparatory form of long education gave access to all the faculties of the university. In Germany, the examination

537

is called the *Abitur*, in Austria the *Matura* and in Scandinavia the *Student* examination. After 1945, a movement grew to open a second way to the universities to students from less academic secondary schools or those who had studied subjects other than classical languages. In 1963 a proposal was considered in the Netherlands to admit persons with any one of the certificates indicating completion of study in a preuniversity school to all faculties of the universities. (Previously, some faculties were restricted to students with classical certificates.) Again, there was a move to make technical diplomas equivalent to university examinations. In Italy, students holding diplomas from certain vocational institutes may be admitted to the appropriate university faculties. Another way of providing entry to the university is to establish special tests for students who have come up through schools other than university preparatory institutions. In some German *Länder*, such tests are given to students from engineering schools who wish to enter higher technical colleges (*technische Hochschulen*).

In England and Wales, the formal requirements for entry to a university were and are based upon success in the General Certificate of Education (GCE) examination, which is administered by a number of university examining boards on the advice of a schools examination council. This examination is at two levels. The O (ordinary) level papers are usually taken by students after five years at a secondary school; the A (advanced) level papers after seven or eight years of secondary education. Passes at the O level are required for entry to colleges of education and are also accepted for entry to some of the higher technical certificate courses. They are, in general, accepted by employers as evidence that a candidate has received a good basic education. The Certificate of Secondary Education (CSE) is intended for less academic pupils in secondary schools. It is intended to introduce a single General Certificate of Secondary Education (GCSE), the so-called 16-plus examination. The minimum university entrance requirements are two A-level passes, presupposing that the student will have passed a number of papers (between five and 10 subjects) at the O level. Each university and department within a university is free to accept students on the basis of GCE results and an interview. Separate entrance examinations to colleges at Oxford and Cambridge universities are being phased out.

Throughout Western Europe, demand for places in universities grew as a consequence of the baby boom and rising expectations. In the early 1960s, more than two applicants were competing for every place in the universities throughout the world. For institutions with very high status, competition for places was far greater. The number of students taking university entrance examinations grew as age cohorts increased. Over the 10 years from 1960 to 1970, the French university population more than doubled—from some 300,000 to 650,000. In West Germany, university enrollments rose from 212,400 in 1960 to 351,000 in 1970, with a further radical increase predicted. In Britain, full-time university students numbered some 104,000 in 1960; by 1970 the figure was 220,000.

To ease the pressure on universities, polytechnics were established in Britain and university institutes of technology were set up in France; and in the mid-1960s, schemes to establish systems of short-cycle higher education were discussed and actively promoted by the Organization for Economic Cooperation and Development (OECD). University enrollments continued to rise, as Tables 6 and 7 indicate.

Table 6
AVERAGE ANNUAL UNIVERSITY ENROLLMENTS, 1937–40

Country	Total population (millions)	University students (thousands)	Students per thousand of population
Belgium	8.5	12	1.4
Britain (England and Wales)	46	55	1.2
France	42	84	2
Italy	45	72	1.9
Netherlands	8.5	9	1.1
Sweden	6.25	9	1.3

Table 7
UNIVERSITY ENROLLMENTS, 1960

Country	Total population (millions)	University students (thousands)	Students per thousand of population
Belgium	9	52	5.8
Britain (England and Wales)	46.25	138	2.9
France	45.5	215	4.7
Italy	49.5	192	3.9
Netherlands	11.5	106	9
Sweden	7.5	37	4.9

An explosion in enrollments is well illustrated by figures for the early 1980s. Although rates of expansion had slowed down and governments throughout Europe were trying, under conditions of slow economic growth, to reduce the total costs of providing higher education for all, the overall figures show a massive increase over those for 1960. Rates of growth far exceeded growths in total population (see Table 8).

Table 8
UNIVERSITY ENROLLMENTS, 1980 (estimated)

Country	Total population (millions)	University students (thousands)	Students per thousand of population
Belgium	10	95	9.5
Britain (England and Wales)	49	407	8.3
France	53.5	870	16.2
Italy	56.5	1,110	19.8
Netherlands	14	149	10.6
Sweden	8.25	204	24.6

While the proportions of university enrollments have not quite reached the levels achieved in the United States, Japan or the Soviet Union, there is no doubt that Western European university expansion has taken place at an unprecedented rate. It has had major consequences in terms of the realization of expectations, the cost of providing education and the internal organization and management of universities. In so far as university teachers have defined worthwhile knowledge and have been able to dictate university entrance requirements, they have had, and continue to have, a profound influence on the content of education in secondary and, indeed, primary schools.

THE CONTENT OF EDUCATION

Traditionally, education in Western Europe has been knowledge-centered. Liberal education in Britain, *culture générale* in France and *Bildung* in Germany express similar, but not identical, concepts. Their aim has been to provide a good general education for those being prepared for leadership.

Two major theories have informed Western European principles of education. One, derived from Aristotle and legitimized by the Roman Catholic church, suggests that a good general education can be provided through seven essential subjects, the liberal arts. They have had a long and distinguished history, and are enshrined today in the highly specialized curricula followed by students in England and Wales. The view that essential subjects should form the basis of a sound general curriculum has been repeated in modified form by a number of English curriculum theorists. The most widely accepted alternative theory may be described as encyclopedism. This theory, advanced by 18th-century French social and educational reformers, suggests that all knowledge should be included in the school curriculum. In practical terms, essentialism legitimizes a curriculum that includes a few carefully selected subjects; encyclopedism justifies the inclusion of as wide a range of subjects as possible.

In the light of these theories, a broad distinction can be drawn between curricula in most continental European schools and those offered in the schools of England and Wales at virtually every level of education. A second difference lies in the freedom given to teachers in English schools to devise their own curricula within the constraints laid down by the examination system. Legally, the curriculum is the responsibility of the LEAs and school governors. In practice, decisions about content, methods of teaching and selection of textbooks are usually left to headmasters and headmistresses and their staffs. The consequence is that in primary schools, the curriculum is often less subject-based than in other European schools. After the first two years of secondary school, pupils are often given a choice and may begin to specialize either in the arts or sciences, or simply choose less academic subjects. The traditional, highly specialized sixth-form courses are much debated. Proposals to broaden the content of preuniversity school education have frequently been thwarted by the demands of university teachers that undergraduates entering their departments should have adequate knowledge of the specialized subjects to be studied.

In France, the ministry prescribes the subjects that must be taught in primary schools. At the first stage of the secondary level of education, there is a core of required subjects, plus a specialized option chosen in the eighth and ninth grades. During the second stage of the secondary level, as pupils prepare in their final three years at school for higher education, they study a core curriculum. To gain a *baccalauréat*, students must pass examinations in four subjects, of which three must be advanced-level subjects. In West Germany, the ministry of education and cultural affairs of each *Land* draws up its own curricula and syllabuses. The basic subjects are studied at all levels, and in the second-level schools further subjects are offered. In Swedish first- and secondary-level schools, the same curricula are offered throughout the whole country, but central control is restricted to the establishment of broad general guidelines. The curriculum in Spanish academic secondary schools is encyclopedic. In the third and final year, in addition to common subjects, pupils may choose either science or humanities. With some variations, curricula in Denmark, Finland, the Netherlands, Portugal and Turkey are encyclopedic.

Curricula trends in Western Europe are clear. First, attempts are being made to gear programs far more to the needs of individual children. In comprehensive schools, this involves the introduction of elective subjects or options. Second, the previous emphasis on Latin and Greek is declining. Continental European schools pay more attention to modern foreign languages. Scientific and technological subjects are also receiving more attention than was previously the case. Mathematics, in all countries except England and Wales, remains central to the concept of a good general education. Finally, in those countries (England and Wales, Scotland, and Northern Ireland are again exceptions) in which vocational schools have played an important part at the second level of education, the content of the courses offered now includes more general, theoretical material—the inculcation of practical skills is postponed until later.

The explosion of scientific knowledge and the development of mass communications have undoubtedly created problems for educators responsible for curriculum design. At the second level of school, Western European curricula are still knowledge-centered. Attempts are being made to reduce the number of required subjects, replace classical studies with modern subjects and allow some freedom of choice. In Britain, there is pressure to increase and modernize the syllabus and introduce approaches that have been adopted by primary school teachers largely on the basis of pragmatic theories developed in the United States. Curricula change slowly in most countries because teachers are understandably unwilling to experiment freely outside the boundaries of the knowledge they have acquired over many years of school and university education. Differences among Western Europe curricula can be explained by reference to the kind of courses followed in universities and teacher training institutions. In the past, the academic secondary school curriculum was regarded as an adequate base of knowledge for teachers going into elementary schools. In recent years, attempts have been made in England and Wales to ensure that all teachers are university graduates. By contrast, this has long been traditional in Scotland. The movement is far less well advanced in continental European systems.

What is offered in university courses has, consequently, a very important influence on the content of education in the rest of the system. British degrees are highly specialized: single honors courses are the norm. In continental Europe it is less usual for applied subjects to be included in university courses than in Britain. Differentiation by type of institution was introduced in Britain when polytechnics were established in the 1960s. Humanistic and technological universities have been common in continental Europe, however, since the 19th century. Admission to any faculty on the basis of a leaving certificate from an academic secondary school is inherent in the European system. (Again, Britain is an exception.) Pressure of numbers on university laboratory and other facilities has made selection from among formally qualified applicants more common.

Only when changes occur in the content of university education will it be possible radically to alter secondary and primary school curricula.

ADMINISTRATION

The implementation of educational policy is the responsibility of personnel in national, regional and local organizations. While too sharp a distinction is frequently made between centralized and decentralized systems of educational administration, the terms may be used to describe continental and British systems respectively.

Most Western European nations have a minister of education, who is de jure responsible for its provision. Officials in education ministries are responsible, as inspectors, for the academic aspects of policy; other officials deal with resources—personnel, equipment and buildings. Regional offices frequently undertake certain administrative duties and may mediate between the national ministry and the local education authorities. Relationships between national, regional and local authorities and teachers vary in accordance with the aspect of education under consideration. Aims are frequently debated and formulated nationally. Teachers may be civil servants, as in France, or hired and paid by local authorities, as in England and Wales.

Since World War II, policy debates about the organization of school systems have been politicized. Leftist politicians have argued that traditional selective secondary schools should be abolished and replaced by comprehensive schools. Rightist parties have accepted the retention of selective schools as a matter of policy. Everywhere, regardless of whether curricula are laid down nationally or determined locally, educators are the principal protagonists in debates about the content of education. By virtue of their position, university teachers have played, and still do play, a decisive role in deciding what should be taught in secondary schools. In turn, secondary school teachers powerfully influence what is taught in primary schools. The complexity of administrative arrangements, however, makes it unwise to generalize about the control of education in Europe.

Under Napoleon, a system of administration was established in France that has been copied throughout continental Western Europe. A powerful national ministry delegated responsibility to regional and local authorities. Publicly maintained secondary schools (*lycées*) were state institutions. Primary schools were communal institutions, and private (Roman Catholic) schools were permitted to exist without financial help from the state. Traditionally, the national administration was divided into sections responsible for the various types and levels of education—elementary, secondary, higher, and youth and sports. A powerful group of national inspectors monitored the implementation of national policies. Legislation, decrees and regulations provided directives for administrators and teachers throughout the system.

In contrast, the administration of education in England and Wales is based on the principle of partnership between national and local authorities. England and Wales, Scotland, and Northern Ireland each has a system of administration and enabling legislation. The 1944 Education Act remains the chief legislative instrument. On many aspects of policy it is vague and permissive, leaving far more room for political maneuver than is usual in educational legislation in the rest of Europe.

Nevertheless, in England and Wales, national salary scales for teachers leave local authorities little room to pay more in response to the demand for teachers in their areas. New state-maintained schools cannot be opened or existing ones closed without the approval of the minister. School-leaving examinations are subject to national policies, although they are administered either by university examination boards or by schools themselves. Finally, an important difference between Britain and the rest of Europe is that curricula are not prescribed nationally. In France, Sweden and Belgium, for example, national curricula have been introduced.

West Germany offers a third model of administration. There, under basic law, the eleven *Länder* have overall responsibility for education. The federal government can issue general legislation on third-level education, scientific research and vocational guidance. A federal commission plans, organizes and manages the schools, while district, city and municipal authorities help to supervise them.

Sweden's national board of education has long exercised considerable control over education. Parliament lays down, usually on the board's advice, a common uniform curriculum and standards for grading pupils in public schools. County education boards have general supervisory, inspecting and consultative functions. The actual provision of school education is a responsibility of local authorities. They undertake local planning and manage buildings, teachers, other school staff, transport, and so on.

In Belgium, education is managed by national, regional and local authorities. Each linguistic and cultural region has its own ministry of education responsible for national education and regional culture. For each of these ministries, the work is coordinated by a secretary-general. Policy is formulated at the national level, but a certain flexibility governs the application of these policies at the regional level.

It should be said that while widely shared principles of democratic administration inform the educational system of Europe, the power of the national, regional and local authorities varies greatly. Clearly, what changes have occurred have been in response to the introduction of comprehensive schools, the expansion of higher education and the widely shared view that teachers should be trained and that preferably all of them should be university graduates. Thus, in France, the sharp division of authority between the directorates has been eroded. The administration of the first and second stages of education in England and Wales has been unified and the divisions between primary, secondary and further education reduced.

Another obvious feature of postwar change has been the attempt to adjust the balance between the responsibilities of the national, regional and local authorities. Formerly, as in France and Sweden, considerable executive power was possessed by the national ministry, but now attempts have been made to increase participation at the local level. On the other hand, in Britain and West Germany, attempts have been made to increase the policy formulating powers of the national agencies of administration. The dilemma facing most Western European governments is how to encourage participation in educational policy making, while at the same time ensuring greater equality of provision. The costs of education make this dilemma difficult to resolve.

In all countries, the universities stand de facto outside the administrative systems responsible for primary and secondary schools. Traditions of academic freedom and university autonomy ensure that university teachers are largely responsible for selecting and examining students, designing curricula and teaching as they think fit. In practice, they decide who should be appointed and promoted, to whom degrees should be awarded and how resources should be allocated.

While the universities of Western Europe share long, powerful and honorable traditions, differences do exist. Whatever the formal system of administration, the pervasive influence of the universities on the operation of schools throughout Western Europe is considerable, and therefore crucially important to any comparative study of school systems.

FURTHER READING

Anweiler, O., and Hearnden, A. G. *From Secondary to Higher Education*. Cologne: Bohlam Verlag, 1983.

Archer, Margaret S. *Social Origins of Educational Systems*. London: Sage, 1979.

Barnard, H. C. *The French Tradition in Education*. Cambridge: Cambridge University Press, 1970.

Betts, R. *The Politics of West German School Reform, 1948–72*. L.A.C.E. Occasional Paper. London: London Institute of Education, 1981.

Boucher, O. *Tradition and Change in Swedish Education*. Oxford: Pergamon, 1981.

Dixon, W. *Society, Schools and Progress in Scandinavia*. Oxford: Pergamon, 1965.

Durkheim, E. *The Evolution of Educational Thought*. London: Routledge and Kegan Paul, 1979.

Eggleston, J. *The Sociology of the School Curriculum*. London: Routledge and Kegan Paul, 1977.

Field, F., ed. *Education and the Urban Crisis*. London: Routledge and Kegan Paul, 1977.

Fragniers, G., ed. *Education Without Frontiers: A Study of Education from the European Cultural Foundation's "Plan of Europe 2000."* London: Duckworth, 1976.

Fraser, W. R., *Reforms and Restraints in Modern French Education*. London: Routledge and Kegan Paul, 1971.

Fuhr, C., and Halls, W. D. *Educational Reform in the Federal Republic of Germany*. Paris: UNESCO, 1970.

Great Britain, Department of Education and Science. *The Education System of England and Wales*. London: HMSO, 1982.

Halls, W. D. *Education, Culture and Politics in Modern France*. 2nd ed. Oxford: Pergamon, 1976.

———. *Society, Schools and Progress in France*. Oxford: Pergamon, 1965.

Halsey, A. H., et al. *Origins and Destinations*. London: Oxford University Press, 1980.

Hearndon, A. G. *Education, Culture and Politics in West Germany*. Oxford: Pergamon, 1976.

———. *Education in the Two Germanies*. Oxford: Blackwell, 1974.

———. *Paths to University: Preparation, Assessment, Selection*. London: Macmillan, 1973.

Holmes, B. *Comparative Education: Some Considerations of Method*. London: Allen and Unwin, 1981.

———. ed. *Diversity and Unity in Education*. London: Allen and Unwin, 1980.

———. ed. *Guide to Education Systems*. Paris: UNESCO, IBE, 1979.

———. *International Handbook of Education Systems*. London: Wiley, 1983.

Husen, T. *The School in Question: A Comparative Study of the School and Its Future in Western Society*. London: Oxford University Press, 1979.

Kallen, D. *The Universities and Permanent Education: A Lost Opportunity*. L.A.C.E. Occasional Paper. London: London Institute of Education, 1980.

Kogan, M. *Education Policies in Perspective: An Appraisal*. Paris: OECD, 1979.

Lawton, D. *The Politics of the School Curriculum*. London: Routledge and Kegan Paul, 1980.

Lynch, J., and Plunkett, H. D. *Teacher Education and Cultural Change: England, France, West Germany*. London: Allen and Unwin, 1973.

Mallinson, V. *The Western European Idea of Education*. Oxford: Pergamon, 1980.

OECD. *Case Studies of Educational Innovation*. Vols I, II and III. Paris, 1973.

———. *Educational Policy and Planning: Sweden*. Paris, 1966.

———. *Reviews of National Policy for Education: Germany*. Paris, 1972.

———. *Short Cycle Higher Education: A Search for Identity*. Paris, 1973.

Simon, B., and Taylor, W., eds. *Education in the Eighties: The Central Issues*. London: Batsford Academic and Educational, 1981.

Van der Eyken, W. *The Education of Three to Eight Year Olds in Europe in the Eighties*. Windsor, Berkshire: Nelson, 1982.

Warnock, H. M., et al. *Special Educational Needs*. London: HMSO, 1978.

THE CHURCHES OF
WESTERN EUROPE

GLEN GARFIELD WILLIAMS

An examination of the exceedingly complicated ecclesiastical structure of Western Europe is simplified if the region is divided into six well-defined areas within which there are, generally, considerable similarities between church life in one country and another. These areas are the Latin countries (France, Belgium, Luxembourg, Italy, Spain and Portugal); the British Isles; the Protestant European mainland (West Germany, the Netherlands and Switzerland); Scandinavia (Norway, Sweden, Denmark, Finland and Iceland); Central Europe (Austria); and the Eastern Mediterranean (Greece and Turkey). Two events have been mainly responsible for the development and consolidation of these areas.

The first event was the Great Schism of 1054, when the churches of the Eastern Orthodox and Roman Catholic traditions sundered their relationships to the thundering of mutual anathemas by Pope Leo IX and the Patriarch Michael Cerularius of Constantinople. After the schism, the Roman Catholics were dominant in all of Western and most of Central Europe. The Orthodox were supreme in the eastern Mediterranean area and in much of Eastern Europe. (Both churches officially expressed their regret over the schism at the Second Vatican Council in 1965.)

The second event was the Peace of Westphalia, which in 1648 terminated the Thirty Years War. In that frightful struggle, the forces of the Protestant Reformation and the Roman Catholic Counter-Reformation fought each other to exhaustion. The result was the clear definition of areas of Roman Catholic, Lutheran and Reformed (Presbyterian) influence. In England, in the meantime, the position of the Anglican church was being consolidated against Presbyterian, Independent and Baptist movements.

The last 300 years have seen little significant change in the ecclesiastical balance of power in Western Europe. The Roman Catholic church is strongest in the Latin countries, in Central Europe and in the Republic of Ireland. Scandinavia and northern and eastern Germany are mainly Lutheran. The Presbyterians are strongest in Switzerland, the Rhine Valley, the Netherlands and Scotland. The Anglicans are in the majority in England and Wales.

Obtaining exact and comparable membership statistics for churches is virtually impossible, partly because precise central records are often not available and partly because churches have differing methods of assessing membership.

The figures quoted here refer, in a general way, to the community covered by the church concerned. They are intended to give some idea of comparative strengths and should not be taken as precise statistics. Further, they do not refer to actual church attendance, but rather to denominational allegiance. In the large churches, especially, church attendance varies from about two to 10 percent of the population, except for special occasions such as Christmas and Easter. Usually, attendance in country areas is relatively higher than in towns.

THE LATIN COUNTRIES

This area is characterized by the overwhelming strength of the Roman Catholic church. In Spain, Portugal, Italy and Luxembourg, some 99 percent of the population is claimed by this church; in Belgium, the percentage is slightly lower, about 97 percent; and in France it is 94 percent. Percentages of practicing Roman Catholics would be considerably lower. It would be erroneous, however, to conclude that similarity of membership percentages implies identity of atmosphere and activity in the Roman Catholic church in these countries. Even before the events of the Second Vatican Council, many French and some Belgian Roman Catholics, both clergy and laity, were much more open to the challenges of the modern world and were less traditionalist than their counterparts in the other countries of the area.

The precise conditions regulating church-state relationships also differ considerably from country to country. For example, a long-standing concordat exists between Portugal and the Vatican. In Spain, a concordat concluded in 1953 was replaced at the beginning of 1979 by a series of four agreements; in Italy a new and in some points radically modified concordat was signed in 1984. Especially in Spain and Italy, provisions for ensuring religious freedom for other Christian churches have made considerable progress in the last 25 years. Thus the Spanish constitution of 1975 declares that the state has a relationship of cooperation with both the Roman Catholic church and other confessions, and in Italy a specific (and historic) agreement was signed in 1984 by the representatives of the Methodist and Waldensian churches and the Italian government.

The degree and methods of exerting influence on political affairs also vary from country to country. In Spain, the Roman Catholic church takes a clear and public part in political affairs; in Italy its influence, although no less real than in Spain, tends to be used in a more covert fashion. This is even truer of Portugal, while in those countries without concordats the influence of the Roman Catholic church is exerted in the form of moral pressure on public opinion rather than direct religious or canonical pressure on governments.

The hierarchical structure in the various Latin countries is similar, with the archbishop of a specific diocese in each country always functioning as primate of the country as a whole. In Italy, the primate is the Pope in his capacity as bishop of Rome. The Second Vatican Council established national episcopal conferences, which assemble all the bishops in each country.

In each of the Latin countries there exist several Protestant churches, which represent at best a small (more generally a very small) proportion of the population. Most of these churches are the result of mission work done by European and American Protestant churches. Until comparatively recently, a number of these missions and churches worked under occasionally severe disabilities.

For its size, Portugal has an unusually large number of Protestant churches and missions, although most have no more than a few hundred members. The more important bodies are the Assemblies of God, Baptists, Brethren, Presbyterians, Methodists, the Lusitanian church (which has close ties to the Anglican communion) and Seventh-Day Adventists. These communities range in number from 2,000 to 5,000. Most of these churches also have small communities in Madeira and the Azores.

In the mid-16th century Spain experienced an indigenous movement of reformation. Small but lively, it also exercised a considerable influence outside Spain, especially in southern Italy, before its obliteration by the Counter-Reformation. Protestant missions first began work in Spain about a century ago, and churches have developed as a result. Apart from several extremely small communities and missions, the largest bodies are the Adventists, Baptists, Brethren and the Spanish Evangelical church, a united church with Presbyterian, Congregationalist and Methodist elements. Each of these bodies probably has between 5,000 and 10,000 members. The Federation of Independent Evangelical Churches and the Assemblies of God number about 4,000 members each, while the Spanish Reformed Episcopal church, affiliated with the Anglican communion, has some 2,000 members.

Religious liberty has been an essential element in the Belgian constitution since 1830. The decades since World War II have been marked by a major effort toward union among the Protestant churches with a longer history of work in Belgium. Thus the former Belgian Protestant Evangelical church, the former Belgian Christian Missionary church and the former Belgian Methodist church are now joined as the United Protestant church, with about 25,000 members. The Belgian Evangelical Mission has some 3,000 members, and there are smaller groups of Seventh-Day Adventists and Baptists, together with several missions.

Luxembourg, where religious affairs are still regulated on the basis of the Napoleonic Code, has a Lutheran church of some 5,000 members, mainly centered near the capital. The southern part of the country is served mainly by the recently recognized Reformed church of Luxembourg, with a membership of about 2,500.

Protestantism in Italy is remarkable for several features. The Waldensian church, which is of the Presbyterian order and has about 30,000 members, is the oldest surviving Protestant church in the world, antedating the other Reformation churches by about 300 years. It is also remarkable how rapidly various Pentecostal communities have taken root, mainly in the south and Sicily, to form, together with the Assemblies of God, by far the largest Protestant groups. There are also Baptist, Methodist, Lutheran and Seventh-Day Adventist churches, whose numbers range from 5,000 to 15,000. In recent years the Waldensian and Methodist churches have begun a process of integration that by 1984 was already very far advanced.

In France, the Lutheran and Presbyterian churches date from the 16th century and give the country a Protestant population of about 1 million. The chief elements here are the Reformed Church of France (400,000 members), the Reformed church of Alsace-Lorraine (50,000), the Lutheran church of Alsace-Lorraine (250,000) and the Lutheran Evangelical church (50,000). Other communities, with memberships ranging from 2,000 to 7,000, are the Mennonites, Methodists, Baptists and Seventh-Day Adventists. A number of independent missions are also very active.

The Salvation Army, which has been particularly affected by the political vicissitudes of this century, is now active in all the Latin countries.

The flow of refugees in Europe following the two world wars has meant the introduction of small Orthodox communities, of Eastern European origin, into the Latin countries. Some of these communities, particularly in France and Italy, have attracted converts from the indigenous population.

THE BRITISH ISLES

Although it is convenient to consider the British Isles as a self-contained area in this study, its definition as an area is based on geographical rather than ecclesiastical considerations. Indeed, the British Isles, including the Irish Republic, present in a comparatively small compass the greatest variety of churches and ecclesiastical practices to be found in Western Europe or possibly anywhere else except the United States. Around the privileged positions of three established or national churches there is a constellation of Free churches of various derivations. The rise, continuity and strength of the various British Free churches is one of the important characteristics of this area.

In England itself, the Church of England (or Anglican church) is at once a national and established church, counting among its baptized members about 65 percent of the population. In its origin, doctrine and practice, the Church of England is not to be identified with the churches of the continental Reformation, even though their development took place contemporaneously during the 16th century. The Anglican church sees itself as a bridge, in some respects, between the churches of the Reformation and the Roman Catholic traditions, and it maintains its claim to preserve the apostolic succession.

The next largest church in England is the Roman Catholic, claiming a community of some 5.5 million and conducting considerable missionary activity.

Among the major Free churches, the largest is also the youngest, since the Methodist church, counting about 2.25 million in its community, came into being at the end of the 18th century when it was separated from the Anglican church. Attempts at reunion of the two churches, although strongly supported, have so far failed. Of the older Free churches, dating from the 16th and 17th centuries, the Congregationalists and Presbyterians merged in 1972 to form the United Reformed church with some 250,000 members; the Baptist Union of Great Britain and Ireland has about 210,000 members.

Added to these there is an active group of various churches and independent congregations of Pentecostalist and revivalist nature, and, particularly as a result of the refugee movements of this century, Lutheran and Orthodox communities. Of more recent date is the establishment of numerous Third World churches and congregations.

In Wales the general situation is similar, and a number of the central church organizations are common to both England and Wales. One or two points should be noted, however. The Anglican church was disestablished there in 1920, when the church in Wales became a separate province of the Anglican communion. There is, moreover, a considerably higher proportion of Free church membership in Wales than in England. Generally, the Welsh-speaking sections of the older Free churches are organized independently of the common central organizations mentioned above.

Scotland has maintained a close relationship with the continental Reformation since the days of John Knox, and Presbyterian influence is strong. Here, the national church is the Church of Scotland—a Presbyterian church of over 1.3 million members. There are four smaller churches of the Presbyterian order constituting a community of 50,000 altogether. The second largest ecclesiastical body is the Roman Catholic, which, mainly as a result of the influx of Irish labor to Scottish industrial areas, numbers nearly 700,000 members. The Anglican church, called the Episcopal church in Scotland, claims some 50,000 members, the Congregationalists follow with 25,000 members, the Baptists with 20,000 and the Methodists with about 13,500 members.

In Ireland, with minor exceptions, church structures cover the whole of the country and do not reflect the political distinction between the province of Northern Ireland and the Republic of Ireland. The dominant church on the Irish scene is the Roman Catholic, which claims 94 percent of the population of the Republic and 35 percent of that of Northern Ireland. (Ever since the establishment of the Irish Free State, later the Republic of Ireland, there has been a marked tendency for non-Roman Catholics to move toward Northern Ireland.) The Church of Ireland, belonging to the Anglican communion, has a membership of over 100,000, the Presbyterian church in Ireland about 140,000 and the Methodist church about 30,000. The Baptists, with a little more than 6,000 members, and the Congregationalists, with some 2,000, complete the roll of the main churches. A considerable number of missions of a revivalist character flourish in Northern Ireland.

THE PROTESTANT EUROPEAN MAINLAND

The Netherlands, West Germany and Switzerland, which comprise this section, are the three countries on the Western European mainland in which the Reformation of the 16th century was strongest and where the main influence is still Protestant. They all, nevertheless, have large Roman Catholic minorities. The main Protestant churches in these countries derive from either the Lutheran or Calvinist Reformation traditions. Churches of the latter order are more generally known in England as Presbyterian and on the Continent as Reformed.

The national church of the Netherlands is the Netherlands Reformed church, with a total community of about 3 million. This church emerged from the bitter struggles of the Dutch against the supremacy of Spain and the Inquisition. Dutch Protestants met in Emden, just outside Netherlands territory, in 1569 and prepared the basis of the church structure, which was confirmed at the Synod of Dordrecht in 1572. Although this remains the largest of the Protestant churches in the Netherlands, there have been several divisions in the church over the centuries. In 1619, the Remonstrant Brotherhood withdrew over the question of predestination. They now constitute a community of about 40,000. In 1982, a larger group withdrew to form the Gereformeerde Kerken, (Re-reformed churches) with a community now of some 800,000.

The Mennonites, now numbering some 60,000, also have a 17th-century origin in the Netherlands. The Lutheran church in the Netherlands is a community of about 50,000. The Netherlands Baptist Union claims 12,000 members and the Union of Free Evangelical Congregations about 18,000. The Salvation Army is also active and there are several much smaller groups, such as the Moravians, the Seventh-Day Adventists and the Society of Friends.

A church that is found in each of the countries of this area, as well as elsewhere, is the Old Catholic, consisting of communities that have separated from Roman Catholicism at different times. The Old Catholic church of the Netherlands withdrew in 1724 and today has some 12,000 members. The Roman Catholic population of the Netherlands is over 5 million and appears rapidly to be reaching parity with the total Protestant population. It is estimated that 17 percent of the Dutch population of 12 million have no specific church affiliation.

In Germany, both in the Federal Republic and the Democratic Republic, the church scene is complicated by the maintenance in church life as well as civil life of the federal structure of the country. Thus each constituent territory (*Land*) has its own territorial Protestant church (*Landeskirche*), which may be of the Lutheran or Reformed traditions, or a union of the two. There are 19 such territorial churches in West Germany and eight in East Germany. In West Germany they benefit from a number of privileges within the state and, while each is completely autonomous, they relate closely in organization and activity. The Lutheran churches have a common organization in the United Evangelical Lutheran church of Germany (VELKD), and six of the United churches form the Evangelical church of the Union (EKU). All the territorial churches in West Germany together form the Evangelical church in Germany (EKiD), a "federation of Lutheran, Reformed and Union churches" constituted in 1948. About half the population of West Germany belongs to the constituent churches of the Evangelical church in Germany.

Together, the Baptists, Methodists and Union of Independent Evangelical Congregations number about 400,000 in West Germany. There are also small Free Lutheran and Free Reformed churches that, on doctrinal grounds, have sought to maintain their independence. There are several Orthodox communities. There are 20,000 Old Catholics whose church, like those of

Switzerland and Austria, seceded from Rome after the promulgation of the dogma of papal infallibility in 1874. The Salvation Army has widespread activity, with an officer staff of about 250. Some 44 percent of the population of West Germany is Roman Catholic. About 2.5 million West Germans claim no religious affiliation at all.

The structure of church organization in Switzerland resembles to some degree that of Germany, since the Swiss political structure is also that of a federation of provinces, or cantons. In Switzerland, however, the main Protestant churches are all of the Reformed order—mainly following the tradition of the Calvinist Reformation, based in Geneva. The cantons of central and eastern Switzerland have remained overwhelmingly Roman Catholic. A considerable proportion of the 3.5 million Roman Catholics in Switzerland—about 53 percent of the population—reside in these areas.

In the Protestant cantons of Switzerland there are 17 state, or cantonal, churches. These are fully autonomous but, together with some of the Free churches, they cooperate closely in the Federation of Protestant churches in Switzerland. The cantonal Reformed churches have together a community of nearly 3 million. In the canton of Geneva there is a Free Evangelical church, which is of Presbyterian order but refuses the privileges of the cantonal church. The Methodist church is the largest of the other Free churches, with 20,000 in its community; and there are small Baptist, Independent Evangelical, Mennonite, Moravian and Seventh-Day Adventist churches. The Salvation Army is also active in many parts of the country. The Old Catholic church of Switzerland is a body of 20,000, and there are also some small Orthodox communities.

SCANDINAVIA

This far-flung area, comprising Finland, Norway, Sweden, Denmark and Iceland, is ecclesiastically the most homogeneous of the European region. All five countries have massive Lutheran Protestant majorities, ranging from 92 percent of the total population in Finland to 97 percent in Iceland. The Lutheran churches in these countries are national, or folk, churches having similar, but not identical, relationships with the state. They are folk churches in the sense that they are more closely related to the people as a national society than to the state as a national institution. The Roman Catholic church is present in the area in minimal proportions.

There exist considerable similarities, too, among the Scandinavian Free churches. There are Pentecostal groups in each country, with communities numbering 250,000 in Sweden, 70,000 in Norway, 50,000 in Finland, 10,000 in Denmark and 2,000 in Iceland. There are also active churches of the Congregationalist order, known as the Mission Covenant churches of Sweden (213,000), Norway (11,000) and Denmark (6,000), and the Free church of Finland (9,000); this group, peculiar to Western Europe, has close relationships with the Congregationalist traditions in Britain.

Together with the Salvation Army, which, with a total community of about 1 million, works in each Scandinavian country, the Baptists, Methodists and Seventh-Day Adventists are present as follows:

	Sweden	Norway	Denmark	Finland	Iceland
Baptists	100,000	12,000	20,000	6,000	200
Methodists	25,000	30,000	6,000	3,000	—
Seventh-Day Adventists	7,000	10,000	7,000	7,500	1,000

Despite so much similarity, some peculiarities in the different national situations may be noted. For example, within the Church of Iceland, where an old-fashioned piety is still practiced, there has also been a very considerable spiritualist movement, which now appears to be waning. In Denmark, in addition to the churches already mentioned, there are very small groups of Quakers and Moravians. Quaker meetings have been held in southwest Norway for over a century, but the community remains only a few hundred strong. The Lutheran Free church of Norway numbers 19,000 persons. Theologically conservative and revivalist movements have strongly influenced Norwegian church life.

In Sweden, where the Church of Sweden claims to have maintained the apostolic succession, the effects of revivalist movements are also noticeable, but have generally been contained within the framework of the national church. On the other hand, similar movements have caused a deep division within the Baptist community. There are also Estonian Lutheran and Orthodox churches in exile.

Finland is the only one of the Scandinavian countries with an Orthodox community of any significant size—54,000 persons. Alongside the national church, there is also a Free Lutheran church, numbering a few thousand adherents. As elsewhere in Scandinavia, revivalist movements have had different results in different parts of the country. Particularly in some of the Free churches, revivalism, along with language problems concerning the use of Finnish or Swedish in the services, has caused tensions and sometimes actual divisions.

CENTRAL EUROPE

Were it not that it would go beyond the geographical framework of this volume, Austria, the sole Central European country to be discussed, should be considered together with Czechoslovakia, Hungary and Poland. This is a clear indication that ecclesiastical pegs will not fit neatly into modern political holes.

Austria has been much disturbed by the political events of the last 40 years. Great streams of refugees from Eastern Europe have passed into or through its territory, and those who have settled there have changed the comparative numbers of the different confessions without basically altering the picture of church relationships.

Nearly 90 percent of the Austrian population is Roman Catholic. Since 1933, a concordat, later followed by a series of specific agreements, has existed between the Vatican and Austria, giving the Roman Catholic church a privileged position. Wide tolerance is extended to other churches, nevertheless, and the Lutheran-Reformed Union church also enjoys certain privileges. This church, the Evangelical church of the Augsburg and Helvetic Confessions in Austria, is the largest non-Roman Catholic community, with some 430,000 adherents. Of these, something over 400,000 are of the Lutheran tradition and the remainder are of the Reformed. The two constituent churches maintain their autonomy on a number of questions, but have a common synod for addressing many major problems.

The Old Catholic church of Austria comprises about 26,000 members, the Methodists and Seventh-Day Adventists about 5,000 each, the Baptists about 2,500 and the Assemblies of God about 1,000. There are also some small Orthodox communities.

THE EASTERN MEDITERRANEAN

As in the previous section, only a part of a geographically larger ecclesiastical area can be considered here. Greece and to a very small extent Turkey constitute the point at which major Orthodox influence enters Western Europe.

Greece is an Orthodox country. Its state church, the Church of Greece, formed a part of the Ecumenical Patriarchate of Constantinople until 1833, when it became a national, autocephalous (autonomous) community claiming some 98 percent of the population. Although this is a state church, whose relationships with the state were redefined in 1923, again in 1943, and in the 1960s and 1970s, the interpretation of these relationships is still disputed at some points. There is a close identification between the Church of Greece and the Greek people, of whom it proved the strong leader during the struggle with the Turks. The second largest Christian community in Greece is the Roman Catholic, of whom some 45,000 members use the Latin rite and some 3,000 to 4,000 are Uniats of recent origin—having an Orthodox tradition but remaining in communion with the Roman Catholic church.

Protestantism is represented in Greece by the Greek Evangelical church, of a Presbyterian-Congregationalist origin and over a century old. It is a community of about 15,000. There is also a very small Free Evangelical church and a number of uncategorized, small missions, mainly of a revivalist nature. These are often run by Greeks who have been converted to Protestantism in the United States and who have taken their new faith back to their native land. The Greek constitution provides for freedom of religion and worship, but Greek laws prohibit proselytizing. From time to time, therefore, the Protestant minorities have serious difficulties in finding a middle way between the constitution and the law.

FORMS OF COOPERATIVE ACTIVITY AMONG THE CHURCHES

One of the most complex problems the non-Roman Catholic churches, both in Western Europe and elsewhere, have had to face during the middle decades of the 20th century has been that of finding forms and methods for the exchange of insights and for practical cooperative activity. To some extent the problem already existed within the individual churches, where thinking was often uncoordinated and valuable ideas were ignored or lost. There has been a considerable increase in the number of study commissions within each church, including the Roman Catholic; and to an increasing degree account is being taken in these commissions of work being done by groups in other churches.

Nowadays, however, many activities are undertaken on a specifically ecumenical basis, officially involving the Anglican, Orthodox, Protestant and Roman Catholic chuches. In Western Europe, such activities usually relate to one or more of the following points:

1. Questions of relationships among the churches. These may take the form of discussions concerning actual union between different churches, but they inevitably involve doctrinal discussions about baptism, intercommunion and the mutual recognition of ministries.
2. Studies of problems directly relating to the life of the churches and the world in which they operate. A great number of theological, sociological, economic, political, international and other kinds of study groups exist in Western Europe. Some of these concern themselves directly with the affairs of the European Community and the European Parliament. Among such study groups, the most important are the Catholic European Study and Information center situated in Brussels and Strasbourg and, for the Protestant churches, the European Ecumenical Commission for Church and Society, at present situated in Brussels but with a planned extension in Strasbourg.
3. Practical social and relief work in all parts of the world, for which the Western European churches are now a major source of means and personnel. Here, again, there is often close cooperation and consultation between non-Roman Catholic and Roman Catholic churches.

Over the last 20 years or so, those churches of Western Europe that are prepared for ecumenical activity have constructed for themselves organs of cooperation and encounter at different levels. Most of the countries treated here have some form of national ecumenical body to which, in some cases, the non-Roman Catholic churches are related. The degree of organization, the powers delegated to the organization and the spheres of activity vary greatly from country to country.

In Europe as a whole, after years of careful preparatory work, a regional ecumenical body was created in October 1964, when the Conference of European Churches was constituted. Most of the major and many of the smaller non-Roman Catholic churches, both in Western and Eastern Europe, belong to this body. The development of regional organizations, independent of, but closely associated with, the World Council of Churches, is a feature of present ecumenical development. In the Roman Catholic church, since the Second Vatican Council, various pan-European structures have been created, the most important of which are the Council of European Bishops' Conferences, the European Conference of Priests and the European Forum of National Laity Committees. There is close cooperation between the Conference of European Churches and the Council of European Bishops' Conferences.

Still other kinds of ecumenical organization are found in the region; some are based on geographical considerations (the Conference of the Churches on the Rhine), some on a cultural factor (the Conference of the Protestant Churches in the Latin Countries of Europe) and some on a common interest (the Churches' Committee on Migrant Workers in Europe).

The forms of cooperative organization are numerous and increasing. There is a recognizable risk of an ecclesiastical Parkinson's Law, but this possibility must not be exaggerated. The multifarious churches of Western Europe, having lived alongside each other for so long, are at last finding each other. Such mutual discovery will inevitably lead to new organizational forms to give it expression.

PROBLEMS FACING THE CHURCHES OF WESTERN EUROPE

Six challenges now facing Western Europe's churches can be defined. First, there is the complicated and ill-defined process of secularization. The term means different things in different ecclesiastical contexts. In general, it includes the steady decline of the influence of the churches and the tendency of Europeans, in particular, to look elsewhere for their salvation. It also involves the gradual challenging of the privileges that churches have enjoyed in many countries for centuries.

Second, directly connected with this and equally deeply rooted in the sometimes long histories of the Western European churches, is the problem of ecclesiastical structural inflexibility in a time of rapid social change. This has many aspects, some of which are questions concerning the role of the congregation, the nature of the ministry, forms of worship, Christian social responsibility in a welfare state or the expression of faith in a technological age.

Third, increasingly urgent problems are posed by the various movements toward integration in Western Europe. People move with increasing ease from country to country in the course of their work—migrant workers, international civil servants and others. It is easier to understand the spiritual needs of these newly uprooted people than to see how to provide for them.

Fourth, the churches in all parts of Europe have become increasingly conscious of Europe's key role in the system of global understandings and tensions. There has been a growth within the churches of the study of Christian responsibility with respect to questions of peace and disarmament; and widespread ecumenical cooperation has been achieved in addressing these questions.

Fifth, the upsurge in Western Europe of other faiths, especially Islam, finds the churches unprepared and often divided in their approaches to this phenomenon.

Sixth, the whole process of increasing mutual awareness is one of the factors contributing to the challenges facing the churches in their ecumenical experience. The Western European churches are not only conscious of this in their relationships with one another, but for many of them the question also has another dimension—that of their involvement in missionary activity on other continents. From this mission work newly independent churches (often, but imprecisely, referred to as "younger churches") have appeared. They are impatient with the old historical divisions, forms and structures of their European forebears. The older churches are being forced to take note of this impatience.

FURTHER READING

Barrett, D. B., ed. *World Christian Encyclopedia*. Nairobi, Oxford and New York: Oxford University Press, 1982.

Cross, F. L., ed. *The Oxford Dictionary of the Christian Church*. London and New York: Oxford University Press, 1957.

Harms, H. H., ed. *Kirchen der Welt*, Stuttgart: Evang. Verlagswerk.

Pro Mundi Vita. Bulletins and dossiers, Brussels.

PART THREE

WESTERN EUROPEAN INTEGRATION

PRINCIPAL WESTERN EUROPEAN ORGANIZATIONS

ANTHONY SHARP*

COUNCIL OF EUROPE

Address: Palais de l'Europe, Strasbourg, France. *Foundation:* May 1949. *Membership:* Austria (1956), Belgium,[1] Cyprus (1961), Denmark, France, Federal Republic of Germany (1951), Great Britain, Greece (August 1949), Iceland (1950), Ireland, Italy, Luxembourg, Malta (1965), Netherlands, Norway, Sweden, Switzerland (1963), Turkey (August 1949). *Function:* Discussion of common interests and problems and discovery of new methods and areas of cooperation between member states.

Organization: The Committee of Ministers consists of one minister—usually the foreign minister—from each member country for the biennial meetings usually held in April and December; ministers' deputies act as permanent representatives at routine monthly meetings. The Council decides with binding effect on all matters of internal organization and may also conclude conventions and agreements. The Consultative Assembly consists of 144 members, weighted in number between member states, either elected by national parliaments or appointed. They are generally parliamentarians and reflect party political strengths in the national parliaments. Members represent public opinion and not their governments. The Assembly meets annually in ordinary session and may submit recommendations to the Committee of Ministers, pass resolutions and discuss reports. The Standing Committee, which represents the Assembly when not in session, meets four times a year. Ordinary Committees deal with the various spheres of cooperation such as social problems, refugees, law, culture, etc. Under the 1950 European Convention, a European Commission is empowered to investigate claims by states (sometimes individuals) that human rights and fundamental freedoms have been violated. Its findings may be examined by the European

* Revised by Richard Mayne.
[1]No date indicates founder member.

Court of Human Rights (founded 1959), whose final and compulsory juris-diction has been recognized by nine Council members or by the Committee of Ministers, which is empowered to take binding decisions by two-thirds majority. The Secretariat serves both the Committee of Ministers and the Consultative Assembly.

NORTH ATLANTIC TREATY ORGANIZATION (NATO)

Address: 1110 Brussels. *Foundation:* April 1949 by the North Atlantic Treaty. NATO is the organizational structure set up to implement the treaty's provisions. *Membership:* Belgium, Canada, Denmark, France,[2] Federal Republic of Germany (1955), Great Britain, Greece (1952), Iceland, Italy, Luxembourg, Netherlands, Norway, Portugal, Spain (1982), Turkey (1952) and the United States. *Function:* To maximize the ability of members indivi-dually and collectively to resist any armed attack upon the territory of any member or a member's occupation forces in the North Atlantic area and to provide means of political cooperation and consultation and economic collaboration among members.

Organization: The Council is the supreme organ of NATO, meeting twice a year at ministerial level and regularly at official level, each government being represented by a permanent representative. The Council is responsible for the implementation of the provisions of the treaty, and may set up perma-nent or temporary committees to assist it in all aspects of its work. The secretary-general of NATO, appointed by, responsible to and chairman of the Council, organizes the work of the Council and directs the international Secretariat and its five divisions: Political Affairs; Defense Planning and Policy; Defense Support; Infrastructure, Logistics and Council Operations; and Scientific Affairs. The secretary-general has direct access to all NATO agencies and to member governments and aids the settlement of disputes between members.

The senior military organ, the Military Committee, is composed of a chief-of-staff of each member country[3] and meets in Brussels at least twice a year at chief-of-staff level, and periodically at the level of permanent military representative. It is responsible for providing recommendations and guidance on military questions to other NATO organs. Subordinate to the Military Committee are the major Commands and Planning Groups: Supreme Allied Commander Europe (SACEUR); Supreme Allied Commander Atlantic (SACLANT); Allied Commander-in-Chief Channel (CINCHAN); Canada-U.S. Regional Planning Group (CUSRPG); and a number of other military agencies. These include the NATO Defense College and the NATO Electronic Warfare Advisory Committee, both in Rome; the Military Agency for Standardization and the Military Committee Meteorological Group, both in Brussels; the NATO Training Group, in Bonn; and the Advisory Group for Aerospace Research and Development, in Paris.

[2] France withdrew from NATO's military command in 1966.
[3] Iceland, having no armed forces, is represented by a civilian. France is represented by a military mission to the Military Committee.

WESTERN EUROPEAN UNION (WEU)

Address: 9 Grosvenor Place, London SW1. *Foundation:* May 1955 by a treaty based on the earlier Brussels Treaty of March 1948. *Membership:* Belgium, France, Federal Republic of Germany, Great Britain, Italy, Luxembourg and the Netherlands. *Function:* The coordination of defense policies and equipment of member countries, and their cooperation in legal, political, cultural and social affairs.

Organization: The Council consists of the foreign ministers or London-based ambassadors of member countries plus an undersecretary at the British Foreign Office, meeting under the secretary-general's chairmanship. It is responsible for policy formulation, the issue of directives to the secretary-general and the organization's agencies, and ensuring close cooperation with the NATO Council. The Agency for the Control of Armaments is responsible to the Council for ensuring that agreements not to manufacture certain weapons are observed, and for controlling the level of armament stocks held by members on the European mainland. The Standing Armaments Committee[4] aims to develop the closest possible cooperation between members in the production and procurement of armaments. The Council has met quarterly since October 1963 to review the political and economic situation in Europe.

The Assembly meets twice yearly in Paris; its members are elected or appointed by member parliaments. It considers defense policy in Western Europe and other common interests of member countries and may make representations to the Council, national parliaments, governments and other international organizations. The Council presents an annual report to the Assembly with special reference to the Agency for the Control of Armaments. The Assembly has a number of permanent committees.

ECONOMIC COMMISSION FOR EUROPE (ECE)

Address: Palais des Nations, Geneva. *Foundation:* 1947. *Membership:* All Western and Eastern European countries (including the Federal Republic of Germany, the Byelorussian SSR and the Ukrainian SSR, and excluding East Germany) and the United States. Switzerland participates in a consultative capacity. *Function:* One of the four regional economic commissions set up by the U.N. Economic and Social Council, the ECE studies European economic and technological problems, collects statistics, furthers the exchange of technical information and makes recommendations.

Organization: The Commission meets annually in plenary session. The various committees are convened for brief meetings throughout the year. The Secretariat services both the Commission and the committees and publishes reviews and surveys.

[4] Address: 43 Avenue du Président Wilson, 75116 Paris.

ORGANIZATION FOR ECONOMIC COOPERATION AND DEVELOPMENT (OECD)[5]

Address: 2 Rue André-Pascal, 75116 Paris. *Foundation:* September 1961 in succession to the Organization for European Economic Cooperation (OEEC) founded in 1948. *Membership:* Australia, Austria, Belgium, Canada, Denmark, Finland, France, Federal Republic of Germany, Great Britain, Greece, Iceland, Ireland, Italy, Japan, Luxembourg, the Netherlands, New Zealand, Norway, Portugal, Spain, Sweden, Switzerland, Turkey and the United States. Yugoslavia also participates in certain matters. *Functions:* To achieve the highest sustainable economic growth and employment among members, to coordinate and improve development aid and to help the expansion of world trade.

Organization: The Council, composed of representatives of the member countries and meeting at both official and ministerial levels, is responsible for general policy and administration. The Executive Committee is composed of the representatives of 11 member countries elected annually by the Council; it meets at least once a week and makes a prior examination of all matters to be submitted to the Council. The Secretariat serves both bodies. In addition, there are a number of standing committees covering specialized economic affairs, the board of management of the European Monetary Agreement (EMA, the successor to the European Payments Union or EPU), and the European Nuclear Energy Agency (ENEA).

NORDIC COUNCIL

Address: The Council has no permanent headquarters. See below under *Organization. Foundation:* 1953. *Membership:* Denmark, Finland (1956), Iceland, Norway and Sweden. *Function:* As a consultative body to increase cooperation between member countries.

Organization: The Council consists of members elected by the member parliaments (Denmark, Finland, Norway and Sweden 16 members each and Iceland five) and also of appointed representatives of each government. It meets annually in ordinary session in the capital of one of the member countries, and may also convene in extraordinary session. For each ordinary session, and for the management of its affairs until the next ordinary session, the Council elects from its members a Presidium consisting of the presidents of the various delegations. Resolutions of the Council take the form of recommendations to member governments, on which the governments must submit annual progress reports to the Council. During each ordinary session the delegates form themselves into five standing committees (economic, cultural, social, communications and legal), each undertaking the preparatory work in connection with matters before the Council. The standing committees may also meet in intersessionary periods, and special committees may also then be formed. The Council has a Secretariat in the capital of each member country; all these countries collaborate closely under the supervision of the Presidium.

Outside the Council there are a large number of official and unofficial Scandinavian committees, enterprises and societies.

[5] See also "The Organization for Economic Cooperation and Development (OECD)," p. 627.

BENELUX

Address: 39 Rue de la Régence, Brussels. *Foundation:* The Benelux Treaty came into force in November 1960 after a number of preparatory agreements. *Membership:* Belgium, Luxembourg and the Netherlands. *Function:* Economic, nonpolitical union of the member countries.

Organization: The Committee of Ministers meets at least once every two months and is composed of no fewer than three ministers from each country. Resolutions must be unanimous (an abstention is not considered a negative vote). The Committee is responsible for decisions relating to the application of the Treaty of Economic Union, ensuring the observance of agreed conventions, and making recommendations for study by and issuing directives to the other Benelux organs. The Consultative Interparliamentary Council consists of 21 members from each of the Netherlands and Belgium and seven from Luxembourg, with no executive role but able to debate general matters concerning the Union. The Council of Economic Union consists of a chairman from each member state and the presidents of the seven committees; the presidents of any of the two special committees may be coopted when their special field is under discussion. The Council of Economic Union ensures the execution of decisions of the Committee of Ministers, passes directives to the committees and special committees, coordinates their work and transmits their and its own proposals to the Committee of Ministers. The Secretariat is headed by a secretary-general who is always Dutch, assisted by a deputy from each of the other member states, all appointed by the Committee of Ministers and directly responsible to the latter's Working Group for the Administration of the Union. The Arbitration Tribunal settles disputes arising from the working of the Union; it consists of two representatives of each member state appointed by the Committee of Ministers. The Economic and Social Advisory Council advises the Committee of Ministers.

EUROPEAN ORGANIZATION FOR NUCLEAR RESEARCH (CENTRE D'ETUDES DE RECHERCHES NUCLÉAIRES, OR CERN)

Address: 1211 Geneva 23. *Foundation:* 1954 on UNESCO's initiative. *Membership:* Austria, Belgium, Denmark, France, Federal Republic of Germany, Great Britain, Greece, Italy, the Netherlands, Norway, Spain, Sweden and Switzerland. Poland, Turkey and Yugoslavia have observer status. *Function:* The collaboration of certain European countries on purely scientific and nonmilitary problems of nuclear research.

Organization: The Council consists of two representatives of each member state. The Committee of the Council has 12 members and comprises the president and vice president of the Council, the presidents of the Finance Committee and of the Scientific Policy Committee, and representatives of member states. There is a Directorate headed by a director general who is assisted by committees.

EUROPEAN SPACE AGENCY (ESA)

Address: 36 Rue Laperouse, 75116 Paris. *Foundation:* 1975; formally established 1980. Formed by the merger of ESRO (the European Space Research

Organization) and ELDO (the European Space Vehicle Launcher Development Organization), both founded 1962 and formally established 1964. *Membership:* Belgium, Denmark, France, Federal Republic of Germany, Great Britain, Ireland, Italy, Spain, Sweden and Switzerland. Austria and Norway have associate status, and there is cooperation with Canada. *Function:* To undertake space research and provide member states with research facilities, and to construct and develop space launcher vehicles on an international basis.

Organization: The Council is the governing body and consists of two representatives for each member state. There are program boards on communication satellites, meteorological satellites, the Ariane launcher, the spacelab and remote sensing. The Council is assisted by the following committees: Administration and Finance, Science Program, Industrial Policy, International Relations, and Space Science, as well as by advisory groups on Satellite Broadcasting, Science and Technology, the Esrange Program, and Documentation.

THE EUROPEAN COMMUNITY (LEGALLY THREE COMMUNITIES: EUROPEAN ECONOMIC COMMUNITY, EUROPEAN COAL AND STEEL COMMUNITY AND EUROPEAN ATOMIC ENERGY COMMUNITY)

Membership: Belgium, Denmark, France, Federal Republic of Germany, Great Britain, Greece, Ireland, Italy, Luxembourg, the Netherlands, Portugal and Spain. More than 100 countries have diplomatic relations with the Community; it has signed agreements with some 120 countries, as well as some 30 multilateral agreements. In Europe, it has association agreements with Turkey, Cyprus and Malta; free-trade agreements with the member states of the European Free Trade Association (Austria, Finland, Iceland, Norway, Sweden and Switzerland). It has also concluded sectoral trade agreements (textiles and steel) with Romania, Hungary, Poland, Bulgaria and Czechoslovakia. In the less developed world; with which it has numerous trade agreements, it has most notably concluded successive Lomé Conventions with 65 states in Africa, the Caribbean and the Pacific. It maintains 78 delegations in nonmember countries, and has information offices in all the member states, as well as in Switzerland and Turkey. Its London office is at 8 Storey's Gate, SW1 P3; its Belfast office at Windsor House, 9/15 Bedford Street BT2 7EG; its Cardiff office at 4 Cathedral Road, CF1 9SG; its Edinburgh office at 7 Alva Street, EH2 4PH. Its Washington delegation is at 2100 M Street, N.W. (Suite 707); its New York delegation (to the U.N.) at 1 Dag Hammarskjöld Plaza, 245 East 47th Street, New York 10016.

For further information, see "The Structure of the European Community," p. 568.

EUROPEAN FREE TRADE ASSOCIATION (EFTA)[6]

Address: 32 Chemin des Colombettes, Geneva. *Foundation:* 1960. *Membership:* Austria, Norway, Sweden, Switzerland. Finland is an associate member. *Function:* To bring about free trade in industrial goods and the expansion of trade in agricultural goods between members.

Organization: The Council is composed of one representative for each member country, meeting at either official or ministerial level. It makes decisions on a wide range of issues including tariffs. Decisions must be unanimous for new obligations, otherwise a majority suffices. There are a number of specialized Council committees. The Consultative Committee comprises a maximum of five representatives per member country. It meets a few weeks before each ministerial meeting of the Council, and may discuss anything within EFTA's sphere of activity. Its chairman reports to the Council. The Finland-EFTA Joint Council is the organ for associating Finland with Council decisions. The Secretariat serves both Council and Consultative Committee.

[6] See also "The European Free Trade Association (EFTA)," p. 612.

THE STRUCTURE OF THE EUROPEAN COMMUNITY

TONY BURGESS*

THE BEGINNINGS

THE European Community (EC) may be defined as an organization set up by a group of Western European countries with the aim of achieving eventual political union through a gradual process of practical economic integration. Although the potential of the Community may have been accepted at the best only tacitly, and as a very long-term objective, by some of the signatories of the founding treaties, the undoubted intention of those who drafted these documents was to establish an institutional framework that could develop, by a process of evolution, into a viable system of government for a European federation, possibly a United States of Europe.

The treaties themselves, however, were never intended to be much more than formal statements of mutually accepted principles—skeletons needing the flesh and sinew of detailed legislation to give them life. In the sense therefore that the emerging shape of the EC has depended, and will continue to depend, on the manner in which its member countries choose to interpret the broadly defined aims of its founders—the manner in which they choose to pad out the skeleton—it is an evolutionary growth. Even the Community's institutions themselves have to a certain extent developed empirically, and in several instances they have been able to reinterpret their terms of reference to meet new or changing situations.

Membership of the Community was at first confined to the six original signatory states of the founding treaties—Belgium, France, the Federal Republic of Germany, Italy, Luxembourg and the Netherlands—although its architects' intentions were that membership should be open to any European state willing and able to accept the obligations of the treaties. In 1961, Britain, Denmark, Ireland and Norway applied to join, but were rebuffed in 1963 when President Charles de Gaulle of France exercised on Britain the veto that all existing members possess over the admission of new members. A similar bid by all four applicants in 1967 was similarly rejected by President de Gaulle. In 1969, however, after de Gaulle's retirement, the six member states agreed to open negotiations. These began in 1970 and

* Revised by Richard Mayne.

568

were completed in 1972. In 1973, Britain, Denmark and Ireland joined, Norway having decided by referendum to reject the agreement. In 1981, Greece became the 10th member of the Community; and Spain and Portugal joined in early 1986.

The Treaty of 1965, creating a single Council and a single Commission for all three European Communities, entered into force in 1967, merging the "executives" of what still juridically remain three "Communities," but leaving intact the respective powers they exercise under the separate Community treaties.

In fact, although for simplicity's sake we have so far referred to "the European Community," the use of the singular is strictly inaccurate, since there are in fact three separate European Communities: the European Coal and Steel Community (ECSC), the European Economic Community (EEC, or the Common Market) and the European Atomic Energy Community (Euratom). Membership in the three Communities is identical, consisting of the countries listed above; and although there are certain constitutional differences between the three organizations, particularly between ECSC on the one hand and EEC and Euratom on the other, similar basic principles are embodied in all three founding treaties.

The establishment of the first of the three Communities, the ECSC, resulted from the Schuman Declaration of May 9, 1950. In this declaration, Robert Schuman, then French foreign minister, proposed that the coal and steel resources of France and Germany should be pooled in an organization open to all European countries. The invitation was accepted by the governments of Germany, Italy, Belgium, Luxembourg and the Netherlands, but the British government replied that it would "reluctantly be unable to accept . . . a commitment to pool resources and set up an authority with certain sovereign powers as a prior condition to joining talks. . . "

The aims of ECSC, which began to operate in 1952 under the terms of the Paris Treaty, were twofold. In the first place, it was intended that the pooling of French and German basic production would achieve the final reconciliation of these two traditional enemies by making further conflict between them impossible on practical grounds. Secondly, ECSC was conceived as the first step toward a new political order in Europe. Out of limited economic integration its founders hoped that political unity would grow. Their choice of a gradualist approach—an attempt to create practical solidarity among European countries through concrete achievements in closely defined fields—was conditioned by disillusionment over previous attempts to unite Europe in one move under more grandiose but basically impractical designs.

The initial success of ECSC, under the leadership of Jean Monnet, who had played a major part in drafting the Schuman Declaration, led very quickly to the first attempt at political union in Europe. Shortly after the signing of the ECSC Treaty, the Community governments signed the European Defense Community (EDC) Treaty, which, by placing the six countries' military resources under joint control, would have solved the problem of German rearmament. At the same time, a plan for a European Political Community was drawn up. These plans came to nothing, however, when the EDC Treaty, ratified by all of the six member states except Italy and France, was defeated on a procedural vote of the French National Assembly.

This failure notwithstanding, the logic of European economic integration, rapidly demonstrated by ECSC, was not to be denied, and the six governments, by their decision to extend the process to the whole field covered by their separate national economies, showed that they had drawn the obvious conclusion. As a result, they concluded two further treaties, the Treaties of Rome, setting up the EEC (which rapidly acquired the nickname of the Common Market, although the earlier Treaty of Paris already referred to "the common market for coal and steel") and Euratom. The aim of the EEC, which with Euratom came into being on January 1, 1958, was to ensure the continued economic expansion of the member countries, and thereby the steady social progress of their peoples, by the creation of a single market for all goods and factors of production in place of the six separate national markets. The Community governments also recognized that the establishment of the thoroughgoing customs union which they envisaged would entail the complete integration of their national economic policies over a very wide front.

Euratom's main aim, given the enormous cost of nuclear research, which it was thought would place a severe strain on the resources of even major countries acting alone, was to ensure the efficient development of a nuclear industry on a Community-wide basis, to the point where it would be capable of making a major competitive contribution to Europe's rapidly expanding power needs. Euratom also concerns itself with medical and biological research in the nuclear field and the industrial uses of atomic energy, but under the terms of the treaty its functions are strictly limited to the peaceful uses of the atom.

THE MAIN INSTITUTIONAL FRAMEWORK

The institutions of the European Community (the reversion to the singular is here deliberate in view of the functional interdependence of the three legally distinct Communities) were constituted by the founding treaties in such a way as to form the basis of a system of government for a Europe ultimately politically united along federal lines. The system already contains an embryonic legislature (the Council of Ministers, the Executive in its policy-making role and the European Parliament), a civil service (the Executive in its administrative role together with its ancillary bodies), and a judiciary (the European Court of Justice). Although considerable development of these bodies' powers, and clearer definition of their functions in relation to each other and to the member governments, will be required before they can fairly be described as a viable system of federal government, the potential exists in the treaties, as the people who drafted them intended that it should. This potential has been clearly recognized and endorsed by the administrators and most, but by no means all, of the statesmen who have been responsible for implementing the treaties.

The Council of Ministers

The Council is made up of ministerial representatives from each member country. In theory, the actual ministers taking part in any particular meeting of the Council vary with the subjects under discussion—ministers of transport when transport policy is on the agenda, ministers of agriculture to discuss farm problems, and so on—but in practice all major Community decisions are taken by a Council consisting of the six countries' foreign ministers. In the minds of observers, and particularly since the merger of the Executives, it is not always obvious how markedly the powers of the Council differ among the three Community treaties. In fact, the Council has most scope when handling EEC matters, and least when dealing with those of the ECSC. On Euratom affairs, its powers are intermediate between the two. While on EEC matters the Council is very much a legislator, filling in the outlines broadly sketched by the treaty, on ECSC and to a lesser extent on Euratom subjects, its main role is to carry out the more detailed decisions already reached by the treaty-making Powers. Although these distinctions have become blurred with the passage of time and the emergence of unforeseen problems, they are important still.

Ministers taking part in meetings of the Council do so as the official representatives of their countries, and a major function of the Council is to ensure that the varying national interests of the member countries are fully taken into account in the shaping of Community policy.

The decision-making machinery set up by the treaties founding the three Communities is based on the acceptance of weighted majority voting in the Councils of Ministers as the norm of Community practice. A unanimous vote is required only where a specific exception to this principle is made in the treaty concerned. In practice, these exceptions may be divided into two groups. There are a few permanent exceptions, of which decisions on the admission of new members and on amendments to the treaties themselves are the most important, and, in the case of the EEC and Euratom, a much larger group of temporary exceptions, applicable during the initial stages of these two Communities.

The temporary exemption from the principle of majority voting under the two treaties of Rome were all meant to terminate at or before the end of the EEC's transition period, i.e., by 1970 at the latest. Some EEC decisions initially requiring a unanimous vote were transferred to the realm of majority voting when the Common Market moved into the second stage of its transition period in January 1962, and most of the remaining temporary exceptions were removed when the Community moved into the third stage of its transition period at the beginning of 1966. The "gentlemen's disagreement" on majority voting—that a majority vote would not be used in practice to override the vital national interests of any member country—which ended the Community crisis of the second half of 1965 and early 1966 does not affect the basic treaty position on this issue.

Except for the rare cases where a simple majority vote of the Council's members suffices, majority voting is weighted. In the Community of Twelve, the weightings are as follows: Britain, France, Germany and Italy, 10 votes each; Spain, eight votes; Belgium, Greece, the Netherlands and Portugal, five each; Denmark and Ireland, three each; Luxembourg, two votes. Out of this total of 76 votes, 54 are needed to approve a Commission proposal. In practice, however, although the Commission has urged more frequent use of majority voting, the Council usually seeks unanimity. This, while safeguarding national interests as conceived by those objecting, has often notoriously delayed decisions.

Chairmanship of the Council is held by each member country in turn (in alphabetical order of the countries' names in their respective languages) for a period of six months. Its meetings are prepared, on a continuous basis, by the Committee of Permanent Representatives, who in one respect are the ministers' deputies at senior official level, and in another their countries' ambassadors to the Community. The Council is serviced by a full-time Secretariat.

The Commission

While the Council represents the national interests of the several member states, the Commission is intended to represent that of the Community as a whole. Its functions are conventionally fourfold: as an executant of Community decisions (an administrative role); as a source of policy proposals; as a mediator in the Council; and as "watchdog of the Treaties," charged with bringing governments, firms and individuals to book (or to court) if they violate the Community's legal requirements.

To ensure that the Commission acts only in the interests of the Community as a whole, its members undertake not to be swayed by the national interests of their own countries, and pledge themselves to independence of their governments, from whom they may not receive instructions. The deliberations of the Commission are secret, and decisions are taken on a straight majority vote. The Commission operates on the collegiate principle, and a decision once reached binds it as a body.

The Commission has its own staff, forming the nucleus of a fully comprehensive international civil service, members of which are responsible only to it, not to the national administrations of their own countries. The duties of the members and staff occupy them on a full-time basis.

On matters of coal and steel, the Commission has inherited the legal powers and duties of the ECSC High Authority. As such, its decisions are directly binding on the coal, steel, iron-ore and ferrous scrap industries of the Twelve, without the need for these decisions to be embodied in national legislation. The initial task of the High Authority, when the ECSC was first set up, was to establish a common market for these products throughout the geographical area of the Six. This it did by abolishing all trade barriers for these products between the member countries, and by removing trade distortions such as discriminatory pricing of coal or steel based on the nationality of the buyer, unjustified government subsidies to national industries and other impediments to rational patterns of trade.

Once a single Community-wide market for ECSC products had been established, the main emphasis of the High Authority's work changed from that of innovation to the administration of the system it had created. In its ECSC capacity, the Commission is now principally concerned with supervising the efficient operation of the common market for coal and steel products, ensuring that the Paris Treaty rules on fair competition between firms are observed, enforcing Community antitrust legislation to prevent any firm or group of firms from attaining or abusing a dominant market position, encouraging investment and research in the Community coal and steel industries, and offsetting the social effects of the changing patterns of employment in the European coal and steel industries. The latter task has become more urgent in recent years as a result of the diminishing importance of the European coal industry; and Community action in this field has taken two main forms: material assistance to new industries that show interest in setting up in declining coal mining areas; and retraining schemes and financial assistance for former workers in ECSC industries who may be obliged to seek jobs in new industries or new areas.

In its Euratom capacity, the task of the Commission is to ensure the establishment within the Community of a viable and efficient industry for the peaceful exploitation of nuclear resources, to encourage nuclear research and the training of atomic scientists, to administer the Supply Agency through which all nuclear fuel used in the Community's civilian atomic industry is channeled, to supervise the common market for all nuclear materials and equipment, and to lay down safety standards for the Community's nuclear industry as a whole. In certain Euratom cases, the Commission can issue regulations that are directly binding on Community firms operating in the nuclear field, and it has wide powers of inspection and control over the use of nuclear materials that pass through the Supply Agency's hands, to make sure that they are being used only for specified and peaceful purposes.

In its main capacity, concerned with the subject matter of the EEC Treaty, the task of the Commission is to supervise the gradual integration of the entire economies of the member countries, a process that involves the removal of unjustified restrictions on the free movement of goods, capital, services and labor, and the working out of common policies in sectors such as agriculture, transport and external trade.

The members of the Commission, at present 17 in number, are appointed unanimously by the national governments. Members hold office for four years, and are eligible for reappointment; their terms of office are concurrent. Not more than two members of the Commission may be of the same nationality. The president and vice presidents of the Commission are appointed from among the members by the governments acting unanimously. Their terms of office are for two years, but they may be reappointed. In the event of the governments failing to agree on the replacement or reappointment of a member or officer of the Commission when the individual's term has expired, the person concerned remains in office until such agreement is reached.

The Commission has an administrative staff of about 10,000 officials, based mainly in Brussels but partly in Luxembourg. One-third of the total is employed in translation and interpretation, made necessary by the fact that, as a legislating body, the Commission must operate in all nine of its member states' main official languages. The (Euratom) Joint Research Centre and other services further employ some 2,800 people.

The European Parliament

The Treaty of Paris which established the ECSC, made provision for a Common Assembly "consisting of representatives of the peoples of the member states of the Community," which would exercise democratic supervision over the actions of the High Authority. When the Common Market and Euratom were set up, this Assembly, which became known as the European Parliament, was given the responsibility of democratic supervision over all three Communities. At present it does not have legislative powers like those of national parliaments, but it has made full and vigorous use of those that it has, and has also extended them.

Since June 1979, when the European Parliament was first directly elected instead of being appointed by and from among the national parliaments, it has consisted of members elected every five years by universal suffrage. With the entry of Spain and Portugal it has 518 members: 81 from each of the four most populous countries, 60 from Spain, 25 from the Netherlands, 24 each from Belgium, Greece and Portugal, 16 from Denmark, 15 from Ireland, and six from Luxembourg.

Perhaps the most significant aspect of the way in which the Parliament operates is the fact that its members have decided, of their own accord, to sit as political groups, not as national delegations. In 1985 there were 131 Socialists; 110 Christian Democrats in the European People's party; 50 European Democrats; 41 Communists and allies; 31 Liberals and Democrats; 29 in the European Democratic Alliance; 20 members of the Rainbow Group; 16 members of the European Right. Six members belong to no group.

The Parliament has a staff of some 2,900 officials, based in Luxembourg. It has 17 standing committees. It holds its plenary sessions in Strasbourg, in the presence of the Commission and the Council, and open to the public.

The Parliament elects its president and officers from among its members. Except in special circumstances laid down in the treaties, the Parliament acts by means of an absolute majority of the votes cast.

The Commission is required to submit an annual report to the Parliament, which can dismiss the Commission by a two-thirds majority vote of censure. So far, it has not used this major weapon, but has concentrated on its other powers. Thus it can and does: supervise the Commission and Council, partly by debating their programs and reports, and partly through incisive written and oral questions; give an opinion on Commission proposals before the Council can decide on them; give a discharge to the Commission on its management of the Community budget; and reject or adopt the draft budget drawn up by the Commission and agreed upon by the Council. In the case of expenditure involving legal obligations to third parties (e.g., agriculture), the Council must have a qualified majority to accept or reject modifications made by the Parliament, whether or not they increase the overall budget. In the case of nonobligatory expenditure, often involving the development of new policies, the Parliament has discretionary powers of amendment within set but periodically negotiable limits. These powers have given rise over the years to regular concerted procedures whereby the Parliament debates financial questions with the Council and the Commission.

The European Court of Justice

The European Court of Justice is the final point of appeal on all matters concerning the interpretation or application of the Community treaties. It has the sole power to rule on the legality of acts committed by the Council of Ministers and the Commission. It can decide on appeals for exemptions from Community regulations, questions of Community procedure, disputes over interpretation of the treaties or their implementing regulations, and cases where Community institutions are alleged to have exceeded their powers. It may also judge cases where the Commission or a member government is alleged to have failed to carry out its responsibilities under the treaties.

Right of appeal to the Court is open to member governments and to Community institutions. Under the Common Market and Euratom treaties, private individuals or legal persons may also appeal to the Court against Community rules that are directed at them, or which concern them directly or specifically. The ECSC Treaty allows firms or associations of firms subject to the treaty's provisions to appeal against particular Community decisions that concern them, or against general decisions that they feel result in injustice when applied in their cases.

The Court may also give judgment and award damages in cases where plaintiffs claim that they have suffered loss as a result of an act of a Community institution. Under certain circumstances, the Court may also decide preliminary issues submitted by national courts in Community countries, where questions of the interpretation of the treaties or the validity of Community decisions are raised in domestic litigation.

The judgments of the Court have direct force of law in all Community countries, without the prior need to be incorporated in the member countries' legislation. They are binding on all parties concerned, whether individuals, firms, national governments, or Community institutions. In the 34 years of the Court's history, there has been no occasion on which its decisions have been resisted by member governments, or on which a government has refused to carry out its rulings.

The Court, which meets in Luxembourg, consists of 13 judges, appointed unanimously by the member governments from among persons of high legal standing in their own countries. The judges are assisted by advocates general, also appointed by the governments, and a clerk appointed by the Court. The judges serve for terms of six years, and may be reappointed. Partial renewal of the membership of the Court occurs every three years, affecting three and four judges alternately. The judges elect from among their number a president of the Court, who holds office for three years.

A simple majority of the judges is sufficient for the adoption of a ruling. No dissenting opinions are published.

THE FORMULATION OF COMMUNITY POLICY

The differences between the Paris Treaty founding ECSC and the later Rome Treaties founding EEC and Euratom are most clearly apparent in the provisions which each makes for the formulation of Community policy. In its ECSC capacity, the Commission has considerably greater power of direct action than in dealing with Euratom and EEC matters. The role of the Council, on ECSC questions, is in many areas confined to putting forward the opinions of governments before the Commission takes decisions that will be binding on the coal and steel industries. However, the Council's prior approval, based on either a simple or a qualified majority vote, depending on the issue, is required for most important decisions. With minor exceptions, unanimous approval by the Council is necessary only for matters outside the strict coal and steel sectors.

On EEC and Euratom matters, there is a far greater degree of interdependence between the Commission and the Council of Ministers in the process of defining Community policy. In these two fields, the Council of Ministers takes the final policy decisions, although it can do so only on the basis of proposals put forward by the Commission. The Council can only modify such proposals by a unanimous vote, even in cases where a majority vote is sufficient to adopt the particular proposal as it stands. In EEC and Euratom, therefore, the Commission has almost the sole right to propose Community policy, while the Council of Ministers retains responsibility for the ultimate decisions on these proposals. Only in certain limited circumstances, on EEC and Euratom matters, does the Commission have the right to take independent action, usually in its administrative role in the implementation of policy already adopted in principle, or under a specific mandate from the Council.

In the process of making proposals for Community action on EEC and Euratom matters, the Commission possesses one important faculty that has greatly facilitated agreement in the Council of Ministers in the past on a number of difficult issues. The Commission has the right to modify its proposals at any time up to the moment when the Council actually reaches a decision. After observing the way in which the debate has gone in the Council on a contested issue, and taking account of the various national positions, the Commission may therefore produce a compromise solution at the psychological moment—a "package deal" in Community jargon.

ANCILLARY COMMUNITY BODIES

The Commission and the Council of Ministers are advised before formulating or implementing Community policy by a number of specialized or general committees. Some of these committees were envisaged in the treaties, others have been set up on an ad hoc basis as the need arose.

The Economic and Social Committee, consisting of some 189 members representing employers' organizations, trade unions, consumers' associations and other social and economic groups, has the right to advise the Commission and Council of Ministers on many aspects of Community policy.

The Consultative Committee, consisting of representatives of producers, traders, workers and consumers, performs a similar task in the field of coal and steel.

In addition, there are very many specialized advisory bodies in scientific, economic, monetary, social, agricultural, regional, transport, banking, budgetary, overseas development and other areas of policy; while professional, trade and trade union federations and associations, as well as national specialist officials, are constantly consulted in the process of preparing Community legislation.

The Community also has four funds to assist its work: The European Social Fund, to prevent or alleviate any social hardship resulting from structural change; the European Development Fund for less developed countries linked to the Community by special agreement; the Agricultural Guidance and Guarantee Fund; and the European Regional Fund. The European Investment Bank has independent status, but fulfills similar roles.

A Court of Auditors, consisting of 12 members appointed by the Council for six years, has extensive powers to supervise the legality and soundness of the Community's budgetary and financial operations.

INSTITUTIONAL REFORM

Dismayed by the slowness of Community decision making and by the imbalance in the institutions, marked by a growing preponderance of the Council and the national governments, a number of actors and observers in the Community process have recently proposed reforms.

The Commission has called for the full recognition of its powers, the use of majority voting in the Council and a strengthening of the role of the European Parliament. The latter has put forward a draft Treaty of Union, which would extend Community action into new fields such as foreign policy, security, European citizenship and monetary union, while sharing legislative power between itself and the Council.

The heads of state and government of the Community—whose periodic meetings are known as those of the European Council—agreed at Fontainebleau in June 1984 to set up an ad hoc committee on institutional affairs to examine ways of improving the way the Community works.

FURTHER READING

Arbuthnot, Hugh, and Edwards, Geoffrey, eds. *A Common Man's Guide to the Common Market*. London: Macmillan for the Federal Trust, 1979.

Armitage, Paul. *The Common Market*. London: MacDonald, 1978.

Bebr, Gerhard. *Judicial Control of the European Communities*. London: Stevens; New York: Frederick A. Praeger, 1962.

Brierley, Caroline. *The Making of European Policy*. London: Oxford University Press, 1961; New York: 1963.

Cocks, Barnett. *The European Parliament*. London: HMSO, 1973.

Coombes, David. *The Future of The European Parliament*. London: PSI, 1979.

———. *Politics and Bureaucracy in the European Community*. London: Allen and Unwin/PEP, 1970.

Lindberg, Leon N. *The Political Dynamics of European Economic Integration*. London: Oxford University Press; Stanford, Calif.: Stanford University Press, 1963.

Noël, Emile. *The European Community: How it Works*. Luxembourg: EC Commission, 1979.

Prag, Derek. *Lobbying the European Community.* London: European Democratic Group, 1983.
Stuart, Mackenzie. *The European Communities and the Rule of Law.* London: Stevens, 1977.
Willis, Virginia. *Britons in Brussels.* London: PSI, 1983.

THE EUROPEAN COMMUNITY: FROM CUSTOMS UNION TOWARD ECONOMIC AND MONETARY UNION

ROY PRYCE

THE program of economic integration set out in the European Economic Community (EEC) treaty signed in 1957 had both short-term and long-term objectives. The core of the treaty was concerned with the former: the creation of a common market, based on a customs union to be achieved over a transition period of 12 years. As the six signatories made clear in the preamble to the treaty, however, this was intended to "lay the foundations of an ever closer union among the European peoples." Once the customs union was achieved in mid-1968 (ahead of schedule), the six nations began to work toward the far more ambitious goal of an economic and monetary union. This has proved to be an arduous undertaking in the difficult economic circumstances of the 1970s and 1980s. The successive enlargements of the Community have also greatly widened the range of national interests to be reconciled. Even the basic common market has come under pressure, and though some progress has been made toward it, economic and monetary union is still a distant target.

THE SIX: CUSTOMS UNION, COMMON MARKET AND ECONOMIC AND MONETARY UNION (1957–72)

The Treaty of Rome was as much the work of politicians as of economists. They had to bear in mind what was feasible, as well as what their advisers told them was desirable. They had little difficulty in agreeing to aim for a common market based on a customs union, rather than the looser free-trade area preferred by the British. They also readily agreed that the common market had to cover agricultural as well as industrial products. But it proved far easier to deal with the latter. The treaty set a detailed timetable for achieving a customs union for industrial goods, providing for the progressive reduction and final abolition—at the end of a three-stage transition period—of quotas and tariffs among the members of the Community, and the replacement of national tariffs toward nonmembers by a common external tariff.

579

In contrast, the provisions concerning agriculture were very sketchy. At that time, 20 percent of the labor force of the Six still worked on the land and farmers were a major political force. Each national group was intensely suspicious of its neighbors. It proved impossible during the negotiations to agree on more than the need for a common agricultural policy and the principles on which it should be based. The rest was left for later negotiation.

The treaty's remaining provisions were strongly inspired by laissez-faire principles. The underlying assumption was of the automatically beneficial effects of a large common market. Major emphasis was therefore placed on measures of "negative integration": the removal of barriers to the movement of goods, persons, services and capital. Fiscal discrimination was to be eliminated, and those national laws and regulations impinging directly on competitive conditions were to be harmonized. Common rules of competition for interstate trade were prescribed. But social provisions were meager; inserted mainly at the insistence of the French, they were designed essentially to level up labor costs in the member countries. A Social Fund was provided, but with the limited function of retraining workers put out of a job by the introduction of the common market. There was nothing included about industrial or regional policy; there were no specific provisions (unlike those in the European Coal and Steel Community/ECSC treaty) to deal with crises. And those provisions relating to cooperation among the member states on general economic policy were very weak.

Rapid early progress

As long as times were good, these gaps in coverage did not much matter. Aided by favorable economic conditions, the Six succeeded twice in the early 1960s (May 1960 and May 1962) in accelerating their timetable of internal tariff cuts and moves toward the common external tariff. They also rapidly settled the tariff levels on a list of previously disputed items. This initial momentum was maintained, and the customs union was formally achieved on July 1, 1968.

These moves were paralleled and indeed only made possible by substantial progress during the same period in the construction of a common agricultural policy. Much of the credit for this belonged to Sicco Mansholt, the Dutch former agriculture minister, then the member of the Commission responsible for agricultural policy. The first breakthrough was achieved in December 1960 with an agreement on the types of market organization to be used for major products and on the mechanisms of market intervention to be employed to maintain price stability. This was then followed by a second major set of decisions that were reached in mid-January 1962 after a marathon negotiation during which, it was reported, "three officials collapsed with heart attacks and stubble-bearded, trigger-tempered delegates fought long into the night, stoked with double whiskies." The outcome was a detailed market organization for grains, pork, eggs, poultry, and fruits and vegetables. Later regulations were approved for beef and veal, dairy products and rice. The first common price levels, however, were only fixed later, beginning in December 1964 with those for cereals. It was these price levels, together with the devices used to insulate the common market from fluctuations in world prices, and the failure to introduce effective measures of structural reform, that set the Community on its course toward self-sufficiency and the overproduction of many farm products that has subsequently proved so burdensome, both financially and politically.

At the time, however, these decisions were accounted a great success. They enabled the Six to move forward over a broad front. High rates of economic growth also helped greatly: they boosted business confidence and created conditions propitious for lifting restrictions on the movement of labor. Steps were taken to ensure that those workers who moved did not lose their entitlement to social security benefits. Details of the application of the treaty's rules of competition were also worked out, and a system of compulsory registration of agreements was decided on in March 1962. External trade policy, too, provided an area for successful common action when the Community took part as a unit in the Dillon (1960–62) and Kennedy (1964–67) rounds of mutual tariff reductions in the framework of the General Agreement on Tariffs and Trade (GATT).

Not all policy sectors proved so amenable. Little progress was made, for example, in implementing the treaty's provisions for a common transport policy. Only slow progress was made in freeing the movement of services and the right of establishment. Many restrictions on capital markets remained. For a while, too, the Community as a whole was brought to a virtual standstill as a result of the crisis precipitated in 1965 by President Charles de Gaulle's objections to Commission proposals for the further development of the Community—and in particular the prospect of wider use of majority voting. Momentum was not restored until after his resignation in April 1969. At the suggestion of his successor, Georges Pompidou, a new summit meeting was held in The Hague in December 1969. A triple formula was adopted for getting the Community moving again, involving measures to complete it, deepen it and widen it. The first category included agreements on the financial regulation for a common agricultural policy and the future funding of the Community; the last category meant reopening negotiations for the entry of Denmark, Ireland and Great Britain. It was in the context of the second category that the achievement of an economic and monetary union now became a new goal for the Six.

A new target: economic and monetary union
Sufficient progress was made at The Hague for the leaders of the Six to declare that the transition period for the achievement of the common market would formally come to an end on December 31, 1969. The focus of attention now became economic and monetary union. There had long been a need for measures of positive integration to complement the removal of barriers on which the treaty had concentrated. In 1962, for instance, the Commission had proposed closer coordination of economic policy and a common monetary policy as objectives for the second stage of the transition period, with monetary union to be achieved in the third stage. At that time, the West German government in particular was against such developments; but two years later agreement was reached on two modest steps, the establishment

of a committee of governors of the central banks of the member states, and of a budgetary policy committee. Both were intended to promote closer cooperation in general economic and monetary policy. The subsequent run on the French franc at the time of the May 1968 student demonstrations, and other signs of growing stress in the international monetary system, increased support for measures designed to underpin the customs union with greater monetary stability. At the Hague summit, the new West German chancellor, Willy Brandt, formally proposed the creation of an Economic and Monetary Union (EMU) in two stages. In March 1970, a working group was set up under the chairmanship of Pierre Werner, prime minister of Luxembourg, to study the details of how it might be achieved. The Werner Report of October 1970 suggested that the EMU should be in effect by 1980, at which point exchange rates among the Community countries would become fixed, their currencies fully convertible and the main levers of economic policy transferred from national to Community level. The report proposed a three-stage transition period, with a gradual narrowing of the margin of exchange-rate fluctuations. It gave rise to sharp differences of opinion within the Community, particularly between the West Germans and the French. The West Germans argued that priority should be given to harmonizing economic policies as a necessary precondition for monetary integration; the French preferred to put monetary policy first. In March 1971, however, the Council of Ministers agreed to embark on the first stage of EMU.

Shortly afterward, in May, there was renewed massive speculation against the dollar. Without consulting their partners, the West Germans decided to let the mark float. Pressure on the dollar nevertheless continued, and in August President Richard M. Nixon ended its convertibility into gold—a move that effectively marked the end of the Bretton Woods system of fixed parities. The Six were unable to reach even the semblance of a concerted response until September. But eventually, after the Smithsonian Agreement (December 1971), which provided for a realignment of the major currencies including a devaluation of the dollar and the adoption of a new "crawling peg" exchange-rate system, the Community countries decided to try again. In March 1972, the Council of Ministers agreed to narrow the exchange-rate fluctuations allowed by the International Monetary Fund to 2.25 percent for the members of the Community, thus establishing what became known as "the Snake in the Tunnel." This new attempt to draw the currencies of the member states closer together soon came under intense pressure. In June 1972, the British, who had agreed to take part in the new arrangements in anticipation of their entry into the Community, left the snake and allowed sterling to float independently. The Irish and (for a time) the Danes followed suit. Nevertheless, at the Paris summit in October 1972, on the eve of the Community's enlargement, the member governments reaffirmed their intention to achieve EMU by the end of 1980, and agreed that its second stage should begin in January 1974. These decisions were part of an extensive package of measures designed not only to extend the scope of common action but also to take the enlarged Community toward an even more ambitious objective: the transformation of the whole complex of their relations into a European Union by 1980.

THE ENLARGED COMMUNITY (1973–84)

In the early months of 1973, the Nine set to work on this new agenda, which included the establishment of a Regional Fund, plans for an expanded social policy to be matched by additional resources for the Social Fund, measures to create a "single industrial base" for the Community, and programs to protect the environment and the consumer. At the same time, the institutions also began working on a tight schedule laid down by the summit to prepare for the second stage of EMU, including the creation, before April 1, of a European Monetary Cooperation Fund. But very soon the clouds began to gather, and the members of the Community found themselves in a much harsher economic environment, having to deal with a new set of problems that were to test severely their capacity to work together.

The impact of recession
The continued instability of the international monetary system was the source of the first of these problems. Early in 1973 there occurred a new exchange crisis and a second devaluation of the dollar. The Italian lira now left the snake, to be followed by the French franc in January 1974. By then, only five of the nine Community currencies remained within it, grouped around the West German mark. The attempt to move to the second stage of EMU was abandoned.

In the meantime, the initial repercussions of the Yom Kippur war (autumn 1973) in the Middle East were felt. Confronted by threats to their oil supplies, the member states, in total disarray, each took individual action. To this initial shock, which badly strained relations between them, were then added the longer-term consequences of the fourfold increase in oil prices. These included strong inflationary pressures in the Community countries, pressures that were countered by policies to reduce demand at a time when demand was also falling in overseas markets. Later, when there were some signs of recovery, the further rise in oil prices in 1979–80 led to a renewed downturn in the level of economic activity.

To add to their problems, the member states had to face at the same time a rapid deterioration in their competitive position. This first became apparent in the 1970s in such traditional industries as steel, textiles and shipbuilding, but it also affected European automobile manufacturers and was equally pronounced in industries based on new technologies. In this last category, the main competition came from manufacturers in the United States and Japan, but a number of newly industrialized countries also made successful, powerful entries into European markets.

The combined effect of these various factors, together with a sluggish European response, was quite dramatic. The rate of growth of the Community's economy, which had averaged 4.6 percent per year over the period 1960–73, now fell to 2.3 percent in 1973–80. Full employment was replaced by rising unemployment: by 1984, the number of those without jobs had risen to over 12 million, of whom some 25 percent were people under the age of 25.

All these problems found their way onto the Community's agenda, as

583

individual countries discovered they were unable to deal with them on their own. Yet although the member states faced common problems, they found it very difficult to agree on common responses. Among the reasons were that rates of inflation as well as levels of unemployment differed significantly from country to country. From 1973–80, for instance, the rate of inflation in West Germany never rose higher than seven percent, compared with peaks of 19.1 percent in Italy, 20.9 percent in Ireland and 24.2 percent in Britain. Luxembourg was able to keep its jobless rate below two percent; on the other hand by 1983 unemployment reached 15 percent in Ireland and over 14 percent in Belgium and the Netherlands.

National policy responses to basic problems also differed. A report in 1975 judged that national economic and monetary policies were more discordant than at any time since the Community was set up. Later, the divergences became even more marked; in 1979 Margaret Thatcher became prime minister in Britain, pledged to strict monetarist policies; two years later President François Mitterrand and a Socialist government attempted Keynesian solutions in France. The latter experiment was soon abandoned, but substantial differences of approach remained, in terms of both general economic policy and the policies of individual sectors.

The Community's increase in size in January 1973 from six to nine, and in January 1981 to 10 with the entry of Greece, made the search for common policies even more difficult. Several of the newcomers proved to be awkward customers—not least because they had been obliged to accept as the price of entry the compact struck among the original Six. The Labour government, which came to power in Britain in February 1974, promptly demanded a renegotiation of the terms. The results were presented as sufficiently positive to persuade 67 percent of those who took part in the referendum in June 1975 to vote in favor of staying in. Even so, opposition to membership continued in the Labour party, and the issue was not settled finally until the party's defeat in the 1983 general election. In the meantime, the rising British contribution to the Community's budget led Prime Minister Thatcher to mount a sustained, truculent campaign to "get our money back." In May 1980, the first of three annual rebates was agreed on, but the British demand for a longer-term solution merged with other unresolved problems at that stage to precipitate a crisis of confidence within the Community.

Uneven development
The record of the Community in subsequent years was very uneven. The customs union was extended over a five-year transition period both to the three newcomers who joined in 1973 and also to Greece when it joined in 1981. Substantial increases in trade with the other members followed; in the case of Britain, whereas trade with the EC had accounted for only about a third of its total trade on entry, by 1981 it had risen to 40 percent. Between 1973 and 1983 an industrial free-trade area was also progressively established with the remaining members of the European Free Trade Association (EFTA).

But within the common market there still remained many barriers to free movement. As far as goods were concerned, these took a variety of forms.

Some resulted from different national levels of value-added tax (VAT), others from complex frontier formalities, administrative requirements or rules concerning technical safety and public health. Governments, under pressure from national producers, were inventive in devising new nontariff barriers to protect domestic suppliers. The British, for example, found ways of keeping out French turkeys and UHT (ultrapasteurized) milk for a while. Similarly, Danish veterinary regulations were invoked to deny access to a range of foreign foodstuffs, including cooked pork. To stem imports of refrigerators, the French suddenly introduced new regulations and a system of prior inspection; to deal with a flood of Japanese videocassette recorders, they insisted on a single, inconvenient point of entry and documentation in their own language. Even the West Germans, erstwhile champions of free trade, mounted a campaign against foreign beers—one newspaper claiming that these beverages could cause impotence. The multiplication of such barriers at last prompted the European Council, in 1982, to support Commission proposals to simplify frontier formalities and ease national restrictions. This support was slow to materialize. In 1984, however, a series of positive developments occurred, including agreement on a uniform document for customs declaration implementation of 15 previously blocked directives harmonizing technical standards. Symptomatic of the new mood were the bilateral agreement between West German Chancellor Helmut Kohl and President Mitterrand on May 28 to remove frontier formalities for European Community citizens at their common borders, and a European Council decision in June to press for a program of measures to achieve a "Citizens' Europe."

There was also a renewed attempt in the 1980s to achieve mutual recognition of university degrees and professional qualifications throughout the member countries. This was a necessary precondition for the movement of professional people throughout the Community. By 1984, only a limited degree of free movement had been achieved for the liberal professions; several proposed directives had been stuck in the Council of Ministers for more than a decade.

During the same period, the common agricultural policy became a major source of tension among Community members. Initially, it was only the British, accustomed to a cheap food policy, who protested the common policy's cost and the surpluses that had begun to appear. The founding members took the view that these were only temporary, that the policy guaranteed supplies for the consumer and a fair price for the producer, and that in any case it was a sacred part of the *acquis communautaire*. When in 1978 the policy began to absorb more than 70 percent of the Community's budget, some efforts were made to curb the annual price rises; but it was not until the early 1980s, when costs threatened to exceed budgetary resources, that pressure for change became insistent. The future of the common agricultural policy then became part of a wider discussion involving the future level of the Community's budget, how it was to be financed and the British contribution to it. In May 1980, the Commission was given a mandate to make proposals on all these matters but, characteristically, was given a leisurely 12 months in which to report. A further three years passed after it had done so before effective action was taken.

The changed circumstances of the 1970s also presented the Community with challenges in new areas, in particular energy and industrial policy. In 1973 oil accounted for 61 percent of the Community's energy consumption, and most of it was imported. The Community was therefore in a vulnerable position when the oil-producing countries succeeded in acting together to raise prices. The Community had great difficulty in adopting a common position toward the Organization of Petroleum Exporting Countries (OPEC), and action to reduce energy consumption and dependence on oil was thereafter undertaken essentially by individual countries, with some agreement on overall targets and strategy but no genuine common policy.

Industrial problems were also tackled piecemeal. To meet the crisis in the steel industry, in which there was a 20 percent fall in production between 1974 and 1981 and an over 30 percent loss of jobs, voluntary production quotas were first tried in 1977. These were replaced in June 1982 by compulsory quotas and minimum prices, as provided for in the ECSC treaty. Steps were taken at the same time to reduce capacity even further, and to negotiate agreements with external suppliers to limit their exports to the Community.

The textile industry also faced severe problems. Between 1973 and 1980 it shed more than 800,000 jobs, well over a quarter of its labor force. Relief was sought through protective trade measures negotiated in the context of GATT's Multifiber Agreement, and there was Community financial help for restructuring and retraining.

While other traditional sectors, like shipbuilding, also had to contract sharply, there was at the same time increasing concern about the Community countries falling behind the United States and Japan in industrial applications of the newer technologies. Belatedly, in early 1984, agreement was reached on a modest European Strategic Program for Research and development in Information Technologies (ESPRIT), jointly funded by the Community and industry. At the same time, initiatives were launched to improve competition in such related fields as telecommunications and biotechnology.

Other positive developments included the creation of a European Regional Development Fund in 1975, although its resources, despite steady increases voted by the European Parliament, remained very modest; agreement in January 1983, after 10 years of tough negotiation, on a common fisheries policy; the quadrupling of the resources of the Social Fund and its gradual reshaping as an instrument of job creation and training for young people; and the creation in 1978 of a new borrowing facility for priority investment projects.

THE EUROPEAN MONETARY SYSTEM

The most important single achievement, however, was the creation of the European Monetary System (EMS). The public initiative for this was taken in October 1977 by Roy Jenkins, president of the Commission, who argued for a renewed attempt at economic and monetary union. The starting point was to be a system narrowing exchange-rate fluctuations among members. One important aim of this would be to increase business confidence in cross-national investment, thus providing a source of greatly needed new jobs.

Strong support for the proposal came from both Helmut Schmidt, the West German chancellor, and President Valéry Giscard d'Estaing of France. They initiated the negotiations leading to formal approval of a detailed plan by the European Council in December 1978, and the entry into operation of the EMS in March 1979.

The system created a new exchange-rate and intervention mechanism; introduced a new European Currency Unit (the ECU), based on a weighted basket of currencies; and reinforced credit mechanisms to sustain exchange-rate stability. The British pound was included in the basket of currencies, but the British did not join in the exchange-rate mechanism (nor did the Greeks when they entered the Community). Nevertheless, during its first five years, the EMS successfully weathered a period of great instability in the international money markets. Two parity adjustments were carried out without major problems, the operation of the system contributed to a convergence of rates of inflation and general economic policies within the Community and there was a substantial growth in the use of the ECU by the private sector. In the international Eurobond markets it became the third most important currency after the dollar and the mark. Disagreement persisted, however, about the development of the EMS, and in particular about the size and role of the embryonic European Monetary Fund. This meant that the second stage of the EMS, due to have begun in March 1981, still had not been introduced by the end of 1984. By that time, strong pressure had developed in Britain for the government to take full part in the system. This was necessary for any concerted action vis-à-vis the dollar, which many in the Community were anxious to achieve.

THE EARLY 1980s

The Community was confronted in the early 1980s by a crisis of confidence. The imminent danger of running out of money at last forced member states to face up to the need to limit spending on the common agricultural policy and to find a way of avoiding annual quarrels with the British over their contribution to the budget. This proved a lengthy and arduous task. A succession of European Council meetings in Stuttgart (June 1983), Athens (December 1983) and Brussels (March 1984) failed to make much progress, and pessimism was pervasive. In April 1984 a *Newsweek* cover story discussed the decline of Europe. "Economic stagnation and political malaise darken the future of a once-proud and powerful continent," went the story, which also quoted a French economist as saying: "Europe has sacrificed the future to the present. We run the risk of becoming as irrelevant as a bunch of Caribbean banana republics." President Mitterrand, speaking in The Hague in February 1984, warned that the Community was in danger of becoming a deserted building site.

Such warnings were heeded. Decisions taken at the Community's annual farm-price review in the spring of 1984 heralded a breakthrough. For the first time a serious effort was made to curb overproduction in the dairy sector. Production quotas were fixed both for the Community as a whole and its individual members, and a superlevy was imposed on those exceeding the quotas; the proceeds of this levy were to be used to finance measures to dispose of surplus milk production. Guaranteed prices for other products were also screwed down. At the next European Council meeting, held in Fontainebleau in June 1984, a package of measures on the other major issues was also agreed to. The Community's budgetary resources were to be increased by raising the contribution from the receipts of VAT from one percent to 1.4 percent by 1986, with the possibility of a further rise to 1.6 percent after 1988. For the British, a lump sum rebate of one billion ECUs (£600 million) for its 1984 contribution was agreed to, as well as a formula for calculating a refund in subsequent years. An early date was also set for concluding negotiations over the entry of Spain and Portugal.

That date was not met, however. The rise in budgetary resources was judged by many to be too little and too late, and bickering continued over details of the budgetary deal. But 1986 was now generally accepted as the date by which the Community should be enlarged from 10 to 12 members, and the Fontainebleau decisions appeared to augur a new and more positive phase in the Community's development. It remained uncertain whether further enlargement would act as another brake on the process of economic integration or would provide an incentive to Community members to build on the successful experiment of the EMS and move on toward economic and monetary union.

FURTHER READING

Albert, M., and Ball, R. J. *Towards European Economic Recovery in the 1980s.* Report presented to the European Parliament, August 1983.

Hodges, M., and Wallace, W. *Economic Divergence in the European Community.* London: Allen and Unwin, 1981.

Holland, S. *Uncommon Market.* London: Macmillan, 1980.

Hopkins, M. *Policy Formation in the European Communities.* London: Mansell, 1981.

Hu, Yao-Su. *Europe under Stress: Convergence and Divergence in the European Community.* London: Butterworth, 1981.

Jeffries, J. *A Guide to the Official Publications of the European Communities.* London: Mansell, 1978.

Lodge, J., ed. *The European Community: Bibliographical Excursions.* London: Frances Pinter, 1983.

———. *Institutions and Policies of the European Community.* London: Frances Pinter, 1983.

Ludlow, P. *The Making of the European Monetary System.* London: Butterworth, 1982.

Swann, D. *Competition and Industrial Policy in the European Community.* London: Macmillan, 1983.

———. *The Economics of the Common Market.* 4th ed. Harmondsworth: Penguin, 1978.

Tsoukalis, L., ed. "The European Community: Past, Present, Future." Special issue of *Journal of Common Market Studies*, September/December 1982.

———. *The Politics and Economics of European Monetary Integration.* London: Allen and Unwin, 1977.

Wallace, H., et al. *Policy-making in the European Community*, 2nd ed. London: Wiley, 1983.

FROM ECONOMIC UNION TO POLITICAL UNION

PIERRE URI

THE aims of the European Community (EC) have always been political. Does this mean that the Community will lead to a political union between the member countries?

GROWTH OF THE EUROPEAN COMMUNITY

Integration started with the pooling of coal and steel, which might seem a strange way to begin, for the freeing of trade in two isolated products for any length of time must cause serious economic distortion. It was a novel approach, which has, however, proved successful; by creating an unbalanced situation, the member countries forced themselves to go a step further in order to restore the balance. Criticism gave a new impetus to the whole operation, by involving the critics in the business of European integration.

Coal and steel both had a symbolic value. Coal was still the main source of power for the manufacturing industries, and steel was, and still is, the mainstay of the armaments industry; together therefore they played a decisive part in peace and war. But above all they provided an opportunity to set up a new kind of institution to administer common interests.

It soon became clear that the idea of a body representing the Community as a whole, which would conduct a sort of dialogue with the member states, was an important one, and could be extended to other spheres. It was next taken up in the project for a European Defence Community (EDC).

In retrospect, EDC was clearly inopportune. Not only was national opinion probably not ready for it, but for years afterward one member of the Community at least (France) was engaged in wars outside Europe, and "exceptional" withdrawals from the proposed integrated force would have been more often the rule than integration. The draft itself, which was copied somewhat unimaginatively from the European Coal and Steel Community (ECSC) Treaty, had several drawbacks. Although putting great emphasis on the supranational principle, embodied in a nine-member Commissariat, it prevented the Commissariat from working because most of the decisions needed the unanimous agreement of the member states.

The difficulty of establishing common forces without a common foreign

589

policy was, however, realized at the time, for without such a policy there could be no decision to use force. Hence the idea of a political community to complement the defense community. The European Assembly's plan to meet this need is not without historical interest, even though it was abandoned when the EDC was rejected by the French parliament. The general structural pattern of an assembly, council of ministers, court of appeal and executive, was copied straight from the Treaty of Paris, but this time the executive was to be elected by the assembly. The powers of the executive were essentially the same as those of the High Authority of the ECSC. As far as diplomacy. was concerned, it could only give advice or suggestions, and though there was a chapter devoted to European laws it gave no indication of their content.

The EDC project thus failed to grasp the basic principle to which the EC owes its success: the direct relationship between the structure of the institutions and their purpose.

The dramatic emergence of the Common Market, after the Treaty of Rome was successfully drawn up five years later (1957), showed that this approach and this type of institution were accepted as sound; indeed, the new Community extended the range of its institutions to take in the whole of the economy.

The objectives of this treaty were again political; economics and politics came together, while the close relationship between institutional structure and aims was made particularly clear in the new treaty's plans for an economic union that would go well beyond the scope of a customs union or free trade area.

POLITICAL QUESTIONS IN ECONOMIC TERMS

It is not easy to determine exactly where a "customs union" ends and "economic union" begins, for the two concepts can be defined in several ways. One definition is that a customs union concerns only the free movement of goods within a given area, and a common tariff at the border; thus according to this definition, any measure which does not strictly concern goods comes under the definition of economic union. This means not only measures such as free movement of labor and capital, but also common rules of competition applying to business concerns or governments, and, of course, common financial resources and common policies.

A narrower definition of economic union is that it requires constructive action as opposed to the mere removal of obstacles to trade; according to this definition, the mere abolition of restrictions on the free movement of capital and labor from one country to the next comes into the same category as measures relating to goods, i.e., a customs union. (This is the position held by some Socialists, who regard any free trade measure as being "right-wing," and who therefore, when the dismantling of tariffs was achieved ahead of schedule in the Common Market, criticized the lack of progress in the creation of common organizations and harmonization of economic conditions to which the Left traditionally attaches importance.)

There is a third possible distinction between a customs union and economic union if the rules of competition, particularly the prohibition of cartels, are considered as an inseparable corollary of free trade. An example of this distinction may be found in the European Free Trade Association (EFTA), which is not an economic union but which, according to the Stockholm Convention, has a few basic rules governing competition; on the other hand, it is not concerned with agriculture and there is no common external tariff, both of which are covered by the Treaty of Rome.

The problems involved in agriculture, transport and foreign affairs, however, cannot easily be classified under any of these definitions of either customs union or economic union. For example, the movement of goods can involve agriculture only if there is a general agricultural policy and marketing system; any rules for transport will involve rules governing transport prices; and a common external tariff rapidly creates the need for a common trade policy, an aspect, in its turn, of foreign policy. In other words, in order to work these largely divergent elements into a coherent whole, an overall plan is essential: there must be an automatic process by which the plan is implemented, leading to the same close interrelation of parts as obtains in an internal or national market. The more the governments are actively involved in the workings of the economy, in order to ensure expansion, stability, full employment and fair distribution of wealth, the more they will be bound to undertake in common, if they are also to establish a common market between their states.

Harmonization and coordination
A question that then arises is how far to take joint action in any given sector. In this connection, "harmonization" and "coordination" are terms that are used frequently and generally treated as synonymous, but it may be useful to define them more precisely. The difference between them (whether it be in connection with tax legislation or monetary policy or anything else) can be demonstrated by their relation to an absolute term: complete unification (of states).

In the absence of such unification, harmonization aims at preventing distortions in competition. Where, for instance, profits taxes differ from one country to another, capital tends to be deflected from economically productive projects into investment on which taxation is less heavy. In a common market, concerted action also has to be taken if competition threatens to bring about harmonization in an undesirable way. For instance, if member countries compete with each other to have the lowest profits taxes, this inevitably leads to increases in other kinds of taxation. This line of argument led to the insertion into the treaties of rules to establish equal pay for men and women and standard working hours to govern the application of overtime rates.

Coordination, on the other hand, does not imply the application of permanent rules. Coordination concerns policies, whether they be policies to deal with the immediate economic situation, or longer-term programs. It does not normally mean that all member countries act in the same way. Instead they often need to act differently, but to complement each other. Rates of interest, for example, may be made to vary from one country to the

591

next according to the balance of payments position; and coordination of regional policy means granting aid to some areas and no aid to others in order to avoid a further concentration of industry in the traditional areas.

Of course, it will always be hard to agree to what extent actions should be based on joint decisions, in the interests of a smoothly operating market or a closer-knit Community. Answers to questions such as how much disparity in taxation systems can be allowed without causing damage to the Common Market; how much autonomy is permissible in trade policy to enable each country to pursue its own foreign policy; which industrial and commercial agreements have a purely local significance and which affect the Common Market as a whole; how much disparity in company law can be allowed between one country and the next—answers to all these questions will depend on individual assessments.

The best and most comprehensive solutions require a much more radical approach. For instance, differing systems of indirect taxation are not incompatible with the Common Market, provided goods carry the taxes of the country of destination. But if this means that exports to another country (even within the Community) are always exempt from tax, and equalization taxes are levied on imports, then fiscal frontiers will always remain, which in practice leads to the same kinds of control that are exercised at customs frontiers today. Leaving aside the question of the effects of these taxes on investment, the standardization of indirect taxation throughout the Community may, therefore, be prompted more by psychological reasons than by strictly economic ones. On the other hand, the opportunity for discussion and comparison that standardization provides leads to schemes sounder economically than many existing national systems that reflect bad habits and outdated traditions.

It always takes time to come to grips with the real, as opposed to the apparent, problems of integration. The absence of European company law or a European type of company has not prevented the existence of a common market nor the formation of joint subsidiaries by companies of different nationalities; the subsidiary companies take the form and abide by the laws of the country in which they are set up. However, the absence of European company law makes mergers between companies of different nationalities practically impossible, with the result that U.S. companies have found it much easier than European ones to reap the benefits of the wider economic area created by the Common Market.

THE POWERS OF THE COMMUNITY INSTITUTION

Logical necessity does not, however, automatically become political reality. In the history of the Community there have been times when progress, instead of being the result of effective and systematic action by the European institutions, as was intended and hoped by the authors of the treaties, was rather at the mercy of whim or the interplay of force, cunning and bargaining between the governments.

The Schuman Plan was based on the new concept of supranationalism. A myth such as this had to be created to arouse public opinion in countries that had long been kept apart and opposed to each other. In the Treaty of Paris, the emphasis is on the powers invested in the High Authority, though almost any decision, apart from the application of the rules of competition, financing the Community and implementing transitional measures, requires the unanimous approval of the Council. The tone is different in the Treaty of Rome. It is written in more modest terms. There is a Commission that, for questions other than those connected with the implementation of the treaty, puts proposals to the Council of Ministers, and it is the Council that makes the decisions. It looks at first sight as if the concept of supranationalism had declined in importance from the Treaty of Paris to the Treaty of Rome, from the ECSC to the European Common Market and Euratom. On closer examination, however, one finds that this power of proposal has given the later institutions even wider powers than the High Authority possessed. Provided that member states are willing to use the possibilities provided for majority voting in the Treaty of Rome, there are hardly any matters over which a majority decision is not ultimately possible, so long as it is based on a proposal from the Commission.

The Commission is of course not the only body to have a common responsibility toward all six countries jointly. The European Parliament, which controls the Executive, and the Community's Court of Justice, which settles disputes, are not simply groups of delegates from the different countries; they too have to define a Community viewpoint. The Parliament has indeed followed this pattern, for its members have grouped themselves according to political view, and not according to country or origin. Even the Council of Ministers has a kind of two-way allegiance: it must not only reconcile the interests of the different governments, but must play its part in establishing a policy for the Community as a whole.

This problem of finding the best method of reaching a collective decision affecting several countries at once is an extremely difficult one today. It presents a kind of dilemma: unanimity seems justified because each national government is responsible for certain interests—each has its own work to do and is answerable to parliament and nation—but unanimity may rule out the possibility of common decisions entirely, because the power of veto creates a potential deadlock.

Those who drafted the Community treaties were wary of prescribing, or trying to prescribe, the immediate application of simple majority voting by the member states. A majority vote between governments is not the same as a majority decision within a country. All the people making up a nation have the same loyalty or responsibility to their country, even though they may hold different opinions. But governments are responsible for various interests and have pledged themselves to differing causes, and they are bound to act in what they consider to be the interests of their country. Thus a majority vote between governments is far from being an objective decision in the sense that it is within an individual country. It provides a risk of coalitions or of underhand bargaining: some member countries may join hands to obtain decisions at the expense of a minority, or there may be compromises by which votes are bought by concessions that have no bearing on the issues at stake.

The European Community (EC)—with its common authoritative body (the Council of Ministers), its rules of procedure laid down in the Treaty of Rome, and its institution (the Commission) for carrying out the decisions of this body by means of discussion and control—is the most original solution yet put forward to solve the problem. The Community does not simply ignore national attitudes, psychological differences and divergent interests; it provides a strictly realistic solution in order to counter the divergences in the initial outlook and circumstances of the countries concerned; a group of people—the Commission—have been appointed to think out and propose new formulas, to create a balanced approach and to provide a concrete idea of the common interest. Supranationalism and cooperation between countries are therefore not contradictory terms in the Community system. It is based on cooperation, but cooperation better organized and made more effective because a body of people can stimulate the parties involved into joint action.

Under the treaty, weighted majority voting was to have been extended by stages until it became, with some exceptions, the general rule, with the stipulation that it would normally require a prior proposal from the Commission, whose proposals could only be altered by itself or by *unanimous* vote of the Council. The point of this last stipulation was to prevent a group of countries forcing the hand of the Commission and of the minority.

In practice, majority voting has always been rare. On matters of major importance for a country in the minority, it would also be inopportune, since on other matters the tables could later be turned. Nor, indeed, would the Commission be acting properly if it proposed a decision cutting across some vital national interest.

These considerations did not prevent President Charles de Gaulle from provoking a crisis on the subject in 1965. France's seven-month absence from all but routine meetings was ended in January–February 1966 by the so-called gentlemen's disagreement, whereby France reaffirmed its unwillingness to join in or to accept a majority vote on "very important matters," while its partners reaffirmed their willingness to try to avoid such a vote. Technically, this meant that henceforth only France and Luxembourg could be outvoted on such very important questions. In practice, it meant increased chariness in the use of majority voting. Only once, in 1982, have majority votes been cast on very important matters; this was when Britain's would-be veto on the adoption of farm prices was overruled, largely because its partners considered the nation's tactics—penalizing farmers in the hope of securing more favorable budget treatment—to be unworthy.

Since then, and particularly since the 1984 summit meeting at Fontainebleau, which set up a committee to consider improvements in the Community's working methods, there have been stealthy signs of greater readiness to apply the treaty as its drafters intended. If this materializes, the vital problem will then be whether the Community institutions can be made to develop gradually and continuously into the institutions needed for a united Europe, and whether economic union may become political union.

THE NATURE OF POLITICAL UNION

There is much ambiguity concerning the extent to which a problem or a decision is political. In a sense, everything that the Community has achieved so far is political, not so much in the achievements of the institutions themselves, where the political content is obvious, but in the sectors of the economy that have been reorganized or given a new framework. To begin with, everything concerning agriculture—production, guidance, maintenance of farm income, the decrease in the farming population—is implicitly political, in the sense that these questions directly affect the electorate. Fiscal reforms, such as the harmonization of the tax systems in the different member countries, are also essentially political measures because the distribution of revenue and economic power between different sections of the population will be deeply affected by them. All this is political also in that the Community's activities have not been based on logic alone but have affected and involved a whole range of national customs, feelings, pressures and arrangements. "When we are agreed," one international civil servant has said, "a problem is economic; when we do not agree then it is political."

Economic problems also of course become political problems the more closely they are related to the general aims and policies of a country. This explains the tension between international agreements and national resistance to their application. Financial policy, credit policy and incomes policy all make up monetary policy, the aim of which is to ensure overall stability, fair distribution of wealth and expansion. This is obviously an essential part of government action, as too (and increasingly) are problems of foreign trade and the Community's policy on such matters as antidumping measures, etc. No less obviously political are the issues involved in such trade-and-aid arrangements as the Yaoundé and Lomé conventions.

One of the difficulties of combining economic and political decision making is that their aims are sometimes contradictory. Apart from the irrationality of the "package" nature of decisions on questions like agriculture, financial or commercial policy—questions that ought in fact to involve as highly logical and scientific an approach as possible—there are some matters in which valid political aims are completed at variance and at times even in contradiction with economic good sense: for instance, the question of associating the Community with one or another of the Mediterranean European countries, for which, practically speaking, the Community gets nothing but bills; or, of course, all so-called problems of prestige. And lastly, there are issues that by their very nature cannot be subjected to the kind of approach the Community uses because they are based on a different set of values, whether valid or not; these are diplomacy and defense, the decisions that affect the continuing existence of the member states as such and determine decisions of peace or war.

There are two basic difficulties before the Community in moving from economic to political union. First is the question of method. In the economic sphere, it has been possible to introduce changes gradually so that their effects are not too severe, and by progressively increasing the number of joint decisions to soften the impact of the Community on national institutions. In diplomacy and defense, however, there seems to be a barrier that has to be broken: it involves the abandonment of all that is fundamental to the separate existence of the national governments, which fear to find themselves reduced overnight to being part of a federation, deprived of international status and with no more autonomy than provinces. The second, and more important, difficulty is that it is not easy for the peoples of the member countries to abandon their traditional national outlooks, which are often different from and even opposed to those of the other members, and accept common objectives.

Clearly, there are some problems such as frontiers, or relations with former colonies or overseas possessions, that are essentially national problems. No country will want to act on the advice of the others when dealing with these, still less hand over decisions on them to others. The only point in discussing them is for consultation or information. The logical line of approach for a country going its own way in these fields would indeed be to cease expecting to have the full support of the others in the name of solidarity. This was shown by both the strength and the limitations of the support given to Britain by its Community partners at the time of the Falklands conflict. Most of these questions have been inherited from the past; some of them have already been settled and others may disappear as times goes on.

However, in the longer term, for countries as small as those of Western Europe, independent foreign policies can only be illusory, unless aims are negative. These countries can independently play a destructive role, refuse to cooperate or break up common institutions, but beyond that all they can do is to strike attitudes or play games. None of them has achieved a special relationship with China, Latin America or the Soviet Union, and indeed they can have no real influence on world affairs except by joining their efforts in some common approach, since alone they have too little to offer.

Political cooperation

Recognizing these facts, but shrinking from their implications, the Community's member states have in recent years established a system of foreign-policy collaboration and coordination known as "political cooperation." It is the successor to the Fouchet Plan of 1961–63. Set up in 1970, this involves regular meetings of the political directors of the respective foreign ministries, which are linked by a special COREUNET telegraph system. Thrice-yearly summit meetings of the European Council, of heads of state and government, and quarterly meetings of their foreign ministers, involve an increasing exchange of once confidential information and an alignment of policy on a number of foreign-policy issues. Agreement is, of course, most frequent on matters of least controversy or moment; but, for a purely intergovernmental arrangement, it works surprisingly well. The question remains whether this method is of a kind that can evolve a true Community foreign policy.

Joint political action

Critics of the Community say that political action must be backed by national feelings, on behalf of which sacrifices can be demanded and made. There is, however, no real disagreement about the fundamental requirements of politics, and no one has ever maintained that anything can be achieved by setting up a disembodied technocracy. Nor has anyone imagined that nations can be merged together immediately, or a European nation born overnight that will command the same affection and loyalty as the traditional mother country.

Nevertheless, it was precisely because the difficulties to be overcome were so great, and were recognized as such, that the founders of the EC set up more than intergovernmental institutions, with the aim of gradually replacing opposing passions by common objectives.

There is an inherent contradiction in the view that political action can be defined as action for which people are prepared to die, and in the sketch of political union, put forward by its supporters, that limits such a union to periodical meetings of heads of state or government, on the grounds that new nations cannot be founded. Take the most typical example of this contradiction in action: the decision to use atomic weapons. It is just possible to conceive of a nation deciding to use them, although in doing so it risks destroying itself; it is even harder to conceive of a collective decision by several countries, although this might be the only kind of decision that would offer them some chance of avoiding disaster. Thus an administrative arrangement of periodical meetings between heads of state would be hopelessly weak in the face of the urgent and dramatic decisions they might have to take.

The question remains whether the existing system of Community institutions can be extended as it stands into the political sphere. One essential prelude to this (though by itself it would not be enough) would be the formation of an independent body to make proposals on long-term European aims, and to instigate concerted action in times of crisis. As far as the procedure for holding meetings is concerned, there is of course a great difference between meetings between governments held at a fixed date and meetings called by a commission to discuss specific proposals worked out in advance. The first is quite likely to achieve nothing except to bring into the open, and possibly aggravate, disagreements. But meetings arranged to work out a policy, or called to deal with specific emergencies, provide an impetus of their own, and their importance can be adjusted according to the importance of the issues at stake—as the history of the Common Market has shown.

The European Parliament, now directly elected, has produced its own draft Treaty establishing the European Union. In some respects it resembles its predecessor of a generation ago. It may suffer the same fate. But it incorporates at least some of the experience gleaned from a generation of Community activity, and it provides a stimulating blueprint for the form that political union might eventually take.

This could not be the final answer, however. Political union is too specific a problem to be solved by preconceived plans. The answer cannot be given in the abstract. European integration since World War II has been a success because instead of following an abstract scheme, it proceeded by sudden bounds. It began by an agreement on coal and steel, and the logical thing would have been to extend integration to other industrial sectors.

Circumstances led instead to the projected EDC, but when this failed the scene of action switched suddenly to general economic integration. The use of a variety of approaches is the key to success.

If the political aims of European integration are to be achieved, it must be understood that unity may develop along lines that seem impossible today. There are several possible approaches that, as often happens in history, could converge at a given time or follow closely on each other. The important thing will be not to miss the opportunity when it arises.

FURTHER READING

Buchan, Alastair, ed. *Europe's Futures, Europe's Choices: Models of Western Europe in the 1970s*. London: ISS, 1969.

Hallstein, Walter. *Die Europäische Gemeinschaft*. Dusseldorf: Econ, 1964.

Lindberg, Leon, and Scheingold, Stuart. *Europe's Would-be Polity*. Englewood Cliffs, New Jersey: Prentice-Hall, 1970.

Mayne, Richard. *The Recovery of Europe*. London: Weidenfeld and Nicolson; New York: Harper and Row, 1970.

Shonfield, Andrew. *Europe: Journey to an Unknown Destination*. Harmondsworth: Penguin, 1973.

Wallace, Helen, et al. *Policy Making in the European Community*. Chichester, Sussex: Wiley, 1983.

EUROPEAN COMMUNITY LAW

NEVILLE MARCH HUNNINGS

ONE of the differences between the European Community (EC) and traditional international organizations is its possession of a fully operative legal system. This has caused confusion in the minds of some British international lawyers, who complain that EC law is not interpreted and applied according to the well-established international-law rules regarding treaty interpretation based on state sovereignty. Instead it is, rightly, regarded by EC lawyers as analogous to a state legal system, and although international-law principles are sometimes used (though not slavishly) as tools with which to construct autonomous EC rules, the approach of the courts is more often influenced by their experience of constitutional law.

The EC itself was created by three classic interstate treaties that instituted its three constituent subsectors, namely the two sectorally specialized systems—for coal and steel (the European Coal and Steel Community/ECSC treaty of 1952) and nuclear energy (the European Atomic Community/ Euratom treaty of 1957)—and the general system embodied in the European Economic Community (EEC) treaty of 1957. Treaties and quasi-treaty agreements between member states are also used for part of the constitutional operation of the Community. Misunderstanding can thus easily arise in the minds of those whose experience of international treaties has not been influenced by a study of the EC itself.

Law created by ordinary international organizations takes the form of treaties, which the member states are free to disregard by not ratifying. The organizations are thus, to that extent, merely treaty-drafting machines. The EC is quite different, for it has its own law-making structure, which is not tied to unanimity and which produces laws having an immediate force on the citizenry. These laws do not require ratification by the member states and are enforceable through the judgments of an EC court, which has compulsory jurisdiction not only over member states but also over their citizens. The nature of that legal system is the subject of this chapter.

SOURCES OF COMMUNITY LAW

The four sources of EC law represent the lowest common multiple of all Western legal systems. Very few countries, and certainly none of the member states of the EC, contain all of them. The EC in this demonstrates its singularity and an analogy with the United States. These four sources are: a written, judicially enforceable constitution; legislation enacted by a legislature especially devised for that purpose; case law as laid down with binding authority by a "supreme" court; and the direct enforceability of legal rules contained in international treaties entered into between the EC on the one hand and non-EC countries or organizations on the other.

Constitutional Treaties

The highest law of the EC system is "the Treaties," that is, the three founding treaties (ECSC, Euratom and EEC) and their later amendments. These latter include the merger treaty, which created a single organization out of the previous triple structure; the budgetary treaty, which created a procedure for adopting the annual EC budget; the second budgetary treaty, which created a Court of Auditors to supervise the financial probity of EC institutions; the Act of Accession, which adjusted the foregoing to the membership of Denmark, Ireland and Britain; the Act of Greek Accession which did the same for Greece; the similar Act regarding Spain and Portugal; and various other documents. Of these last, the more important are the Luxembourg compromise, by which the member states agreed not to insist on the majority rule for the adoption of legislation (the precise constitutional status of this document is controversial); the 1970 decision on EC finance, which abolished the old system of national annual block grants and replaced it by the EC's "own resources"—direct revenue that, although collected by the member states, forms part of the EC's funds as soon as collected from customs duties, charges and levies, and from the proceeds of a one percent value-added tax levy; and the 1976 decision on direct elections to the European Parliament.

These texts form the written constitution of the EC, against which all other laws are tested through judicial review proceedings. That is a classic function of written constitutions, particularly in federal and quasi-federal states. The EC treaties are, however, peculiar in that they also contain rules of substantive law in addition to general principles. So, whereas in national systems the constitution is usually more of a shield than a sword and affects mainly governmental acts (with the possible exception of a bill of rights), in the EC system it contains a considerable number of rules that impose both rights and obligations directly on individuals, and which form the basis for major and discrete branches of law. Competition law and equal pay are two examples of this.

Legislation

The EC treaties, like any other constitution, lay down the form and procedures for community legislation—secondary law. The term *secondary legislation* is often misused as a synonym for this (the treaties are not legislation; they are primary *law*). The term should be used only for subordinate legislation—legislation issued by inferior organs.

Primary legislation is, thus, that which is enacted by the Council, the supreme lawmaking institution of the EC. If one uses, loosely but helpfully, the image of the Commission as the executive branch of Community government, then the legislature—the equivalent of a parliament—is a three-chamber system. It comprises the European Assembly, which has arrogated to itself the name European Parliament in an attempt to acquire a greater legislative role; the Economic and Social Committee, equivalent in many ways to the function of the House of Lords as a chamber of magnates; and the Council. The two former have at present, advisory powers only, while the Council, the "upper house," alone may enact legislation. The equivalent to statute law, acts of Parliament, *lois, Gesetze*, etc., is Council legislation issued with its plenitude of authority. This authority derives directly from the treaties and even extends beyond any remit specifically made in them to embrace any action that "might prove necessary to attain, in the course of the operation of the Common Market, one of the objectives of the EC," where the treaty has not provided the necessary powers (see Article 235 EEC).

Such laws, which rank second in the EC hierarchy, follow a complex itinerary through the various legislative organs, sometimes in the public view, sometimes not—just as in national systems. There is, at least in theory, ample opportunity for public opinion, whether general or specialized, to influence the outcome. Under the ECSC treaty, however, the position is slightly different, reflecting a greater acceptance of supranational solutions in 1952. Plenary legislative powers in matters covered by the ECSC rest not only with the Council but with the Commission (previously the High Authority), which legislates by "general decision," a form similar to a Presidential decree under the present French constitution or an Order in Council under the Royal Prerogative of the British Crown, and which avoids exposure of its drafts to normal parliamentary processes.

As with all parliamentary democracies, the executive also has legislative power that is controlled by parliament in the form of enabling legislation. The Council may thus enact a law delegating power to the Commission to legislate in detail on the matter. Apart from one or two very exceptional instances, the Commission derives no legislative power direct from the treaties, and must therefore always rely on a delegation of power from the Council; there is no equivalent of the Italian *decreto-legge*. Commission legislation ranks third in the hierarchy of laws; like most executive lawmaking, it is not usually exposed to the public prior to promulgation. In some particularly sensitive areas, however, the Council enabling law does require the Commission to publish in the *Official Journal* of the Community an advance draft of its proposal, so that public opinion can be given a formal part to play. This was particularly so in the case of the so-called block exemptions, where the Council, by Regulation 19/65, permitted the Commission itself to legislate to exempt whole categories of commercial agreement from the prohibition against restraints of competition laid down in Article 85 EEC.

EC legislation takes two forms, described in Article 189 EEC. *Regulations* are the standard statutory form, directly applicable to the citizen and equivalent to national legislation at whatever level. After adoption by the Council or, if delegated, by the Commission, and after translation by EC lawyer-linguists into the nine languages of the EC, they are published in the *Official Journal*, and may not come into force until so published. *Directives* are more complicated. They are indirect legislation, imposing an obligation on member states to transform them into national law by means of national legislation. For this purpose, each directive contains a time limit—usually a year but sometimes as long as six years—within which it must be implemented in the member states. Like regulations, directives are published in the *Official Journal*, but because they do not, at least in theory, impose obligations on individuals directly but are addressed to states only, publication is not a condition of their validity or enforceability.

Case law

The countries influenced by the French Civil Code do not, in theory, admit the lawmaking effect of judicial decisions. Judgments are addressed to the dispute at issue and do not have any wider consequences. In practice, the judgments of the supreme courts of cassation do tend to have a more general effect. But that is far removed from the rule underlying the English common law, that the principles stated by senior judges as the basis of their decisions are to be followed by their colleagues in inferior courts. French lawyers and some French courts have therefore had difficulty in accepting the broader approach of the European Court of Justice and in agreeing to be bound by the latter's interpretation of EC law—not for the particular case (that causes no difficulty), but also as a binding rule to be applied to all similar future situations.

Nevertheless, the judgments of the European Court of Justice do, like those of common-law countries, contain general principles of law that are applied by the Court consistently to all later cases and that consequently can have what might appear to be a lawmaking effect. This is most dramatic when the Court "creates" a legal principle out of the legal atmosphere of Europe and embeds it in EC law. Examples of this process are the principle of "proportionality" (*Verhältnismässigkeit*), borrowed from German constitutional-administrative law, and the rulings that respect for fundamental rights is a basic principle of EC law, which was derived from the adoption by all member states of the European Convention on Human Rights. This is a natural process in the early stages of any new legal system and has enabled the European Court gradually to build a coherent legal structure which does not depend slavishly on texts that, normally, leave a large number of gaps. Although the main function of the Court is to interpret and apply existing EC "black letter" law, the principles it enounces form separate legal rules in their own right, which are to be added to those set out in the texts described above.

The European Court is the only EC legal tribunal. The Commission, however, also performs some quasi-judicial functions, particularly in the field of competition law. Although its position as a tribunal is in doubt (and in any case it has no judicial status at all vis-à-vis the European Court), the Commission's decisions on competition matters are intended to be consistent and to guide business people. Consequently, all business lawyers active in competition law regard the Commission's decisions as laying down the general legal principles the Commission intends to follow (and which businesses should also follow), at least until the European Court rules otherwise. To that extent, therefore, these decisions also form an interstitial source of law in the single, but important, area of competition.

Treaties, international and legislative

The case law of the European Court finally settled the question of whether international treaties entered into by the EC constituted a direct source of EC law, or whether they only bound the EC as such, the citizenry being affected only when their rules were translated into EC legal forms (regulations and directives). In October 1982, in the case of *Kupferberg* (104 / 81), the Court clearly adopted the former solution. International treaties may, therefore, in appropriate cases, also constitute sources of EC law.

There is, however, another form of treaty to be found in the structure of EC law. It is used as a variant form of legislation and so may be called a legislative treaty. Because it is a cumbersome method of creating law it has been used only four times (although other drafts are under discussion). It was used in the 1968 Convention on Jurisdiction and Enforcement of Judgments in Civil and Commercial Matters (the Judgments Convention); in the 1968 Mutual Recognition of Companies Convention; in the 1975 Community Patent Convention; and in the 1980 Convention on the Law Applicable to Contractual Obligations. Of these, only the first named is in force. None of the others has yet received sufficient ratifications from the member states.

Treaties thus appear in EC law in three different guises: as constitutional treaties (between all member states), as legislative treaties (between some or all member states), and as international treaties (between the EC as such and nonmember states).

Information

All these sources form part of the overall corpus of law that the citizen, whether individual or company, must know and comply with, in addition to (or sometimes in contradistinction to) national law. One of the greatest difficulties at present is to ensure that the citizen is aware of these laws. Texts of the treaties are, of course, published by the EC itself, by government printers and by private publishers. Legislation, international treaties and Commission decisions are all published in the *Official Journal* and by private publishers, legislation being covered also by loose-leaf encyclopedias in most member states. European Court case law is contained in the Court's own reporter, *European Court Reports*, which is published in several languages, and in the privately published British *Common Market Law Reports* and U.S. *Common Market Reports*. Much of this material is also available on-line in the two private computerized data bases, EUROLEX and LEXIS, and also in the EC's own data base, CELEX. The latter, however, is intended primarily for use of EC institutions themselves.

CONTENT OF EC LAW

The content of EC law derives in part directly from the treaties themselves and also from external developments having only an originating link (if that) with the treaties, which themselves confer the ultimate power to create or state particular sets of legal rules. There is no way in which this can be described as a complete system of law. Matters may be the subject of extended or partial treatment—either because they have obvious effects on the common market; or because the treaties provide that national law shall to a large extent be replaced by EC rules; or because individual Commission officials, with or without the prompting of persuasive pressure groups, have become convinced of their importance; or because member states have been generally in agreement, and therefore have not blocked progress. The pattern at any one time is therefore haphazard. It is possible, nevertheless, to give it a certain degree of shape, derived in the first place from the structure of the treaties, particularly Part Two of the EEC treaty, entitled "Foundations of the Community."

The four freedoms

The EC is at once a customs union, a common market and a community. All these depend on the concept of a single area with no internal barriers to movement. To make this a reality, the EEC treaty provides for freedom of movement of goods, persons, services and capital.

Of these freedoms, the two latter are at present underdeveloped. Neither investment capital nor financial services may move freely across national borders, although transfers of money related to the movement of goods are free. There is practically no case law or legislation on movement of capital.

With regard to services, it has been established that restrictions based on nationality are prohibited. But a greater hindrance lies in differing national requirements for technical or professional qualifications and thus for permission to work. This has been remedied in part by the enactment of directives on compulsory recognition of qualifications in individual occupations, but progress is slow, particularly in the professions. Two recent developments foreshadow a major expansion of this freedom. In early 1984, in *Luisi and Carbone* (286/82 and 26/83), the European Court held that tourism was a service and that the freedom included that of tourists to travel in order to *receive* tourist services from hoteliers and others. Also in 1984, the Commission produced a discussion paper, *Television Without Frontiers*, in which the concept of freedom of services was divorced from the movement of persons supplying or receiving them and applied to the movement of the disembodied services themselves, such as television signals.

The other two freedoms have been the subject of much greater attention. The right of personal movement, both as a potential employee and to set up in business on one's own account, and now also as a consumer of services, has been developed in detail by the Court's case law on the appropriate treaty provisions. In this it has impinged on aliens law and labor law. This has led to three very important pieces of legislation: Regulation 1612/68, which proscribes discrimination against foreigners in access to and treatment at work; and possibly the most complex EC legislation of all, regulations 1408/71 and 574/72, which attempt to ensure to workers, as they move about the EC, the full benefit of their social security schemes by providing elaborate rules for portability and cumulation of workers' insurance contributions, wherever they have paid them.

Free movement of goods covers customs barriers, and gave rise to one of the earliest leading judgments of the Court, *Van Gend and Loos* (26/62), in which the power of individuals to enforce their rights under the treaty was first laid down. Apart from questions of customs procedure, there is also a large body of cases defining the meaning of the different customs headings (is the caribou, for example, a wild or domestic animal?), mostly referred from the very active fiscal courts of West Germany. More important, however, is the extensive case law that has built on Article 30 EEC, which refers to "quantitative restrictions" on imports, interpreted as equivalent to "nontariff barriers," and including restrictions operating at the point of sale within a member state long after the article has passed through customs, if the restriction on sale has a discriminatory effect against imports.

The four "policies"
While freedom of movement is a necessary part of a common market, the EEC treaty also lays down four "policies" in sectors of the economy in which EC law is especially concerned. The most important of these is the common agricultural policy (CAP), which sets up an elaborate scheme of import levies, export subsidies, production quotas, prices and aids aimed at insulating the EC market from world prices and ensuring the farmer a guaranteed standard of living. The foundation of this is contained in 10 articles of the EEC treaty and 21 produce marketing regulations, each governing production and first marketing of a different group of agricultural products, supplemented by a further series of regulations on farming structure covering such matters as farm modernization, cessation of farming, farm investment, producer groups, and farm management and accounts. On the basis of these Council regulations, a continuous stream of Commission regulations pours forth, supplemented in turn by substantial litigation and resultant case law.

The second important EC policy is called the common commercial policy, although in fact it relates only to foreign trade. It is this part of the treaty that underlies the large number of commercial treaties entered into by the EC with the rest of the world. As does the CAP, this policy too has a preemptive effect, in that matters the EC has begun to regulate are thenceforth removed altogether from member state legislative powers. Trade treaties do not normally lead to litigation or need much implementing legislation, so this policy would not be an important area of law were it not that it covers antidumping. This latter, a form of judicialization of international trade disputes, has led through the General Agreement on Tariffs and Trade (GATT) to an important Council regulation, recently reenacted in codified form, on the basis of which a large quantity of quasi-judicial decisions are being taken by the Commission, leading to a slowly increasing case law.

The common transport policy has, largely through failure to enact the necessary basic legislation, remained embryonic even in the original areas of road, rail, and river/canal transport. Air and sea transport are still excluded from the policy itself. Social policy, on the other hand, is a growing area of law—partly through the directives and case law on sex equality and partly through some important legislation in the field of worker safety and protection.

Special sectors

Of the three industrial sectors covered by the two specialized Communities (ECSC and Euratom) one, nuclear energy, has produced virtually no law. Coal gave rise to a certain amount of case law in the early days, but this never amounted to much. Steel, however, has been a potent stimulator of law, both legislation and cases. In the EC's first decade and a half, this was linked to a form of quasi-fiscal self-financing based on the use of iron scrap called the scrap equalization scheme and the scrap equalization levy. In more recent years, over-capacity in the steel industry has led to international disputes involving the antidumping laws and to directorial involvement by the Commission in the industry. The Commission has attempted to reduce global capacity through production quotas backed up by heavy fines for overshooting.

Harmonization

Article 100 EEC requires the Council to enact directives to harmonize such national laws as "directly affect the establishment or functioning" of the common market. Specific provisions elsewhere in the treaty provide for harmonization of certain named branches of law. This is a fertile source of EC legislation, but it is mostly in the form of directives, not of case law, since most of the disputes occur at national level and relate to the national implementing legislation, which frequently does not reveal its EC origin.

Apart from a large number of uniform standards directives (some 30 relating to motor vehicle construction alone) and the adoption of the new international standards for weights and measures, this part of EC legal activity moves deep into some major areas of national law and is thus of great importance to lawyers. The concept of harmonization is taken broadly and often borders on law reform or innovation rather than on the ironing out of differences in national rules. Thus the fifth Company Law Directive (not yet enacted) adopted the controversial two-tier board system (management board and supervisory board) for company management and control on the sole basis of the existing West German system. Harmonization is therefore used as a basis of authorization for ordinary legislation by the EC on aspects of law that do not fall within any particular EC interest. In this way, there has emerged a major series of directives on company law and stock exchange law—directives that already occupy a large part of the total national law in those fields. Similar legislation has begun in the fields of banking and insurance. The EC Patent Convention covers most of the detail of patent law and will eventually replace most national patent law. Proposals for a similar coverage of trademark law are well advanced toward enactment. Copyright is also likely to be brought into the picture. A draft convention to harmonize bankruptcy law has been under discussion for many years. Other areas of law are affected less systematically by EC harmonization— criminal procedures, for instance, in combating frauds against the EC itself.

New areas of law

The heads of government in summit meetings (now called the European Council) proposed that the EC should adopt elaborate programs of legislation in the two popular fields of consumer and environmental protection. To some extent these can be based on harmonization (Article 100), but often it is necessary to use the catchall legislative authority of Article 235. Most of the proposed consumer protection legislation is highly controversial and still in draft; it covers such matters as manufacturers' liability for defective products, and retail sale of goods other than in shops, such as by mail order or by door-to-door sales. Much environmental legislation is, however, in force, particularly on water pollution.

To these two branches of law covered by legislation should be added a third, which was created entirely by the Court of Justice through its case law. Human rights are part of EC law—not as an independent set of rules, but as an adjunct to EC law and a test to which EC law must conform.

Restrictive practices
Both the ECSC and the EEC treaties contain strong rules aimed at preventing restrictive agreements between traders or abusive exercise of a dominant position. The treaty rules are themselves detailed and have been supplemented, for the EC, by an array of further Council and Commission regulations. In particular, these have led to a large number of quasi-judicial Commision decisions, many of which have been appealed to the Court. For EC lawyers this is the most important and productive area of all EC law.

Full faith and credit
The creation of a single legal area, to match the common market in goods and people, has been restricted to free movement of legal decisions. Under the 1968 Judgments Convention, decisions by a court anywhere in the EC are directly enforceable in all other member states as if they were decisions of their own courts. The rules apply to judgments and court orders in the field of civil and commercial law; they are not intended to be a form of enforcement of EC law but rather of ordinary national law. As a necessary adjunct to such automatic recognition, the Convention contains far-reaching rules on jurisdiction that replace existing national rules. In the field of legal procedure, the Convention is of exceptional importance to all lawyers, whether or not they specialize in EC law, and it has given rise to considerable case law both in the European Court and in national courts.

APPLICATION OF COMMUNITY LAW

Direct effect
The central feature of the EC legal system is the role of the individual. The system's essential precondition was a form of law that affected the individual with as little interference as possible. The EC devised a variety of techniques to do this, adjusting the solution nicely to the different types of situation. The most direct and simplest method was the regulation, directly applicable to everybody, to governments and governed alike. The least direct technique was the directive (and to some extent the legislative treaty), requiring implementation by state instrumentalities and only affecting the citizen

"as through a glass darkly"; for the most part, the citizen does not know that it is EC law that is touching him or her. This indirect method also has the disadvantage that it relies upon positive action by member governments, action that tends to be somewhat dilatory. It may therefore be only after considerable delay that this form of EC law reaches the citizen at all. To solve this, and fill the gap, the European Court devised a new principle, that of direct effect.

At first, this applied only to the treaties themselves. It was argued by the Dutch government in *Van Gend and Loos* in 1962 that the EEC treaty was intended only to impose duties on and give rights to the member states (just like any ordinary international organization). If, therefore, the Dutch government imposed customs duties on imports when the treaty said it should not, only the member state of export could complain (a pure international law argument). But governments are slow to enforce rights at law against other governments. Giving such a right to the injured individual, therefore, provided the basis for all future development of EC law. The Court was nevertheless cautious. Each provision in each article of the treaty would have to be separately examined to find whether it had such a direct effect, the test being whether it was clear, unconditional, complete in itself and leaving no discretion to the member state. Even 20 years later, only a minority of the treaty provisions had been thus scrutinized, and not all of them had been granted such effect, although most of the more important provisions had been. Through this the treaty became a living body of law, not only for lawyers but also for the people whose conduct it was intended to influence.

From there it was but a step, although a bold one, to apply the rule to directives. If, when the time limit for implementation had expired, the member state had not implemented a directive, then individuals might directly enforce their rights under it. As with the treaty, however, each provision of the directive would be tested to see whether it was appropriate to give it "direct effect." Even if the directive had been implemented, it would still be possible to refer to it in interpreting the relevant national legislation.

The same principle was then applied, but much more guardedly, to international treaties as well.

EC law and national law
The relationship between EC law and national law is complex. In a very real sense EC law is an autonomous legal system coexisting by the side of, but separate from, national law. And yet there are so many links between them that their mutual interrelation cannot be disregarded when considering either. This is a reflection of the whole EC political system, and can be seen at its most obvious in the concept of the directive. Nevertheless, if the European Court of Justice was to become anything like a supreme court it was inevitable that a hierarchical relationship would have to be established. From the EC's side it came early. In 1964, in *Costa* v. *Enel* (6/64), the Court held that EC law, of whatever rank, prevailed over inconsistent national law. This was regarded as essential to the cohesion of the EC, and no exceptions have been recognized to that absolute rule. To be effective, however, it was necessary to gain the cooperation of the various national courts,

since they owed primary allegiance to their national legal systems and national constitutions, and it was they that would give effect in practice to any concept of EC superiority. Gradually, the supreme courts of all the original six member states stated their acceptance of the primacy of EC law, with the exception (until recently) of the French supreme administrative court, the Conseil d'Etat, and with the West German and Italian constitutional courts insisting that the protection of human rights entrenched in their constitutions would take priority over contrary EC law if a conflict were to arise before the EC had itself acquired an adequate and enforceable bill of rights.

None of the new member states has yet reached that stage, although both the Irish Supreme Court and the British House of Lords have given indications that they do accept the dominance of EC law, at least as a working hypothesis. The British constitutional principle of the sovereignty of Parliament has not, however, yet been put to the test or judicially questioned.

ENFORCEMENT OF COMMUNITY LAW

Police

It is a basic working principle of the EC system generally that the EC creates law but the member states apply it. This separation of function exists in the judicial field also. Apart from high constitutional issues between member states and EC institutions, it is expected that the main burden of applying EC law will be borne by the national courts.

Administrative enforcement, likewise, is primarily the obligation of the member states. In three major areas, however, there is direct EC enforcement: competition, antidumping and steel.

The Competition Department of the Commission (DG IV) is responsible for all policing of the antitrust laws in Articles 65 and 66 ECSC, Articles 85 and 86 EEC and related regulations. These cover: investigation; execution of EC search warrants, seizure of incriminating evidence; issuance of an indictment, called a statement of objections; oral hearing in a quasi-judicial but predominantly administrative procedure presided over by a full-time hearing officer; and issuance of a judgment in the form of a Commission decision, appealable to the European Court. DG IV is also responsible for enforcing the prohibition against state aids (Articles 92 and 93 EEC).

Antidumping is a similar responsibility of the Foreign Affairs Department of the Commission (DG I), but forms only a small part of that department's responsibility—unlike DG IV, which has no other duties.

The powers of the Commission in relation to management of the steel industry are greater and are not confined to mere policing. During the period of the scrap levy, however, it did use an outside (Swiss) agency, under contract, to carry out inspections and investigations on its behalf; now, enforcement of the production quotas and imposition of fines form part of its duties.

These functions may be contrasted with the Commission's lack of power to enforce the common fisheries policy. The European Court has gone very far in transferring direct sovereignty over the living resources of the sea from the coastal states to the EC; but the EC has no coast guard or navy of its own, nor any means of policing the seas to protect this resource. It has therefore provided finance to the coastal states to continue their earlier fisheries protection duties, but, as it were, on behalf of the EC.

Courts

Judicial enforcement of EC law is primarily the function of the national courts, which are expected to be capable of handling it with the same expertise as their own domestic law. In doing this, they are assisted by a unique facility (Article 177 EEC) to make sideways reference to the European Court for guidance in the form of authoritative interpretation of any relevant point of EC law. Final courts of appeal are required to make such a reference. The European Court in such a situation does not decide the case; it is not a court of appeal sitting over the national courts. It does not even say whether the national law is compatible with EC law. It merely interprets the latter. But it does so in such a way that the national court, on receipt of the ruling, can then apply the law to the facts before it and give a judgment that is proper in terms of the EC. This system has enabled the Court to keep firm, if discreet, supervision over the day-to-day application of EC law, while maintaining a friendly and correct relationship with its judicial opposites and allowing the national courts to play their active part in working the EC's judicial machine.

The European Court itself receives its personal litigation primarily through the indirect means of the Article 177 reference. It also hears appeals by enterprises from decisions of the Commission in competition matters, or indeed in the many other areas in which its decisions affect individuals, particularly agriculture and, at present, steel. A smaller number of cases involves direct action between the member states and the Commission (both ways) and even between two different organs of the EC itself, as when the European Parliament sued the Council for not passing legislation to implement the common transport policy, or when the Commission sued the Council for the right to take part on behalf of the EC in international treaty negotiations on road transport matters within the auspices of the U.N. Economic Commission for Europe. This high-level litigation seems to be increasing; but personal litigation is rising at an even greater rate, and the productivity of the 10-judge Court stands at some 200 judgments a year.

FURTHER READING

Brown, L. Neville, and Jacobs, F. G. *The Court of Justice of the European Communities.* 2nd ed. London: Sweet and Maxwell, 1983.

Collins, L. *European Community Law in the United Kingdom.* 3rd ed. London: Butterworth, 1984.

Hartley, T. C. *The Foundations of European Community Law.* Oxford: Clarendon Press, 1981.

Lasok, D. *The Law of the Economy in the European Communities.* London: Butterworth, 1980.

―――, and Bridge, J. W. *Introduction to the Law and Institutions of the European Communities.* 3rd ed. London: Butterworth, 1982.

Usher, J. *European Community Law and National Law: The Irreversible Transfer?* London: Allen and Unwin, 1981.

Wyatt, D., and Dashwood, A. *The Substantive Law of the EEC.* London: Sweet and Maxwell, 1980.

THE EUROPEAN FREE TRADE
ASSOCIATION (EFTA)

C. M. W. VASEY

EFTA is a remarkably successful organization, the success of which goes beyond its own membership. It has contributed to the establishment of an industrial free trade area in Western Europe with a population of more than 300 million and 40 percent of world trade. Through EFTA, those European countries unable or unwilling to accept the aims of economic and political integration within the European Community (EC) have been able to play a full part in the establishment of a single European market, thus avoiding the economic division of Western Europe that was once feared might result from the creation of the European Economic Community (EEC) in 1958.

Unlike some other regional groupings, EFTA has never considered the establishment of free trade or the promotion of closer economic relations between its members as its sole aim. The association was set up and has developed in the shadow of the EC. Indeed, the EFTA countries have always been as much if not more concerned with what was happening within the EC as with their own relatively trouble-free progress. Of the seven founder members, two joined the EC in 1973 (Britain and Denmark), one attempted to do so (Norway) and one was scheduled to do so in 1986 (Portugal). The existing EFTA countries are tied to the EC by a network of bilateral agreements covering not just free trade but also sectoral questions (steel, agriculture, fisheries, scientific and technical cooperation), and they see their future in terms of establishing closer relations with the EC, both bilaterally and as a group.

HISTORY

To understand how EFTA has developed and its role in Western European economy, it is first necessary to recall the origins of the association. It was set up in May 1960 on the basis of the Stockholm Convention, signed in July 1959. The seven founding members were Austria, Britain, Denmark, Norway, Portugal, Sweden and Switzerland[1].

[1]Finland acquired associate status in 1961, and Iceland joined in 1970.

These countries, whatever their collective importance as trading nations, could hardly be described as forming a natural economic unit. The origins of EFTA are to be sought in the formation of the European Economic Community in January 1958, bringing with it the threat of tariff discrimination against those countries left outside. What brought the Seven together in Stockholm in July 1959 was the breakdown in December 1958 of the negotiation on the British plan for setting up a multilateral free trade area embracing the whole of Western Europe, which would have come into existence concurrently with the common market that the six countries of the EC were proposing to create among themselves. The ostensible reason for the breakdown was the French refusal to accept a free trade area without a harmonized external tariff and a more extensive coordination of economic and social policies than the British, the Scandinavians and the Swiss were prepared to accept. The real reason lay somewhat deeper—in the existence of two divergent approaches to European integration, one based essentially on trade liberalization, the other on the creation of common policies over most aspects of the economy.

The immediate purpose of EFTA was to establish an industrial free trade area by means of the progressive elimination of tariffs and quotas on goods produced in the member states. It was confidently assumed that a pragmatic system of intergovernmental cooperation would be adequate to deal with any nontariff problems that might arise. The ultimate purpose, however, was to persuade the Six to agree to a multilateral trading arrangement that would prevent the economic division of Europe, while allowing the EC to pursue its own development. From this point of view, the formation of EFTA was essentially a political maneuver, designed to facilitate an overall settlement and at the same time put pressure on the Six. It was noticeable that the British, to whom EFTA meant a relatively small accretion of strength, were always less enthusiastic than the Swiss and the Swedes. Indeed, EFTA had hardly come into existence before Britain began to have second thoughts about the wisdom of this collective approach to the problem of tariff partnership with the EC as opposed to a direct request for membership, even though this involved a greater degree of integration than the British had hitherto been prepared to envisage.

The 13 years during which Britain was a member of EFTA were in fact dominated by London's growing obsession with joining the Common Market of the Six. The first application by the British government to join the EC was made in June 1961, barely a year after the Stockholm Convention came into force. Although it was agreed that EFTA would be kept in being until satisfactory arrangements had been concluded with the EC to meet the legitimate interests of the various EFTA countries so that they could all participate from the same date in an integrated European market, the British decision was the signal for a general move to abandon EFTA. Britain, Denmark and Norway formally applied for membership of the EC; Sweden, Switzerland and Austria applied for association. Finland and Portugal never specified what kind of arrangement they would seek, but it could only have been some form of association.

The breakdown of the negotiations between Britain and the EC in January

1963 gave EFTA a new and unexpected lease on life. Faced with the prospect of being excluded from the EC for an indefinite period, the Seven had no choice but to make the most of their own organization, which had cooperated fairly smoothly on the economic level. (Tariffs on inter-EFTA trade had already been reduced by 50 percent from their original levels by January 1963, though under the initial timetable for tariff reductions, tariffs need only have been cut by 30 percent.) The result was a program of measures adopted at Lisbon in May 1963, which included among other things a revised timetable for the remaining tariff reductions, a general review of the inadequacy of the EFTA rules of competition and new activities in the field of agriculture and economic development.

The progressive internal development of EFTA following the Lisbon meeting left unresolved, however, the problem of the economic division of Western Europe, which became increasingly acute with each new tariff reduction within the EC. Early in 1965, the Seven decided to take the initiative again. At a meeting in Vienna in May, it was decided to approach the Six with an offer of permanent collaboration between EFTA and the EC on a number of concrete nontariff problems, such as patents and industrial standards. The immediate purpose of the proposal was to attenuate some of the harmful side effects of the economic division of Western Europe, but it was also hoped to lay the foundations for an eventual overall settlement. In fact, the whole "bridge-building exercise," as it was generally called, was overtaken by events. The situation was transformed by the internal crisis in the EC over the nature of the integration process, which for a time effectively put an end to any hopes of opening a dialogue with the Six, and then by the British decision, announced in April 1966, to begin diplomatic soundings on the possibilities of obtaining satisfactory terms of admission to the EC. The Austrian government had in fact been negotiating separately with the Six for association with the EC since 1964, while the Danish government had for some time been under considerable pressure from its farmers to obtain membership separately. The British decision had the effect of swinging the whole association behind a policy of direct contact with the EC, even if Sweden and Switzerland still remained dubious.

The continuing deadlock within the EC between France and the other five member states meant that the EC was unable to either to develop into an integrated supranational grouping that no British government could have hoped to join, or to respond to overtures from Britain and the other EFTA countries for membership or simply for closer trade relations. The Wilson government, like the Macmillan government before it, came up against the continuing opposition of the French under General Charles de Gaulle.

In spite of the EC's undoubted success in removing tariff barriers ahead of schedule, it became clear to the Six themselves that the future economic and political development of the EC was dependent on its enlargement to include Britain and the other EFTA countries that wanted to join. Once de Gaulle left the scene, events began to move rapidly. At the Hague summit in November 1969, the French conceded the principle of *élargissement* as part of a triptych including *consolidation* (meaning essentially complete EC financing for the common agricultural policy) and *approfondissement* covering the development of common policies in fields other than trade). Britain, Denmark, and Norway immediately applied for membership as in 1961, and negotiations with the British government, now under Edward Heath, began in June 1970. The Treaty of Accession was signed in Brussels in January 1972, although Norway subsequently withdrew its applications following a No vote in the referendum called to approve the results of the negotiation. On January 1, 1973, Britain and Denmark formally withdrew from EFTA to become members of the EC, while a series of bilateral free trade agreements came into force between the remaining EFTA countries and the EC either simultaneously or shortly afterward.

When EFTA was first set up, it was assumed that it was a temporary arrangement, which would sooner or later disappear as its members achieved membership or association with the EC. By the time the EC finally agreed to admit Britain and Denmark and to establish an industrial free trade area with the other EFTA countries, there was no longer any question of EFTA's disappearing. The association emerged with a reduced membership and a slimmed down secretariat, but with a permanent role in the European trading system. Since 1973, it has continued to provide the legal basis for the free trade arrangements among its members, as well as a forum for discussing general problems of trade policy and coordinating its members' bilateral relations with the EC, which remains, of course, the hub of the European trading system.

THE EUROPEAN TRADING SYSTEM

EFTA's main achievement has always been the breaking down of import barriers in Western Europe. The European trading system, which now embraces 18 countries—all the democratic market-economy countries of Western Europe[2]—was achieved in three stages.

The first stage was the progressive removal of customs tariffs and import quotas on all goods except those of agricultural or marine origin, between the founder members of EFTA and the EC respectively. The original time-table laid down in the Stockholm Convention, which was based as far as possible on that of the EC, providing for an initial tariff reduction of 20 percent on July 1, 1960, to bring EFTA into line with the EC, followed by three reductions of 10 percent at intervals of 18 months and five at intervals of one year. The target date for the final abolition of tariffs was thus January 1, 1970, as in the Treaty of Rome. This timetable was repeatedly modified to keep pace with the acceleration of the EC tariff-cutting schedule, with the result that the first three tariff cuts of 10 percent were brought forward to July 1961, March 1962 and October 1962 respectively, by which time

[2] The six EFTA countries and the 12 EC member states. This enumeration excludes Turkey, Cyprus and Malta, which all enjoy tariff-free access to the EC market for their industrial exports and preferential tariff arrangements for their agricultural exports, but are unlikely to seek full membership of the EC, at least in the foreseeable future. None of these three countries has any preferential trade relations with EFTA. It should be noted that Yugoslavia has signed cooperation agreements with both the EC and EFTA, and benefits from preferential access to their respective market under the Generalized System of Preferences for developing countries.

EFTA was more than two years ahead of schedule. A revised timetable for the remaining tariff cuts was adopted at Lisbon in May 1963, under which the date for the final removal of customs duties on inter-EFTA trade was fixed at December 31, 1966, 18 months ahead of the date for the final removal of tariffs in the EC.

Exceptions to the general elimination of tariffs in EFTA reflected the differing levels of industrial development within EFTA. Thus Norway and Finland were authorized by the Council to delay the final removal of tariffs in certain sectors until 1970, so as to give the industries concerned further time to adapt to free trade.[3] Portugal, which was only included in EFTA through British influence, was always treated as a special case, and retained some tariff protection for her existing and potential infant industries. In addition to the progressive removal of import duties, the Convention provided for the progressive elimination of quotas and other import restrictions, except those required for noncommercial reasons, the enforcement of national laws on marketing and the protection of state monopolies. The date for the final elimination of quotas was the same as that for the removal of tariffs. In fact, both Portugal and Finland were allowed to retain a limited number of quotas, Portugal to protect its automobile assembly industry, Finland in connection with its system of bilateral trade agreements with the Soviet Union. The Convention also allowed the temporary reimposition of import quotas during the transition period if the progressive elimination of tariffs and quotas resulted in an appreciable fall in production in a given industry or region—a provision that was never used.

The second stage began with the accession of Britain and Denmark to the EC in 1973. The Accession Treaty provided for the progressive removal of all tariffs between the Six and the new member states in five equal stages beginning on April 1, 1973, and ending on July 1, 1977. Parallel to the Accession Treaty, the Community concluded bilateral agreements with each of the remaining EFTA countries providing for the establishment of a separate industrial free trade area with each of them.[4] These agreements provided for the removal of tariffs and quotas between the seven EFTA countries and the six EC countries and Ireland (which had joined the EC at the same time as Britain and Denmark), according to the same timetable as that laid down in the Accession Treaty, while allowing Britain and Denmark to avoid reintroducing customs duties on trade with their former partners. As an exception to the general rule, complete free trade was not finally established till the beginning of 1984 for a limited number of products, mainly paper products and certain nonferrous metals.

The third stage was reached with the enlargement of the EC toward the Mediterranean at the beginning of the 1980s. The accession of Greece in 1981 meant that the EC's free trade agreements with the EFTA countries had to be adapted accordingly so as to provide for the removal of tariffs and quotas on imports from Greece as well as on EFTA exports to that

[3]Iceland, which joined EFTA only in 1970, was given until 1980 to remove tariffs and quotas on imports from other EFTA countries.

[4]For legal reasons, each EFTA country had to conclude two agreements, one with the EEC and one with the ECSC.

country. As regards Spain, an agreement was signed in June 1978 under which the EFTA countries obtained the same treatment for their industrial exports as the EC countries already received for theirs under the 1970 preferential trade agreement. In return, the EFTA countries agreed to grant the same tariff concessions as the EC on Spanish exports. This should enable a smooth transition to complete free trade between Spain and the EFTA countries following Spanish accession to the EC in 1986. It will also enable EFTA to avoid repeating the difficulties experienced with Greece as a result of the fact that Greece enjoyed a preferential trading relationship with the EC prior to accession under its 1961 association agreement. Portuguese accession to the EC, also in 1986, will not cause any particular problems to the other EFTA countries, since Portugal has been a member of the association since the beginning, though it is clear that the Portuguese economy will continue to require tariff protection against imports from the rest of the EC and EFTA, which it will enjoy during the transition period.

Neither the Stockholm Convention nor the individual free trade agreements concluded by the EFTA countries with the EC require a common external tariff or common trade policy toward third countries, as is the case with the Treaty of Rome establishing the EEC. In order to ensure that goods are not imported from outside the area into the member country with the lowest external tariff and then reexported free of duty into another member country with a higher external tariff, it was necessary to lay down a complicated set of rules defining those products that are deemed to originate in the area and hence qualify for preferential tariff treatment. These rules have always been subject to constant dispute and revision. During the 1958–59 negotiations about a possible Europe-wide free trade area, it was seriously argued on the EC side, particularly by the French, that it was impossible to define workable origin rules without a prior harmonization of external tariffs: indeed, this was one of the ostensible reasons for the breakdown in negotiations.[5] The origin rules laid down in the Stockholm Convention (which incidentally took up three times as much space as the rest of the convention) provided basically that goods traded between the

---

[5] It is probably true, however, that by the very nature of things a free trade area does tend to encourage the downward harmonization of tariffs on imports from outside the area. This is illustrated by the dispute over "tariff drawback" (refund of import duty paid on imported raw materials of semimanufactures subsequently reexported). The Convention provides that once free trade has been reached, member states may refuse the benefit of EFTA tariff treatment to imports from other member states that have benefited from drawback. This rule was finally confirmed by the Council, but only after a minority of member states had made a determined effort to get the rule rescinded on the grounds that it would penalize industry in high-tariff countries. The experts' view, which was shared by the majority of the member states, was that drawback, like any other export subsidy, was incompatible with a free trade area, and that the remedy for any country that found its export industries penalized by high duties on imported raw materials was to reduce the level of the duties in question. The multilateral reduction of tariffs as a result of the Kennedy and Tokyo rounds of trade negotiations in the General Agreement on Tariffs and Trade (GATT) in the 1960s and 1970s has considerably reduced the significance of external tariffs in both the EC and EFTA.

member states would qualify for EFTA tariff treatment if the EFTA component was more than 50 percent by value or, alternatively, if certain prescribed processes had been performed in the exporting member state. In order to minimize the risk of trade deflection at the expense of traditional outside suppliers, an extensive list of industrial raw materials and semimanufactures in which EFTA is deficient was classified as of EFTA origin even if imported from outside the area. These rules worked even more smoothly than expected, and the safety-valve provisions of Article 5 of the Convention, which allow a member state to take safeguard measures in the event of industrial production being affected by trade deflection, were never invoked.

When the EC was enlarged in 1973, EFTA was forced reluctantly to abandon its own rules and adopt the system devised by the EC, not only for trade between the two groups but also for intra-EFTA trade. To benefit from EFTA tariff treatment, a product must either have been wholly produced in the exporting country or have undergone sufficient processing to ensure that it falls under a different tariff heading in the Brussels Nomenclature for the customs classification of goods. This general principle is modified in two ways in its detailed application to particular products. In some cases the change of tariff heading is not considered sufficient, and other specific conditions have to be met, for example the use of a particular production process or a percentage criterion. In other cases a change of tariff heading is not required, but the rules specify the processing that must be done in an EFTA country or the percentage requirements that have to be met.

The new origin system also made provision for cumulative origin. Expressed in simplified terms, cumulative origin allows a product or component originating in an EFTA country (or in the EC) to be further worked or processed in one or several other EFTA countries (or in the EC), even if this further working or processing on its own would not suffice to give the final product originating status.

The new origin rules, which were generally considered more protectionist and also more burdensome to firms because of the complicated requirements for separate accounting, have been subject to a continuous process of revision to take account of practical difficulties for particular products as well as of technological change. The EC has always been reluctant to envisage a general review of its system, which is applied to all its preferential tariff arrangements.[6] The EFTA countries on the other hand have been pressing since 1975 for the simplification of the origin rules, in particular by the introduction of an alternative percentage criterion and by improved rules for cumulative origin. The EC did agree, however, to introduce an alternative percentage criterion for products covered by chapters 84 to 92 of the Brussels Nomenclature as from April 1983. The effect has been to give companies in the engineering sector the possibility of claiming duty-free treatment on the basis either that the appropriate processing rules have been fulfilled or that no more than a certain percentage (in most cases 30 or 40 percent)

[6] These involve not only the EFTA countries, but also the preferential trading agreements with most Mediterranean countries, the associated developing countries in Africa, the Caribbean and the Pacific (ACP) and the Generalized System of Preferences for the developing countries.

of the ex-works value of the product is accounted for by raw materials or components from third countries.

The free trade areas established under the Stockholm Convention and under the bilateral agreements between the EFTA countries and the EC do not, of course, include either agricultural or fisheries products as such, though a large number of processed agricultural products are classified as industrial goods and so qualify for duty-free treatment. Agricultural markets were regulated by a variety of price-support mechanisms throughout Western Europe, making it impossible to remove tariffs and other import restrictions without prior harmonization of support policies.

Rather than propose a common agricultural policy as provided for in the Treaty of Rome, but for which EFTA lacked either the economic basis or the institutional machinery, the authors of the Convention merely laid down that one of the objectives of the association should be the expansion of trade in agriculture so as to provide "reasonable reciprocity" for those member states whose economies were dependent on their exports of farm produce. This meant, in practice, Denmark and Portugal. The problem was dealt with essentially by means of bilateral agreements, which were considered an integral part of the Convention, any tariff concessions they contained being extended to all EFTA countries. The best known was the Anglo-Danish agreement giving free access to the British market for Danish bacon and butter, which was the price of Danish membership of EFTA.

In May 1963, it was decided to set up a standing committee to carry out an annual review of EFTA trade in agriculture and to study ways and means of increasing it. In addition to seeking further tariff concessions, the Danes also argued strongly for EFTA solidarity vis-à-vis the EC, even going so far as to threaten to leave the association if their partners would not cooperate. This meant, in the first place, that the latter should refrain from subsidizing exports to traditional Danish markets in Germany and the rest of the Six, which were being rapidly eroded under the impact of the common agricultural policy of the EC. In the second place, the Danes argued insistently for a common policy against dumped or subsidized agricultural exports to EFTA markets from nonmembers, which in practice meant the EC and Eastern Europe. The other member states merely referred to the GATT provisions on dumping, but were unwilling to envisage coordinated action even on that basis.

The problem of reciprocity for Denmark was finally solved when that country joined the EC in 1973. The six EC countries, which during the 1958–59 negotiations had argued that agricultural produce must be included in the free trade system if reciprocity was to be ensured, dropped this demand once Britain had opened up its enormous market to EC agricultural exports by joining. Indeed, in its concern to preserve the autonomy of the common agricultural policy, the EC was the first to insist that the agricultural aspect of the free trade agreements be limited to ad hoc tariff or quota concessions, negotiated bilaterally. At the same time, new rules were introduced concerning the measures that the EFTA countries and the EC were permitted to take in order to offset differences in the price of agricultural raw materials, including compensatory taxes and variable import levies.

This approach effectively solved the agricultural problem. The only significant concessions made by the EC as the price of industrial free trade concerned Portugal (agricultural products such as wine and processed tomatoes) and Iceland (fisheries products), implementation of the latter being delayed to 1976 as a result of the dispute over fishing rights with Britain and West Germany. Austria, which has concluded special arrangements with the EC on beef and wine, has sought unsuccessfully to negotiate a global preferential trade agreement in the agricultural sector to offset its trading deficit with the EC in the industrial sector. However, no other EFTA country is interested in going beyond the present ad hoc approach, which also limits the tariff concessions they can be expected to make to the EC's southern partners, Greece, Portugal and Spain.

EFTA'S INTERNAL DEVELOPMENT

The Stockholm Convention was drawn up in the summer of 1959. It is a highly pragmatic document, in which virtually the only specific provisions are those dealing with the removal of tariffs and quotas and the rules of origin. The other articles merely lay down a series of general rules designed to ensure that the proper functioning of the free trade area is not interfered with as a result of government action or inaction in other fields. The only institution established by the Convention is a purely intergovernmental Council with no supranational powers.

Although EFTA refrains on principle from any interference with member states' domestic arrangements not directly related to tariffs and quotas, the Convention nevertheless recognizes that government action or inaction in certain fields—such as the right of establishment of foreign firms, restrictive business practices, the commercial activities of public authorities, state export aids and dumping—can nullify the benefits of free trade. Member states are accordingly free to invoke the consultation and complaints procedure, which is the normal means of settling disputes, if they feel their interests are being jeopardized. In addition, the Convention gives the Council power to lay down more detailed rules for dealing with these problems in the light of experience. One of the main decisions taken at Lisbon in May 1963 was, in fact, to review all the relevant provisions of the Convention before the end of the transition period.

The "rules of competition," as they are commonly known, may be divided into two kinds. In the first place, member states may be required to refrain from certain practices. Thus Article 13 of the Convention forbids the use of a whole range of direct and indirect export subsidies, as well as any aid to industry the main effect of which is to nullify the benefits of trade liberalization for industry in other member states; Article 14 bans commercial practices by public bodies that provide the same sort of protection for domestic producers as would be banned under the Convention if obtained through the use of tariffs and quotas or state aids.

The rules of competition of the second category assume some form of positive government action. Thus Article 15 deals with cartels or restrictive business practices that frustrate the benefits "expected" from free trade;

Article 16 outlaws restrictions on the establishment or operation of firms that are applied in a discriminatory way for the same purpose; and Article 17, besides confirming member states' rights under GATT to deal with cases of dumping by means of countervailing duties or import restrictions, also provides that they may be asked to take action against the dumping on their markets of non-EFTA goods that threaten the interests of other member states.

The Lisbon review did not result in the establishment of a detailed set of legal rules and principles to be applied throughout the association, comparable to the body of legislation built up by the EC. EFTA's approach has been rather to review national legislation and administrative arrangements in order to identify possible problems, and then to devise suitable procedures for handling complaints or agreed-upon criteria for applying the rules in concrete cases. The approach remains a purely intergovernmental one, more like the GATT system than the legal enforcement machinery of the EC.

The removal of tariffs and quantitative restrictions on imports threw into relief the problem of technical barriers to trade resulting from divergent national regulations and industrial standards. As early as 1964, the EFTA Council agreed that governments should provide notice of all new regulations in advance of their implementation, so as to give time for consultation with EFTA governments. The "INST" procedure, as it is called, was strengthened and its application widened in 1975. In April 1968, the Council approved general guidelines for cooperation in this field, under which EFTA countries agreed to inform and consult each other on new compulsory technical regulations, and to ensure as far as possible nondiscriminatory treatment in testing and approval procedures. They also agreed to work together in the appropriate international bodies.

As a matter of policy, EFTA has eschewed any attempt at harmonizing standards or technical regulations, but it has negotiated a series of mutual recognition schemes and conventions, under which tests and inspections may be carried out in the exporting country according to the procedures prescribed by the authorities of the importing country. The aim is not to establish common test methods, but to ensure conformity of the goods tested with the regulations in force in the importing country. There are six such schemes: they concern pressure vessels (1971), ships' equipment (1971), agricultural machines and tractors (1972), gas appliances (1972), lifting appliances (1978) and heating equipment using liquid fuel (1978). The two conventions concern the manufacture of pharmaceutical products (1970) and the control and marking of precious metals (1972). Although the various schemes and conventions are serviced by the EFTA secretariat, they are legally independent of the Stockholm Convention. Various non-EFTA countries—including Britain, West Germany, the Netherlands, Denmark and Ireland—take part in one or another of these arrangements.

The benefits of free trade are likely to be jeopardized not merely by competitive distortions, but also by conflicting economic and financial policies. Under Article 30 of the Convention, the member states recognize that their individual economic and financial policies may affect the economies of the other members, and state their willingness "to pursue those policies in a manner which serves to promote the objectives of the Association." The means for implementing this provision, apart from the possible recourse to the consultation and complaints procedure implicit in the wording of the article, are periodic exchanges of views and recommendations by the Council. In fact, these provisions remained in abeyance until the sterling crisis of October 1964, when Britain unilaterally imposed a 15 percent surcharge to protect its balance of payments. The resulting crisis spurred EFTA into setting up an Economic Committee, which keeps a regular watch on short-term developments in the world economy and in the member states, and their likely effects on EFTA trade, as well as on more general economic problems. Since the 1964 clash with Britain, the committee has had to deal with balance-of-payments crises in Finland, Iceland and Portugal, leading to the temporary imposition of import-deposit schemes or tariff surcharges. The committee has provided a useful forum for discussing the impact of the measures in question and possible forms of assistance by other member countries. The principal forum for reviewing member governments' economic policies and subjecting them to a certain degree of international supervision remains the OECD.

From the beginning, EFTA was faced with the problem of how to ensure that the benefits of free trade were evenly spread among member countries with different levels of development. Tariff measures of the sort adopted in favor of Portugal, Norway and Finland, giving these countries further time to adapt their more backward industries to free trade, were partial and temporary solutions. In May 1963, the Council set up an Economic Development Committee, which carries out development studies with particular reference to problems arising from the removal of tariffs and, more important, acts as a forum for promoting technical and financial cooperation among the member states, mainly at nongovernmental level.

EFTA'S INSTITUTIONAL SYSTEM

The EFTA Council operates in practice at two levels. The major political decisions are taken at ministerial meetings held two or three times a year in one or another of the national capitals. The day-to-day administration of the association is left to a committee of the heads of the permanent delegations in Geneva.

To assist in its work, the Council has set up a number of permanent committees, composed of national officials, to deal with various aspects of EFTA activity. The Customs, Budget and Trade Experts committees have existed almost from the beginning. To these were added the Agricultural Review and Economic Development committees (May 1963) and the Economic Committee (November 1964). In 1972, the Agricultural Review Committee became the Committee on Agriculture and Fish, and in 1974 the Customs Committee was renamed the Committee of Origin and Customs Experts, reflecting its enlarged role in administering the origin rules in the EC–EFTA free trade agreements. The Council has also made frequent use of ad hoc working parties to look at particular problems, ranging from the elimination of quotas to the revision of the rules of competition.

The whole system of permanent committees and ad hoc working parties is organized and served by a Secretariat under the command of a secretary-general. Although without any formal right of initiative, the secretary-general plays an important role in the decision making process and as speaker for the association in contacts with other international organizations. The Secretariat has never sought to acquire any of the EC Commission's enforcement powers, which remain foreign to the EFTA system.

Finally, there is the Consultative Committee, composed of independent experts and representatives from both sides of industry in the different member countries. This was set up by the Council in February 1961 to advise on the affairs of the association as a whole. There is also a Committee of Members of Parliament of the EFTA countries, which grew out of the earlier EFTA parliamentarians' group, a purely informal body composed of delegates from the EFTA countries to the Consultative Assembly of the Council of Europe. Neither of these two institutions has any real powers, however.

Unless the Convention specifically provides otherwise, decisions of the Council have to be unanimous.[7] Within the limits of the objectives of the association, the Council's legislative powers are very wide indeed, since it has the right, and in some cases the duty, either to supplement or amend almost all the substantive provisions of the Stockholm Convention, from the rules of origin to the rules of competition. This power has not, however, been used to transform the Convention. Apart from the operative provisions directly related to the free trade area, the Convention is essentially a good-conduct code, and the supplementary rules adopted by the Council have never gone beyond agreed interpretations of the way in which the various articles are to be applied.

The Council is also the judicial organ of the association. Disputes about the proper implementation of the Convention are settled through the consultation and complaints machinery, which may be set in motion by any member state that feels that the objectives of the association or the benefits expected from the liberalization of trade are being jeopardized. If the normal bilateral and multilateral consultations yield no results, the injured member state may make a formal complaint to the Council, which sets up an examining committee to establish the facts of the case. The Council then decides the case by a simple majority vote. To enforce its ruling, the Council may issue appropriate recommendations to the offending member state or authorize the other member states to suspend the application of specified treaty obligations, also by a simple majority.

In practice, the association works in such a way that disputes rarely reach the formal complaints stage. The tendency was initially for the member states to settle difficulties between themselves on an ad hoc, bilateral basis. Subsequently, it was decided to make greater use of the provisions for multilateral consultation in the Council, while the secretary-general was given the power

[7]As a general rule, decisions are taken by a simple majority in cases where a member state asks to be relieved from, or refrains from complying with, its obligations under the convention. No new obligation can be imposed on a member state by majority decision.

to draw the Council's attention to bilateral settlements between the member states that involved a danger of divergent interpretations. In practice, when faced with unilateral safeguard measures, as happened in 1976 with Austria (over women's tights) and Sweden (over footwear), the other member countries concentrated on obtaining the withdrawal of the offending measures as soon as possible.

EFTA VIS-À-VIS THE EC

In the course of the decade following the first enlargement of the EC in 1973, there was a transformation in relations between the EC and EFTA. This reflected changes in Community attitudes much more than those of EFTA countries.

When the enlargement was being negotiated, the EC resolutely ignored EFTA as such. The EC negotiated virtually identical free trade agreements with each EFTA country, independently, with parallel joint committees and origin rules. There was no consideration of the possibility of negotiating a single agreement with EFTA, presumably because Brussels had not forgotten the ill-fated attempt to merge the EC in a Europe-wide free trade area in 1958–60; nor was the EC prepared to establish institutional links with EFTA as a group. Even official contacts with the EFTA Secretariat were eschewed as an infringement of EC autonomy. The consequences of this attitude can still be felt in the form of unnecessarily complicated customs procedures and origin rules, as well as extraordinarily cumbersome procedures for managing the free trade system, since decisions have to be simultaneously adopted in identical wording by all seven joint committees.

This did not prevent informal cooperation developing between the two organizations. Customs and origin problems were almost from the beginning dealt with jointly by EC and EFTA experts, even if the formal decisions had to be taken on a separate bilateral basis. Coordination meetings between the EFTA Secretariat and the EC Commission take place regularly.

Formal recognition of the special relationship between the EFTA and EC countries reflected the growing consciousness of the importance of the European trading system achieved almost without pain between 1973 and 1977, at a time when the international economic environment was becoming harsher.

In 1977, on the initiative of the Austrian chancellor, Bruno Kreisky, EFTA countries held a summit in Vienna, following an institutional pattern already introduced by the EC. The EFTA leaders called for closer cooperation between the two groupings to accompany the achievement of free trade, and to ensure that its benefits were not jeopardized as a result of divergent economic policies. It was made clear that this cooperation should proceed on a practical and pragmatic basis.

Evidence of growing EC interest in improving relations with EFTA was provided by the EC Council's decision to conduct a yearly survey of the state of cooperation with the EFTA countries, beginning in 1978. The 10th anniversary, in July 1982, of the signing of the free trade agreements was the occasion of a declaration by the EC Council, indicating the EC's willingness to undertake cooperation additional to the free trade agreements in the mutual interests of the EC and the countries concerned, to which the EFTA countries replied with a similar declaration in November 1982. These initiatives culminated in a joint ministerial meeting between the EC and its member states and the EFTA countries, which took place in Luxembourg in April 1984. The resulting declaration called for further steps to consolidate and strengthen a single European economic area—language unimaginable 12 years earlier—as well as emphasizing the importance of continuing flexible and pragmatic cooperation outside the free trade agreements as such. The president of the Commission and the vice president responsible for external relations had a meeting with EFTA ministers in Geneva in November 1984 to review progress in following up the Luxembourg declaration.

In the first instance, the two sides agreed to concentrate on the establishment of a single European market through action in three priority sectors: the abolition of technical barriers to trade, the simplification of customs formalities and procedures, and the further simplification of the origin rules.

As regards the problem of industrial standards, the intention is to work together as far as possible through the existing Europe-wide bodies, such as Comité Européen de Normalisation (CEN) and Comité Européen de Normalisation Electrotechnique (CENELEC). National standards institutions in both groups will cooperate on the same basis as regards the exchange of information on new national rules and standards, though as far as legislative harmonization is concerned, it is clear that the EFTA countries will have to align on Community rules and procedures.

As regards the administrative procedures hindering the free movement of goods, the ideal solution would be the establishment of a single accompanying document for all merchandise. Agreement having been reached in the first place for intra-EC trade, it should be relatively easy to negotiate its extension to trade between the EC and EFTA.

For all questions not directly concerned with the function of the free trade agreements, bilateral cooperation between the Community and the industrial countries will remain the order of the day. A network of bilateral agreements already exists concerning agricultural trade (with Austria, Finland, Iceland, Norway and Switzerland), fishing rights (with Finland, Iceland, Norway and Sweden) and access to the EC market for steel products (with Austria, Finland, Norway and Sweden). In addition, EFTA countries are also signatories to various research projects in the COST framework and most of them are now included in EURONET, the EC's data-transmission network.

In addition to frequent ministerial visits, there are now regular bilateral contacts between officials to discuss matters outside the competence of the joint committees. The subjects discussed range from general economic and monetary policy and industrial questions, which interest virtually all the EFTA countries, to transport and transit formalities (of particular concern to Austria and Switzerland), as well as energy policy and development aid (Norway), industrial safety, the protection of the environment and consumer protection (Norway and Sweden) and insurance (Switzerland).

Although cooperation is extensive and likely to grow over the coming years, the EFTA countries remain essentially in a satellite position with regard to the EC. It is not that the EC has ever sought to dominate its neighbors economically or politically. But inevitably it is the EC that determines the speed with which Western Europe moves toward a unified economic area, the main concern of the EFTA countries being to ensure that the process of integration does not leave them out in the cold or create new barriers at their expense. As far as bilateral cooperation is concerned, the desire for closer relations has always been felt more strongly on the EFTA side than on that of the EC.

This is the inevitable consequence of the basic nature of the EFTA system: a grouping of small countries united only by their desire to obtain the benefits of industrial free trade among themselves and with the EC, which continues to absorb half their total exports. Unwilling to accept the political commitments of EC membership or to create a similar organization for themselves, incapable of negotiating with the EC on a footing of relative equality, they must be content with adapting to the EC as it develops and expands, while exercising as much influence as they can from outside. This pattern is unlikely to change much in the future.

THE ORGANIZATION FOR ECONOMIC COOPERATION AND DEVELOPMENT (OECD)

SALOMON WOLFF and MICHAEL DURAND

ORGANIZATION FOR EUROPEAN ECONOMIC COOPERATION (OEEC)

THE Organization for Economic Cooperation and Development (OECD) has a long and eventful history, some knowledge of which is necessary if we are to appreciate the Organization's present work and future prospects. OECD comprises Western Europe, the United States, Canada, Japan, Australia and New Zealand, and is often taken today to represent the economic interests of the rich industrial countries. However, it must not be forgotten that it arose in the wake of another international organization—the Organization for European Economic Cooperation (OEEC), a union of the Western European states ruined in World War II, which was formed to promote the best allocation of Marshall Plan dollars for the recovery of their shattered economies.

On June 5, 1947, the U.S. secretary of state, General George C. Marshall, made his famous speech announcing massive American aid toward the economic reconstruction of Western Europe, on condition that the countries concerned pooled their efforts in attacking the problems involved. This offer was to have a far-reaching effect on the postwar development of the area. Just over a month later, on July 12, 1947, representatives of 16 European countries met in Paris to discuss acceptance of the American offer. From this conference emerged the Committee for Economic Cooperation, which was given a double task—to make a detailed report to the U.S. Congress on the state of the European economy and to lay the groundwork for a permanent system of European economic collaboration. The conference that launched OEEC was held early in 1948, and on April 16 of the same year the new organization started work. A short time afterward it moved its headquarters to the Château de la Muette on the edge of the Bois de Boulogne, which was also to be the seat of its successor, OECD.

Of the many international organizations that arose in the postwar period probably none succeeded as well as OEEC in carrying out its allotted tasks. It had 18 member states—all the countries of Western Europe with the

627

exception of Finland. Its contribution to the economic reconstruction of Western Europe can hardly be overestimated. When it started work, the whole of the Western European economy lay in ruins. Thirteen years later, when OEEC was succeeded by OECD, most of the OEEC countries had reached a degree of prosperity they had never known. In these 13 years the total production of these countries had more than doubled. Not only were their budgets balanced but they could show substantial surpluses into the bargain, with the result that by the end of 1958 it was possible to introduce convertibility of currency. The standard of living in these countries had attained undreamed-of heights. Western Europe, which in 1948 had stretched out a begging hand to Washington, was now once again a factor to be reckoned with in the world economy.

A major factor in the "economic miracle" that had taken place in Western Europe was certainly the generous extent of Marshall Plan aid. But even when this aid came to a stop in June 1953, the economic recovery of Western Europe continued to take big strides. There can be no doubt that it was the flood of dollars from the United States, the distribution of which among individual countries was organized by OEEC, that made the first steps easier and indeed made them possible. But OEEC's most striking success was the result both of the close degree of collaboration between the member countries and of the basic principles governing this collaboration. Very soon after its foundation, OEEC began to urge upon its member states the desirability of free international trade and a multilateral payments system. Dismantling of the trade and payments restrictions that had been built up during the war and the period of shortages that followed it provided the basic element in Western European economic recovery.

Liberalization of foreign trade and the foundation of the European Payments Union (EPU) were the most important tools in this recovery. "Liberalization of foreign trade" meant the deliberate and progressive removal of quota restrictions, first of all between member states themselves and then from trade between them and other countries including the United States. Gradually, this liberalization policy was extended to "invisible" trade services and, to some extent, capital movements. A "Code of Liberalization" for trade was complemented by a "Code of Liberalization of Current Invisible Operations."

Free development of European trade presupposed, however, the existence of corresponding financial measures in the monetary field which had to be cleared of restrictive bilateral agreements. Thus there arose within OEEC the idea of a European clearing house, the duty of which would be to meet creditor nations' demands in a strong currency and to accord debtor nations a credit in the same currency. In the role of clearing house there appeared the European Payments Union (EPU), which started work on July 1, 1950 and was not liquidated until convertibility of the European currencies was introduced in late 1958. (Its place was then taken by the European Monetary Agreement, EMA, which had been drawn up as far back as 1955 with an eye to this contingency.) EPU practice was based on the "unit of account," of the same value as the U.S. dollar. Surpluses and deficits of any one country vis-à-vis its trade partners were calculated on a reciprocal basis. In this way, credits or deficits were no longer reckoned against any particular country but against EPU, which gave partial credit to debtor countries. The means for these credits were provided partly by the creditor countries and partly by the United States.

THE TRANSITION TO OECD

It might at first sight appear that the success of OEEC proved its own undoing, in that it made itself superfluous by carrying out its allotted task—the economic reconstruction of Europe—to everyone's satisfaction. In reality, however, the crisis in OEEC that led to its reorganization was sparked by deep-set differences of opinion among the member states about the path Western Europe should tread in the future. The OEEC member states were split into two groups. The first group, led by France, wanted to push on beyond the progressive integration of their economies to a politically united Western Europe, a United States of Europe; the other group, led by Great Britain, felt that the most that could be aimed at was collaboration in certain restricted fields between sovereign states.

The Treaty of Paris creating the European Coal and Steel Community (ECSC) was signed on April 18, 1951. This organization formed by six countries—France, West Germany, Italy, Belgium, Holland and Luxembourg—owed its inception to the initiative of the French foreign minister, Robert Schuman. As long as economic integration remained restricted to the coal and steel industries it had little effect on the activity of OEEC. The attempt, which soon followed, to turn the "Six" into a European Defense Community was finally defeated by the resistance of the French parliament. The move some years later to establish a European Economic Community (EEC) was crowned with a good deal more success. By the Treaty of Rome of March 25, 1957, the Six laid the basis for the integration of their economies in a Common Market by means of a customs and economic union.

About the middle of 1956, even before the Common Market took definite shape, Britain started working within OEEC for the formation of a European free trade area, which would comprise all the member states and thereby largely offset the protectionist element in the Common Market of the Six. These negotiations went on until November 1958 when they were broken off at France's instigation, which led to a serious crisis within OEEC. Soon afterward, however, at the end of 1958, the Western European currencies were able to move toward full convertibility as a result of the stabilization of the French franc. At the same time a start was made with the implementation of the Treaty of Rome by reducing tariffs between the six member states. Not long afterward, negotiations started between Britain, Sweden, Norway, Denmark, Switzerland, Austria and Portugal on the formation of the European Free Trade Association (EFTA), which finally came into being by the Treaty of Stockholm, signed on January 4, 1960. The creation of EFTA—which was intended by its promoters mainly as a means of putting pressure on the Six to get them to reconsider the question of negotiations over a multilateral association of other European countries with EEC—was not likely to improve relations between the two camps within the framework of OEEC.[1] The future of the Organization had therefore become problematical.

It was the United States, the original prime mover behind OEEC, that now provided a solution. When the Atlantic Economic Conference opened in Paris early in 1960, Douglas Dillon, the U.S. undersecretary of state, proposed that OEEC should be so modified as to include the United States and Canada. The decision to do so transformed a purely European organization into an Atlantic one. As the accession of the new members involved extensive rethinking of the whole idea of the Organization, its nature and its tasks, almost a whole year passed while negotiations went on over the necessary changes. A preparatory committee was entrusted with drawing up the new articles; presided over by the newly appointed secretary-general of OEEC, Professor Thorkil Kristensen of Denmark, it produced not only a new convention but also a report in which the various questions involved were set out in detail. This report and the convention itself were approved at the ministerial conference held in Paris on December 13 and 14, 1960, the report forming an integral part of the convention. The convention on the setting up of the OECD was signed on December 14, 1960 in Paris by the representatives of 20 countries—Belgium, Denmark, West Germany, France, Greece, Ireland, Iceland, Italy, Luxembourg, the Netherlands, Norway, Austria, Portugal, Sweden, Switzerland, Spain, Turkey, Britain, the United States and Canada. The convention came into force on September 30, 1961 following ratification by the signatory powers. In April 1964, Japan joined the Organization, thus becoming its 21st member. Finland followed in January 1969, Australia in June 1971 and New Zealand in May 1973.

The convention establishing OECD is couched in very general terms. U.S. constitutional and executive practice had to be borne in mind, as questions of economic policy in the United States are subject to the approval of Congress to a far greater extent than they are in Europe. The aims of OECD are set out as follows in Article I of the Convention:

> The aims of the Organization for Economic Cooperation and Development shall be to promote policies designed:
> (a) to achieve the highest sustainable economic growth and employment and a rising standard of living in Member countries while maintaining financial stability, and thus to contribute to the development of the world economy;
> (b) to contribute to sound economic expansion in Member as well as in non-Member countries in the process of economic development;
> (c) to contribute to the expansion of world trade on a multilateral, non-discriminatory basis in accordance with international obligations.

Economic policy, development aid and world trade are thus stated as the main preoccupations of the Organization; the rest of the convention is concerned with basic principles for running the Organization.

INTERNAL STRUCTURE OF OECD

Internally, OECD is modeled essentially on OEEC. Binding decisions can be taken only by unanimous approval of the supreme organ, the Council,

[1] For details of EEC and EFTA, see the chapters "The Structure of the European Community" (p. 568) and "The European Free Trade Association (EFTA)" (p. 612).

in which all members are represented. Any member, however, has the right to abstain. If a country announces that it is not concerned with, or interested in, the question being discussed, a decision may be taken without its participation; such a decision is then not binding on the nonparticipating country. The only substantial difference between OEEC and OECD is that in the latter the position of the secretary-general is stronger; this officer not only heads the Secretariat but is also president of the Council whenever the Council is composed not of cabinet ministers but of permanent delegates from the member countries. The work of the Council is prepared for it by the Executive Committee which is formed by 10 member states appointed annually by the Council.

The secretary-general heads an international staff of some 500 to 600 economists and experts in other disciplines, backed by about 800 statistical, clerical and secretarial assistants. The staff is, by statute, independent, owing its loyalty to the OECD as a 24-nation entity. Drawn from the member countries, it reflects the international canvas of the OECD area as a whole. In this context, perhaps the most important fact about OECD is that it has no supranational element. The secretary-general, although chairing its sovereign body, the Council, when it is not meeting at ministerial level, is entirely subject to their collective will. In other words, the secretary-general has the power to propose but not to dispose. In theory, at least, not only the biggest countries—the United States, Japan, Germany—hold a power of veto on any action, but also the smallest—Iceland, Ireland, Portugal. In fact, it rarely comes to anything of the sort; the principle of unanimity holds, but is hardly ever met head-on in the Council. It has usually been anticipated in a special working party or committee, when the project or program in question is either adapted without excessive loss or dies a death lamented by its main sponsors. This may be any number of governments, the Secretariat, or most likely a mixture of the two.

OECD carries out its work mainly through its special committees. Of particular importance is the Economic Policy Committee, which is composed of high officials of member states and which meets three or four times a year. Its discussions aim at closer coordination of the economic policies of OECD members. This committee is helped in its work by three working parties formed by a limited number of member states. Working Party 3 is particularly influential, in that it deals with currency and balance of payments questions and exercises an unmistakable influence on the monetary policy of the leading industrial powers. The other two working parties are concerned with policies for the promotion of economic growth and with production costs and prices. In addition, there is the Economic Development and Review Committee, which is specially concerned with the annual review of the economic situation of individual member states. The results of this review are published by the Organization in the form of separate reports on each country, which usually arouse a great deal of public interest. Assessment of economic development is based not only on memoranda supplied by member states but also, and to a greater extent, on documentation prepared by the Economics and Statistics Department of the Secretariat. This department is organized in exemplary manner and its work is of great service in promoting better understanding of economic and financial matters. Even though some of the statistics prepared by OECD are intended for confidential internal use only, the main body of information assembled is regularly released. Each year the Organization publishes some 10,000 statistical tables that are at the disposal of governments, parliaments, professional associations, trade unions, market study groups and other research institutes.

The handling of development aid problems falls within the competence of the Development Assistance Committee (DAC)—which carries on from the Development Assistance Group (DAG), a body created even before OECD was established.

Developing countries need not only financial means but also technical know-how. Also working within the framework of OECD is the Technical Cooperation Committee, which is devoted to carrying out technical assistance programs for the benefit of member countries such as Greece, Iceland, Portugal, Spain and Turkey. Turkey is something of a problem for the Organization in that it requires very extensive financial aid, and a special consortium is concerned with the administration of this aid. A similar consortium has been created to deal with Greece's problems.

A special Working Group of Technical Cooperation is concerned with technical aid to nonmember countries, and about one-fifth of the funds made available by the donor countries in the shape of bilateral donations are spent on such aid.

The other activities of the Organization are of lesser scope than its work in the two main fields of economic policy and development assistance. A Trade Committee follows developments in international trade; however, while the old OEEC was able to do a lot of good work in this field, after it was transformed into OECD trade policy was deliberately pushed into the background, as it was generally agreed that thenceforward world trade should develop according to the principles laid down by the global General Agreement on Tariffs and Trade (GATT). Since then the Trade Committee has concerned itself mainly with the problems created by trade between the industrial states and the developing countries. World trade was further promoted by the work of the Fiscal Committee, which was in particular responsible for a "Draft Convention for the Avoidance of Double Taxation with respect to Taxes on Income and Capital," which has served as a model for the conclusion of many bilateral agreements of the same kind.

A Committee on Capital Movements and Invisible Transactions seeks to remove obstacles in the field of international trade in services and capital. To this end it worked out a "Code of Liberalization of Capital Movements" and "Code of Liberalization of Current Invisible Operations" and sees that they are observed.

When the European currencies went over to convertibility at the end of 1958, there came into force, as has already been mentioned, the EMA to which only the European members of OECD belong. The work of EMA, which is run by a board of management, has however grown less and less important since its inception, as international monetary policy has gravitated more and more to other international organizations. Thus EMA's activity has in recent years been confined mainly to granting Turkey credits from

STRUCTURE OF OECD

COUNCIL

EXECUTIVE COMMITTEE

SECRETARY GENERAL

INTERNATIONAL SECRETARIAT

International Energy Agency (IEA) Governing Board

Nuclear Energy Agency (NEA) Steering Committee

Center for Educational Research and Innovation (CERI) Governing Board

Development Center

Special Programs***

Economic Policy*

Committee for Energy Policy

Development Assistance Committee

Technical Cooperation Committee

Trade Committee

Financial and Fiscal Affairs**

Manpower and Social Affairs Committee
Education Committee

Environment Committee
Ad Hoc Group on Urban Problems

Committee for Information
Computer and Communications Policy
Committee for Scientific and Technological Policy
Industry Committee ● Steel Committee

Committee for Agriculture
Fisheries Committee

* Economic Policy Committee, Economic and Development Review Committee, Consortium for Turkey.
** Committee on International Investment and Multinational Enterprises, Committee on Capital Movements and Invisible Transactions, Payments Committee, Insurance Committee, Committee on Financial Markets, Committee on Fiscal Affairs, Committee of Experts on Restrictive Business Practices, Committee on Consumer Policy, Maritime Transport Committee, Tourism Committee.
*** **Cooperation in Road Research**, Club du Sahel, Cooperative Research in Food Production and Preservation, Control of Chemicals.

the European Fund which forms part of it. In these circumstances it is not certain whether EMA will be preserved or, if so, in what form.

The Manpower and Social Affairs Committee has, on the other hand, a very extensive field of action. It was at this committee's instigation that OECD decided to summon its member states to review their labor market policies and to make these a part of the machinery to promote economic growth. The committee has launched several investigations, among which those dealing with mobility of manpower are specially important.

The Industry Committee deals with questions concerning the progress and expansion of industry. It comprises a whole series of subcommittees devoted to special problems of single industries such as steel, chemicals, textiles, cement, etc. Similarly, the Energy Committee supervises the work of the special committees for coal, electricity, oil and gas. These committees devoted to single branches of industry and energy are described as "vertical" committees; they publish regular and comprehensive reports on developments in their respective fields.

Agricultural problems are in the hands of the Committee for Agriculture, which meets regularly at ministerial level and so provides the ministers of agriculture of the member states with an opportunity for keeping in close personal touch with each other and with each other's problems. Although this committee is not empowered to exercise any direct influence on the agricultural policies pursued by individual countries, its researches and the discussions carried on within it make a valuable contribution to better mutual understanding. This is especially so since most of the member states have the same sort of agricultural problems to cope with, arising from the rethinking necessary in agriculture as a result of increased industrialization and technical progress. There is also a separate Fisheries Committee.

OECD's field of activity extends also to scientific problems in so far as there is any connection between these and the central questions of economic and development policies. Scientific questions are dealt with by two committees—the Committee for Scientific and Technological Policy and the Committee for Scientific Research. Some attempt is made in this connection to establish what contribution scientific research and training have to make to economic advancement.

OECD has several more committees in addition to those above mentioned, e.g., the Insurance Committee, the Maritime Transport Committee, the Committee of Experts on Restrictive Business Practices, the Tourism Committee and also several special subcommittees. A Budget Committee prepares the decisions of the OECD Council on the internal finances of the Organization; its expenditure is covered by the contributions made to it by member states.

OECD inherited from OEEC the European Nuclear Energy Agency (ENEA), an autonomous organization aiming at promoting the use of atomic energy for peaceful purposes in Western Europe.

PAYING THE PIPER

An important body, which does not figure on the organigram, p. 633, is the Budget Committee. The OECD budget is about $70 million. The bill is footed by the 24 member governments, with the United States paying 25 percent and the others in proportion to their gross national product (GNP). Fifteen years ago, U.S. GNP accounted for 50–51 percent of the total OECD GNP; in 1984, even with a soaring dollar, it equalled less than 40 percent. The budget committee, composed, like all other committees, of national delegates, not only imposes an overall ceiling on spending for the coming year but also often questions the value—and so the cost—of a particular program or project. It is acting under instruction from the Council, so translating into budgetary terms the politico-economic stances expressed—probably through the voices of ambassadors—in the superior body. If there are roadblocks ahead, they will be broadly known at this stage. As will be seen from the organigram, the Organization's activities extend to almost all sectors of the economy, the overriding aim being to foster and promote the economic growth of member states and of developing countries alike.

However, OECD has little power to exercise any decisive influence on the economic policies of its member states. A considerable gap lies between, on the one hand, the size of the job OECD is expected to do and, on the other, the practical means it has of doing it. While the parent organization, OEEC, had certain specific functions, initially in the distribution of Marshall Plan aid and later in the field of European trade and monetary systems, OECD operates in no well defined or specific field of activity. On the contrary, in almost every domain of its activity it finds itself in competition with other international organizations that are much better equipped for practical action. Thus, questions of financial policy belong to the sphere of the International Monetary Fund (IMF) and the "Group of Ten"; problems of trade policy come under GATT; while EC and EFTA are concerned with changes in the economic structure of Europe. And these are only the most important rival organizations. OECD, it has become clear, is not well adapted to making firm decisions requiring practical implementation.

But one must guard against underestimating the importance of OECD's activities. OECD is making a decisive contribution to economic collaboration in the Western world by providing a forum where the industrial states of the West meet to investigate and discuss their common economic problems. In this way, OECD plays the part of a joint study and research organization where ideas, plans and information can be exchanged and where questions of principle as well as day-to-day problems can be studied, always with an eye to improving coordination between individual member states.

Established at a time of prosperity and growth, OECD has recently had to weather, as have all other international institutions, a period of stagflation and of radical changes in the world economy resulting from two oil crises, with the consequent shift of emphasis from demand to supply economics, and the steady emergence of the so-called NICs (newly industrializing countries) as a new industrial and commercial force in the world. On both fronts, the OECD Secretariat produced prompt and valued analyses, although OECD's report on the NICs was delayed for about a year by the government of what has been described as its own most advanced super-NIC, Japan. Clearly, this is what the member governments expect from OECD: that it should provide analyses that help them face the truth of a new or emerging situation and, accordingly, adopt the policies best suited to coping with it—and that from an international as well as a narrowly national standpoint. This by no means always entails or even implies common action. Within the spirit of the common approach, which may be expressed as a Council-endorsed decision, recommendation, or set of principles or guidelines, governments prefer in the OECD context to keep their hands free to act in the way that best suits their legislative scene and immediate circumstances. OECD's main function, in the eyes of these paymaster governments, is to help them react skillfully to (ideally, of course, to anticipate) new, externally imposed economic policy challenges. So the face of OECD has to evolve all the time.

RECENT CHANGES

Inflation, on which OECD issued an unambiguous warning in 1970, was the first big economic threat of the period. Preceding the first oil crisis, it was probably the first manifestation of the new challenge of the epoch to capitalist societies, whether almost unadulteratedly free-market, largely managed, or otherwise mixed. It affected exchange rates and the pattern of payments balances, as well as knocking individual living standards or, more precisely, the purchasing power of those probably least able to compensate themselves against it. With the 1973 oil shock, combining depressed demand and unemployment with sharper inflationary pressures, and the undermining of the Phillips curve, liberal economics were forced to enter a new phase; even in the traditionally affluent industrialized countries, economic policy had to treat supply as seriously as demand. OECD responded, stage by stage, to this evolving challenge, seasoning hallowed Keynesian demand recipes with a sprinkling of monetarism in face of the evident supply crisis.

The creation in 1974 of the International Energy Agency (IEA) as a semi-autonomous wing of the organization brought a new dimension to OECD, in two senses: it added to OECD's store of analysis and potential policy; the IEA was also accorded a status not enjoyed by OECD as a whole, having a weighted majority system that enables it, at least in theory, to act without unanimity in the event of a specified (seven percent) oil supply shortage. This was in keeping with the strong political impulsion of the oil-consuming countries immediately following the 1973 oil price rise; in the case of the United States, this further took the form of an initial preference for establishing the IEA in Brussels, perhaps with a link to NATO, and clear of the action-shy and sometimes clogging processes of OECD. In terms of action, it is doubtful whether the political cohesion of the IEA in the event proved more dynamic than that of OECD in general. The special emergency oil supply system has never in fact had to be fully triggered off—though there have been many dummy runs—and the bulk of the IEA's work —on conservation, alternative energy sources and oil market reports—has proved to be of a traditional OECD type: the marshaling of facts and figures, leading to analyses with built-in policy pointers for its member governments to treat in their preferred ways.

However, when OECD launched its program on so-called positive adjustment policies (PAP) in 1978–79, it looked to be somewhat out of step with what was politically feasible at that moment in most countries. It denounced all defensive measures, such as the shoring up of weak firms and sectors in face of the still growing economic crisis; indeed, it criticized narrowly sectoral actions in general as too often unbalancing or even undermining economic strategies at the national level. All such defensive measures would, the OECD Secretariat stressed, only make recovery—when it came—more precarious and so jeopardize its sustainability. At that stage it was several years away, even in the United States. In other countries, notably pre-Barre Giscardist France, PAP's stern message was very badly received. But the program was pressed through, in a specially set up working group of the economic policy committee; and by the time of the final report, it was pretty well accepted wisdom. In May 1982, a special statement issued by OECD foreign and finance ministers referred to the alternatives of a "virtuous circle of macroeconomic stability and microeconomic flexibility or a vicious circle of instability and rigidity." And the positive adjustment theme has figured in all OECD's work—stepped up in the current decade—on microeconomic questions, on innovation, on adaptation to new technologies and, stemming from them all, on old and new forms of protectionism.

OECD, insofar as it can be treated as an entity in its own right, has a highly delicate balancing act to perform. Even when the performance is wanted, the acrobatics must be discreet, and it is part of the contract that OECD does not look for applause.

FURTHER READING

Adam, H. T. *L'Organisation européenne de coopération économique*. Paris: Librairie Générale de Droit et de Jurisprudence, 1949.

L'Huillier, J. A. *Théorie et pratique de la coopération économique internationale*. Paris: Editions Génin, Librairie de Médicis, 1957.

Kristensen, T. "The OECD: a landmark of international co-operation," *NATO's Fifteen Nations*. December 1962–January 1963.

Marjolin, Robert. *Europe and the United States in the World Economy*. Durham, N.C.: Duke University Press, 1953.

Message from the President of the United States transmitting a copy of the Convention on the OECD, signed at Paris on December 14, 1960. The White House, Washington, 1961.

OECD. Rules of Procedure of the Organisation. Paris, 1963.

OECD Convention of 14th December 1960. Report of Preparatory Committee. Related Document. Paris: OECD, 1960.

The OECD: History, Aims, Structure. Paris: OECD. (Periodic.)

The OECD Observer. (Bimonthly.)

Partnership for Progress. Paris: Atlantic Institute, 1964.

Report of the Committee on Foreign Relations, United States Senate on Executive E., 87th Congress, 1st Session. Washington, D.C.: U.S. Government Printing Office, 1961.

THE TRADE UNIONS AND INTEGRATION

COLIN BEEVER

BACKGROUND AND STRUCTURE

TRADE unions are well established in most countries of Western Europe and they usually have long histories and traditions. One exception to this is West Germany, where the original trade union movement was dismantled under the Hitler regime and built anew on quite different lines after 1945. The other exceptions are also countries that have no continuous tradition of democratic government—Spain, Portugal, Greece and Turkey; unions here are, generally speaking, less well established. The main trade union strengths are to be found in the European Community (EC) countries and in Sweden, Norway and Austria.

Broadly speaking, trade unions consider themselves political as well as industrial bodies and have usually tended to ally themselves with one political party or another. Where there has been a significant ecclesiastical element in national politics, the unions are usually divided, but where there has been no active political battle involving the church (mainly in Protestant countries), the unions tend to be united. Another element having an important bearing on the divisions of trade unions is the strength of the Communist parties in the countries concerned. This might itself be influenced, of course, by the presence of the ecclesiastical factor in politics. Thus Social Democratic, Christian Democratic and Communist parties all have their own philosophies about the role of trade union movements. They support, sometimes financially, the setting up and maintenance of movements built in their own image. All pay lip service to the ideal of trade union unity, but all equally firmly reject that unity if it is not on their own terms.

The countries with a broadly united trade union movement, where most individual unions are affiliated with a single national center irrespective of political sympathy, are Britain, Ireland, Denmark, Sweden, Norway, Austria and Greece. Those with more than one main national center are France, Italy, Germany, Belgium, the Netherlands, Luxembourg, Switzerland, Spain and Portugal.

The country-by-country position of the unions in the EC is as follows. Initials in parentheses are of the three internationals which will be defined

638

and discussed later, to which the trade union national centers are affiliated. Only major national centers are included here.

West Germany

Most trade unions are united in the Deutscher Gewerkschaftsbund, or DGB (ICFTU), which dominates the trade union scene although not all unions are affiliated with it. The DGB is Social Democratic in orientation, but has a large minority of Christian Democratic supporters. There is also a separate small Christian national center, the CGB (no international affiliation), which describes itself as nondenominational and has no party affiliation. There is also the DAG, which represents the interests of salaried employees, but whose approaches do not differ radically from the DGB's. The West German trade union movement is one of the strongest in Europe.

Britain

Britain has the largest trade union movement in Europe and it is united in one national center, the Trades Union Congress, or TUC (ICFTU). It gained fairly consistently in stature and influence until the 1980s, when governments began to pay less attention to it and to its representatives on many national and public bodies. Economic recession, high unemployment and changes in the law have all eroded its organizational strength. It has a close affinity with the Labour Party, in that many of its members are also party members or supporters, and the unions contribute massively to party funds.

France

The various attempts at unity that have been made by the trade unions have come to little, and France has one of the most divided labor movements in Europe. It is split five main ways. The largest national center is the Confédération Générale du Travail, or CGT (WFTU). This has adhered more closely than any other center in Europe to international Communist policies, industrial and political, but in recent years has loosened its ties with the WFTU, which may portend a softer line. The second largest national center is the Confédération Française Démocratique du Travail, or CFDT (no international affiliation), which used to be Christian Democratic but is now Social Democratic in orientation. The third largest is the Force Ouvrière (ICFTU), originally a breakaway from the CGT in the early postwar years, and strongly anti-Communist although it asserts its independence of all political parties. The fourth largest is the Confédération Française des Travailleurs Chrétiens, or CFTC (WCL), which is a fragment of the original Christian-oriented center from which the CFDT broke away in 1964. Finally, there is the Confédération Générale des Cadres, or CGC (no international affiliation), composed of professional employees who have reached a certain hierarchical level. Although the French unions appear weak in membership numbers, despite their divisions they do carry industrial and political weight and are occasionally capable of changing the minds of governments, in particular by organizing mass demonstrations.

Italy
Again, the largest national center is Communist-oriented, though like the Italian Communist party itself it adopts a "soft" approach and entirely rejects the Soviet line in international matters. This center is the Confederazione Generale Italiana del Lavoro, or CGIL (WFTU). The second-largest national center is the Confederazione Italiana Sindacati Lavoratori or CISL (ICFTU), which is Christian Democratic in orientation but affiliated, nonetheless, to the largely Social Democratic international rather than to its Christian Democratic counterpart. The smallest, the Unione Italiana del Lavoro, or UIL (ICFTU), is Social Democratic. The unity against fascism that had previously united all these trade unions broke down in the late 1940s after the pacts between the democratic parties had also come to an end. By the early 1970s, however, there was a strong desire for unity of action, and the three national centers agreed to dissolve themselves and reestablish as a single confederation by 1972–73. This never happened, mainly because of various party political pressures against it. A "federative pact" took its place, bringing together the three confederations without dissolving them. The confederations delegate power to the pact organizations working together at regional and provincial level, so that all bargaining or strikes, involving the government, for instance, are now jointly managed on the union side.

Belgium
One of the highest densities of European trade union organization is to be found here. There are two main national centers, the Roman Catholic Confédération des Syndicats Chrétiens, or CSC (WCL), which is the largest, and the Fédération Générale du Travail de Belgique, or FGTB (ICFTU), which is Social Democratic in orientation. Their main strengths are, respectively, in Flanders and Wallonia, although each has substantial minority representation elsewhere. Both centers are fairly influential politically.

Luxembourg
Trade union affiliations here are split between the Confédération Générale du Travail, or CGT (ICFTU), which is Social Democratic in orientation, and the LCGB (WCL), which is Christian Democratic.

Netherlands
There is a higher degree of trade union unity in the 1980s than there was a decade previously because of the merger in 1976 of two unions, one Social Democratic in orientation, the other Roman Catholic. The new organization, the Federatie van Nederlandse Vakbeweging, or FNV (ICFTU), is the dominant national center. The others are the Christelijk Nationaal Vakverbond, or CNV (WCL), which is Protestant-oriented, and the Vakcentrale voor Middelbaar en Hoger Personeel, or MHP (no international affiliation), which exists for supervisory and managerial staff. The national centers of the unions have had significant political influence in the country since World War II, mainly because of their membership the Social and Economic Council. This tripartite body represents government, employers' organizations

and workers' organizations and advises the government on all measures planned by public authorities in the field of social and economic policy.

Denmark

The predominant national center is Landsorganisationen i Danmark, or LO (ICFTU), which organizes about half the working population. The other main center is the Joint Council of Danish Public Servants and Salaried Workers Organizations, the FTF, which is white-collar and has about 75 percent of its members in the public sector. The Danish trade union movement, which is historically highly craft-based, is very strong organizationally, with considerable industrial and political influence.

Ireland

Since 1959 the unions in Northern Ireland have been united with those in the Republic in the Irish Congress of Trade Unions, or ICTU. The majority of unions affiliated to it are Irish-based, but a significant minority have their headquarters in England. A number of unions affiliate to the British TUC as well as to the ICTU. The ICTU itself is nonsectarian and nonpolitical, although a number of its important constituent unions are affiliated to the Labour party in Ireland. The ICTU has been a unifying factor in Ireland; because it is strongly organized, its influence on the government is significant. The Northern Ireland committee of the ICTU has played a leading role in the affairs of the North and has brought to bear strong influence to prevent the trade union movement from dividing along sectarian lines.

Greece

The trade union movement has had a checkered career because of several periods of political repression. Since the fall of the dictatorship in 1974, the Greek General Confederation of Labor, or GSEE (ICFTU), has operated with greater freedom, but is still under heavy government influence. Following a change of government from right to left, there was a court decision invalidating the GSEE's 1981 congress on the grounds of its lack of democracy. The court replaced its administrative board with temporary appointees. The European Trade Union Committee (ETUC) suspended the GSEE's affiliation until a new board was installed at the 1983 congress, and its affiliation rights have now been restored. The movement has subsequently been sympathetic to the Socialist government.

Spain

The largest trade union national center is the Union General de Trabajadores, or UGT (ICFTU). A smaller center is the STV/ELA in the Basque region, also ICFTU affiliated. The other national center is the Comisiones Obreras, which has close links with the WFTU.

Portugal

The largest national center is similarly named to its Spanish counterpart and is known by the initials UGT-P (ICFTU). The other national center is the Inter Sindical (WFTU).

THE THREE INTERNATIONALS

The International Confederation of Free Trade Unions (ICFTU)

The trade union international with by far the most affiliates, membership and influence in Western Europe is the ICFTU. It is located in Brussels and in July 1983 it had, worldwide, 136 trade union center affiliates from 96 countries, representing 85 million members. It organizes throughout Europe and is almost wholly Social Democratic in orientation. Its main affiliates in Western Europe set up their own organization in 1973 to coordinate policies respecting the EC and the European Free Trade Association (EFTA), as well as to comment on European matters generally. This organization, the European Trade Union Confederation, or ETUC, was set up in co-operation with Christian national centers, which are also members; one Communist national center in Italy has subsequently joined.

The World Confederation of Labour (WCL)

The WCL is a much smaller organization than the ICFTU and the bulk of its affiliated membership is in Western Europe. Its most significant national centers are in France, Belgium, the Netherlands, Luxembourg and Switzerland. It is Roman Catholic in orientation, though it has a minority of Protestant affiliates, and it too has its headquarters in Brussels. Formerly called the International Federation of Christian Trade Unions, its practical differences with the ICFTU are mainly organizational, but its trade union policies, especially on European issues, are very similar. Its European affiliates, except for the French, take part in the work of ETUC.

The World Federation of Trade Unions (WFTU)

The WFTU has the largest world membership of the three internationals, the great bulk of its affiliates are in the Soviet Union and Eastern European countries, or in other countries showing solidarity with them. Its headquarters are in Prague. The WFTU has a history of political opposition to the EC, yet it has in affiliation the largest trade union centers in Italy (CGIL) and France (CGT). The CGIL has always rejected the anti-EC line of the WFTU and has in fact cooperated with non-Communist unions as an affiliate of ETUC. The French CGT has not joined ETUC and has generally maintained the Soviet line against the EC, although this policy has softened in recent years.

UNION INFLUENCE IN WESTERN EUROPE

The social-provisions chapter of the Treaty of Rome setting up the EEC encourages unions to use their influence directly, and they do so. They are seated on the EC's Economic and Social Committee and on its Standing Committee on Employment, among other EC bodies. The provisions of the social chapter, as well as some of the broader treaty commitments, make clear that the EC is an organization the job of which, in part, is to improve the living and working conditions of its citizens. This corresponds to a role in which the unions are themselves expert.

Most of the trade union national centers in Europe have always been enthusiastic about European integration and eager for the EC to be the main instrument for achieving integration of the national economies and of economic and social policies. The exceptions are the two Communist unions in France and Italy (although the latter is halfway there) and the British TUC, which has advocated that Britain relinquish its membership of the EC. The TUC is now unique among European national centers in striking this national attitude. The other national centers, while supportive in principle, are critical of the practical operations of the EC and particularly of national government control of it through the Council of Ministers, which they regard as clumsy and lacking in drive.

With such a high degree of consensus about Europe, it was natural that the unions should want to set up their own organization to coordinate and integrate their policies and efforts on behalf of their members. This is the rationale behind ETUC, which in 1984 had 34 affiliates representing 43 million members in 20 countries.

ETUC's headquarters are in Brussels. Its affiliates are mainly ICFTU national centers, although its WCL affiliates include national centers in Belgium, Luxembourg, the Netherlands and Switzerland, and the WFTU affiliate in Italy is also a member. ETUC's congress meets at least every three years to decide future policy and to elect an executive and principal officers. All affiliated trade union centers are represented on the executive, and this body meets at least six times a year to decide on the implementation of resolutions and action programs adopted by the congress.

The secretariat is headed by a general secretary, and is otherwise composed of his deputy and four policy secretaries. The secretariat coordinates the activities of ETUC, prepares meetings of standing committees and working groups, represents ETUC at many conferences and consultations within the EC, EFTA and the Council of Europe, and makes proposals to ETUC's executive committee.

ETUC's aims, set out in its constitution, are to "represent and promote the social, economic, and cultural interests of workers at the European level in general and, in particular, in respect of all European institutions. ..." Affiliated organizations will also "work to safeguard and strengthen democracy in Europe." In 1978 ETUC set up the European Trade Union Institute (ETUI), a center for education, research and documentation in support of the European trade union movement. This institute has produced several well-researched publications on economic and social policies in Europe.

Detailed references to ETUC's policies and work may be found in the chapter "Industrial Relations in Western Europe," p. 508. It may be noted here that ETUC has recently demonstrated its continuing support for further and faster integration in Western Europe by calling for the admission to the EC of Spain and Portugal simultaneously and within a fixed timetable. These admissions, ETUC held, needed to be accomplished in the context of "a global Mediterranean policy."

THE PROBLEMS OF INTERNATIONALISM

The new moves toward internationalism have posed special problems for the trade union movement. One of the most pressing of these is how unionism is to develop a supranational movement as opposed to the high degree of national coordination it has by now achieved. Unions will eventually find that they cannot keep calling for faster relinquishing of national sovereignty by EC member governments unless they are prepared to relinquish more themselves to the international trade union movement.

This problem has two parts. First, there is the difficult process by which autonomous national centers transfer their authority to a body like ETUC, which at present is little more than the highest common factor of agreement among them. In this respect, ETUC is rather like the Council of Ministers of the EC itself, but with considerably less authority to commit its constituent parts to genuine change. A considerable extra commitment of resources and time by senior national trade union figures would be required to bring such changes about. Also required would be a conscious decision to transfer responsibility for some aspects of collective bargaining, instead of merely lobbying activities, to ETUC and its expanded secretariat.

Areas for transfer would largely concern overall economic and social problems and the type of fringe benefits that are provided by national law or by EC regulations or directives. These are the only areas where there would be competence to bargain collectively within EC institutions, because the Community itself is not an employer in any general sense. Matters relevant to particular industries or to multinational companies would normally have to be processed through the ICFTU's international trade secretariats (ITSs) or their equivalents elsewhere, as the appropriate bodies dealing with specialist industry matters outside Community jurisdiction. One of the aspects of this sort of international bargaining is that multinational companies operating in Europe are often owned outside it; others, owned in Europe, may operate outside the region. To bargain with them, the unions therefore need bodies with areas of competence wider than Europe.

The second aspect of the problem of union supranationalism is the adjustment needed to bring about a truly unified labor market throughout the EC. This would involve increased international mobility of trade union members through free migration and there are associated problems of how, through the EC Social Fund, to cushion local labor markets against the shocks of recession and redundancy.

Labor migration

Recent international migration statistics show impressive numbers of foreign workers in EC countries—a total of 4,712,000, of whom 1,294,000 came from other EC countries and 3,418,000 from nonmember countries. These figures in Table 1 center on 1980, with the actual national survey dates varying between October 1979 and April 1981.

Of the three main host countries, West Germany takes most migrants from Turkey, Yugoslavia, Italy and Greece, in that order; France takes them from Portugal, Algeria, Morocco, Italy and Spain; and Britain gets them

Table 1
FOREIGN EMPLOYEES BY NATIONALITY, EARLY 1980s *(000)*

EC member countries	From member countries	From nonmember countries	Total	Number of Emigrants from
West Germany	557.7	1,364.3	1,922.0	47.4
France	161.8	1,111.5	1,273.3	103.1
Italy	2.9	13.1	16.0	555.1
Netherlands	69.4	123.1	192.7	65.7
Belgium	126.1	69.4	195.5	50.9
Luxembourg	32.2	18.2	50.4	3.0
Britain	312.7	466.7	779.4	88.1
Ireland	15.0	3.5	18.5	231.5
Denmark	10.8	28.6	39.4	7.7
Greece	5.1	20.1	25.2	139.1
Nonmember countries				
Portugal				444.2
Spain				235.1
Turkey				674.4
Yugoslavia				387.5
Norway				8.0
Finland				4.7
Sweden				6.9
Algeria				295.2
Morocco				196.5
Tunisia				71.7
Others				1,094.5

Source: European Commission, *Eurostat 1983*, Table III/10.

from "Others" (mainly Commonwealth countries), from Ireland and from Italy. Belgium also has significant numbers of immigrants from Italy, France and Morocco; the Netherlands from Turkey, Morocco and Belgium.

There is virtually complete freedom of movement and residence within the EC for nationals of every member country. They may move to take jobs actually offered or to seek jobs. Their families can move with them, and their social security rights are largely protected and transferable. The position of migrants from nonmember countries is in most cases quite different, however. No EC laws protect them in the same way, although national laws do so in some respects and in some countries. Non-EC nationals may be paid the same money as others who are prepared to do the same jobs (usually toward the bottom of the wages table), but they have few of the other rights or freedoms of EC internal migrants, as respects changing jobs, social security or residence terms. This applies particularly to those from non-EC European countries. But legal migrants to Britain from Commonwealth countries, or to France from former colonies, may well have intermediate-level rights, and they do not usually have the language problems that Europeans experience.

Some serious disabilities, then, are experienced by migrants from European countries outside the EC where lower living standards prevail.[1] There were 674,000 Turks in the EC in the survey period, the great bulk of them in West Germany. As the recession hit and jobs dried up, great pressures were put on the Turks to return home. Their continued presence often caused resentment in local communities, with many instances of ethnic prejudice directed against them. Many of these migrants were housed in totally male hostel communities, in itself a recipe for major social friction. Yugoslav migrant workers, of whom the great majority of the EC's 387,000 also went to West Germany, experienced some of the same problems. Theirs were perhaps less severe, if only because of their greater facility with the German language.

There were 444,000 Portuguese, mostly in France, and 235,000 Spaniards, also mostly in France but with a big minority in West Germany. Most of these people have traditionally taken nonindustrial jobs, so that they have not been as concentrated in particular communities and the same problems have not arisen. Their migrant rights are now enhanced by Spanish and Portuguese membership of the EC.

This level of international migration has put trade unions in a difficult position. They have had to recruit as many migrants as possible in order to protect them against exploitation by employers and undercutting of the wage and benefit levels of national and other EC workers. In some areas they have also had to contend with hostility to the migrants on the part of their traditional members. This hostility has not been directed entirely at workers from outside the EC, but has occasionally also affected Italians and Greeks, who have also emigrated in large numbers, especially to West Germany.

At the national and international levels, unions have striven hard to contain and eliminate this hostility and any acts of prejudice. ETUC, for instance, has adopted a statement on ways of combating racism and xenophobia in Western Europe. It made the point that there was a danger of racism's gaining ground against migrants in host countries as unemployment increased.

One of the features of our industrial society is that it causes migration, both nationally and internationally, toward the main centers of competitive industry, leaving other areas relatively depressed, both as regards the industry and the size of the working population it can maintain. There is a parallel process of people moving out of agriculture and out of manufacturing industry, as they become more capital-intensive, into the service sector. The proportion of employees working in the EC's service sector rose steadily between 1970 and 1982 from 47.3 percent to 57.5 percent, and no member country deviated from this pattern. Agricultural employment declined from 10.3 percent to 6.8 percent, again without national deviation, and the proportion employed in manufacturing industry declined from 42.4 percent to 35.7 percent. Only in Greece and Ireland did the proportion engaged in manufacturing industry marginally increase.

[1]For further discussion of this problem from an economic point of view, see "Foreign Labor in Western Europe," p. 486.

All these factors show the need for special measures to cushion the impact of job fluidity geographically, industrially and commercially. People move within their own countries, within the EC and from outside to within the EC. They also move from one job sector to another in increasing numbers. Many special measures operate at national or regional levels to help smooth these transitions, and there is also one special international measure, the EC's Social Fund. The fund has undergone a number of alterations to meet changing circumstances since it was set up by Articles 123–128 of the Treaty of Rome; its main use, however, has been to subsidize retraining in new skills for employees who have been, or otherwise would be, out of work because of changes in industrial and commercial patterns. From 1984, when further changes were introduced, three-quarters of the fund's resources were to be concentrated on promoting employment for young people under 25 (who comprise 40 percent of the total of unemployed people), and most of the rest was to serve the needs of the long-term adult unemployed, those becoming redundant, women wanting to reenter employment, the handicapped, migrant workers and those needing retraining to keep abreast of new technologies and methods. There was to be a concentration on underdeveloped regions. Five percent of the fund was to go for experimental projects and on monitoring and measuring results, with priority given to work on measures to reorganize and reduce working time.

The trade unions and ETUC have made the terms of reference and operations of the Social Fund a special area of interest and concern. This is because it complements their own policies, first of bringing up the standards of the less-privileged wage and salary earners, and second of mitigating the social disruption brought about by technical change, recession and the gradual integration of Europe's huge labor market. The unions see their primary role as protecting the interests of their members and of workers in general. But they also believe they have a mission to promote the integration of the national economies into a European economy. They believe the member countries of the EC will thereby be more competitive in the world, will expand at a faster rate and will bring higher levels of gainful employment. The British TUC may not subscribe to all these sentiments, but there is no doubt that they are the philosophy of ETUC as a whole. The unions have therefore played their full part in the Economic and Social Committee and in the Standing Committee on Employment, which advise the European Commission on future policy initiatives. In many other ways they have made their presence felt in matters relating to the integration of the labor market, including migration and the operations of the Social Fund.

Social policy in the Community is, naturally, much wider than the above implies. Article 118 of the EEC treaty outlines the aim of promoting "close collaboration between member states in the social field, particularly in matters relating to: employment, labor legislation, and working conditions; occupational and continuation training; social security; protection against occupational accidents and diseases; industrial hygiene; the law as to trade unions, and collective bargaining between employers and workers." The unions are naturally very active in insisting that nobody accept a lower standard of living and that all achieve better conditions in all these fields. It is an enormous and complex undertaking for the Community to try to harmonize national laws and policies in all these matters, but the process is gradually succeeding.

COLLECTIVE BARGAINING

The manner in which the unions have set up their own new machinery in the EC, and in which they have been thrown together in their work at EC headquarters and seated on official bodies, has had a significant effect on their activities and on their ordinary industrial negotiations. They have got used to thinking in Community rather than in national terms, both in their policies and planning and in their collective-bargaining techniques. The flow of information has greatly increased among member countries' unions; major concessions won in one country immediately become a basis for comparison in others.

There is a marked tendency in the Community to improve social and fringe benefits and narrow the national gaps between them. Some of these movements come about through national legislation, in which trade union pressures play their part; but others, such as shorter hours and longer holidays, more often come about through collective bargaining in industry. One variable, social security expenditure, as a percentage of gross domestic product during the 1970s, is shown in Table 2.

Table 2
GROWTH IN EXPENDITURE ON SOCIAL SECURITY, 1970–80
(<i>Percentage of Gross Domestic Product</i>)

	1970	1980	1980 as % of 1970
Belgium	18.5	27.7	149.7
Denmark	19.6	28.0	142.8
West Germany	21.4	28.3	132.2
France	19.2	25.8	134.4
Ireland	13.2	22.0	166.7
Italy	18.4	22.8	123.9
Luxembourg	16.4	26.5	161.6
Netherlands	20.8	30.7	147.6
Britain	15.9	21.4	134.6

Source: European Commission, *Eurostat, Social Protection Statistics, 1970–80.*

Some caution must be exercised in interpreting the statistics in Table 2 because of the rise in unemployment and therefore the unemployment benefits paid over the period. This would partly account for the high rises in Belgium, Ireland and the Netherlands, for example, which have been hit particularly hard by unemployment. It is equally apparent that Italy and Britain, despite higher than average unemployment, have slipped badly in this regard over the decade. Britain was next to the bottom in 1970 and in 1980 was firmly at the bottom of the EC in the proportion of its spending on social security.

648

Measuring living standards
It is also interesting to look at hourly earnings and labor costs in manufacturing industry side by side with disposable income.

Table 3
EC HOURLY EARNINGS AND LABOR COSTS
COMPARED TO DISPOSABLE INCOME

			Manufacturing industry				Whole company Net national disposable per capita income at current prices and exchange rates, in ECUs[2]	
	Average gross hourly earnings of manual workers in current PPS[1]		Hourly labor costs, manual and nonmanual					
			ECUs	ECUs	PPS	PPS		
Country	1975	1981	1973	1981	1973	1981	1973	1981
Belgium	2.87	6.14	3.77	12.16	3.40	12.42	3,414	7,758
Denmark	3.49	6.51	n.a.	9.63	n.a.	8.68	4,323	8,807
West Germany	2.72	5.43	4.25	10.94	3.40	10.56	3,977	8,558
France	2.02	4.24	3.31	9.63	2.90	9.55	3,507	8,411
Ireland	2.48	4.84	n.a.	5.99	n.a.	7.24	1,670	4,085
Italy	2.48	5.17	2.94	7.40	3.63	9.82	2,098	4,967
Luxembourg	3.62	6.70	4.08	10.29	3.80	11.13	4,366	11,426
Netherlands	2.89	5.20	4.11	10.83	3.80	10.66	3,356	7,904
Britain	2.80	4.69	2.11	7.45	2.66	7.04	2,358	6,998
Greece	1.24	3.11	n.a.	3.83	n.a.	5.30	1,480	3,319

[1] PPS: Purchasing Power Standard units.
[2] ECUs: European Currency Units, in which the Community keeps its accounts.
Source: European Commission, *Eurostat, Tables 1983 and 1984.*

Table 3 shows that in 1981 the countries having the lowest hourly labor costs in money terms were by and large those having the lowest manual earnings in terms of purchasing power and also the lowest disposable per capita income—Greece, Ireland, Italy and Britain. (French manual workers also had low purchasing power but French employees in general had a middle position in terms of labor costs.) The converse of this is that, on the average, workers in countries with the highest labor costs also have the greatest purchasing power. This is a factor of considerable interest to trade unions, and one that might at first sight encourage them to believe that high wages and high costs automatically go with high living standards. That would be a mistaken conclusion. What has to be scrutinized are the relative trends over a period of time and not any static position.

If the trends from 1973 or 1975 are examined, the position is much less clear-cut. There is no apparent correlation between the level of increase

649

of hourly labor costs and the level of increase of purchasing power or disposable income per capita, although the situation is made even less clear by the lack of available labor-cost data for the earlier period from Denmark, Ireland and Greece. The example shows, however, that while the country with the sharpest increase in labor costs, Britain at 253 percent, was also the country with the sharpest increase in disposable per capita income (197 percent), it was also the country with by far the lowest increase in purchasing power, 67 percent (although this figure was measured over a period two years shorter).

Belgium, on the other hand, which had the next highest increase in labor costs (222 percent), had a relatively low rate of increase in disposable income per head (127 percent), but one of the highest rates of increase in purchasing power (114 percent).

The contrast between the two countries seems, at first sight, remarkable. Both have sustained heavy increases in unemployment rates over the same period, so that the different patterns cannot be entirely explained by the redistribution of wealth through the social security system. That undoubtedly has some effects, though, that would put the relative rate of increase of purchasing power and disposable per capita income out of phase. The probable explanation of the variations is the different patterns of net national savings per capita and net fixed capital formation within the gross domestic products of Britain and Belgium (net fixed capital formation per capita is the amount that goes into increasing a country's stock of plant and equipment, with depreciation deducted). While the British have consistently saved much less per capita than the Community average, the Belgians saved much more than that average until 1980 onward, when unemployment bit deep. It is the same with net fixed capital formation—the British have consistently scored lower and the Belgians consistently higher than the Community average.

This explanation seems to be confirmed by an examination of the consumer price index for the period 1973–81. Britain's increase was 217 percent against Belgium's 86 percent. It is likely that the very low saving and investment rates, complemented by the high rate of inflation as shown by the price index, were responsible for the very low improvements in purchasing power of British workers in this period, in spite of the heavy earnings push by their trade unions. Conversely, other European countries, of which Belgium is the prime example, have saved and invested better, thus keeping down their rate of inflation. They have made much better progress in increasing the purchasing power of those in employment, although disposable income, on the average, including that of those not employed, may have declined relatively. This is partly dependent on social security levels.

Although the conclusions drawn for other European countries cannot all be as sharply differentiated as those for Britain and Belgium, the tendencies are generally valid. The conclusions to be drawn by trade unions should be that, to improve the real standards of living of their members, they must support high personal savings and a high investment rate from industry from its own savings in the form of undistributed profits. The unions must also strive to keep the general level of inflation down and pay levels up. In broader terms this means that, to benefit their members, most unions need to help restrict the level of pay increases commensurate with real increases in national productivity or efficiency. This also requires that employers and public authorities should guarantee to invest at a higher rate as a compensatory mechanism to the settlement of pay demands at lower than traditional levels.

These kinds of messages are difficult to get across at local union levels. Initiatives need to funnel down from international and national levels if they are to stand any chance of success in becoming a countervailing force to the normal intense pressures at local or industry level. The international research offices of trade union and employer organizations, in particular, ought to be pointing out these stark facts of life to their affiliates.

FUTURE PROSPECTS

Further developments in trade union structure and policies in Western Europe depend on a variety of factors. One of these is the political complexion of the governments of Community members, and particularly their economic policies. The unions feel that in recent years there has been a hardening of attitudes in the Council of Ministers, which has a monetarist background. Governments, it is felt, have been prepared to let unemployment drift upward in the wake of world recession, without doing enough in terms of public expenditure to hold in check the effects of unemployment or to provide adequate levels of social compensation. The Commission has been more responsive to union pressures, as has the European Parliament; but the Council of Ministers holds the ultimate reins of power and determines the rate of progress. This hardening of resistance to union pressures, in order to retain control of costs at national or industry level, inevitably holds back further integration of the unions' own efforts at the international level. International collective bargaining with the Community itself is still a long way off.

The unions hoped that with the advent of a directly elected European Parliament, the political left would be in the ascendancy. The opposite has been the case since the 1979 and 1984 elections. The unions have relatively few friends on the right, which holds sway in the parliament. Nevertheless, the parliament has become an additional lobby for the unions, and they have used it to some effect. The employers' organizations have shown that in terms of effective lobbying they can more than counterbalance the unions when the need arises.

The policies so far pursued by the unions at national and international levels in Western Europe are forward looking and take the broad view on economic and social affairs. Unions fully appreciate the benefits, and what they believe to be the inevitability, of European integration—economic, social and political—and they want to speed up the process.

The unions are, by and large, a major unifying factor in the integration of Europe. They have created their own integrated organization in ETUC and have pursued much more united policies through it than politicians have often managed within the Council of Ministers. They have had a unifying effect within particular countries as well. Their attempt to unify the Italian trade movement, frustrated largely by Italian politicians, is one example. Another is the operation of the ICTU national center, bridging the sectarianism that divides the Irish Republic from Northern Ireland and Catholic from Protestant.

If European unions were to lose influence it would be a setback for democratic processes. The EC has the unions to thank for much of the popular and articulate support it enjoys. Unions have consistently spoken for the people in support of integration; their opposition would certainly have made things more difficult. Governments have been remarkably slow to recognize the value of this support for a united Europe.

One additional step that unions could take for greater unity would be to support the issuance of an international union membership card, paralleling the forthcoming European passports and the portable social security benefit entitlements, already in existence. Such a move would be both symbolic and practical, and could be used to guarantee union rights and the acceptability of migrants throughout the Community.

FURTHER READING

Beever, Colin. *European Unity and the Trade Union Movements*. Leyden: Sythoff, 1960.

European Communities, Brussels. *Eurostat* statistical series, especially *Social Statistics, 1982–84*.

European Communities, Brussels. Selected monographs from the *European File* series, especially those on social aspects of EC policy, 1981–84.

European Communities. Trade Union Information Division, Brussels. Separate monographs on the trade union movements in Britain, Denmark, France, West Germany, Ireland, Italy, the Netherlands, 1982–83.

European Trade Union Confederation, Brussels. Constitution, congress reports, press releases and European Trade Union Institute studies, 1981–84.

Jacobs, Eric. *European Trade Unionism*. London: Croom Helm, 1973.

Kendall, Walter. *The Labour Movement in Europe*. London: Allen Lane, 1975.

Stewart, Margaret. *Trade Unions in Europe*. Epping, Essex: Gower, 1974.

BUILDING A
COMMUNITY OF TWELVE

DAVID SPANIER

No one is in any doubt that the further enlargement of the European Community (EC), the opening to the South, will impose very great strains on its ability to function as a Community. At the same time, everyone recognizes that this change is the most important development of the Community since 1973.

The tensions caused by the first enlargement—the accession of Britain, Ireland and Denmark—have after all barely been absorbed 13 years after the event. Can anyone involved suppose that in a Community of 12 the institutions, the way in which the Community is organized to make decisions, will work more smoothly? That the agricultural markets will be better organized? That economic and monetary union will have been brought significantly closer to achievement? On the contrary, it is perfectly plain that everything, or almost everything, is now likely to work a good deal worse—at least that the Community will be more cumbersome and, in fundamental ways, more troubled. True, the long-awaited settlement of the British budget dispute, in the summer of 1984, raised hopes that at long last the Community might look forward and outward, instead of being perpetually involved in internal wrangling. But as of this writing, that was only a hope; the essential tasks all remain to be fulfilled. It is virtually axiomatic, in short, that the Community will be encumbered by its new Iberian dimension.

Yet at the same time it is paradoxical, for this extension was taken for granted. Whatever obstacles were thrown up in the negotiations for Spanish and Portuguese entry, and notwithstanding quite distinct reservations about Spain's membership on the part of France in the mid-1970s and the consequent delay in the timetable, the so-called Iberian enlargement remained on course. It was a political decision, reflecting the strength and solidity of the Community as it is, with all its faults. The decision confirmed for the Community's founding members and later entrants alike its centrality and power of attraction. Looking back from, say, the year 2000, or even 1990, this further enlargement will probably seem no more than an unremarkable, perfectly natural process of growing.

Growth, however, is often painful. It was observed well before the

653

negotiations,[1] when any further enlargement was only a gleam in the candidates' eyes, that a less homogeneous Community with a larger number of members, the newest of which would not have been "socialized" into the Community's accepted customs and conventions, would necessarily find its institutions harder to operate and agreement more difficult to achieve. This was a lesson of the enlargement in membership from six to nine nations; further enlargement to include less homogeneous political and economic systems could be expected to reinforce this conclusion.

On the economic front, new Community members with substantial populations and economic potential will clearly alter the balance of common policies. "Generalizations as to their effects are difficult," Edwards and Wallace wrote, "but certain common features are significant. All four countries (Greece, Spain and Portugal, and Turkey) have a large, if declining, population engaged in agriculture; and a large proportion of consumer expenditure is devoted to food. Each is also economically dependent upon the Community. Their foreign trade statistics show a remarkable consistency; some 40–50 percent of their trade is done with the Community."

Integration in the Community has been dominated by the concept of liberating trade flows between members. Yet, the study went on:

> it is less clearly appropriate to the circumstances of semideveloped or developing economies, where there is a need for protection against low-cost imports from established industrial producers in the interest of protecting domestic industries. The enlargement of the Community to include countries in this intermediate position between highly industrialized and underdeveloped economies creates particular difficulties. It is difficult to envisage, for example, an enlarged Community being able, or even attempting, to secure roughly equal benefits for both potential and existing members.

Agriculture was the key; the basic problem would be the demands of the potential new members for protection and support similar to that given to the more northerly producers. The potential strain on an unreformed common agricultural policy (CAP) would be immense. "The direct effect of enlargement on the Community's budget," concluded Edwards and Wallace, "will depend upon the extent to which it adds to or reduces surpluses and upon the relationship between world and CAP prices. Deficits in cereals and meat are likely to be increased while greater surpluses in citrus fruit, wine, olive oil, tobacco etc. are probable." While the pressures for the reform of the CAP are increasing, and cannot be too long delayed, the entry of Spain, in addition to that of Greece, could well produce the extra burden that brings the entire edifice crashing down.

[1]"The problem of implementation may well be of considerable importance. The Community rests upon the supremacy of Community law and its acceptance and implementation by member governments. The current members have not always lived up to their commitments, partly because of political weakness or opposition and partly due to administrative inadequacy. There must be some doubts on both counts for the potential candidates; certainly their administrative apparatus is likely to be severely stretched." Geoffrey Edwards and William Wallace, *A Wider European Community? Issues and Problems of Further Enlargement*, A Federal Trust Paper, London, 1976.

APPLYING FOR MEMBERSHIP

Spain applied for membership in July 1977, barely six weeks after its first democratic elections in 40 years. Portugal had applied four months earlier. Portuguese negotiations opened in October 1978, Spain's the following February. The tone was set when the first secretary of the Spanish Socialist party, Felipe González (who became prime minister in 1982 and saw the negotiations through to their conclusion in 1984), remarked to the president of the Commission, Roy Jenkins, that for Spain the Community's enlargement is a "global, historical, and fundamental project." Jacques Chirac, courting right-wing and farming interests in France, offered a less rosy view. Spain must be merely an associate member, he declared, because its presence as a full member would be intolerable for French agriculture. More prudently, President Giscard d'Estaing contented himself with expressing certain reservations. The Portuguese prime minister, Mario Soares, commenting on Benelux hesitations, roundly stated: "I am for a political Europe and real supranational institutions. I judge the entry of countries from southern Europe would represent an enormous contribution to such a Europe." Prime Minister James Callaghan of Britain expressed "total support" for Portugal, Britain's oldest ally, and he could hardly have done less. Even António Salazar, the former dictator, had seen Portugal as an integral part of Europe— hence its membership of NATO and the European Free Trade Association (EFTA). When Soares told the Portuguese parliament that entry was the logical sequel to the revolution of April 1974, his remark was greeted by prolonged applause. The opening of Spain's negotiations was something of a relief. "With Brussels we have been rather like a man standing impatiently in the rain on a doorstep," said Leopoldo Calvo Sotelo, then minister for European affairs. "Now that the door has opened and we have been admitted to the waiting room, we can be more patient." Spanish public opinion regarded membership as a good thing, questioning it but little.

There were disparities, and serious ones. The Portuguese economy, obviously, was no "threat" to the Community; its output could be absorbed without, in effect, anyone's noticing it. But Spain is, so to speak, a major minor European power. And so far as agriculture was concerned, Spain is a major producer. Spanish membership increases the area of usable agricultural land in the Community by 27 percent, irrigated farmland by 80 percent, the active farm population by 28 percent and the number of farming units by 30 percent. French reservations, from this point of view, were perfectly understandable. In general terms, Spanish membership enlarges the farming sector by a third. But at the same time, the number of consumers has risen by a mere 13 percent (36 million), and their per capita income is only half the Community average. By comparison, Portuguese membership enlarges the agricultural area by a mere four percent and the number of consumers by slightly less than that. Moreover, under the terms of the first enlargement, and thanks to Portugal's membership in EFTA, arrangements had already been made to eliminate tariffs on industrial goods between Portugal and the Community.

In the preamble to the Treaty of Rome, which gave birth to the European Economic Community (EEC), the founder members declared themselves "resolved by thus pooling their resources to preserve and strengthen peace and liberty," and called upon "the other peoples of Europe who share their ideal to join in their efforts." The Commission recalled this resolution when reviewing the further enlargement. "Therefore," its report concluded, "once Spaniards, Greeks and Portuguese had taken the political decision to apply for Community membership, the Community could not very well refuse them without denying the principles of its existence—or, for that matter, acting against its own interests. The nine Community countries are not unaffected by the political, economic and social stability of their European neighbors. The consolidation of democracy in Greece, Spain and Portugal is, therefore, a factor in the stability of the EEC as a whole." The Commission added, to show it was not insensitive to criticism, the fact that the three applicant countries had not yet reached the same stage of economic development as the other members. Such statements should help change the Community's image, particularly in the Third World, by making it less accurate to describe it as a "rich man's club."

Roy Jenkins, when president of the Commission, had summed up the hopes and aspirations of the Community back in 1977. He held that enlargement would be successful only if the Community was consolidated and enriched in the process. This meant that it must look to the implications for its institutions, traditions, habits and working methods, and its stated objectives. Enlargement meant that if the Community did not go forward, it would go backward; if it could not cope with enlargement, that would stultify its ability to cope with much else. Enlargement was a gathering-in of European civilization and would give the Community its proper European dimension.

The first step on the way to becoming a member of the Community, after the Council of Ministers has pronounced itself in favor of a new applicant, is for the Commission to give its opinion. The wheels of the bureaucracy turn slowly, so that this process takes some months to complete. The Commission's opinion provides the essential framework for entry negotiations proper, which follow over a period of years. Finally, on completion of negotiations, a further year or so is allowed for parliamentary ratification, by all the countries involved, of the new treaty of accession.

THE COMMISSION'S OPINION

The Commission said yes to Spain's application. In November 1978 it expressed its opinion on Spain at some length. It began by welcoming the prospect of a democratic Spain becoming part of Europe. ("Europe," in the Commission's terminology, means of course the Community.) It recommended that negotiations should start as soon as possible and be conducted with determination to find satisfactory solutions. Success implied that Spain's economy should be integrated with that of the Community without intolerable strains on either, with Spain being able to bridge progressively the gap still separating it from the Community. Once the process of integration was complete, the Community was to emerge strengthened, not "diluted."

The Commission then set out the problems under a number of headings. In industry, three requirements needed to be met: (1) elimination of the present imbalance in the dismantling of tariff and nontariff barriers between the Community and Spain, imbalance which had resulted from the application of the preferential trade agreement; (2) harmonization of the basic conditions of competition, notably from the angle of taxation and state aid; and (3) the speedy involvement of Spain in industrial restructuring schemes and the common disciplines adopted for industries in crisis.

In agriculture, the problems arose primarily from the level of self-sufficiency to be achieved by the enlarged Community for a variety of products, notably Mediterranean produce. The mechanisms of the common agricultural policy, such as price levels and guarantees, would be bound to boost Spain's production capacity. Enlargement also raised problems of structures in the size of farms and farmers' incomes. Other issues raised by the need to harmonize the conditions of competition came under regional and social policy, the idea being, in parallel with the negotiations themselves, that a concerted effort be made to coordinate Spanish and Community policies in order to reduce the impact of accession. Restructuring measures in industrial sectors, both in Spain and in the Community, coupled with the acceleration of the rural exodus, would inevitably have appreciable repercussions on employment in the initial stage. The size of the problems made it even more necessary that special attention be paid to employment in the Community's coordination of member states' economic and social policies, to ensure that unemployment did not cause widespread migration.

Turning to external relations, the Commission noted that Spain's membership would have a dual impact. First, it would further reinforce the Community's commercial power; second, it would affect certain aspects of external policy, chiefly toward Mediterranean countries. The consequences of Spain's accession would be relatively severe for certain of the Community's Mediterranean partners whose exports compete most strongly with those of Spain, since Spain's exports of the products concerned would tend to grow after accession. It recommended that the Community should discuss restructuring trade with the countries most affected.

All this—restructuring Spanish industry, rationalizing Spanish agriculture and implementing regional development programs—would require time and mobilized resources. The Commission believed that such action must be launched without delay as soon as negotiations were opened, for if a common market was to be established between Spain and the existing Community without political, economic or social disturbance, the measures in question must have produced their effects. The Commission therefore recommended a transitional period sufficient to liberalize intra-Community trade and the free movement of workers.

Here the Commission, naturally enough, hedged its bets. The transitional period must not be too long, and certainly not indefinite. For individual sectors it could be determined in the negotiations. In any case, it should be tailored to the problems and kept to the minimum compatible. The Commission considered that while it would be possible to undertake fairly rapidly the dismantling of tariffs and similar measures and the alignment of agricultural prices in the context of Spain's immediate adoption of the common agricultural policy, the introduction of common disciplines and coordination measures involving Spain were bound to take time. The mutual interest of the parties in ensuring that integration went smoothly meant that during this time measures permitting an orderly transition, and in particular a general safeguard clause, would need to be maintained. The Commission considered that in delivering its opinion on Spain's accession it must reiterate that all these measures should be put into effect within a period of up to 10 years.

Portugal, on whose application the Commission had pronounced in March 1978, was an easier case. Calling for negotiations to start as soon as possible, the Commission noted that democracy in Portugal was now an established political fact. The country had already ridden out testing times, owing to the aftermath of the revolution and the problem of reabsorbing refugees from Angola and Mozambique, with the result that the new democracy had rapidly gained indisputable international authority.

Reviewing the economic problems of accession, the Commission believed the impact would be very limited, because of the relatively small size of the Portuguese economy. The problems liable to arise would stem primarily from the fact of appreciable disparities in development, which would accentuate the Community's diversity. For Portugal, the prospect of accession made it all the more necessary to remedy certain shortcomings in its economy.

The country's society and economy, according to the Commission, showed major structural weaknesses in all sectors of activity. Twenty-eight percent of Portugal's working population was still employed in agriculture, which, however, accounted for only 14 percent of gross domestic product. Its industrial structure was dominated by traditional sectors at present depressed all over the world. Services, despite the country's great tourist potential, represented only a comparatively small proportion of output. Accession, the report went on, by completing the process begun under the 1972 agreement to open the Portuguese market to competition from Community industry, would be liable to aggravate Portugal's economic difficulties. Accession could force enterprises not yet fully developed to go out of business altogether, and it could further accentuate regional disparities.

In agriculture, the repercussions would be less clear cut. Extension of the Community system of price support might benefit some Portuguese production lines. On the other hand, opening the market to products from member states and nonmember countries having preferential agreements with the Community would mean keener competition, and this could hit the less competitive production lines very hard indeed.

In view of these problems, the Commission argued that it was urgent for the Portuguese government to effect radical economic and social reforms to bring about the country's necessary restructuring. In support of Portuguese structural reform, the Commission proposed that the Community should play an active part, first by financial assistance, and beyond that by cooperating in various development programs in both the industrial and agricultural sectors. If necessary, import restrictions on Portuguese goods should be lifted.

The transitional period for Spain and Portugal, curiously enough, was to be inspired by a principle quite different from that which applied to the first enlargement of the Community. When Britain, Denmark and Ireland joined, the transition period was designed for the new members to adjust to existing Community legislation (*acquis communautaire*). This was essentially the same for all sectors and featured fixed, relatively short timetables. The solutions to be devised for further enlargement of the Community, the Commission noted, must promote the integration of countries with a level of development well below the Community average; they must allow for an additional effort to reorganize structures within the existing Community; and they must be conceived in such a way that the enlarged Community could be consolidated without impeding progress. Similarly, rather different or more extreme problems arose on the institutional side. For political reasons, the only adjustments made to provisions of the original treaties by the first accession treaty in 1972 were those directly reflecting the increase in the number of member states. With the new accessions, there would be twice as many member states as in the Community as originally constituted. The Community would find itself less homogeneous as a result of the different political, economic and social structures of the new members, and would find it more difficult to reach joint decisions and apply them properly.

Experience in the changeover from six to nine members had already revealed that it was difficult or even impossible to act and react in concert. With 12 members, the institutions and decision making procedures would be considerably strained; holdups and second-best compromises would be inevitable if the Community's modus operandi were not improved. The main change, so the Commission hopefully proposed, would be to make greater use of majority voting on matters that practical experience had shown to be suitable for it, to have the Commission, as a rule, exercise administrative and executive functions and to take greater care in deciding which of the legal instruments provided for by the treaties was to be used in each case and how it would be implemented.

GENERAL REACTIONS

The prevailing view was that among the Big Four, Britain was the country likely to be least affected by the further round of enlargement. In a 1978 article by Loukas Tsoukalis, it was noted, however, that the Labour government had expressed the fear that the decision to speed up Greek entry might be at the expense of Spain and Portugal.[2] There were, in turn, widespread fears on the Continent that the Labour government might see enlargement as a means of diluting the Community. Certainly, the British government did not share the view of the Benelux countries, Ireland and the Commission that major institutional reforms should take place in anticipation of enlargement. The weakening of the institutions and of the cohesion of the Community in general had been the main cause of worry for the small members, with the possible exception of Denmark. Ireland had also been concerned

[2] Loukas Tsoukalis, "A Community of Twelve in Search of an Identity," *International Affairs*, Vol. 54 (1978), pp. 437–51.

about financial transfers to the three new applicants and their possible effect on its own net share of the Community budget.

A good point was made by Tsoukalis, in the article just referred to, about strengthening parliamentary institutions. "In a world where political and economic democracy is becoming rather a rarity," he wrote, "the Community would play an extremely valuable role if it contributed to the survival and improvement of democracy in Western Europe. But the survival of democratic institutions depends much more on economic conditions than on declarations of principles."

The most interesting account of the British attitude to enlargement was given in early 1978 by David Owen, then foreign secretary, in oral evidence to the House of Lords Select Committee on the European Communities. Enlargement was the greatest issue facing the Community, he declared. The dominant reason why the three applicant countries had asked to join was their belief that membership would buttress their democracies. He then addressed the very tricky question of what happens if a member state ceases to become a democracy and takes on "an authoritarian cast." The Council of Europe, he pointed out, which took a tough line with the Greek colonels' dictatorship, has a provision for nonparticipation. The Community did not have such a provision. He suggested "a declaration of democracy," to be mentioned in the treaties of accession, but admitted it would be only window dressing. Against a provision for suspension, which he personally favored, there were arguments that such action would cause enormous disruption. As an initial response, he felt, an offending state might be suspended from political cooperation.

Turning to the central dilemma of enlargement, Owen raised the question whether by further enlargement the members were delaying or moving away from the achievement of greater unity, and resigning themselves to becoming only a free trade area. There had always been a choice, to some extent mutually reinforcing, between economic unity and political unity, he suggested. They went together, but the priorities sometimes varied. The founders of the Community had chosen economic unity and economic organization as their first basis, but their prime purpose had still been political.

GIBRALTAR

Gibraltar did not figure in the Spanish negotiations, but it was always at the back of British and Spanish minds. Spain, of course, wanted sovereignty and no less, but the attitude of the civilian governments that succeeded Franco was far less harsh and, from the British viewpoint, more sensible. The British objective was to avoid trouble over the Rock, without really expecting that a settlement could be achieved acceptable to the parties concerned. The official Whitehall view was that it was inconceivable that a country could, one day not too far in the future, join the Community if, at that moment, it was blockading a part, however tiny, of another member state's territory. The Spanish understood this but were not prepared to relinquish their claims. Routine diplomatic contacts had been going on for some time, occasionally at the foreign minister level; and in 1980, Lord Carrington seemed to have squared the circle. At an agreement signed in Lisbon, Spain agreed to lift the restrictions imposed on Gibraltar, which had sealed it off from Spain for a decade, in return for the simultaneous opening of negotiations with Britain on the future of Gibraltar, without preconditions. In other words, Spain was free to raise its demand for sovereignty while Britain nominally refused to discuss any such thing. But the agreement was only on paper; when it came to implementing it, successive Spanish governments found it too much to swallow, and let each date for raising the siege slip by. Britain's ferocious defense of the Falkland Islands, in the South Atlantic war of 1982, put a further strain on Spanish sympathies. Two years later, when a new, civilian Argentine president paid a much-publicized official visit to Spain, Prime Minister González signed a joint declaration of support. "Spain and Argentina," it read, "which are the victims of an anachronistic colonial situation, support their claims over the Malvinas Islands and Gibraltar to restore the integrity of their national territories through peaceful means in conformity with the relevant resolutions of the United Nations." The British remained patient, confident that, in due course, the Spanish would come around. And eventually, some of the restrictions were lifted, allowing foot traffic between Gibraltar and the mainland and open borders as of early 1985. There was no final settlement of the dispute, however, but only a feeling that, in the end, the issue would not be allowed to deflect the course of Spain's historic return to the European fold.

TURKEY

The case of Turkey, an associate member state of the Community since 1963, was not in immediate view, but was perceived as a further aspect of Mediterranean enlargement in the distant future. (The association agreement envisaged full membership by 1995.) The economic link with Turkey was the crux of the overall Western effort to help the country overcome its endemic poverty and so bind it (on the subsequent record, with only partial success) to the European masthead of democratic rule. To this end, the Commission recommended, back in 1979, across-the-board trade and medium-term financial assistance to Turkey, to fill out the association agreement. In 1981, the National Security Council, which held power in Ankara, decided to start preparatory work on Turkish accession as a full member. It was well understood that this could happen only when Turkey had established a freely elected parliament; but in the meanwhile, special EC divisions were set up in the various ministries with a coordinating role played by the foreign minister. In short, measures to restore democratic rule and economic preparations for membership were to proceed in parallel. Turkey, in the Commission's view, had always held a special political status among the Community's partners, "identical" to that of Greece; accordingly, care was to be taken that the negotiations for Greece's entry, then in train, should not be achieved "at Turkey's expense." And of course there were political factors to be taken into account: the strategic position of Turkey, the quarrel over Cyprus and, inflamed by the partition of that unhappy island, the consequent deterioration of relations between Ankara and Athens.

MIDTERM REPORT

By the end of December 1982, which might be taken as roughly the halfway mark in the entry negotiations, the Commission reported progress to the European Council. The picture was patchy. The main drawback was that economic growth, in the applicant countries and the member states, had slowed down. Continuing recession had hampered the expected process of adjustment between the two. And the Community itself was beset by painful problems of internal restructuring. Nevertheless, three principles were confirmed: clarity of the terms of accession; adoption of the *acquis communautaire* in full; simultaneous accession of Spain and Portugal. The Commission affirmed that clarity of the terms of accession must be confirmed by the Community, particularly with regard to the nature and content of the transitional period.

Previously, the Commission had envisaged a transition in stages; in view of the difficult budgetary and trade problems facing the Community and the applicant countries, the idea of adopting only part of the *acquis communautaire* seemed an attractive solution. In practice, it now said, this option would merely defer the problem, giving rise to even greater new difficulties and perhaps subverting the principle of gradual integration. A further complication would face the institutions in making decisions for policies that would no longer be common.

The third principle was perhaps the most significant for the two applicants. The Commission held that simultaneous accession for Portugal and Spain was preferable for both the Community and the applicant countries. Even if the issues varied and the progress made in the negotiations differed, this goal could be achieved. For historic and cultural reasons, Portugal and Spain had pursued their candidacies separately; now they were linked together, which meant in practical terms that Portugal, if necessary, would have to wait for Spain.

Discussing the internal obstacles to their accession, in terms of their own resources, the Commission returned to a favorite theme. For a number of years the Community had been living with a budget under which expenditure was dangerously near the ceiling, despite more effective management of the common agricultural policy and the favorable trend of prices for agricultural products on the world market. It was not until the summer of 1984 that the Community finally resolved the long-running row over the British budget contribution and at the same time agreed to increase the one percent value added tax ceiling on own resources to 1.4 percent; and even then bitter arguments about financing current expenditure continued.

The cost of enlargement to include Portugal and Spain, the Commission calculated, would not place an intolerable financial burden on the Community and could not be regarded as disproportionate to the political importance of enlargement. The size of the budget, as it then was, would increase by between 15 and 20 percent; the two new members would receive net transfers that, on the basis of a notional budget (Community of Twelve) for 1981, would have amounted to between 850 and 1,400 million European currency units (ECUs) equivalent to between four and six percent of the budget of the enlarged Community.

Turning to the working of the Community institutions, the Commission urged the case for more effective voting, citing yet again the difficulties caused by the deadlock in the decision-making process. Enlargement to a Community of Twelve would obviously intensify this immobility unless steps were taken to streamline the machinery. But how? The Commission put forward various ways in which decision making could be made more flexible: most simply, by greater use by the Council of the scope available to it under Article 155 of the EEC treaty for devolving executive powers on the Commission; a more systematic use of the vote by qualified majority, as provided for in the treaties; and, more optimistically, extension of majority voting in certain cases where the Treaties at present require unanimity (for example, in areas covered by Article 100).

The Commission also took into account the significance of a directly elected European Parliament. Its opinions should be given a specific role in the attempt to make decision making more flexible, the Commission's suggestion being that the Council should adopt a text by qualified majority if it was in accordance with the proposal from the Commission and the opinion of the Parliament. Last but not least, the Commission promised to take a new look at its own operations and makeup, including the use of languages.

Under the heading of obstacles thrown up by the negotiations, the Commission noted that many of the difficulties involved in enlargement were "traditional." They arose from the fears engendered in the member states by the prospect of change, the increased openness of their markets to external competitors and the corresponding adjustments required. Such difficulties, the Commission thought, tended to obscure the structural advantages of economic integration (increased size of markets, improved conditions of competition, and so on). Transitional measures would ensure the process was a gradual one; in the accession negotiations, most of the difficulties had been, or would be, resolved by this procedure, itself traditional.

All was very hopeful; however, the Community was also faced with intensified difficulties, in various sectors of the economy, from the similarity between the Community's own problems and specialization trends in the applicant countries. The difficulties, as was only too well known, related mainly to Mediterranean agricultural products, fisheries, textiles, and iron and steel. The sectoral difficulties had two main characteristics. First, they might relate to surpluses—whether existing or potential, the important point being that the phenomenon was not temporary, especially as the consumption of certain products could not be increased beyond certain limits in present circumstances. Second, such difficulties mainly affected the Community's less favored regions (the Mediterranean), those already in trouble, such as regions with declining industries or, in the case of fisheries, coastal regions. A renewed effort to reduce surplus production capacity was essential, given the significant increase in the Community's self-sufficiency rates that enlargement would bring in olive oil, fruit and vegetables, and wine.

The Commission concluded that since the heads of state or government had clearly confirmed the political purpose of enlargement, a concerted effort had now to be made to find the means of achieving enlargement. It sought a clear response from the European Council on the principal choices that held the key to the successful conclusion of the negotiations.

"A VIEW FROM THE BRIDGE"

Reviewing Mediterranean enlargement at length at around this time, Loukas Tsoukalis gave a sympathetic judgment, so far as the Community's performance was concerned. "In a period of prolonged economic recession and growing unemployment, it is remarkable that the *acquis communautaire* has been preserved; even more so, that the Community is prepared to open the doors to three semi-industrialised countries on the European periphery. At the same time, it appears to the other side an 'inefficient and unsympathetic negotiator' because of the slowness and the unwieldiness of its internal decision-making system."[3]

From the applicant countries' point of view, their negotiating strength lay in their economic weakness and in the threat of a radical reorientation of their foreign policy, an argument that had been used by the Karamanlis government and that became even more credible when espoused by big opposition parties. However, as Tsoukalis noted, "given the economic character of the European Community and the nature of the accession talks, high policy considerations have to be translated into bargaining about custom duties and support prices for agricultural products. After all, the history of the Community is full of examples where high and low politics are closely intertwined."

On the other hand it was certainly unrealistic to think that institutions and policies intended for a Community of six, or even nine or ten, could remain unchanged after the entry of new members with different interests and problems.

It all seemed very hard going. Yet by the end of 1983, the Commission could report that after about 40 negotiating sessions with each candidate country, this process was almost complete in several areas: transport, regional policy, economic and financial questions, capital movements, taxation, harmonization of laws and the right of establishment for private citizens. In the case of Portugal, negotiations were almost complete on the customs union in industrial goods, coal and steel, Euratom and external trade. The main areas still to be negotiated were agriculture, fisheries and social affairs; nevertheless, considerable progress had been made, considering the delicate nature of the subjects already dealt with. This was a tribute to the positive political will displayed by all sides. The Commission considered that enlargement was not simply a symbol of the vitality of the Community, but offered new hope for the European ideal.

THE FINAL OBSTACLES

The candidates themselves, naturally enough, were becoming more than a little frustrated, in fact openly irritated, by the slow pace of negotiations.

[3] Loukas Tsoukalis, *The European Community and Its Mediterranean Enlargement*, London, Allen and Unwin, 1981.

Public opinion in Portugal, unmoved and unconcerned by the technicalities, had taken membership for granted; it was not a matter of argument. Indeed, Gaston Thorn, as president of the Commission, had gone so far, during a visit to Lisbon in 1982, as to remind his hosts that "We didn't apply to join Portugal, Portugal applied to join us." Spain was a different case; its volatile reactions during the course of the talks in Brussels alternately cast the negotiations into light or consigned them to darkness. The Spanish public was committed to Europe, certainly; only the extremes on the left and right, which carried very little weight in the new democracy, were opposed. But the Spanish were eager and impatient and did not conceal their feelings. Moreover, there was always the anxiety on the part of Spain's friends in the Community, shared by cautious defenders of the new democracy in Madrid, that an upset in Brussels could undermine the country's political stability. Spain, unlike Portugal, was not yet a member of NATO. It was an open question how far the new constitution had taken root. Such fears were not imaginary, and indeed the whole point of the accession negotiations—delayed if not stalled—was to remove such fears for ever. "If the bride keeps putting back the date, the wedding may be called off," a leading businessman summed up the mood in the early days. Hence the alarm. It was manifested most obviously in vague Spanish threats of some unspecified alternative solution—presumably a tilt to the Soviet bloc—if the negotiations failed. It seemed improbable, to say the least; the reality, which belied talk about Europe being "a difficult sweetheart," was that there was no other match in sight.

But the Spanish repeatedly gave vent to such imprecations. Even the Portuguese, phlegmatic as they were, were driven to speak of "alternatives," though there was no known alternative to the preaccession aid, totaling 625 million ECUs, which Portugal had received from the Community between 1975 and 1983. As late as 1984, papers like *El Pais*, the independent daily, were urging the Ten not to "bring Spain to its knees," while Manuel Marín, the Spanish minister responsible for European Community affairs, could describe the Community's fishery proposals as "a monumental insult." "The EEC sets Spain on a road without an exit," protested the daily *Diario 16*. "The proposals of the EEC are unacceptable.... the Community is disarming our industry, destroying our agriculture and gives us no fish," it quoted Sr. Marín again.

The Commission was aware of the frustration in the applicant countries. For the EC, the Commission noted, reviewing the Athens summit of December 1983, it was a matter of considerable importance that negotiations should be completed quickly. More than six years had elapsed since the request for membership had been made, and in both candidate states there had been signs of annoyance at the delay. Greek membership had taken only five years to settle.

What, in fact, were the remaining difficulties that had to be resolved? They arose, the Commission noted, from the impact of the negotiations on the general structure of the Community and the need to adapt the Community itself to change. The first difficulty concerned the size of the Community budget. Although the accession of Portugal and Spain did not imply a very great financial burden, nonetheless it seemed likely to carry Community expenditure over the existing ceiling. An increase in the Community's resources, therefore, would be necessary before Portuguese and Spanish entry, even if there were no need for the new expenditure to cope with economic difficulties resulting from enlargement.

Moreover, the Commission originally held that a return to sufficiently rapid and lasting growth was a major condition for resolving the serious economic policy problems to be overcome. It was now clear that this could not be expected. It would therefore be necessary to make funds available, not only to restructure some sectors of the Portuguese and Spanish economies, but also to aid those regions badly affected. Typical of the difficulties was olive oil. Because of the large Spanish production, in a Community of 12 states there would be a surplus of some 230,000 tons (implying a Community self-sufficiency of 122 percent). This would harm previous Community suppliers, which included Tunisia, Morocco and Turkey, and it would mean a rise in the cost of the CAP of 800 million ECUs. The surplus would be partially caused by a reorientation of consumer demand toward cheaper types of vegetable oil. Enlargement would therefore create difficulties with states outside the Community—both those producing olive oil, whose exports would be cut, and those producing cheaper vegetable oils which might have to be subject to taxation. Similar difficulties appeared likely for wine, fruit and vegetables.

Fisheries were a separate problem because of the size of the Spanish fishing fleet. Directly or indirectly, the fishing industry occupied about 700,000 people (compared with 600,000 in the Community). Indeed, with over 17,000 vessels, the Spanish fishing fleet is one of the largest in the world. Spain is also a major consumer of fish. So despite the size of the fleet and the extent of the catch, there was an overall deficit in fishery products. National fishery resources being fairly limited, Spain had attempted, with some difficulty, to adopt the Community's own fishing agreement extending members' Atlantic and North Sea fishing limits to 200 miles, and to conduct a series of bilateral agreements with non-Community members in order to gain access to foreign waters. The problem was therefore twofold: adoption of these bilateral agreements by the Community, and the impact of Spain's access to Community waters where stocks were already depleted.

As to industry proper, the obstacles were inherent in the two new members' adjusting to a common internal market. Following trade agreements in 1970 and 1976, Spain and Portugal had both had access to the Community market, and the effect of their industrial exports had largely been absorbed. On the other hand, the industries of both these countries had been protected (heavily, in the case of Spain) and might find it hard to adjust to a new situation. The Commission found the difference in industrial productivity between these countries and the Community to be over 40 percent. The position was still more difficult in the case of such industries as steel and textiles, where there was considerable overproduction. For instance, with Spanish steel exports accounting for 45 percent of total production at the beginning of the 1980s, the Community was faced with absorbing Spanish production into its own contracting steel industry. For textiles, the position was reversed; it was Portuguese production that aroused alarm.

What this meant, taking the European budget and all the other outstanding issues together, was that the Community had become dependent, for its own inner health and future well-being, on the success of enlargement. Spanish and Portuguese entry was, by now, as essential to the Ten as it was for the Two. The Commission held that the demand for membership by the two states had the almost accidental effect of a catalyst the operation of which would determine the development of the Community over the years to come. It was clear that, whatever the difficulties, the EC and its institutions could not refuse this particular challenge. The way to a successful future lay through enlargement: no retreat was possible.

A partial breakthrough occurred in an indirect or unexpected way, as so often happens in the Community, through the settlement of a seemingly minor wrangle among the Community's agricultural experts on ways of marketing produce from the Mediterranean regions. This accord was a precondition of meaningful discussions with the two applicants. It was probably not a coincidence that it came the day after a summit meeting of Socialist prime ministers in Athens, when both Dr. Soares and Sr. González had complained about the slow progress of the accession talks: their French, Italian and Greek opposite numbers evidently got the message. Thanks to concessions by these three countries in the Council meeting that followed, a new arrangement was made for Mediterranean produce. Under it, ways of marketing fruit and vegetables were laid down, covering citrus fruits, tomatoes, apricots and eggplants—on such homely products are the foundations of Europe built. In a wider framework, the Community had already approved an extended calendar of meetings in a concerted attempt to rescue the Community from its impending bankruptcy as the budget resources became exhausted and overspent.

Even so, the negotiations did not prove as easy or quick as had been forecast. The timetable envisaged completing all the outstanding dossiers by the end of 1984, allowing 1985 for ratification, with entry to take place on January 1, 1986. A Commission résumé of progress drawn up in mid-1984 spoke of the negotiations entering the decisive phase, and predicted that if swift and decisive progress was made in July, it would still be possible to keep to the provisional timetable. Spain and Portugal would then become members of the Community, the Commission declared, on July 1, 1986—this was the first time this late date, six months after the publicly proclaimed date of January 1, had been mentioned. (Quite a surprise, but merely, so one was assured, a misprint! If so, it seemed highly prescient.) For as the summer of 1984 came and went, and the negotiations resumed in the autumn, it became clear that there was not the slightest hope of winding everything up by the end of 1984. Spring of 1985 seemed a more realistic target, and even that would require some luck, given that a dozen key issues were still outstanding and several others scarcely broached.

The new delay was a further disappointment to the candidates. Spain was particularly gloomy. France, once again, was seen as the stumbling block; and Portugal, too, realized it would have to wait for its larger neighbor. "Let the French block our negotiations; if they think we are going to back down they are mistaken,"·a senior Spanish negotiator remarked hotly. The outlook was not improved by a bumper olive harvest in Spain of almost 600,000 tons as against 235,000 the year before, and an expected surplus of five billion liters (5.3 billion quarts) of wine. France and Italy, the two largest producers of wine and olive oil in the Community, were unable to reconcile their views on how to control surplus production, with the result that the Community as a whole was unable to reach a common position to present to the Spanish side. Britain and West Germany, on the other side of the financial ledger, were resisting all moves to extend unlimited price guarantees to producers. Unless both Spain and the Community showed more flexibility, warned the Irish chairman of the Council of Ministers, the negotiations as a whole might break down. Sr. Morán, the Spanish foreign minister, thought that the talks might drag on for seven or eight months more; but the position would be no better then, he added. He also referred to the need for Spanish membership to be ratified by the French National Assembly during 1985, while the Socialists still had a majority—the implication being that Spain itself was very far from seeking delays.

Recalling themselves to their duty, the EEC foreign ministers, meeting in emergency session in Dublin, gave a new impetus to the stalled negotiations, leaving all matters of detail, however, to the experts to be dealt with in the weeks ahead. It seemed clear that, with one final heave, the outstanding issues would be resolved, so that Spain and Portugal could become members of the Community in 1986.

Was it all worth it? Some had even wondered whether a Community of Twelve was a contradiction in terms. And would the process of enlargement stop there? Austria, Sweden and Switzerland might be debarred by neutrality; Turkey by political and economic conditions. But Sweden and Norway might start reconsidering their relations with the Community; and Turkey, if once restored to democracy, might want to follow the precedent of Greece. Was there not a danger that the Community might expand so far as to disintegrate?

Not an easy question to answer; in fact, the proof of such a pudding will obviously lie in the eating, in the years ahead. And in the nature of things, it will be a "Yes, but" answer.

The possibility, evoked on so many occasions by the ever-hopeful Commission, that the accession of the new member countries might act as a catalyst for internal Community reforms that were essential, irrespective of any increase in membership, has to some extent taken place. But what has been achieved, notably on the budget, was hardly achieved under the stimulus of further enlargement, even though that prospect cast a forward shadow. The clearing up of the British budget dispute was a necessary and very protracted act of internal accountancy. It was the kind of negative achievement that lifted a constraint, rather than added to the luster of the European ideal. Beyond it still lay the costs and contradictions of the CAP; reforms were supposed to be under way but, like the weather, were regarded as something agricultural ministers talked about rather than took action on. The prospect, on the contrary, was for still bigger surpluses in Mediterranean produce. On the industrial side, the Community continued in the early

1980s to work through the global recession; but evidence of new thinking, either in economic and monetary policies, or in technological cooperation or, on the human side, in combating mass unemployment, was hard to come by. Fine words, small deeds. So far as the institutions themselves were concerned, the hopes of streamlining decision making have not, as yet, been fulfilled; the European Council of Heads of States and Government remained the heavy motor of all major policy decisions—slow to move. Only in foreign policy, in the framing of common positions on the Middle East, in reviews of the European Security Conference, and on various international issues of the day, did the Community seem to be acting in a more coherent and cohesive way. Even then the maverick line of its newest member, Greece (pro-Soviet, i.e., anti-Turkish) was a hindrance and sometimes an embarrassment. The strength of the Community derived actually from its performance of its everyday work, its functioning as a trading block, its network with Third World countries, its representative capacity as a partner of the United States without any short-term hope of becoming a United States of Europe. In this sense, the expansion from 10 to 12 will certainly enhance and extend the role and influence of Community Europe.

FURTHER READING

Bailey, Richard. *The European Community in the World*. London: Hutchinson, 1973.

Edwards, Geoffrey, and Wallace, William. *Issues and Problems of Further Enlargement*. A Federal Trust Paper. London: Federal Trust, 1976.

Pepelasis, A., et al. *The Mediterranean Challenge*. Brighton: Sussex European Research Centre, 1980.

Tsoukalis, Loukas. "A Community of Twelve in Search of an Identity," *International Affairs*, Vol. 54 (1978), pp. 437–51.

———. *The European Community and Its Mediterranean Enlargement*. London: Allen and Unwin, 1981.

THE FUTURE OF INTEGRATION

RICHARD MAYNE

"WE don't know where we're going—we only know we're going there together." The words may seem reminiscent of one of the British army's less intelligent marching songs; they were in fact the answer given by a very wide-awake official of the European Commission to a journalist who asked him about the European Community's long-term future. *Journey to an Unknown Destination* was likewise the subtitle chosen by the late Sir Andrew Shonfield for his BBC Reith Lectures on the Community in 1972, when Britain, Denmark and Ireland were about to join.

Both descriptions sounded vague and unusual; but most political ventures, however cautious, are in fact leaps in the dark. The future is ipso facto unknowable, until it becomes the present—and even then ... What makes the future of the European Community so difficult to predict, however, is the fact that so many participants are involved, all with divergent objectives, while the goals formally assigned or agreed on by consensus have themselves evolved over time. The dust kicked up by the winding column of Eurocrats and others further obscures the horizon; and if its advance guard of scouts has occasional glimpses of the promised land, there are always skeptics to denounce it as a mirage.

CONFUSED UTOPIAS

The earliest days of European unification, in the late 1940s and early 1950s, were marked by a degree of semantic confusion perhaps unrivaled since the *filioque* controversy. What was "Europe?" What was "unity?" The failure to ask these fundamental questions, or at least to agree on the answers, led to much fruitless debate: "federalists" and "functionalists," in particular, charged regularly past each other in the verbal tournaments of the Council of Europe; and the "European Movement" grouped under its multicolored banners the partisans of several mutually exclusive political creeds. Academic students of the period may tend to smile in retrospect, forgetting that their own clarity of vision owes much to the accumulated efforts of busy, preoccupied people who had to think out what they were doing while they were trying to do it.

What visions of Europe's future, then, guided those who pioneered her

670

unity? Perhaps the simplest was a rejection of the past. "Europe was not built," said the Schuman Declaration of May 9, 1950, "and we had war." The aim was more than simply to prevent war between France and West Germany. In 1950, with Hitler's defeat only five years away and trouble brewing over the Ruhr and the Saar, this in itself was no mean ambition; yet beyond lurked vaster, vaguer prospects. "For peace to have a real chance, there must first be a Europe." "The contribution that an organized and living Europe can bring to civilization is indispensable to the maintenance of peaceful relations." What, at that time, did such phrases mean?

For Jean Monnet, initiator of the Schuman Plan, the ultimate vision seemed then to be a federation of the West. It was the time of the beginnings of the cold war, and with them the first steps toward "Atlantic" groupings. If the Schuman Declaration spoke of "the European federation which is indispensable to the maintenance of peace," it was a federation conceived in a wider Western framework, perhaps even as a first model for some kind of universal order.

In so far as European unity was thus regarded as the germ of law and order in the world, it clearly harked back to its own theoretical origins. The various unsuccessful utopians who throughout the centuries had preached the unity of Europe had most often had in mind a universal system: the reason was simply that for them Europe was the heart of the world. By the end of World War II such cosy illusions were no longer tenable; but in the first days of the peace, from the Bretton Woods and San Francisco agreements onward, attempts were made to achieve some kind of unity on a world scale. It was natural, therefore, that some of those who later championed federalism in Europe should speak and write in terms which suggested that they saw it as a pilot plant for federalism in the world. Again, it would be easy to deride such notions, particularly in Great Britain, where the word *federalism* seems often to be associated with crankiness, despite the federal solutions so frequently offered by British governments to postcolonial problems. Nonetheless, it can hardly be denied that the success of quasi-federal organization in Europe would do much to vindicate the notion, and that some at least of its lessons might later stand a chance of being applied elsewhere. If, for example, a quasi-federal system succeeded in reconciling France and West Germany only a few years after they had been at each others' throats, the advocates of such systems would have a partial answer to the reproach that they were starry-eyed in supposing similar progress one day possible in relations between East and West.

Already, however, exegesis of even so primitive a nature probably makes too explicit the ultimate aims of the federalist wing of early "Europeans." For the time being, and in the unpromising cold-war context of the early 1950s, they were content to act where action was possible. This, essentially, was in the territory of the six countries that adopted the Schuman Plan— France, Germany, Italy and Benelux. "Europe," for the moment, was what its detractors then called "Little Europe"; and its theoretical model was at first fairly simple. The original Schuman Plan invested most of its political capital in the High Authority, based partly on the International Ruhr Authority, a short-lived organization that was created in 1949 by Britain, the United

States and France. To begin with, there was no provision even for a Council of Ministers, although this emerged very early in the Schuman Plan negotiations. "Authority" was the key word; and the High Authority's own publicists later stressed this aspect of the organization with almost forbidding relish. "Supranational" was another favorite expression at the time. In some degree it was justified as a dramatization of what was, after all, a striking novelty; but it led to misapprehensions—among the champions of European unity as well as its opponents—about the likely shape of united Europe's political future. Even federalism, so often regarded in Britain as impracticably extremist, in fact prescribes decentralized as well as centralized decision making.

THE SINGLE-STATE HYPOTHESIS

A close study of the political institutions of the United States might have helped to avoid some misunderstanding of this sort; but the slogan "The United States of Europe" was often employed in the early 1950s by those whose vision of the future was based on the single-state hypothesis, as it may be called. The supposition, that is, was that as Europe advanced toward political unity, through the Schuman Plan, the European Defense Community, and so on, the member countries of the Community would gradually assume the characteristics of a single nation, perhaps with a European patriotism or even nationalism to complete the analogy with the nation-states of the past.

Monnet himself never espoused this particular doctrine. His own view of Europe, as expressed in his writings and speeches, from the first laid greater emphasis on the "organizational" aspect of Europe and its exemplary value as embodying common rules and institutions. He did, however, liken the acceptance of law and order by nations in international affairs to its acceptance by the citizens of any one country in their relations with each other, and this may at times have seemed to support the single-state hypothesis with which he disagreed. Others, moreover, and especially the various promoters of Europe's cultural unity, tended to display in mild forms a European patriotism that in politics might have seemed less innocuous.

Similar tendencies emerged later in some of the theorizing about the Common Market. Here the aim was clearly enough to establish among the six member countries a single market and a single economy comparable to those of a single state. From this to the single-state hypothesis of Europe's political future was not an enormous step. Even today, some such assumption seems to underlie much of what is said and written about the future of Europe, notably in the field of defense. Up to a point, it has its justification, since a European Defense Community would undoubtedly require machinery for rapid collective decision making. If Europe were to evolve an autonomous collective defense capacity within the Atlantic Alliance—what used to be called the "twin pillars" or "dumb-bell" concept—that logic seems hard to escape. What seems less certain is whether, for this very reason, the member states and their citizens would be prepared in the foreseeable future to take that step.

EUROPE AS A THIRD FORCE

This question notably failed to trouble 1950s champions of a cognate hypothesis: Europe as a "Third Force." What precisely the phrase meant was open to dispute even then. A Gaullist deputy, speaking in the European Parliament, even claimed that it implied no more than the emergence of Europe as an economic power following the United States and the Soviet Union. Not everyone was lulled by such a bland interpretation; for the phrase's original context made fairly clear that what its advocates had in mind was a status for Europe comparable with that which Pandit Nehru sought for India—independence from both East and West. Even that description, however, remained ambiguous. If "independent" meant "no longer dependent"—for example on U.S. aid—or "no longer subordinate" in the Atlantic Alliance, few Europeans would have rejected it; nor, on its record and its repeated assertions, would the United States. But when the term was used by Gaullists, as it still sometimes is, the implication seemed to be a Europe without permanent attachments. This, if opinion polls are to be credited, has never found widespread support from the public, even in President de Gaulle's France.

EUROPE OF THE STATES

Gaullism contained many paradoxes. Not the least of them was the fact that many who adhered to the third-force hypothesis of an independent Europe not only rejected the single-state analogy with which it seemed to have affinities, they also spurned both supranationality and integration. Was this not a contradiction in terms? In practice, Gaullist France helped to promote the economic integration of Europe; but right from the beginning, the spokesmen of the regime insisted that Europe could be united only by the collaboration of sovereign states. Their opponents, with some justice, retorted that a "Europe of the States" of this kind would find it hard to achieve "independence," and that those who sought both objectives at once were wanting the end without willing the means.

No explicit or coherent answer to this objection was ever forthcoming: the most that Gaullist theory would concede was that "one day" Europe might become "an imposing confederation." The difference between this and a federation, in the eyes of its sponsors, appeared to be more than a matter of three letters. It certainly seemed to exclude a European constitutional structure similar to that of the United States. Faced with this contradiction, one could only conclude that Gaullist philosophy was incoherent, or seek some other explanation.

One such explanation, however unworthy, was that General de Gaulle intended to provide Europe's leadership himself. This, of course, would have been the negation of the careful balance enshrined by the treaties in the Community institutions. Instead of safeguarding everyone from domination by a single major member state, it would have returned to the bad old habits of national hegemony over a gaggle of clients too disunited to stand up for themselves. From the viewpoint of the country ruling the roost, there would be no need for political integration since the ultimate decision making center would be the ruler's national capital.

Curiously enough, some such political arrangements were foreseen a century ago by Victor Hugo, when he wrote that "in the 20th century there will be an extraordinary nation. . . . This nation will have Paris as its capital, and will not be called France: it will be called Europe"—a point of nomenclature that the general might have disputed. His Community partners, and West Germany in particular, were hardly to be blamed if they found such a prospect unattractive. In an "independent" Europe of the States on this model, some states would have been a great deal more independent than others. What was more, so contradictory a model would only have led to continual jockeying for position in the old pre-Community way.

UNITY OR UNION

These ancient debates are less irrelevant than they may seem. A veteran of past Euroconstitutional controversy, returning to Britain from abroad in the 1980s, would have a curious and sad impression of *déjà vu, lu et entendu*. While the British government has not espoused or repeated any of the theses propounded by General de Gaulle, it has sought to avoid any commitment to "union," as suggested by the European Parliament, some European governments and a number of pro-European activists. What, it asks, does "union" mean? The unspoken fear seems to be that it might imply greater delegation or merger of sovereignty—perhaps an extension of the present Community institutions from the economic to the political or foreign-policy sphere. The end of such a road, it is true, might be the single-state hypothesis. To that extent, British doubts may be understood. But when government ministers voice their preference for "unity" rather than "union," they provoke the plausible suspicion that what they seek in Europe is little more than the status quo.

THE INEVITABILITY OF GRADUALNESS

Immobility, in fact, has never been an option for the EC. Some have likened it to a bicycle, in that if it stops, it can only fall. Jean Monnet realized the optimistic alternative: that having once set the process in motion, governments would gradually come to accept as feasible further steps that they would have refused indignantly had the moves been proposed at the start. To advocates of European integration, this seemed no more than the normal working out of gradual change. To its opponents, however, it seemed what the former French premier Michel Debré, for long the lone Gaullist opposition in the Community's Parliament, had called the *engrenage*. This untranslatable word usually means "the works" or "gear wheels"; here, with reference to the Community, it has the implications of "sausage machine." M. Debré was anxious that France should not be swallowed up by the process of integration.

The notion was somewhat as follows. To solve the problem of the Ruhr, the Schuman Plan had created a common market in coal and steel. To remedy the disequilibria caused in the member countries' economies by the integration of these basic products, it was necessary either to deintegrate them or to integrate the rest of the economy in a common market for all goods. Such a general common market would only produce its full fruit if the factors of production were integrated too, and freedom of movement was accorded to capital and labor. Once this measure of integration was on the way, it would be logical and indeed necessary to harmonize taxes, legislation, and so on, and to adopt common policies not only in such sectors as transport and agriculture, where pure competition was not enough, but also, ultimately, in most fields of economic and monetary policy. To achieve all this, and to administer the resultant economic union, some political machinery would be necessary; when it was established and fully operative, the member nations would be ready to take further steps in political integration that could lead them to the "ever closer union" prescribed by the Treaty of Rome. Steadily and ineluctably, the practical fusion of interests and pooling of sovereignty would lead to full political union.

In practice, of course, so neat a pattern was too good to be true. As time went on, some of the earlier and simpler models and hypotheses were modified. The High Authority set up by the Schuman Plan seldom acted by diktat, but in fact engaged in a permanent dialogue with the national governments represented in the Council of Ministers, in order to find solutions to common and often unforeseen problems. The further steps in economic integration that seemed so logical required not only long negotiation but also immense administrative labors even when in principle the governments were agreed. Europe was being built piecemeal and untidily, with crises and setbacks and lacunae along the way. At the center of the whole process, however, there remained the dialogue between a European body responsible for seeking solutions to common problems and the Council of Ministers responsible for defending national interests and taking the final decisions together. This institutional system was confirmed by the treaties of setting up Euratom and the Common Market. It differed from the original simple blueprint for the Schuman Plan, from the single-state analogy, from political federalism, from Europe of the States; it was novel and sui generis; it had evolved. At the same time, it promised to give the advantages of each of the earliest, simpler hypothetical systems. It was capable of reaching difficult decisions, like a true Authority. It was able to create a single economy out of six. It maintained and protected the rights of the states, but pointed the way toward possible federal developments in the political field.

In a joint declaration in Bonn on June 1, 1964, Jean Monnet's Action Committee for the United States of Europe, comprising the majority of the political parties and all the non-Communist trade unions of the Six, spelled out what still remains the most articulate rationale of how the existing Community might extend its methods into new fields and at the same time develop a more satisfactory relationship with the United States. It looked forward, as the Action Committee added in a further statement, to

a new period in which European nations will gradually come to treat foreign policy and defence as joint problems, as they already deal with economic questions in the Common Market. This intermediate period is necessary for real progress to be made in the organization of Europe. Once they have transformed relations between them in this way and come to speak with one voice on the essentials of policy, the European nations will be able to open the great debate which will ultimately enable them to decide what form a democratic government of Europe is to take.

Nothing ultimate was prejudged, therefore; but the way ahead seemed clear.

Equally clear, at least to Monnet's committee, was the future posture of Europe vis-à-vis the United States. It was neither subordination nor "independence" in the Gaullist, third-force sense; nor was it now conceived as dissolution into an "Atlantic Community," federal or otherwise, since this would have presupposed American willingness and ability to undertake Community-style obligations. What was envisaged, rather, was a relationship of equals between the United States and united Europe in the making—something more enduring, and more self-confident on both sides, than the traditional alliance of one vast and many smaller powers. This new relationship of equals would extend in time into the field of defense. Thus united in equal partnership, Europe and the United States would be in a better position to come to terms with the Soviet Union, without any move toward a détente producing, as now, nervousness in Europe—especially in West Germany—which in turn could lead to impatience in the United States. The emergence of a politically united Europe, moreover, would facilitate a détente by making unilateral national action impossible and by furnishing a political framework within which the German people could be safely and peacefully reunited without reconstituting a single and separate German state. Finally, the resultant settlement between the West and the Soviet Union would create a climate of peace that would promote and facilitate the peaceful evolution of the rest of the world. United Europe would thus have started a ripple that would carry a very long way.

THE REAL WORLD

Nothing, of course, was ever likely to turn out so pat. When the first edition of the present Handbook was published, the EC had just been rocked by crisis; there seemed no prospect of Britain and other countries joining it; France had left NATO, and NATO was leaving France. Gloomy scenarios seemed in order; more hopeful possibilities were proffered with diffidence and apology.

By comparison with 1967, the present may seem a far more propitious time. Gaullism may not be dead, and may have migrated to London or Washington or both; but pragmatism seems in the ascendant. The Community has been enlarged three times, to include not only Britain, Ireland and Denmark, but also Greece, Spain and Portugal. The member states have reaffirmed their desire to achieve "European union." They have established a "European Council"—thrice-yearly meetings of the heads of state and government—and a system of political cooperation between their foreign ministries, linked by a special telex net.

The same old headaches recur in the Common Market: agriculture, the budget, "harmonization," minor pinpricks of every sort. Half the British population remains lukewarm about Europe; there is reluctance in Denmark and opposition in Greece.

But gradually, alluvially, the EC is consolidating itself. Its critics claim that it moves too slowly: it does—especially in matters of high technology. Yet at last it is mounting an all-out attack on the nontariff barriers that still divide the "common market," so-called. It is planning to make itself more attractive, with an array of popular measures to create "a citizens' Europe." And in several ways—bilaterally, in procurements, but also multi-laterally, within Western European Union—some of its member states are inching their way toward joint European action on security: disarmament and defense.

The "partnership" side of the equation remains less satisfactory—largely, but not wholly, because in crucial areas the Community countries have not yet "got their act together." They can hardly speak with one voice in monetary matters while their European Monetary System remains rudimentary, and their European Currency Unit is still not a real currency. They can hardly expect to be treated as an equal partner in security matters when there is no European Defense Community, as there might have been in the 1950s. They can hardly match the political maneuverability of the United States when they have no political institutions to speak with a single voice. Every such shortcoming on the European side compounds American tendencies to act alone, and they are many and powerful.

Undoubtedly, the climate for joint action in Europe was more propitious when Europe and the world were booming. Progress may be easier when the present recession recedes. But, paradoxically, it is in hard times that joint action is most needful. There are many signs that Europeans are aware of this. When will their governments have the vigor and imagination to break out of the vicious circle? They can only succeed together.

FURTHER READING

Camps, Miriam. *What Kind of Europe?* London and New York: Oxford University Press, 1965.

Duchêne, François. *Beyond Alliance*. Paris: Atlantic Institute, 1965.

Kohnstamm, Max and Hager, Wolfgang, eds. *A Nation Writ Large?* London: Macmillan, 1973.

Mayne, Richard, ed. *Europe Tomorrow*. London: Collins Fontana, 1972.

———. *Postwar: The Dawn of Today's Europe*. London: Thames and Hudson, 1983.

Shonfield, Andrew. *Europe: Journey to an Unknown Destination*. Harmondsworth: Penguin, 1973.

Wallace, Helen, et al., eds. *Policy Making in the European Community*. Chichester, Sussex: Wiley, 1983.

INDEX

679